Chronology of the Birth of Cinema 1833–1896

This book is for Anette, whose unwavering support got me through it, however slowly.

Chronology of the Birth of Cinema 1833–1896

DEAC ROSSELL

LE GIORNATE DEL CINEMA MUTO

JL

CHRONOLOGY OF THE BIRTH OF CINEMA 1833–1896

British Library Cataloguing in Publication Data

Chronology of the Birth of Cinema 1833–1896

Rossell, Deac

A catalogue entry for this book is available from the British Library

Paperback ISBN: 0 86196 716 2
EPUB: 9780 86196 964 7
EPDF: 9780 86196 965 4

Front cover image: One of six double-sided phenakistiscope disks prepared by Simon Stampfer and published in 1833 by Matthias Trentsensky in Vienna. [Werner Nekes Collection.]

Published by
John Libbey Publishing Ltd, 205 Crescent Road, New Barnet, Herts EN4 8SB, United Kingdom e-mail: john.libbey@orange.fr; web site: www.johnlibbey.com

Distributed Worldwide by
Indiana University Press, Herman B Wells Library—350, 1320 E. 10th St., Bloomington, IN 47405, USA. www.iupress.indiana.edu

Printed and bound in the UK by Short Run Press Ltd.

Contents

Introduction

This account of the origins and first full year of the cinema is intended to be reliable, inclusive, verifiable, and comprehensive. In its earlier version, published in *Film History* in 1995 and long out of print, several historical errors that were deeply embedded in published film histories were corrected; the present account, surprisingly, has found more longstanding errors that have been accepted without demur by the authors of early- and pre-cinema narratives. Those corrections alone are justification for this book, as its fixed text with its multiple sources should provide a stable guide to the many strands of innovation and experimentation that led to the year 1896 and the blooming first full year of early cinema.

The attempt to provide an inclusive account means in the first place that this text looks equally at all nations and disregards national prejudice in citing its material findings. More subtly, in the second place it means that no undertaking towards establishing moving pictures has been discarded because it was a technological, or social, or economic dead end. There are some surprisingly workable technologies, in their own time, that have been ignored or overlooked at later points because they did not lead directly to the successfully-resolved technology that came to be known as the cinema. Prominent amongst them is the Schnellseher viewing apparatus of Ottomar Anschütz which gave nearly 50 exhibitions across Europe and North America between 1887 and 1895, the majority of them public exhibitions for fee-paying audiences. As it is clear that the Anschütz sequence photographs for his viewer directly influenced early films for the Edison Kinetoscope, as well as some of Birt Acres's early film work, the Schnellseher and its exhibitions cannot be justifiably rejected on technological grounds from any account of the evolution of cinema in its first phases.

The attempt here has been to make every entry verifiable, giving citations to each individual item. While many of the materials collected here come from single scholars working regionally or locally, every effort has been made to reliably check the sources for the events recorded, and dubious items have, in theory, been weeded out or corrected with further bibliographic citations. It is sometimes difficult to judge the veracity of an event, but an unrelenting effort has gone into checking the events collected here, including those long-established in early- and pre-cinema histories. As a result, it is hoped that the present account reflects a more stable, true, and consistent record than any individual prior work.

This account attempts also to be wholly comprehensive in its approach to the origins of the cinema. Nothing has been deliberately left out because it did not 'fit' some preconceived notion or because it was thought to be less relevant than other material. One result of this principle, apart from the resulting international character of the work, is that the astounding diversity of early cinema (and many of its direct predecessors) is present throughout. There are exhibitions in restaurants, at concerts, and in private homes as well as in established and temporary theatres or fairgrounds and markets. And there are patents from known and unknown inventors whose apparatus turns out, in many cases, to have been a practical contribution to the narrative of emerging cinema. Some circles of early adopters are well known, for example the links between the magicians David Devant, Georges Méliès, Carl Hertz and the Isola Brothers, Vincent and Émil. But there are other circles noticeable here, preferences for specific apparatus on the French Fairgrounds, preferences for bundled 'complete outfits' in lesser German cities, or preferences for local suppliers in the British midlands. These associations, which cannot be seen or found by studying only the cinema that emerged in large urban theatres, or the cinema that was attached to early cinema's most prominent figures, became the backbone of the introduction of cinema across the wider culture and internationally, and tell a story that cannot be reduced to an historical dispute between the Lumière brothers and the team of Thomas Edison. Early cinema, and its inventive predecessors, are too robust, too chaotic, and too opportunistic to be distilled into a single narrative that easily contains all the elements of the story.

The glue, the interstices, the fabric that holds together the events collected here is missing from this account in one important respect: the magic lantern culture that existed from about 1670 until early in the 20th century. The projection and storytelling culture of the magic lantern, later called the sciopticon lantern or optical lantern, was not so much a 'precursor' of the cinema, as it was the environment into which the cinema was born, the milieu which nursed the cinema through its extended period of invention until just after the turn of the century, and the context which provided the cinema's first business and aesthetic practices. The story of magic lantern culture and its relationship to cinema has yet to be properly written, but it is slowly gaining substance and credibility as lantern culture sheds an abundance of nostalgia and gains historical insight. The magic lantern began to develop its own narrative and pictorial vocabulary at least from July 1672, when the early German scientific instrument maker Johann Franz Griendel in Nürnberg gave an elaborate magic lantern show to the French traveler Charles Patin. "For in a moment I saw the Air fill'd with all sorts of Birds, almost after the same manner as they are usually painted round about Orpheus," Patin reported, "and in the twinkling of an Eye, a Country-Wedding appear'd to my view, with so natural and lively a representation that I imagin'd myself to be one of the Guests at the Solemnity. Afterward the Horizon of my sight was taken up with a Palace so stately, that nothing like it can be produc'd, but in the Imagination; before which there were divers Personages running at the Ring: these Heroes seemed to be the Gods that were adored by Antiquity, and among them 'twas pleasant to observe Momus mounted upon a Barbary-Horse, and making Satyrical Reflections upon Jupiter, who had made a false step amidst so jolly a company."[1]

The many implications of moving slides in Griendel's lantern show turned into actual moving slides elsewhere across the first quarter of the 18th century. A number of moving slides of various types were collected, sold, or exhibited at this early moment of projection: a slide of two goats butting, and another of a bear that reared up on its hind legs and attacked a man dressed in Swiss clothing with its front paws;[2] a moving carriage with rotating wheels made of brass and moved by a thread, a Cherub working at a spinning wheel, also moved by a thread, and a shooting gun, which was worked by a rapidly withdrawn paper slip that revealed the reddish firing discharge and speeding bullet.[3] An elaborate description of

1 Charles Patin, *Quatre Rélations Historique*. Basel: 1673, p. 238. The text here is taken from the English edition of 1696 which repeats in full the Basel description: Charles Patin, *Travels thro' Germany, Swisserland, Bohemia, Holland and other parts of Europe*. London: 1696, pp. 233ff.

2 Bonifacius Heinrich Ehrenberger [or: Samuel Johann Rhaenus], *Novum et Curiosum Laternae Magicae augmentum ....* (Jena, 1713), p. 7. On the authorship of this thesis, Ehrenberger or Rhaenus, see Hauke Lange-Fuchs, "On the origin of Moving Slides", in *The New Magic Lantern Journal*, Vol. 7, No. 3, p. 10-14, esp. 11-2.

3 Zacharias Conrad von Uffenbach, *Merckwürdige Reisen durch Niedersachsen, Holland und England....* (Frankfurt/Leipzig/Ulm, 1753-4: Stettinische Buchhandlung), p. 62–63.

a moving slide appeared in 1705 when Johann Conrad Creiling published his thesis *Phaenomena Laternae Magicae*, where he gave an example of the proper way to begin a magic lantern show, beginning with extinguishing the lights and removing the cap over the lantern lens, at which point "the figure of the prologue appears on the wall, moving strangely and in a curious habit, and opens the scene, greeting the spectators by bowing and courteously removing his hat; then he disappears again and his place is quickly occupied by other movements which follow consecutively one by one".[4]

The most widely illustrated early set of moving slides, five different images each demonstrating a different method of moving the two slide glasses involved, was published in Petrus van Musschenbroek's *Beginselen der natuurkunde.* of 1736.[5] Musschenbroek was part of a family running a famous instrument workshop in Leiden, and most likely constructed these five moving slides himself. Until he left home in 1714 on his studies, Petrus spent much of his time in the workshop painting and making lantern slides, and when in early 1711, von Uffenbach also visited the Musschenbroek workshop, and had already bought a magic lantern from the family, he complained about the work of Petrus in making slides: "We hear that the youngest brother makes the figures for it [the magic lantern]. But they are not as faultless as those the father had made."[6] One of Musschenbroek's moving slides, of the turning sails of a windmill motivated by a thread wrapped around a second wheel with a crank, was an image that would remain an essential part of the lantern showman's repertoire for the next 150 years or more, with additional effects like swans feeding in the millpond added after the discovery of dissolving views in the 1840s. The other four slides also became part of the standard lantern repertoire: they depicted a man drinking from a goblet whose arm is moved by a lever, a man whose hat and wig can be removed or replaced at will that were individually moved by two drawbars, a tightrope walker moving with his balance pole from end to end of his rope who was slid across a panoramic background, and a finely dressed lady who makes a polite curtsey when she is moved in her hinged glass by a lever underneath.[7]

In 1770, Edme-Gilles Guyot gave instructions on how to use two panoramic slides to represent a storm at sea, with one slide containing the action of the waves "from its least movement through to the terrifying storm" and a second slide containing "ships of different aspects and sizes and at various distances, along with a few clouds." This became one of the most widely circulated instructions on work with moving slides as the method and its images were reprinted in a German edition in 1772, in a pirated Engish edition by William Hooper in 1774, and in another account by Johann Christian Wiegleb in 1779.[8] Passing the two slides through the lantern simultaneously produced the effect of a growing or diminishing storm populated with wave-tossed ships. Guyot also reminded the lanternist that "One must take care that the

4 Johann Conrad Creiling, *Phenomena Laternae Magicae ....* (Tubingae, 1705), p. 4.

5 Petrus van Musschenbroek, *Beginselen der natuurkunde, Beschreven ten dienste der Landgenooten* (Leiden, 1736: Samuel Luchtmans). The often cited 1739 date for these slides is for the French translation of this work issued by the same publisher under the title *Essai de physique*.

6 Zacharias Conrad von Uffenbach, *op. cit.*, (Note 3), entry for 20 January 1711, p. 433. The father mentioned would be Johan Joosten van Musschenbroek (1681-1707). See Peter de Clercq, *At the Sign of the Oriental Lamp. The Musschenbroek workshop in Leiden, 1660–1750.* (Rotterdam, 1997: Erasmus Publishing). The workshop had been making magic lanterns since at least 1675.

7 A catalogue of 1748 mentions a slide with a man forging iron. See de Clercq, *op. cit.* (Note 6), p. 248.

8 See Edme-Gilles Guyot, *Nouvelles Récréations Physiques et Mathématiques* (Paris, 1769-1770: Gueffier), Tome III [1770], p. 184; Johann Christian Thenn, *Neue physikalische und mathematische Belustigungen, oder Sammlung von neuen Kunststüchen und Vergnügen, etc.*, (Augsburg, 1772: Kletts)[Guyot translation, with additions by Thenn], pp. 184-87 & Tab. 21; William Hooper, *Rational Recreations ...* (London, 1774: L. Davis/J. Robson/B. Law/G. Robinson), p. 39-40; Johann Christian Wiegleb, *Unterricht in der natürlichen Magie* (Berlin/Stettin, 1779: Friedrich Nicolai), pp. 152–154 & Tab. VII. See also Deac Rossell, "The Magic Lantern and Moving Images before 1800," in: *Barockberichte* (Salzburg), 40–41 (August 2005), pp. 686–693.

various representations are not sharply divided from each other, but on the contrary grow step by step and are progressive. It is easy to see that this must all be very carefully painted, since the beauty of the representation depends on this alone … ."

It was in the middle of the next century, however, when the lantern and its mechanical movements became truly ubiquitous. A combination of the slides from the new medium of photography, and the invention of an efficient, inexpensive lantern by E. J. Marcy in Providence, Rhode Island brought the lantern into common use. This new sciopticon lantern had a new fuel, kerosene (or paraffin oil), which was affordable to all, and had a burner that gave a safe, bright light so that it could be used to good effect in medium-sized halls everywhere. Across the 1870s, it became widely available across North America, Europe, and beyond. The sciopticon was easily manageable and was used by the widest possible assortment of amateurs, churchmen, public speakers, educators, showmen and photographic clubs. It is hard to imagine the universality of the magic lantern, or sciopticon, in western culture by the end of the 19th century. Terry and Debbie Borton carefully accounted for all of the lantern shows in Middletown, Connecticut, during the first three months of 1895, and then extrapolated their result to the entire population of the United States, which implied about 150,000 lantern shows for the entire year across the US, given by about 60,000 different lecturers. Applying a conservative perspective to their mathematical findings, they estimated that somewhere between 75,000 and 150,000 lantern shows were given by 30,000 to 60,000 lecturers annually, including many amateur shows.[9] Magic lantern culture had by then established major lending libraries for slide sets and accessories, with circulating catalogues of 250-plus pages, and the lantern was not a stranger to any public venue. The lantern was a familiar accompaniment to many kinds of fairs, markets, and public events, so much so that very early cinematographic exhibitions were sometimes advertised as "not a magic lantern show." This was the magic lantern culture into which the cinema was born, first as experimental apparatus, then as cutting-edge photographic processes, and finally as its own medium of moving images. And it is an account of this evolution of moving picture work, supported by magic lantern culture, that is the core of the present book.

One startling, decisive difference between movement in magic lantern shows and movement in even the earliest cinematographic shows, is the direction of the movement. Movement in lantern shows was always particular: one element of the image moved and the rest stayed impermeably still. If a drinker lifted his drink to take a sip, and possibly in the most complex slides then rolled his eyes in pleasure, then nothing else in the painted scene moved. If a fishing boat left harbour on a stately breeze, then its only possible action was to return to harbour in reverse in the same manner. Movement in projected slides was also characterised by being always in a flat plane, across the screen. Mechanical slides could not move in depth, or towards or away from the viewer and the screen. So when an early reviewer wrote about the Lumière film *Feeding the Baby* in Rochester, New York in February 1897, the reporter specially noted features of the film that are hardly noticed by a modern viewer: "So intent is the spectator usually in watching the proceedings of the happy trio at table that he fails to notice the pretty background of trees and shrubbery, whose waving branches indicate that a stiff breeze is blowing. So it is in each of the pictures shown; they are full of interesting little details that come out one by one when the same views are seen several times."[10]

9 Terry and Debbie Borton, "How Many American Lantern Shows in a Year", in Richard Crangle, Mervyn Heard, and Ine van Dooren, eds, *Realms of Light. Uses and Perceptions of the Magic Lantern from the 17th to the 21st Century* (London, 2005: The Magic Lantern Society), pp 105–115.

10 George Pratt, *Spellbound in Darkness* (Greenwich, CT, 1973: New York Graphic Society Ltd.), p. 18, where the film is called *Baby's Breakfast*.

This was a major shift in perception for the audience: movement across the entire screen, rather than only in specified portions of the image. Perhaps an even greater shift came with movement on the screen that was towards the audience, whether of a train entering a station or waves breaking against a pier. There are reports from early cinema exhibitions of audiences reacting vigorously when this kind of movement appeared, as movement in this direction had not been seen by audiences over the previous 200 years of optical projection. Movement in depth, towards a spectator, had been seen only live and in the real world, not in its projected gloss. This phenomenon in early cinema has been widely examined as 'the train effect' on spectators.[11] In fact, both movement across the whole image and movement towards the spectators are exemplified in one of the most common of early cinema films, *Workers Leaving the Lumière Factory* of 1895.[12] The workers are spread across the open gates of the factory, and each worker moves independently towards the spectator or takes a turn to their right to exit the screen space. A simple film used in many of the earliest Lumière exhibitions, the universal all-across-the-screen movement, plus its movement in depth instead of in a flat plane across the screen, was radical and startling to early audiences, as it is no longer to us today. When the film was shown on 22 March 1895 by Louis Lumière at the Société d'encouragement pour l'industrie nationale, one of the few press reports of the showing commented that the 'animated view' was "very curious ... showing in complete motion all these people hurrying into the street, producing a most shocking effect so that a repetition of the projection was required by the wholly astonished audience".[13] As Yuri Tsivian has written, "... it was not so much the Lumières as the viewer personally who authored the train effect. The film survives, but we have lost its viewer."[14] The viewer who has been lost is the viewer raised in magic lantern culture, whose experience of projected movement was gained wholly from the limitations of mechanical moving slides.

The present account is an attempt to record with exactitude the evolutionary steps that distinguished cinematographic work from the mainstream of magic lantern culture across the 19th century to the end of 1896. As such there are many surprises along the way, and it is hoped that every reader will be able to engage with substantial material that will, in the end, enlarge the sense of how the cinema came into existence.

Deac Rossell
London 2022

11 A thorough empirical survey of these early cinema movements is in Stephen Bottomore, "The Panicking Audience?: Early cinema and the 'train effect,'" in *Historical Journal of Film, Radio and Television*, 19:2, pp. 177–216. See also Martin Loiperdinger, "Lumière's Ankunft des Zugs: Grundüngsmythos eines neuen Mediums" in *KINtop* 5 (1996) pp. 37–70. Note that neither of these authors approach audience reaction to screen movement from the perspective of magic lantern culture. Instead they respond to early cinema materials directly and extrapolate from later cinematic viewing habits.

12 A view of workers leaving the Lumière factory in Lyon, *Sortie d'usine*, was actually made three times: on 26 May 1895, on 10 March 1896, and on 15 August 1896. A fourth version was shot in February 1897. The overall view is the same in each version, but the details vary, particularly of which workers move in which direction, whether there is a black horse visible (version 2), or how a worker with a bicycle moves. See Michelle Aubert and Jean-Claude Seguin, *La Production cinématographique des Frères Lumière* (Paris, 1996: BIFI/Editions Mémoires de cinéma), pp. 214–215, Nos. 685–688.

13 *Bulletin du Photo-Club de Paris*, April 1895, p. 125. See also Laurent Mannoni, *Le grand art de la lumiere et de l'ombre. archeologie du cinema.* (Paris, 1994: Nathan) pp. 393–394.

14 Yuri Tsivian, *Early Cinema in Russia and its Cultural Reception* (London, 1994: Routledge), pp. 144–145.

Acknowledgements

According to the inscription on the dedication page, it was in June, 1965 that my inspirational first film teacher, David Shepard, gave me a copy of Philippe Esnault's *Chronologie du cinéma mondial, des origines à nos jours* (Les grands films classiques, 1963). Little did he, or I, recognize at the time how prophetic a gift had been given. Since that time, many, many people have contributed to the genesis of this work over a long period of time. I am constantly reminded of the generosity of the community of early cinema scholars and consider myself lucky to be counted amongst their ranks. I would, nonetheless, like to point out initially a few remarkable contributors, none more significant, or more patient, than my publisher, John Libbey, who has been waiting with a gracious tolerance for a manuscript for some years now, whereafter his improved structure and clear design made the work more useful and more readable. Without his support, the work would never have come close to being finished. I am also most appreciative of support for this book from the *Giornate del cinema muto*, encouragement that is to me especially poignant since this central meeting of the early cinema community was very influential at the outset of my work in early cinema three decades ago.

There are two other colleagues who will be very much missed and that I would like to acknowledge as well. Richard Brown, recently deceased and the co-author of two major books on British cinema with Barry Anthony, was a genuine English eccentric, unwaveringly devoted to his typewriter and to the Royal Mail. My correspondence files show more than 130 pages from his antique writing machine. I did not carry on such an intense correspondence with Paul Spehr, the retired Smithsonian Institution historian of early cinema who died shortly before Richard, but our correspondence and contact goes back even further, to 1979 when he came to lecture for me on early cinema at the Museum of Fine Arts, Boston.

My most unrepayable debt, of course, is due to the laborious hours of page-turning of those previous historians whose works are noted in the bibliography. It is a debt of which, in my own page-turning, I am more and more conscious, and one that I acknowledge wholeheartedly and with gratitude. My own work was first encouraged by the late Douglas Edwards at the Academy of Motion Picture Arts and Sciences, and later spurred on by Stephen Herbert of the Museum of the Moving Image in London. Each of the following acknowledgments, listed alphabetically, recognizes those across at least two generations who sent books, information, hard questions, articles and/or materials which made a direct contribution to the present work, and who often surprised me with unanticipatedly generous offerings: Barry Anthony, Richard Balzer, Bill Barnes, John Barnes, Jürgen Berger, Camille Blot-Wellens, Stephen Bottomore, Carlos Bustmente, Peter Domankiewicz, Marguerite Engberg, Tony Fletcher, Jean-Paul Goergen, Tom Gunning, Richard Koszarski, Paul Kusters, Hauke Lange-Fuchs, Martin Loiperdinger, Laurent Mannoni, Pamela Müller, Charles Musser, Aurelio de los Reyes, Ursula Reichert-Nekes, Jens Ruchatz, Walter Schobert, Lester Smith, Vanessa Toulmin, Yuri Tsivian, Herbert Tümmel, Merten Worthmann.

PART 1: CHRONOLOGY

1833

January 20:

The Belgian scientist Joseph Plateau publishes in *Correspondence mathematique et physique de l'observatoire Bruxelles* the results of his research undertaken at the end of 1832 in a letter with this date titled "Sur un nouveau genre d'illusion, d'optique", which describes his phenakistiscope,[15] a disk the where phases of painted movement, incorporating between them thin radial slots, when spun and observed in a mirror created an illusion of motion for the viewer. Plateau, a physicist engaged with light and vision, had also studied art and drew his own disks containing between 15 and 19 phases of movement, the earliest a dancer in sixteen phases. By July 1833 the London publisher Rudolph Ackermann had marketed a set of disks drawn by Plateau under the name Phantasmascope. Two further series followed from Ackermann in the same year, drawn by Thomas Talbot Bury in 8 to 10 phases, and Thomas Mann Baynes in 12 to 16 phases, for a scientific toy then called the Fantascope.

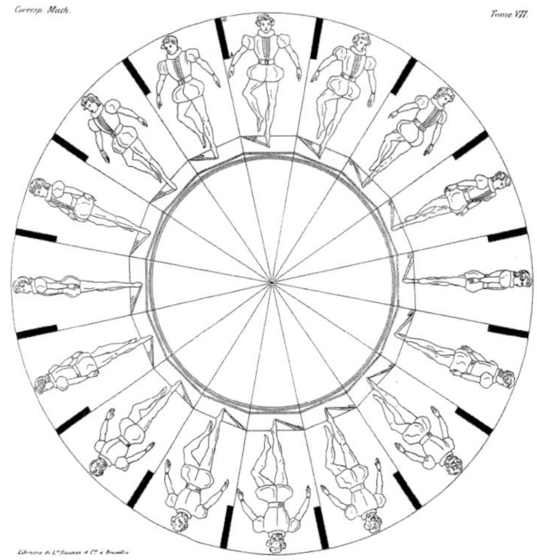

Plateau's first phenakistiscope disk, a dancer drawn by himself in 16 phases and exhibited in 1832, was published by Rudolph Ackermann in London in 1833. [Mannoni, Campagnoni & Robinson, *Light and Movement*, 228.]

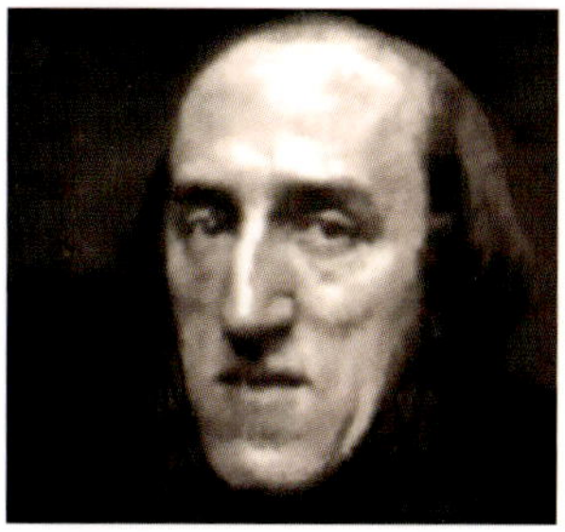

Joseph Antoine Ferdinand Plateau in 1843, a decade after his first publication of the phenakistiscope. [Wikipedia.]

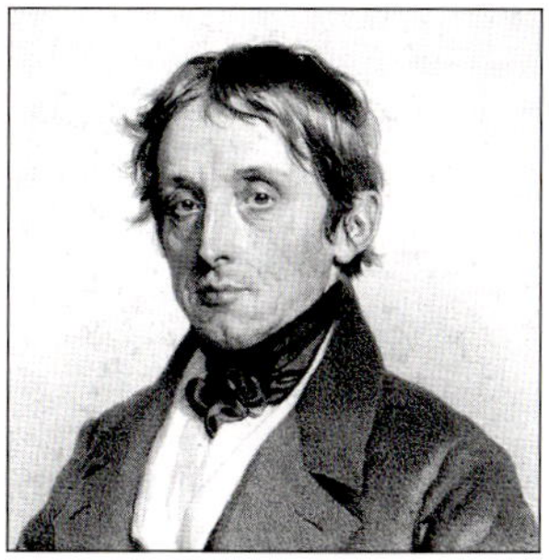

Simon Stampfer in 1842, nine years after describing his phenakistiscope device, called the Stroboskop. [Lithograph by Joseph Kriehuber, 1842. Public Domain.]

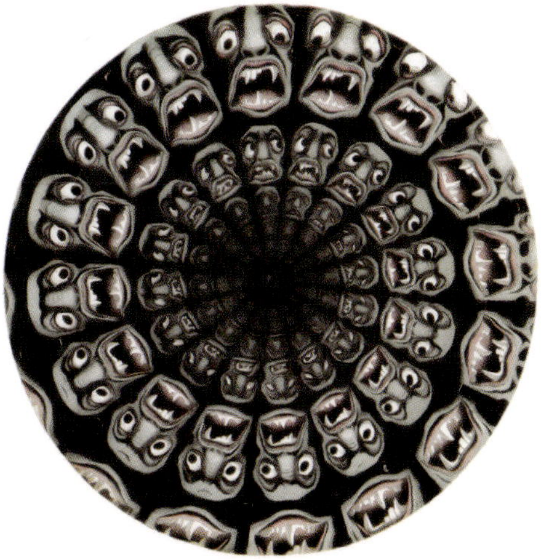

This demon drawn by Plateau was a part of one of the three sets of phenakistiscope disks published in 1833 by Rudolph Ackermann in London. [Werner Nekes Collection.]

April 24:

Completing research begun in December 1832, the Austrian Professor of Geometry Simon Stampfer at the k. k. Polytechnischen Institute in Vienna requests a patent (Privileg) for his *Stroboskop*, a phenakistiscope viewer for animated images. A disk with phases of painted movement, incorporating between them thin radial slots, when spun and observed in a mirror created an illusion of motion for the viewer. By February 1833 Stampfer had prepared six double-sided disks, and his *Privilegium der österreichischen Monarchie Nr.1920* was granted on 7 May 1833 for two years. A viewer and a set of double-sided disks 28–29 centimeters in diameter each containing from 8 to 13 images was quickly published by the firm of Trentsensky & Vieweg in Vienna, with

15 The phenakistiscope is also in some places spelled phenikistiscope, phenakistoscope, or phenikistikop, and at times appears under further names such as Fantaskop, Stroboscope or Stroboskop, or Phorolyt, amongst many others. Throughout this text the proprietary name will be noted if possible, but the device is always identified as a phenakistiscope.

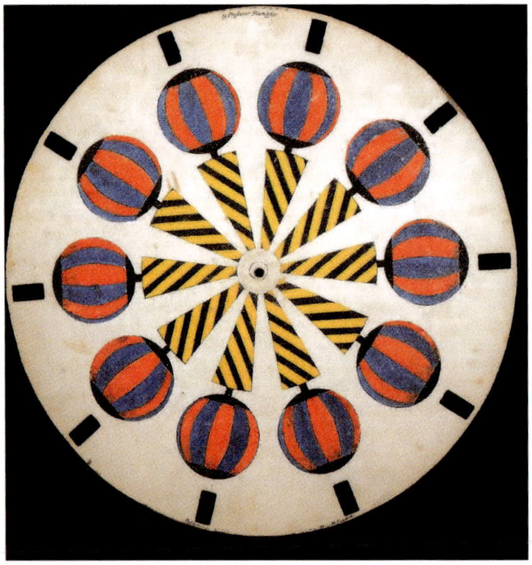

One of six double-sided phenakistiscope disks prepared by Simon Stampfer and published in 1833 by Matthias Trentsensky in Vienna. [Werner Nekes Collection.]

a second set of disks following in the same year. Stampfer's patent clearly understood all of the implications of his stroboscopic display and its possibilities: "... in this way it will be possible not only to represent the workings of machinery of various kinds, for example wheels and forges, rolling wagons and rising balloons, but also the most diverse gestures and movements of humans and animals can be surprisingly shown. Also, through the application of the same principles by means of other mechanical arrangements self-constructed actions can be shown, for example theatrical scenes, workshops captured in action, etc., just as through slides of the usual sort drawn pictures may be represented."

1834

(1.) Wherever the observer is placed, whether near the cylinder or remote from it, *all the objects* depicted on the inner surface of the cylinder are visible to him at one and the same time. This is a highly paradoxical phænomenon; but the explanation of it is involved in the deductions already made. For, if we assume P to be coincident with A, or make $\vartheta = \pi$ and $\psi = \frac{1}{2}\pi$, we have $\phi = \frac{\pi}{2} + \sin^{-1}\frac{a}{d}$, which is equivalent to the arc TBD, contained between the tangent ET and the diameter AD. Consequently the point T is the projected place of the point A, and TBD, the portion concave toward the eye, is the projection of the whole semicircle ABD. And so of the other semicircle AtD, which is projected on tD. But the thickness of the material will obstruct the view of a small portion adjacent to T and t.

(2.) Wherever the eye is placed, the divisions of the projected picture are sensibly equal in breadth, especially toward the central parts. For since $\sin^{-1}\frac{a \sin\psi}{d} = \frac{a\psi}{d} - \frac{a(d^2-a^2)\psi^3}{6d^3}$ &c., if we neglect the second and following terms, which are evidently small, we have $\phi = \vartheta - \psi + \frac{a\psi}{d}$ exceedingly near;

Excerpt from William George Horner's mathematical analysis of the zoetrope in his publication in the *London and Edinburgh Philosophical Magazine* of January, 1834. William George Horner, *The London and Edinburgh Philosophical Magazine and Journal of Science*, Vol. 4, January–June 1834, pp. 36–41. [Public Domain.]

January:
The British mathematician William George Horner describes the zoetrope in optical detail for the first time, as a rotating hollow cylinder with vertical slots in its high rim through which drawn phases of movement mounted on the interior of the cylinder could be "displayed to unlimited numbers [of viewers] at once". This was an adaptation of the phenakistiscope that did not use a mirror, but his design became widely known only in the 1860s. Horner's description of the instrument, which he called the Daedaleum, was predominantly a mathematical discussion of the visual principles involved in stroboscopic vision.[16]

16 In 1833, Simon Stampfer had published a brochure describing a rotating cylinder with images mounted inside its rim that were viewed through slots. He further described an endless band of images mounted between slots in the band and rotated between two horizontal rollers. The brochure was included with the second edition of his phenakistiscope disks sold by Trentsentsky & Vieweg, and republished in 1834 in the *Jahrbücher des k. k. polytechnischen Instituts* (Wien), v. 18, pp. 237–258; see esp. p. 244.

1841

January 27:
Jan Evangelista Purkyně (or Purkinje) lectures to the Schlesischen Gesellschaft für vaterländische Kulture in Breslau on the operation and use of his Phorolyt, a phenakistiscope with separate picture and shutter disks rotating on the same axis, thusly eliminating the need for a mirror when using the device. This small adaptation in the Phorolyt also brings an independent shutter (the closer disk with slots) into use in stroboscopic viewing for the first time. Noting the work of Stampfer, Paris, Horner and others, Purkyně also suggested the use of three-dimensional moving photographs in the device. The apparatus was marketed publicly in two sizes for Christmas 1841.[17]

Phorolyt disk of a hand with a quill pen writing the letter 'a' in 8 phases. The disk is 12,3 cm in diameter and was published by Ferdinand Durst in Prague. [Cinématheque française, Inv. AP-94-0366.]

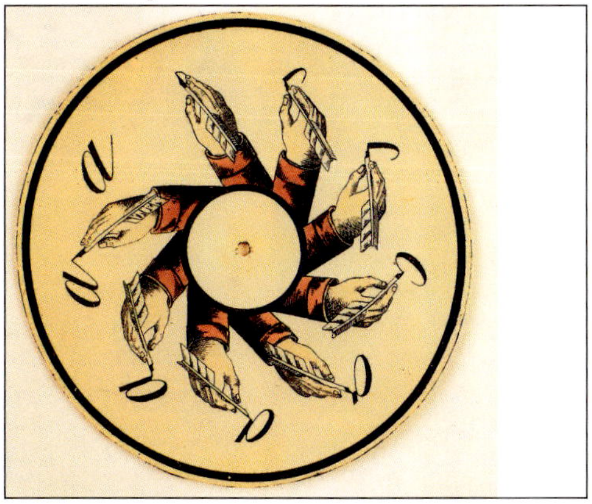

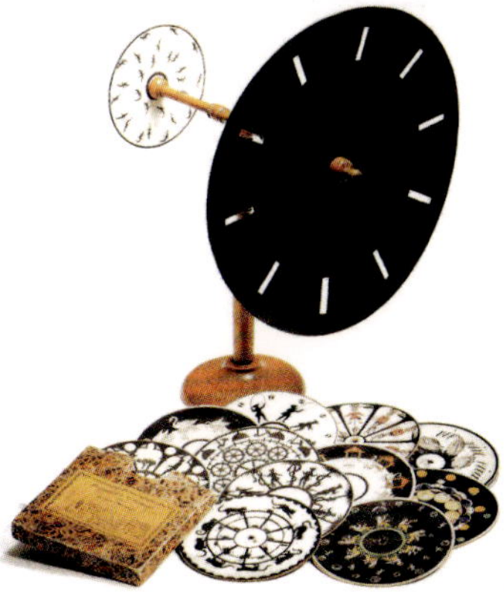

Phorolyt with its retail box and 12 disks, published by Ferdinand Durst in Prague. [Deutsches Museum, Munich.]

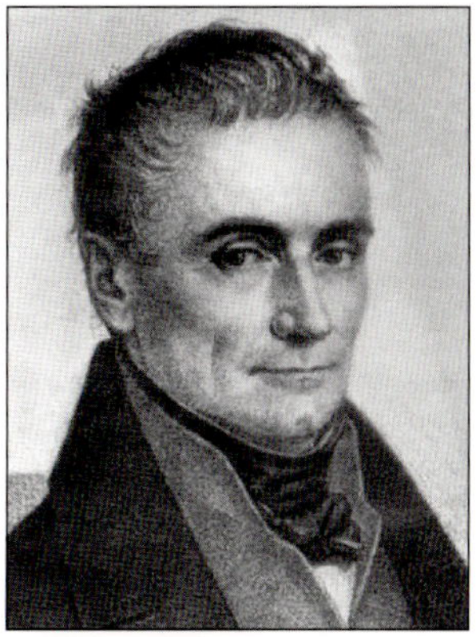

Jan Evangelista Purkinjě in Breslau, 1837. [Public domain.]

February 19:
Jan Evangelista Purkyně lectures again to the Schlesischen Gesellschaft für vaterländische Kulture in Breslau on the principles on which the Phorolyt was constructed.

1843

February 12:
T. W. Naylor of Newcastle-upon-Tyne writes to *The Mechanic's Magazine, Museum, Register, Journal and Gazette,* which publishes his description of a "Phantasmagoria for the Exhibition of Moving Pictures", a projecting phenakistiscope; the magazine published the letter on April 15. The apparatus combined imagery from published phenakistiscope disks with a magic lantern, the images traced in transparent inks onto a glass disk which was rotated between the lantern's condenser lens and its objective lenses. Between the two objective lenses a shutter disk rotated on the same axle. The *Mechanic's Magazine* article was reprinted in Germany and led both Franz Freiherr von Uchatius and Leopold Ludwig Döbler to their own projecting phenakistiscopes. Naylor, who remains obscure, preferred tracings of the phenakistiscope disks of Rudolph Ackermann, 96 Strand, London, which sometimes had two animated images of 12 phases each on either side of a single disk. Naylor's letter mentions specifically: a fat man eating, with a dog jumping up to snatch his food; a nest of serpents gliding sinuously from the centre off the edge of the disk; a lady and gentleman waltzing; quadrille dancers; an Indian juggler; a pair of duellists; a drummer; and a bell-ringer.[18]

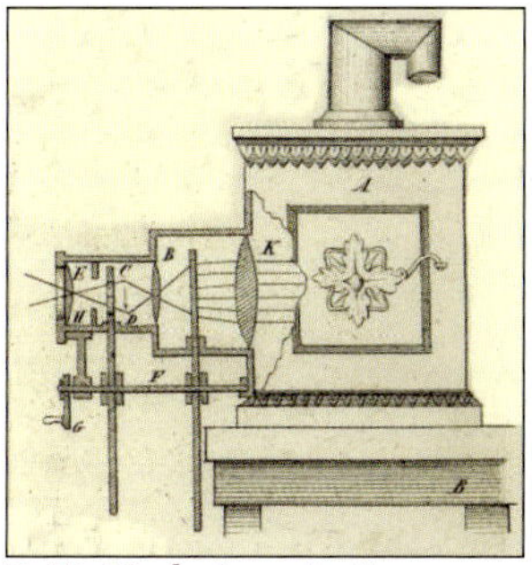

T. W. Naylor's projecting phenakistiscope, as published in *Dinglers Polytechnisches Journal* (Tübingen) in January, 1844. [*Dinglers Polytechnisches Journal*, January 1844. Public Domain.]

17 Purkyně was an eminent scientist, working at universities in Prague and Breslau (today Wrocław) who made lasting contributions to vision and the structure of the eye, the circulation of blood, the physiology of the heart and the characteristics of the nervous system. It is the Purkinje fibres which he described in the heart which today transmit the signals of a pacemaker. He also identified the unique structure of fingerprints, and saw their usefulness in solving crimes.

18 Reports on Naylor's projecting phenakistiscope were published in *Dingler's Polytechnisches Journal* (Tübingen) in January, 1844, and in the *Illustrierte Zeitung* (Leipzig) on 11 May 1844. A later correspondent to *Mechanic's Magazine* queried whether "there is any mistake of the printer, the engraver of the diagram" after having tried to construct the apparatus himself and "found it will not answer the representations of Mr. N." (*Mechanic's Magazine*, v.38, 17 June 1843, p. 505)

1845

Franz Freiherr von Uchatius produces his first projecting phenakistiscope, built by the Vienna optician and instrument maker Wenzel Prokesch. This was a modification of Naylor's apparatus with transparent images on a glass disk mounted behind a shutter disk, both rotated on the same axle and now both placed between the lantern condenser lens and its two objective lenses, using a fixed oil lamp illumination. According to Uchatius' own account in 1853 (see below) the device produced very dim images of only about 6 inches diameter. According to Hecht (p. 119, No. 210) the images from Naylor's apparatus would have been sharper and brighter because of the placement of its shutter disk at the optical convergence point between the two objective lenses, in contrast to the much wider optical path interrupted in this machine of Uchatius.

Franz Freiherr von Uchatius in 1881 at the end of his long career, in the uniform of a Field Marshall. [Drawing by Mathea K , Österreichische Nationalbibliothek.]

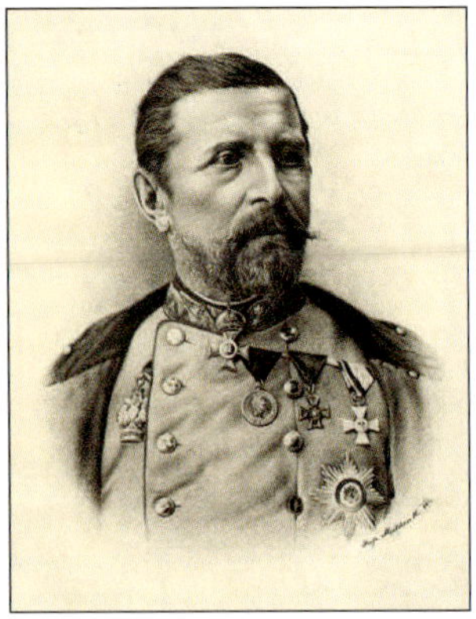

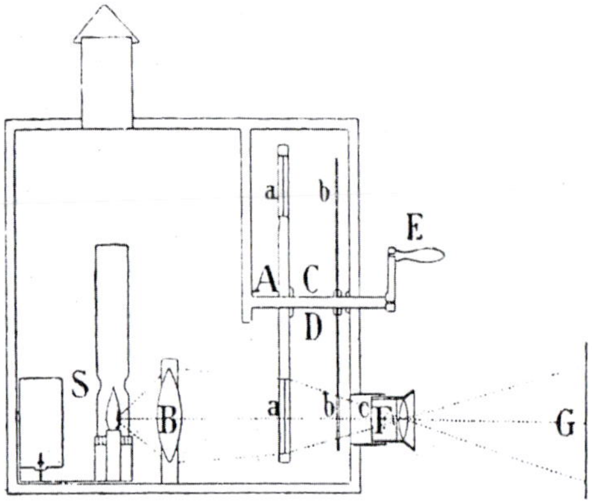

The first projecting phenakistiscope of Franz Uchatius, powered weakly by an oil lamp. [*Sitzungsberichte Wiener Akademie der Wissenschaften, mathematisch-naturwissenschaftlichen klasse*, v10 (1853), opposite p. 484. [Public domain.]

1847

January 3:
Imperial Austrian patent [Privilegium] submitted by Leopold Ludwig Döbler for his projecting phenakistiscope, called Phantaskop. Granted as No. 4829 on 23 January 1847 for a period of two years, and assigned by Döbler to Wenzel Prokesch. The device used 12 fixed lenses in front of 12 transparent figures painted on a glass plate. Illumination from a fixed limelight burner passed in succession through each projection lens by means of a rotating mirror and two interior lenses. The apparatus was built by the Vienna firm of Wenzel Prokesch, Laimgrube 47, at a reputed cost of more than 4000 Gulden, and although Prokesch was assigned the patent, no further copies of the machine are known to have been made. The sequenced images were painted by Hr. Geyling. This was a modification and improvement on both the 1843 apparatus of T. W. Naylor and the 1845 apparatus of Franz Freiherr von Uchatius.[19]

Leopold Ludwig Döbler in 1847. [Oil painting by either Joseph Matthias Aigner or Johann Christian Schoeller, Historical Museum, Vienna.]

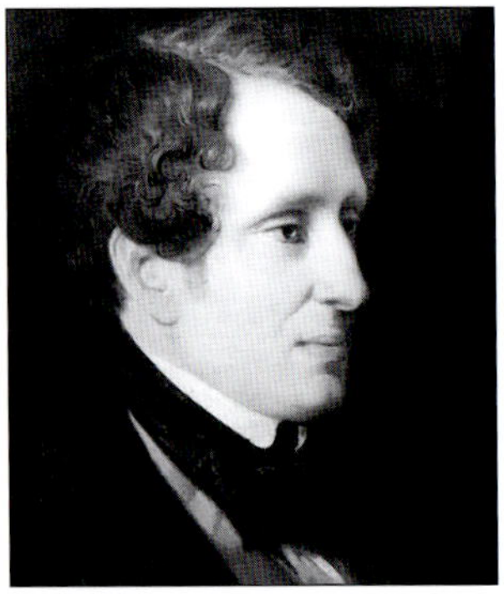

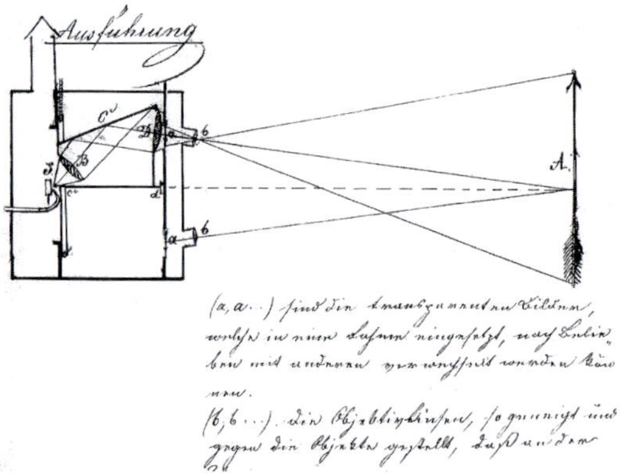

Excerpt from Döbler's patent application with his drawing of the Phantaskop, showing its rotating illuminant that passed by 12 lenses and images in succession.
[Wiener Stadt- und -Landesbibliothek, Handschriftensammlung.]

19 There is a great deal of confusion in almost all printed accounts of the relationship of Döbler and Uchatius, with many erroneously reporting that the Döbler projecting phenakistiscope had been bought from Uchatius and was in use for more than a decade.

January 16:
Phantaskop of Leopold Ludwig Döbler opens at the Josephstadt Theatre, Vienna, for 25 performances through 8 February. The phenakistiscope projections were preceded by a series of dissolving views and followed by a display of chromatropes. Music used throughout was by court composer Anton Emil Till. The Austrian emperor, Ferdinand I, attended on 22 January, along with Archduke Franz, the Prince of Salerno, and other dignitaries. The shows were frequently sold out, but detailed reviews were not impressed with the quality of the Phantaskop images. The eight sequenced images, painted by Hr. Geyling, included *The Turkish Conjuror*, *The Ring Jumper, Small Parade*, *The Woodcutter*, *The Chinese Conjuror*, *The Strutting Dancer*, *The Tightrope Walker* and *The Duellists*.[20]

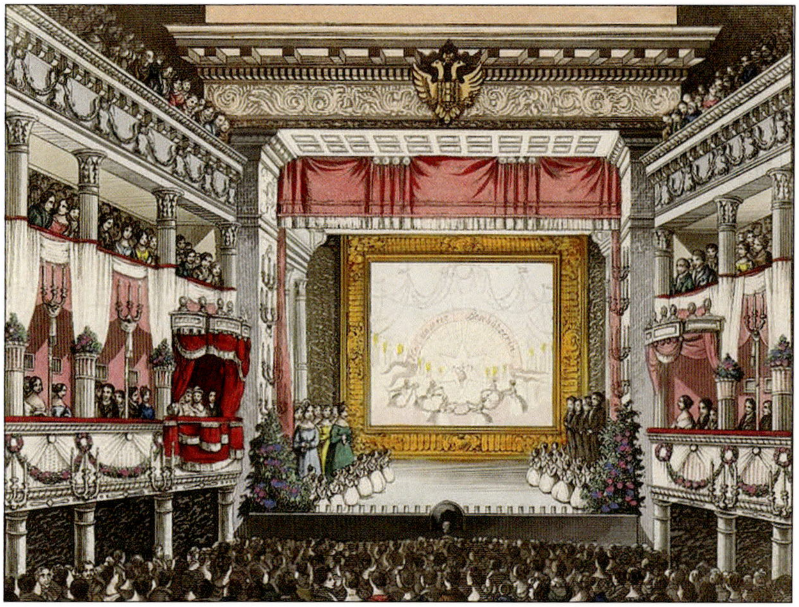

Interior of the Theater in der Josefstadt, 1844. The smallest private theatre in Vienna, it had 1004 seats. [*Costumebild der Theaterzeitung*, Vienna. Wikimedia Commons. Public Domain.]

March 7 or 8:
Phantaskop of Leopold Ludwig Döbler at the theater in Brünn (today Brno) for two performances. In Brünn, Döbler gave a benefit performance for the St. Cyrill children's hospital, collecting 328 Gulden, 21 Kreuzer.

Facade of the Reduta Theater in Brünn (today Brno), built in 1787.
[Photo: Petr Šmerkl, Wikipedia. Public Domain.]

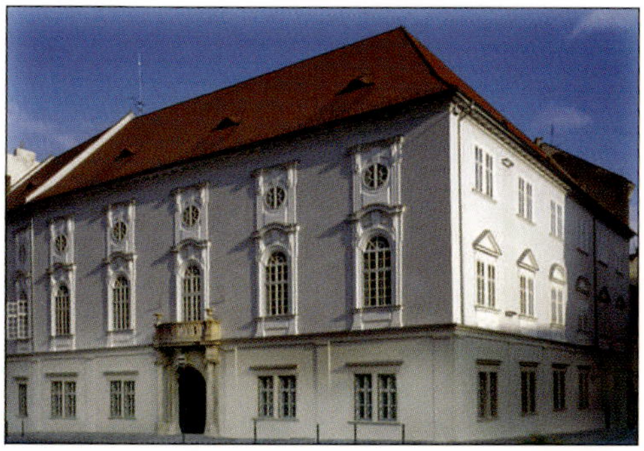

March 22:
Phantaskop of Leopold Ludwig Döbler re-opens at the Josephstadt Theatre, Vienna, likely for one week. For these shows Döbler combined his Phantaskop disks with dissolving views projecting changing background scenery.

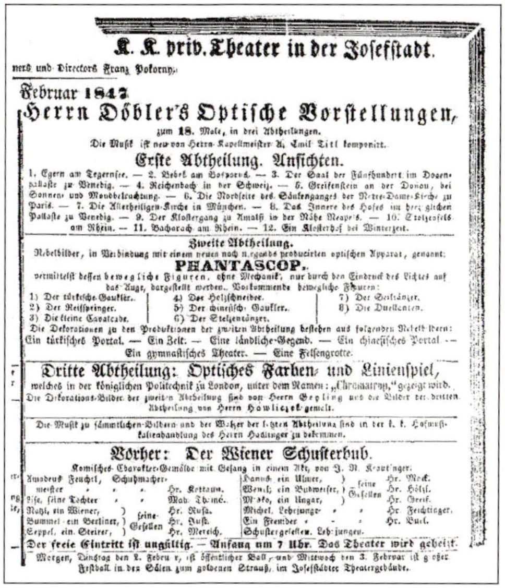

K. K. priv. Theater in der Josefstadt.

ners und Directors Franz Pokorny.

Februar 1847

Herrn Döbler's Optische Vorstellungen,

zum 18. Male, in drei Abtheilungen.

Die Musik ist neu von Herrn Kapellmeister A. Emil Titl komponirt.

Erste Abtheilung. Ansichten.

1. Egern am Tegernsee. — 2. Bebek am Bosporus. — 3. Der Saal der Fünfhundert im Dogenpallaste zu Venedig. — 4. Reichenbach in der Schweiz. — 5. Greifenstein an der Donau, bei Sonnen- und Mondbeleuchtung. — 6. Die Nordseite des Säulenganges der Notre-Dame-Kirche zu Paris. — 7. Die Allerheiligen-Kirche in München. — 8. Das Innere des Hofes im herzoglichen Pallaste zu Venedig. — 9. Der Klostergang zu Amalfi in der Nähe Neapels. — 10. Stolzenfels am Rhein. — 11. Bacharach am Rhein. — 12. Ein Klosterhof bei Winterzeit.

Zweite Abtheilung.

Nebelbilder, in Verbindung mit einem neuen noch nirgends producirten optischen Apparat, genannt:

PHANTASCOP,

vermittelst dessen bewegliche Figuren, ohne Mechanik, nur durch den Eindruck des Lichtes auf das Auge, dargestellt werden. Vorkommende bewegliche Figuren:

1) Der türkische Gaukler.	4) Der Holzschneider.	7) Der Seiltänzer.
2) Der Reifspringer.	5) Der chinesische Gaukler.	8) Die Duellanten.
3) Die kleine Cavalcade.	6) Der Stelzentänzer.	

Die Dekorationen zu den Produktionen der zweiten Abtheilung bestehen aus folgenden Nebelbildern: Ein türkisches Portal. — Ein Zelt. — Eine ländliche Gegend. — Ein chinesisches Portal. — Ein gymnastisches Theater. — Eine Felsengrotte.

Dritte Abtheilung: Optisches Farben- und Linienspiel,

welches in der königlichen Politechnik zu London, unter dem Namen: „Chromatrop," gezeigt wird.

Die Dekorations-Bilder der zweiten Abtheilung sind von Herrn Geyling und die Bilder der dritten Abtheilung von Herrn Howliczek gemalt.

Die Musik zu sämmtlichen Bildern und der Walzer der letzten Abtheilung sind in der k. k. Hofmusikalienhandlung des Herrn Haslinger zu bekommen.

Vorher: Der Wiener Schusterbub.

Komisches Charakter-Gemälde mit Gesang in einem Akt, von J. N. Krautinger.

Amadeus Feuchtl, Schuhmachermeister		Hr. Kettauer.
Lise, seine Tochter		Mad. Thomé.
Natzl, ein Wiener,	seine Gesellen	Hr. Rusa.
Bummel, ein Berliner,	seine Gesellen	Hr. Rust.
Seppel, ein Steirer,	seine Gesellen	Hr. Mereich.
Hannes, ein Ulmer,	seine Gesellen	Hr. Meck.
Wenzl, ein Budweiser,	seine Gesellen	Hr. Hölzl.
Misko, ein Ungar,	seine Gesellen	Hr. Greif.
Michel, Lehrjunge		Hr. Feichtinger.
Ein Fremder		Hr. Buel.
Schustergesellen. Lehrjungen.		

Der freie Eintritt ist ungültig. — Anfang um 7 Uhr. Das Theater wird geheizt.

Morgen, Dingstag den 2. Februar, ist öffentlicher Ball, und Mittwoch den 3. Februar ist großer Festball in den Sälen zum goldenen Strauß, im Josefstädter Theatergebäude.

Detail of the programme for Döbler's performance at the Theater in der Josefstadt, Vienna, on 7 February 1847. [Vienna Stadt- und -Landesbibliothek. Public Domain.]

June 5:
Phantaskop of Leopold Ludwig Döbler opens at the Royal Court-Theatre, Munich.

1847 undated:
possible additional Döbler Phantaskop performances in Olmütz, Hamburg, Budapest, Graz.

20 The two main sources here, by Kaldy-Karo and Debler, have slightly different accounts of these shows, based on their separate use of original newspaper sources. Both need to be consulted in seeking further information on Döbler and his Phantaskop, and both also list unresearched shows. As perhaps due to the annual hometown appearance of one of Europe's most famous conjurors, the reviews were sometimes ecstatic, but some close observers disagreed. Siegfried Reissek at the Academy of Sciences contended that "the Turkish juggler threw his balls around so randomly that one could not tell how they might return to his hands ... *The Ring Jumper* is not properly drawn in his individual images ... the same failings are again found in *The Chinese Conjuror* ...", etc. The original titles of the projected disks are: 1. *Der türkische Gaukler*. 2. *Der Reifspringer*. 3. *Der kleine Cavalcade*. 4. *Der Holzschneider*. 5. *Der chinesische Gaukler*. 6. *Der Stelzentänzer*. 7. *Der Seiltänzer*. 8. *Die Duellanten*. It is clear again here that the subjects were often inspired by published phenakistiscope disks.

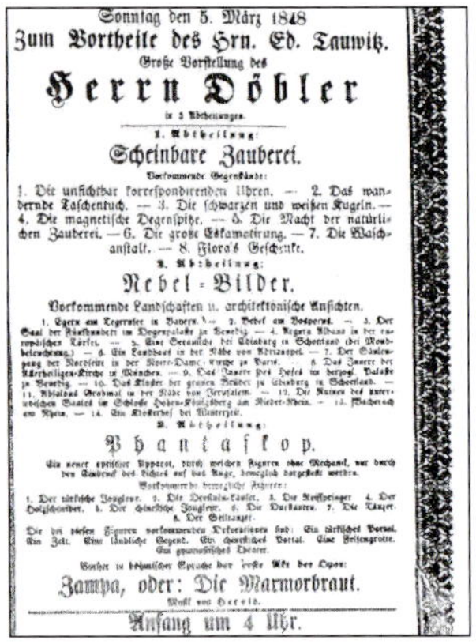
Sonntag den 5. März 1848
Zum Vortheile des Hrn. Ed. Tauwitz.
Große Vorstellung des
Herrn Döbler
in 3 Abtheilungen.

1. Abtheilung:
Scheinbare Zauberei.
Vorkommende Gegenstände:
1. Die unsichtbar korrespondirenden Uhren. — 2. Das wandernde Taschentuch. — 3. Die schwarzen und weißen Kugeln. — 4. Die magnetische Degenspitze. — 5. Die Macht der natürlichen Zauberei. — 6. Die große Eskamotirung. — 7. Die Waschanstalt. — 8. Flora's Geschenke.

2. Abtheilung:
Nebel-Bilder.
Vorkommende Landschaften u. architektonische Ansichten.
1. Egern am Tegernsee in Bayern. — 2. Nebel am Bosporus. — 3. Der Saal der Fünfhundert im Dogenpalaste zu Venedig. — 4. [illegible] in der europäischen Türkei. — 5. Eine Seeansicht bei Edinburg in Schottland (bei Mondbeleuchtung.) — 6. Ein Landhaus in der Nähe von Adrianopel. — 7. Der Säulengang der Nordseite in der Notre-Dame-Kirche zu Paris. — 8. Das Innere der Allerheiligen-Kirche in München. — 9. Das Innere des Hofes im herzogl. Palaste zu Venedig. — 10. Das Kloster der grauen Brüder zu Edinburg in Schottland. — 11. Absolons Grabmal in der Nähe von Jerusalem. — 12. Die Ruinen des unterirdischen Saales im Schlosse Hohen-Königsberg am Nieder-Rhein. — 13. Bacherach am Rhein. — 14. Ein Klosterhof bei Winterzeit.

3. Abtheilung:
Phantaskop.
Ein neuer optischer Apparat, durch welchen Figuren ohne Mechanik, nur durch den Eindruck des Lichtes auf das Auge, beweglich dargestellt werden.
Vorkommende bewegliche Figuren:
1. Der türkische Jongleur. 2. Die [illegible]. 3. Die Reifspringer. 4. Der Holzschneider. 5. Der chinesische Jongleur. 6. Die [illegible]. 7. Die Tänzer. 8. Der Seiltänzer.
Die bei diesen Figuren vorkommenden Dekorationen sind: Ein türkisches Portal. Ein Zelt. Eine ländliche Gegend. Ein chinesisches Portal. Eine Felsengrotte. Ein [illegible] Theater.
Vorher in böhmischer Sprache der erste Akt der Oper:
Zampa, oder: Die Marmorbraut.
Musik von Herold.

Anfang um 4 Uhr.

1848

March 4:
Phantaskop of Leopold Ludwig Döbler opens at the Bohemian National Theatre, Prague, with a benefit for the theatre's chorus.

March 5:
Phantaskop of Leopold Ludwig Döbler opens at the Bohemian National Theatre, Prague, with a benefit for the retiring actor Ed. Tauwitz.

1848 undated: Possible additional Döbler Phantaskop performances in Prague, Brünn, Stuttgart, plus performances in Vienna (private) and Klafterbrunn (private).

Detail of the programme for Döbler's benefit for the actor Ed. Tauwitz in Prague. The other half of the programme was given in Polish.
[Archive of the Museum für Unterhaltungskunst, Vienna.]

1852

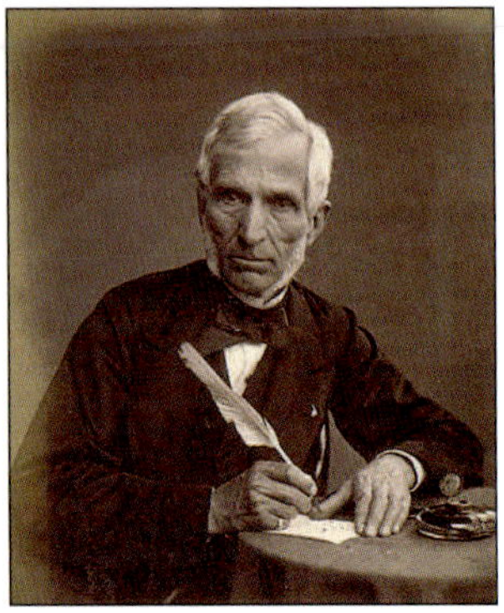
Antoine Claudet, c1860.
[Photo: Thomas Rodger, c1860, St Andrews University Library.]

May 22:
Antoine Claudet writes to *La Lumiére* that he has constructed a stereoscope for moving pictures, showing "for example a woman working with a needle and making all the appropriate movements". Claudet would make the same claim again, using the same image description and also citing the date of 1852, in a letter to *The Photographic Journal* of November 16, 1865.

November 12:
Addition to French patent 13,069 of February 16, 1852, *Système d'instrument dit stéréoscope, faisant paraître en relief des images photographiques faites sur des surfaces planes, même sur des matières transparents, du verre, etc., et pouvant projeter les images agrandies sur des écrans,* of Jules Duboscq for alterations to his stereo viewer to allow the viewing of animated stereoscopic photographs. Twelve or more pairs of images were mounted around a cardboard disk which was then viewed in the stereoscope by means of two small angled mirrors. This device was a handy evolution of Wheatstone's stereo viewer, advertised by Duboscq in several models, and was one of his array of stroboscopic devices produced in the early 1850s, including several variants of projecting phenakistiscopes which could be set in front of a magic lantern.

1853

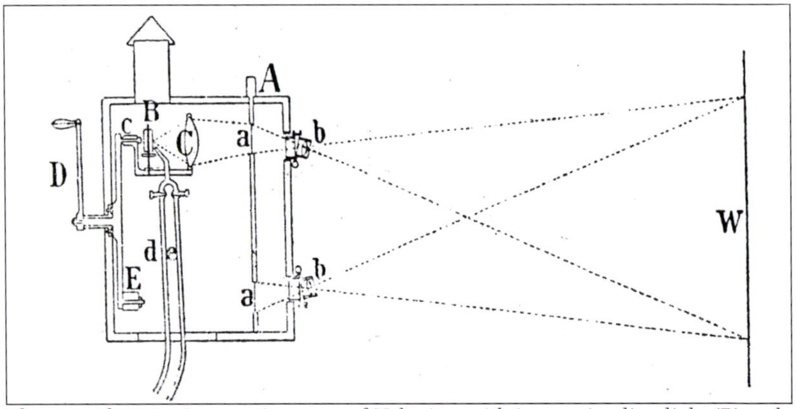

The second projecting praxinoscope of Uchatius, with its rotating limelight (B) and condenser lens (C), passing in front of 12 painted images (a) and lenses (b).
[*Sitzungsberichte Wiener Akademie der Wissenschaften, mathematisch-naturwissenschaftlichen klasse*, v10 (1853), opposite p. 484. Public domain.]

April 21:
Franz Freiherr von Uchatius demonstrates the second model of his projecting phenakistiscope at a meeting of the natural sciences branch of the Royal Academy of Science, Vienna. Built by the Vienna instrument maker Wenzel Prokesch, this was an improvement of Döbler's 1847 apparatus, now also using limelight illumination. Twelve images painted on a fixed glass plate were arranged in front of 12 lenses, and a unit consisting of the small limelight burner and a condenser lens was rotated inside the lantern housing so that each image was illuminated in turn. The projected image was now up to as much as two meters in height with significantly brighter illumination.

July 12:
Franz Freiherr von Uchatius demonstrates the second model of his projecting phenakistiscope at his home in Vienna for a half-dozen guests, including Ludwig Leopold Döbler and his wife Elise.[21]

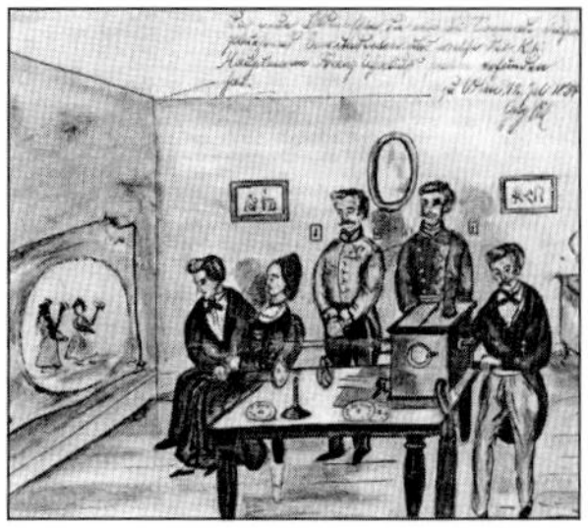

Franz Uchatius demonstrating his second projecting phenakistiscope for friends at his home in Vienna, probably including Ludwig Döbler and his wife Elise.
[Robert Kaldy-Karo, *Ludwig Döbler, genius des biedermeier*, p. 207.]

1855

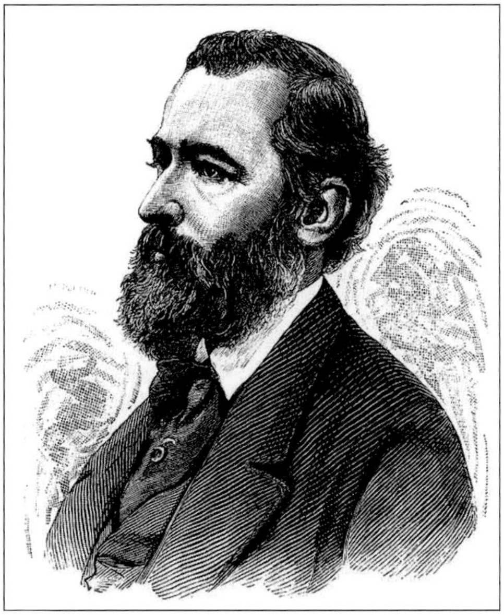

Johann Nepomuk Czermak in 1873.
[Wikimedia Commons. Public Domain.]

January 18:
Johann Nepomunk Czermak addresses a meeting of the Natural Science branch of the Royal Academy of Science in Vienna and presents 20 papers on his physiological studies, one of which describes his Stereophoroscope viewer, a combination of Purkyně's Phorolyt and a stereoscope. Czermak had studied with Purkyně at Breslau, and this device derived from his teacher's instruments comprised a horizontal octagonal drum of prisms with a large-diameter octagonal band of images facing the mirrors. When rotated, and seen with a hand-held stereo viewer through horizontal slots cut into in the outer band, a three-dimensional impression of a moving subject was observed. Something like a vertical zoetrope with mirrors, Czermak stated that he had used the instrument "for a long time", and that recent progress in photography, especially in Paris, would make the device easier to use in physiological investigations of vision. This apparatus is the ancestor, if not the direct inspiration, for Reynaud's praxinoscope (see below).[22]

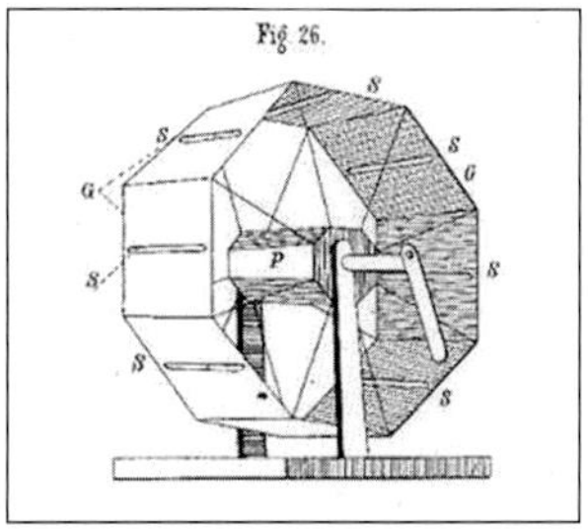

The Stereophoroscope of Johann Czermak, announced in 1855 but "in use for a long time".
[Johann Czermak, *Physiologische Studien*, Taf. III, Fig. 26. Public Domain.]

1860

February 27:
United Kingdom patent 537, *Improvements in Apparatuses for Exhibiting Photographic, Stereoscopic, and other Pictures, Models, Figures, and Designs*, to Peter Hubert Desvignes for a series of cylindrical stroboscopic viewing devices including variants of vertical and horizontal zoetropes, a phorolyt, and a viewer with a long band stretched over two cylindrical hubs. The patent is an unusual summary of stroboscopic design and knowledge, involving precise descriptions and construction details for two dozen viewers, some illuminated by sparks or electrical lights and intended for projection. Although first described in the 1830s, the zoetrope was only

21 The dated watercolour by Georg Dill that establishes this private demonstration of the apparatus is the only known image of any projecting phenakistiscope in use. The drawing was published in black-and-white in Kaldy-Karo, *Ludwig Döbler, genius des biedermeier*, p. 207, who cited a private collection. I traced the collector, who had since died, and the two institutions who divided his extensive collection of prints, the Stadtmuseum Munich and the Historisches Museum, Hannover, but both contend that the original watercolour is not in their possession. Original presumed lost.

22 The connection to the praxinoscope is as follows: Czermak was the outstanding advocate of the use of audio-visual tools in education in Germany. In France, the same public advocacy of audio-visual education was most prominently led by the Abbé François Moigno. These two public politicians for visual education undoubtedly knew of each other's work, although no-one has yet looked for a direct relationship or for correspondence. At the beginning of his career, Charles-Emile Reynaud attended a course of lectures on projection given by Moigno in Paris in July, 1864, and rapidly became a friend of Moigno and then his assistant, preparing slides and working in Moigno's laboratory until December 1865 when he and his mother left Paris. There is more work to be done here, but knowledge of Czermak's Sterephoroscope could have had a very direct route to Reynaud while he was working with Moigno.

now achieving widespread popularity, as Desvignes brought his own design to market in Britain just as zoetropes made by the Milton Bradley Company in America also appeared.[23]

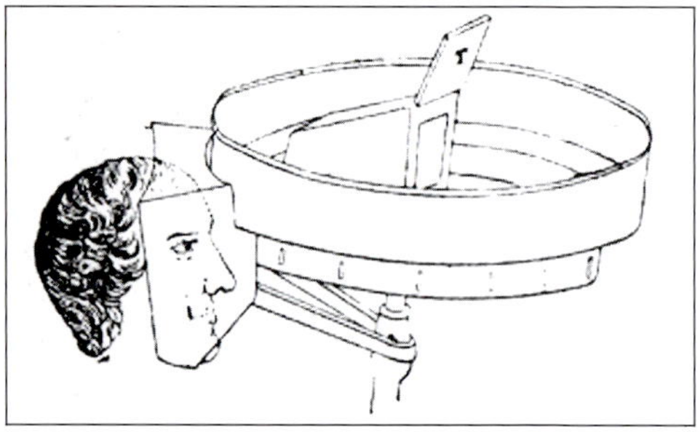

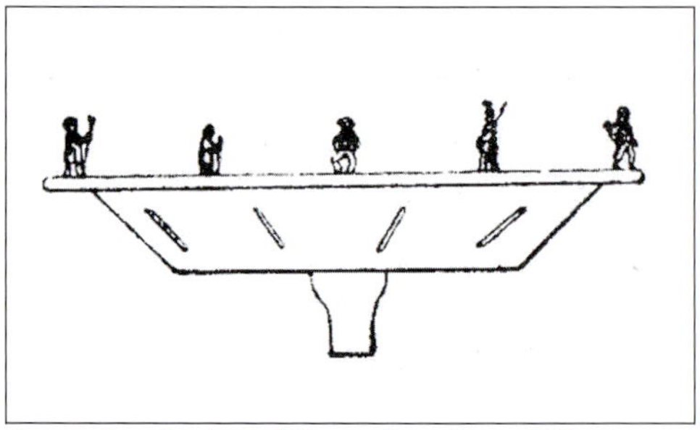

Two of Desvignes' many suggestions in his patent. A zootrope with the slots below the image band, viewed through an immobile interior channel that limited the field of vision, and another using three-dimensional figures mounted on the rim of the cylinder. [United Kingdom patent 537 of 1860, Figs. 5 & 22.]

May 22:
United Kingdom patent 1260, *Improvements in Thaumatropes or Phenakistoscopes*, to William Thomas Shaw, for a stereo phenakistiscope based on Wheatstone's reflecting stereoscope, where an elaborate gearing system synchronizes the rotation of two phenakistiscope disks outfitted with stereo photographs and two shutter disks. When activated, three-dimensional objects appear in motion. No reduction to practise is known, but this patent reflects the intense interest in moving stereoscopy at mid-century.

1861

February 5:
United States patent 31,357, *Exhibiting Stereoscopic Pictures of Moving Objects*, to Coleman Sellers of Philadelphia, for his Kinematoscope, a rotating drum with stereo photographs mounted radially and viewed through an eyepiece as a peep-show. Related to a vertical zoetrope, the device was intended to rotate fast enough to allow the individually posed photographs to represent limited motion. Produced as a toy and used in his home, images for the Kinematoscope included Sellers hammering and his wife sewing. In 1941 his grandson wrote "My recollection is that the motion was very smooth...".[24]

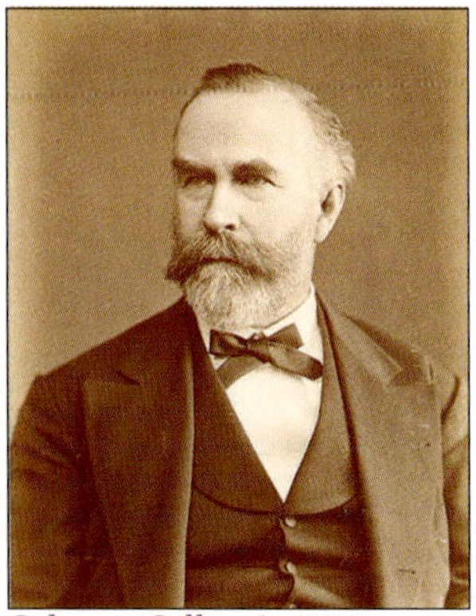

Coleman Sellers in 1875. [Photograph by W. Curtis Taylor, 1875. Public Domain.]

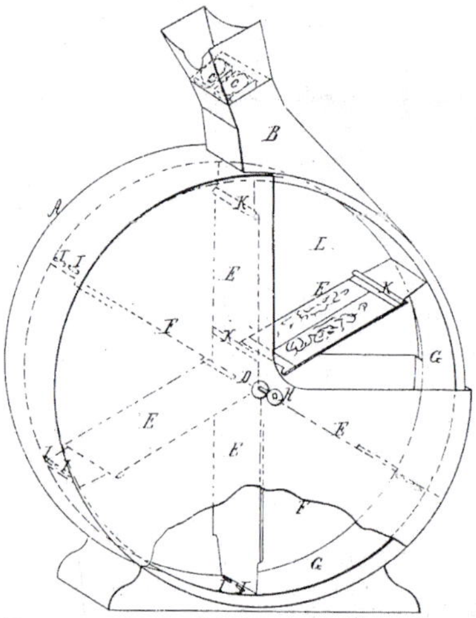

The Kinematoscope of Coleman Sellers, for producing the effect of motion from stereographic photographs. Fig. 1 from his US patent. [United States patent 31,357, Fig. 1.]

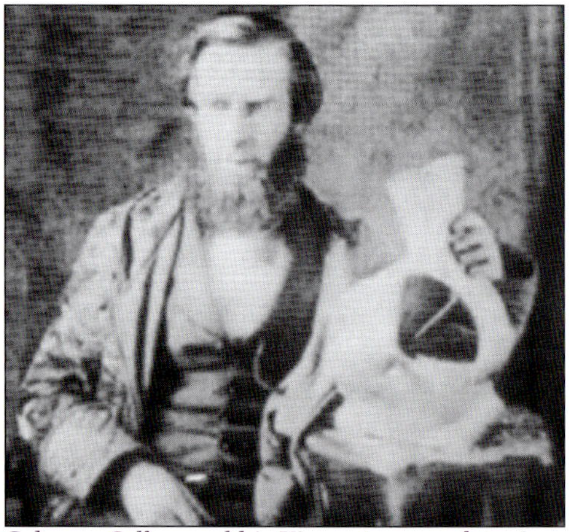

Coleman Sellers and his Kinematoscope, later in life. (c1890?) [Fernando Camarero Rioja, *Los Animales y la Invención del Cine*, p. 134.]

23 Born in Constantinople in 1804, Desvignes grew up in London, was educated at the Royal Academy of Arts, and then was a pupil of the architect William Atkinson. He became a noted architect and interior designer, working for over a decade on the refurbishment of the Stadtpalais Liechtenstein in Vienna, the residence of the principality's ruling family and a project costing (then) some 11 million Gulden. Returning to England in 1849 and settling in Lewisham, Desvignes may have continued working on house interiors for the aristocracy, but this detailed patent of optical devices is the major known artifact of his last 30 years.

24 Coleman Sellers was an experienced machine tool designer and manufacturer who later turned to electrical work and oversaw the construction of the first electrical generating plant at Niagara Falls, New York. An active officer of the Franklin Institute, as was his friend Henry Heyl, he was President of the institution from 1870 to 1874. The patent was assigned to Sellers and G. Burnham of Philadelphia.

June 8:
UK patent 1457, *A Photographic Apparatus, having for Object to Reproduce the Successive Phases and Shiftings of a Motion*, to Henry Du Mont, for a novel photographic camera either using plates affixed to a drum in motion, or plates arranged vertically and dropping rapidly by means of gravity. This was a first attempt at producing a camera for sequence photography, but the idea was defeated by the available photographic processes of the time: wet collodion plates could not be prepared and stored in advance, and dry plates were very insensitive and unable to photograph movement.

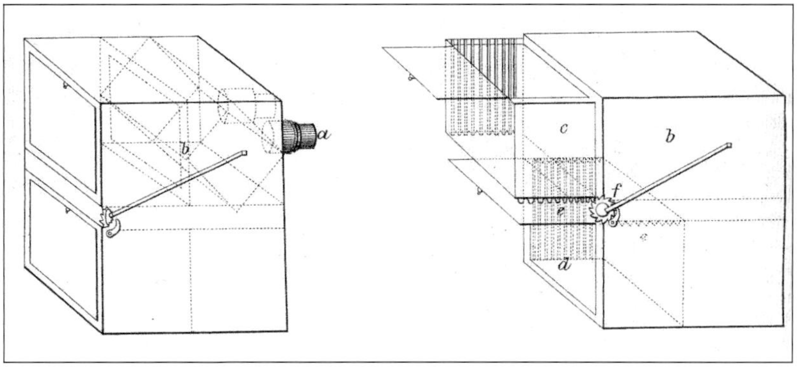

Two views of Du Mont's gravity-fed camera for fast plate changes. It was still too slow to produce an illusion of movement with the photographic chemistry of its day. [United Kingdom patent 1457 of 1861, Figs. 1 and 2.]

June 24:
Jan Evangelista Purkyně demonstrates his improved phenakistiscope, now called the Kinesiskop, to a meeting of the Natural Sciences division of the Königlichen böhmischen Gesellschaft der Wissenschaft in Prague. This was a renamed and slightly modified Phorolyt, with a much larger diameter shutter disk and a significantly smaller picture disk holding nine photographs of individually taken phased motion. A disk demonstrating the phases of the beating heart of a sheep was shown at the meeting, and a disk with Purkyně's own head slowly revolving is also known. He used the Kinesiskop (then called Kinescope) for over a decade in his teaching, and the Vienna optician Ferdinand Durst manufactured the device for sale.

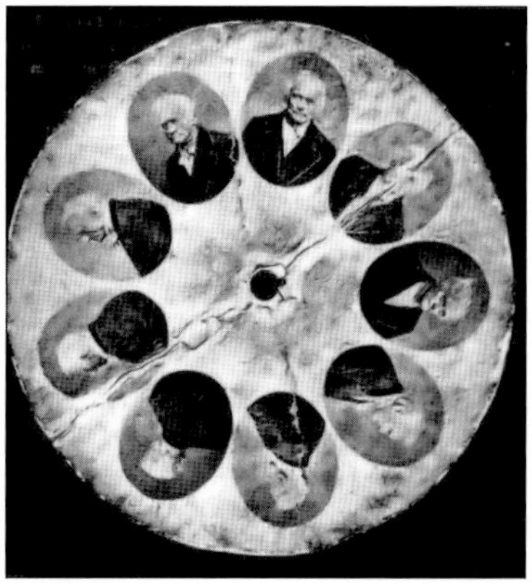
Kinesiskop disk of Purkinje turning his head. The apparatus used still photographs posed in sequence to generate an illusion of movement.
[Karel Smrz, *Dějiny Filmu*, p. 155.]

1862

June 13:
James Liang writes to a friend that yesterday (June 12) he had the first satisfactory results with his Motoroscope, a device for exhibiting stereoscopic views in motion. Liang, the Dundee inventor of a flax-spinning frame, a pneumatic oil can, and other devices, experimented at first with a zoetrope using both slots and stereoscope lenses for viewing, but found the number of pictures too limited to raise the desired effect, and began working with a long band holding the slots (on the outside) and pictures (on the inside) that revolved around two vertical rollers and was viewed through a rectangular stereo lens. Liang, whose work is today cited only by Stephen Herbert, is representative of a number of figures who attempted to blend stroboscopic disks, the zoetrope, and stereo vision together in a new optical device.

1864

March 14:
The Motoroscope of Dundee inventor James Laing is presented to the Royal Scottish Society of Arts at their meeting in Edinburgh. The device consisted of a long band revolving around two vertical rollers, viewed through a rectangular lens and intended to exhibit stereoscopic moving pictures. Under sporadic development for at least two years, the Motoroscope was essentially an extended zoetrope that could theoretically display an unlimited number of stereo photographs. The only known image for the device was of an animated wooden village, with revolving windmill sails and smoke drifting from a cottage chimney. Liang predicted that the difficulty of producing sequenced photographic stereo images would be overcome in future by "the hands of a willing and skillful photographic artist". Liang's paper was read in his absence, and the device was demonstrated by the Secretary, which "excited considerable interest", and after some discussion the paper was "remitted to a Committee".

1865

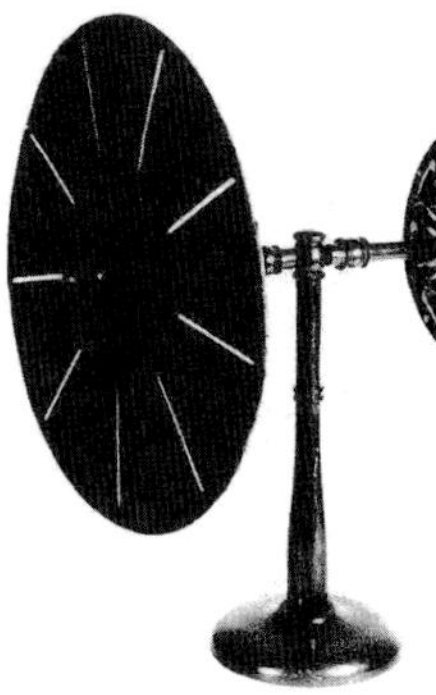

August 31 – September 3:
Jan Evangelista Purkyně lectures with his Kinesiskop, now rearranged for projection by means of a magic lantern, at the 11th Congress of Hungarian Doctors in Pressburg (today Bratislava). The lecture on the operation of the heart and its valves caused a sensation at the conference, not least because of the large-scale moving illustrations of a pumping heart that accompanied it.

The Kinesiskop of Jan Evangelista Purkinje, here with a disk of the beating heart of a sheep that was part of his university lectures in Prague for many years.
[Fernando Camarero Rioja, *Los Animales y la Invención del Cine*, p. 132.]

1867

March 6:
United Kingdom patent 629, *An Improved Mode of and Means for Producing Optical Illusions*, to Henry Watson Hallett for a zoetrope with an adjustable stand to facilitate both viewing and the illumination of the images in the drum. This patent seems to stem from the Milton Bradley company in Springfield, Massachusetts, as Hallett's address is given first as Springfield and "now of No. 8, Southampton Buildings, Chancery Lane, in the county of Middlesex", and then is referenced as "A communication from abroad by Milton Bradley, of Springfield". This patent strands as a recognition of the popularity of the Zoetrope at the time.

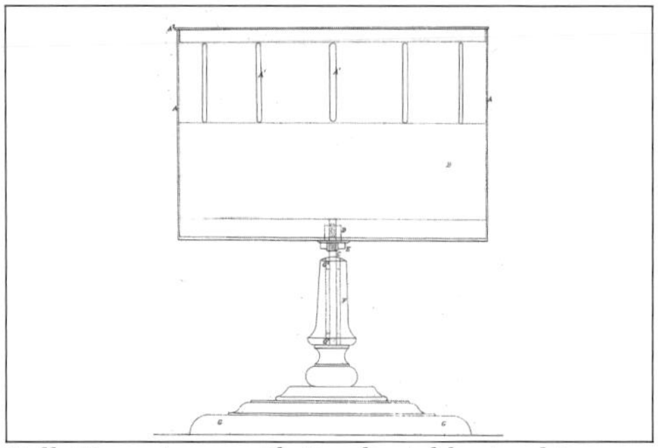

Hallett's zoetrope with its adjustable stand to facilitate both viewing and the illumination of the drum.
[United Kingdom patent 629 of 1867, Fig. 2.]

April 23:
United States patent 64,117, *Toy*, to William E. Lincoln of Providence, Rhode Island, for a zoetrope, using the term for the first time. This is a very basic patent for the device, adding only a patterned disk at the bottom of the cylinder, and where it is belatedly claimed that "the great advantage of this invention over all other toys based on the same optical illusion is, that with this any number of persons can, by placing it in the centre of the room, be able easily to see, at the same time, all the movements". The patent was assigned to Milton Bradley & Co., Springfield, Massachusetts.

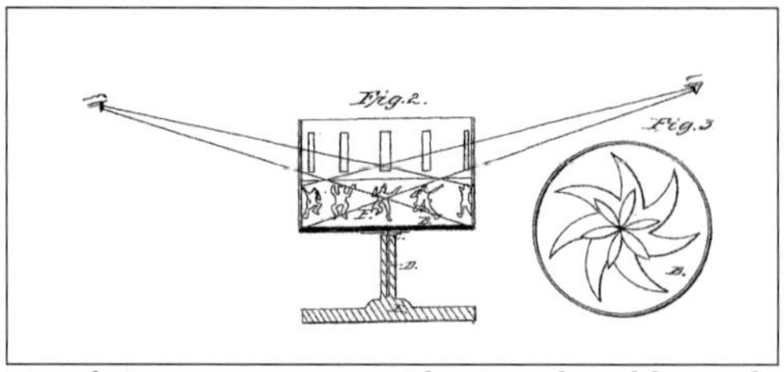

Lincoln's zoetrope patent, showing the additional imagery he suggested for the base of the zoetrope cylinder.
[United States patent 64,117, Figs. 2 and 3.]

1868

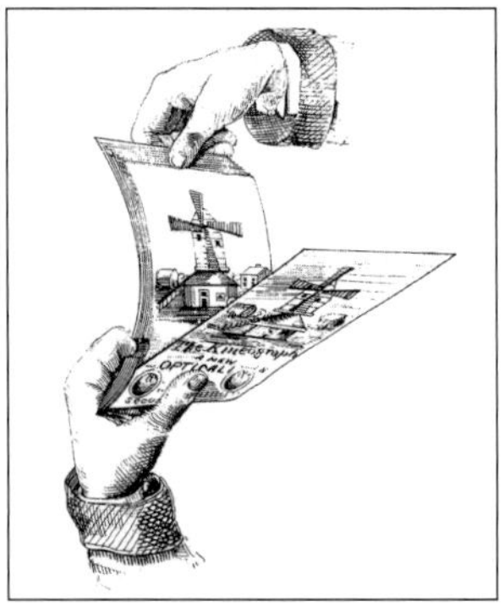

March 18:
United Kingdom patent 925, *Improvements in the means of producing Optical Illusions*, to John Barnes Linnett, a printer in Birmingham, for a flip book with drawn phases of movement, which he called The Kineograph. He also provided for the use of photographic images in flip books, as well as double-sided printing to provide two moving pictures in each book, and suggested "the said leaves, sheets, or cards may be turned over by mechanical means with the same effect". The patent illustration shows the turning sails of a windmill, an image of movement available for the magic lantern since at least 1736 when Petrus van Musschenbroek published the image of a windmill in his selection of moving slides. Linnett published about a dozen Kineograph booklets, including the windmill, a jumping skeleton, a sailor dancing a jig and removing his hat, two duellists, and others.

March 27:
Joseph Maurice leaves his specification for *Improvements in the Means or Method of Producing Optical Illusions* at the UK Patent Office. Maurice received provisional protection only for a device using a phenakistiscope, zoetrope, or similar "motion apparatus" combined with a "transparent mirror or glass" placed onstage so that a strong light on the images in the motion apparatus will find them reflected on the glass. Maurice's text implies he has been using this stage effect for some time; it seems to be a miniature version of Pepper's Ghost, but also implies the (reflected) projection of stroboscopic imagery.

1869

August 10:
United States patent 93,594, *Optical Instrument*, to O. B. Brown of Malden, Massachusetts, for his projecting phenakistiscope, which he called the Phœnocinopticon. A small disk painted with phased movement was intermittently moved by a linked gear motivated by a revolving pin. A two-bladed shutter disk revolved in front of the projection lenses of a magic lantern, and the entire unit was built to fit into a standard lantern slide stage. An adjustable aperture mounted inside the lamphouse before the lens opening insured that only one picture at a time was projected by the intermittent unit. The patent refers to the work of Naylor, Duboscq and others. Obediah Brown advertised his patent for sale at least twice, and exhibited the machine at an industrial exhibition in Boston in 1870. The instrument entered the historical literature very early as "the first moving picture projector", which it clearly is not, and this phrase continues to be used in error widely today on the Internet in conjunction with references to Brown's patent.

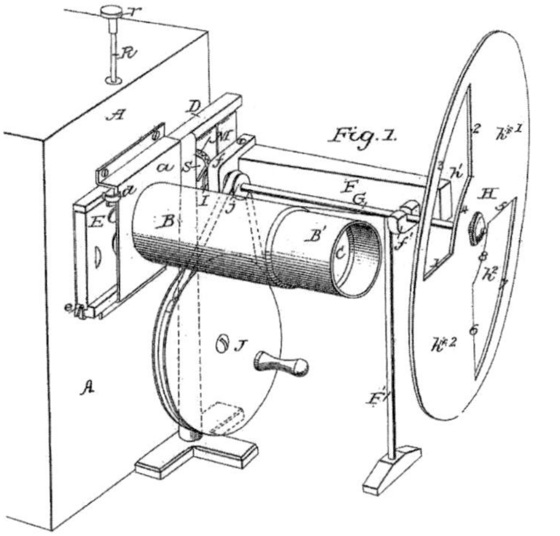

Left: The projecting phenakistiscope of O. B. Brown, with its mechanical intermittent mounted in the slide stage of a standard magic lantern. [United States patent 93,594, Fig. 1.]

The Phœnocinopticon—An application of the principle of the Zoetrope to the Magic Lantern. Patent for sale. Send for circular. O. B. Brown, 126 Tremont st., Boston.

Below: One of Brown's advertisements for the sale of his patent. [Courtesy Peter Domankiewicz.]

1870

February 5:
Modern research by Peter Domankiewicz shows that the Phasmatrope of Henry Heyl purportedly exhibited at the Academy of Music, Philadelphia on this date, did not actually take place. Although this date (and the following one on 16 March), are deeply ensconced in the history of moving pictures, there is no contemporary evidence of this apparatus in 1870. Heyl claimed in an 1898 letter that this performance was "the origin of the movies", a claim evidently accepted for the last 121 years. His letter claimed three separate projections using disks showing a couple dancing a waltz, a Japanese acrobat performing a somersault, and Brother Jonathan (as the US mascot Uncle Sam was then known) making a speech, which would have been a sensation at the time. The programme of the event at which Heyl claimed his Phasmatrope was in use makes no mention of the device, and there are no contemporary newspaper reports of the Phasmatrope in use.[25]

March 16:
Modern research (see above) shows that there is no record in the minutes of the Frank-

25 Henry Heyl was a professional inventor, most notably of the first practical wire office stapler for paper, and of a method of using wire staples instead of thread in bookbinding, which when combined with new printing technology led to the mass production of inexpensive books. He was an officer of the Franklin Institute, as was his friend Coleman Sellers. His Phasmatrope and the disk of the waltzing couple was sold to the Franklin Institute after his death, and was recently 'mislaid' and unavailable to researchers. Peter Domankiewicz has looked at Heyl extensively, and finds no contemporary sources for this event, apart from Heyl's own later claims in 1898. There is also no record of the Phasmatrope being demonstrated at the regular monthly meeting of the Franklin Institute on 16 March. In 1898 Heyl wrote to the *Journal of the Franklin Institute* recalling these screenings and suggesting they were the origin of moving pictures. See Peter Domankiewicz, *Was the Phasmatrope a Phantoscope Phantasy? Henry Heyl and Moving Pictures.* (Privately circulated, intended for publication soon.)

lin Institute, or in press reports of their monthly meeting on this date, that would confirm that the Phasmatrope of Henry Heyl was demonstrated on this date at the Franklin Institute in Philadelphia. The only claim for the Phasmatrope on this date comes from a letter Henry Heyl wrote to the Franklin Institute in 1898. (See footnote above.)

1876

July:
The *British Journal of Photography* publishes a description of the first known photographic sequence that records a physical body in motion in real time, achieved by the phototographer and painter James Ross of Edinburgh. Three images of a boy jumping over a large stone. A weighted drop shutter with a small opening was used on a strip of three 'medallion' lenses in a multi-lens camera made for the taking of multiple copies of the same subject. Ross was interested in 'instantaneous' photography, recording a girl skipping rope and a girl on a swing at its apogee, but the three images of a boy jumping a large stone could qualify as the earliest known chronophotograph.

November 9:
Provisional UK patent 4344, *Improvements in Apparatus for Taking a Succession of Photographic Pictures and for Exhibiting Such Pictures*, to Wordsworth Donisthorpe for a linked plate changer and lens shutter that would "facilitate the taking of a succession of photographic pictures at equal intervals of time" so that a subsequent printed paper strip of the recorded movements could be used in a zoetrope or phenakistiscope. The patent was never carried to a full specification.

1878

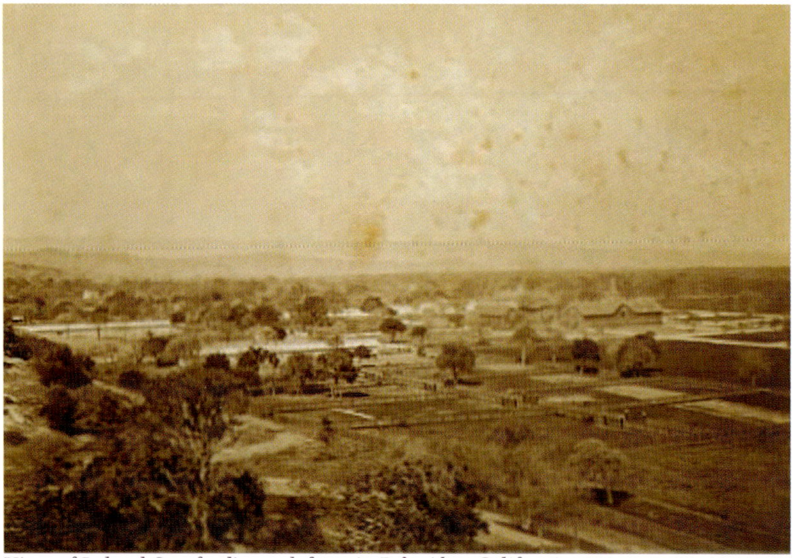

View of Leland Stanford's stock farm in Palo Alto, California, c1881. [Library of Congress, public domain.]

Patent detail of the electrical release for Muybridge's spring-loaded double-acting shutters in use at Palo Alto. [United States patent 212,865, Sheet 2, Figure 1.]

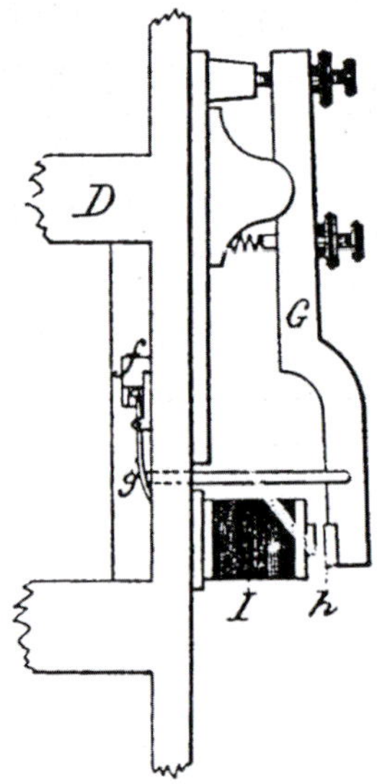

June 11:
Eadweard Muybridge takes the first sequence photographs at Leland Stanford's ranch at Palo Alto, using 12 Scoville cameras with Dallmeyer stereo lenses. This was the first session of his chronophotographic work at Palo Alto in 1878–79.

June 27:
US patent 212,865, *Improvement in the Method and Apparatus for Photographing Objects in Motion*, to Edward J. Muybridge for his double-acting shutters motivated by electro-magnets and released by wires strung across the track at Palo Alto. The patent also covers Muybridge's painted backdrop with its numbered vertical lines "to show the position and progress of the horse and his posture at each exposure".[26]

July 11:
US patent 212,864, *Improvement in the Method and Apparatus for Photographing Objects in Motion*, to Edward J. Muybridge for his spring-loaded double-shutter for instantaneous photography, plus his arrangement of series cameras including the shutter-releasing strings across the horse track at Palo Alto.

Patent detail of Muybridge's spring shutter release used in Palo Alto, tripped by wires strung across the horse track.
[United States patent 212,864, Figure 2.]

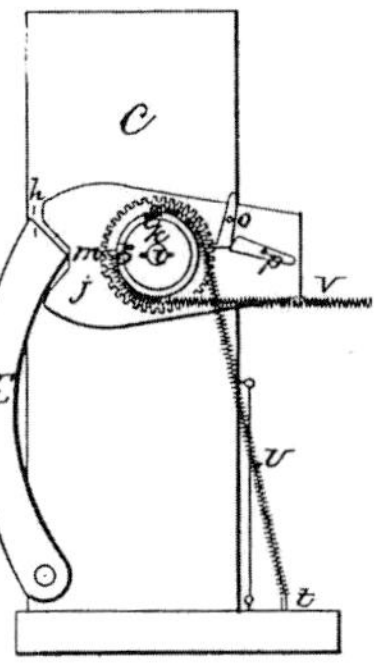

1879

January 25:
L'Illustration (Paris) reports that the expert horseman Emile Duhousset has mounted Muybridge series photographs in a zoetrope with good results. The same issue offers for the zoetrope several bands of Muybridge silhouette photographs at a cost of 10 francs. A few zoetropes from this period survive.

June 28:
The editor of *The Field* (London), W. B. Tegetmeier, reports in his issue of this date that he, too, had satisfactorily mounted Muybridge series photographs in a zoetrope. Tegetmeier may also have offered these zoetrope bands for sale in England under his own copyright.[27]

Late Autumn:
Eadweard Muybridge, debut of the Zoogyroscope, later called the Zoopraxiscope, at the home of Leland Stanford. Over the last weeks of the year, the apparatus was exhibited several times for Stanford and his guests.

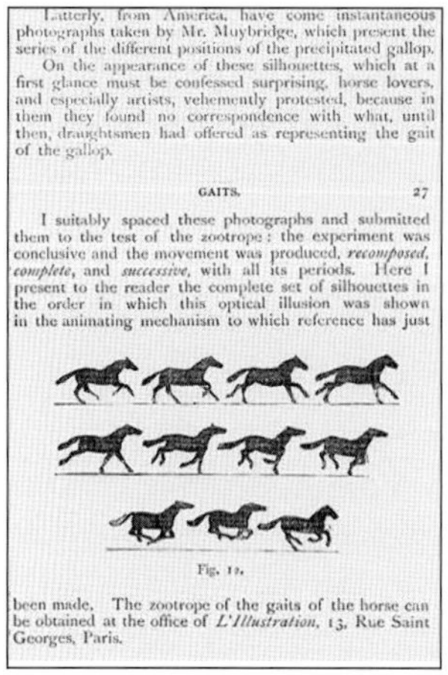

Latterly, from America, have come instantaneous photographs taken by Mr. Muybridge, which present the series of the different positions of the precipitated gallop.

On the appearance of these silhouettes, which at a first glance must be confessed surprising, horse lovers, and especially artists, vehemently protested, because in them they found no correspondence with what, until then, draughtsmen had offered as representing the gait of the gallop.

GAITS. 27

I suitably spaced these photographs and submitted them to the test of the zootrope: the experiment was conclusive and the movement was produced, *recomposed*, *complete*, and *successive*, with all its periods. Here I present to the reader the complete set of silhouettes in the order in which this optical illusion was shown in the animating mechanism to which reference has just

Fig. 12.

been made. The zootrope of the gaits of the horse can be obtained at the office of *L'Illustration*, 13, Rue Saint Georges, Paris.

Silhouettes of a galloping horse as photographed by Muybridge and used by Emile Duhousset to demonstrate the gait in a zoetrope.
[Emile Duhousset, *The Gaits, Exterior and Proportions of the Horse* (English edition), 1896. Courtesy Stephen Herbert. Public domain.]

1880

16 January:
Eadweard Muybridge demonstrates the Zoopraxiscope, then called the Zoogryoscope, in the ballroom of the home of his patron Leland Stanford, on Nob Hill in San Francisco. One of several projections at Stanford's home, including another on 20 January.

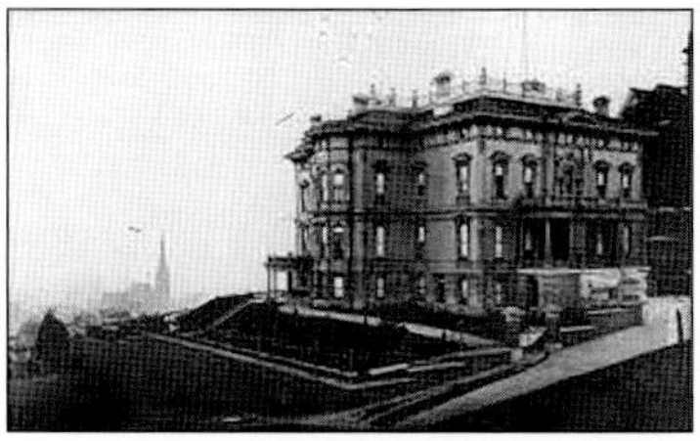

Leland Stanford's new mansion on Nob Hill at 905 California Street, San Francisco soon after its completion in 1877.
[Photograph by Eadweard Muybridge. Public domain.]

March 21:
Eadweard Muybridge demonstrates his Zooprazicope for visitors to Stanford's establishment at Palo Alto.

26 The Muybridge patents have generated much controversy right from the start, and have divided the literature which reports on them. The issue is how the sophisticated electrical shutter was developed, and the best explanation seems to be that it was John D. Isaacs, a young draftsman at Leland Stanford's Central Pacific workshops in Oakland, California, who made the first suggestion to use electricity on Muybridge's original design of the shutter, and then made working drawings. Isaacs had been called in, along with Arthur Brown, who suggested "some mechanical contrivance to work automatically, as the horse passes along", after Muybridge took a wooden model of his shutter to Stanford, who suggested Muybridge take the model to the chief engineer of his Central Pacific Railroad Company, Samuel Montague, and seek his help. Montague organized Isaacs and Brown to work with Muybridge, and the final model of the shutter was produced by Paul Seiler of the California Electrical Works in San Francisco. Isaacs was the one member of the team who thought he was short-changed, and threatened to sue Muybridge over the patent, but was restrained by his foreman at Central Pacific, Arthur Brown. See Haas 1976, 139; Prodger 2003, 147-9.

27 It is nearly impossible today to ascribe the surviving zoetropes of the period to either Duhousset or Tegetmeier. One of these zoetropes, from a private collection on the Continent, was in the exhibition I curated for the Filmmuseum Düsseldorf in 2001; another is in the Stadtmuseum München.

May 4:

Eadweard Muybridge with his Zoopraxiscope at the San Francisco Art Association, 313 Pine Street, the public debut of the apparatus. This was a press preview for Muybridge's lecture at the Art Association the next day. The presentation included series of horses as well as athletes, a bull, a deer and a dog, plus flying birds. Reporting on the event, the *Alta California* declared "Mr. Muybridge has laid the foundation of a new method of entertaining the people...".

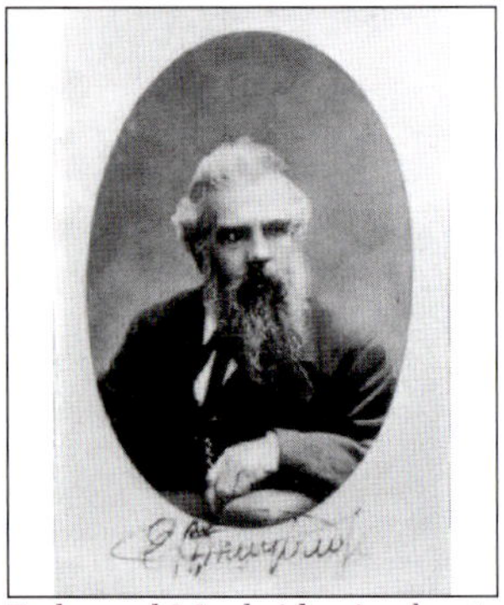

Eadweard Muybridge in about 1876, just before he began his chronophotographic studies for Leland Stanford.
[Trade card published by Bradley and Rulofson, San Francisco. Public domain.]

May 5:

Eadweard Muybridge lectures with his Zoopraxiscope for members of the San Francisco Art Association, 313 Pine Street, repeating the material shown to the press the previous day.

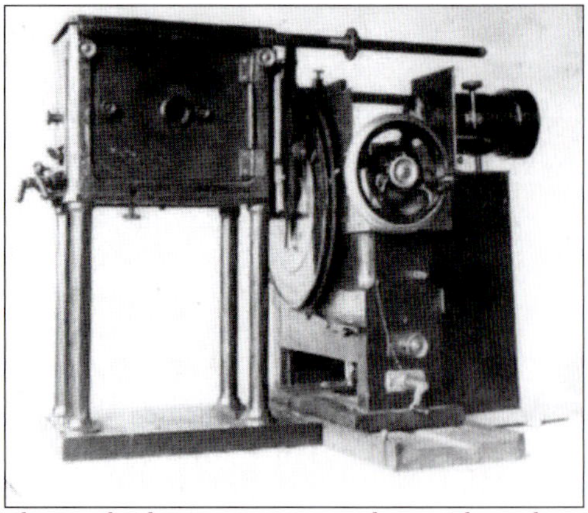

The Muybridge Zoopraxiscope, here without the crinkled chimney top from his magic lantern that was later mistakenly added to the instrument. [Photo by Eadweard Muybridge, from a lantern slide in his bequest to the Kingston Museum and Heritage Service.]

1881

August 31:

US patent 279,878, *Method of and apparatus for Photographing Changing or Moving Objects*, to Edward J. Muybridge for improved weight-driven and electrically-released double shutters for series photography.

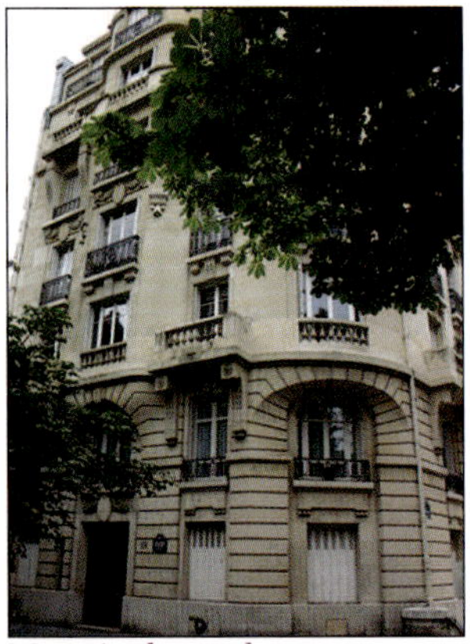

Marey's elegant house at 11 Boulevard Delessert, where he lived from 1881 to 1904, and where Muybridge gave the first European demonstration of his Zoopraxiscope. [Photo by Luca Borghi.]

September 26:

Eadweard Muybridge demonstrates the Zoopraxiscope at a reception in Paris organized by Étienne-Jules Marey, where he is the guest of honour at Marey's new home on the Boulevard Delessert. The guests included the German physician and physicist Hermann Helmholz, the Norwegian physicist and meterologist Vilhelm Bjerknes, the Mauritian physiologist and neurologist Charles-Edouard Brown-Séquard, the French physicist and researcher Eleuthère Mascart, the French physicist and physician Jacques-Arsène d'Arsonval, the French photographer and caricaturist Nadar (Gaspar-Félix Tournachon), and the French chemist and adventurer Gaston Tissandier, among others. Muybridge's trip to Europe was sponsored by Leland Stanford.

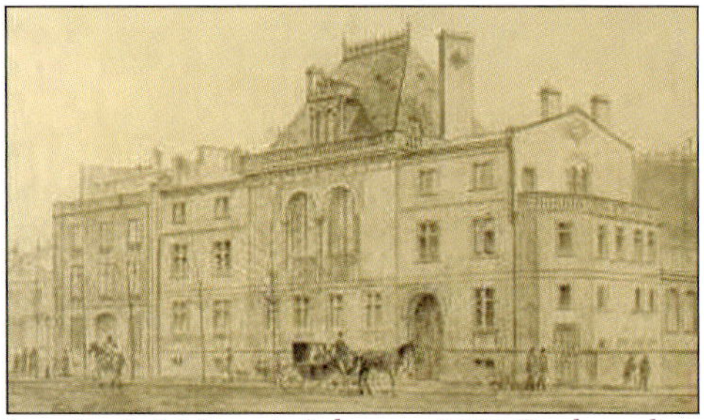

Jean-Louis Meissonier's house at 131 Boulevard Malesherbes, in a sketch by Alphonse Trimolet from January, 1882. [Les Musées de la Ville de Paris.]

November 3:

Eadweard Muybridge demonstrates his Zoopraxiscope at the home of the painter Jean-Louis Ernest Meissonier, 131 Boulevard Malesherbes, Paris, to a group of invited guests.

November 26:

Eadweard Muybridge demonstrates the Zoopraxiscope at a gala reception for 200 guests from the Parisian artistic world organized by Jean-Louis Ernest Meissonier at his home, 131 Boulevard Malesherbes, Paris. Guests included the painters Léon Bonnat, J. B. E. Detaille, and Jean Léon Gérôme, plus the author Alexandre Dumas. The projectionist for this demonstration was the scientific instrument maker and projection specialist Alfred Molteni.

December 14:

Eadweard Muybridge demonstrates the Zoopraxiscope for the Cercle de l'Union Artistique, Paris. Meissonier served as the interpreter for Muybridge.

1882

February 11:
Eadweard Muybridge lectures with the Zoopraxiscope at the Ecole des Beaux Arts, Paris, just before he leaves France for England.

March 6:
Eadweard Muybridge rehearses his upcoming lecture with the Zoopraxiscope at The Royal Institution, Albemarle Street, London.

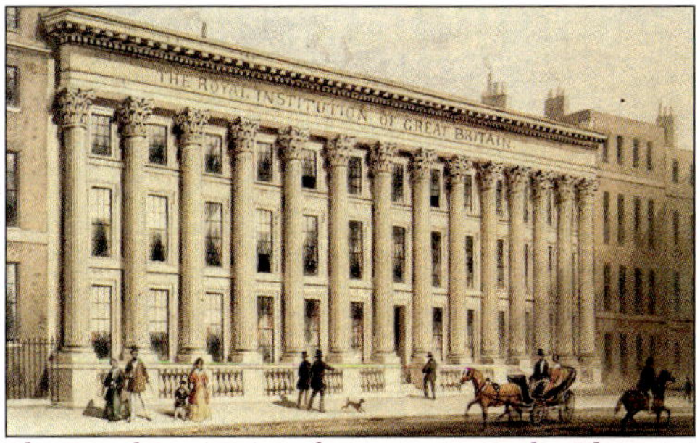

The Royal Institution, from a painting by Thomas Hosmer Shepherd. The building still stands and is in use today. [Painting by Thomas Hosmer Shepherd, 1838. Public domain.]

March 13:
Eadweard Muybridge lectures with the Zoopraxiscope at 5 p.m. at The Royal Institution, Albermarle Street, London, for an invited audience including royalty and figures from the worlds of literature and science, who included the Dukes of Westminster, Sutherland, Argyll, and Richmond. The poet laureate, Alfred Tennyson was also present, as were the biologist Thomas Henry Huxley and Prime Minister William Ewart Gladstone. The RI's patron and honorary member The Prince of Wales chaired the meeting. Due to the intense demand for seats, a second show was organized for the same evening.

March 16:
Eadweard Muybridge lectures with the Zoopraxiscope at the Royal Academy of Arts, Burlington House, London.

March 18:
Eadweard Muybridge lectures with the Zoopraxiscope at the Savage Club, Lansdown Hall, London.

April 4:
Eadweard Muybridge lectures with the Zoopraxiscope at the Royal Society for the Encouragement of Arts, Manufactures, and Commerce, John Adam Street, London.

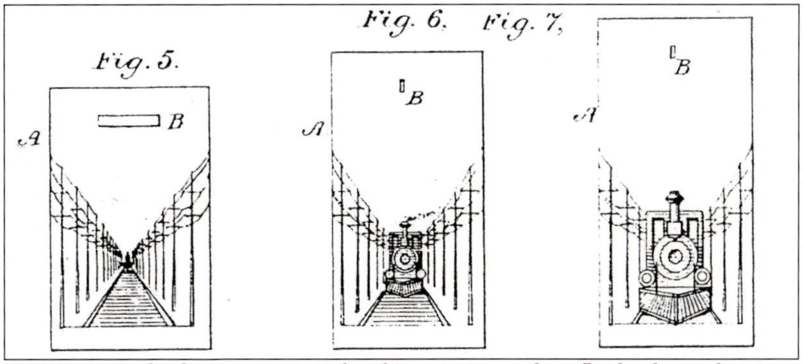

Figures 5, 6 and 7 from van Hoevenbergh's 1882 patent for a flip book, pre-figuring a major image of early cinema. [US Patent 258,164, Figures 5, 6 and 7.]

April 5:
Eadweard Muybridge lectures with the Zoopraxiscope at the South Kensington Science and Art Department [later, the Science Museum], London.

April 7:
United States patent 258,164, *Optical Toy*, to Henry van Hoevenbergh of Elizabeth, New Jersey, for a flip book. This first US patent for a flip book is very similar to previous European ones. One set of drawings illustrates an onrushing locomotive.

May 24:
United States patent 259,950, *Optical Toy*, to Henry van Hoevenbergh of Elizabeth, New Jersey, for a flip book improving his April 7 patent (above) by combining several image sequences in the same booklet.

June 5:
Eadweard Muybridge lectures with his Zoopraxiscope at the Liverpool Art Club, Upper Parliament-street. The lecture and illustrations "of a very interesting character" were seen by "a large gathering of ladies and gentlemen".

June 8:
Eadweard Muybridge demonstrates his Zoopraxiscope for a number of scientists, artists, photographers and others at the private residence of John J. Atkinson, 140 Upper Parliament-street, Liverpool. The demonstration included a shortened version of Muybridge's standard lecture, and he suggested that the results of his next experiments in America would be published in association with Jean-Ernst-Louis Meissonier and Etienne-Jules Marey, under the auspices of Robert C. Johnson, a patron of the arts in San Francisco. No such publication is known to have appeared.

July 30, or August 1:
Eadweard Muybridge, returning to America, lectures with the Zoopraxiscope in the theatre of the Newport Casino, a 500-seat hall in an athletic and cultural center at 186–202 Bellevue Avenue, Newport, Rhode Island.

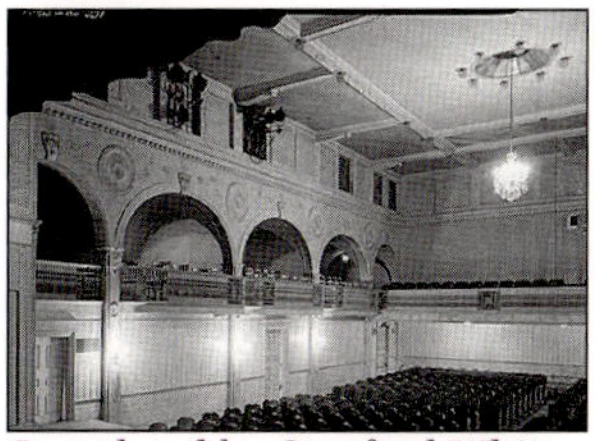
Completed by Stanford White in July 1880, the Newport Casino Theatre also hosted a lecture by Oscar Wilde in 1882.
[Photographer unknown; posted to Cinema Treasures.]

October 19:
Eadweard Muybridge lectures with the Zoopraxiscope at the Society of Arts of the Institute of Technology [later MIT], Berkeley Street, Boston, Massachusetts.

October 23:
Eadweard Muybridge lectures for the public with the Zoopraxiscope at Union Hall, Boston. For an admission of 50 cents for adults and 25 cents for children, performances were held daily on 23, 24, 26, 27 and 28 October at 8pm, with matinees on Wednesday and Saturday. Muybridge was paid a fee by Kelley's Musical and Literary Bureau, who arranged these public performances.

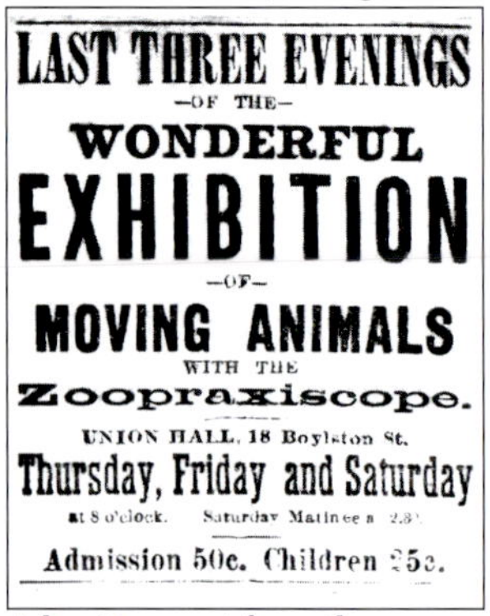

Advertisement from the *Boston Daily Globe* for Muybridge's lectures in October, 1882. [Courtesy Kingston Museum, Kingston upon Thames.]

November 17:
Eadweard Muybridge lectures with the Zoopraxiscope at the Turf Club, Madison Square, New York City.

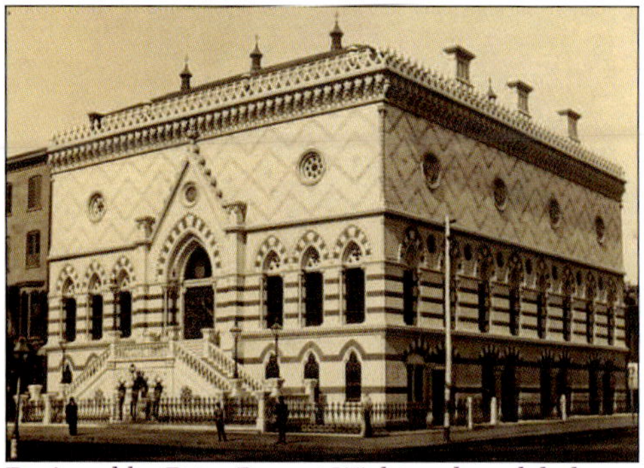

Designed by Peter Bonnet Wight and modeled on the Doge's Palace in Venice, the building for the National Academy of Design was ready in 1866 and demolished in 1901. [Photograph by Maurice Stadtfeld, 1866. Public domain.]

November 28:
Eadweard Muybridge lectures with the Zoopraxiscope at the National Academy of Design, 23rd Street and Fourth Avenue, New York City.

December 22:
Eadweard Muybridge lectures again with the Zoopraxiscope at the National Academy of Design, 23rd Street and Fourth Avenue, New York City.

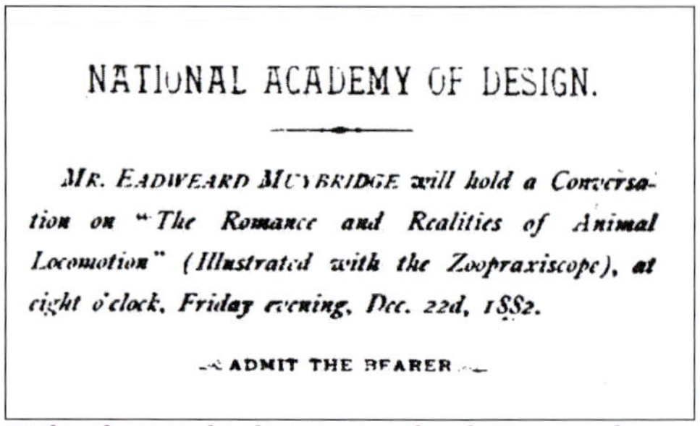

Ticket for Muybridge's December lecture at the National Academy of Design, New York City. [Courtesy Kingston Museum, Kingston upon Thames.]

1883

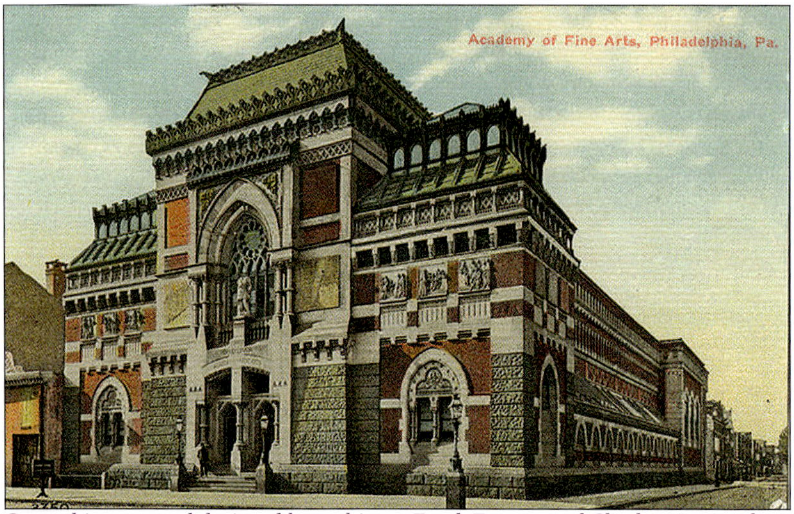

Opened in 1876 and designed by architects Frank Furness and Charles Hewitt, the Pennsylvania Academy of the Fine Arts building is seen here in a lithographed postcard from about 1900. [Postcard c1900 issued by the Souvenir Post Card Company of New York. Public domain.]

January 9:
Eadweard Muybridge lectures with the Zoopraxiscope at the Union League Club, Fifth Avenue and West 39th Street, New York City.

February 12:
Eadweard Muybridge lectures with the Zoopraxiscope at the Pennsylvania Academy of the Fine Arts, corner of Cherry Street and Broad Street, Philadelphia. The painter Thomas Eakins, who was himself a chronophotographer, had been teaching at the Academy since 1876, was its Director from 1882.

February 13:
Eadweard Muybridge lectures at the Franklin Institute, 15 South 7th Street, Philadelphia (the building is now the Philadelphia History Museum). At the time of Muybridge's lecture,

Coleman Sellers was a past President of the Institute, and Henry Heyl a prominent member.

February 15:
Eadweard Muybridge lectures with the Zoopraxiscope at the 2,500-seat Academy of Music, 240 South Broad Street, Philadelphia.

February 16:
Eadweard Muybridge lectures with the Zoopraxiscope again at the Pennsylvania Academy of the Fine Arts, Philadelphia.

August 7:
A meeting in the office of William Pepper, provost of the University of Pennsylvania decides to offer Muybridge the use of the grounds of the Veterinary Hospital "for the prosecution of his work on the investigation of animal motion". Attending were the physicist George Barker, the publisher J. B. Lippincott; Coleman Sellers, and others. This was the initiation of the massive study of locomotion published in 1887 in 781 plates, and would restrict Muybridge's lectures for the next four years.

September 20, or 21:
Eadweard Muybridge lectures with the Zoopraxiscope at the Swain Free School (later Swain School of Design), New Bedford, Massachusetts, for an audience of art students and local citizens.

November 9:
Eadweard Muybridge lectures with the Zoopraxiscope at Boylston Hall, Harvard College, Cambridge, Massachusetts.

November:
Muybridge publishes zoetrope strips of his series photographs.

Undated:
further Muybridge lectures in America, including Cooper Union (NYC), the Photography Section of the American Institute (NYC), plus a lecture for the Scientific Society of the University of Pennsylvania (August?).

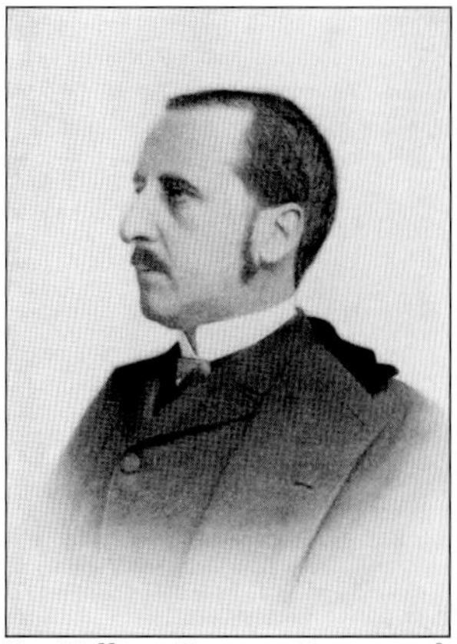
Dr. William Pepper, Provost of the University of Pennsylvania, in 1896. [*Popular Science Monthly*, Vol. 49. Public domain.]

1884

February 8:
Eadweard Muybridge lectures with the Zoopraxiscope at Association Hall, Philadelphia.[28]

August:
Eadweard Muybridge lectures with the Zoopraxiscope for the Scientific Society of the University of Pennsylvania, at the university chapel, Philadelphia. According to Thomas Anschutz, a university student and assistant to Muybridge, the lecture was "the same he gave us last year but not so well given".

1885

April 30:
Eadweard Muybridge lectures with the Zoopraxiscope at the Scientific Society of the University of Pennsylvania, Philadelphia.

Undated: several Muybridge lectures on his work to students at the University of Pennsylvania.

1886

November 2:
United States patent 376,247, *Method of and Apparatus for Producing Animated Pictures of Natural Scenery and Life*, to Augustin Le Prince of New York City for his 16-lens camera and projector using "glass, canvas, or other Prepared Surfaces" to support the photographs. The patent was issued on 10 January 1888, on the same day Le Prince's application for the same device was made in Great Britain, as UK 423 of 1888.

28 It is likely that this lecture is the one mentioned in the Annual Report of the Philadelphia Art Museum (No. 9, 1884) as given at the Pennsylvania Museum and School of Industrial Art. William Pepper, provost at the University of Pennsylvania who initiated Muybridge's work in Philadelphia, was President of the Museum and School. Housed in the only surviving building from the Centennial Exhibition of 1876, the building in Fairmont Park is a National Historic Landmark and today houses the Please Touch Museum.

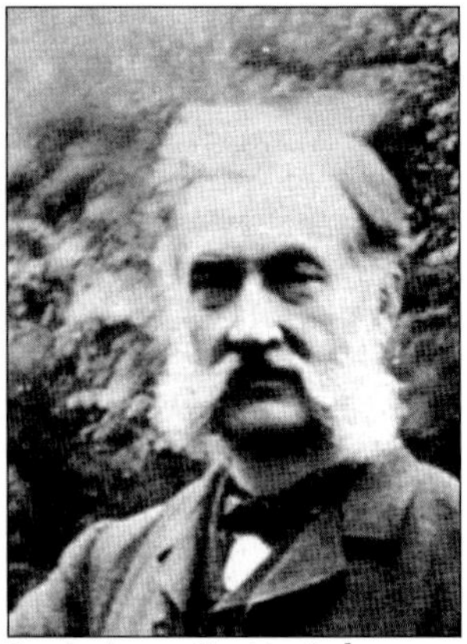

Louis Augustin Aimée le Prince, c1889. Christopher Rawlence, *The Missing Reel* (1990), Plate II, facing page 19.

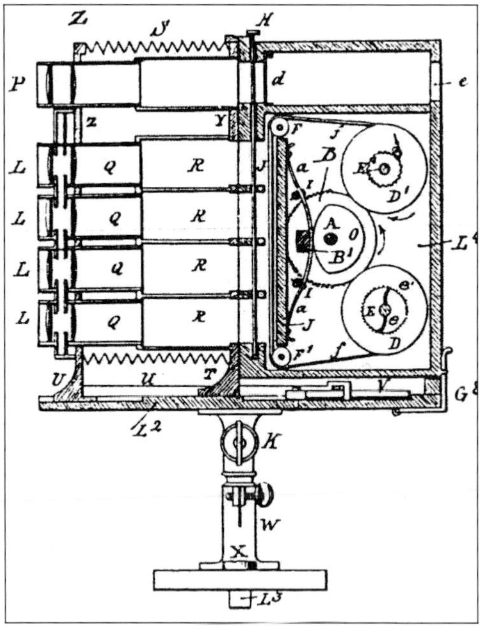

A sectional view of Le Prince's 16-lens camera. At right, the image bands traveled from the lower drum D through the apertures to the upper drum D'. At left, the lower block of four lenses was repeated four times across the width of the camera, while the upper lens assembly was used to focus the apparatus by means of the lever V at the bottom. [United States patent 376,247, Sheet 2, Figure 3.]

November 4: Dr. William Gilman Thompson reads a paper on "The Movements of the Heart and Intestines Illustrated by Photography" at a meeting of the New York Academy of Medicine. Directly inspired to use photographic methods by the chronophotographs of Muybridge, he devised with Robert Dempsey Gray a chronophotographic camera with images mounted on a disk moved intermittently by an arrangement of cogwheels turned by a handle. The report of the meeting concluded that "the results were very interesting, and the movements, changes of form, and pulsations of the heart were distinctly shown". Along with precise medical descriptions of his experiments, emphasizing the accuracy of the photographic method which he and Gray had devised, Thompson noted the "facility with which the action of various cardiac and intestinal stimuli could be illustrated before classes of students".

November 17:
United Kingdom patent 14,917, *An Improved Toy or Picture Book*, to Arthur Andrew Melville for a flip book he called *The Living Picture Book*, with two images printed back-to-back. Melville also suggested binding three images in a triangular book and four in a cross-shaped book.

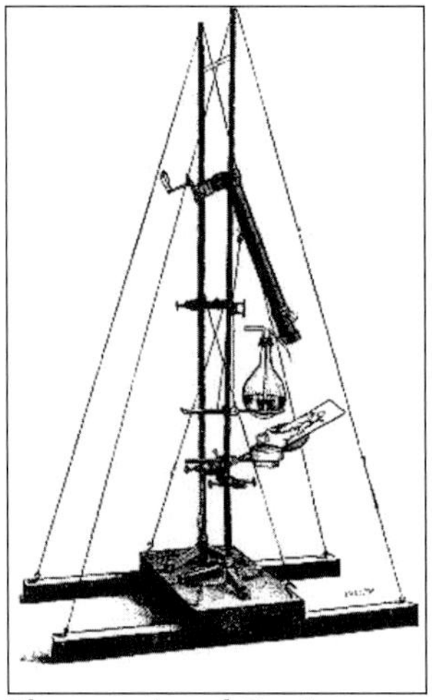

Thompson's and Gray's chronophotographic camera mounted and ready for use. The hand crank to operate the camera is at the top left; the subject is held on the platform at the middle right. [*Scientific American Supplement*, Vol. XXII, No. 564, 2 October 1886, Figure 1. Public domain.]

Dr. William Gilman Thompson in an undated photograph.
[U.S. National Library of Medicine, Digital Collections. Public Domain.]

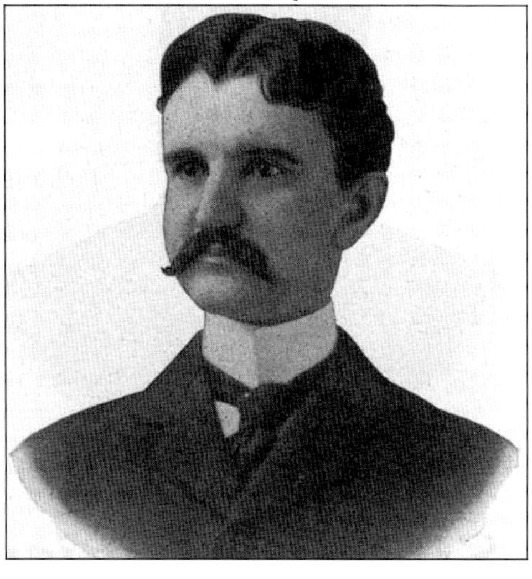

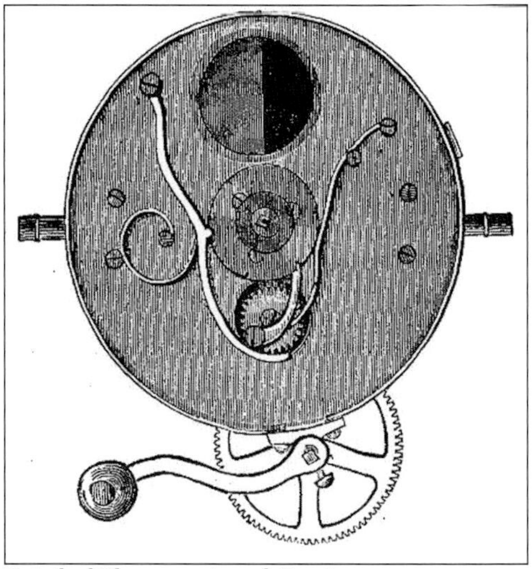

Detail of Thompson's and Gray's chronophotographic camera of 1886, which recorded six phases of movement. [*Scientific American Supplement*, Vol. XXII, No. 564, 2 October 1886, Figure 2.]

1887

March 19:

Ottomar Anschütz demonstrates the first model of his Schnellseher in the mezzanine of the Culture Ministry, Unter den Linden 4, Berlin. This was the first public appearance of the apparatus, and the demonstrations continued on March 20 and 21, from 12 noon to 3pm, under the auspices of Culture Minister von Goslar. The invited audiences were made up of scientists, politicians and photographers. Disks shown were various horse gaits from the summer 1886 series taken at the Militär Reitinstitut, Hannover.

Mid-June:

Anschütz Schnellseher exhibited daily to a paying public at Stadtbahnbogen No. 21 adjacent to the Ausstellungspark (Exhibition Park), Berlin. The exhibitions lasted until mid-September at this railway arch facing the popular amusement park.

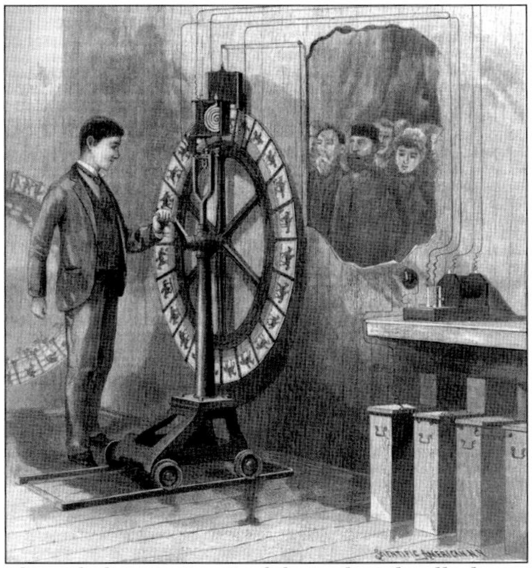

The only known image of the early Schnellseher was published in *Scientific American* in November 1889, and shows the typical presentation: The Schnellseher and its operator were divided from the viewers, who saw the images of movement in small groups of four to seven persons at a time. Note the rails that allowed the instrument to be pulled back from the wall to change its disks (leaning against the wall in the background), and the row of electrical batteries below the Ruhmkorff coil that supplied the Geissler tube at the top of the Schnellseher. [*Scientific American*, 16 November 1889. Public domain.]

September 20:

Anschütz Schnellseher demonstrated for the annual convention of natural scientists (Naturforscherversammlung), September 18–22, in Wiesbaden.

September:

Eadweard Muybridge lectures with the Zoopraxiscope in Albany, New York. This was an early presentation in Muybridge's planned three-year world tour exhibiting his new series photographs from the Pennsylvania project, and was intended to generate further subscriptions for the published work. The majority of these lectures were now unpaid, with Muybridge considering it "desirable to accept invitations, as of indirect benefit to the University and *–Animal Locomotion*".

October 3:

Anschütz Schnellseher demonstrated at the *Verein zur Pflege der Photographie und verwandter Künste*, Frankfurt am Main. The apparatus was shown twice, accompanied by a short lecture, and the meeting saw "many" chronophotographic disks exhibited "with the greatest interest" before the session ended.

October 10:

Anschütz Schnellseher opens for the public at the Polytechnic Hall, Frankfurt a. M., for 5 days.

December:

Eadweard Muybridge lectures with the Zoopraxiscope in the studio of the sculptor and painter Thomas Shields Clark, Pittsburgh, Pennsylvania.

December:

Eadweard Muybridge lectures with the Zoopraxiscope at the Art Institute of Chicago.

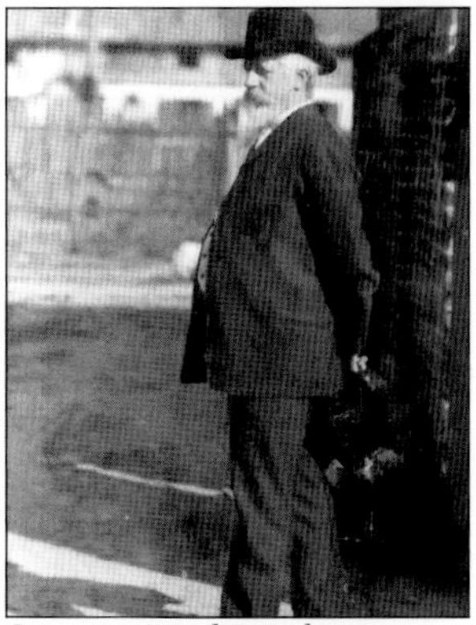

Ottomar Anschütz about 1904, most likely on a return visit to Lissa. [Deac Rossell Collection. Public domain.]

He later wrote to the secretary of the University of Pennsylvania's provost that "I did pretty well in Chicago. 14 ($100) subscribers, and 2 complete series ($600 each) and expect some more when I return".

Undated: further Anschütz Schnellseher demonstrations at the Kunstgewerbehalle, Dresden; others.

Undated: further Muybridge lectures at the Union League Club, New York; the Studio of William Merritt Chase, New York City; Milwaukee, WI; Madison, WI; Minneapolis, MN; St. Louis, MO; Denver, CO; others.

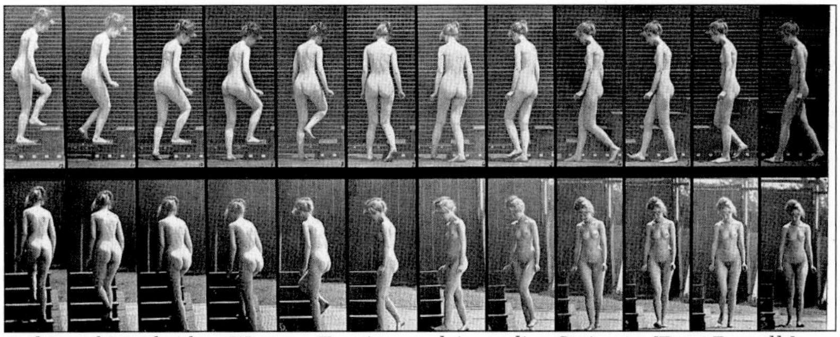

Eadweard Muybridge, *Woman. Turning, and Ascending Stairway*. [Deac Rossell.]

1888

January 10:
UK patent 423, *Improvements in the Method of and Apparatus for Producing Animated Photographic Pictures,* to Louis Aimé Augustin Le Prince of New York City, presently in High Holborn, London, for his 16-lens camera and projector.

January 11:
French patent 188,089, *Méthode et appareil pour la projection de tableaux animés,* to Louis Aimé Augustin Le Prince for his 16-lens camera and projector.

February:
Ottomar Anschütz installs a Schnellseher permanently in a room at his photography studios, Charlottenstrasse 59, Berlin. Demonstrated frequently in 1888-1892, there seem to have been various models of the Schnellseher in occasional use at Anschütz's studio headquarters until about 1902.

February 25:
Eadweard Muybridge lectures with the Zoopraxiscope at the New England Society, Orange, New Jersey. Thomas Edison attended the Saturday evening lecture with his wife Minna.

February 27:
Eadweard Muybridge meets with Thomas Edison on Monday morning at the new laboratory in West Orange, New Jersey. Muybridge shows some of his photographs, and suggests marrying the Zoopraxiscope to the Edison phonograph to produce sound moving pictures.[29]

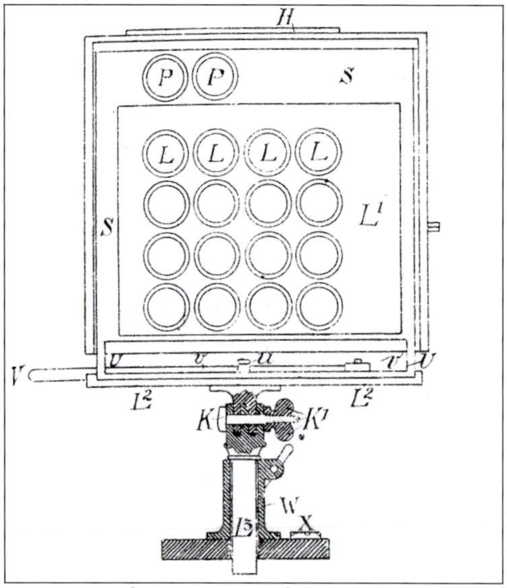

Front view of Le Prince's 16-lens camera, with the focusing lenses at the top and the focusing lever, V, at the left bottom. [United Kingdom patent 423 of 10 January 1888, Figure 1.]

April 23:
Eadweard Muybridge lectures with the Zoopraxiscope at the School of Drawing of the Museum of Fine Arts, Boston, presenting his new Pennsylvania series photographs. This lecture at the predecessor to the School of the Museum of Fine Arts was held in the Drawing Studio at the rear of the museum building in Copley Square.

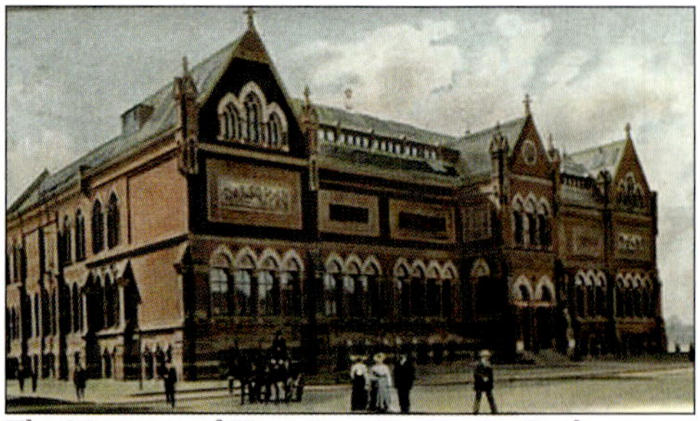

The Museum of Fine Arts, Boston, in Copley Square before 1909. The School of Drawing was incorporated in the main museum building, and Muybridge lectured there just seven years after the building opened. [Vintage postcard. Public domain.]

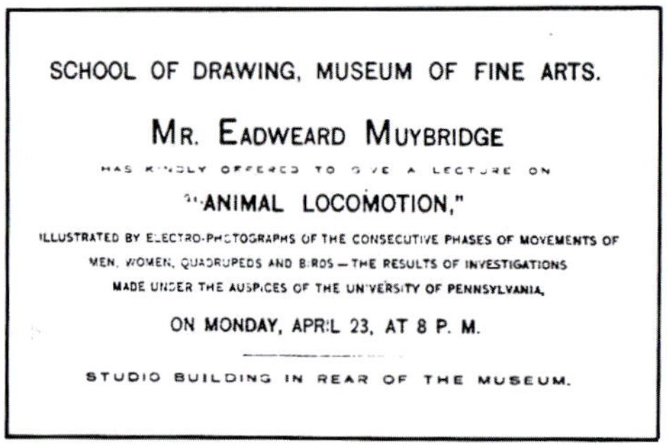

SCHOOL OF DRAWING, MUSEUM OF FINE ARTS.

MR. EADWEARD MUYBRIDGE

HAS KINDLY OFFERED TO GIVE A LECTURE ON

"ANIMAL LOCOMOTION,"

ILLUSTRATED BY ELECTRO-PHOTOGRAPHS OF THE CONSECUTIVE PHASES OF MOVEMENTS OF MEN, WOMEN, QUADRUPEDS AND BIRDS – THE RESULTS OF INVESTIGATIONS MADE UNDER THE AUSPICES OF THE UNIVERSITY OF PENNSYLVANIA.

ON MONDAY, APRIL 23, AT 8 P. M.

STUDIO BUILDING IN REAR OF THE MUSEUM.

Ticket for Muybridge's lecture at the Museum of Fine Arts, Boston. [Courtesy Kingston Museum, Kingston upon Thames.]

May 4:
Eadweard Muybridge lectures with the Zoopraxiscope for the benefit of a Free Library, at the Music Hall in Orange, New Jersey. This visit initiated correspondence between Edison and Muybridge over the purchase of plates from *Animal Locomotion*, which arrived at the Edison laboratory in November.

June 21:
Eadweard Muybridge lectures with the Zoopraxiscope in the Hall of the Milwaukee College, Wisconsin, presenting his new Pennsylvania series photographs.

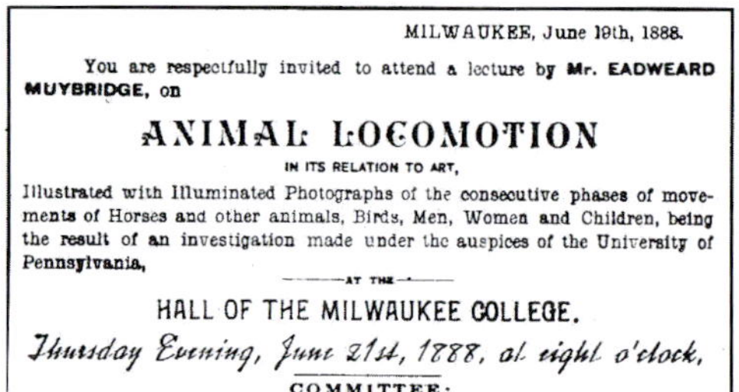

MILWAUKEE, June 19th, 1888.

You are respectfully invited to attend a lecture by Mr. EADWEARD MUYBRIDGE, on

ANIMAL LOCOMOTION

IN ITS RELATION TO ART,

Illustrated with Illuminated Photographs of the consecutive phases of movements of Horses and other animals, Birds, Men, Women and Children, being the result of an investigation made under the auspices of the University of Pennsylvania,

AT THE

HALL OF THE MILWAUKEE COLLEGE.

Thursday Evening, June 21st, 1888, at eight o'clock,

COMMITTEE:

C. S. FARRAR. MRS. S. S. FRACKELTON. E. C. ELDRIDGE.

Ticket for Muybridge's lecture in Milwaukee, 21 June 1888. [Courtesy Kingston Museum, Kingston upon Thames.]

29 Edison later denied that this meeting ever took place, and had Terry Ramsaye excise references to it in the manuscript of his history *A Million and One Nights*. Paul Spehr (2008, 75) makes the fair suggestion that W. K. L. Dickson also very likely attended the Muybridge lecture. There are extensive discussions of this meeting in both Hendricks (1961, 4–14) and Spehr (2008, 75–77).

July 14:

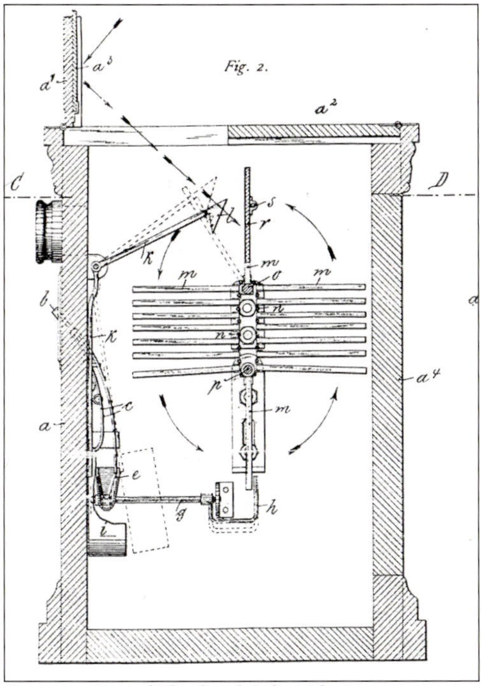

Cross-section of Eberhard Schneider's automat for stereo card viewing. The device is typical of many stereo automats of the period. [German patent 46 561 Figure 2.]

German patent 46561, *Selbsteinkassirender Schaustellungsapparat*, to E. Schneider in Oberhausen for an automat operated stereoscopic viewer. This is a patent by Eberhard Schneider, who later also claimed to have worked on moving picture apparatus at the Krupp works in the early 1890s. Schneider was an active exhibitor and manufacturer of cameras and projectors in New York City from 1897 to about 1904, when he was sued by Edison.

December 1:
French patent 194,482, *Appareil dit Théâtre optique,* to Emile Reynaud for his Théâtre

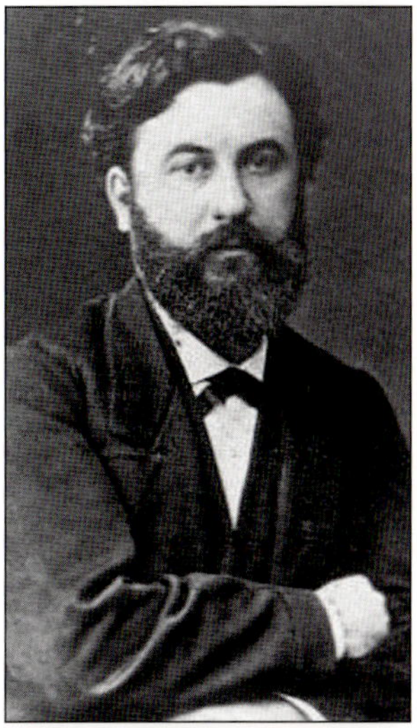

Émile Reynaud, schoolteacher, inventor of the Praxinoscope and operator of the Pantomimes Lumineuses, in c1875. [Photographer unknown. Public domain.]

Optique. There were additions to this patent on 6 January 1889 and 26 August 1889. This device using reflective mirrors to project onto a screen not only later (see below) became a very successful public exhibition of moving images painted on a flexible band, but also solved one important element in reducing flicker and blurring on the screen to which many subsequent photography-based inventors would only slowly return: the use of perforated stock and its firm registration of movement by the use of sprockets projecting

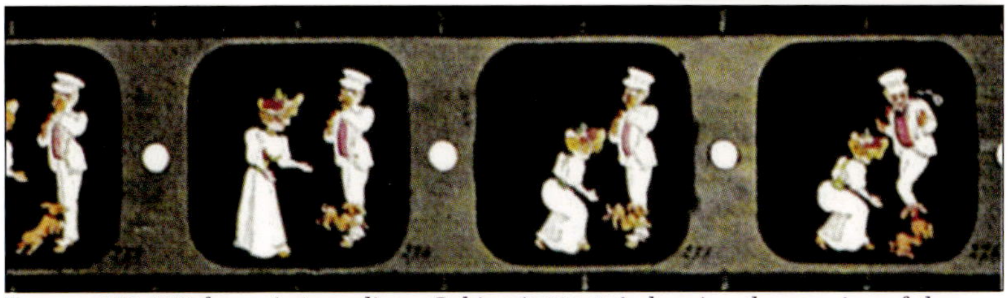

Frames 273-276 from *Autour d'une Cabine* (1893-94) showing the spacing of the images and the large perforations used in Reynaud's *Théâtre optique*. [Dominique Auzel, *Emile Reynaud et l'image s'anima*, page 61.]

from a wheel. Reynaud's band was about 65mm wide, with images 50mm wide and 40mm high. There were large spaces of about 25mm between each frame, and the perforations were circular 6mm holes in the middle of the film band between the images, reinforced with metal ringlets.

Late 1888:
Anschütz Schnellseher exhibited at the international photography exposition held as a part of the *Grand concours internationale des sciences et de l'Industrie* in Brussels. Disks of Horse and rider jumping a hurdle, *Gymnast leaping over another from a springboard*, and *Horse and rider at the gallop* were shown, amongst others. For this exhibition the Schnellseher was called an Electro-Tachyscope, a name frequently used thereafter.

Undated: further Anschütz Schnellseher exhibition at photography exhibition in Florence, Italy.

Undated: further Muybridge lectures with the Zoopraxiscope.

1889

January 22:
William Friese-Greene demonstrates a magic lantern of his design with automatically changing photographic slides at a technical meeting of the Photographic Society of Great Britain in London. Using twin lanterns with slides linked together by a kind of chain and advanced by a clockwork mechanism to create an impression of motion, the device was also exhibited at the Crystal Palace Photographic Exhibition in March.

February 9:
Eadweard Muybridge lec-

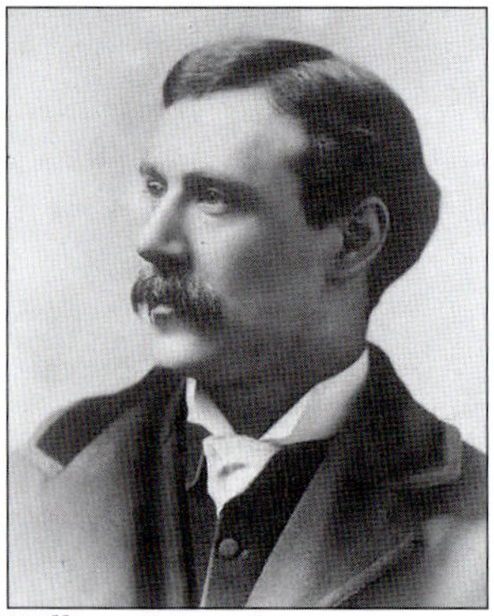

William Friese-Greene, a significant pioneer and at times considered the inventor of the cinema, c1890. [Science Museum London.]

tures with the Zoopraxiscope at a soirée at the home of the painter Sir Lawrence Alma-Tadema, 44 Grove End Road, St. John's Wood, London.

Mid-March:
Eadweard Muybridge lectures with the Zoopraxiscope at the South Kensington Art and Science Department (later Science Museum), London.

March 22: Eadweard Muybridge lectures with the Zoopraxiscope at the regular Friday meeting of the Royal Institution, 21 Albemarle Street, Mayfair, London, replacing Dr. Edgar Crookshank on microbes due to Crookshank's illness. The Zoopraxiscope showed horses jumping, galloping and trotting, "But it was generally acknowledged that the most wonderful of all was the illustration of the flying of a bird...". For this new tour of Europe, Muybridge normally presented both still photographs and zoopraxigraphic moving images in a lecture called *Animal Locomotion in its relation to Design in Art.* He travelled with Ernest Webster, from Berkhamstead, who operated the lantern and the Zoopraxiscope.

March 23:
Eadwead Muybridge lectures with the Zoopraxiscope in the Lecture Theatre of the South Kensington Museum, London, at 3pm. Admission 1 shilling. This was the first of two lectures at the museum.

April 9:
United States patent 417,202, *Manufacture of Flexible Photographic Films,* to Henry M. Reichenbach, a chemist for George Eastman, for producing rolls of transparent, flexible film made of nitro-cellulose and camphor. Although virtually the same process as that filed earlier by Hannibal Goodwin, Reichenbach's patent included the exact chemical proportions necessary to produce the thin celluloid film, which Goodwin's did not.[30]

☛United States patent 306,284, *Improvement in Flexible Photographic Film,* to George Eastman for the process of manufacturing flexible celluloid film.

May 2: Eadweard Muybridge lectures with the Zoopraxiscope at the Royal Institution, 21 Albemarle Street, Mayfair, London, beginning a set of two lectures at 3pm for an admission of half a guinea.

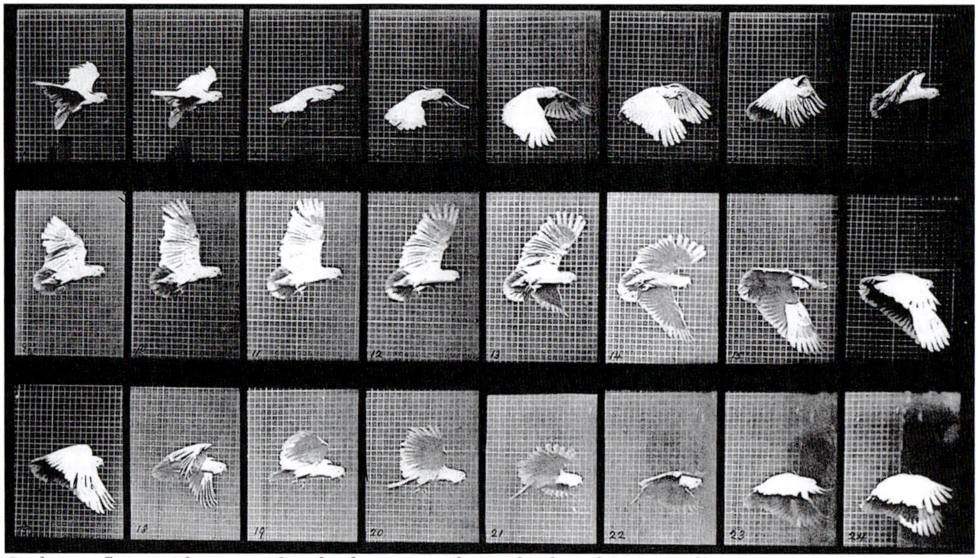

Cockatoo; flying. Often considered a favorite with Muybridge's lecture audiences. [Plate 759 from *Animal Locomotion*, 1887. Public domain.]

30 The Rev. Hannibal Goodwin, a clergyman in Newark, New Jersey, held several photographic patents from the late 1870s and 1880s. His patent specification for nitrocellulose film was filed 2 May 1887, and was amended seven times over the next 13 months. The patent's subsequent history, and the interferences it ultimately created with George Eastman's patents, is an epic of bureaucratic fumbling and legal entanglement. According to Carl W. Ackerman's biography *George Eastman* (London, 1930: Constable and Company, pp. 61–62 and 89–90, Eastman had written to his lawyer, J. B. Church in Washington, D. C. On 3 March 1889 that "... I can lay no claim to the chemical part of the process. The mechanical part only is mine & the chemical part Henry M. Reichenbach ... As the claims are presently drawn, neither Reichenbach nor myself could father them, as they combine the chemical & mechanical features, which are separate inventions ... I should like very much to have Reichenbach's name connected with this application and think it would please him."
Two additional patents for the manufacturing process actually used by the Eastman Dry Plate and Film Company were issued to both Reichenbach and Eastman on 22 March 1892 and 19 July 1892. On 31 December 1892 Eastman discovered that Reichenbach and two other employees were conspiring to begin a rival company manufacturing film using the secret processes; on New Year's Day 1893 all three were summarily dismissed. Reichenbach and various associates formed two new photographic companies in the succeeding years, but both failed. In Spring 1909, Reichenbach asked Eastman for a job again, but Eastman, in a polite note, declined to re-employ him.

May 8:
Eadweard Muybridge lectures with the Zoopraxiscope at the Royal Society, Burlington House, Piccadilly, Mayfair, London.

May 9:
Eadweard Muybridge lectures with the Zoopraxiscope at the Royal Institution, 21 Albemarle Street, Mayfair, London, at 3pm, completing his course of two lectures.

June 15:
Founding in Great Britain of the *Optical Magic Lantern Journal and Photographic Enlarger*, later the *Optical Lantern and Cinematograph Journal* (from 1904), and the *Kinematograph and Lantern Weekly* (from 1907), the major film trade paper in England until it closed on September 25, 1971.

June 19:
Eadweard Muybridge lectures with the Zoopraxiscope at a Ladies' Night gathering at the Royal Society, Burlington House, Piccadilly, Mayfair, London.

June 21:
British patent 10,131, *Improved apparatus for taking photographs in rapid series*, to William Friese-Greene and Mortimer Evans for a camera for 'taking photographs automatically in a rapid series with a single camera and lens'. Using unperforated film 63mm/ 2 ½ inches wide and initially geared to produce two pictures per turn of the driving handle, this camera was rapidly improved to take four pictures for each turn, delivering a maximum of about 10 frames per second.[31]

July 26:
Eadweard Muybridge lectures with the Zoopraxiscope at a conversazione in Blackpool.

August 10:
Anschütz Schnellseher demonstrated at the

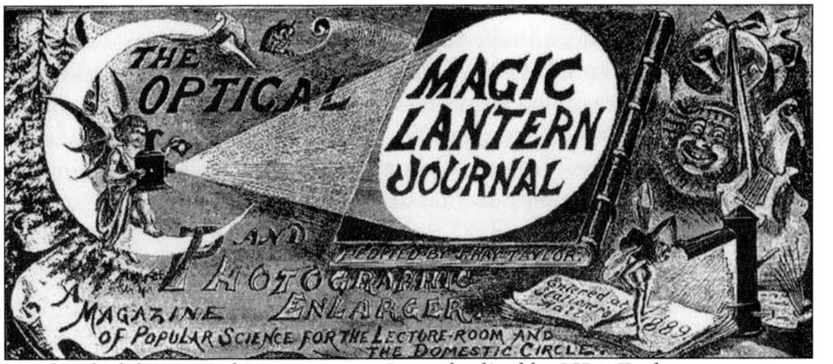

Masthead of the *Optical Magic Lantern Journal*, edited by J Hay Taylor.
[Deac Rossell Collection.]

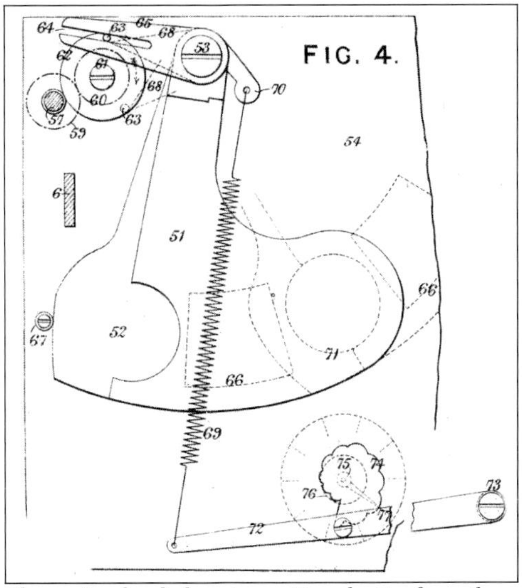

The spring-loaded reciprocating shutter from the patent of Friese-Greene and Evans, Figure 4. The complicated device worked slowly, but was considered by some to be the basic patent for cinema cameras.
[UK patent 10,131 of 21 June 1889, Figure 4.]

Exhibition of Photographic Dealers and Manufacturers, Boston, by C. B. Richards & Son of New York. To operate the machine and change its disks, Richards had imported the German technician Adalbert Bennecke.

Mid-August to mid-September:
During the photographic Jubilee Exhibition in Berlin, Anschütz exhibited many of his photographs, and advertised that his Schnellseher was available to be seen at his business premises, Charlottenstrasse 59, Berlin.

August 15:
British patent 12,921, *Improvements in the production and representation of instantaneous photographic pictures*, to Wordsworth Donisthorpe and William Carr Crofts for the Kinesigraph camera, an apparatus also useable as a projector, with a continuously moving paper film band and with the intermittent supplied by moving the entire film transport assembly upwards at the same speed as the downwards moving film band during the exposure of the film before the lens. This large, floor-standing apparatus was capable of taking 8 to 10 images per second, which were intended to be shown on a projector with a similar mechanism. Each image was circular, 2 ½ inches in diameter, and

31 Also, German patent 56 503 of 25 February 1890, Swiss patent 2054 of 3 March 1890, Spanish patent 10541 of 24 February 1890, Canadian patent applied for 22 February 1890, Italian patent 221 444 of 1890, New South Wales (Australia) patent 2121 granted 31 March 1890, Victoria (Australia) patent 7618 granted 4 June 1890. Friese-Greene went on to hold many patents in different fields, including for mass photographic printing, photo-typesetting, an airship with a hybrid engine and several early colour film processes.

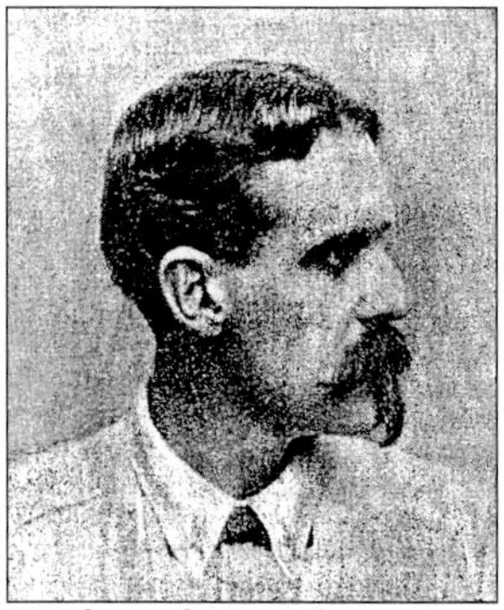

Wordsworth Donisthorpe in 1890. [*The Chess-Monthly*, December, 1890.]

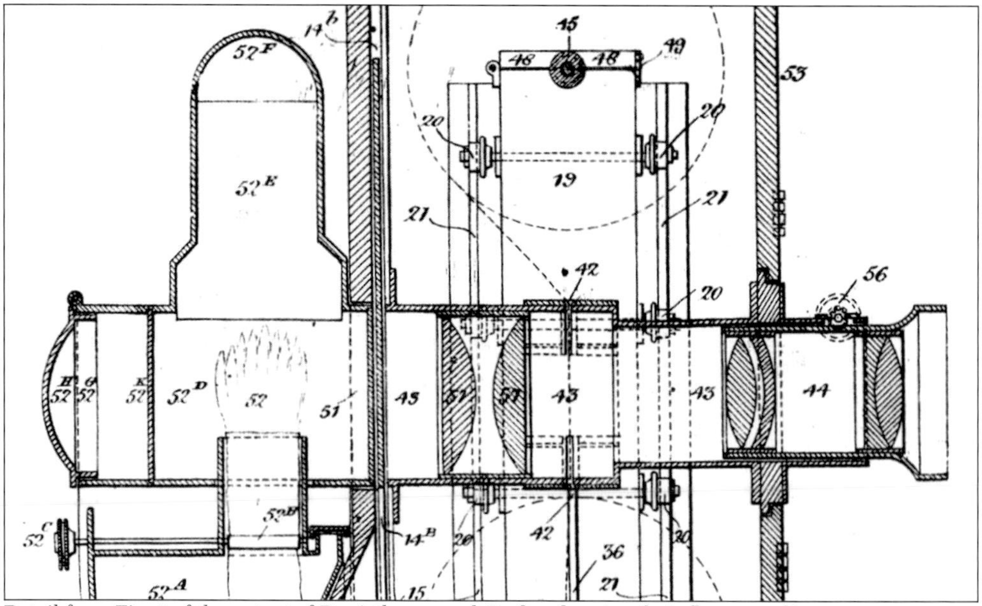

Detail from Fig. 5 of the patent of Donisthorpe and Crofts, showing their floor-standing apparatus as a projector. The oil lamp is at the left, No. 52 below the chimney 52E and above the wick regulator 52C. The film enters in front of condensors 57-57 at 42 as shown by the dotted line, with projection lenses at the right. Although pictures were taken, and survive, the projector never worked. [UK patent 123,921 of 15 August 1889, Fig. 5, detail.]

placed on 3 1/4 inch wide film. Eastman stripping film with a celluloid secondary backing was later used in the camera. Failing to raise capital after two 'experts', a painter and a magic lantern maker, dismissed the idea, Donisthorpe never developed the apparatus further.[32]

☛Anschütz Schnellseher demonstrated at the Photographic Exhibition at the Königlichen Kriegsakademie, Dorotheenstraße, Berlin, Germany.

August 19:
A dinner given by the Société française de Photographie at the Hotel Continental in Paris, at the end of an international congress, celebrates the 50th Anniversary of the invention of photography. Among the distinguished guests at the dinner were Thomas Alva Edison (the guest of honor), Jules Janssen, Georges Balagny, Albert Londe, Étienne-Jules Marey, Paul Nadar, Louis Pasteur, and the three Lumières, Antoine, Auguste, and Louis.

August 21:
Eadweard Muybridge lectures with the Zoopraxiscope at the Photographic Convention of Great Britain, St James's Hall, London, where he was received with "tremendous applause" for presenting "the most wonderful revelation of the age". Muybridge gave one lecture as part of the convention's series of presentations.

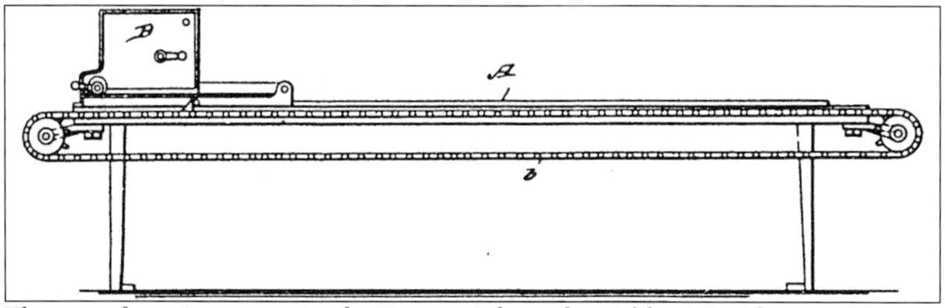

The manufacturing apparatus for Eastman's long glass tables (A). A hopper (B) containing first the celluloid and, when dried, the emulsion was drawn along the glass table (A) by a belt or chain (b). The original tables were either 80 feet or 100 feet long. [US patent 417,202 of 10 December 1889 (H M Reichenbach), Figure 4.]

August 27:
The Eastman Company produces the first flexible celluloid film for public sale, at their new manufacturing plant. A nitrocellulose solution was poured onto glass tables three and one half feet wide and fifty feet long and allowed to dry overnight; the photosensitive emulsion was then poured over the celluloid backing and also allowed to dry, before the combined

32 Also, French patent 209,174 of 28 October 1890, *Perfectionnements dans la production et la représentation des images photographiques instantées*; German patent 58166 of 9 November 1890. *The Photographic News* of 12 June 1891 reported on the taking of photographs of moving objects with this apparatus 'at a rate of from 8 to 12 per second ... a maximum speed of 12 per second need not be exceeded in order to secure the effect of continuous and natural motion'. Nine frames of celluloid film of Trafalgar Square, London, exposed during 1890 are in the collection of the National Museum of Photography, Bradford, England, and one (continuous) frame is in the collection of the Cinémathèque française, Paris.

sheets were stripped from the tables and cut into saleable sizes. The delicate process, prone to many flaws in manufacture such as spots, static electricity streaks, and bubbling, made both flexible roll film for the Kodak cameras and sheet film as a substitute for glass plates.

September 2:
W.K.L. Dickson pays for a roll of George Eastman's celluloid film, 3/4" wide and 50 feet long, the first order for Eastman's new product from West Orange. Six further rolls were received at the laboratory in November, and another six rolls in December.[33]

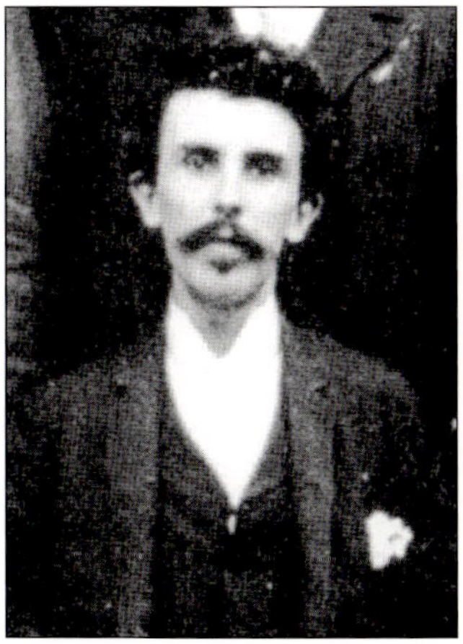

William Kennedy Laurie Dickson in 1893. [Detail from a photograph of Edison's staff in 1893, from Samuel Hawley, *The Fight that Started the Movies* (2016), after p. 124.]

September 5:
German patent 53840, *Photographischer Serien-Apparat*, to Ludwig Meyer in Berlin for a chronophotographic camera taking seven sequential images on a single glass plate. The apparatus contained seven lenses with focal-plane shutters tensioned by a long rubber band that was tripped in sequence by turning a crank, which could be adjusted to regulate the intervals between exposures. Meyer intended his device for photographing fast-moving objects such as birds in flight.

September 12:
Eadweard Muybridge lectures with the Zoopraxiscope at a conversazione arranged by the British Association in the Natural History Museum, Newcastle.

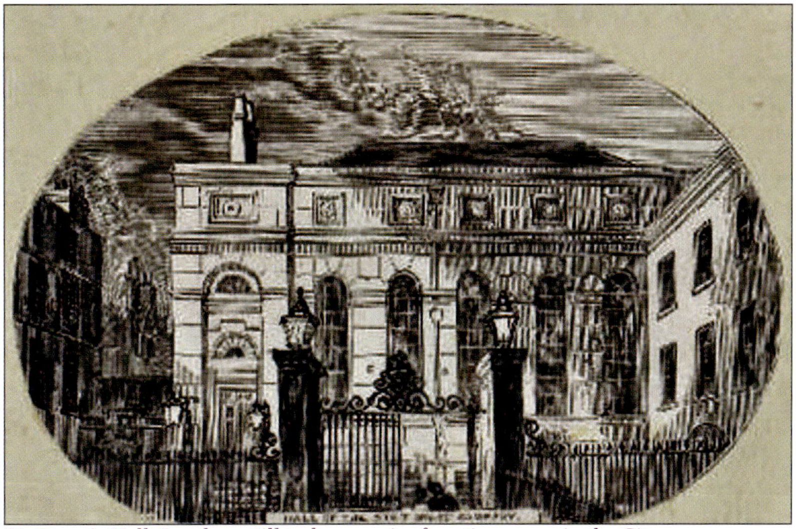

Stationer's Hall, London, still today a major function space in the City. [London Metropolitan Archives.]

September 17:
Eadweard Muybridge lectures with the Zoopraxiscope again at a conversazione arranged by the British Association in the Natural History Museum, Newcastle.

October 2:
Eadweard Muybridge lectures with the Zoopraxiscope at a conversazione held as part of the annual meeting of the Library Association, Stationer's Hall, London

October 28:
Eadweard Muybridge lectures with the Zoopraxiscope at the Literary and Philosophical Society, 7.30 pm, the Music Hall, Surrey Street, Sheffield. Without quoting a price, patrons were warned in the advertising: "No admission without ticket".

November 7:
Eadweard Muybridge lectures with the Zoopraxiscope at the Bristol Naturalists' Society, Victoria Rooms, Bristol

November 9:
Eadweard Muybridge lectures with the Zoopraxiscope at the University Museum, Oxford.

November 15:
Anschütz Schnellseher demonstrated at the premises of C. B. Richards & Son, photographic suppliers, 3 East 14th Street, New York City. The exhibitions continued sporadically through November "for interested parties". Shown was the series *Horse and Rider Jumping a Hurdle* and others. The apparatus was also demonstrated in Philadelphia, the center of the American

33 The earliest order for photographic celluloid at Edison's laboratory was for sheet Zylonite from the American Zylonite Company of North Adams, Massachusetts, which arrived on 11 May 1889. On June 25, a dozen sheets of Vergara Ivory film arrived from Allen & Rowell in England along with a dozen sheets of celluloid from John Carbutt in Philadelphia. The Carbutt film was used in early experiments on a cylinder-type Kinetoscope. See Spehr 2000 and Spehr 2008.

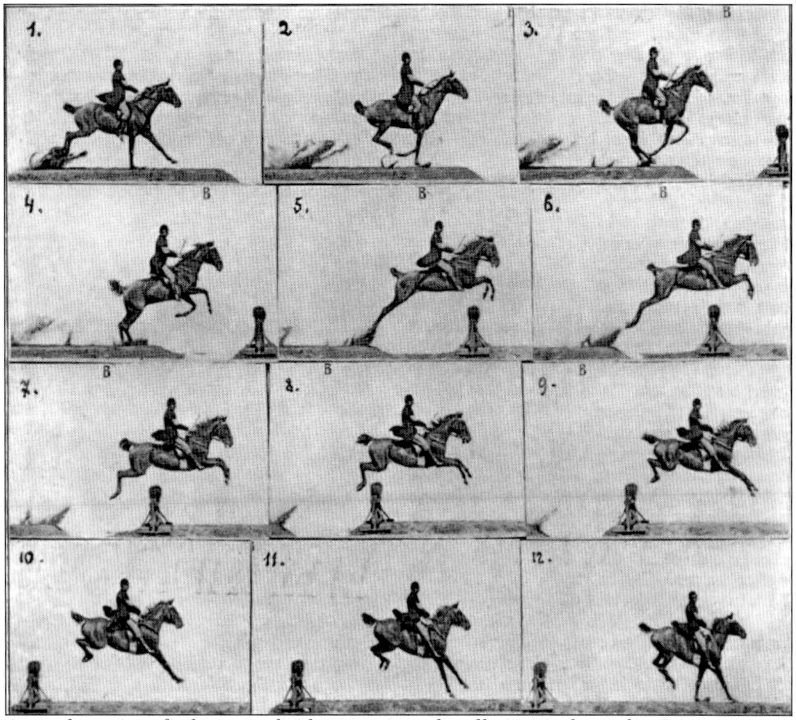

An early series of a horse and rider jumping a hurdle in 12 phases by Ottomar Anschütz. A signature image for Anschütz, it is difficult today to ascertain which particular series was in use in 1889. [Deac Rossell Collection.]

photographic business at this time.

November 16:
Anschütz Schnellseher (Electrotachyscope)[34] is described and illustrated in a long article in *Scientific American*, the first technical description of the machine outside Germany and its only known illustration. The article also illustrates six phases of a javelin thrower, and refers to the public exhibition at C. B. Richards & Co. of 3 East 14th Street, New York City.

November 21:
Eadweard Muybridge lectures with the Zoopraxiscope to student members of the Natural Science Society, the Wellington School (later Wellington College) Crawthorne, Berkshire.

November 27:
Eadweard Muybridge lectures with the Zoopraxiscope to the Leeds Mechanics' Institution and Literary Society, Leeds.

November 28:
Eadweard Muybridge lectures with the Zoopraxiscope for the Yorkshire Philosophical Society at the Festival Concert Rooms, York. The Archbishop of York was in the chair for this presentation.

December 2:
Eadweard Muybridge lectures with the Zoopraxiscope at the Assembly Rooms, Bath, under the auspices of the Mayor and the Presidents and Officers of the local scientific and arts societies..

December 12:
Eadweard Muybridge lectures with the Zoopraxiscope at the London Institution, Finsbury Circus, London.

Late December:
Anschütz Schnellseher demonstrations move to the United States Photographic Supply Company, also of 3 East 14th Street, New York City. Shown were *Horse and rider jumping a hurdle*; *Gymnast jumping over another's back*; athletic sports [javelin thrower, stone thrower]; "various positions of various birds and animals"; jumping dogs; climbing monkeys.

Undated: further Muybridge lectures at the Royal College of Surgeons, the Royal Geographical Society, the Zoölogical Society, the school of military engineering at Chatham, others.

Undated: further Anschütz Schnellseher exhibitions at the Hunting, Fishing and Sports Exhibition, Kassel; in Massachusetts; at a photography exhibition, St. Petersburg, Florida.

34 There is some understandable confusion in the literature about the various Anschütz machines, as he, like C. Francis Jenkins with his Phantoscope, tended to call all of his devices by the same name. At the same time the German literature invariably refers to his Schnellseher, whilst the English-language literature usually uses the term Electrotachyscope. This patent is for the operating principle of the machine, shared by 8 of the 9 models of Schnellseher: transparent images were fixed around the rim of a revolving disk and were illuminated briefly from behind as they passed a viewing aperture by an intermittent light provided by a Geissler tube. The first public model of the Schnellseher had a picture-disk diameter of some 150cm, and was a free-standing machine turned by a crank that was viewed by a small circle of people on the other side of a wall. Other versions included a long (c. 4 m) cylindrical apparatus, still hand-cranked, for multiple viewing, and an automat version with 65cm diameter disks. Altogether about 170 Schnellsehers were made, some 152 of them the automat version produced for Anschütz by the electrical firm of Siemens & Halske in Berlin. The original apparatus was patented by Anschütz in England (British patent 23,042 of 14 December 1892) under the name Electric Wonder. The patent suggests an alternative use of a strip or band of photographs in a coin-operated apparatus. Hopwood (No. 40) also mentions this strip-photographic device as the Electric Wonder.

1890

January 8:
Eadweard Muybridge lectures with the Zoopraxiscope at the twelfth annual Associated Soirée of the city's literary, scientific, and art societies at St. George's Hall, Liverpool. Introduced by the mayor, Muybridge's presentation was one of five given in the evening at rooms with elaborately installed collections and displays organized by the twenty sponsoring societies of the city.

January 16:
Anschütz Schnellseher demonstrated in a new model, a long cylindrical drum able to show six series photographs simultaneously, at the Photographische Verein zu Berlin. Anschürtz is now actively attempting to commercialize his moving picture apparatus, and he suggested in his talk devising an apparatus that would display 5–600 phases of movement, allowing "20 or 30 seconds of movement to be brought to lifelike movement".

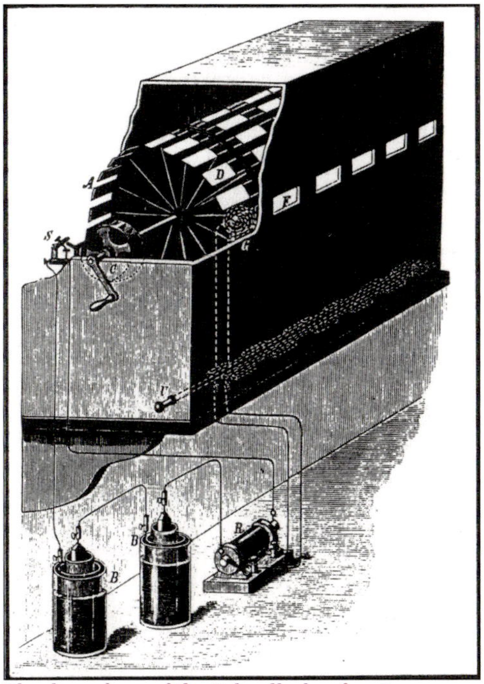
The drum form of the Schnellseher for six viewers, an attempt to commercialize the moving picture device that was briefly used in 1890. [Deac Rossell Collection.]

☛An improved model of the original Anschütz Schnellseher, making it more portable, was also shown at the same meeting in Berlin. This machine demonstrated Anschütz's *Speaking Portraits* (Sprechende Porträts) for the first time in public.

January:
Anschütz Schnellseher demonstrates *Speaking Portraits* for Kaiser Wilhelm and his family at the Berlin City Palace.

February 3:
Eadweard Muybridge lectures at the Scientific Society, in the Lecture Hall at Tower Street, Ipswich, England, with his Zoopraxiscope.

February 8:
British patent 2295, *Improvements in Apparatus for the Production of Optical Illusions* to Emile Reynaud for his Théâtre Optique.

February 11 and 13:
Eadweard Muybridge lectures twice with the Zoopraxiscope at the Belfast Natural History and Philosophical Society, in the Hall of the YMCA, Belfast, Ireland for the Society's Popular Lecture Series, with the mayor taking the chair. Reserved seats, 2*s*, unreserved 1*s*, lecture at 8pm. A second lecture was given on the 13th, alternating with his appearances in Dublin.

February 12 and 14:
Eadweard Muybridge lectures twice with the Zoopraxiscope in the theatre of the Royal Dublin Society, Leinster House, Kildare Street, Dublin, Ireland. The lecture was at 4pm, the first of the 1890 series of 14 afternoon popular lectures by the Society. A second lecture was given on the 14th, alternating with his appearances in Belfast.

February 17:
Eadweard Muybridge lectures with the Zoopraxiscope sponsored by the Photographic Society of Ireland, in the Ancient Concert Rooms, Dublin, Ireland. The public lecture was quickly arranged after the success of Muybridge's two presentations to the Royal Dublin Society, and was given "to a very large audience".

February 23:
George Eastman asks the Board of Directors of the Eastman Dry Plate Company to approve the manufacture of flexible celluloid film, intended for use in his hugely successful Kodak camera system. Transparent celluloid would replace the opaque paper backing of his film rolls, thereby drastically reducing the labour and expense of developing the film and printing positive images from it. By this time Eastman and his chemist Harry Reichenbach had developed both a formula and a manufacturing process for the material, and had identified sources and costs of raw materials. The drawing up of patent applications was also now begun. The Board approved manufacture of the new material, and plans for a new factory building were drawn up.

February 25: William Friese-Greene demonstrates his improved "machine camera", capable of recording up to 10 frames per second, at the Bath Photographic Society. Developed with Mortimer Evans, Friese-Greene told the society at the presentation: "Mr. Mortimer Evans has improved and improved on it so much that I am positive that the results will have a tendency in bringing forward a new kind of photography". The camera is thoroughly reported in *Scientific American* on April 19 and Friese-Greene sends details to Edison.

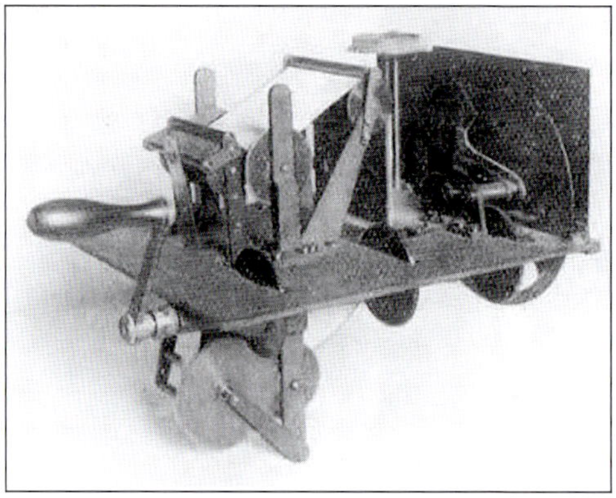

The machine camera of Friese-Greene and Evans, 1889. [*Kinematograph and Lantern Weekly*, 8 July 1909.]

February 26:
Eadweard Muybridge lectures with the Zoopraxiscope at the Queen's Rooms, Glasgow, for the Glasgow Philosophical Society. Public interest was so great that Muybridge delivered two additional lectures.

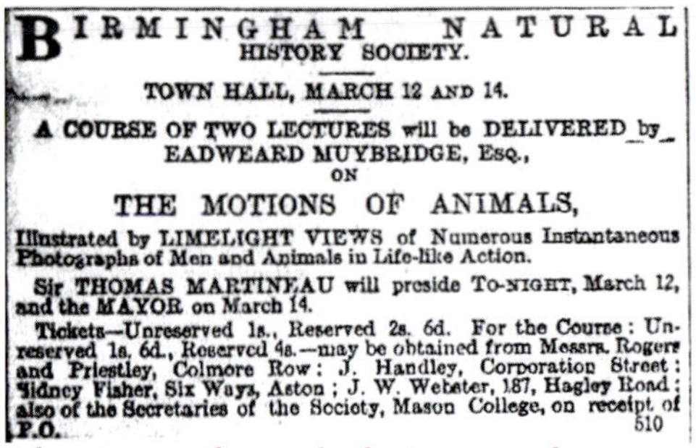

BIRMINGHAM NATURAL HISTORY SOCIETY.

TOWN HALL, MARCH 12 AND 14.

A COURSE OF TWO LECTURES will be DELIVERED by EADWEARD MUYBRIDGE, Esq., ON

THE MOTIONS OF ANIMALS,

Illustrated by LIMELIGHT VIEWS of Numerous Instantaneous Photographs of Men and Animals in Life-like Action.

Sir THOMAS MARTINEAU will preside To-NIGHT, March 12, and the MAYOR on March 14.

Tickets—Unreserved 1s., Reserved 2s. 6d. For the Course: Unreserved 1s. 6d., Reserved 4s.—may be obtained from Messrs. Rogers and Priestley, Colmore Row; J. Handley, Corporation Street; Sidney Fisher, Six Ways, Aston; J. W. Webster, 187, Hagley Road; also of the Secretaries of the Society, Mason College, on receipt of P.O. 510

Advertisement for Muybridge's course of two lectures in Birmingham in March, 1890. [Kingston Museum, Kingston upon Thames.]

March 8:
British patent 3730, *Improvements in or applicable to photographic cameras*, to Mortimer Evans for variations to the intermittent drive mechanism of his earlier joint patent with William Friese-Greene of 21 June 1889.

March 12 and 14:
Eadweard Muybridge lectures twice with the Zoopraxiscope at the Town Hall, Birmingham, for the Birmingham Natural History and Microscopial Society, with the Mayor presiding. "There was last night a large audience. The committee of the society desire us to express their exceeding regret that, owing to an unexpectedly great demand for seats at the last moment, sufficient room was not reserved for holders of "reserved" tickets and that care will be taken to prevent this occurring on Friday evening", for the second lecture.

March 15:
Anschütz Schnellseher demonstrated for the press at the United States Photographic Supply Company, 3 East 14th Street, New York City. Shown were disks of a horse and rider jumping a hurdle, a gymnast jumping over another from a springboard, birds in flight, dogs jumping a ditch, and various athletes. The *New York Times* reporter noted, "The legs of the horse move according to his gait, the dust is seen rising, the motion of the animal's ears, his mane and tail flying, and even the distention of the nostrils is noticed".

March 26:
UK patent 4704, *Improvements in Cameras for Photographing Objects in Motion*, to Frederick H. Varley in London for a single or twin-lens camera for taking sequential photographs on film. Only the stereoscopic version is known to have been constructed, producing images 3 inches square on 6 3/4 inch wide film; Varley also suggests transparent positives could be projected with the same device. Part of a series of collaborations with Friese-Greene, it is a variation on the Friese-Greene & Evans cameras. After the two men fell out, the Varley patent was published as 'Patent opposed'.

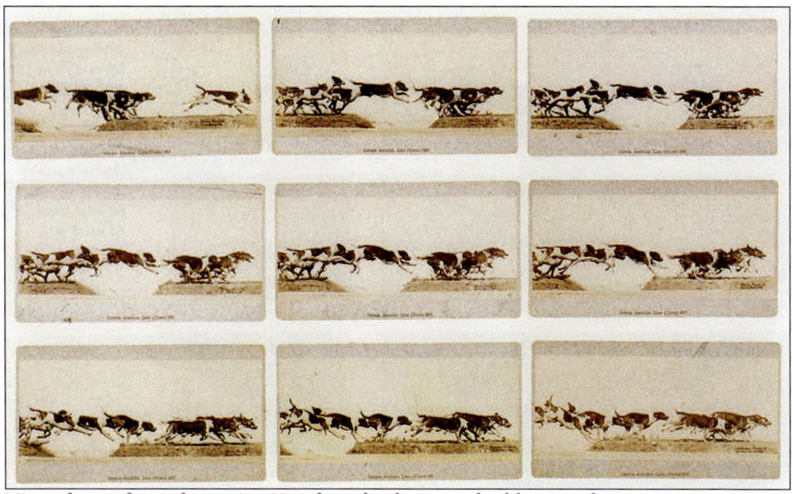

Nine phases from the series *Hundemule* photographed by Anschütz in 1887. [Agfa Photohistorama, Cologne.]

☛Étienne-Jules Marey publishes *Le vol des oiseaux*, including his classic study of pigeons in flight, photographed with his 1887 paper-ribbon camera at 60 frames per second. The apparatus, along with zoetropes utilising Marey's chronophotographic images of flight, had been exhibited at the Paris Exposition in the summer of 1889, where they were seen by Thomas Edison in August or September, and were explained at that time by Marey when the two men met.

March 31:
UK patent 4978, *Improvements in Toys, Shades, and Advertising Devices, and in Methods of Actuating or Exhibiting the same*, to Edwin Burbage Phillips and Henry Courteen, for a zoetrope seated on the chimney of a lamp that was rotated by the lamp's rising hot air. This patent is representative of a number of suggestions in the 1890s for using moving imagery in advertising.

April 7:
The Lenox Lyceum Exhibition, in the former Panoramic Building at Madison Avenue and 59th Street, New York City, opens to the public with an elaborate installation of Edison's achievements and products. As part of this exhibition, there is an unsolved mystery about whether W. K. L. Dickson produced a version of an Anschütz-style Schnellseher to project moving images on the ceiling of the hall. Gordon Hendricks originally proposed this early exhibition, but recent work by Paul Spehr shows that it is very unlikely to have taken place.[35]

April 10:
Anschütz Schnellseher gives another private demonstration for the family of Kaiser Wilhelm II at the Berlin City Palace. Shown were disks of an eagle owl in flight, running hounds, fencing soldiers, mounted soldiers riding, gymnastic exercises, and a few street scenes in the Berlin district of Kölln.

April 21 & 22:
Anschütz Schnellseher, in its drum form, demonstrated for Karl Maria Eder at the k. k. Graphischer Lehr- und Versuchsanstalt, Vienna. Disks shown were Hound in full run, Funny Journey (Lüstige Fahrt), Four marching soldiers, Horse and rider jumping a hurdle, Gymnast jumping over another by means of a springboard.

Late April:
Anschütz Schnellseher exhibited daily at a guest house at Parkviny 2, Vienna. The showings ran from 10 am to 8 pm for an admission of 30 Kreutzer for each viewer, for at least a week. Advertised as "Living Photography" and "not to be confused with the well-known Stroboscope", visitors were urged to contemplate "the electrical wonder of movement, as it has never before been seen". As there was only one drum-form Schnellseher in existence, the showings probably ended when the apparatus needed to move to its next proposed engagement.

May 9:
Eadweard Muybridge lectures with the Zoopraxiscope at both 3pm and 8pm at the Royal Concert Hall, Hastings, England, sponsored by the Hastings and St. Leonard's Photographic Society. The weather was poor, and so was the attendance.

June 26:
William Friese-Greene gives a demonstration talk at the Chester Photographic Convention about his motion picture cameras and lantern (projector), however he says the latter was damaged in transit. The only moving pictures seen are of a hand opening and closing, on a device with a built-in screen.

September 16:
Louis Aimé Augustin Le Prince, holder of the first British patent for a cinema device (10 January 1888), and a candidate for the inventor of the cinema, visits his brother in Dijon, where he boards the train to Paris and mysteriously disappears with his moving-picture apparatus. By 1888 Le Prince, using an awkward but practicable camera with sixteen lenses exposing two alternating rolls of paper negative film, could produce images at a rate appropriate for synthesizing movement and for its subsequent projection, although the slightly overlapping images had poor registration. It was with a rumored significantly improved single-lens device that he disappeared whilst on his way to Paris.

September 30:
Frederick H. Varley demonstrates a stereoscopic camera for taking serial pictures to the Photographic Society of Great Britain in London. Friese-Greene exhibits sequences taken with it.

35 The assumption of a major projection on this date is in Gordon Hendricks, *The Edison Motion Picture Myth*, pp. 84–92. Showing that it is nearly impossible to have occurred, but that interest in moving projections was intense and that what actually happened at the exhibition remains a mystery, is the analysis of Paul Spehr in *The Man Who Made Movies: W. K. L. Dickson*, pp. 180–182. Repeated attempts were made to convert the Anschütz Schnellseher in its second model (called Tachyscope in the US) into a projector, but all were failures and the apparatus was not capable of projecting its images over any significant distance. Anschütz's later device, the Projecting Electrotachyscope, which was indeed capable of large-scale projection, was not patented until November 1894 (see below), although there is a convincing report that it, or a predecessor apparatus, was demonstrated nearly a year before the patent.

October 1:
George Eastman begins construction of Kodak Park, a new manufacturing facility outside Rochester, New York, with a groundbreaking ceremony for the first three buildings: a testing laboratory, a power plant, and a new film factory. Necessitated by the strong demand for flexible celluloid film for roll-system cameras, the new factory was initially equipped with twelve glass coating tables, each 200 feet in length. Within six months of its opening in June 1891, enlargement was begun, and the capacity was doubled by 1892.

October 3:
French patent 208, 617, *Appareil photo-chronographique*, to Étienne-Jules Marey for his chronophotographic apparatus using a film band. The 90mm wide, unperforated, sensitized paper film band was held by a pressure plate momentarily in the camera's aperture, while double rotating disc shutters allowed the light to expose it. The film travelled between two spools enclosed in the camera, and could move at a speed of 1,80 meters per second.

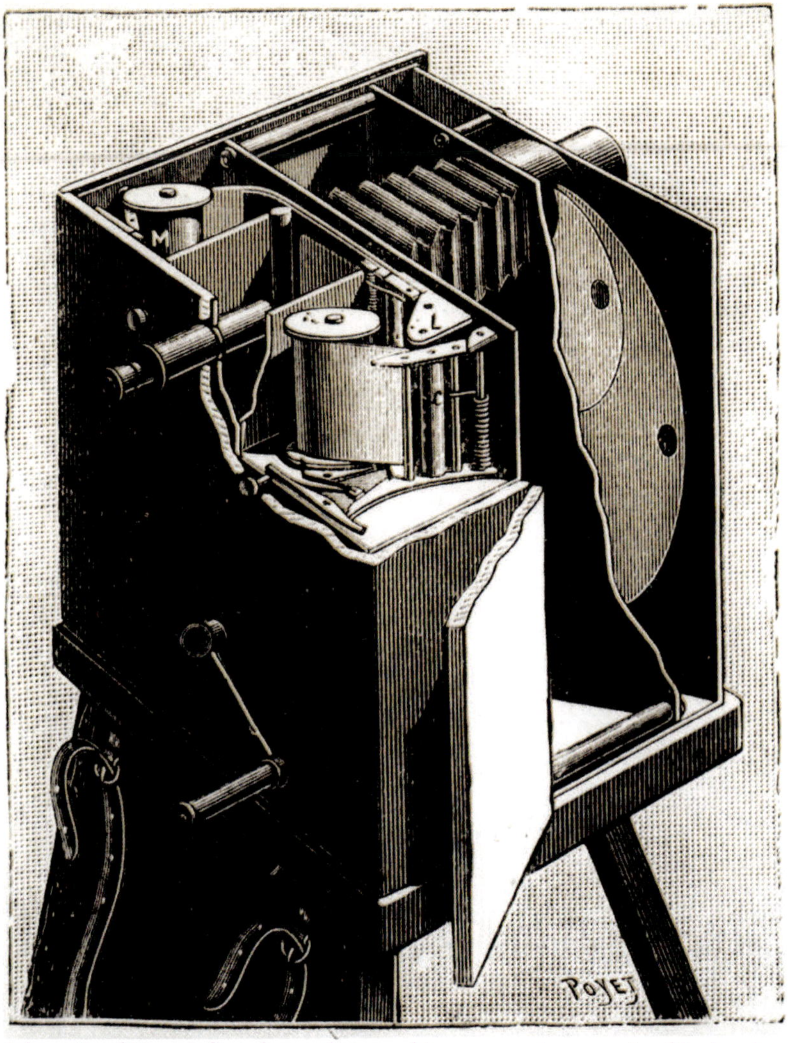

Schematic of Marey's first chronophotographic camera using a moving film band 1,60 meters long, 1890. [*La Nature*, No. 911, 15 November 1890, p.377.]

October 8:
German patent 57 133, *Photographischer Apparat für Serienaufnahmen*, to Ernst

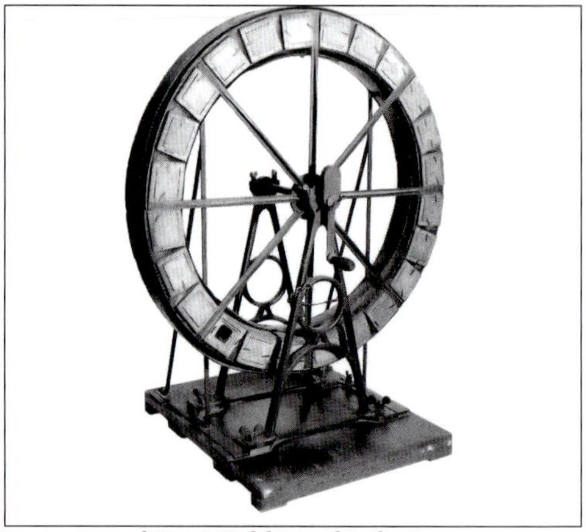
Rear view of Ernst Kohlrausch's first chronophotographic camera, showing the 24 individual plate holders and the operating crank. [Deutsches Museum, Munich.]

Kohlrausch for his chronophotographic apparatus allowing the taking of sequence photographs for the analysis of movement. The device had 24 cameras mounted on a vertical wheel; when set in motion each camera passed an aperture through which light from the subject was allowed to fall upon the photosensitive plate, thus avoiding parallax in the taking of series photographs. An eminent gymnast and physical education teacher, Kohlrausch intended this apparatus and its subsequent projector to be used in the teaching of proper gymnastic exercise.[36]

36 In 1893 (or 1894?) Kohlrausch described an improved apparatus, evidently not patented, in which four lenses are attached to a rotating disk, with the 24 photographic plates attached to a rotating wheel in motion continuously behind the lenses. The disk and the drum are connected by gears so that the individual lenses and plates are precisely aligned when a lever is thrown to release the shutters and record a full series of images. Both cameras and their projectors survive in the collection of the Deutsches Museum, Munich.

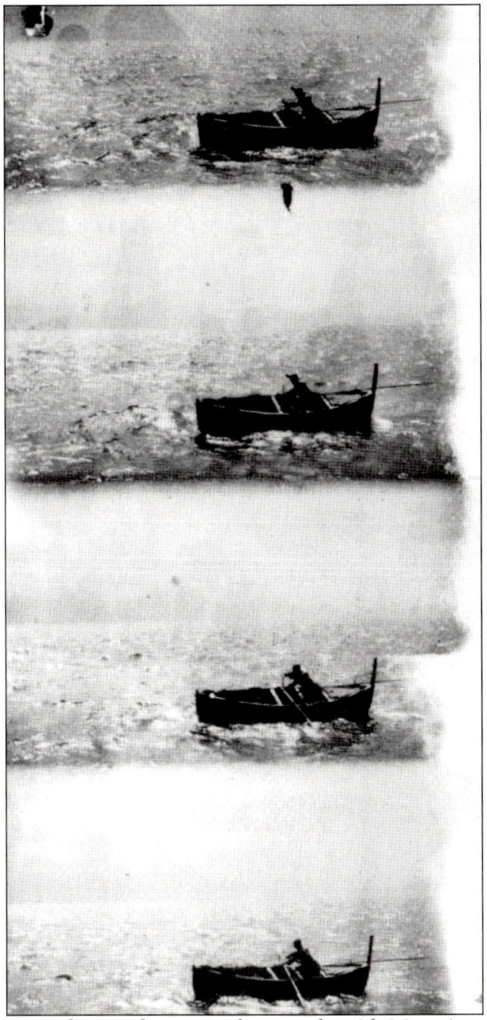

Four phases of a rowing boat made with Marey's film band camera in 1890.
[Archives of the Collège de France.]

☛Eadweard Muybridge lectures with the Zoopraxiscope for the Bristol and West of England Amateur Photographic Association in Colston Hall, Bristol. A second lecture was given on Friday, October 10, when "As on Wednesday evening, the attendance was decidedly not large".

October 13:
Eadweard Muybridge lectures at the Midland Institute, Birmingham, England, with his Zoopraxiscope.

October 20:
Eadweard Muybridge repeats his lecture at the Midland Institute, Birmingham, England, with his Zoopraxiscope.

October 21:
William Friese-Greene demonstrates two stereoscopic cameras to the North London Photographic Society, one of which has been adapted to be used as a lantern for projection. He hands around strips of negatives from the camera, one being 23m (75ft) long.

October 28:
Eadweard Muybridge lectures with the Zoopraxiscope at the Sheffield Literary and Philosophical Society, 7.30 pm at the Music Hall, Surrey Street. "No admission without ticket."

☛French patent 209,174. *Perfectionnements dans la production et la représentation des images photographiques instantanées*, to Wordsworth Donisthorpe and William Carr Crofts for their Kinesigraph combination camera and projector.

November 3:
Étienne-Jules Marey demonstrates his improved sequence camera for the Académie des Sciences in Paris. Using George Eastman's new flexible transparent celluloid film, and with a six-pointed star wheel intermittently clamping the film before the lens during its continuous transport, the camera was able to expose sequence photographs at rates up to 100 pictures per second, for the close analysis of movement.

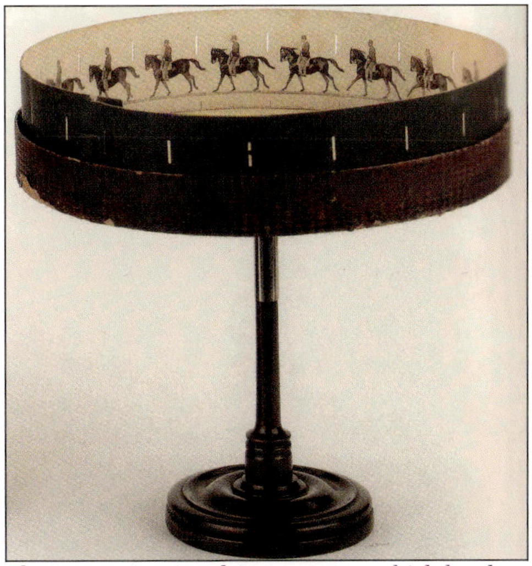

The innovative Anschütz zoetrope, which he also called a Schnellseher, that allowed any number of movement phases to be used.
[Georg Füsslin Collection.]

November 7:
Eadweard Muybridge lectures with the Zoopraxiscope at the Bristol Naturalists' Society, in The Victoria Rooms, Bristol, England.

November 9:
German patent 58 166, *Vorrichtung zur Erzeugung und Vorführung von Augenblicksbildern*, to Wordsworth Donisthorpe and William Carr Crofts for their Kinesigraph camera and projector.

November 11:
US patent 452,966, *Method of Producing Instantaneous Photographs*, to Wordsworth Donisthorpe and William Carr Crofts for their Kinesigraph camera and projector.

November 15:
German patent 60285, *Stroboskopischer Apparat (Schnellseher)*, to Ottomar Anschütz for an improved zoetrope where individual photographs are separated by narrow viewing slots, and then form the cylindrical wall of the zoetrope when it is attached to the rotating

base of the device. This allowed any number of phases in a chronophotograph to be used, as the number of viewing slots was determined by the number of photographs, and not by the inflexible apertures of a normal zoetrope. This was intended to use Anschütz's series photographs to reconstitute the impression of continuous motion, whcre the first and last images in any strip matched so that there was no interruption in the fluid motion of the image. The thin viewing slots ensured the clarity and crispness of the moving image.

November 27:
H. Smith of the Eastman Company demonstrates flexible celluloid roll films, a new product of the company, at the Bath Photographic Society. The celluloid film was on sale in England from January, 1890.

☛Frederick Varley describes, but does not show, a stereoscopic camera, at a meeting of the London and Provincial Photographic Association. Friese-Greene exhibits strips of film shot with the camera.[37]

☛Eadweard Muybridge lectures with the Zoopraxiscope as part of a series of six Armistead Lectures at Kinnaird Hall, Dundee, Scotland. The 8pm lecture was preceded by an organ recital at 7.15. Tickets for the course, First Seats 2*s*, Second Seats 6d; individual tickets after 7.45, 6d and 1d.[38]

December 4:
Eadweard Muybridge lectures with the Zoopraxiscope for the Mechanic's Institution, Burnley, England.

December 8 and 9:
Eadweard Muybridge lectures with the Zoopraxiscope at the Corn Exchange, Gloucester, England. On the 8th the sponsor was the Literary and Scientific Association, and the Exchange was crowded. While praising the lecture, the *Gloucester Citizen* complained strenuously: "The corporation ought really to keep their rats in better order than to allow them to career about the Corn Exchange on public occasions. The appearance of these rodents (whom a long succession of corn markets seems to have rendered enterprising to a most impudent and unpleasant degree) upon the screen last night would have been appropriate, and they might have served a useful purpose as illustrations of Mr. Muybridge's points; but their practical demonstrations on the floor of the laws of animal locomotion – whatever relation it may have borne to their design and art – not only proved somewhat terrifying to ladies in the audience, but distracted attention from the lecturer and his subject." On the 9th, under the auspices of the Natural Science Society, "the attendance was but scanty".

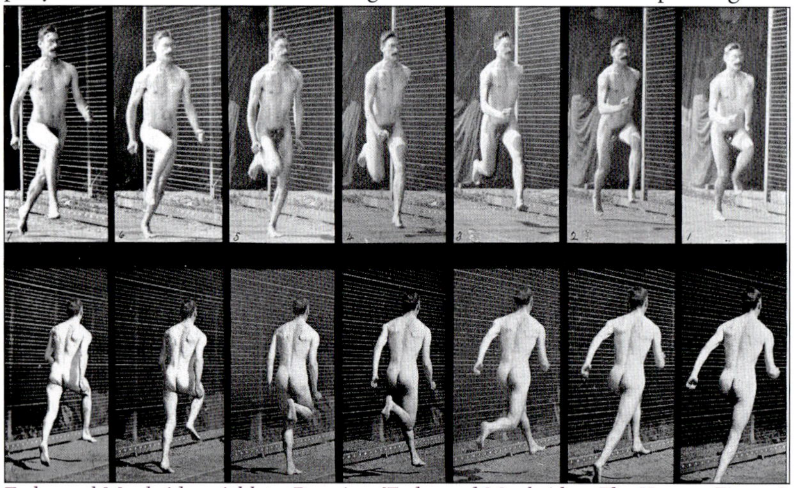

Eadweard Muybridge, *Athlete. Running.* [Eadweard Muybridge, *The Human Figure I Motion*, Fifth Edition, 1919, p. 37.]

December 12:
Eadweard Muybridge lectures with the Zoopraxiscope at the Town Hall, Bootle, with the mayor presiding. Lecture 8pm, admission 2*s* 6d, 1*s*, or 6d.

December 16:
Eadweard Muybridge lectures with the Zoopraxiscope at Co-Operative Hall, Darwin, as the third in the series of Huntington Lectures.

December 17:
Eadweard Muybridge lectures with the Zoopraxiscope at the Town Hall, Manchester, in a meeting chaired by the Mayor.

Undated: further Anschütz Schnellseher exhibitions at the Tagung des Deutschen Photographen-Vereins, Weimar;

Undated: further Muybridge lectures in Hull, Portsmouth, Chatham, the Royal College of Surgeons, the Royal Geographic Society, others.

37 Friese-Greene was declared bankrupt in 1891 and was not seen at photographic or scientific societies for five years. Nonetheless, he held on to most of his motion picture equipment and around the middle of 1893 he shot a film of the street outside his wife's photographic studio at 35 King's Road, London, on perforated 65mm celluloid, with a 4:3 picture ratio. There are several personal accounts of projection in his basement workshop there, but no public demonstrations. In 1896 he made a successful comeback and was involved with key early film figures including Birt Acres, John Wrench, John Alfred Prestwich and Esme Collings.

38 The following lecture, on Friday, December 5, was given by C. R. C. Steytler on the topic"Edison's Latest and Most Perfected Phonograph"

1891

January 9:

Ernst Kohlrausch demonstrates his chronophotographic apparatus before the Verein zur Förderung der Photographie in Berlin. Between 1890 and 1893 Kohlrausch took series photographs of gymnastic exercises which were considered 'completely sharp and finished'.

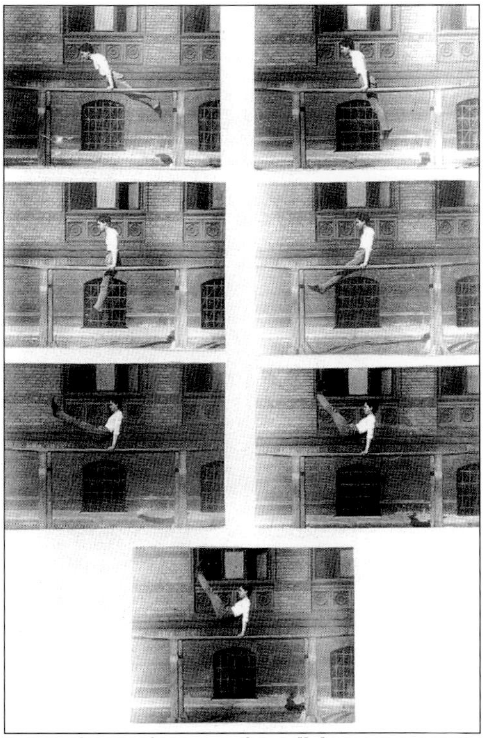

Seven phases of *Swings of Parallel Bars*, 1891, taken in front of the Gymnasium where Kohlrausch taught. [Deutsches Museum, Munich.]

January 24:

Eadweard Muybridge lectures with the Zoopraxiscope at the Hotel de la Société de Geographie, Paris, France. The hall was filled and many artists were present.

February 27:

Eadweard Muybridge lectures with the Zoopraxiscope in Manchester, England.

March 9:

Eadweard Muybridge lectures at the Urania Theatre, Berlin, before an audience of 500 persons, including Minister of Culture von Goslar, members of the Academy of Science and Arts including Adolf Friedrich Erdmann von Menzel, members of the Art Association, and other prominent dignitaries and physicists. He projected his drawn series pictures with his Zoöpraxiscope after Ottomar Anschütz refused to make photographic series transparencies available for the demonstration.[39]

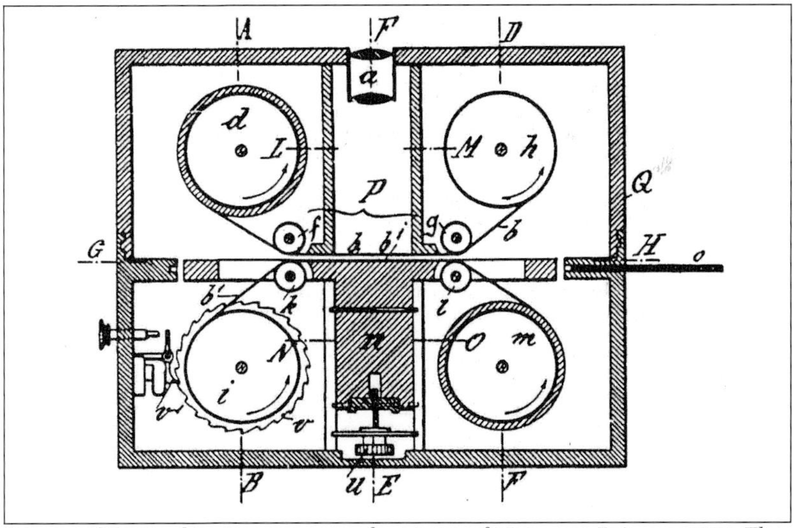

Scheme of the combination camera and projector of Victor von Reitzner, 1891. The upper band of celluloid moves steadily from left to right, and the lower metal shutter band moves from right to left intermittently.
[German patent 59390 of 22 March 1891, Fig. 1.]

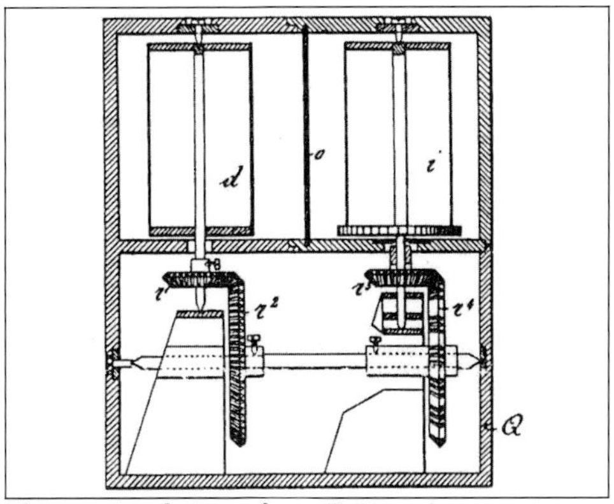

This sectional view of von Reitzner's apparatus shows the wide film band on the left driven by the same crank shaft as the gap-toothed intermittent on the right.
[German patent 59390 of 22 March 1891, Fig. 2.]

March 22:

German patent 59390, *Aufnahme- und Projektionsapparat für bewegliche Objekte*, to Victor von Reitzner of Vienna, for a chronophotographic camera and projection apparatus with a continuously moving paper or celluloid film band. The device had an unusual intermittently moving shutter at the focal plane, an opaque band with slightly trapezoidal slots ('so that in taking a picture, the sky is exposed

39 In contrast to the impressed scientists, who received Muybridge warmly, Anschütz was critical: "they interested me very much ... my judgement is this: those projected pictures which were technically competent, are accomplishments which everybody is capable of copying. The rest leaves much to be desired."

less on the film') moving in the opposite direction to the film. Intermittent movement was produced by means of an unusual gap-toothed gear wheel very similar to the one later used by George William de Bedts in 1896, who had been von Reitzner's Paris sales agent.

May 20:
A prototype Edison Kinetoscope has its first demonstration for outsiders at the West Orange laboratory, when it is shown to 147 delegates of the National Federation of Women's Clubs after their luncheon at the Edison home, 'Glenmont'. Press reports followed when journalists from New York City saw the apparatus a week later. This early model used film 19mm wide with perforations along one side, and the film featured Edison employee W. K. L. Dickson, doffing his hat and nodding a greeting to the viewers of his image on film.

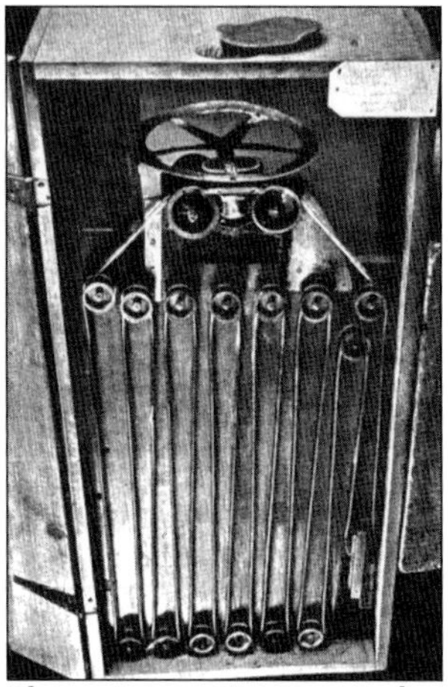

The prototype Kinetoscope for 19mm wide film used for the exhibition to Mrs. Edison's friends at her luncheon for the National Federation of Women's Clubs.
[Hans Traub, *Als man anfing zu filmen* (1940), p. 63.]

July 18:
Anschütz Schnellseher opens to the public at Stadtbahnbogen 21, a railway arch in the Berlin Exhibition Park. The exhibition ran daily until December. Precise figures for 18 July to 25 August record 14,858 viewings at 10 Pf. each; there were over 17,000 viewings to 31 August. Anschütz used the success of this exhibition of his original model Schnellseher to try and convince Siemens & Halske to construct the automat version of the apparatus at their own expense, an offer which they declined. The exhibition ran until December.

July 27:
The Phonoscope of Georges Demenÿ is presented at the Académie des Sciences, Paris. The device used twenty-four sequential images fixed to the outer rim of a glass disc, which was then placed between a strong light source and a lens. A second counter-rotating disk with slots provided an intermittent shutter. Demenÿ's main subject was a man pronouncing words and phrases. Later, he hoped that his 'speaking portraits' (*portraits parlants*) would replace still photography for family albums, a suggestion already demonstrated by Ottomar Anschütz.

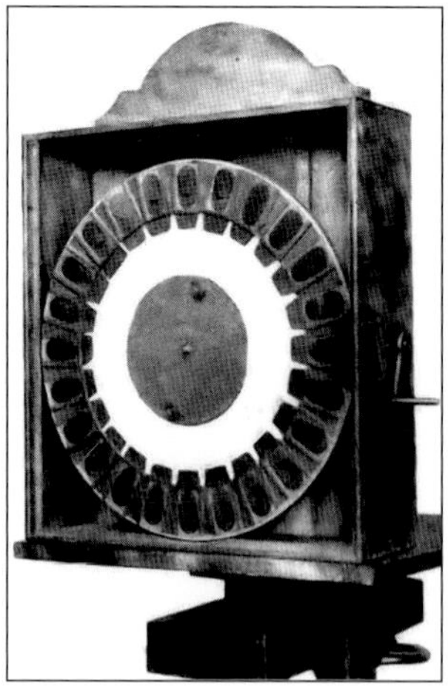

Interior of the Demenÿ Phonoscope, with a disk of 24 images mounted.
[Karel Smrz, *Dejiny Filmu* (1933), p. 173.]

August 8:
Anschütz Schnellseher, in its new model as a coin-fed automat, exhibited in the Halle für Wissenschaft und Medicine at the Internationale Elektrotechnische Ausstellung in Frankfurt am Main. This was the first public appearance of the automat version of the Schnellseher, and was installed in the Siemens & Halske display at this major electrical exhibition that had opened in May and ran through October. Siemens & Halske ultimately produced over 150 automat Schnellsehers for Anschütz. A disk of a horse and rider jumping a hurdle was shown from 10am to 9pm.

August 24:
Thomas Alva Edison files three United States patent applications regarding his motion picture apparatus.[40] US patent 403, 534 covered

40 These three patent applications follow four motion picture 'caveats', whose dates have been sometimes cited as dates of patent or invention. A 'caveat' in the American patent system is a description of current work in progress, held privately at the Patent Office and valid for one year. It could be used as a bar to other applications regarding the same work. The Edison caveats were: Motion Picture Caveat 1, 8 October 1888; Motion Picture Caveat II, 3 February 1889; Motion Picture Caveat III, 2 May 1889; and Motion Picture Caveat IV, 2 November 1889. Edison had learned early in his inventing career of the importance of utilising the US patent process on behalf of his clients, and the multiplicity of his inventions comes to a large extent from his interest (and that of his financiers) in blanketing coverage of any area of investigation so widely as to inhibit the ability of others to enter the field with competitive apparatus. As a young inventor, Edison had been initiated into this modern big business practise by some of the largest and toughest American corporations. On 2 December 1872, William Orton, president of Western Union and Edison's main client at the time, wrote to Edison that he should 'invent as many processes as possible [in order] to anticipate other inventors in new modes and also to patent as many combinations as possible.' By 1876, under a new contract with Western Union that gave Edison the resources to build his Menlo Park laboratory, he was working for clients on improvements to the telephone, with the express purpose of finding ways to get around the patent of Alexander Graham Bell of Boston.
By the time Edison began his prolonged and rather low priority work on motion pictures, this style of legal manipulation was as important a component of his overall business stance as his undoubted genius for innovation. Along with Edison's public prominence, his ability to seduce journalists, his financial security and his unparalleled record as an inventor, Edison's knowledge of how to manoeuvre within the patent and

the method of taking the pictures and subsequently reproducing them.[41] US patent 403,535 covered the method and apparatus for taking the pictures.[42] US patent 403,536 covered the apparatus for reproducing the pictures in an exhibiting machine.[43] These broad claims had great difficulty over many years in the U. S. Patent Office, with various claims being rejected in favour of priority by Le Prince, Donisthorpe & Crofts, Friese-Greene, Southworth & Hawes, and several others. While work continued at Edison's laboratory that increasingly changed the technical nature of the equipment covered by these patent applications, Edison's lawyers were in heated negotiation with the patent office and all three were finally issued between 1893 and 1897, some in quite radically changed form. The camera patent became the most important of the three, as US patent 589,168 issued on 31 August 1897, the basis of Edison's many later attempts to claim a monopoly on all motion picture production.

December 6:
Georges Demenÿ demonstrates his Phonoscope at the Conservatory of Art, Paris, before 1200 people. It is unclear whether the Phonoscope itself was demonstrated, as its tiny aperture and modest illumination were inadequate for such a large audience, or whether the thirty diapositives with sound that were exhibited were seen on a magic lantern or other apparatus.

Undated: further Muybridge lectures May and June at the Technische Hochschule, Munich; Technische Hochschule, Vienna; Society of Artists, Vienna; Turin, Italy.

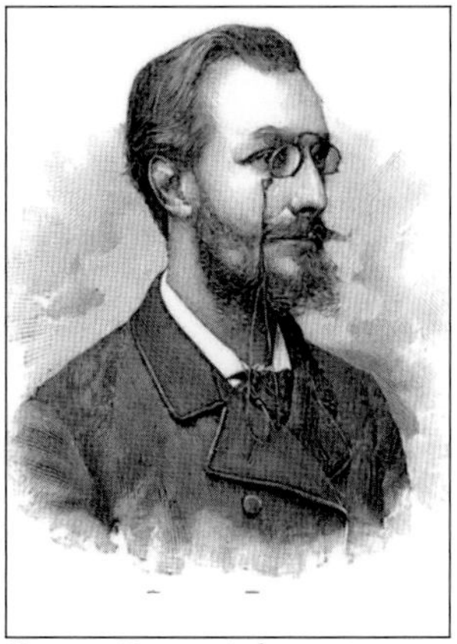

Georges Demenÿ about 1885. [Photographer unknown. Public domain.]

1892

February 12:
French patent, *Appareil photographique instantané pour l'obtention automatique et sans interruption d'une série de clichés analytiques du mouvement ou autres dit le Cinématographe Léon Bouly*, to Léon Bouly for a photographic apparatus to take a row of analytical pictures, called Cinématographe Léon Bouly – the first appearance of the word "cinématographe". Designed for film somewhere between 38mm and 48mm wide, with a friction intermittent mechanism provided by broken rollers intermittently gripping the film and pulling it down, Bouly's equipment does not seem to have been demonstrated and no film survives.

March 3:
French patent 219,830, *Appareil dit Phonoscope reproduisant l'illusion des mouvements de la parole et de la physionomie par*

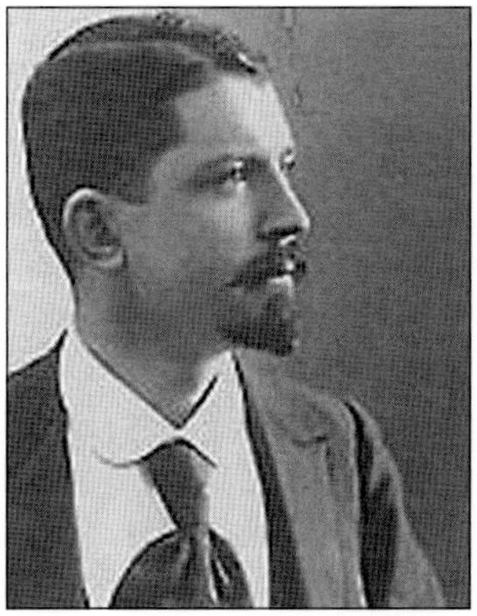

Léon Bouly in c1895. [Photographer unknown.]

legal systems may have been even more important in charting the course of development of the motion picture in America than has heretofore been acknowledged, even by the 'anti-Edison' authors, who somewhat miss the point. The aggressive drive not only to invent and to succeed, but equally to inhibit competitors and to drive them from the arena had been a part of Edison's normal practise as an inventor for at least two decades before the birth of the movies.
There is undoubtedly further work to be done in examining the process of the invention of movie apparatus in America in the 1890s from this perspective, especially as the American invention history in this decade is so different from that of France, Britain, or Germany. The necessary work is not an anti-Edison exercise, but one that re-evaluates and re-examines all of the factors involved that make the history of moving pictures in America so different from the equivalent histories in western Europe.

41 All claims for this patent were rejected on both 2 January 1892 and 15 October 1895. On the last day possible for an appeal, 18 October 1895, a new set of specifications was put forth, creating a patent interference case with the Biograph company, which they lost on 26 March 1897. Biograph's petition to appeal was declined on 31 July and the patent 589,168, *Kinetographic Camera*, was issued to Edison a month later. Biograph vigorously contended that fraud had occurred over this patent, which was then actively used against many companies, including the International Film Company, Maguire and Baucus as agents for Lumière, Sigmund Lubin, and Edward H. Amet. This patent was one of Edison's primary contributions to the Motion Picture Patents Company, which continued to sue on its basis (among others) as late as mid-1914.

42 Twenty-two of twenty-three claims in this application were rejected on 4 January 1892. A claim for a stop-motion intermittent device was divided from the patent and filed separately on 26 March 1892, with all four of its claims rejected on 18 June 1892. Changing their phrasing, the Edison lawyers finally succeeded in persuading the Patent Office to issue the amended text as US patent 491,993, *Stop Device*, on 21 February 1893.

43 All but two of the 19 claims in this application were rejected on 13 November 1891. After lengthy correspondence and further changes, the patent was issued as US patent 493,426, *Apparatus for Exhibiting Photographs of Moving Objects*, on 14 March 1893.

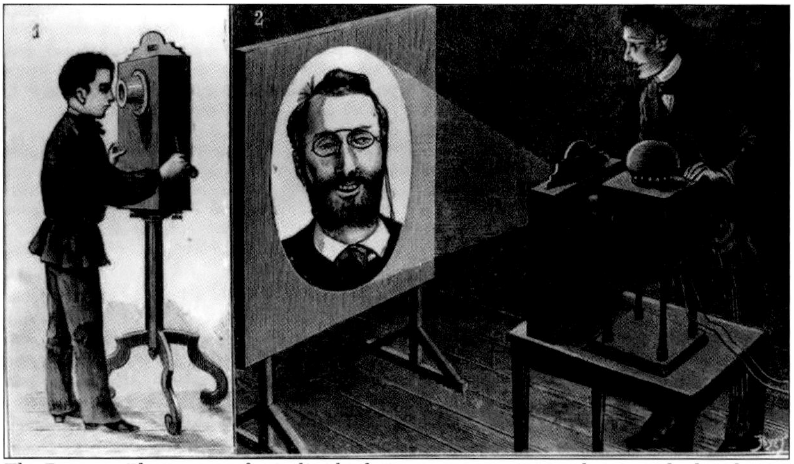

The Demenÿ Phonoscope for individual viewing or projection, here an idealized projection of a portrait of Demenÿ himself.
[*La Nature*, No. 985, 16 April 1892, p. 312, Fig. 2.]

vision directe ou par projection au moyen d'une lumière, to Georges Demenÿ for the Phonoscope, a chronophotographic apparatus developed in the laboratory of Étienne-Jules Marey using a disc of 24 or 30 images rotated in front of a second rapidly and synchronously moving shutter disk, for 'reproducing the illusion of movement in speech and physiognomy by direct vision and by means of light.' The device could be viewed individually through a lens, as a peepshow, or adapted for projection using a Molteni lantern as illumination. Demenÿ intended the apparatus to be used to teach the hearing-impaired to speak. Displayed at the International Photographic Exhibition at the Champ de Mars in Paris, *Le Radical* reported: 'I must tell you that this is something amazing. ... Some day or other, industry will get hold of this happy invention, and then present-day photography will get the elbow. The animated portrait is certainly the photography of tomorrow.'[44]

April:
Anschütz Schnellseher installed at the Zoologische Garten, Bremen. Five automat models were installed at this zoo where Anschütz had for several years undertaken instantaneous photography of animals.

April 18:
Eadweard Muybridge lectures with the Zoopraxiscope at the Academy of Sciences, San Francisco, California.

April 22:
Eadweard Muybridge lectures with the Zoopraxiscope at the art Association, San Francisco, California.

May 2:
Étienne-Jules Marey writes a letter to the Académie des Sciences, describing a projector he was working on for his sequenced photographs and his intention to demonstrate it at a future meeting. The demonstration never took place, in part because the registration of the images in his camera was uneven and the mechanism of his projector was too abrupt for the film bands to survive. He achieved only some ragged projections at the laboratory, of individual images cut apart and reassembled onto a rubberized fabric.[45]

May 3:

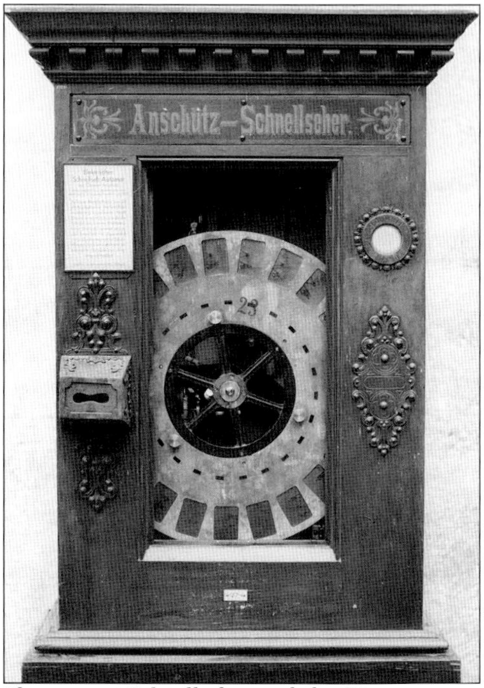

The automat Schnellseher made by Siemens & Halske, Berlin in over 150 examples. The viewing port is on the left, the coin entry slot at the upper right. The works were exposed so that viewers could witness the operation of the marvel.
[Deutsches Museum, Munich.]

44 There were additions to this patent on 25 August 1892, 2 May 1896, 18 June 1896, and 24 July 1897. British patent 15,709 of 1 September 1892; German patent 71339 of 20 November 1892. The French and German patents also include a suggestion for an entirely different apparatus: series pictures are mounted in a spiral on an opaque drum operated by a crank, with a lens fixed opposite the drum. The axle of the drum is a helical screw, which moves each image past the lens in succession, with the intermittent provided by a circular shutter powered through the same geared crank revolving synchronously in front of the light source, which is directed to each image by a mirror.

45 At the end of 1893, in his book *Le Mouvement*, Marey rejected the idea of projection. However, in his paper for this meeting, Marey says: 'It is possible to give the eye the sensation of real movement by projecting images in succession on to a screen by means of an instrument which I shall have the honor of presenting to the Academy at an upcoming meeting,' but Marey never fulfilled this promise.

Anschütz Schnellsehers shipped to the Hohenzollern Galerie, Berlin. Four machines were installed later in May by the Siemens & Halske mechanic Zander, and were exhibited to the pubic at this prestigious gallery through June.

June:
Anschütz Schnellseher installed at the Berlin Ausstellungpark with four automat machines, running for five months. The Schnellsehers were probably transferred from the nearby Hohenzollern Galerie, and were possibly a return to Stadtbahnbogen 21. Anschütz kept good records of the visitors to this exhibition, which saw the apparatus viewed, at 10 Pfg. per viewing, 16,618 times in June, 17,271 times in July, 9,978 times in September, and 3,517 times in October.

June 5:
German patent 66346, *Kontrolvorrichtung für Selbstverkäufer*, to Ottomar Anschütz for a coin-operated mechanism for a free-standing automat. Siemens & Halske were irritated with Anschütz for applying for this patent, as they had done most of the work on the device during the development of the automat Schnellseher.

June 13:
Anschütz Schnellseher installed at the Crystal Palace, London, by the UK Siemens & Halske agents. The exhibition was limited to only a few weeks because of the planned disconnection of electricity supplied by Siemens & Halske to the exhibition hall.

July 21:
Extra disks for the Anschütz Schnellseher were shipped to the Zoologische Garten, Berlin, where four machines were running for public visitors, at least through September.

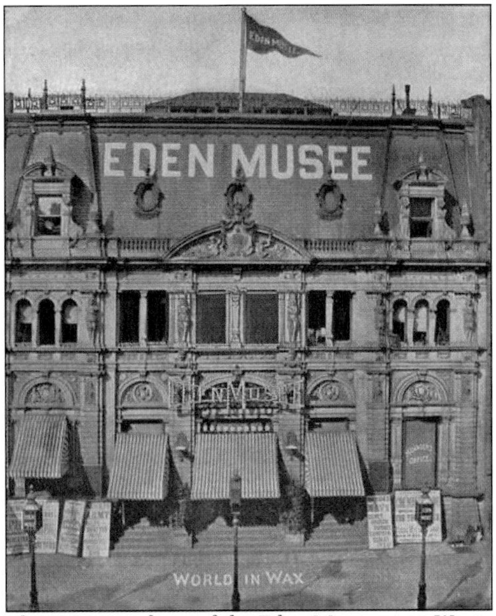

The imposing front of the Eden Musee at 55 West 23rd Street, New York City, in 1899, taken during the Dewey celebrations. Most likely a publicity photo from the Musee itself.
[*The New York Times*, 20 June 1915.]

September 1:
Anschütz Schnellseher exhibited at the Eden Musée, 55 West 23rd Street, New York City. Two machines, the first of five exhibited, were running on this date. Disks shown included *Boxers*, later also known as *Boxers in the Ring*. These Schnellsehers were part of a shipment of 26 machines that were sent to the United States by Siemens & Halske in August. The Siemens and Halske mechanic E. Zander oversaw the installation and operation of the machines in New York and elsewhere.[46]

September 24:
United States patent 525,991, *Series Photographic Camera*, to Max Mayer of Munich, Germany, for his chronophotographic camera using either a ring holding sensitized plates or a moving band of paper film. The intermittent was provided by an ingeniously shaped tappet acting on a ring of twenty-one shaped teeth; when cranked, an off-center arm on a slave gear motivated the tappet. Twenty-five to fifty exposures per second were possible. A particularly interesting point of this unusual apparatus, which is nearly unrecorded, is that Mayer specifically intended the pictures to be used to reproduce motion 'in a stroboscope, magic-wheel, disk or similar instrument.'[47]

September 29:
Anschütz Schnellsehers exhibited at an unknown location for the Am. Inst. Dur. Produkts in New York City. Twelve Schnellsehers were exhibited.

October:
Emile Reynaud opens his show of living pictures, Pantomimes Lumineuses, at the

46 This exhibition is reported inaccurately (especially with regard to its dates) in both Talbot's *Moving Pictures*, p. 47 (1912 & 1923) and Ramsaye's *A Million and One Nights*, Vol. 1, pp. 182–183 (1926). Talbot says in 1923 that the apparatus was "exactly the same" as the Kinetoscope, which was not patented in Europe, which is an egregious error.

47 Only Zglinicki, *in Der Weg des Films*, p. 229, mentions a patent to Max Meyer [sic.] of Munich. A letter from Mayer in 1911 in the Oskar Messter legacy in the Bundesarchiv (Folder 87, old numbers), says the apparatus was patented in the United States to avoid the high fees of patenting in Germany, and contains a typical claim of priority, saying the device was first worked out in December 1872 and January 1873. Although the device seems not to have been publicly demonstrated, and is still a question for further research, the patent was published on 11 September 1894, and it is also interesting that Mayer located the purpose of his device more in the world of entertainment and amusement than in the realm of science and motion analysis. His apparatus is also an example of how widespread the idea of reconstituting motion was in the 1890s, and of how the development of chronophotographic apparatus that was only a half-step away from the cinema was not confined to a tight circle of professional scientists and physiologists.

Théâtre Optique, in the Cabinet Fantastique of the Musée Grevin, 28 Boulevard Montmartre, Paris. A singer accompanied by a piano player interpreted the serenade of Colombine by Pierrot, and an original score throughout was composed by Gaston Paulin.[48] Between 1892 and 1900 there were some 12,800 performances seen by over 500,000 visitors, at an admission price of 50 centimes.[49]

October 10:
Anschütz Schnellseher exhibited at Koster & Biall's Music Hall, Broadway and 34th Street, New York City. This apparatus was part of the 26 automat Schnellsehers that had arrived in New York in August.

Mid-October:
Tachyscope of M. J. Steffens and E. E. Fiora exhibited at

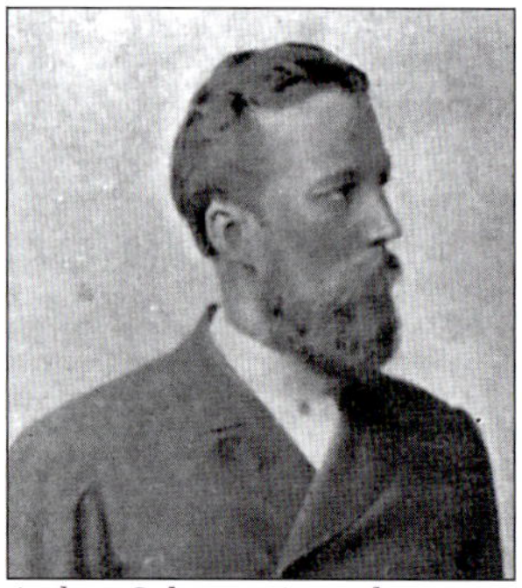

Arthur Schwarz in early 1893, just after he became head of the Electrical Wonder Company.
[*The Practical Photographer* (London), 1 January 1893, courtesy Richard Brown.]

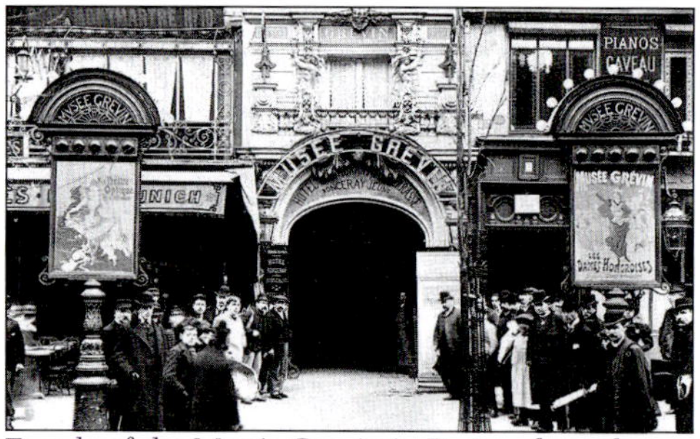

Facade of the Musée Grevin in Paris, where the Pantomimes Lumineuses of Émile Reynaud was exhibited for eight years from October, 1892.

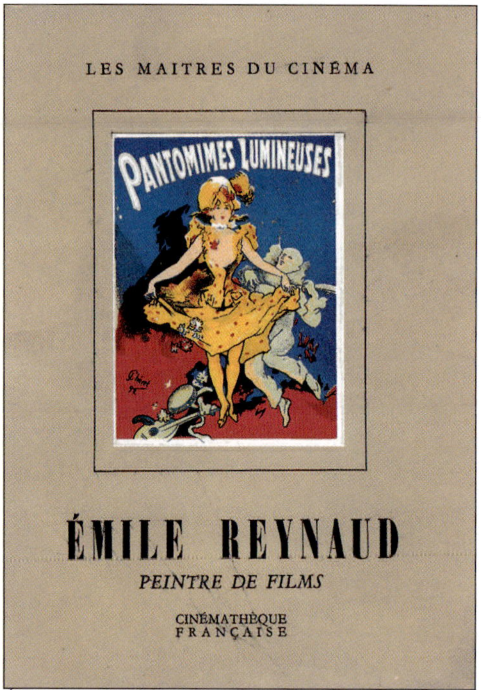

Émile Reynaud and his Pantomimes Lumineuses were valorized by the Cinématheque française in their first publication in 1946.
[Deac Rossell collection.]

Chapin and Gore's restaurant, Monroe Street, Chicago. This apparatus was most likely a pirate copy of the Anschütz Schnellseher.

November 12:
Founding of the Electrical Wonder Company (EWC) in London, consolidating world-wide rights (outside Germany) for the exploitation of the Anschütz Schnellseher. Arthur Schwartz

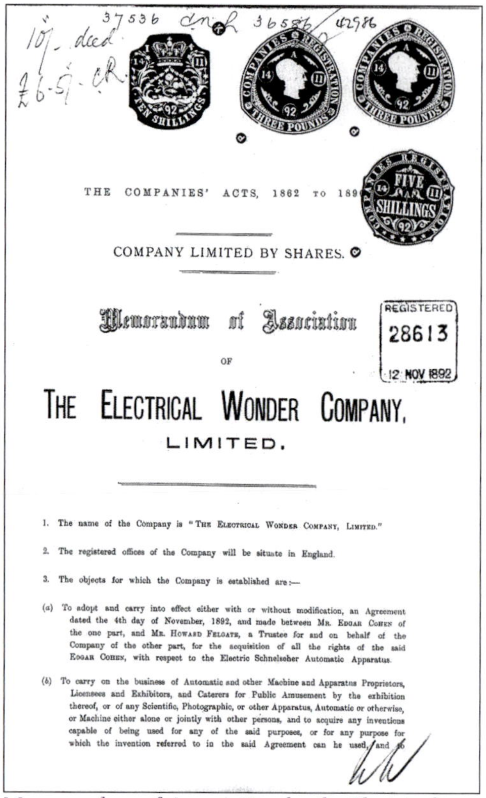

THE COMPANIES' ACTS, 1862 TO 189

COMPANY LIMITED BY SHARES.

REGISTERED 28613 12 NOV 1892

Memorandum of Association
OF
THE ELECTRICAL WONDER COMPANY,
LIMITED.

1. The name of the Company is "THE ELECTRICAL WONDER COMPANY, LIMITED."

2. The registered offices of the Company will be situate in England.

3. The objects for which the Company is established are:—

(a) To adopt and carry into effect either with or without modification, an Agreement dated the 4th day of November, 1892, and made between MR. EDGAR COHEN of the one part, and MR. HOWARD FELGATE, a Trustee for and on behalf of the Company of the other part, for the acquisition of all the rights of the said EDGAR COHEN, with respect to the Electric Schnelseher Automatic Apparatus.

(b) To carry on the business of Automatic and other Machine and Apparatus Proprietors, Licensees and Exhibitors, and Caterers for Public Amusement by the exhibition thereof, or of any Scientific, Photographic, or other Apparatus, Automatic or otherwise, or Machine either alone or jointly with other persons, and to acquire any inventions capable of being used for any of the said purposes, or for any purpose for which the invention referred to in the said Agreement can he used, and

Memorandum of Association for the Electrical Wonder Company, the London firm that would undertake world rights - outside Germany - for the Anschütz Schnellseher.
[Courtesy National Archives, Kew.]

became the head of this company that melded various contracts between Anschütz and Howard Felgate, Edgar Cohen, Joe Livingston, and others in the previous few weeks.

November 19:
The Blair Camera Company of Boston raises the price of its celluloid roll film to the trade. Founded by Thomas Henry Blair in 1879, this manufacturer of photographic cameras and apparatus began to make celluloid roll film in late 1891, and Blair was the sole supplier of celluloid roll film for parts of 1892 and 1893, largely due to the Eastman Company's difficulties in manufacture. Blair film was used almost exclusively for positive prints for the Edison Kinetoscope, since the celluloid

48 Gaston Paulin had also composed the music for a shadow play presented at the Musée Grevin by Louis Morin in 1891.

49 The Théâtre Optique closed on 1 March 1900, replaced by John Hiewelt's puppet show accompanied by an all-female orchestra from Hungary.

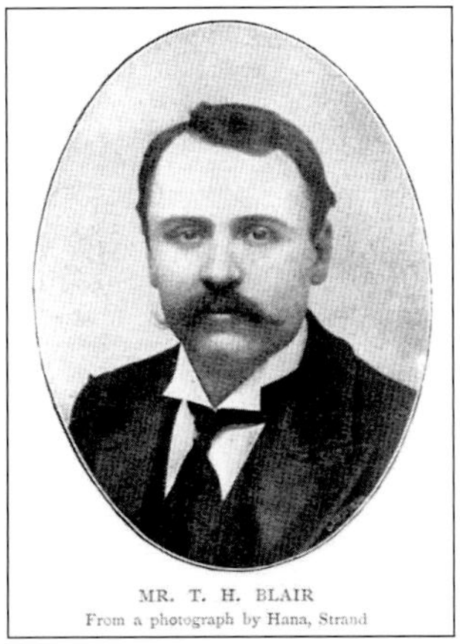

Thomas Henry Blair in 1895. [*Black and White*, 20 July 1895.[

base, which was purchased by Blair from the Celluloid Manufacturing Company of Newark, New Jersey, was semi-transparent with a slightly frosted appearance that was particularly suitable for viewing by transmitted light, as in the Kinetoscope. Blair film was also widely used in Europe by most of the English and many Continental inventors and film-makers through 1896.[50]

December 14:
UK patent 23,042, *Improvements in Coin Freed Apparatus for Exhibiting Optical Illusions*, to the Electrical Wonder Company in London for the Anschütz apparatus patented in Germany in June. EWC was now the world-wide agent (outside Germany) for the Schnellseher.

December 19:
Anschütz Schnellseher parlour with 12 automat machines opens at No. 425, The Strand, London. The exhibition continued until 30 March 1893. Disks shown include two different dancers, row of marching soldiers, horse and rider jumping a hurdle, boxers in the ring, group of trotting sulky riders, woman rider trotting, athlete performing a headstand, Uhlans on horseback, high jump, boys exercising, others. This was an exhibition by the newly-formed Electrical Wonder Company (EWC), who ultimately acquired world-wide rights to the commercial exploitation of the Schnellseher.

December 20:
Founding and first meeting of the Société Française du Phonoscope, created by Georges Demenÿ, Ludwig Stollwerck and William Gibbs-Clarke to exploit the Phonoscope for animated portraits, animated projections in combination with a phonograph, and as an automat viewer. Étienne-Jules Marey's laboratory chief and assistant for many years, Demenÿ founded his new venture while Marey was on his usual long Winter vacation in Naples.[51]

1893

January 13:
US patent 509,362, *Toy*, to Herman Casler of Syracuse, New York, for a combination toy and puzzle involving the placement of numbered small balls into numbered pockets. The toy is intended for amusement that requires both patience and study of its operation.

March 1:
US patent 509,841, *Photographic-camera Shutter*, to Herman Casler of Syracuse, New York, for a pivot-mounted small spring-driven shutter for a miniature detective camera.

☛US patent 517,539, *Camera*, to Herman Casler (one half assigned to Harry N. Marvin) for a small detective camera about the size of a pocket-watch, able to take six hexagonal exposures 13mm wide on a 44mm (1.75 inch) disc of film. This camera, known as the Photoret, was jointly designed by Casler and W. K. L. Dick-

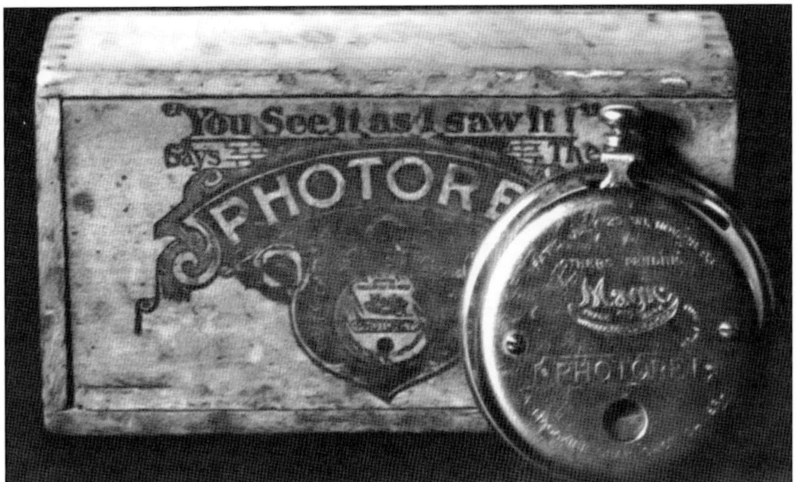

The Photoret pocket-watch camera, designed by Hermann Casler and W. K. L. Dickson. [Michel Auer, *The Illustrated History of the Camera* (1975), p. 99.]

50 While products of the Blair Camera Company had been available in England throughout the 1890s, the European Blair Camera Company was a wholly separate firm, begun by Thomas Henry Blair after he was removed from the management of his American concerns by disgruntled investors in 1895. European Blair, with manufacturing facilities at St. Mary Cray, Kent, and offices at 9 Southampton Street, High Holborn, London, sold a wide range of photographic equipment, dry plates, and celluloid films. They were an important supplier of celluloid films to both British and Continental inventors and pioneers through 1902.

51 The associates of this company were Georges Demenÿ, 3 rue Saussier Leroy, Paris; Ludwig Stollwerck, of Stollwerck Brothers, Cologne; and William Gibbs Clarke of Lausanne, who was represented by François-Henri Lavanchy-Clarke, also of Lausanne. The capital was fixed at 20,000 Fr., equally supplied by Stollwerck and Clarke, and the profits of the company were to be split evenly in thirds between the three partners.

son; Marvin likely provided some financing. It was successfully marketed for the Christmas season of 1893 by the Magic Introduction Company of New York, owned by Elias B. Koopman. In its positive review, *Scientific American* said of the Photoret that it "eclipses for compactness and novelty anything of the kind that has come to our note...". These four friends would ultimately go on to form the KMCD group, and then launch the American Mutoscope and Biograph Company.

March 11:
Anschütz Schnellseher exhibited at the Eleventh Annual Building Exhibition, Royal Agricultural Hall, Islington, London. The Schnellseher ran through 25 March.

March 21:
Anschütz Schnellseher parlour opened by the Electrical Wonder Company at 91 Brompton Road, London. The exhibition ran through 1 April.

March 24:
Anschütz Schnellsehers permanently installed by the EWC at the Crystal Palace, London, where they were called The Electrical Wonder. Continuous exhibitions ran from 10am to 9pm in the Entertainment Hall. The EWC went bankrupt on 2 December 1893, but the liquidator kept this exhibition open as it regularly returned over £2 per week. Possibly including a sale of eight machines and disks to the Crystal Palace itself in late January 1894, the exhibition remained open and advertised in the press until the end of May, 1895.

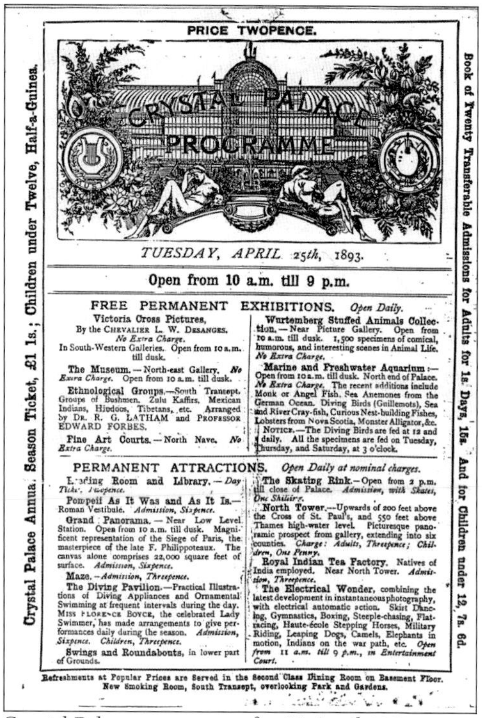

PRICE TWOPENCE.

CRYSTAL PALACE PROGRAMME

TUESDAY, APRIL 25th, 1893.

Open from 10 a.m. till 9 p.m.

FREE PERMANENT EXHIBITIONS. *Open Daily.*

Victoria Cross Pictures, By the CHEVALIER L. W. DESANGES. *No Extra Charge.* In South-Western Galleries. Open from 10 a.m. till dusk.

The Museum.—North-east Gallery. *No Extra Charge.* Open from 10 a.m. till dusk.

Ethnological Groups.—South Transept. Groups of Bushmen, Zulu Kaffirs, Mexican Indians, Hindoos, Tibetans, etc. Arranged by DR. R. G. LATHAM and PROFESSOR EDWARD FORBES.

Fine Art Courts.—North Nave. *No Extra Charge.*

Wurtemberg Stuffed Animals Collection.—Near Picture Gallery. Open from 10 a.m. till dusk. 1,500 specimens of comical, humorous, and interesting scenes in Animal Life. *No Extra Charge.*

Marine and Freshwater Aquarium:—Open from 10 a.m. till dusk. North end of Palace. *No Extra Charge.* The recent additions include Monk or Angel Fish, Sea Anemones from the German Ocean, Diving Birds (Guillemots), Sea and River Cray-fish, Curious Nest-building Fishes, Lobsters from Nova Scotia, Monster Alligator, &c. NOTICE.—The Diving Birds are fed at 12 and 5 daily. All the specimens are fed on Tuesday, Thursday, and Saturday, at 3 o'clock.

PERMANENT ATTRACTIONS. *Open Daily at nominal charges.*

Reading Room and Library.—*Day Ticket, Twopence.*

Pompeii As It Was and As It Is.—Roman Vestibule. *Admission, Sixpence.*

Grand Panorama.—Near Low Level Station. Open from 10 a.m. till dusk. Magnificent representation of the Siege of Paris, the masterpiece of the late F. Philippoteaux. The canvas alone comprises 22,000 square feet of surface. *Admission, Sixpence.*

Maze.—*Admission, Threepence.*

The Diving Pavilion.—Practical Illustrations of Diving Appliances and Ornamental Swimming at frequent intervals during the day. MISS FLORENCE BOYCE, the celebrated Lady Swimmer, has made arrangements to give performances daily during the season. *Admission, Sixpence. Children, Threepence.*

Swings and Roundabouts, in lower part of Grounds.

The Skating Rink.—Open from 2 p.m. till close of Palace. *Admission, with Skates, One Shilling.*

North Tower.—Upwards of 200 feet above the Cross of St. Paul's, and 550 feet above Thames high-water level. Picturesque panoramic prospect from gallery, extending into six counties. *Charge: Adults, Threepence; Children, One Penny.*

Royal Indian Tea Factory. Natives of India employed. Near North Tower. *Admission, Threepence.*

The Electrical Wonder, combining the latest development in instantaneous photography, with electrical automatic action. Skirt Dancing, Gymnastics, Boxing, Steeple-chasing, Flat-racing, Haute-école Stepping Horses, Military Riding, Leaping Dogs, Camels, Elephants in motion, Indians on the war path, etc. *Open from 11 a.m. till 9 p.m., in Entertainment Court.*

Refreshments at Popular Prices are Served in the Second Class Dining Room on Basement Floor. New Smoking Room, South Transept, overlooking Park and Gardens.

Crystal Palace Annua. Season Ticket, £1 1s.; Children under Twelve, Half-a-Guinea.

Book of Twenty Transferable Admissions for Adults for 1s. Days, 15s. And for Children under 12, 7s. 6d.

Crystal Palace programme for 25 April 1893, including the Anschütz Schnellseher, here called The Electrical Wonder. Some of the listed picture disks were not taken by Anschütz and were more likely copied from Muybridge. [Thanks to Richard Brown for a copy of this programme.]

April 11:
Eadweard Muybridge lectures with the Zoopraxiscope to art students at the Athenaeum Hall, Chicago, Illinois, prior to the opening of the World's Columbian Exposition in the city and during the construction of his Zoopraxigraphical Hall at the Exposition. The lecture was repeated again two days later on 13 April.

April 15:
The Electrical Wonder Company issues a call on shareholders due to their receipt of a concession to exhibit the Anschütz Schnellseher at the World's Columbian Exhibition in Chicago. The concession allowed the exhibition of up to 50 machines on the grounds of the Fair, where it was labelled The Electrical Wonder, and Chicago issued the concession promptly after Edison declined to make his Kinetoscope available, as his machine was unfinished.

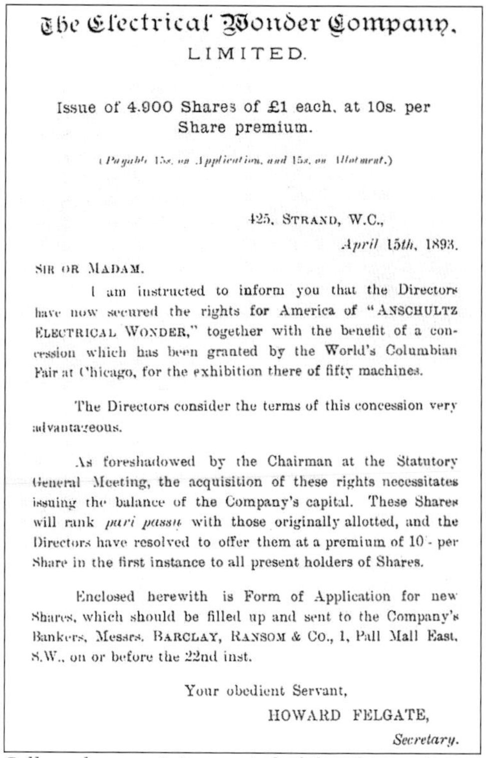

The Electrical Wonder Company,
LIMITED.

Issue of 4.900 Shares of £1 each, at 10s. per Share premium.

(*Payable 15s. on Application, and 15s. on Allotment.*)

425, STRAND, W.C.,
April 15th, 1893.

SIR OR MADAM.

I am instructed to inform you that the Directors have now secured the rights for America of "ANSCHULTZ ELECTRICAL WONDER," together with the benefit of a concession which has been granted by the World's Columbian Fair at Chicago, for the exhibition there of fifty machines.

The Directors consider the terms of this concession very advantageous.

As foreshadowed by the Chairman at the Statutory General Meeting, the acquisition of these rights necessitates issuing the balance of the Company's capital. These Shares will rank *pari passu* with those originally allotted, and the Directors have resolved to offer them at a premium of 10/- per Share in the first instance to all present holders of Shares.

Enclosed herewith is Form of Application for new Shares, which should be filled up and sent to the Company's Bankers, Messrs. BARCLAY, RANSOM & Co., 1, Pall Mall East, S.W., on or before the 22nd inst.

Your obedient Servant,
HOWARD FELGATE,
Secretary.

Call on the remaining capital of the Electrical Wonder Company as a result of their concession at the World's Columbian Exposition in Chicago. [UK National Archives, Kew.]

April 27:
German patent 74792, *Photographischer Serienapparat mit nur einem Objectiv*, to Richard Brandauer in Stuttgart for a chronophotographic device arranged as a series of camera backs mounted on a vertical wheel inside a light-tight housing using a single objective lens. Each camera back had an individual shutter that was cocked before the wheel was rotated; as it turned, the device triggered each shutter in front of the single lens and produced a series of instantaneous photographs. This apparatus was a further development of Kohlrausch's device of 8 October 1890.

May 1:
Anschütz Schnellseher opens at the World's Columbian Exposition in Chicago, under the auspices of the EWC. Probably no more than two dozen machines were in use, installed on the main floor of the Electricity Building (German Department), and on the Midway Plaisance under the viaducts of Stoney Island Avenue, Woodlawn Avenue and Midway Avenue. The EWC printed a special brochure for the exhibition, which listed the disks shown: *The Trained Elephant, Steeple Chase, Sitting Bull Dance, Acrobats, At the Riding Academy, Gymnastic Exercises, The Ballet Dancers, The Jumping Dog, Marching Soldiers, Riding at the Park, Prize Fighters in the Ring*, others. Both Thomas Armat and Adolph Zukor saw their first moving pictures on the Schnellseher at the Chicago fair.[52]

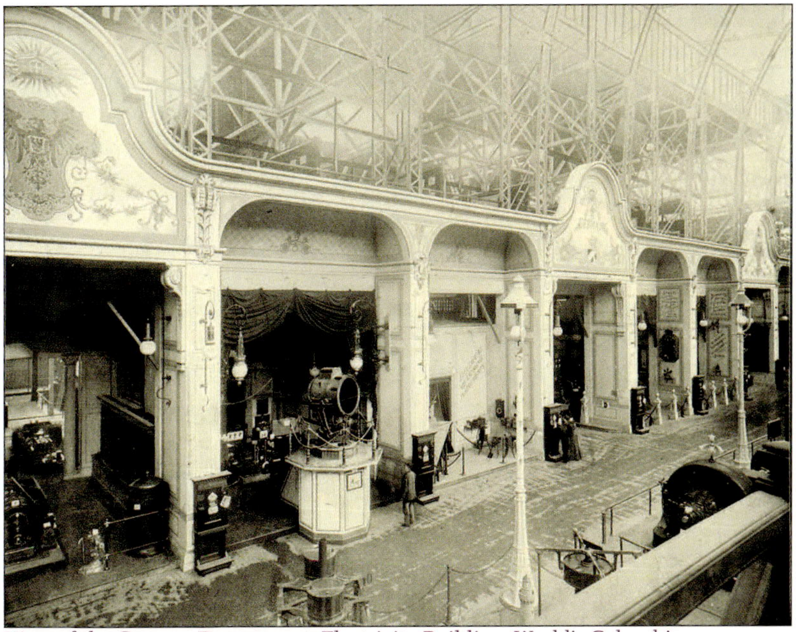

View of the German Department, Electricity Building, World's Columbian Exposition, 1893, showing seven Schnellsehers, installed at the base of each column. [World's Columbian Exposition publicity photograph by the Werner Co., Chicago, 1893.]

May 9:
Edison Kinetoscope demonstrated for 400 people at the monthly meeting of the Department of Physics at the Brooklyn Institute in New York City. George M. Hopkins, president of the Physical Department, explained the principles of the machine and projected Choreutoscope images with a magic lantern as well as images from a device similar to the Zoöpraxiscope before using the lantern to project and examine single-frame images from the Edison film *Blacksmith's Shop*. When, at the very end, the audience was invited to view this film on the Kinetoscope itself, this final portion of the event took over three hours to complete.[53]

May 10:
Eadweard Muybridge lectures with the Zoo-

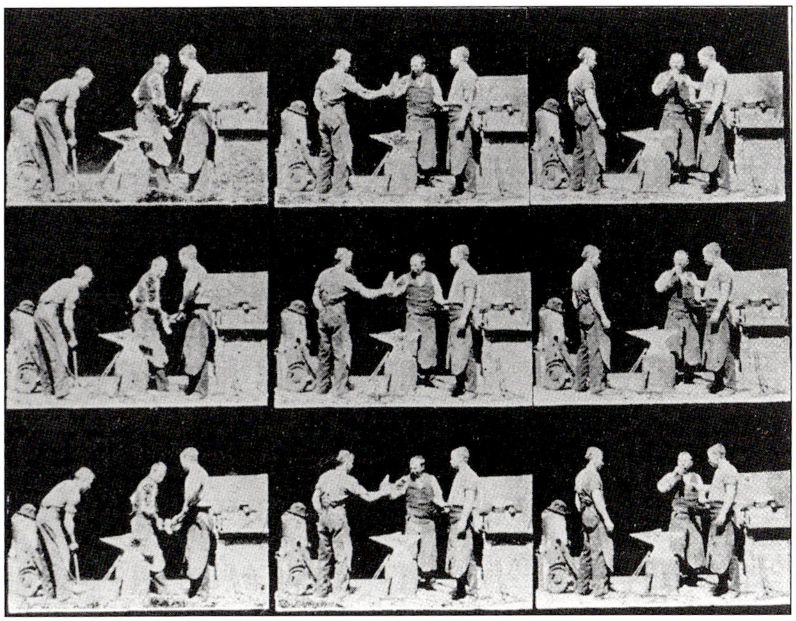

Nine frames from *Blacksmith Scene*, featuring Edison employees at the Black Maria studio. A widely used early Kinetoscope subject, the film was one of two exhibited at the first public demonstration of the apparatus in Brooklyn a few days after it was shot. [Charles Musser.]

52 The appearance of the Schnellseher at the Chicago Fair is the reason that so many historical sources were confused for so long about the Kinetoscope being at the fair, which had been widely advertised but which never appeared. I have not traced all the false claims about the Kinetoscope, but anyone who made a clear claim to see the Kinetoscope undoubtedly saw the Schnellseher under its deliberately deceptive name of The Electrical Wonder.

53 This first version of the film now called *Blacksmithing Scene* (or, *Blacksmiths*) was shot by William Heise in the newly-completed Black Maria studio at Edison's premises in West Orange, just a few days before the Brooklyn demonstration. As the Eastman Company was at this time unable to supply celluloid film, the picture was shot on Blair Camera Company celluloid supplied in 50-foot lengths. See also Charles Musser, *Edison Motion Pictures*, p. 83, No. 16.

praxiscope at Jackson Park, Chicago, Illinois, immediately adjacent to the site of the Midway Plaisance of the World's Columbian Exhibition, while he awaits the completion of his Zoopraxigraphical Hall. The lecture was free.

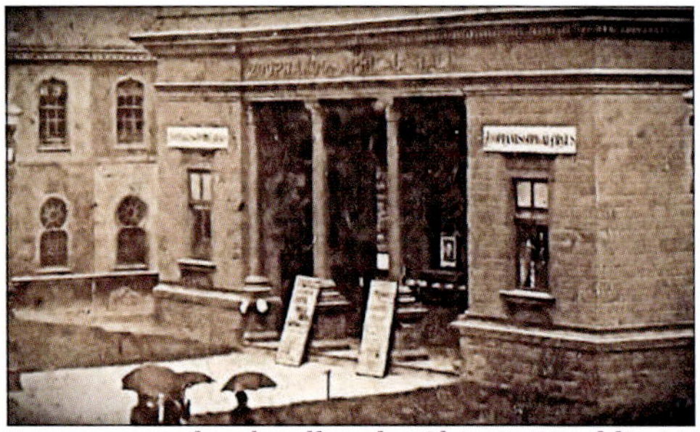

Zoopraxographical Hall at the Chicago World's Fair, 1893. Muybridge made only $213.41 profit for the entire fair to 31 October.
[Detail of a wide view of the Midway Plaisance courtesy Stephen Herbert.

June 17:
Staff and musicians "of all the Denizens of the Midway Plaisance" parade into Jackson Park at 2pm, in a symbolic opening of the entertainment district of the World's Columbian Exposition in Chicago, Illinois, the main sections of which had opened on May 1. Eadweard Muybridge's attraction on the Midway, Zoopraxigraphical Hall, was noted in the announcement of the parade, and most likely opened at about this time. The building designed by Thomas Wing of Chicago, was a 50 foot by 80 foot exhibition hall constructed of wood and iron with a brick façade, that was torn down when the Exposition closed on October 30. Muybridge advertised that his Zoopraxiscope exhibitions and lectures were sponsored by the United States Government Educational Bureau, the University of Pennsylvania, and the National Board of Education. There are newspaper reports that attendance was scant, and the venture seems to have been a failure for Muybridge, despite his efforts in promoting his work through a new edition of *Descriptive Zoopraxography* and a set of 50 phenakistiscope cards.

June 26:
Thomas Alva Edison signs a contract with craftsman James Egan for the construction of 25 Kinetoscopes. Egan was to work at the West Orange laboratory and to build everything but the motor, mirror, lens and the coin-operating device, but he was to assemble and test the entire apparatus and deliver finished products to Edison. His model was a Kinetoscope made in the shop of patternmaker John Valentine of Newark, New Jersey. Egan did not fulfill his contract, and in the end, the order was completed by Edison employee William Heise. Ten machines were ready by the end of March, 1894.

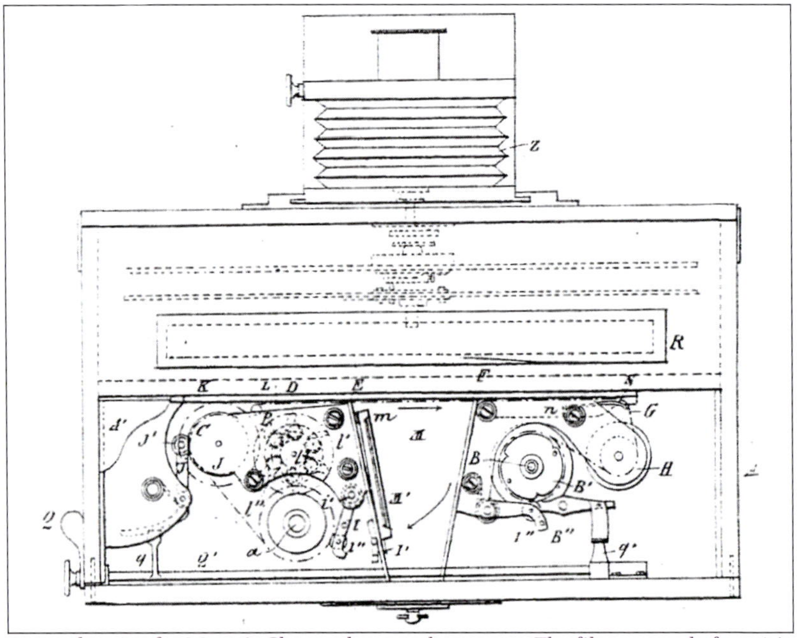

Patent drawing for Marey's Chronophotographe camera. The film unspools from 'a' and winds up on spool B, which also supplies the intermittent movement of the band. Two shutters, both revolving in the same direction but one five times faster than the other, are seen from the top above R in the lens case.
[French patent 231,209 of 29 June 1893, Fig. 2.]

June 29:
French patent 231,209, *Appareil chronophotographique applicable à l'analyse de toutes sortes de mouvements*, to Étienne-Jules Marey for a chronophotographic camera. Using the same basic mechanism as his 1890 camera, Marey proposes here a 'double useage' machine where either a paper film band or a rigid glass plate holder could become the recording medium. The number of exposures was regulated by changing the number of teeth on a wheel operating a pressure intermittent on the film, and at the same time changing the number of openings in the two contra-rotating disc shutters. Exposures of up to 60 images per second were possible, at speeds of about 1/22 to 1/2500 second.

June 30:
French patent 231,232, *Disques à images positives pour phonoscopes et leur mode de préparation* to Georges Demenÿ for Phonoscope disks.

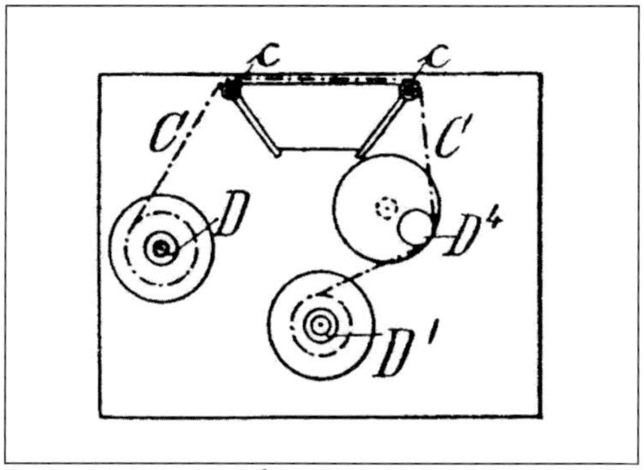

Demenÿ's important 'beater' intermittent movement that was widely used in early cinema apparatus. The revolving cam at D4 pulled a single frame of film forward at each revolution for exposure in either a camera or a projector. [German patent 80 424, Figure 8.]

October 10:

French patent 233,337, *Appareil destiné à prendre des séries d'images photographiques à des intervalles de temps égaux et très rapprochés sur une pellicule sensible*, to Georges Demenÿ, now working independently of Étienne-Jules Marey, for an improved chronophotographic camera for his Phonoscope. With a new film transport mechanism, this was a transitional machine improved in only a few weeks. The improvements are first found in Swiss patent 7703 of 11 December 1893, German patent 80424 of 12 December 1893, and British patent 24,457 of 19 December 1893. The improvements added an eccentric cam intermittent movement (beater) to the apparatus, which pulls each frame of film down and leaves a bit of slack, or a loop, greatly relieving the strain and wear on the film band. It was an important movement that was used by many manufacturers of cameras and projectors in the early years of the cinema. The camera, called the Chronophotographe, used 60mm wide film and was marketed with some success by Léon Gaumont in 1896, after alterations by Demenÿ and engineer Léopold René Decaux.

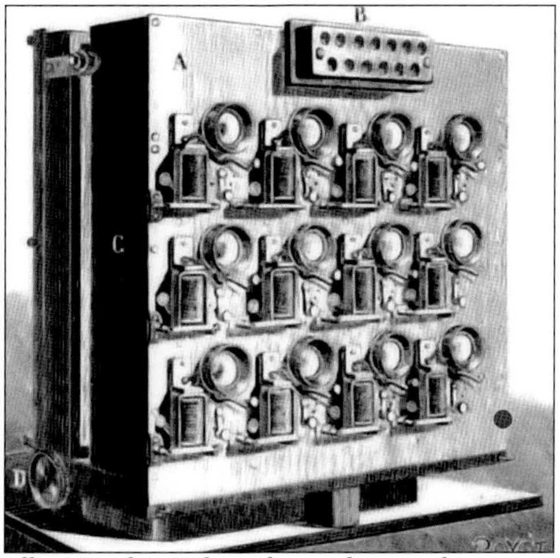

Albert Londe's 12 lens chronophotographic camera with electrically-released shutters. [*La Nature*, No. 1067, 11 November 1893, p. 373.]

November 3:

Albert Londe demonstrates his chronophotographic apparatus with 12 lenses and shutters released by electromagnetic switches at the *Société française de photographie* in Paris. In use from 1891, the camera could expose twelve images each 70mm by 70mm on a plate 24cm by 30cm in any range from several seconds down to one-tenth of a second. Working in a laboratory at the Salpêtrière hospital where most of his sequence photographs supported medical and psychiatric research into fits and seizures, Londe's wide-ranging interests and influence across instantaneous photography is much underrated in most recent chronophotographic literature. In this presentation, Londe showed sequence photographs of athletic movements, waves breaking on a shore, studies of various animals, and Mlle. Barenco of the nouveau Cirque in graceful movement with an umbrella.[54]

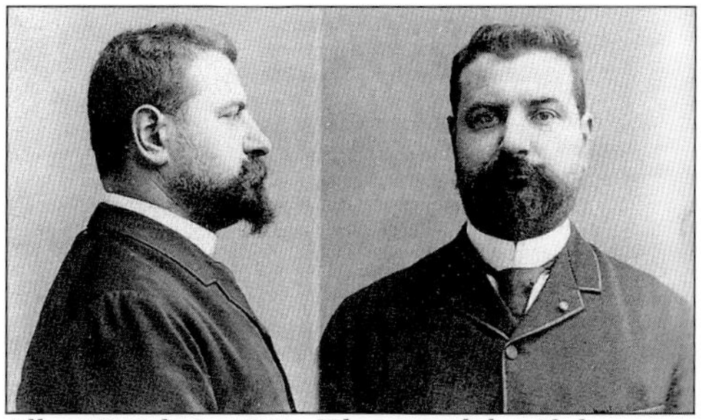

Albert Londe in 1892. [Photograph by Alphonse Bertillon, 1892. Public domain.]

November 6:

Albert Londe repeats the demonstration of his 12 lens chronophotographic apparatus for the Photo-Club de Paris. At the beginning of January, 1894, he would demonstrate it again at the Société d'encouragement pour l'industrie nationale.

December 8:

UK patent 23,670, *Apparatus for Exposing Successive photographic Plates, and for Exhibiting Magic Lantern and other Slides*, to Birt Acres in Barnet for a device allowing multiple photographic plates or lantern slides to be successively exposed or exhibited. Essentially a slide stage with a reservoir of plates/slides that could be quickly changed, this patent confirms Acres's early interest in capturing or exhibiting continuous motion.

54 Londe also collaborated with Paul Richter, Professor of Anatomy at the Ecole des Beaux-Arts on *Physiologie artistique de l'homme en mouvement*, published in 1895, and made a series of chronophotographs for Gustave Le Bon, published in *his L'Equitation actuelle et ses principes*. In his famous painting *Nu descendant un escalier* of 1912, Marcel Duchamp combined a series of nine Londe chronophotographs with Marey's graphic methods from single-plate chronophotographs.
This was Londe's second chronophotographic apparatus. The first, developed in 1883, had nine lenses arranged in a circle with the shutters tripped by a metronome. In 1898 Londe acquired a 35mm cine camera (a Chronophotographe Demenÿ) and used it in his researches in parallel with his 12-lens camera.

December 14:
UK patent 24,0321, *An Improved Musical Toy*, to Charles Henry Davy in London for a combination of a small zoetrope and a small musical box arranged so that the figures in the zoetrope appear to be dancing to the music from the attached box. Both the barrels that provided the music, and the images in the zoetrope were changeable so that a quadrille, polka, waltz or other dance could be performed.

December 27:
French patent 235,100, *Appareil réversible de photographie et d'optique pour l'analyse et la synthèse des mouvements dit le Cinématographe Léon Bouly*, to Léon Bouly for a combination camera and projector for taking and projecting pictures of movement. The practical design used a 'mutilated roller' intermittent movement, in which part of a continuously moving roller was cut away, allowing the film to be momentarily clamped stationary at the aperture for exposure. Mechanically sound, the device suffered from the common problem, prior to the introduction of perforations in the film band, of accurate registration.

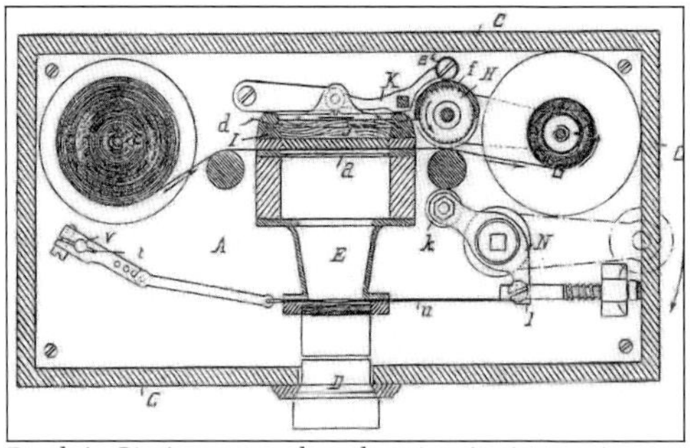

Bouly's Cinématographe, showing its intermittent movement (f, H) and clamping friction drive (K) that in use would place images irregularly on the film band. [French patent 235,100 of 27 December 1893, Fig. 2.]

Undated: further Anschütz Schnellseher exhibitions in Charing Cross, London; various seaside towns and piers; in shops along the Strand and Oxford Street.

1894

February 25:
The great deception: Jean Aimé Le Roy claims projection of Edison Kinetoscope films at Riley Opticians, 16 Beekman Street, New York City, on his own equipment. Le Roy never patented his apparatus, and this disputed projection was not reported in the press at the time, but only later reported by witnesses. If it happened, it would be the first public projection of Edison films, and the first known public projection in the world. Le Roy claimed repeat showings at Verona Hall & Bijou Theatre, Brooklyn; the Opera House, Clinton, NY (22 February 1895); the Opera House of March Chuck (5–10 March, 1895); Harrington's Theatre Wonderland (19–24 March 1896), which are cited as well in several sources. There are no independent records of these exhibitions. Modern scholar H. Mark Gosser asserts that extant advertisements for these later shows were 'probably printed years later by opponents of the Motion Picture Patents Company to gain priority over the Edison patents'. One of the most disputed and least documented of early cinema dates.

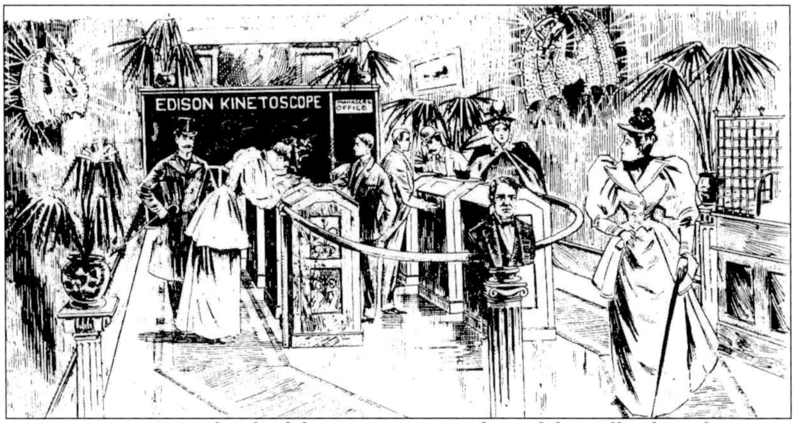

An imaginative 1894 sketch of the Kinetoscope parlour of the Holland Brothers at 1155 Broadway, New York City, emphasizing the bourgeois appeal of the new apparatus. [Antonia and W. K. L. Dickson, *History of the Kinetograph, Kinetoscope and Kineto-Phonograph* (1894), p. 59.]

March 6:
Eugene Sandow, the Austrian strongman, is photographed for the Kinetoscope in the recently completed Edison studio at West Orange, the Black Maria. Instead of taking his $250 fee for the filming, Sandow asked to meet Mr. Edison, which was then arranged.

April 14:
First public Kinetoscope parlor opened, at 1155 Broadway, New York City, by George and Andrew Holland, with ten Edison machines. Admission was 25 cents for a ticket to see one row of five machines. The first day's receipts, before any advertising or notice had appeared, was about $153. By the end of May, the parlor was staying open on Sundays to accommodate the crowds.

Films included: *Sandow, Horse Shoeing, Barber Shop, Bertoldi (Mouth Support), Wrestling, Bertoldi (Table Contortion), Blacksmith's Shop, Highland Dance, Trapeze, Roosters.*

May 17:
Kinetoscope parlor opened in the Masonic Temple, 148 State Street, Chicago, by George and Andrew Holland, with ten machines.

June 1:
Kinetoscope parlor using five machines opens at 946 Market Street, San Francisco, at Peter Bacigalupi's phonograph parlor.

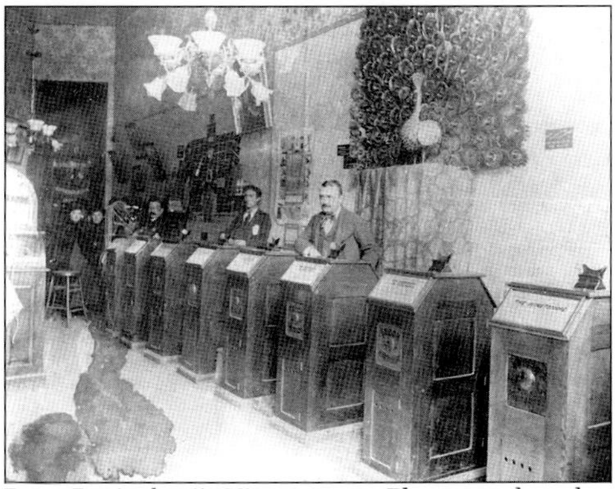

Peter Bacigalupi's Kinetoscope, Phonograph and Graphophone Arcade, 946 Market Street, San Francisco, CA. with its row of eight Kinetoscopes. [Edison National Historic Site, National Park Service, US Department of the Interior.]

June 14:
Anschütz Schnellseher demonstrated in the Committee Room at the Conversazione of the Camera Club, London.

June 15:
Michael Leonard and Jack Cushing are filmed in a six-round boxing match at the Black Maria for the Kinetoscope Exhibition Company of Otway Latham and his associates, who probably also suggested increasing the Kinetoscope capacity to 150 feet of film, and slowing the speed of the camera to 30 frames per second, thereby allowing an increased viewing time which sufficed for one-minute boxing rounds. When exhibited, the special admission for this highly publicized event was ten cents per round, or 60 cents to see the entire fight. Owing to the availability of capital from partner Samuel Tilden, Jr., this group became very active in both Kinetoscope exhibition and in production of films for the apparatus, made through the Edison organization.

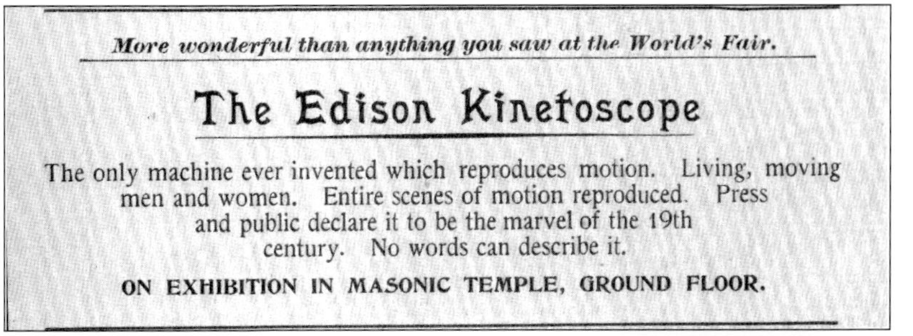

Advertisement for the Edison Kinetoscope exhibition of the Holland Brothers at the Masonic Tempole in Chicago. [International Cinema Museum, Chicago.]

July 6:
A report in *The Photographic Times* (Vol. 25, p. 2) in New York City contains a picture of the Phantoscope camera of C. Francis Jenkins, and reproduces a series of pictures made with it, indicating that the Phantoscope had produced experimental films before July 1894.

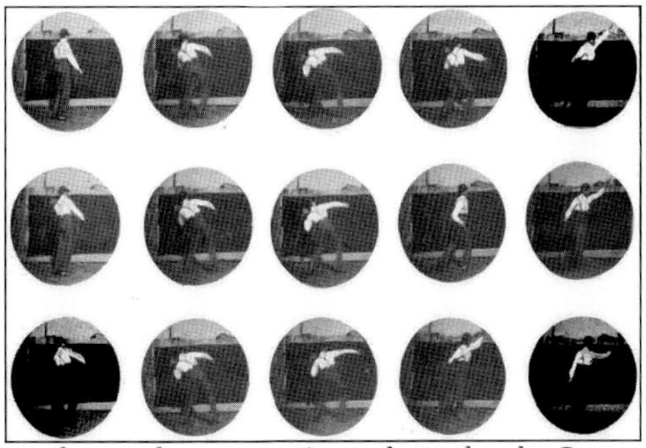

15 phases of a man putting a shot, taken by C. Francis Jenkins on his Phantoscope camera. Originally 50 images, the sequence was edited to allow a card of images to be reproduced. [*The Photographic Times*, vol. 25 (1894), p. 2.]

July 8:
Edison Kinetoscope opens at an amusement park in Eagle Rock, New Jersey, where it became 'the most popular feature ... this season' according to the *Orange Journal.*

July 16:
Edison Kinetoscope opens at the Salle des Dépêches of the journal *Le Petit Parisienne*, 20 Boulevard Montmartre, Paris, France, its first appearance in Europe. The shows were organized by George A. Georgiades, Demetrius Anastas Georgiades,

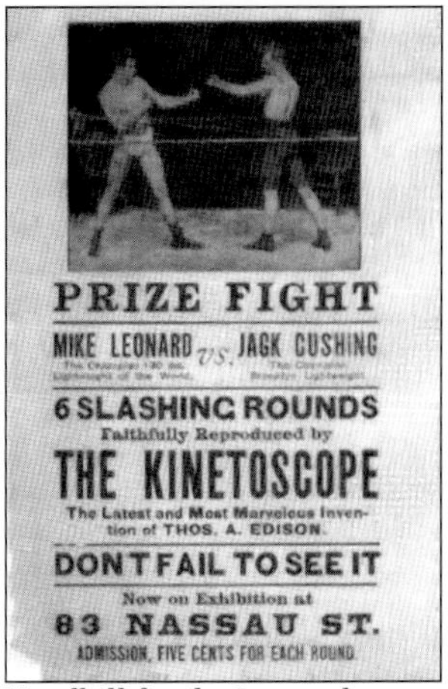

Handbill for the Leonard - Cushing fight, filmed at the Black Maria for the Latham brothers. [Collection Dan Streible.]

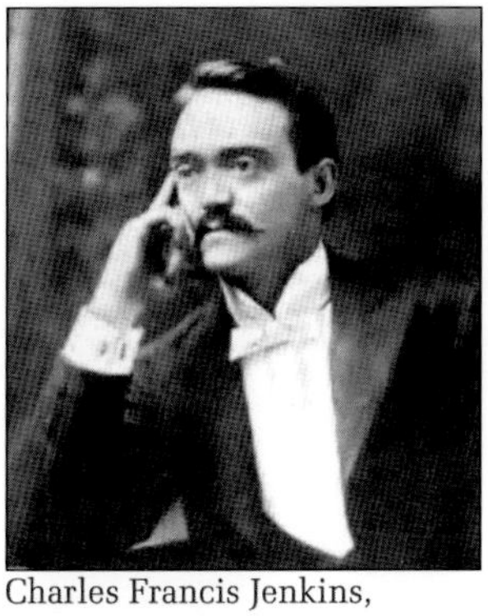

Charles Francis Jenkins, c1897. [Charles Francis Jenkins, *Animated Pictures* (1898), Frontispiece.]

and George John Tragidis, all naturalized American citizens from the Greek community in Turkey, who purchased their Kinetoscopes early on in New York City but exhibited them in Paris and London.[55]

July 27:
Addition to French patent 233,337, of Georges Demenÿ for improvements to his apparatus of 10 October 1893, including his 'beater' intermittent movement. This is the French addition to the basic patent (see above) incorporating the improvements made in earlier German and British patents, and proposing in addition to the beater movement a take-up reel in order to enhance the registration of the images.

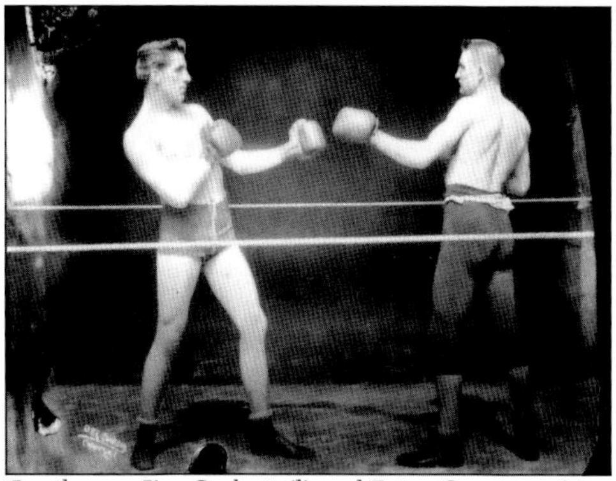

Gentleman Jim Corbett (l) and Peter Courtney (r) pose for W K L Dickson before their fight for the Lathams at Edison's Black Maria. [Edison National Historic Site.]

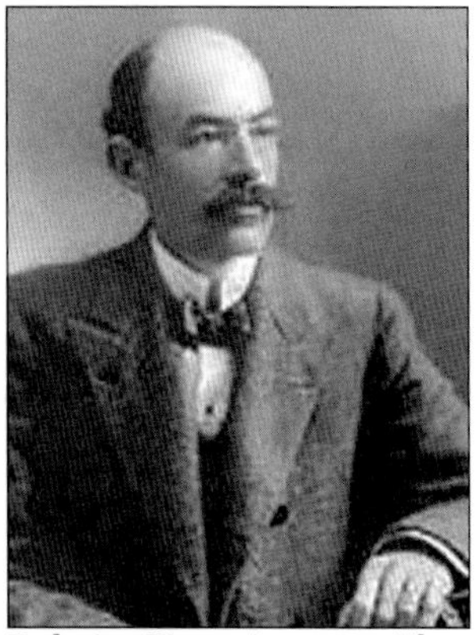

Federico Figner in c1905. The Czech-born immigrant was a traveling phonograph exhibitor who opened a Kinetoscope parlour in Buenos Aires and then also made the first films in Argentina before founding an important recording company, Odeon. [Unknown photographer; published in Guillermo Caneto, etc., *Historia de los Primeros Años del Cine en la Argentina* (1996), p. 29.]

August 4:
US patent 539,799, *Lantern for Bicycle-Riders*, to William K. L. Dickson of Orange, New Jersey, for a battery-powered bicycle light and reflector. This patent is a good example of Dickson's independent work while he was part of the Edison laboratory, here work that was not on moving picture apparatus.

August 9:
Edison Kinetoscope opens in Philadelphia, as an attraction on board the steamer *Republic*, which made regular excursions to the Delaware Bay ocean resort of Cape May, New Jersey. The season ended on 23 September.

September 7:
Gentleman Jim Corbett and Peter Courtney stage a fight in the Black Maria, resulting in a uniquely long film of six minutes duration. As boxing was illegal in New Jersey at this time, Edison told an investigating Grand Jury a few days later, 'I was not there. ... . I did not understand a prize fight was to take place ... . I should certainly not permit any fight to a finish in my place under any consideration.'

September 18:
Edison Kinetoscope parlour hosts a special screening for the press in Buenos Aires, Argentina. Entrepreneur Federico Figner had obtained six machines and a phonograph from Edison while he was in New York City, and the public exhibitions continued until 4 November, after which the group of Kinetoscopes moved around the city, first to calle Suipacha 334, then to a storefront between San Martin and Florida streets, ending the year at calle Florida 81. Admission was A$1, and all of the exhibitions were accompanied by demonstrations of X-rays.

October 1:
Michel and Eugène Werner, Edison's French concessionaires, open the first Kinetoscope parlor in Paris with ten machines, at 20 boulevard Poissonniere, not far from the Musée Grevin. Admission, 25 centimes. Later in the month they open another parlor at their office, 85 rue de Richelieu. The important pioneer Henri Joly saw the Kinetoscope for the first time at one of these exhibitions.

Films include: *Blacksmith Shop*, *Cock Fight*, *Annabelle Serpentine Dance*, *A Bar Room Scene*, *Carmencita*, *Wrestling Match*, and *Barber Shop*.

October 5:
Georges Demenÿ writes to August and Louis Lumière and asks them to participate in the Société Française du Phonoscope, established to exploit his invention, thereby beginning a long correspondence on the merits of his equipment and leading years later to his claims to be the true originator of the cinema. Demenÿ and Louis Lumière met in Paris in November, but without Lumière seeing the Phonoscope.

October 6:
Kinetoscope parlor opens at the Columbia Phonograph Musical Palace, 919 Pennsylvania Avenue, Washington, D. C. The inventor C. Francis Jenkins sees his first Kinetoscope here.

55 Themistocles John Tragidis and George Malamakis (or Malamackis) may also have been involved in this adventure. Richard Brown's dogged research to reveal the identities and origins of these briefly active but most significant figures in early cinema has been published in *The Kinetoscope. A British History* (East Barnet, 2017: John Libbey Publishing Ltd.).

October 9:
Alexander Black presents his first completed 'picture play,' *Miss Jerry*, at the Carbon Studio of arts patron James Lawrence Breese at 5 West 16th Street, New York City, where many of the interior scenes for the play were photographed. The play, about a novice reporter who meets a string of characters and solves a crime before falling in love with her editor, consisted of about 300 glass magic lantern slides projected by a modified sciopticon onto a screen at a rate of three or four a minute. Black recited the text of the nearly 2-hour play himself, while John Hyatt Brewer provided improvised music on the piano and organ, and Tracy Tisdell operated the lantern. Following this successful presentation, Black toured with *Miss Jerry* and his subsequent picture plays (*A Capital Courtship*, *Miss America*, others) steadily on the lyceum circuit until 1904.

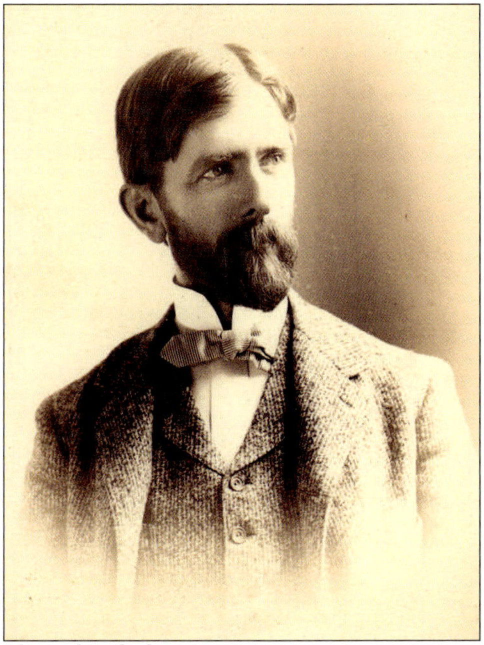

Alexander Black in 1894.
[Photograph by Richardson Brothers, Brooklyn, NY. Public domain.]

October 18:
Edison Kinetoscope opens at 70 Oxford Street, London, in the headquarters of the Continental Commerce Company, just founded by the Edison agents Maguire and Baucus, the machine's first appearance in England.

Films include: *Annabelle – Serpentine Dance*, *Barber Shop*, *Blacksmith Shop*, *Carmencita*, *Cock Fight*, *Wrestling Match*.

November 3:
Schnellseher of Ottomar Anschütz opens at the Swedish photographic exhibition in Stockholm. The Edison Kinetoscope will open at the same industrial exhibition on 4 February 1895.

November 6:
German patent 85791, *Projektionsapparat für stroboskopisch bewegte Bilder*, to Ottomar Anschütz for his Projecting Electrotachyscope, the last of his nine models of Schnellseher. The apparatus allowed enlarged projection of series photographs with the individual images arranged alternately on two large disks holding 12 images each and moved intermittently before each of two lenses by a 14-sided Maltese Cross gear. A deeply saw-toothed disk acted as a before-the-lens shutter to mask the alternating images, and was driven synchronously with the image disks. Sixteen images per second were shown, with each disk and lens providing half; illumination was by means of a pair of 110 Volt/40 Ampere electrical arc lamps. Anschütz consulted on the design of this apparatus with Anton Verständig at Siemens & Halske, and it was built by the mechanic Bödecker.[56]

November 10:
Edison Kinetoscope opens at 206 South Spring Street, Los Angeles, by showman Thomas Tally.

☛Edison Kinetoscope opens on Congress Avenue, Austin, Texas.

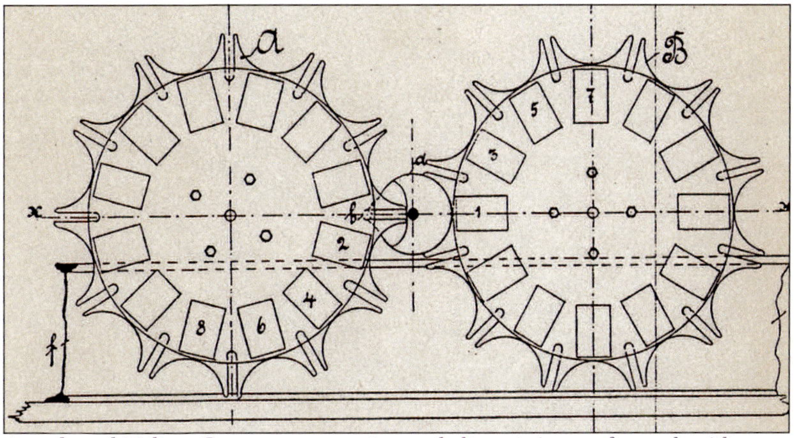

An enlarged Maltese Cross arrangement moved alternate images forward, with each of the two disks providing up to 12 phases of movement. Powerful arc lamps meant the projected images were up to 25 feet wide, significantly larger than most early cinema exhibitions. [German patent 85791 of 6 November 1894, Fig. 1.]

56 French patent 242,886, *Procédé de projection d'images à mouvement stroboscopiques*. W. H. Harrison, an experienced technician and correspondent for *The Optical Magic Lantern Journal*, reported in the issue of 1 December 1893, p. 196, that an unidentified screening of this apparatus "avoided the jerkiness sometimes seen in such projections with which we are now familiar" and noting that "something of the same kind was recently exhibited in the Strand, but without optical projection, and with the light of an intermittent discharge through a vacuum tube, instead of by a powerful discharge in air as is necessary in optical projection".

November 11:
Edison Kinetoscope parlor opens at 101 Woodward Avenue, Detroit, under the management of Charles Urban. The dynamic Urban migrated to England in 1897 as manager of the London branch of Edison's agents Maguire & Baucus, which he transformed into the Warwick Trading Company, one of the leading early film concerns in Britain.

November 12:
Phantoscope of C. Francis Jenkins exhibited at the Pure Food Exposition, Washington, D. C. This was Jenkins's peep-show kinetoscope, developed for the Columbia Phonograph Company of Washington, D.C., who had the Edison Kinetoscope concession for Washington and Atlantic City but who could not acquire enough Kinetoscopes from Edison and asked Jenkins to make a version of the Edison machine.

November 21:
United States patent 549,309, *Mutoscope*, to Herman Casler for a hand-turned card device intended as a toy to supplement Edison's electrically-driven Kinetoscope. The device was developed by Casler with Harry Norton Marvin, Elias Bernard Koopman, and W. K. L. Dickson; the latter supplied critical advice, secretly, as he was still working for Edison at the time.[57]

November 24:
United States patent 536,569, *Phantoscope*, to C. Francis Jenkins for his peep-show viewer using no shutter and continuously moving

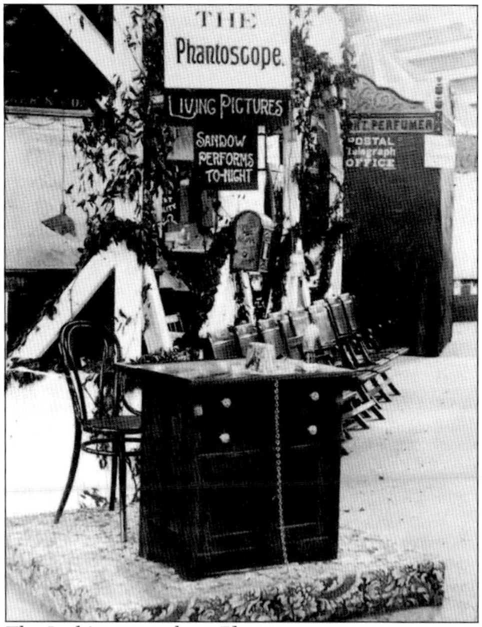

The Jenkins peepshow Phantoscope was exhibited at the Pure Food Exposition in Washington, D C, 1894.
[Franklin Institute, Philadelphia.]

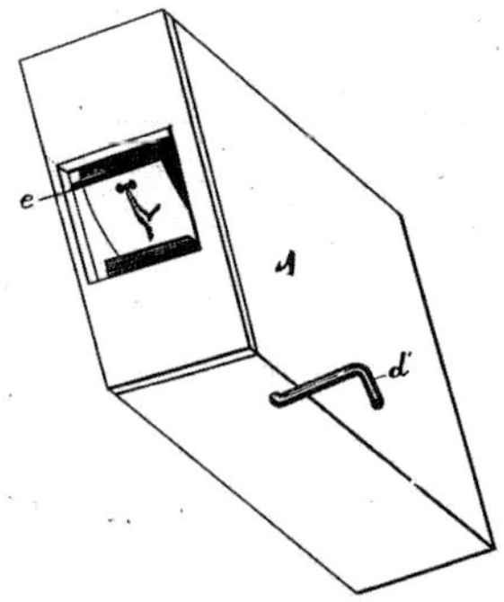

The Mutoscope began as a lightweight, inexpensive toy for which this was the basic patent, referred to in many later, more complex patents and devices.
[US patent 549,309 of 21 November 1894, Fig. 1.]

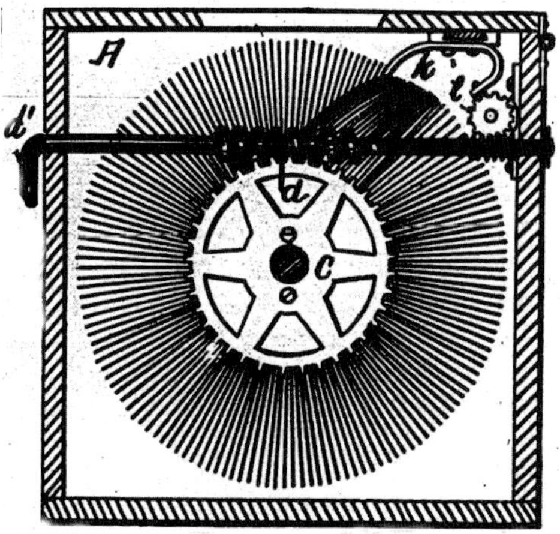

Inside the box, the crank d' turned a worm gear d, which rotated the image cards, while a wire stub k held back each card to display it to the viewing port at the top. The stub was itself wiggled by another worm gear on the same shaft acting on the wheel t. Ingenious, simple, and the beginnings of a robust worldwide business when later improved. [US patent 549,309 of 21 November 1894, Fig. 8.]

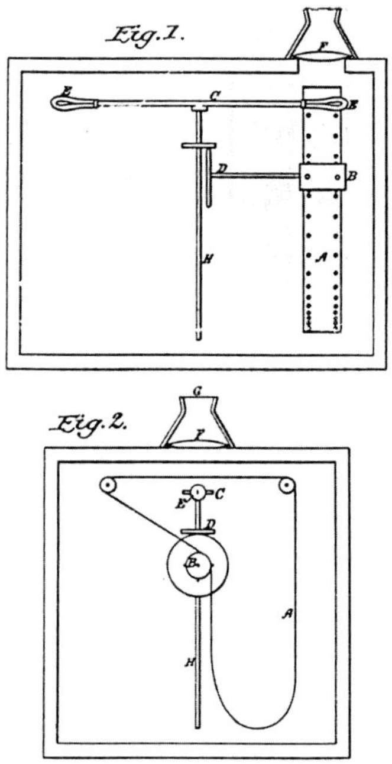

The Jenkins peep-show Phantoscope was significantly simpler than Edison's Kinetoscope as it tried to provide more economical moving picture viewing. [US patent 536,569 of 24 November 1894, Figs. 1 & 2.]

57 British patent 14,439 of 30 July 1895, French patent 249,286 of 30 July 1895, and German patent 89058 of 31 July 1895. On 26 May 1896 the original US patent was divided, and new applications made for two smaller flip-card devices. The first, issued as US patent 614,367, *Mutoscope* on 15 November 1898 described a simple hand-held Mutoscope with the cards extending from the top of a wooden handle and 'flipped' by a simple wire crank extended into the shape of a sidewise 'U'. The second, issued as US patent 584,305 *Mutoscope* on 8 June 1897, described a small hand-held box, viewed through an opening at the top, where the cards stood upright in a rack which had a sliding knob on the bottom to flick the cards.

film. The device is a Kinetoscope-type apparatus with the intermittent awkwardly provided by two incandescent lamps mounted on a revolving arm. Like all of Jenkins' various moving picture machines it was called a Phantoscope, leading to some confusion in the literature.

November 25:
Anschütz Projecting Electrotachyscope demonstrated for the first time at the large auditorium of the Post Office Building at the corner of Artilleriestrasse and Oranienburgerstrasse, Berlin. The apparatus used two intermittently-moved disks connected by a Maltese Cross gear and two 40-ampere carbon arc lamps. The resulting life-sized animated pictures were seen on a screen measuring 6 by 8 meters. The morning lecture and projection was for invited guests of Culture Minister von Goslar, and the afternoon lecture was for members of the Photographische Verein zu Berlin. The scientific press noted the imprecise registration of the images caused by the parallax of Anschütz' camera battery, which was accentuated by the great size of the projected images. Anschütz had forty different picture series available for showing; the precise titles exhibited included: *Kürassier im langsamen Trabe, Parademarsch; Schnellfeuer, schreitendes Kamel, Lang-Bocksprung eines Turners über das Pferd, Einseifen beim Barbier, Zwei Zimmerleute früstuckend, Skatspieler, Rauchende Jungen.*

November 26:
Edison Kinetoscope parlor opens at 1436 Broadway, at the corner of 40th street in New York City, running from ten in the morning until midnight. This was at least the sixth Kinetoscope parlor in New York, with other exhibitions already open at 1155 Broadway; 39 Park Row; 144 East 14th Street; 158 East 125th Street; and one at an unknown address. By the first of February 1895 two more Kinetoscope parlors would open in New York, at 943 Broadway and 587 Broadway.

November 29 & 30:
Anschütz Projecting Electrotachyscope opens to the public in the large auditorium of the Post Office Building at the corner of Artilleriestrasse and Oranienburgerstrasse, Berlin. Admission was 1 Mark and 1.50 Mark, with a selection of the 40 prepared disks presented.

November 30:
Edison Kinetoscope opens in a converted shop at 148 Pitt Street, Sydney, Australia, organized by J. C. Williamson and George Musgrove in association with the Macmahon brothers.[58] A phonograph, the Bell-Tainter Graphophone, was added to the exhibition from 22 December. Admission 1 Shilling to see five machines. By 3 January 1895 the show had attracted some 25,000 patrons; the exhibition closed on 29 January.

Films included: *Annabelle Skirt Dance, Cock Fight, Blacksmith Shoeing a Horse, Comical Barbershop Scene, Juan Caicedo Dancing on the High Wire.*

December 3:
Edison Kinetoscope opens at Seaver E. Olson's "Mammoth Department Store" in Minneapolis, MN, as a special holiday attraction. Foreshadowing later department store practise, Seaver rented space in his store to the exhibitors, presumably representatives of Raff & Gammon. Admission 15 cents for adults to see five machines, 10 cents for children.

December 5:
Michel Werner opens an additional Edison Kinetoscope parlor and sales office, in the house at 6–8 place de l'Opera, at the corner of the boulevard des Capucines, Paris.

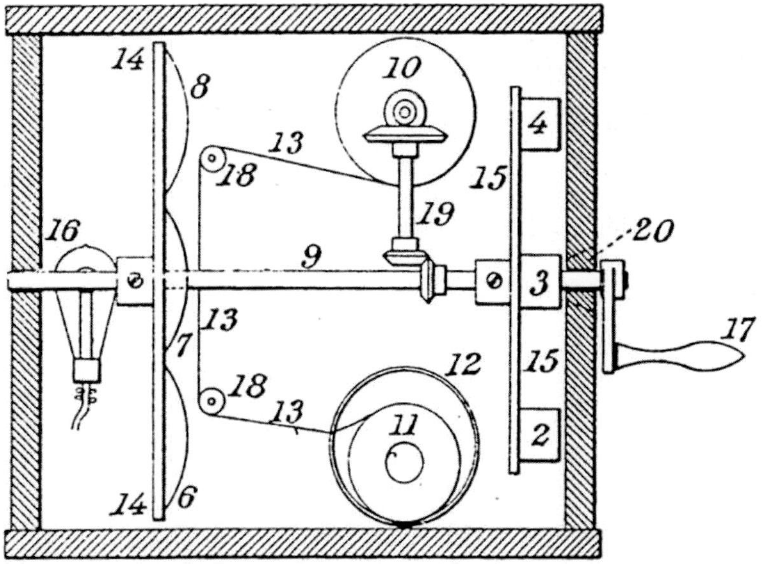

The Jenkins combination camera and projector of late 1894. The four rotating lenses are at the right (2,3,4), and when in use as a projector the electric light (16) at the left is illuminated. The device used continuously moving film and had no shutter. [US patent 531,556 of 12 December 1894, Fig. 1.]

58 James, Joseph and Charles Macmahon were Australian theatrical entrepreneurs involved in many aspects of early cinema. James managed six American theatrical tours of the actress Mrs. Scott Siddons and later leased several theatres in Australia's capital cities. With his brother Charles he managed the first concert tour of the Edison phonograph in 1890, with lectures given by British showman Professor Douglas Archibald, beginning a long association with the Edison interests.

December 12:
United States patent 560,800, *Kinetographic camera*, to C. Francis Jenkins for a chronophotographic apparatus used as a camera and projector. Four rotating lenses mounted on a circular disk moved synchronously with continuously moving transparent flexible film about 3" wide; the device did not have a shutter. Projection was accomplished by threading a developed positive print of the film on the reels of the apparatus and lighting an electric lamp fixed behind a second disk holding four condensing lenses and fixed to the same drive shaft as the objective lenses. The results could be viewed directly on a ground-glass plate or projected on a screen, although such images were probably not very large and quite blurred.
(*See image on previous page.*)

December 13:
Edison Kinetoscope opens at the Clarendon Hotel, Port Jervis, New Jersey, by the proprietor James Joyce. It was shown in the public room of the hotel, where it became a great local attraction. Admission ten cents. The opening film was *Blacksmith's Shop.*[59]

December 16:
Edison Kinetoscope opens at Lauritz Vilhelm Pacht's Panorama, in Copenhagen, Denmark. The Panorama presented Edison phonograph concerts, Dioramas and other attractions. Admission 50 Øre, children 25 Øre.

December 17:
Edison Kinetoscope opens at Oswald Stoll's Panopticon, Philharmonic Hall, St. Mary Street, Cardiff, Wales, as part of the theatre's second "Mammoth Xmas and New Year Carnival". Three machines were exhibited.

December 27:
Edison Kinetoscope opens in Regulierbreestraat, Amsterdam, The Netherlands, by Karel van Egmond and H. F. Degens. Admission ten cents for each film.

Films included: *Een Smederij in Werking*; *Gevecht in een Bar*, *Anne Belle Serpentine Danseres.*

☛Additional Kinetoscopes opened quickly in the reception hall of the newspaper *De Telegraaf* and at the Rijksmuseum; also at the end of April 1895 in Nijmegen.

☛UK patent 25,100, *Improvements in Kinetoscopes*, to John Anderton and Alfred Lomax for a device to allow more than one person to simultaneously view a Kinetoscope. The apparatus was an attachment whereby a prism allowed one person to view the moving images directly through the prism mounted over the viewing aperture of the machine, whilst another viewed the image horizontally in reflection from the prism's silvered base. The patent further suggests that a second or third prism may also be attached to increase the number of simultaneous viewers. Anderton was a scientific instrument manufacturer in Birmingham who held several patents on magic lantern accessories, and Lomax was a Blackpool exhibitor of the Edison kinetoscope and other entertainment devices. The patent specification was left just six weeks after Lomax received his first kinetoscope. It is not known if the device was reduced to practise.

December 28:
Still seeking backing for his Phonoscope and its eccentric cam intermittent movement, Georges Demenÿ pleads with Louis Lumière to 'find a practical solution in order to use the work which I have already produced', and asks that Lumière meet with his associate François-Henri Lavanchy-Clarke.[60]

☛Anschütz Schnellseher opens at the Esposisço Imperial in the Avenida Palace Hotel, Lisbon, by travelling exhibitor Carlos Eisenlohr.

59 Other North American cities where the Edison Kinetoscope was publicly exhibited by the end of 1894 included: Binghamton, NY; St. Louis, MO; Cincinnati, OH; Albany, NY; San Antonio, TX; Newark, NJ; Dallas TX, Portland, OR; Allentown, PA; Tacoma, WA; Jersey City, NJ; Denver, CO; Austin, TX; Jackson, MI; Atchison, KA; Waco, TX; Boston, MA; Columbus, OH; Montreal Canada; Paterson, NJ; Sherman, TX; St. Paul, MN; Raton, NM; Charleston, SC; St., Thomas, Ontario, Canada; Minneapolis, MN. Helena MT; Davenport IA; Pittsfield, MA; Louisville, KY; Bangor, ME; Atlanta, GA; Memphis, TN; Savannah, GA; Galveston, TX; Morristown, NJ; Halifax, Nova Scotia, Canada; Milwaukee, WI; Springfield, MA; Rochester, NY; New Orleans, LA; Syracuse, NY; Seattle, WA; Rutland, VT; Burlington VT; Omaha, NB.
North American cities with 1895 Edison Kinetoscope openings include: Trinidad, CO; Indianapolis, IN; Macon, GA; Scranton, PA; Hot Springs, AR; Evansville, IN; Butte City, MT; Ottawa, Canada; Duluth, MN; Lafayette, IN; Montgomery AL; Richmond, VA; Lawrence, KA; Williamsport, PA; Niagara Falls, NY; Chattanooga, TN; Portage, WI, Watertown, NY; Jackson, MS; Huntsville, AL; Monett, MO; Great Falls, MT; Baker City, OR; Glens Falls, NY; Little Rock, AR; Utica, NY; Port Huron, MI; Lake Park, MN; Gardiner, ME; Wilmington, DE; Gloucester, NJ; New Haven, CT; New Bedford, MA; Huntington, PA; Augusta, ME; Canastota, NY; Olympia, WA; Tyrone, PA; Long Branch, NJ; Salem, MA; New Bedford, MA; Coney Island, NY; Amherst, VA; Cyrene, WY; Riverside, RI; Steubenville, OH; Pontiac MI.
The openings in both Boston and Philadelphia were in department stores: Jordan Marsh Company in Boston, and Gimbel's in Philadelphia. Both used the new apparatus as an attraction for customers, prominently displayed on the ground floor of the establishments. In 1895, after the end of the Summer season, and apart from a few replacement machines to early exhibitors, only three new orders for Kinetoscopes were received by Raff & Gammon from 1 September 1895 through the end of the year.

60 In May, 1896, Lavanchy-Clarke, a resident of Switzerland, would obtain the concession to exhibit the Lumière Cinématographe at the Geneva Exposition.

1895

January 1:

The *Pantomimes lumineuses* of Emil Reynaud reopens at the Musée Grevin. The show had closed on 28 February 1894 so that Reynaud could renovate his equipment and prepare new painted image bands, with the sleight-of-hand magician Carmelli (Auguste-Joseph Coëne [Cohen]), a long-time employee of the Musée Grevin, occupying the Cabinet Fantastique in the interim. Maintenance of the apparatus and preparation of new scenes was a serious problem for Reynaud, not least because his daily exhibition schedule was so intense. The return of the *Théâtre Optique* was triumphant, proving the show had lost none of its popularity.

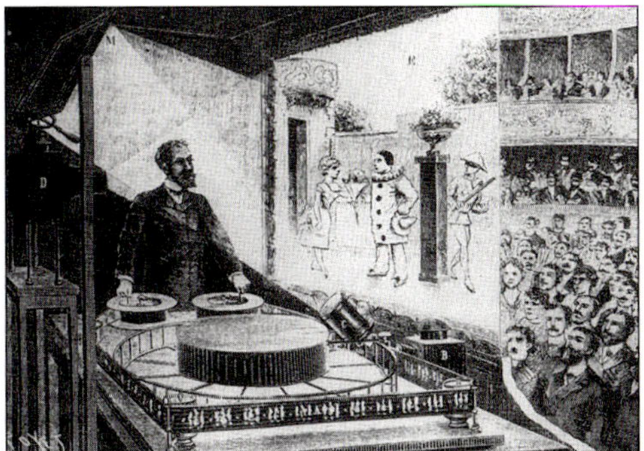

A depiction of Émil Reynaud operating his Théâtre Optique at the Musée Grevin. [*La Nature* No. 999, 25 July 1892, p. 128.]

January 3:

British patent 182, *Improvements in or relating to the Kinetoscope*, to Cecil Wray of Bradford, for his device allowing a Kinetoscope image to be enlarged and projected on a screen. The awkward apparatus uses two mirrors and a prism to direct the intensified light of a Kinetoscope through a magic lantern condenser and lens arranged horizontally so as to project the image from the film onto a vertical screen.

January 6:

Edison Kinetoscope opens at the candy and sweet shop of J. George Smith, St. Paul, MN, for at least two weeks. Smith combined the Kinetoscope with an Edison phonograph and visitors could hear non-synchronous music while they watched the films. Edison's *Barber Shop Scene* was accompanied by a band playing *Pomp and Circumstance*, or by a barbershop quartet singing *Oh, the Bullfrog in the Pond.*

January 14:

Edison Kinetoscope opens on the balcony of Mannheimer Bros. department store in St. Paul, MN, for one month. The five machines, tickets, films and other materials for the exhibition were supplied by H. D. Higbee of Chicago, an agent who had purchased machines from Raff & Gammon. Films were changed weekly, and opening week films included gaiety girls dancing, Annie Oakley, a wrestling match between a man and a dog, Japanese girls dancing, and a boxing match. Admission to see all the films was 10 cents for adults and 5 cents for children.

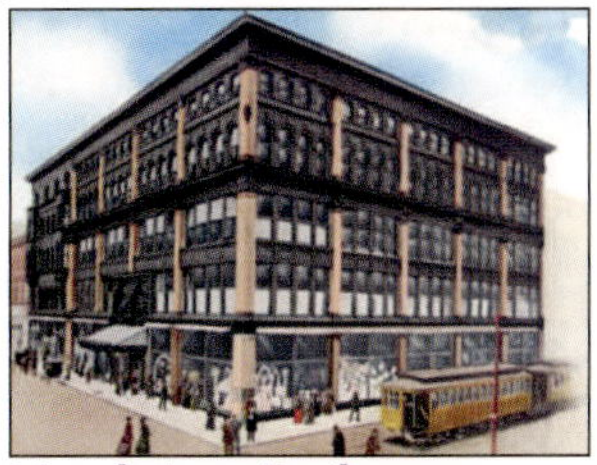

Mannheimer Brothers department store, St. Paul, MN, about 1910. [Souvenir postcard c1910. Public Domain.]

January 20:

Edison Kinetoscope opens in Mexico City, Mexico with a reception for President General Porfirio Dias and his wife.

February 4:

Edison Kinetoscope opens at the Palace of Industry, Valhalla Way, Stockholm.

February 5:

Edison Kinetoscope opens in the Main Hall, Tasmanian Exhibition, Domain, in Hobart, Australia. Organized by the Macmahon brothers, five machines were shown through March 12.

February 13:

French patent 245,032, *Appareil servant à l'obtention et à la vision des épreuves chronophotographiques*, to Louis and August Lumière for the Cinématographe, a compact device that could be used as a camera, a projector, or a printer, using 35mm film and with an intermittent movement provided by a pair of claws that gripped circular perforations at the side of each frame and pulled it into place for exposure.[61]

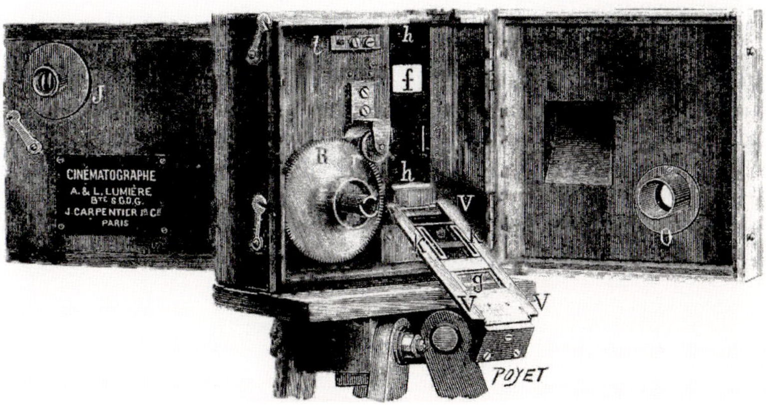

View of the Lumière Cinématographe from the rear, open. The objective lens is on the panel to the left, and the film gate and transport path is folded down. [Trutat, *Le Photographie animée* (1899), p. 74.]

February 22:
Anschütz Projecting Electrotachyscope opens to the public at the old Reichstag building, Leipzigerstrasse 4, Berlin. Assisted by his son Guido, Anschütz began regular showings of 'Living Pictures' ('*Lebende Bilder*') in a lecture hall holding 300 persons, with an admission of 1 – 1.50 Marks. The exhibitions lasted through the end of March 1895, and the income amounted to 5400 Marks.[62]

Films included: *Einseifen beim Barbier, Sprung des Hundes über den Graben, Zwei Zimmerleute früstuckend, Skatspieler, Rauchende Jungen.*

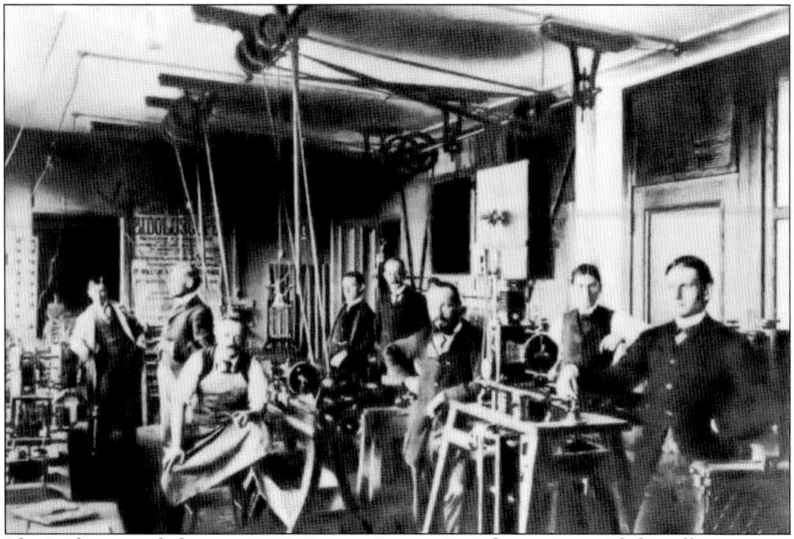

The Latham workshop in 1895. Eugene Lauste is at the centre, with his elbow on an apparatus, Otway Latham is at the right, and Gray Latham is between them. Father Woodville Latham is in profile on the left, looking out the window. [Courtesy Film Stills Library, the Museum of Modern Art, New York.]

February 26:
Eugene Lauste, W. K. L. Dickson, and Otway and Gray Latham film a swinging light in their workshop at 35 Frankfort Street, New York City, as a test of their newly constructed camera, a device with continuously moving film 50mm wide and no intermittent, called the Panoptikon, later called the Eidoloscope. This nighttime filming was the first full use of an apparatus that had been in development since September, 1894.[63]

March 1:
Otway Latham operates an improved camera and shoots a film of his father, Woodville, his brother Gray, Kleinert and Eugene Lauste and his son on the roof of the Scott Building, 35 Frankfort Street, New York City.

March 2:
Herman Casler tests the Mutoscope (Biograph) camera developed with key surreptitious advice from W. K. L. Dickson, at the machine shop of C. E. Lipe, 208 South Geddes Street, Syracuse, New York, using a strip of blank

61 Additional French patents for this device to the Lumières and/or their builder Carpentier on 15 February, 30 March, and 6 May 1895 and on 28 March and 18 November 1896. German patents 84722 of 11 April 1985; 90850 of 27 February 1896; and 98931 or 31 December 1896. British patent 7187 of 8 April 1895. For United States patent 579,882 see entry for 6 September 1895 below. The Cinématographe was normally equipped with an unnamed 50mm focal length symmetrical lens of 16mm front diameter costing 50 Francs. In the early literature this was known as the lens for taking negatives. A better lens was also offered at 126 Francs: it was made by Zeiss and had a 54mm focal length and an aperture of 1:6.3 with an iris adjustment.

62 The presentations in Berlin, and another in Hamburg, are the only known public exhibitions of the Anschütz Projecting Electrotachyscope. The Edison Kinetoscope reached Berlin also in March 1895, and it is possible that Anschütz finally saw the potential in working with flexible celluloid film instead of his normal individual glass plates, around which his entire system for taking and reproducing chronophotographs was built. According to Oskar Messter in 'Ottomar Anschütz: zu seinem 90. Geburtstag', in *Die Kinotechnik*, Vol. 18, No. 8, 20 April 1936, pp. 123–126, as cited in Hermann Hecht, *Pre-Cinema History*, No. 540I, pp. 377–378, Anschütz knew of the existence of Eastman's celluloid film strips, but preferred 'on principle' to use German manufactured materials; as there were no German celluloid film band manufacturers at this time, he continued to use glass plates in his camera. Hecht comments further that "With all due respect ... it is much more honest to say that he [Anschütz] failed to see the advantage of using film-bands ... Yet in spite of Messter's laudatory remarks and chauvinist attitude, he underestimates Anschütz's real contribution to pre-cinema history." Anschütz, with his unbending commitment to high photographic quality, may also have found the photographic emulsions of celluloid film bands unsatisfactory for his purposes.

63 Although it is clear that Edison later felt 'betrayed' by Dickson, and that Dickson was perhaps impatient with the long gestation (some five years) of the motion picture work at Edison's laboratory, Dickson's secret work with both the Lathams and with Biograph cannot be seen today as a wholly unethical association. In the machine shops of the day, it was common for a skilled mechanic to hire out to other entrepreneurs whilst remaining an employee of a particular shop, just as it was common practise for an employer, as Edison frequently did, to use 'inside contracts' with special pay to his mechanics to manufacture a small batch of devices or to assemble a particularly elaborate apparatus. A senior machine shop craftsman of this time had a considerable freedom of action in determining his working day and pace; Edison's 'invention factory' in its atmosphere and working practises maintained many of these traditional freedoms, although not all of them. Dickson was, in his work with Latham and Biograph, at least in part, reflecting the shop traditions within which he had been raised. Dickson also seems to have had enough individuality to want to be personally more prominently known for his work in motion pictures, and as an inventor in his own right. For further information, see 'Machine Shop Culture and Menlo Park' by Andre Millard, and 'Telegraphy and Edison's Invention Factory' by Paul Israel, both in William S. Pretzer, ed., *Working at Inventing: Thomas A. Edison and the Menlo Park Experience*, (Dearborn, MI, 1989: Henry Ford Museum & Greenfield Village). See also Paul Spehr, *W. K. L. Dickson: The Man Who Made Movies* (New Barnet, Herts, 2008: John Libbey Publishing Ltd.).

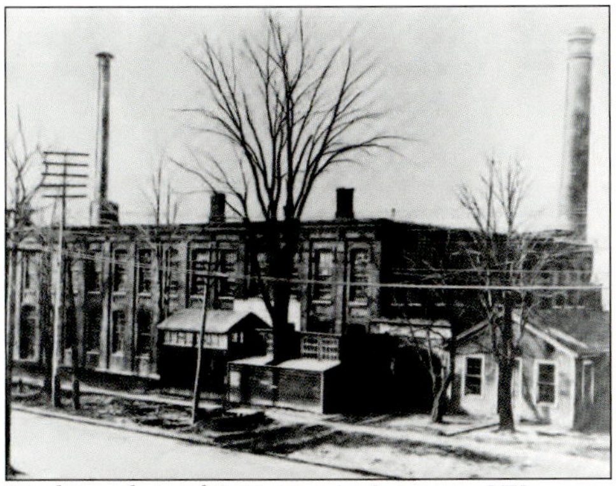

Machine shop of C. E. Lipe in Syracuse, NY, c1898, where early work on the Biograph system was undertaken. [Hendricks, *The Beginnings of the Biograph* (1964), Illus. 1.]

paper. The device had a friction intermittent movement and a film pathway 68mm wide.

March 6:

Edison Kinetoscope opens at the Haunted Swing Premises, Bourke Street East, Melbourne, Australia. Organized by the Macmahon brothers, five machines were shown through June 8.

☛George A. Georgiades opens a Kinetoscope parlor in Lisbon, Portugal, after the dissolution of his partnership with George John Tragidis (and James Hough) following their loss of a court case in London for "passing off" replica Edison Kinetoscopes made by Robert W. Paul.

March 9:

US patent 540,545, *Series Photographic Camera*, to Robert Dempsey Gray in New York City for his combination moving picture camera and projector. The unusual apparatus had a single lens and a single band of flexible film, with a rotating semi-circular mirror behind the lens that exposed frames of the image onto two areas of the film band perpendicular to each other as the film band wound its way around the apparatus. The film ran over toothed sprocket wheels with the intermittent provided by a spring-controlled claw motivated by a master-slave gear. For projection, two lamp houses at right angles to each other illuminated the film bands with the revolving mirror performing its duties in reverse, reconstituting the image for the single lens. Although ingenious, Gray's system put a great strain on the film band and on its perforations. His apparatus was much improved in only a few weeks; see entry under 2 June.

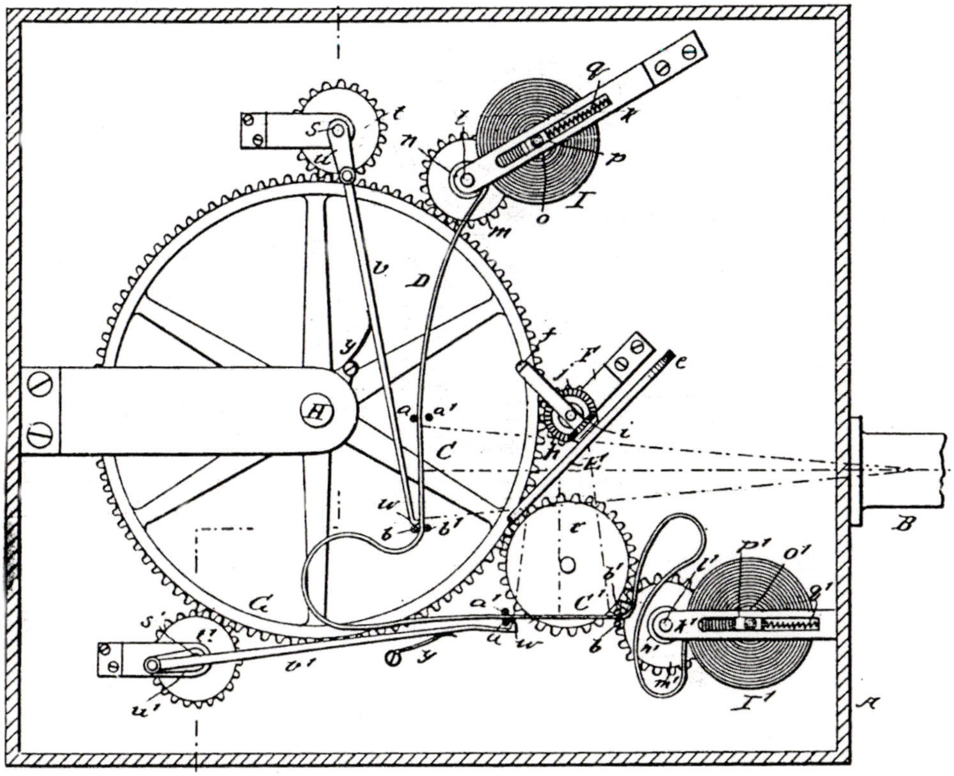

In Gray's combination camera and projector, the rotating half-mirror is at E and e, which reflects the image from lens B straight down onto the moving film at C1 and then allows it to pass through to the film at C. [US patent 540,545 of 9 March 1895, Fig. 1.]

March 11:

Edison Kinetoscope opens in a Salle de Dépêches in Brussels. Two machines were installed, showing *Une Bagarre dans un bar â New York* [Bar Room Scene] and *La Loïe Fuller* [Annabelle Serpentine Dance].

March 13:

Edison Kinetoscope opens on the rue Haldimand, Lausanne, Switzerland.

March 20:

Edison Kinetoscope opens to the public in Münster at the concert hall Centralhof. Admission, 30 pfennig to see three different scenes.

March 22:
Lumière Cinématographe demonstrated by Louis Lumière before the Society for the Encouragement of National Industry, 44, rue de Rennes, Paris (at 4 place Saint-Germain-des Prés), where it was called a 'Kinetoscope de projection'. One film was shown: *La sortie des ouvriers de l'usine Lumière*, and several experimental colour still photographs in the Lumière autochrome process were projected with a magic lantern. There were only a few press reports, noting some technical information and commenting that the 'animated view' was "very curious...showing the movement among the people as they hasten towards the street, producing a most shocking effect so that a repetition of the projection was required by the wholly astonished audience".

March 23:
Edison Kinetoscope opens in Utrecht, The Netherlands, for 2 weeks.

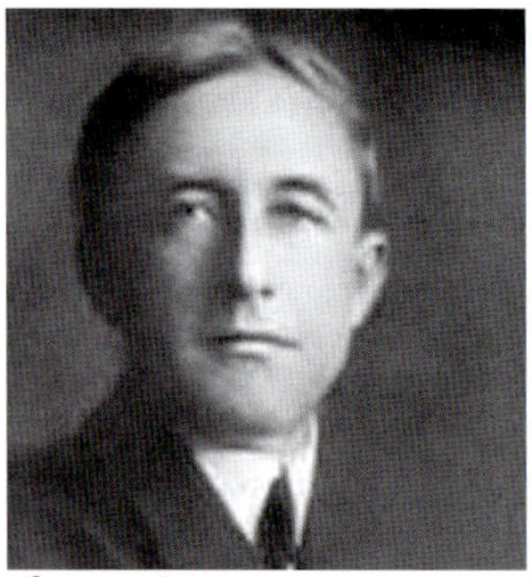

Thomas Armat, c1915. [Photograph by Arnold Genthe, c1915. Public Domain.]

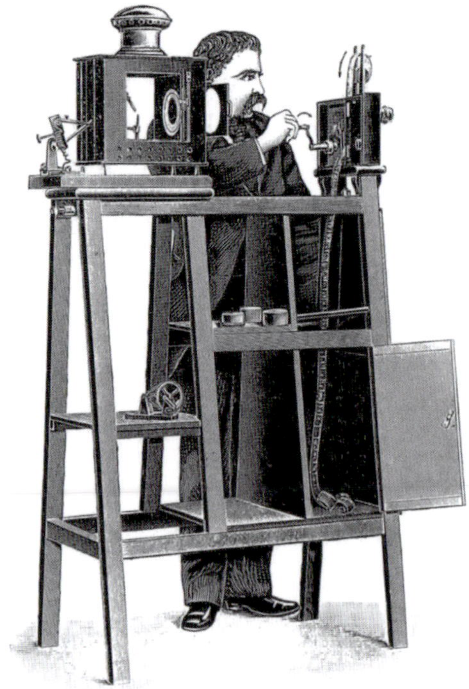

The Lumière Cinématographe in use as a projector, at first called a "Kinetoscope de projection". [Courtesy Archives Château Lumière, Lyon.]

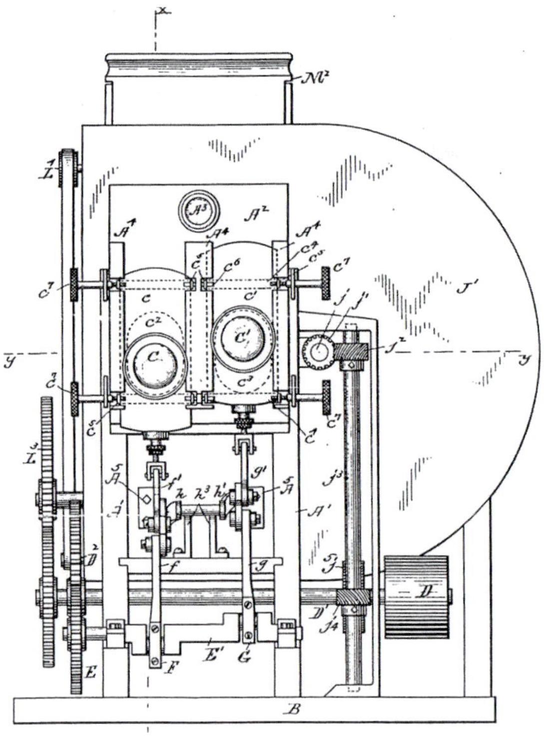

Front view of the Eames camera and projector. The twin lenses are at C and C' and move vertically in the plates c and c' through a camshaft at E'. [US patent 546,093 of 25 March 1895, Fig. 1.]

March 25:
United States patent 546,093, *Camera-Lantern*, to Owen A. Eames in Boston for his Animatoscope, a chronophotographic apparatus using a pair of reciprocating lenses and double-width film to record or project series photographs. The apparatus used reciprocating lenses, each running at half the needed speed to reduce strain on the film.

☛Thomas Armat and C. Francis Jenkins sign a partnership contract to exploit Jenkins' various apparatus designs using Armat's capital. Although Armat brought the money to the partnership, he was also an experienced mechanical inventor, holding several patents on electrical apparatus for railways.

March 29:
Robert William Paul sends a sample strip of film shot by Birt Acres to Thomas Edison in New Jersey, offering to produce additional English scenes for the Edison Kinetoscope. Edison replied on 16 April 1894 rejecting the

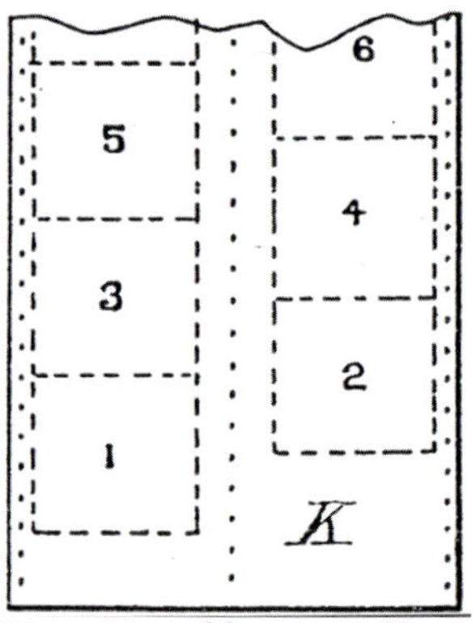

Disposition of frames on film in the Eames camera and projector. [US patent 546,093 of 25 March 1895, Fig. 7.]

offer. The film was taken outside Acres's home at Clovelly Cottage, Barnet, and features Acres's assistant, Henry Short. It implies that by this date Acres had all the means necessary to take and reproduce motion pictures in the Edison size and standard. This early camera used an intermittent clamping plate to hold the film steady in the aperture during exposure, as the film ran between upper and lower spools.

March 30:
Birt Acres begins making films for Robert W. Paul, who is supplying the Kinetoscope parlor of George A. Georgiades and George John Tragidis, including *Oxford and Cambridge University Boat Race* (March 30), and *The Epsom Derby* (May 29). Two earlier trial films were *Cricketer Jumping over Garden Gate* (February) and *Incident Outside Clovelly Cottage, Barnet* (March).

☛French patent 246,246, *Appareil ou projections de photographies instantanées de scènes animées sur bandes pelliculaires dénommé Cynégraphe*, to Jules Carpentier for his Cynégraphe projector, an apparatus with an intermittent movement and two lenses using toothed sprockets to move alternately two perforated bands of film.[64]

☛Addition to French patent 245,032 of 13 February (above) of Auguste and Louis Lumière modifying the cam that motivates the claw intermittent into a triangular shape set in an oval framework, and naming the apparatus the Cinématographe for the first time.

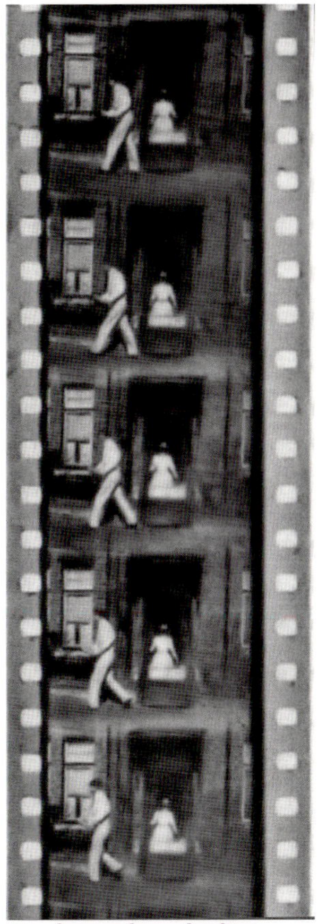

Five frames from the first successful film made in the United Kingdom, *Incident Outside at Clovelly Cottage, Barnet*, by Birt Acres. [Talbot, *Moving Pictures* (1912), opposite p. 36.]

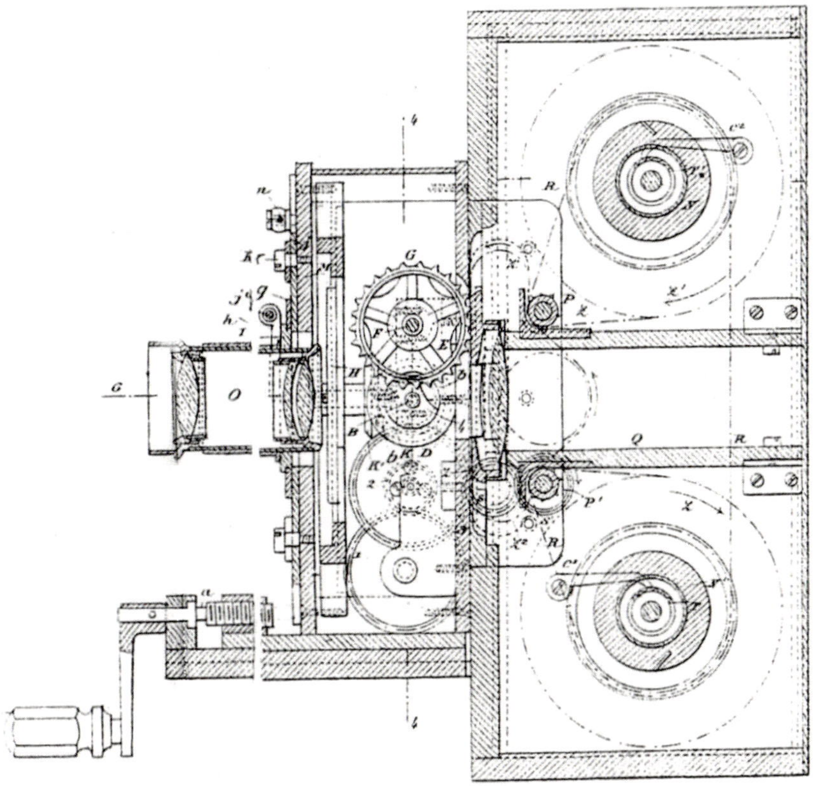

Section through Carpentier's twin-lens camera and projector of March, 1895, showing the film path (R) and intermittent system (B, b, E). [French patent 246,246 of 30 March 1895, Fig. 13.]

April 1:
Owen A. Eames lectures at the Camera Club of Boston about his twin-lens continuous-filmstrip camera and projector, the Anima-

64 In 1892 Carpentier patented an early 'vest-pocket' still plate camera for images 45 x 60mm, the Photo-Jumelle, which was very popular. He received a British patent on 6 April 1892 for a similar camera with a push/pull plate-changing mechanism. In late Autumn 1895, Carpentier began making the first 25 copies of the Cinématographe for the Lumière brothers in his shop at 20 rue Delambre, Paris, where he had specialized in constructing optical, electrical, and precision instruments since 1878.

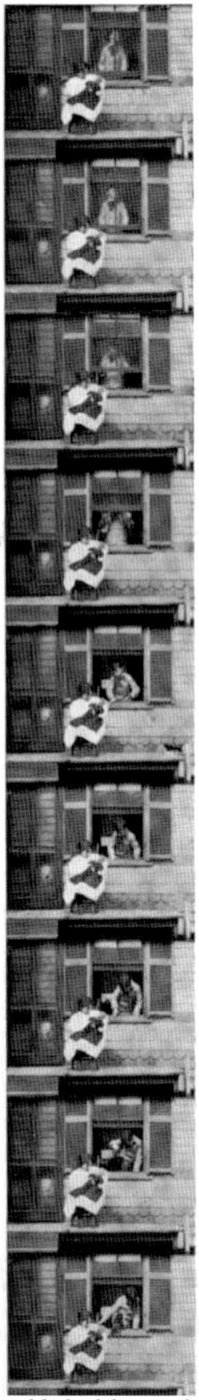

Nine published frames from the Animatoscope, taken in front of Eames's home in Brookline, MA. [*The Photographic Times*, July 1896, p. 331.]

toscope. Using film wide enough to carry two side-by-side images, Eames's apparatus used alternating vertically moving lenses to follow the continuously moving film. He employed different shutters for his camera and the projector, recognizing the shorter exposure for taking negatives in relation to the longer exposure in exhibiting positives. At this lecture he described the machine as "nearly ready". Nine published frames taken by the Animatoscope are evidence of the practical working of the apparatus

April 2:
W. K. L. Dickson leaves the employ of Thomas Alva Edison, in a dispute with Edison's recently-installed business manager, William Gilmore. At a meeting with Edison, the pair sought to sort out long-standing differences, but Dickson lost his temper and resigned on the spot. He may have stayed at work at West Orange until around April 20, and it was only at the end of the month that newspapers reported publicly that he had left Edison after 12 years.

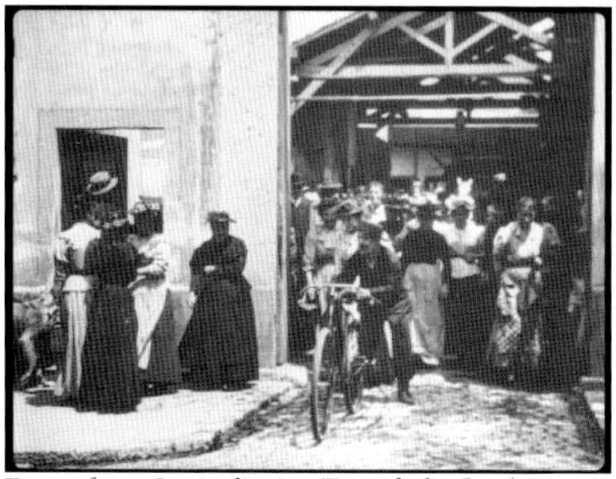

Frame from *Sortie d'usine* (I) made by Louis Lumière. [Frame from Michelle Aubert and Jean-Claude Seguin, *La Production cinématographique des Frères Lumière*, Cat. 685.]

April 17:
Lumiére Cinematographe demonstrated in the ampithéâtre of the Sorbonne, Paris. One film was shown: *Sortie d'Usine*.[65]

April 18:
Creation of the Deutsche-Österreichische-Edison-Kinetoskop-Gesellschaft, as the agency to represent and exploit the Edison Kinetoscope in Germany and Austria. One of the partners in this group was the Stollwerck chocolate company, through their automatic vending machines subsidiary, the Deutsche Automaten-Gesellschaft Stollwerck & Co.

April 21:
Having completed a projector for their 50mm wide film system, still called the Panoptikon and soon to be known as the Eidoloscope, Woodville, Gray, and Otway Latham, with Eugene Lauste and W. K. L. Dickson, give a press showing of their apparatus at 35 Frankfort Street, New York City, screening a film

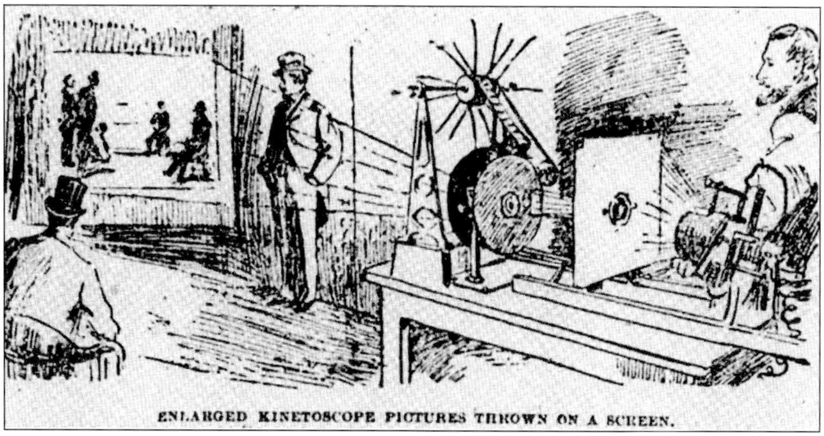

Sketch of the press showing of the Eidoloscope, then called the Panopticon, from the New York *Sun*, the day after its first appearance. [The New York *Sun*, 22 April 1895, p. 2.]

65 Michelle Aubert and Jean-Claude Seguin, in *La Production cinématographique des Frères Lumière*, tentatively date the production of the first version of *Sortie d'usine* as 26 Mai 1895, but production must have occurred a few weeks earlier for the film to have been shown in Paris on this date. See film No. 685, p. 214.

made on the roof of the workshop building, the first known public projection of motion pictures in the United States. The *New York Sun* reported blandly on the antics of boys tumbling at play, although admitting "even the puffs of smoke could be plainly seen, as could also a man's movements when he took a handkerchief from his pocket". Edison belittled the screening in the same news report, calling the machine "a rearranged Kinetoscope" and promising to sue if any screenings continued.

☛Edison Kinetoscope opens at via Roma 2 in Turin, Italy.

May 1:
Edison Kinetoscope parlour installed by the Deutsch-Oesterreichischen Edison-Kinetoskop Compagnie (DOEKCie), in a rented pub at Wilsdrufferstrasse 13, Dresden, Germany, managed by the actor Richard Erhardt. The parlour remained open until 30 April 1896.

May 4:
Gray and Otway Latham film a boxing match between Young Griffo and Charles Barnett on the roof of Madison Square Garden, New York City, with their Eidoloscope camera. The device contained a loop in the continuously moving film mechanism, later patented as the "Latham loop" and the subject of much later legal dispute. This alteration allowed a largely unlimited capacity for continuous filming, in this case so that the entire eight minutes of the fight could be photographed without stopping.

May 5:
Edison Kinetoscope opens in a bar on the Place de Cataluña in Catalogne, Spain.

May 6:
Addition to French patent 245,032 of 13 February 1895, of Auguste and Louis Lumière, adding a roller to receive the film above the gate of the Cinématographe.

May 11:
Anschütz Schnellseher opens to the public at the Italian Exhibition, Hamburg, under the auspices of Siemens and Halske. This exhibition was a reluctant attempt by Siemens to recover some of the unpaid bills for the construction of the apparatus. Thirty machines were installed, running until 13 December. There were 2348 viewings of the Schnellsehers in the first five days of the exhibition, and 56,645 viewings during the exhibition, at a time when both the Edison Kinetoscope and the Anschütz Projecting Electrotachyscope were running in the city.[66]

May 16:
Edison Kinetoscope parlor opens in the 'elegantly furnished side room' of the house at Gänsemarkt 2, Hamburg. Five machines were installed, with films changing every two weeks; admission 50 Pfennig. The kinetoscope ran until April, 1896.

May 18:
British patent 9881, *Improvements in means for viewing a series of pictures for the purpose of obtaining from same an appearance of movement*, to Phillip Middleton Justice, as agent for James Edward Hough of New York City, for a Kinetoscope-type device. A series of photographs were mounted as a helical band on a drum which is moved on a screw axle: a slotted shutter is turned synchronously between the images and a viewing objective, with illumination transmitted to the images by a funnel at the side. The patent was "a communication from abroad" by J. E. Hough, a phonograph pirate who was involved with R. W. Paul in

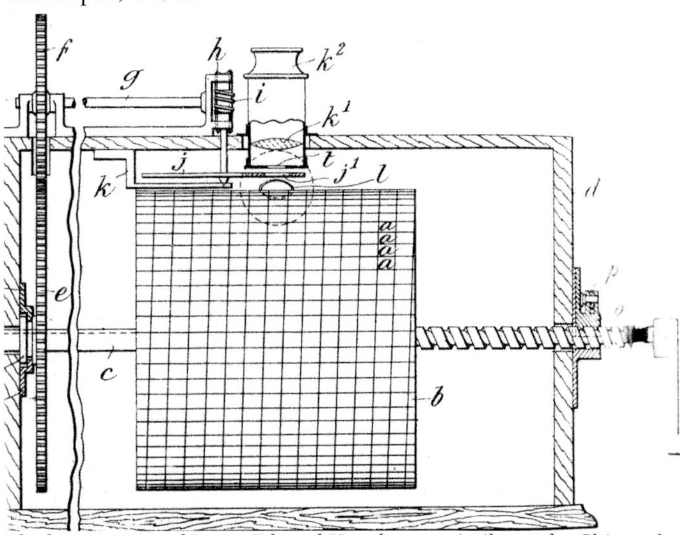

The kinetoscope of James Edward Hough, very similar to the Chinnock kinetoscope, where a band of images (a,a,a,a) was wound around a drum and seen through an eyepiece (k1, k2). An intermittently driven shutter (j, j1) was between the eyepiece and the image band, which was moved across the eyepiece by a helical screw. [UK patent 9881 of 18 May 1895, for Phillip Middleton Justice on behalf of James Edward Hough, Fig. 1.]

66 The Siemens & Halske agent in charge of the exhibition wrote back to the main office in Berlin every day with a count of the tickets sold, helpfully attaching to each letter the bank deposit ticket for the correct amount, providing an early exhibition record of unparalleled veracity.

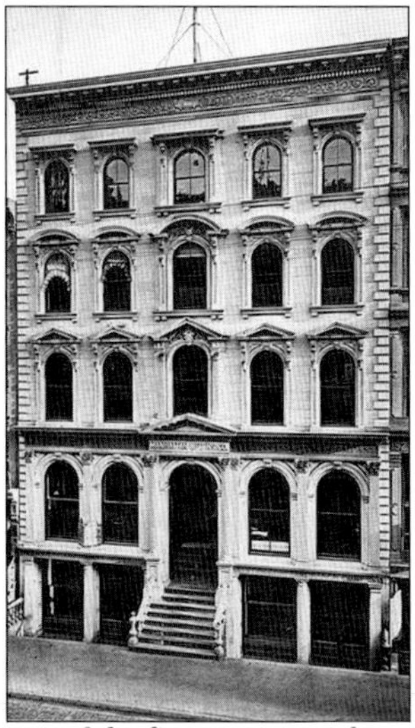

Site of the first commercial moving picture exhibition in the United States, 156 Broadway, New York City, probably in the sub-basement on the left.
[Heliotype by James R Osgood, Boston, MA, 1893, courtesy of Barry Anthony.]

the supply of replica Edison Kinetoscopes. This apparatus was very similar to the unpatented Chinnock Kinetoscope widely used in the U. S. from early 1895, with which Hough was also reportedly involved.[67]

May 19:
Charles Pathé announces the availability of his counterfeit kinetoscopes made by Robert Paul in London, in *L'Industriel forain* (No. 302). Priced at 1700 Francs, Henri Joly came to buy one, initiating his long association with Pathé.

May 20:
Latham Eidoloscope opens in a rented shopfront at 156 Broadway, New York City, to exploit their boxing film *Young Griffo – Battling Barnett,* beginning the first fully commercial run of projected motion pictures to the public. Shows were given every fifteen minutes, and lasted 12 minutes each. "You'll see people and things as they really are", suggested one journalist. The canvas screen was about 9 feet by 5 feet, and the image projected by the continuously running film with a narrow-slot shutter was very dim. "Quite a crowd of people visit the store at each performance", wrote *The Photographic Times*, "many making their exit wondering 'how it's done.'"

Films included: a boxing match, a horse race.

May 21:
Edison Kinetoscope opens in "the elegant exhibition rooms" at Friedrichstrasse 65, Berlin, accompanied by an intense advertising campaign. Part of the presentation established by the Deutsch-Oesterreichische Edison-Kinetoskop-Compagnie was a very noticeable tall, thin doorman from Dar-es-Salaam in native dress named Benjamin Franklin. The exhibitions ran until 31 August.

May 23:
By this date copies of the Edison Kinetoscope manufactured by Robert Paul were open to the public in an arcade in Leather Lane, London, managed by the eccentric 'Viscount' Hinton.

May 25:
Addition to French patent 233,337 of 10 October 1893 of Georges Demenÿ for improvements to his Chronophotographe, adapting the camera for projection using 60mm wide film. This was now a fully viable cinema apparatus, but was enmeshed in the failure of Demenÿ's Phonoscope Company, for which he could not raise any money. His new device would lie fallow until modified by Demenÿ and Léopold-René Decaux after the success of the Lumière Cinématographe and brought to market by Léon Gaumont in 1896, still using the 60mm film width. Adapted to 35mm film, it remained Gaumont's primary apparatus until 1900.[68]

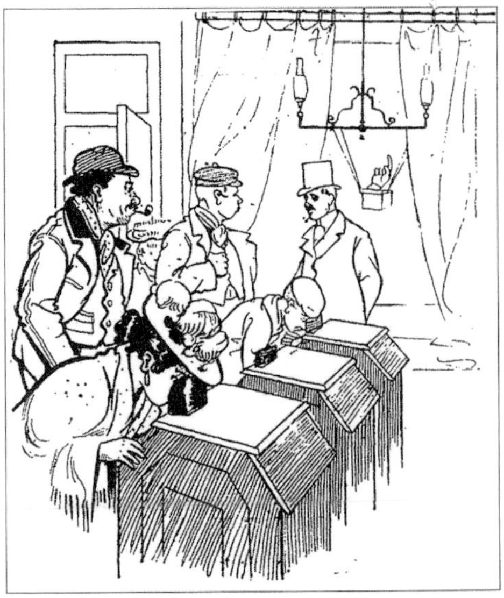

Viscount Hinton (William Turnour Thomas Poulett; at rear in top hat) presides over the exhibition of Robert Paul pirate kinetoscopes in Leather Lane, London. [Richard Brown and Barry Anthony, *The Kinetoscope, a British History* (2017), p. 127.]

May 27:
British patent 10,474, *Improved apparatus for enabling photographic images to be taken, projected, or viewed in rapid succession*, to Birt Acres for his kinetic camera, also adaptable as a projector, using the intermittent movement of his earlier apparatus, a spring-roller

67 Gordon Hendricks, in *The Kinetoscope*, p. 169, makes an unclarified reference to "the Werner and Hough agreement" drawn up by Alvah Chinnock and signed on 3 May 1895, which "activated the North American Kinetoscope Company, which exhibited the Chinnock Kinetoscope". For Hough's involvement with R. W. Paul, see Richard Brown, "A New Look at old history – the Kinetoscope: Fraud and market development in Britain in 1895," in *EPVC*, v10 n4 (November 2012), pp. 407–439.

68 Demenÿ wrote: "I brought well-known capitalists to my laboratory at Levallois, I showed them animated projections of galloping horses, wrestlers, gymnasts, talking portraits. They considered this invention as a childish recreation, they could not be turned from their intention to leave, and did not advance a thousand francs to follow it up."

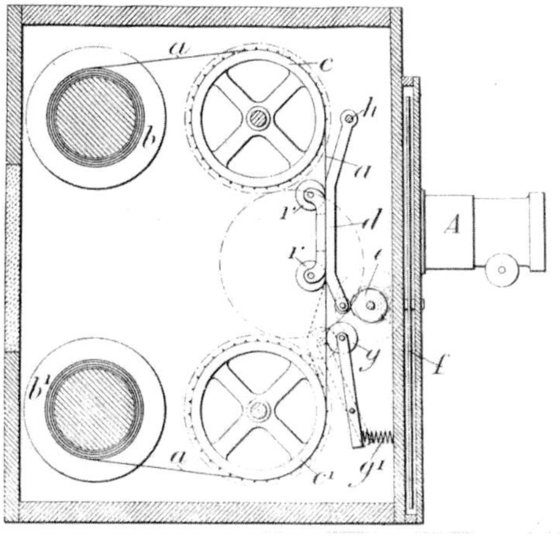

The kinetic camera of Birt Acres. An intermittent spring-loaded clamp (d) stopped the film at the camera gate for exposure after a synchronized spring-loaded roller (g) deflected the film so the continuously turning sprockets (C, C') did not break it. A delicately balanced mechanical movement that made the first films in Britain. [UK patent 10,474 of 27 May 1895, Fig. 1.]

momentarily clamping each frame in the aperture for exposure, with a spring-loaded roller to deflect the film below the aperture to relieve tension on the film while it is momentarily exposed for exposure or projection.

May 29:
Birt Acres films the Derby at Epsom.

☛Anschütz Projecting Electrotachyscope opens to the public at Carl Henckel's Concert Hall, Hamburg, Germany. The exhibitions, accompanied by lectures, ran through 12 June.

May 30:
Edison Kinetoscope opens at the Salon Edisson [*sic.*], Carrera de San Jeronimo, Madrid.

June 1:
Edison Kinetoscope opens in a salon of Sr. Moccia, via Vittorio Emanuele 151, Palermo, Italy.

Films include: *Danza Buffalo*, *Contorsionista Bertholdi*, *Una bottega da falegname*.

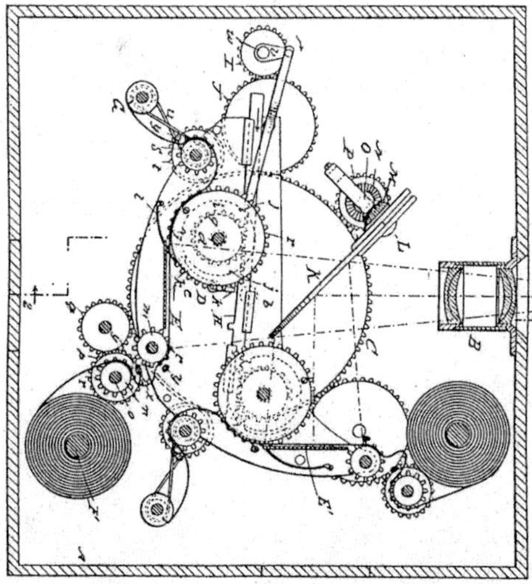

For the improved Gray camera and projector, two intermittently activated sprockets are motivated by the base plate C, and each draws one band of film across a focal plane at E and E' so the half-mirror K can reflect alternate images, much reducing strain on the film. For projection, illumination was placed behind E and E' with the mirror now sending the alternate images to the projection lens.
[German patent 92809 of 2 June 1895, Fig.1.]

June 2:
German patent 92809, *Serien-Apparat mit zwei Filmbändern*, to Robert Dempsey Gray in New York City, for his combination camera and projector. This is a practical improvement of Gray's earlier U. S. Patent 540,545 of 9 March 1895 for a single-film-band movement based on the same concept, indicating that a machine was in serious development. The improvements here include the use of two separate film bands instead of a single band, reducing the strain on each and reducing the speed with which each needed to move through the apparatus. The film path is also less bendy. This patent clearly indicates that a practical device was in active development by Gray, but no further information is currently available about the ultimate development or use of this apparatus.[69]

June 10:
Lumière Cinématographe demonstrated for the *Congres des Sociétés Françaises de*

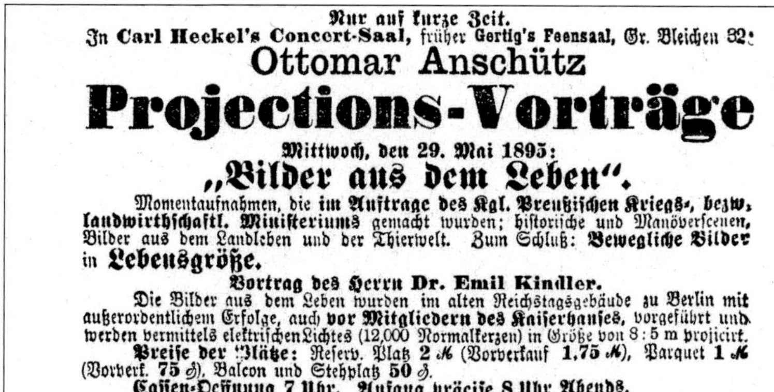

Nur auf kurze Zeit.
In Carl Heckel's Concert-Saal, früher Gertig's Feensaal, Gr. Bleichen 32:
Ottomar Anschütz
Projections-Vorträge
Mittwoch, den 29. Mai 1895:
„Bilder aus dem Leben".
Momentaufnahmen, die im Auftrage des Kgl. Preußischen Kriegs-, bezw. landwirthschaftl. Ministeriums gemacht wurden; historische und Manöverscenen, Bilder aus dem Landleben und der Thierwelt. Zum Schluß: Bewegliche Bilder in Lebensgröße.
Vortrag des Herrn Dr. Emil Kindler.
Die Bilder aus dem Leben wurden im alten Reichstagsgebäude zu Berlin mit außerordentlichem Erfolge, auch vor Mitgliedern des Kaiserhauses, vorgeführt und werden vermittels elektrischen Lichtes (12,000 Normalkerzen) in Größe von 8 : 5 m projicirt.
Preise der Plätze: Reserv. Platz 2 ℳ (Vorverkauf 1,75 ℳ), Parquet 1 ℳ (Vorverk. 75 ₰), Balcon und Stehplatz 50 ₰.
Cassen-Oeffnung 7 Uhr. Anfang präcise 8 Uhr Abends.
Vorverkauf bei: Käse, Alsterarcaden, Kimmelstiel, Neuerwall, Crone & Martinot, St. Pauli, Sophienstraße 49, Hercules Hinz, Altona, Königstr. 65, v. Inten, Steindamm 21, Rathhausstr. 16, und Oberstedt & Schering Nachf., Brandstwiete 13.

Advertisement for the Hamburg exhibition of the Projecting Electrotachyscope at Carl Heckel's Concert Hall. [*Hamburger Fremdenblatt*, 29 May 1895.]

69 Robert Dempsey Gray was a photographic technician working in lower Manhattan and living in Brooklyn. He developed and patented a widely sold concealed, or 'detective,' camera in late 1885, and a roll film camera (with H. E. Stammer) in 1887. Perhaps more pertinently, he devised a chronophotographic apparatus with medical surgeon Dr. William Gilman Thompson to make sequential records of the human heart under various conditions, a device capable of producing six images on a circular plate in the period of one second. See Coe 1978, 55& 82; Rossell 2013, 18–25.

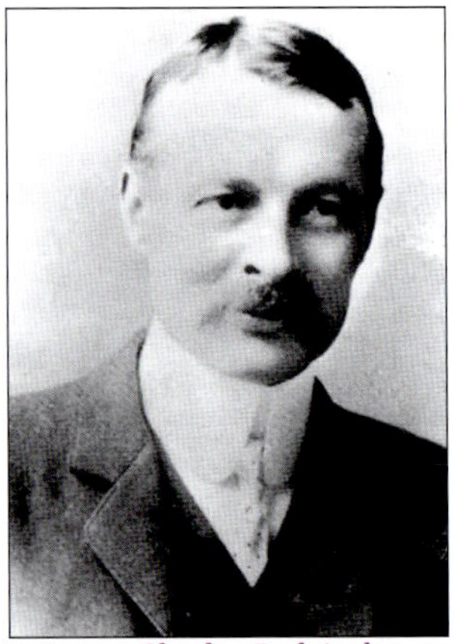
A young Charles Pathé, about 1912. [Photographer unknown. Public domain.]

Photographie, chez Berrier and Millet, Place Bellecour, Lyon. Eight films were projected and two films were also taken at the Congress, the latter projected on the following day (see below).

Films included: *La sortie des usines Lumière*, *Une leçon de voltige*, *Les Forgerons*, *La Pèche aux poissons rouges*, *Attaque du feu (Pompiers)*, *Le repas de bébé*, *Place des Cordeliers*, *Le jardinier et le petit espiegle*.

June 11:
Edison Kinetoscope opens at the Albion Chambers, View Street, Bendigo, Australia. Organized by the Macmahon brothers, five machines were shown through June 17.

June 12:
Projection of two Lumière Cinématographe films taken at the *Congres des Sociétés Françaises de Photographie* in Lyon, at the end of the banquet closing the congress. The films had been taken the day before, and were not later included in Lumière catalogues.

Films included: *L'Astronome Janssen s'entretenant avec M. Lagrange, Conseiller general du Rhone* and *Les membres du Congres debarquant d'un bateau-mouche a Neuville-sur-Saone.*

June 13:
Charles Pathé, impatient for more new films for his Kinetoscope parlor, concludes an agreement with Henri Joseph Joly to manufacture a cinema camera.

June 18:
French patent 248,254, *Appareil permettant de voir les photographies animées*, to Eugène Werner for 'a new type of apparatus' for viewing 'a series of photographs reproduced on an endless film, animated with a continuous movement'. This was an outright piracy of the Edison Kinetoscope with only a few details changed, for example a shutter made of a rotating cylinder pierced with four windows.[70]

June 19:
Edison Kinetoscope opens at the Academy of Music, Lydiard Street South, Ballarat, Australia. Organized by the Macmahon brothers, five machines were shown through June 26.

June 20:
Birt Acres films the opening of the Kiel Canal with his Kinetic Camera, in Kiel, Germany.

☛Edison Kinetoscope opens in the field next to the amusement slide in the Holtenauerstrasse, Kiel, as part of the International Marine Festival organized for the opening of the Kiel Canal. Along with Birt Acres filming the opening of the canal, Ottomar Anschütz was also present to document the event. Specialty acts, concerts, show booths and exotic restaurants were all a part of the festivities, admission to which was 20 Pfennig, children half-price, military free.

June 28:
Edison Kinetoscope opens at the Exhibition Theatre, Geelong, Australia. Organized by the Macmahon brothers, five machines were shown through July 2. The exhibition included a phonograph demonstration on a Bell-Tainter Graphophone.

July 1:
Anschütz Schnellseher opens to the public at an exhibition in Lübeck, Germany under the auspices of Siemens and Halske. Twelve machines were installed, running through 2 October. This was a further attempt to recover their investment in manufacturing costs of the apparatus.

July 5:
Edison Kinetoscope opens in the Calle Legazpi in Donostia-San Sebastian, by Manuel Galindo, representing the Paris agency Eliseo-Express. Galindo will later exhibit a Kinetografo in Bilbao and the area around the Bay of Biscay.

July 11:
Lumière Cinématographe demonstrated for an audience of 150 persons who sat in a tower room on either side of the screen at the publication *Revue Générale des Sciences Pures et Appliquées*, Paris. Films were the same as at the *Congres des Sociétés Françaises de Photographie*, above 10 June.

July 20:
Max Skladanowsky demonstrates his Bioskop projector at the Gasthaus Sello, Berliner Strasse 27, in Pankow, a suburb of Berlin. This was a private invitational screening to test the new projector, held in the main hall of the establishment. The Skladanowsky films

70 At the time, Eugène Werner seems to have separated from his brother Michel and his father Alexis, as their Kinetoscope business was rapidly changing and rapidly declining, but they were still the exclusive French agents for the Edison Kinetoscope. See Laurent Mannoni, '1894 – 1895, les années parisienne du Kinetoscope Edison', in *Cinémathèque* 3, Spring/Summer 1993, pp. 47–57.

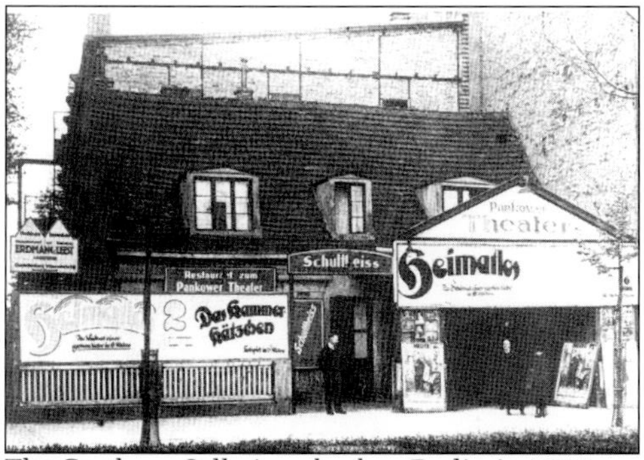

The Gasthaus Sello in suburban Berlin in 1927, after it had been turned into the Pankow Theatre. It would later become the Tivoli cinema. [Courtesy Märkisches Museum, Berlin.]

had been shot in the beer garden of the same Gasthaus at the beginning of May. The screening was attended by Franz Dorn and Julius Baron, directors of the Wintergarten Theatre, Berlin, who immediately made a contract for a November public premiere with the conditions that the 'Doubleprojector' not be demonstrated to anyone or the patent applied for until the Wintergarten showing on 1 November 1895.

Films included: *Bauerntanz, Jongleur, Komisches Reck, Erfinder des Bioscops, Kamarinskaja, Ringkampf, Die Grunatos, Das boxende Känguruh.*

August 5:
The Mutoscope (Biograph) camera takes its first 'official' film in Canastoda, New York, of Professor Al Leonard and Bert Hasler in a boxing match.[71]

August 10:
Léon Gaumont, an engineer formerly employed by Jules Carpentier and by the precision instrument makers Félix and Jules Richard, establishes his own photographic equipment company, L. Gaumont et Cie., with a group of investors including Gustave Eiffel, Joseph Vallot, and Alfred Besnier.

August 13:
Edison Kinetoscope opens at Organ Hall, Bowen Park Exhibition Grounds, Brisbane, Australia. Organized by the Macmahon brothers, five machines were shown through 16 August, when the exhibition moved to the Telegraph Chambers, Queen Street, through 26 August.

August 22:
Georges Demenÿ signs an agreement with Léon Gaumont licensing the latter to publicly exploit his Phonoscope. This contract comes after Demenÿ and George William de Bedts, the French representative of the raw film manufacturer the European Blair Camera Company, mutually abandon long negotiations whereby de Bedts would exploit the Phonoscope as a private portrait device, and Demenÿ would use it for public projections.

August 24:
Demenÿ Phonoscope exhibited at the Stollwerck automat hall in Cologne. An Edison Kinetoscope, like the Phonoscope arranged as an automat, was also installed at the opening of this hall that featured Stollwerck's automats dispensing chocolates. This installation is the only known commercial exploitation of the Phonoscope for viewing animated photographs.

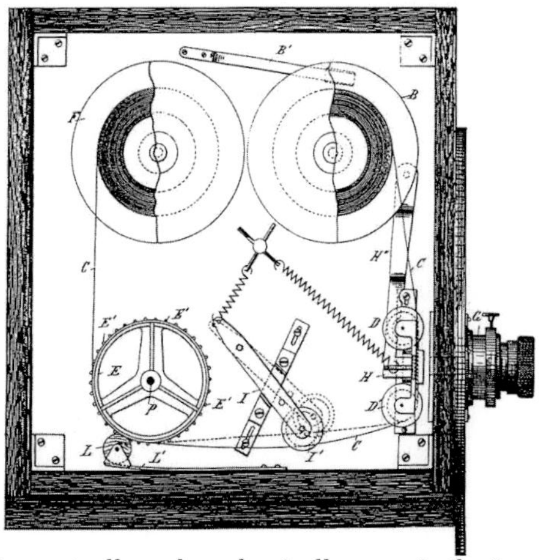

Conceptually and mechanically very similar to the Acres UK patent for his kinetic camera, this German version illustrates the flexibility of the artifact in early cinema work. The deflecting arm has been moved and the gate-clamping device is now also spring-loaded, with a single sprocket wheel driving the mechanism, instead of two sprockets acting in tandem.
[German patent 92247 of 25 August 1895, Fig. 1.]

August 25:
German patent 92,247, *Vorrichtung zur Aufnahme und Projektion von Reihenbildern*, to Paul Müller for the kinetic lantern camera and projector of Birt Acres. Müller was an employee of Ludwig Stollwerck, with whom Acres had concluded a contract for the exploitation of his apparatus in Germany.[72]

August 26:
The Latham Eidoloscope projects for one week at Chicago's Olympic Theatre, then moving directly to Kohl & Middleton's Clark

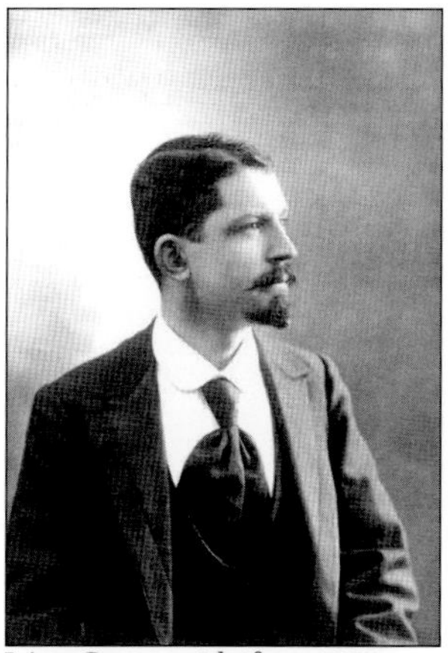

Léon Gaumont before 1890.
[Courtesy Musée Gaumont.]

71 In mid-June 1895, the Mutograph shot as a test film a mock boxing match between Herman Casler and Harry Marvin behind the C. E. Lipe machine shop, 208 South Geddes Street, Syracuse, New York.

72 Both Zglinicki, p. 231 and Hopwood, p. 103, have previously noted the striking similarities of the Müller patent to the apparatus of Birt Acres.

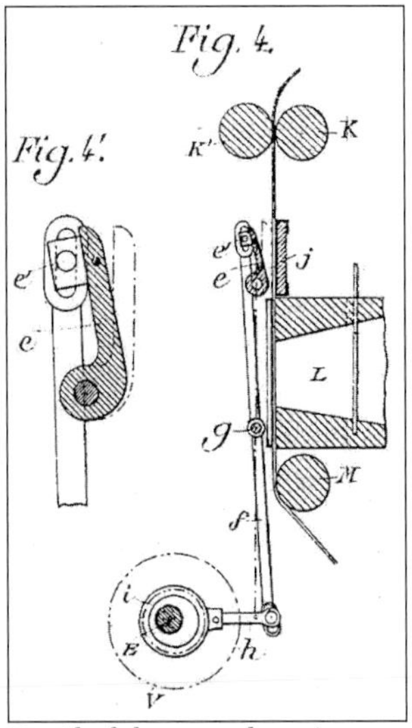

Detail of the gate-clamping mechanism in Joly's first camera (Fig. 4) and its motivating arm (Fig. 4'). [French patent 249,875 of 26 August 1895, Figs. 4 and 4'.]

Street Dime Museum, where it remained for three weeks.

☛French patent 249,875, *Nouvel appareil chronophotographique*, to Henri Joly for his first cinematographic camera and projector, developed in April-May 1895, and equipped with a sprocket roller similar to that of Birt Acres. With this camera Joly photographed films for the Edison Kinetoscopes of Charles Pathé. Also: UK patent 18,695 of 1895 by international convention.

August 28:
United States patent 586,953, *Phantoscope*, to Thomas Armat and C. Francis Jenkins for their Phantoscope projector. The intermittent mechanism was a simple cam which engaged multiple segments of a star wheel, a kind of 14-sided Maltese Cross movement called a Boston Gear, and the apparatus also used a 'loop' to reduce tension on the moving film.

September 2:
Edison Kinteoscope opens in Townsville, Australia. Organized by the Macmahon brothers, five machines were shown through 6 September.

September 6:
US patent 579,882, *Kinetographic Camera*, to Auguste and Louis Lumière for their Cinématographe. This is the American version of F 245,032. By filing this patent in the U. S. belatedly, a week later than Armat and Jenkins, the latter patent was given priority for its claims in the U. S., a costly mistake for the Lumière Company similar to the widely noted failure of the Edison Manufacturing Company to take out European patents on the Kinetoscope.

September 7:
Edison Kinetoscope opens on Mosman Street, opposite Collins' Exchange Hotel in Charters Towers, Queensland, Australia. Organized by the Macmahon brothers, five machines were shown through September 21, with the Australian premiere of three Kinetophones added on 16 September.

Kinetophone films included *Albert Chevalier singing a 'Coster Ditty'* and two unknown titles.

September 21:
Lumière Cinématographe demonstrated privately for family and friends by Antoine Lumière at his home La Ciotat, in Clos du Plages, France. There were about 150 guests, and the invitations specifically included whole families, including children.

Films included: *Baignade sur la plage, Goûter de Bébé, L'arrivée du train, L'arroseur arrosé, La sortie des usines.*

September 22:
The K. M. C. D. Group, as they informally referred to themselves, met at Herman Casler's home in Canastoda, New York. The group included Harry Marvin, W. K. L. Dickson, and Elias B. Koopman and would be the foun-

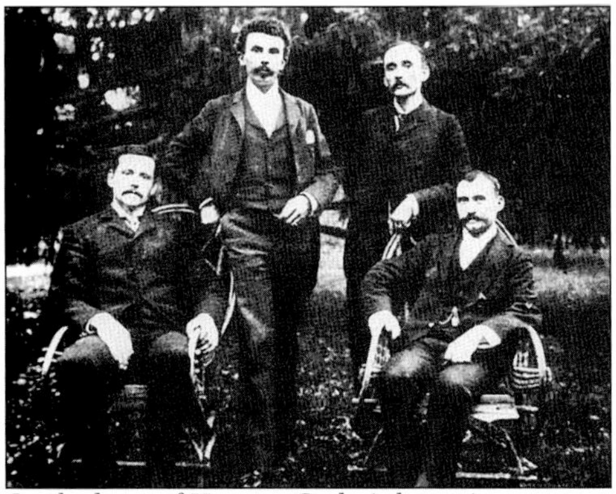

On the lawn of Herman Casler's home in Canastota, New York, the friends who would establish the American Mutoscope Company later in the year: (from left) Harry Norton Marvin, William Kennedy Laurie Dickson, Herman Casler, Elias B. Koopman. [Museum of Modern Art Film Stills Archive.]

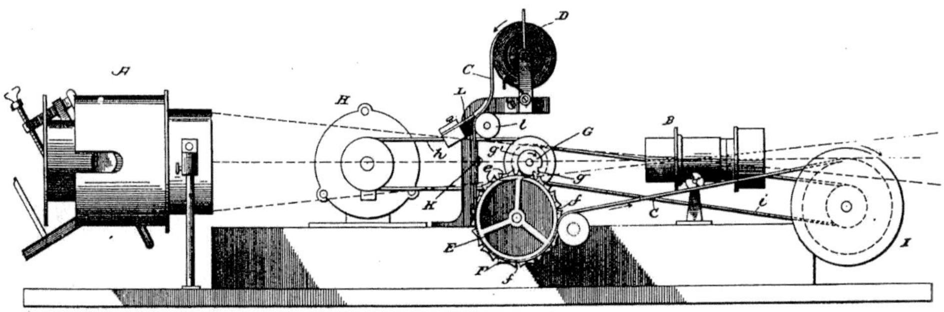

The Phantoscope of Armat and Jenkins in 1895. The 'Boston gear' is at E, its rotating cam spur is at G and g'. [US patent 586,953 of 28 August 1895, Fig. 1.]

ders of the American Mutoscope Company when they formally incorporated in late December. At this time work was well advanced on both the Mutoscope flip-card viewer and a single-lens camera for taking series photographs.

September 26:
Edison Kinetoscope opens at the Café de Vereeniginng, Utrecht, The Netherlands.

September 27:
Edison Kinetoscope opens in East Street, opposite the Argus office, Rockhampton, Australia. Organized by the Macmahon brothers, five machines were shown through October 3. On October 4, three Kinetophones opened in the same premises through October 12.

Kinetophone films included: *Madame Patey singing 'The Holy City'*, *Harry Rickards singing 'E Dunno Where 'E Are*, and *The American Auctioneer*.

September 29:
The Phantoscope projector of Thomas Armat and Charles-Francis Jenkins is exhibited at the Cotton States Exposition in Atlanta, Georgia, in a space next to the Hagenbeck Animal Exhibit near the extreme east end of the midway. Jenkins and Armat divided their exhibition stall in half, and used two projectors to allow reasonably continuous shows at 25 cents admission, with a third projector in reserve in case of breakdown. The Phantoscope used Edison Kinetoscope films acquired from E. F. Murphy of the Columbia Phonograph Parlor in Washington, D. C. According to the *Atlanta Journal*, which reviewed the show on 21 October 1895, as "The most wonderful electric invention of the age", the show presented "a perfect reproduction, full life size, of the living originals, every act and motion absolutely perfect, even to the wink of an eye".

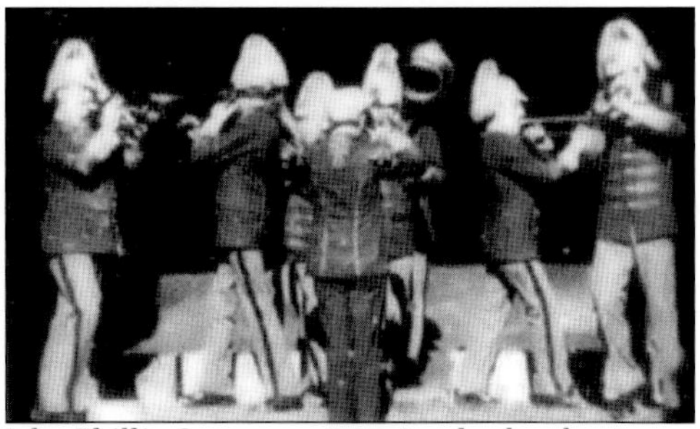

John Phillip Sousa was notoriously shy about filming his band, believing that a film would cut into the bookings for his incessantly touring musicians. So the picture exhibited at Atlanta was more likely *Band Drill*, a scene from the play *The Milk White Flag*, but indicating also that Jenkins and Armat had a keen appreciation of celebrity as they promoted their invention. [Musser, *Edison Motion Pictures*, No. 102, p. 160.]

Films included two acts from *Trilby*, one act from *1492*, *Carmencita*, *Sousa's Band*, dances, a fist fight, *Annabelle in the Sun* and Serpentine dances, a cock fight and others. The shows ran about 18 days, until a fire broke out on that end of the midway on October 15.[73]

October 13:
Charles Pathé announces the availability of Henri Joly's kinetoscope for four viewers in *L'Industriel forain* (No. 323). According to Pathé only a few were sold for use on the fairgrounds. Their availability came three weeks before Joly's patent (See November 8).

October 16:
Eadweard Muybridge lectures with the Zoopraxiscope at Ipswich Public Hall, Ipswich, England, under the auspices of a special committee led by W. Vick.

October 18:
Eadweard Muybridge lectures with the Zoopraxiscope at the Surrey Street Music Hall, Sheffield, England, under the auspices of the Sheffield Literary and Philosophical Society.

October 24:
British provisional patent 19,984, *A novel form of exhibition or entertainment, means for representing the same*, to William Paul for a film projector in a hall built to resemble a Pullman car, which he called "a machine to explore time". Paul had been inspired by reading H. G. Wells' *The Time Machine*, first published in 1895. This patent, which was abandoned, may have been a collaboration between Paul and Wells. Years later re-invented by George Hale and popularized from 1904 as Hale's Tours.

October 29:
C. Francis Jenkins exhibits the Phantoscope at his brother's jewelry store in Richmond, Indiana, while on his way home from the Cotton States Exhibition in Atlanta, having brought one of the three Atlanta machines with him as he stopped at home for his brother's wedding.[74]

November 1:
Bioskop of Max and Emil Skladanowsky opens at the Wintergarten Theatre, Berlin, in a side alcove off the main lobby, at the theatre then located in the Martin Luther Straße, the first projections of film in Europe to a paying audience. The filmed variety acts from their

73 The Latham Eidoloscope and the Edison Kinetoscope were also at the Cotton States Exhibition, and Armat, Gray Latham, and Jenkins, as well as Frank Harrison of the Raff & Gammon Kinetoscope agents, all discussed their equipment and exhibitions.

74 Jenkins' later claims of a successful projection of an early model Phantoscope in Richmond, Indiana, on 6 June 1894, are false and a later fabrication produced for a variety of claims and counter-claims about precedence of invention. This incorrect date was printed as fact as early as 1918 by Homer Croy in *How Motion Pictures are Made*, and the date appears in many later histories.

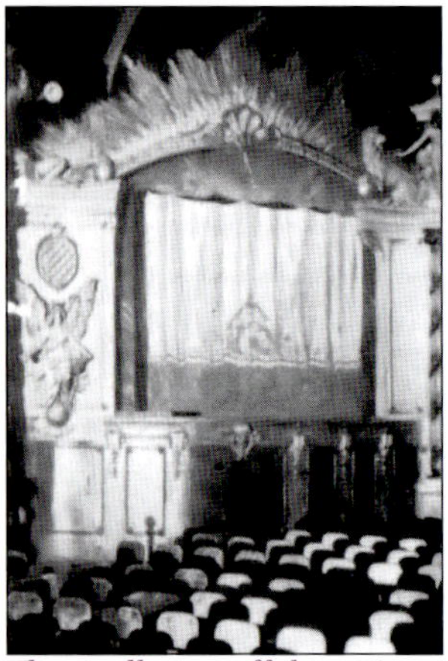

The small stage off the main lobby of the Wintergarten Theatre where the Skladanowsky brothers gave the first performance of their Bioskop, in rear projection with a screen kept wet for transparency. [Anon., *Festschrift Wintergarten 1888–1938*, p.103.]

private projection of 20 July are repeated, as the last presentation of the new November programme. The presentation used rear projection, and to help the transparency of the screen stagehands kept it wet during the performances. The films also had original scores

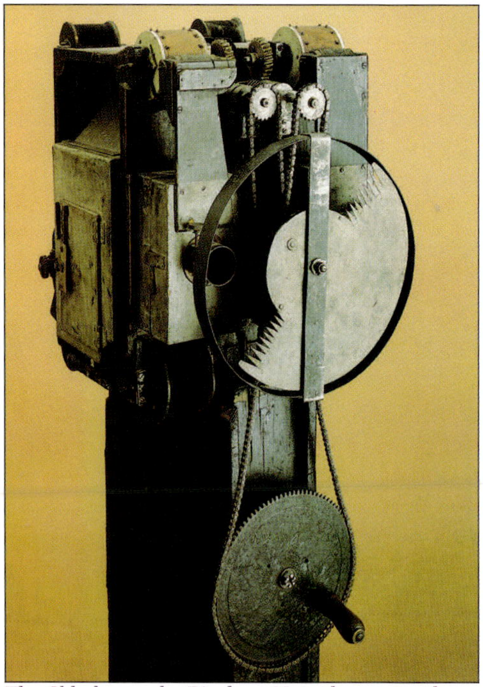

The Skladanowsky Bioskop. Note the sawtooth shutter blade, derived from magic lantern dissolving view practice, that blended the images from the two separate film bands. [Jürgen Ristow, *Vom Geisterbild zum Breitwandfilm* (1986), p. 43.]

played live and composed by Hermann Krüger. Film titles were given on a slide projected by a magic lantern. Each film lasted about six seconds, and was repeated several times. The presentations at the Wintergarten continued through November 30.

Films included: *Italienischer Bauerntanz, Komisches Reck, Serpentine Tanz, Der Jongleur Paul Petras, Das boxende Känguruh, Akrobatisches Porpourri, Kamarinskaja, Ringkampf, Apotheose.*

☛German patent 88599, *Vorrichtung zum intermittirenden Vorwärtsbewegen des Bildbandes für Photographische Serien-Apparate und Bioskope*, to Max Skladanowsky for the intermittent movement of his Bioskop projector. The patent is dated 1 November since the contract between the Wintergarten Theatre and the Skladanowsky brothers for one month's run at 2250 Marks specified that the Bioskop could not be otherwise seen or known prior to the engagement. A double-projector showing alternate frames from two strips of film each running at 8 frames per second for a combined 16 frames per second rate on the screen, the Bioskop used film 54mm wide with images 40mm wide and 30mm high, perforated at the sides. A worm-gear intermittent and toothed sprockets fed the film. Illumination was by means of two 6-Ampere arc lamps, and a half-circular shutter with deeply incised teeth mounted before the lenses and run synchronously with the film bands smoothly blended the alternately projected images from the two separate film strips. Like Reynaud, the Skladanowskys reinforced the film perforations with metal ringlets.[75]

75 Skladanowsky's camera, developed in 1892 with his brother Emil, used unperforated 65mm wide roll film, and ran at a speed of 8 frames per second but had very poor image registration. To produce filmstrips for his projector, the negatives were cut up and laid out alternately (1, 3, 5, 7... and 2, 4, 6, 8 ... etc.) on sheets of magic lantern slide celluloid 1.5 meters square. The celluloid sheets were then cut into strips 1.5 metres long, producing strips of about 48 images each, which were then glued together to make each of the two film bands for the Bioskop double-projector. Although Skladanowsky's projector is frequently denigrated in the classical literature of early cinema invention, it was a logical development of his fundamental experience with dissolving magic lanterns, with which both he and his father, Carl, had earned a part of their livings. The Skladanowsky Bioskop closely parallelled the mechanical principles of dissolving views, and the use of twin lenses for the optical blending of alternate images from two simultaneously moving image sources, was found not only in lantern practise but also in the Projecting Electrotachyscope of Ottomar Anschütz. The Bioskop also had the advantage over projectors made for the next few years of being virtually without flicker: the deeply saw-toothed before the lens shutter, taken from dissolving view shutters for the magic lantern, fully blocked with appropriate gradations the continuous light from each lens in turn during the change of images, so there was no intermittent period of blackness on the screen – the apparatus ran without sharp periods of light and dark. Additionally, again as in dissolving magic lanterns, each frame was quickly blended on top of the next without interruption.

Skladanowsky's reputation is also hindered by the prints of his films preserved by the major archives like the Cinémathèque française, Paris, the Museum of Modern Art, New York, the National Film Archive, London, and others. Reprinted twenty or more years after their original creation and specially circulated as a preservation reel, these film prints are very simple unaltered dupes of Skladanowsky's original material intended for showing on his double-projector. As such, they can no longer be seen as they were in 1895: each title 'repeats' itself twice, showing on a modern projector each of the two bands of Skladanowsky's films consecutively. Since each of the two film bands contains only half of the individual images of the work, only one-half of the necessary images for smooth reproduction of movement are seen in each of the two 'repeats': on screen today the movements seem to be jerky and rough, not at all as they would have been when the alternate images from both bands were combined and projected continuously in Skladanowsky's apparatus. Not only interested viewers but also many archivists seem unaware of the nature of the prints of Skladanowsky's films which today mis-represent his achievements in all contemporary screenings of his film work.

November 8:
French patent 251,549, *Photozootrope à un ou plusieurs oculaires*, to Henri Joly for a kinetoscope-type device weighing 35 kilos suitable for four viewers and with two horizontally moving film bands each 110 meters long, called the Photozootrope. The device had been

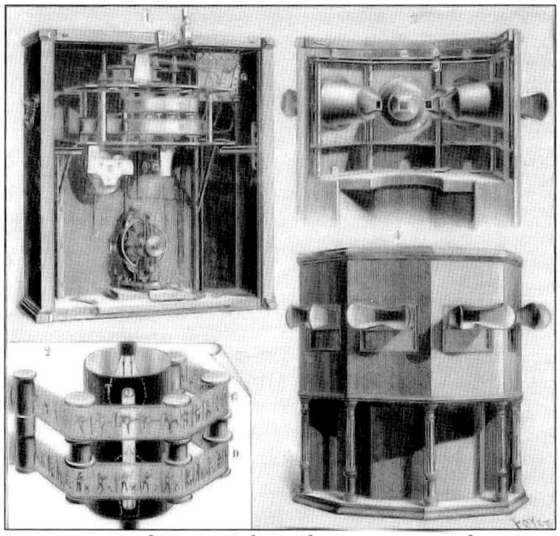

Four views of Henri Joly's Photozootrope showing its inner workings, one of the several attempts to expand the number of viewers beyond the single person allowed at the Edison Kinetoscope.
[*La Nature*, No. 1196, 2 May 1896, p. 357.]

ordered by Charles Pathé, who sold them at a price of 390 Francs, as opposed to the 800 Franc cost of the reproduction kinetoscopes made by R. W. Paul, and the 1,500 Franc price of a genuine Edison Kinetoscope.[76]

☛Edison Kinetoscope opens at a YMCA festival in Jubilee Hall, Adelaide, Australia. Organized by the Macmahon brothers, five machines were shown, moving to Hindley Street on 11 November and to a shop on Rundle Street on December 3. The five machines were exhibited for one day only (December 28) at Glenelg Town Hall and then returned to Rundle Street, closing on 6 January 1896.

November 10:
Lumière Cinématographe demonstrated for the Association Belge de Photographie at the Ecole Industrielle of the city of Brussels, Belgium, by Charles Moisson and his assistant Charles Ducom from the factory of A. Lumière et Fils, Lyon. The prototype cinématographe was called in the press 'a practical application of the Edison Kinetoscope,' and about 130 members were present. Eight films were shown.

Films included: *La sortie des ateliers Lumière à Lyon*; *Le saut à la caserne*, *Le bébé* et *les poissons rouges*, *Les forgerons*, *Le tête-à-tête de M. Janssen*, *L'incendie*, *Les baigneuses (si amusantes dans leurs ébats)*, *La place des cordeliers à Lyon*.

November 11:
Italian patent 40,128, *Kinetografo Alberini*, to Filoteo Alberini for his combination camera, projector, and printer, the Kinetografo Alberini. The idea and technology of this minor apparatus was derived from the Lumière Cinématographe. Alberini, in partnership with Dante Santori, later became a pioneer manufacturer of apparatus and owner of a

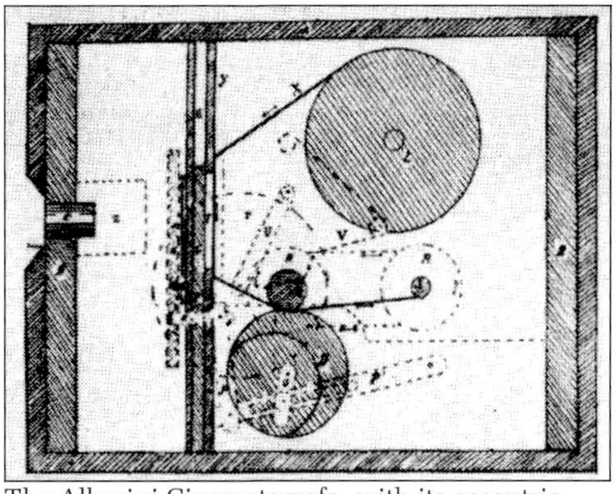

The Alberini Cinematografo, with its eccentric cam intermittent clearly shown.
[Aldo Bernardini, *Cinema muto italiano*, V. 1 (1980), p. 156.

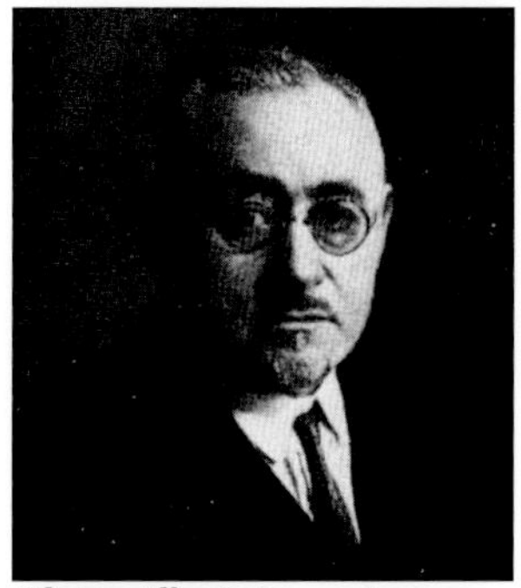

Filoteo Alberini, a major pioneer of Italian cinema.
[Aldo Bernardini, *Cinema muto italiano*, V. 1 (1980), p. 156.]

small studio in via Appia Nuova, Rome. This patent was granted 21 December 1895.[77]

November 12:
Lumière Cinématographe presented to the Literary & Artistic Circle, Brussels, by Charles Moisson from the factory of A. Lumière et Fils, Lyon.

November 13:
Lumière Cinématographe demonstrated in Louvain, Belgium, at the Musée de Physique de l'Université Catholique de Louvain, for the Association Belge de Photographie, by Charles Moisson from the Lumière factory in Lyon. The screening was organized by Prof. F. De Walque, one of the founders of the Association and president of the Cercle Industriel de l'Université.

76 This apparatus embodies a curious similarity to the Birt Acres Electroscope: both machines have two bands of horizontally-running film, one of which is viewed while the other is rewound. Joly remains closer to the original Edison Kinetoscope, with the mechanism fully enclosed in a free-standing cabinet and viewed through individual hooded apertures. Acres's machine, at Ludwig Stollwerck's urging, was an eye-level rear-projection device with a very short throw that allowed up to half-a-dozen or so viewers to see the film simultaneously.

77 This early patent seems not to have produced a significant working apparatus or to have exerted much influence. But in 1897 Alberini, who was an important pioneer exhibitor and filmmaker, joined with Anchise Cappelletti and Lionello Ganucci-Cancelleri to produce a new apparatus, the Cinesigrafo, or 'Cinesigrafo a serie', using a wide film similar to the American Biograph and publicly exhibited for the first time in May 1899 at the Italian Photographic Exposition in Florence. The device received French patent 291,835 on 18 August 1899.

Films included: *La sortie des ateliers Lumière à Lyon, Le saut à la caserne, Le bébé et les poissons rouges, Les forgerons, Le tête-à-tête de M. Janssen, L'incendie, Les baigneuses (si amusantes dans leurs ébats), La place des cordeliers à Lyon.*

November 14:
US patent 584,228, *Mutoscope*, to Harry Norton Marvin for a cylindrical toy mutoscope where the motive power is provided by the viewer's breath directed against the image cards from a long tube. According to Marvin, his device does not depend on the elasticity of the cards or their support, as in the toy mutoscopes of Herman Casler and W. C. Farnum.

☛US patent 584,311, *Mutoscope*, to Harry Norton Marvin, for a toy mutoscope where the motive power is provided by the viewer's breath, directed through a short tube running along the edge of the longitudinal box holding the image cards.

November 16:
Lumière Cinématographe demonstrated at the Sorbonne, Paris, for the reopening of the Faculté des Sciences, in the presence of eminent scholars and professors including MM. Darboux, Lippmann, Bouty, Troost, and Front.

November 25:
C. Francis Jenkins, after a falling-out with Thomas Armat, files a patent interference claiming the Phantoscope was his exclusive invention. The joint Armat-Jenkins patent (28 August 1895, above) was granted only after Armat bought out all of Jenkins' interests in the Phantoscope, for cash, and Jenkins withdrew his interference. It was this arrangement that allowed Armat to sell the Phantoscope to Raff & Gammon, who obtained Edison's backing for the device to be re-named and marketed as the Edison Vitascope. It was also this arrangement that Jenkins broke by repeatedly exhibiting the Phantoscope under its original name and loudly claiming its superiority to the Vitascope.

☛Latham Eidoloscope opens at Kohl & Middleton's Palace Museum, Minneapolis, MN, for an undetermined number of shows. "Instead of looking into a tiny aperture and seeing small figures going through grotesque motions", *The Minneapolis Tribune* reported, "you sit comfortably in your seat and see the figures thrown up life size on an immense screen ... They dance, wrestle, engage in prize fights, and do all the other things men and women do. So complete is the deception that one can scarcely realise that these figures do not live but are mere shadows thrown up on the screen by the powerful aid of electricity."

November 29:
Edison Kinetoscope opens at Bartlett's Studio, Queen Street, Auckland, New Zealand, with four machines organized by Alfred Henry Whitehouse. The exhibition continued until 15 February 1896, when the machines went on a tour of the North Island.

Films included: *Fire Rescue Scene, Comical Barbershop Scene, The Chinese Laundry, Annabelle's Butterfly Dance.* A new set of films was exhibited from 20 December 1895, including: *Highland Dance from 'Rob Roy', The Boxing Cats, Scene from Hoyts' 'Milk White Flag', Princess Ali Dance.*

December 7:
UK patent 560,367, *Apparatus for Exhibiting Successive Photographs*, to Ademor N. Petit, assigned to himself and Joseph Livingston of New York, for an unusual projector using photographs mounted on a sensitized belt that are passed in front of a synchronized cylindrical shutter. Livingston was deeply involved with the Anschütz Schnellseher, at one point in 1892 holding all North American rights to the machine.

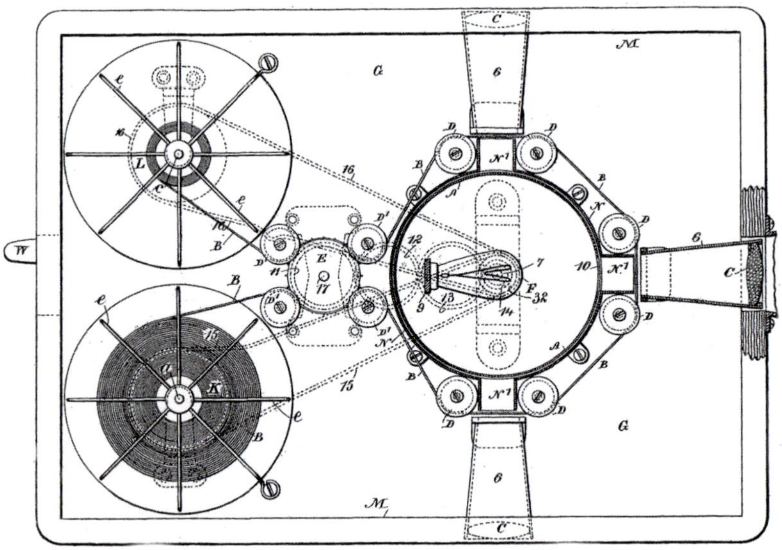

Petit's exhibiting improved exhibiting device is clearly meant to be another multiple-viewer peep show; the image band moved from the lower reel K to the upper reel L, passing around rollers D, D, D, D while a drum shutter A provided intermittency and rotated past any number of viewing ports C, C, C. Another example of the flexibility of the artifact in early cinema.
[US patent 560,367 of 7 December 1895, Fig. 1.]

December 18:
C. Francis Jenkins demonstrates the Phantoscope at the Franklin Institute in Philadelphia, just one week before the Lathams' Eidoloscope opens at Keith's Bijou Theatre. Two years later, after a flawed committee report from the Franklin Institute, Jenkins would receive the Elliott Cresson medal as the sole inventor of projected motion pictures.

December 20:
Edison Kinetoscope opens in the central railway station, next to a billiards parlor, in Münster, Germany, 'For a short time only.' Admission 30 Pfennig fur three different scenes. The apparatus remained on public view until the end of January.

December 21:
Skladanowsky Bioskop repeats the Wintergarten programme at the Concerthaus Ludwig in Hamburg, running for five days.

December 23:
Latham Eidoloscope opens at Keith's Bijou Theatre in Philadelphia for one week. The machine had been purchased from the Lathams by a Mr. Vandergrift.

☛Elektroskop of Birt Acres exhibited at the automat-parlour of the Deutsche Automaten-Gesellschaft, Königin-Augusta-Halle 17-21, Cologne, Germany. A rear-projection device with a screen about two feet wide, the Elektroskop exhibited one 35mm film while simultaneously rewinding a second film on a parallel set of works; then the mechanics shifted and the second film was exhibited while the first picture rewound. This was Acres's attempt to provide Stollwerck with an automat exhibition device that could be seen simultaneously by more viewers than the Kinetoscope. The apparatus was never patented.

Two films by Birt Acres were shown, the 1895 *Derby* and a *Three-Part Serpentine Dance.*

December 27:
The American Mutoscope Company is founded in Jersey City, New Jersey, by Herman Casler, W. K. L. Dickson, Elias Koopman and Harry Marvin, with a capital of $2 million, to publicly exploit their long-developing Mutoscope and to define the group previously known informally as KCMD. Company papers were signed by the principals on this date, the company was incorporated on 30 December and began operations on January 1, 1896.

December 28:
Lumière Cinématographe opens for its first commercial public exhibition, at the Salon Indien, a small hall in the basement of the Grand Café, 14 Boulevard des Capucines at the corner of the rue Auber, Paris. Seating about 100 persons on café chairs, the Salon Indien had its own direct entrance from the boulevard. The screening was arranged by Antoine Lumière and his old friend, the photographer Clément-Maurice; the projector was operated by Charles Moisson, with a Molteni lantern providing electric arc illumination and attended by the photographer

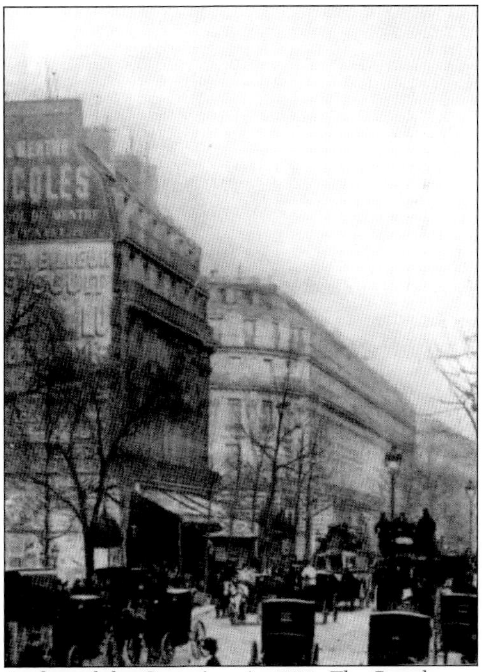

Boulevard des Capucines in 1895. The Grand Café is in the basement of the building just to the left of the white horse at the lower centre of the photograph. [Maurice Bessy and Lo Duca, *Louis Lumière, Inventeur* (1948), p. 106.]

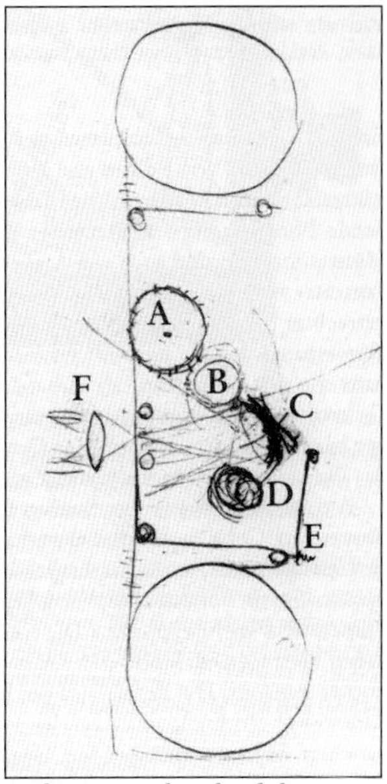

Preliminary sketch of the Electroscope by Birt Acres, made in a meeting with Ludwig Stollwerck in early June 1895. This was a rear-projection automat holding two films; the mirror at C shifted to illuminate only one film at a time. [Courtesy Martin Loiperdinger.]

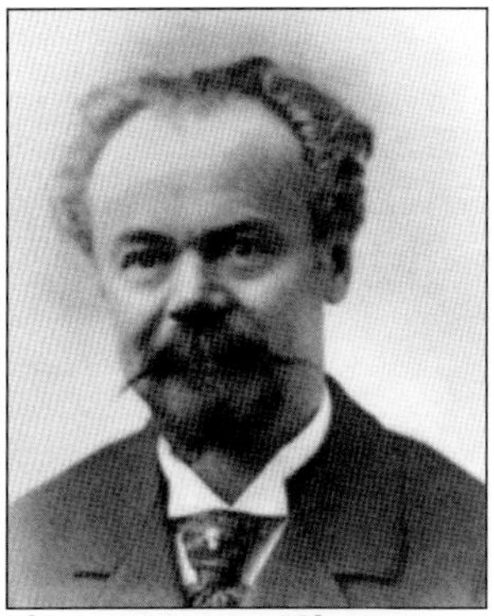

Clement Maurice (Clement Gratioulet), who organized the Grand Café premiere with Auguste Lumière. [Michelle Aubert and Jean-Claude Seguin, *La Production cinématographique des Frères Lumière* (1996), p. 412.

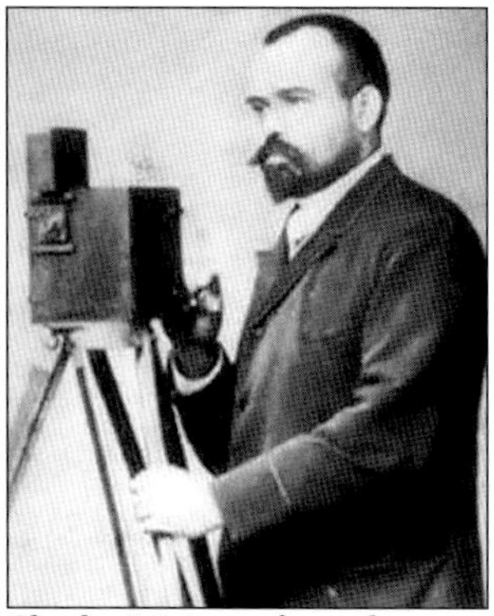

Charles Moisson from the Lumière factory in Lyon was the operator for the premiere at the Grand Café. [Michelle Aubert and Jean-Claude Seguin, *La Production*

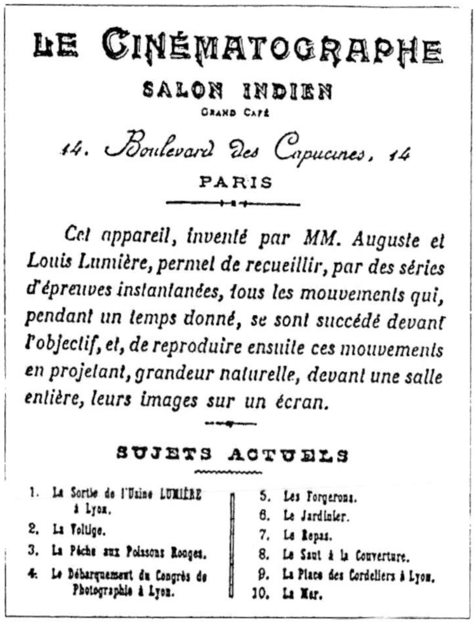

LE CINÉMATOGRAPHE
SALON INDIEN
GRAND CAFÉ
14, Boulevard des Capucines, 14
PARIS

Cet appareil, inventé par MM. Auguste et Louis Lumière, permet de recueillir, par des séries d'épreuves instantanées, tous les mouvements qui, pendant un temps donné, se sont succédé devant l'objectif, et, de reproduire ensuite ces mouvements en projetant, grandeur naturelle, devant une salle entière, leurs images sur un écran.

SUJETS ACTUELS

1. La Sortie de l'Usine LUMIÈRE à Lyon.
2. La Voltige.
3. La Pêche aux Poissons Rouges.
4. Le Débarquement du Congrès de Photographie à Lyon.
5. Les Forgerons.
6. Le Jardinier.
7. Le Repas.
8. Le Saut à la Couverture.
9. La Place des Cordeliers à Lyon.
10. La Mer.

Premiere programme with a list of the films shown, plus an explanation of the Cinématographe. [Maurice Bessy and Lo Duca, *Louis Lumière, Inventeur* (1948), p. 107.]

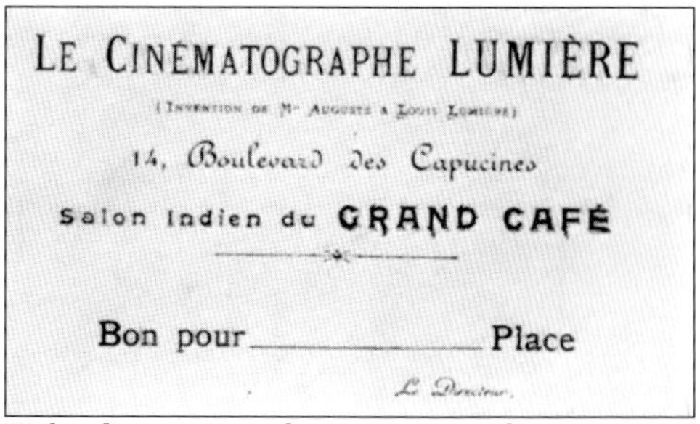

LE CINÉMATOGRAPHE LUMIÈRE
(Invention de MM. Auguste & Louis Lumière)
14, Boulevard des Capucines
Salon Indien du GRAND CAFÉ

Bon pour ______ Place

Le Directeur.

Ticket for entrée to the premiere performance, reserving a place in the small hall. [Maurice Bessy and Lo Duca, *Louis Lumière, Inventeur* (1948), p. 107.]

Jacques Ducom. The invited audience included writers for scientific and popular publications, and directors of Paris theaters, along with friends of Antoine Lumière. For the subsequent performances, admission was one Franc; by early January 1896 a policeman was on hand to control the crowds. In mid-January, after rave press reports, the receipts were 2,500 to 3,000 Francs daily for the 15-minute shows. While this most famous early cinema event is not the first screening of motion pictures to a paying audience, the careful strategy of the Lumière brothers and their father in demonstrating their invention to significant audiences of scientists and photographers over the preceding months ensured that, in Beaumont Newhall's words, the Cinématographe became "the first projector to meet with instant success".[78] At the first promotional screening ten films were shown, with title slides projected by a magic lantern.

Films included: *La Sortie de l'Usine Lumière à Lyon*, *La Voltige*, *La Pêche aux Poissons Rouges*, *Le Débarquement du Congrès de Photographie à Lyon*, *Les Forgerons*, *Le Jardinier*, *Le Repas*, *Le Saut à la Couverture*, *La Place des Cordeliers à Lyon*, *La Mer*. Later performances included a variety of further titles from the Lumière stock.

December:
Brander Matthews publishes a short story 'The Kinetoscope of Time' in *Scribner's Magazine*, pp.733-44, in which a man views scenes from the past in a kinetoscope and is then offered the opportunity to see future scenes as well, but declines.

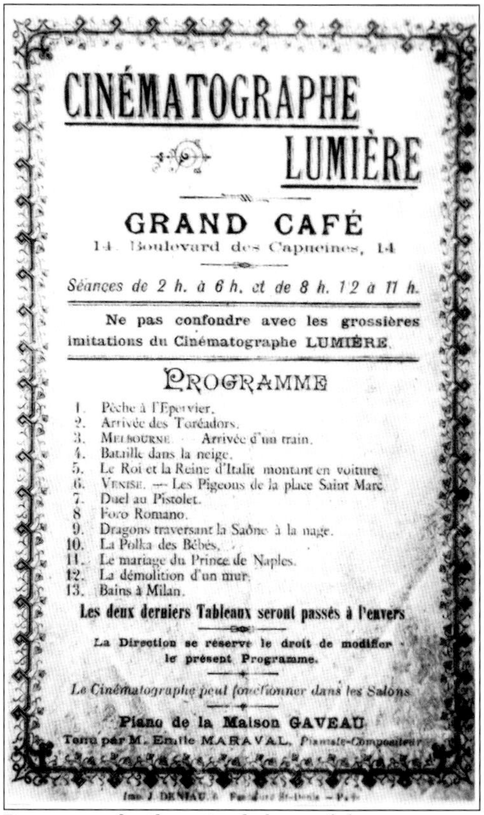

CINÉMATOGRAPHE LUMIÈRE
GRAND CAFÉ
14, Boulevard des Capucines, 14
Séances de 2 h. à 6 h. et de 8 h. 1/2 à 11 h.
Ne pas confondre avec les grossières imitations du Cinématographe LUMIÈRE.

PROGRAMME

1. Pêche à l'Epervier.
2. Arrivée des Toréadors.
3. MELBOURNE. Arrivée d'un train.
4. Bataille dans la neige.
5. Le Roi et la Reine d'Italie montant en voiture.
6. VENISE. — Les Pigeons de la place Saint Marc.
7. Duel au Pistolet.
8. Foro Romano.
9. Dragons traversant la Saône à la nage.
10. La Polka des Bébés.
11. Le mariage du Prince de Naples.
12. La démolition d'un mur.
13. Bains à Milan.

Les deux derniers Tableaux seront passés à l'envers

La Direction se réserve le droit de modifier le présent Programme.

Le Cinématographe peut fonctionner dans les Salons

Piano de la Maison GAVEAU
Tenu par M. Emile MARAVAL, Pianiste-Compositeur

Programme for the extended run of the Cinématographe at the Grand Café. [Jacques Rittaud-Huitenet, *Le Cinéma des Origines* (1985), p. 39.]

78 Beaumont Newhall, *The History of Photography* (New York, 1964: The Museum of Modern Art), p. 9. Max and Emil Skladanowsky and their Bioscop were in Paris at the time, contracted to open in January at the Folies Bergère, and they attended the Salon Indien screening of the Cinématographe on 29 December, with the Director of the Folies, after which, although they were paid for the month, their engagement was cancelled and they returned to Berlin without exhibiting.

1896

January 1:
Edison Kinetoscope opens in via Garibaldi 176, Messina, Italy, by Attilio Dogheria, running for six weeks until approximately 19 February.

January 5:
Skladanowsky Bioskop opens in Pankow, a northern district of Berlin. The screenings ran until 29 January.

January 8:
German patent 93743, *Serien-Apparat met rotierendem Cameraträger*, to Heinrich Plump in Berlin for a chronophotographic device with a single lens and a series of cameras arranged on a large vertical wheel. This is a modification of the apparatus of Ernst Kohlrausch from 1890, as later improved by Brandauer in 1893. Plump's adaptation has a focal plane shutter which is automatically set and then triggered by the movement of the wheel during the recording of a sequential movement.

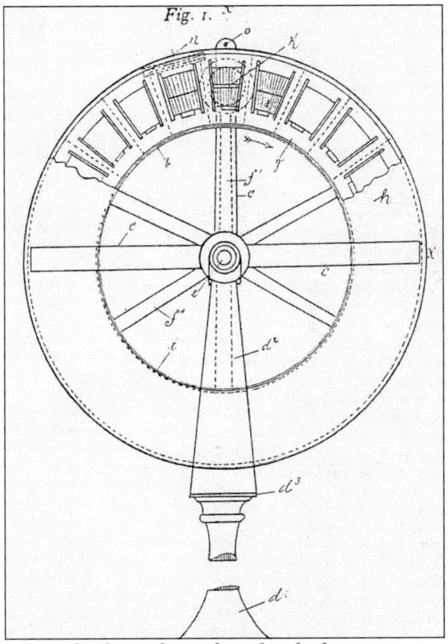

Heinrich Plump brought a focal-plane shutter, seen at *K*, for the sharp capture of movement to Ernst Kohlrausch's chronophotographic apparatus. [German patent 93743 of 8 January 1896, Fig. 1.]

January 10:
French patent 253,103, *Poinonneuse destinée au perforage des films ou pellicules utilisées pour la photographie et la reproduction des images mouvementées*, to George William de Bedts for a stamping machine used to perforate film strips used for the photography and reproduction of moving images.[79]

☛Kinetic Lantern of Birt Acres is demonstrated to the Lyonsdown Photographic Society, Barnet, England.

Films included: *The Derby*, *Skirt Dancers*, *Opening of the Kiel Canal.*

January 14:
Kinetic Lantern of Birt Acres is demonstrated for the Royal Photographic Society, 14 Hannover Square, London. The projection apparatus was a development of his Kinetic Camera.

Films included: *Boxing Match*, *Dancing Girls*, *Derby of 1895*, *Rough Sea at Dover*, *Emperor's Review of Troops.*

☛French patent 253,195, *Système de mécanisme à mouvement intermittent applicable aux appareils chronophotographiques et aux appareils pour projections animées*, to George William de Bedts for his Kinetographe de Bedts, a combination projector, camera and printer incorporating an unusual intermittent system of a mutilated gear where a three-toothed wheel engaged cams on another wheel to bring the film into place for either exposure or projection. This intermittent was derived from one used by Victor von Reitzner in his chronophotographic apparatus of 1891; de Bedts had been von Reitzner's agent in Paris. The Kinetographe featured light weight (5 kilograms) and easily reversed the film during projection for comic effects. The apparatus could also be used for direct viewing like the Kinetoscope.[80]

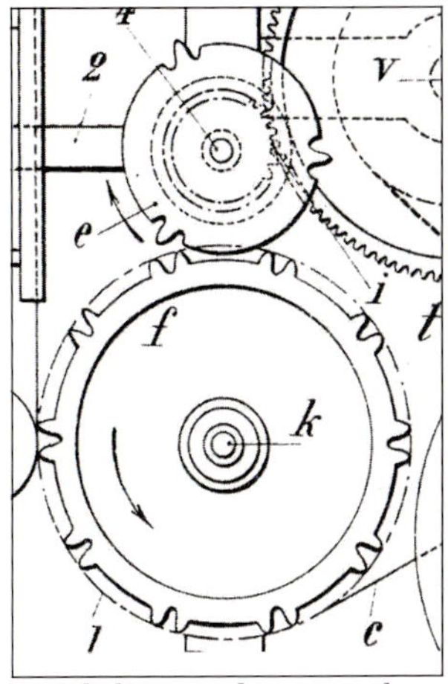

Detail showing the unusual intermittent movement of the de Bedts Kinetographe, very early on the open market in 1896. [United Kingdom patent 6503 of 24 March 1896, Figure 1, detail.]

79 George William de Bedts, an overlooked pioneer of the cinema, had a working reversible camera and projector by November, 1895, whose film and entrainment was based strictly on the dimensions of the Edison Kinetoscope. He had been the Paris agent for the chronophotographic apparatus of Victor von Reitzner, and in 1894 for that of Georges Demenÿ. In late 1895 he unsuccessfully negotiated with Henri Joly to take over his apparatus, and he was known as well to Jules Carpentier, the manufacturer of the Cinématographe for the Lumière brothers. See below for the public sale of his equipment. For the entire story, see Laurent Mannoni, *Le grand art de la lumière et de l'ombre: archéologie du cinéma*, especially pp. 417ff, and Laurent Mannoni, *George William de Bedts et la commercialisation de la chronophotographie*, in the collected papers of 'Les Vingt premières années du cinéma français', Paris, 1995.

80 Also patented in the UK as patent 6503 of 24 March 1896, *Improvements in the mechanism of chrono-photographic, kinetoscopic, and lantern-projection apparatus.*

January 15:

Having already reached agreement with Thomas Armat to become the sole agents for the sale, lease, and use of the Phantoscope, the business agents Raff & Gammon, whose Kinetoscope business was struggling, meet with Thomas Alva Edison and his business manager William Gilmore to obtain their cooperation to manufacture Armat and Jenkins's device and supply films for it. The Phantoscope will henceforth become the Edison Vitascope projector. Meanwhile, C. Francis Jenkins will continue to exhibit the Phantoscope under its old name, until it is seized by legal action, and will continue to claim its superiority over the renamed 'Vitascope'.

☛Kinetic Lantern of Birt Acres is demonstrated to the Photographic Club at Anderton's Hotel, 162-5 Fleet Street, London.

Films included: *Emperor's Review of Troops, Dancing Girls, Boxing Match, The Derby, Rough Sea at Dover, Boxing Kangaroo.*

☛George William de Bedts founds the first purely film company in France, the Société G. De Bedts et Cie, 368 de la rue Saint-Honoré, Paris, with a capital of 15,000 Francs. His associates were André Castelni, a publicist, and Guillaume Sabatier, director of the publication *Quotidien illustré.*

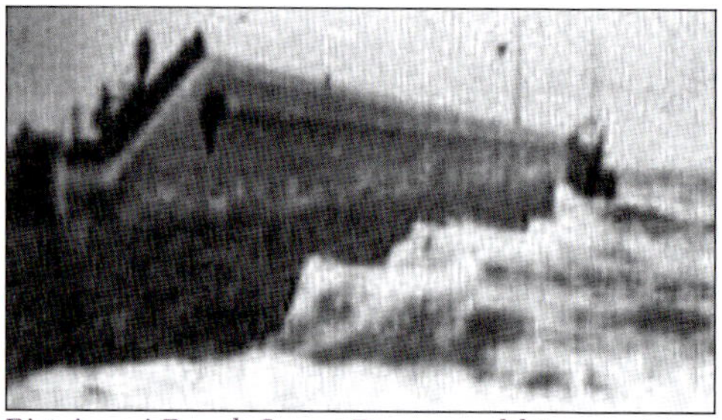

Birt Acres' *Rough Sea at Dover* would turn out to be one of the most popular of all early films, shown widely in Britain, Europe and America. [Deac Rossell.]

January 20:

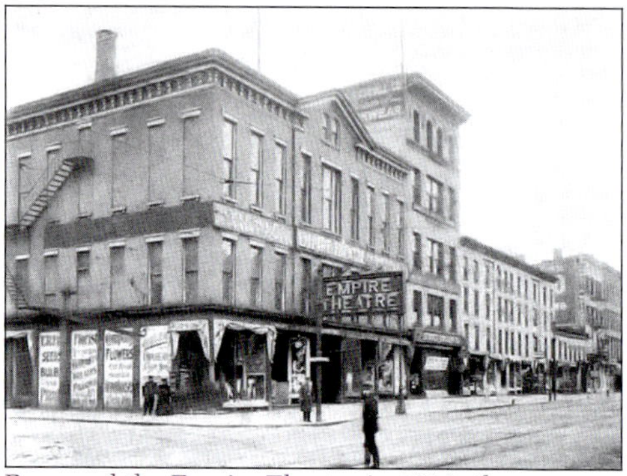

Renamed the Empire Theatre in 1899, the Wonderland Musee Theatre was located at the corner of East Main Street and North Clinton Avenue from 1894. Built as Washington Hall in 1860, the building was demolished in 1904. [http://cinematreasures.org/theatres/55724.]

Latham Eidoloscope opens at the Wonderland vaudeville theatre in Rochester, New York, for two weeks. D. C. Porter had purchased this apparatus from the Lathams. In reporting on the exhibition, the *Rochester Democrat and Chronicle* notes that while "extremely interesting", the Eidoloscope pictures, like magic lantern pictures, "increase in size in proportion to the distance of the lens from the screen and the stage of the Wonderland is so shallow that the moving figures in eidoloscope pictures shown there cannot be made more than a foot or so in height", strongly implying that the entire show, including rear projection, was given from the stage of the theatre.

January 22:

United States patent 571,496, *Kinetoscope*, to Adolph Pettenkofer of Brooklyn, NY, for a tabletop peep-show viewer. This is a variant of the mutoscope with pictures individually mounted on a long supporting band that is cranked by hand through the apparatus. Pettenkofer sought a simpler, more economical machine displaying a greater number of pictures.

January 25:

Lumière Cinématographe opens at 1 rue de la Republique, Lyon, France, with an invitational screening. Marius Perrigot, Felix Mesguich and Felicien Trewey were the operators. Billed as "La Photographie Animée", the screenings opened regularly to the public from 26 January and ran without interruption until the end of 1898.

☛Lumière Cinématographe opens in the foyer of the Paris Opera, Paris, France, during

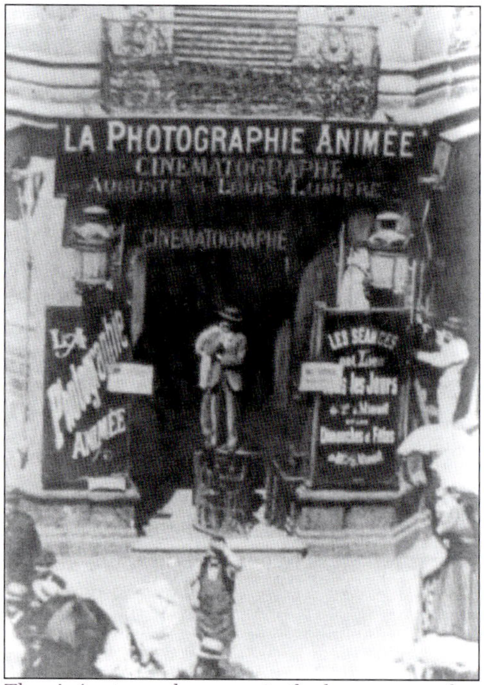

The cinématographe opens in the home town of the Lumières at 1 rue de la République, Lyon.[Jacques Rittaud-Hutinet, *Antoine, Auguste et Louis Lumière* (Lyon, 1994: Éditions Lyonnaises d'Art et d'Histoire, p. 44.]

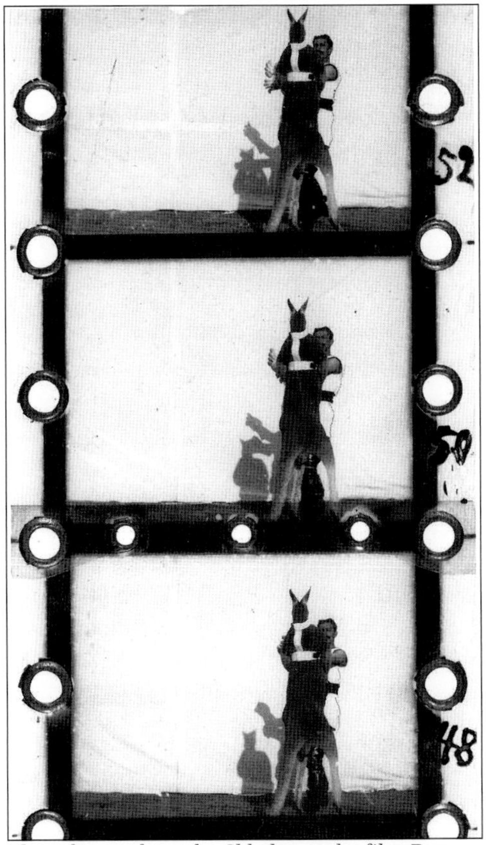

Three frames from the Skladanowsky film *Das boxende Känguruh*. Note the metal ringlets forming the perforations on both sides of the image, and the frame numbers (48, 50, 52) indicating the alternate images used for one of the two film bands in the Bioskop projector. [George Eastman House/International Museum of Photography and Film, Rochester.]

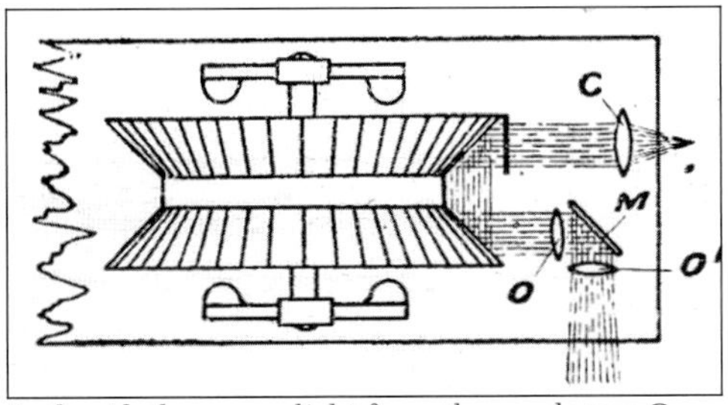

In the Alethoscope, light from the condenser C passes through the continuously moving film and onto a set of mirrors which turn it at a right angle to a second set of mirrors and through two elements of the projection lens at O and O^1 as it is turned again at right angles by the mirror M. The system was intended to drastically reduce wear and tear on the exhibitor's most expensive item, the celluloid films. [Henry Hopwood, *Living Pictures*, p.171.]

a masked ball. *Le Monde* in Paris reported on "the machine that has recently conquered the enthusiastic attention of the public: the Cinématographe of MM. Lumière". This high society exhibition not only reached a different public than the ongoing screenings at the Salon Indien of the Grand Café, but also initiated the use of the cinema at public fancy-dress events that would eventually culminate in the disastrous fire at the Charity Bazaar on 4 May 1897.

February 1:
Skladanowsky Bioskop opens in the Walhalla Theatre in Halle. The screenings ran until 15 February, and were accompanied by a programme of dissolving views.

Films included: *Italienischer Bauerntanz, Komisches Reck, Akrobatisches potpourri, Das boxende Känguruh, Jongleur, Kammarintzky, Ringkampf Greiner – Sandow, Apotheose.*

February 17:
French patent 254,090, *Appareil dénommé Aléthoscope, destiné à enregistrer photographiquement les scènes animées et à les reproduire soit par projection, soit par vision directe avec ou sans illusion du relief,* to Paul Mortier in St. Etienne for his Aléthoscope, an apparatus for taking and projecting animated scenes which used no intermittent, instead having continuously running film and an arrangement of revolving mirrors. The apparatus could also be used for direct viewing in a manner similar to the Kinetoscope.[81]

81 Georges Sadoul, in his *Histoire général du cinéma*, Vol. 1, p. 112, calls this apparatus the aléthorama and suggests it was derived from Emile Reynaud's *Théatre Optique*. It would certainly seem logical that with the well-known audience success of Reynaud's exhibitions, and on the evidence of the many varied forms of early cinematic apparatus, that optical solutions to the issues of film cameras and projection would have been widely attempted. Emil Mechau's splendid film projector, first demonstrated in 1912 and successfully manufactured by Leitz in its improved version from 1921 with over 500 examples made, must have itself had some predecessors. But while optical solutions to the issues of reproducing movement with multiple lenses, mirrors, prisms, etc. are discussed thoroughly if they were proposed before 1896, there is almost no discussion of this branch of cinema technology in the literature about those proposed from 1896 onwards, a splendid example of scholars seeing the development of a technology through the rear-view mirror: once one knows how the technology stabilizes, all one has to do is retrace the antecedents of the successful line of investigation. This 'wrong end of the telescope' view gives a particularly false image of the context of invention in the 1890s. One exception is Karl Forch, *Der Kinematograph und das sich bewegende Bild,* (Vienna/Leipzig, 1913): see pp. 96–118. Interestingly, and scarcely documented, Auguste and Louis Lumière took out a patent on an optically structured film apparatus in a time when most biographies and histories have them completely devoted to work in photography and the creation of the Autochrome color process. Having 'lost' whatever control or headstart they had in the film business they were central to creating, did the brothers think that with a wholly new and fully patent-protected approach that they could once again establish an ascendancy in the young medium? French patent 323,667 of 12 August 1902, *Cinématographe à movement continuée la pellicule,* and German patent 157698 of 19 August 1902, both of which describe a cinématographe with a continuously moving film band, where the intermittent is provided by a pair of right-angled mirrors shifted in and out of the light path by a curved cam gear. An earlier German patent, 103 314 of 3 August 1898 (Swiss patent 17,621) described their apparatus for a continuously moving film band with the intermittent provided by a rather esoteric flexible water-filled prism.
The ongoing momentum behind the continuous stream of optical intermittent apparatus was not simply an attempt by newcomers to break into the young cinema business, but was a response to the damage done by any type of physical intermittent movement to the exhibitor's most costly and short-lived accessory: the films themselves. The whole area of optical movements remains one for further research. Paul Mortier held several German patents on optically arranged apparatus: see German patents 117 025, 330 867 and 388 933; British patent 23,564 of 1901. See also apparatus from A. Musger (German patents 180 944 and 240 457; Austrian patent 23,608; French patent 387,407); F. Schmidt and Haensch

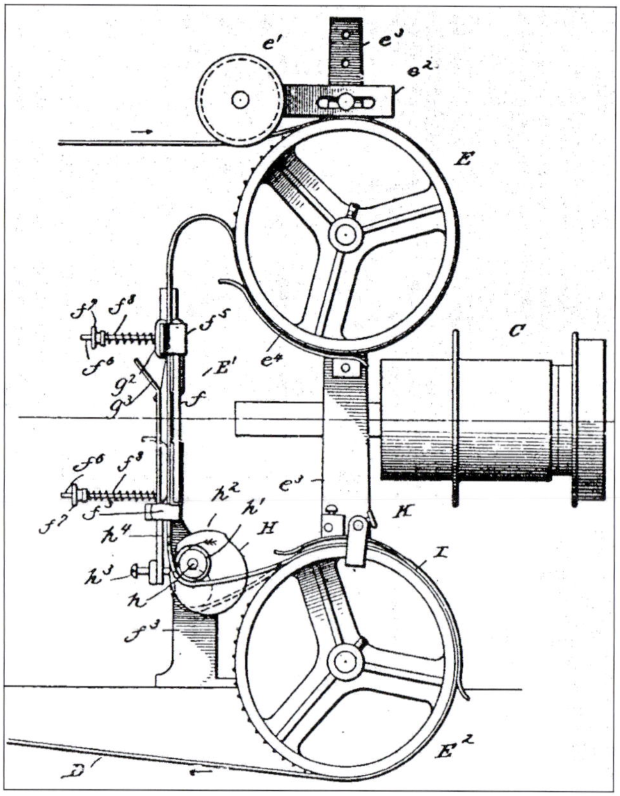

The Vitascope patent of Thomas Armat, showing the beater movement below the film gate at H. Two further variants for the beater intermittent were also included in this patent. [United States patent 673,992, *Vitascope*, of 19 February 1896, Fig. 2.]

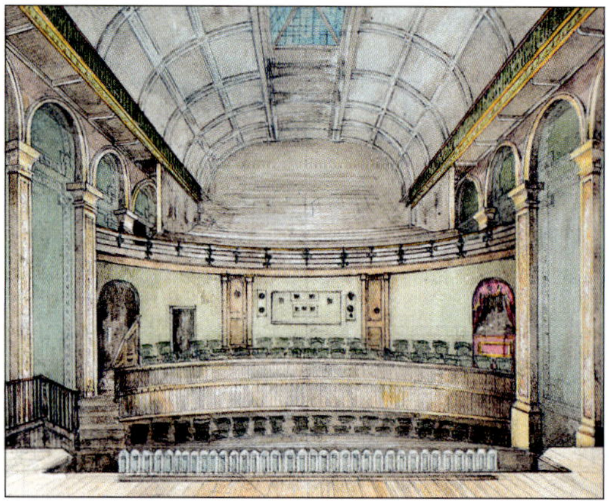

View from the stage of the large theatre, Regent Street Polytechnic in a watercolour from 1881. The windows of the projection box for thc Polytechnic's elaborate magic lantern shows is below the balcony seating; for its premiere, the Lumière Cinematographe was operated from the floor of the theatre itself.[Brenda Weeden, *The Education of the Eye. History of the Royal Polytechnic Institution 1838–1881*, p. 44.]

February 19:

British patent 3777, *A new or improved means for giving intermittent motion to a strip of film for taking or exhibiting photographs*, to Henry William Short in London for an intermittent movement utilizing a sprocket wheel intermittently turned by a helix- or worm-gear in continuous motion, with a portion of the works cut away.[82]

☛United States patent 673,992, *Vitascope*, to Thomas Armat for a re-named Phantoscope. An improvement of the Armat/Jenkins device with its continuously-moving film, this patent added a beater intermittent movement and spring tensioned velvet-covered film gate to the Phantoscope. A minor improvement to the earlier machine was a small tensioned roller just above the upper sprocket wheel which acted as a guide in feeding film from the upper reel. By the time of this patent application, Armat had already concluded an agreement (see above, 15 January) with Kinetoscope agents Raff & Gammon for the exploitation of the machine under Edison's name. Armat had suggested the name 'Zoescope' for the machine. By the end of the year (see below, 22 September) a Maltese Cross intermittent was added to the apparatus.[83]

February 20:

Theatrograph of Robert William Paul is demonstrated for the first time at Finsbury Technical College, Leonard Street, London, the school where he obtained his early technical training. The college had a reputation for innovative engineering and electrical studies, first as a feeder school for the City and Guilds

(German patent 124 932); Holst (German patent 97 217); W. Stroud (British patent 4661 of 1898); E. A. Bréard (German patent 154 141, French patents 323,497 & 323,089); Emil Busch Aktien-Gesellschaft (German patent 241 124); J. Kraus (German patent 104 441); H. Tönnes (German patent 134 534); J. Bianchi (US patent 867,185); Th. J. Harback (German patent 176 302, US patent 708,303); John Nevill Maskeleyne (British patent 11,639 of 1896, German patent 100 559); Huet and Daubresse (US patent 721,954); Emil Mechau (German patent 242 128); J. L. Terrisse (German patent 217 326 & French patent 387,894 plus additions 11,787 & 12,519); Deutsches Mutoskop und Biograph Gesellschaft (German patent 107 356); Ch. M. Campbell (German patent 116 454); A Rosenberg (British patent 9291 of 1901); The Rotary Photographic Company and V. Von Madaler (British patent 8791 of 1911); L. Thurstone (US patent 982,904); C. R. Uebelmesser (US patent 994,043); W. H. Reid (US patent 672,710); M. Barr (German patent 114 920 & British patent 8245 or 1899); Corobtsoff and Himuli (French patent 434,805); W. K. L. Dickson (British patent 6793 of 1899); W. Wahlmann (German patent 204 720).

82 Short also received provisional protection for two other patents which were not published: No. 4166, 25 February 1896, for a 'method of exhibiting or displaying consecutive photographs or pictures of moving objects or figures', and No. 10,276, 13 May 1896, for 'improvements in or relating to the manufacture of book forms of kinetoscopes'. Short successfully manufactured a pocket kinetoscope, called the Filoscope, patented on 3 November 1898, No. 23,158, but this early registration shows his long interest in the device. See also note to entry of 27 August 1896.

83 The beater movement and gate assembly was also patented in Germany, patent 99042 of 18 April 1896.

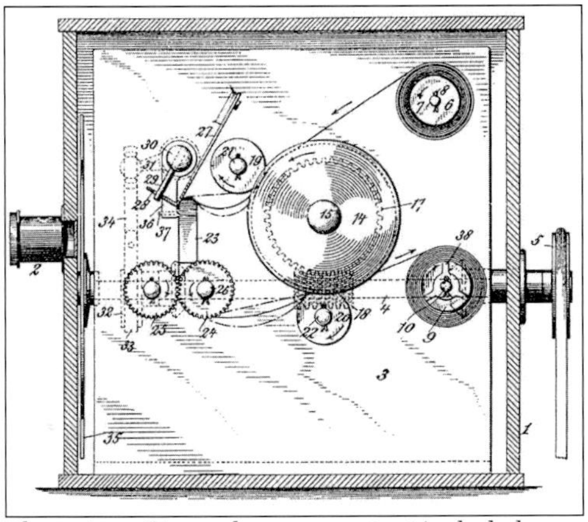

The unique Biograph camera patent included provision for punching holes in the film so that either Mutoscope cards or celluloid films could be printed from the negatives. Here, a side view of the two punches is at 37, attached to the rocking shaft 29 moving on spindle 30 which also holds the film in place for its exposure by means of a light spring 27 as the celluloid moves through the device.
[United States patent 629,063, *Kinetographic Camera*, of 26 February 1896, Fig. 1.]

of London Institute and then in 1910 incorporated into Imperial College, University of London. Paul's first machine, using an intermittent sprocket wheel only below the film aperture, was not patented.

Films included: *Rough Sea at Dover*, *Trilby*.

☛Lumière Cinématographe presented at the Regent Street Polytechnic (now Westminster University), London, by magician Felicien Trewey to an invited audience of press and leading artists. Lecturer George Francis accompanied the screenings. Trewey was an outstanding magician and master of 'shadowgraphy', or reciting witty stories accompanied by his own hand-shadows, and

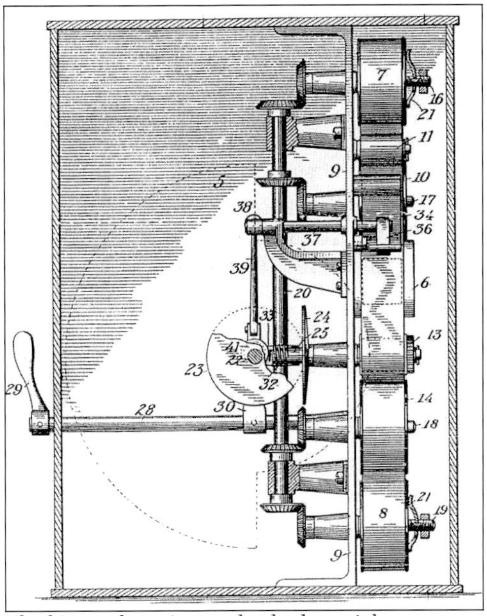

The biograph projector also had special requirements, due to its friction intermittent, so Casler designed another ingenious solution to keep the film regularly 'in frame' on the screen. Here, the handle 29 adjusts a rotating circular drive wheel, 23, so that it moves toward the centre or towards the rim of a second circular wheel, 24, slightly slowing or speeding up the movement of the film through the device and keeping the image on the screen centred.
[United States patent 666,495, *Consecutive View Apparatus*, 26 February 1896, Fig. 1.]

was of retirement age when he obtained the rights to the Cinématographe in England. He had also been present at the first showing at the Salon Indien as a friend of Antoine Lumière, and appeared in several of the early Lumière films, including *Chapeau à Transformation*, *Assiettes Tournantes*, and, famously, in *La Partie d'Écarte*, where he is the card-player at the right of the table.[84]

Films included [in order shown, with Lumière catologue numbers]: *Cordeliers Square, Lyon [cat.128]; Photographic Delegates Disembarking at Neuville-sur-Saône* [not in cat.]; *Arrival of a Train at a Station* [cat.653]; *Fishing for Gold Fish* [cat. 69]; *Spinning Plates* [cat.1]; *Blacksmiths at Work* [cat. 51]; *Game of Cards* [cat 73]; *Sea Bathing* [cat. 11]. Also shown in the evening to the public: *Serpent*; *Baby's Dinner* [cat. 88]; *Prize Fighters* [cat.16]; *Dinner-Hour Exodus from the Factory* [cat. 91].

February 21:
Lumière Cinématographe opens to the public at the Regent Street Polytechnic, London, by Felicien Trewey, running through 14 July. Admission, 1 Shilling, Polytechnic members, half price. In October the Polytechnic began its own public cinema shows, calling itself "the Home of Animated Photographs'.

February 25:
French patent 254,249, *Nouvel appareil Photographique pouvant également être employé comme*

84 A 1936 programme honoring Louis Lumière in London claims that the director of the Polytechnic, Quintin Hogg, visited Paris, saw the Lumière Cinématographe, and requested the show for London, a logical step as the Polytechnic had long been famous as a venue presenting elaborate and technically unique multiple magic lantern projections. Since Trewey was rejected by the Alhambra in late February 1896, and had to give two test performances before the management of the Empire would take up a regular booking, the attitude of English theatrical managers toward the Cinématographe seems to have been quite different and much more reluctant than that of the science- and projection-oriented Polytechnic. Precisely where the Lumière Cinématographe projections took place at the Polytechnic is undetermined. A supplement to the *Polytechnic Magazine* of 4 March 1896 (p. 125) says "... we have taken advantage of an opportunity to let our Great Hall for the next three months for the exhibition of a new invention, called the "Cinématographe" ... the Small Lecture Hall and the Marlborough Rooms will be freed for the use of those sections which have hitherto met in the Great Hall'. The report on the invitational screening in *Photography*, 27 February 1896, p. 143, says 'The exhibition was given to the press in the large hall of the Polytechnic, Regent Street...' It also noted 'the very poor illumination of the pictures..'. The Marlborough Hall is nonetheless mentioned in almost all early public reports. Under Quintin Hogg's management, from December 1881, the Polytechnic's Large Theatre became the Great Hall, while the latter was turned into a gymnasium. New and thorough research by Jeremy Brooker, in *The Temple of Minerva*, [p. 152] suggests convincingly that the Lumière Cinématographe opened in the old Large Theatre, then called the Great Hall and subsequently moved to the smaller Marlborough Rooms during its four-month run.

appareil cronophotographique dit Photothéagraphe, to Ambroise-François Parnaland, for the Photothéagraphe, an awkward chronophotographic camera using non-perforated film advanced by the push of a button.

February 26:
United States patent 629,063, *Kinetographic Camera*, to Herman Casler for the Biograph camera, using wide-gauge celluloid film 68mm wide with image frames 54mm high and a mutilated roller intermittent. The camera also punched a single perforation in each frame of the film at the time of exposure, to aid in registration during printing for Mutoscope flip-card viewers or on film strips for projection. Extensive legal battles with the Edison company were not resolved, controversially, until March 1897, and both camera and projector (see below) had wide circulation throughout the world as their high optical and mechanical quality compensated for the unusual guage of the film bands and the unusual intermittent movement.[85]

☛United States patent 666,495, *Consecutive-view apparatus*, to Herman Casler for the Biograph projector, using wide-gauge celluloid film 68mm wide with image frames 54 mm high and a mutilated roller intermittent. One mechanical reason for the success of this unusual apparatus was the clever frame adjustment for the broken-roller intermittent. The speed of the intermittent sprocket, and therefore the relationship between the speed of pulling a frame into the projection gate and the speed of the constantly fed and taken up film from the projector's reels, was maintained by a friction wheel driven by the motor running on a second friction disk set at right angles and connected directly to the intermittent sprocket. The driving friction disk could be adjusted to run slightly more towards the outside rim, or towards the axle, of the disk controlling the intermittent sprocket, thereby increasing or decreasing its speed and maintaining the correct framing of the image in the gate and on the screen.[86]

February 28:
Theatrograph of Robert William Paul demonstrated for the second time, at the library of the Royal Institution, Albemarle Street, London.

☛Lumière Cinématographe demonstrated privately at the Empire Theatre of Varieties, Leicester Square, London, by Felicien Trewey.

☛Lumière Cinématographe opens at the Eldorado, Nice, France. The showings ran through April 22.

February 29:
Lumière Cinématographe shown to the press in Brussels, at 7, galerie du Roi.

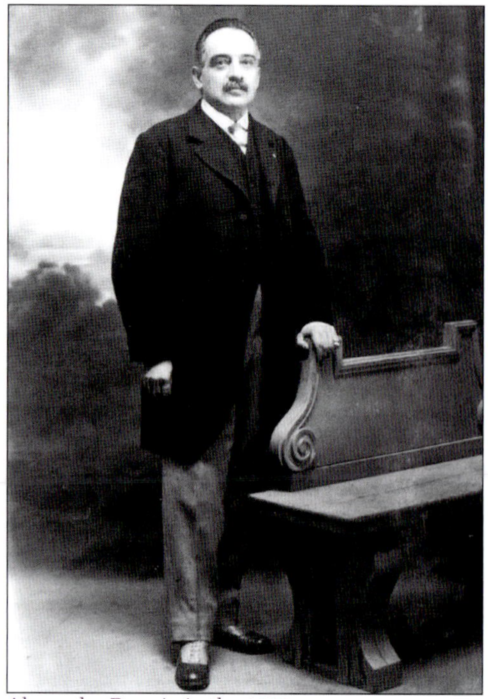

Alexander Promio in the 1920s.
[Jean-Claude Seguin, *Alexandre Promio ou les énigmes de la lumière*. Paris & Montréal, 1999: Éditions L'Harmattan / L'Harmattan Inc.]

☛Edison Kinetoscope opens at Streatham Hall in London, England.

March 1:
Lumière Cinématographe opens to the public at 7, galerie du Roi, Brussels. The operator was Francis Doublier, who had been offered a room in the center of the city by a Brussels newspaper. Admission 1 Franc.

☛Alexander Promio, an assistant to the optician Boulade in Lyon, quits his job and joins the firm of A. Lumière et Fils, where he becomes one of the most important of the Lumière cinema ambassadors, in charge of

85 On 17 December 1895 Herman Casler patented another still camera in Britain, manufactured by Casler and E. B. Koopman: the Presto, which was an all-metal miniature roll-film apparatus shaped like an oval with squashed ends, which took 32mm square pictures. A changeable back allowed it to be fitted with a carrier for four small glass plates. The simple drop shutter was reset by inverting the camera.

86 Maintaining the proper framing of the image in projection, and therefore the proper image on the screen, was a significant problem in early projection equipment, especially as the films were prone to frequent breakage and splicing, even over their very short lengths. Although many solutions were tried, the issue of adjusting the frame in the projection aperture while the projector was running was not fully resolved until 1899 or later in various machines. Due to the variation of pull-down by the friction-based gripper intermittent of the Biograph apparatus through wear, through unstable friction in different atmospheric conditions, and through inconsistencies in the thickness of the celluloid film, the framing of the Biograph projector required constant and subtle attention from the operator during use.

training Cinématographe operators (along with Marius Perrigot), and photographing with and exhibiting the Cinématographe in Italy, Russia, Spain, the United States, Turkey, and other locations.

☛Skladanowsky Bioskop exhibited at the Concert-Haus in Cöthen, Germany, until 8 March as part of an elaborate dissolving view show that included *Snow White and the Seven Dwarves*; views of ruins and pyramids; and a balloon trip around the world. There was also a demonstration of Röntgen's X-rays. On opening night the hall was sold out, with large audiences predicted for the following days; at the end of the run on 8 March the town mayor personally congratulated the Skladanowskys on their achievement. The Bioscop was exhibited alternatively with a programme of dissolving views.

Films included: *Italienischer Bauerntanz*, *Komisches Reck*, *Akrobatisches potpourri*, *Das boxende Känguruh*, *Jongleur*, *Kammarintzky*, *Ringkampf Greiner – Sandow*, *Apotheose*.

☛Lumière Cinématographe opens in Bordeaux, at 10, Allée de Tourny, at the corner of rue Jean-Jacques-Bel, organized by the Lumière general agent M. Shavanon and the former pharmacist Billard. The impressive building was the home of the Académie des Sciences, Belles-Lettres et Arts de Bordeaux from 1712 to 1890. The showings ran until the end of October, from 2pm until 11pm, admission 1 Franc, in sessions of 20 minutes each.

March 2:
British patent 4686, *Improvements in apparatus for projecting kinetoscope pictures on the screen*, to Robert William Paul in London for an improved version of his Theatrograph projector (the earlier model, unpatented, was used at Finsbury, February 20, above), with a double sprocket intermittent drive mounted both above and below the film aperture, each driven by a seven-sided Maltese Cross/spur gear, and a take-up reel operated by a sliding belt.[87]

87 German patent 93120, 18 April 1896.

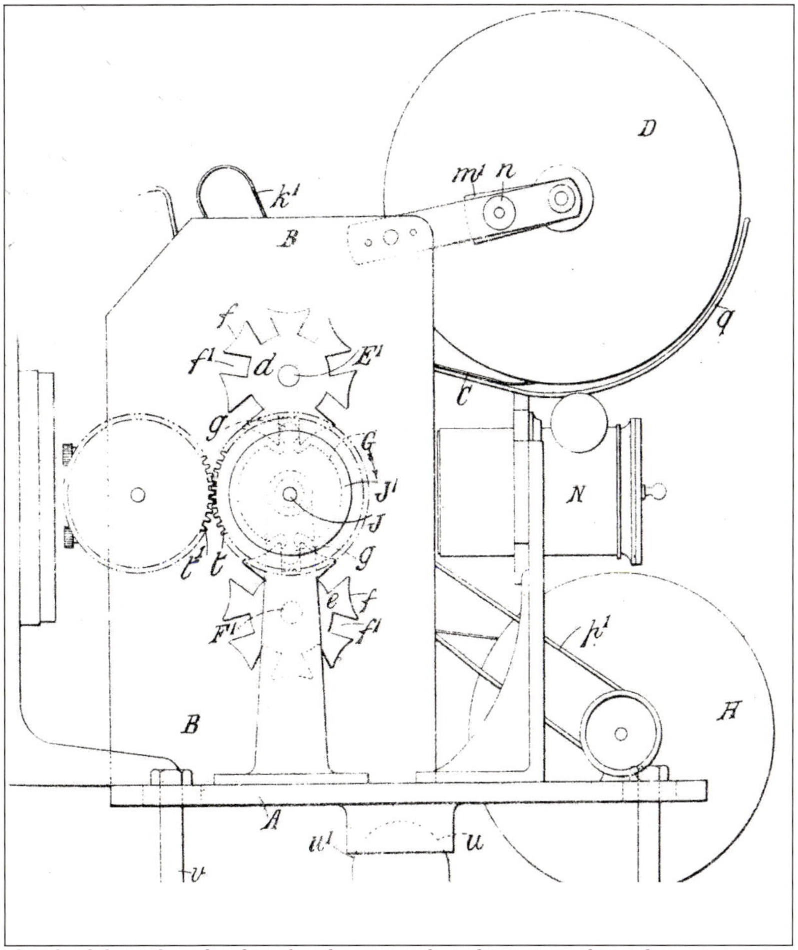

Sketch of the right side of Paul's Theatrograph, in his patent of March 1896, showing the double-Maltese-Cross intermittent at E and F, with its spur gear behind J. The gears t and t1 continuously rotate the projector's barrel shutter, adjacent. [United Kingdom patent 4686, *Improvements in Apparatus for Projecting Kinetoscope Pictures on the Screen*, 2 March 1896, Fig. 2, detail.]

☛French patent 254,394, *Cinographoscope Pipon Frères*, to Alexandre Jules Pipon and Jules Alexandre Pipon for their Cinographoscope, a combination camera and projector. Manufacturers of photographic apparatus, the Pipon brothers were quickly involved in moving pictures and their apparatus proved popular with French showmen.

March 3:
UK patent 4841, *Improvements in means of apparatus for exhibiting pictures of moving objects by projecting them onto a screen or other surface*, to James Yate Johnson as communicated from abroad by Woodville Latham of New York, for the Eidoloscope projector, incorporating the "Latham loop", formed by an extra sprocket roller which induced a slack loop preventing the intermittent movement from jerking the

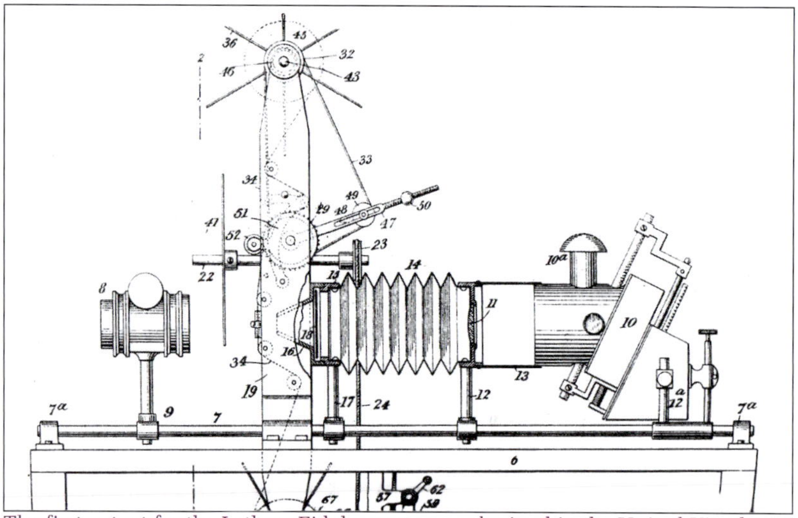

The first patent for the Latham Eidoloscope was submitted in the United Kingdom on 3 March 1896, for a projector that had been in use in public since 20 May 1895. The light source is at the far right, and the film moved from the bottom reel through the apparatus to be rewound at the top. [United Kingdom patent 4841, *Improvements in Means or Apparatus for Exhibiting Pictures of Moving Objects by Projecting them onto a Screen or other Surface*, 3 March 1896, Fig. 1, detail.]

entire reel of film during projection. In its later US patent, the apparatus was called a "Projecting Kinetoscope".[88]

March 5:
French patent 254,515, *Appareil appelé le Phototachygraphe Sanson*, to Raoul Grimoin-Sanson for improvements to his Phototachygraphe Sanson. He designed an 'inverted' four-sided Maltese Cross intermittent which changed individual frames in the aperture of the projector much more quickly than before, permitting a great reduction (to 85^0) in the size of the shutter and an increase in the brightness of the image on the screen.[89]

☛French patent 254,540, *Appareil de reproduction de scènes animées d'aprèes des vues enregistrées chronophotographiquement, dit le Kinébléposcope*, to Ambroise-François Parnaland for his Kinébléposcope, a device for the individual viewing of chronophotographs mounted on the circumference of a rotating disk.

March 6:
Lumière Cinématographe opens at the Salle sur la Canebière, 3 rue de Noailles, Marseille. The screenings ran thorugh November 14.

March 7:
Lumière Cinématographe in a trial public showing during a matinee performance at the

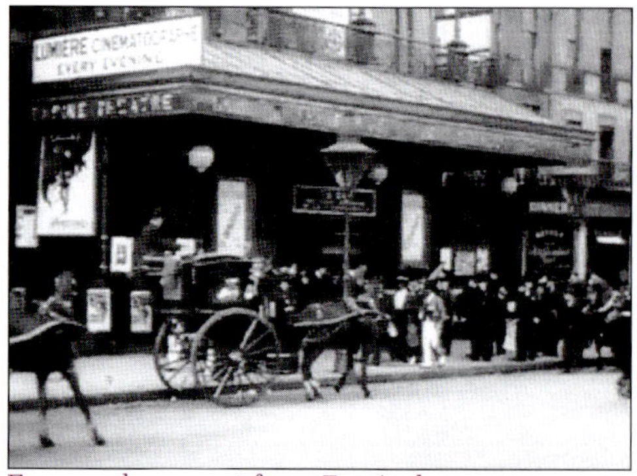

Frame enlargement from *Entrée du cinématographe*, taken in Leicester Square, London, during the spring 1896 Lumière engagement at the Empire Theatre. [Michelle Aubert and Jean-Claude Seguin, *La Production cinématoghraphique des frères Lumière* (Paris, 1996: Editions Mémoires de cinéma / Bibliothèque du Film (BIFI), film 1024, p. 287.]

Empire Theatre of Varieties, Leicester Square, London, by Felicien Trewey.

March 9:
Lumière Cinématographe opens to the public at the Empire Theatre of Varieties, Leicester Square, London, by Felicien Trewey, at first using the same machine that is projecting at Marlborough Hall. The Empire showings were phenomenally successful, forcing the addition of matinee performances in the theatre's Grand Foyer at 3, 4, and 5 o'clock daily. The shows continued until May, 1897.[90]

Films included: *Arrival of Train at Station, Bathers in the Mediterranean, Workers Leaving the Lumière Factory, Tea Time for Baby, Blacksmith at Work, Game of Cards, Children at Play, Gardener's Hose Trick, Trewey's Serpentine Ribbon, La Place des Cordeliers à Lyon.*

March 12:
Lumière Cinématographe opens at 220 Kal-

88 This was the first patent for the Eidoloscope, preceding both French patent 255,171 of 31 March 1896, and US patent 707,934 of 1 June 1896. There was much litigation and claim over the 'Latham Loop', and the Latham US patent was later declared invalid due to "prior reduction to practise by Thomas Armat".

89 The Phototachygraphe Sanson was used continuously and successfully at the Exposition Nationale et Coloniale in Rouen in April and May, 1896, where it won a Gold Medal, and became one of the major competitors to the Lumière Cinématographe on the French market, along with the Joly-Normandin apparatus.

90 The Lumière Cinématographe used at the Empire Theatre was later acquired by collector Will Day (Catalogue No. 119) and is now in the Musée Henri Langois of the Cinémathèque français. Inv. AP-95-1414 (W. Day), see Mannoni, *Le mouvement continué*, p. 370.

verstraat, Amsterdam, The Netherlands. Admission 50 cents, children 25 cents. Organized by Camille Cerf of the Société de la Photographie Animée in Brussels, assisted by Lumière operator Francis Doublier. The screenings ran until the end of May. The playing of music during the performances was forbidden by the local authorities.

Films included: *Het uitgang der fabrieken Lumière te Lyon, De Besproeier, De Kinder-maltijd, Een omvallende muur, De aankomst van het Spoor, Eene Vechtparty, Het Kaartspel, De Zee, Eena les in de Photographie, Kinderenvermaak, De veranderlijke Hoed.*

☛Lumière Cinématographe opens at the Studio Le Lieure in Rome, Italy. The shows ran until 10 May.

March 13:

Lumière Cinématographe opens in the piazza Colonna, in a storefront at via del Mortara 17, Rome, next door to the photographic studio of Henri Le Lieure at via del Mortara 19, continuing until April 29. A week after the opening, on 19 March, the Cinématographe showings were supplemented with panorama views of far-off and imaginary places projected with a magic lantern.[91]

Films included: *Arrivée d'un train en gare, Baignade en mer*, (Una) *via di Parigi.*

March 17:

French patent 254,836, *Appareil chronophotographique pouvant également servir à la projection des positifs*, to Henri Joly for a chronophotographic device to be equally capable of the projection of positive prints, using a ratchet intermittent and an open loop to reduce wear on the film similar to the 'Latham loop'. One of the most practicable machines of its time, it became in France the main competitor to the Lumière Cinématographe, along with the Phototachygraphe of Grimoin-Sanson. The patent was bought by Ernest Normandin and the Joly-Normandin projector was available for sale by October 1896.[92]

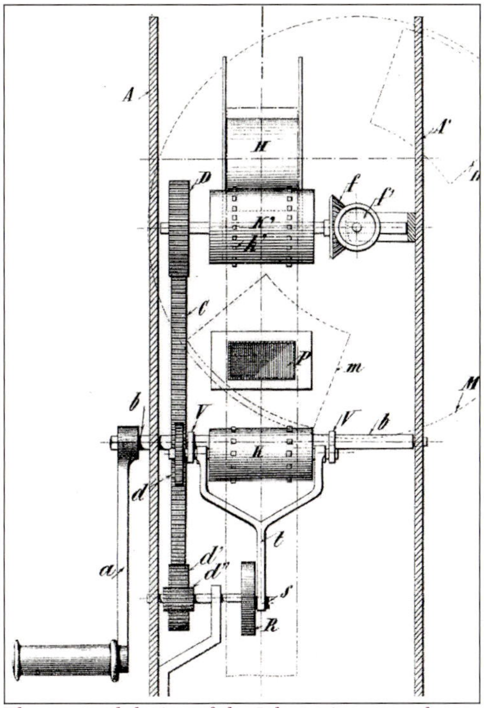

The unusual design of the Joly projector used an intermittently moved lower sprocket roller *K* driven by an eccentric pin on the lowest roller *R*, while the top sprocket *K'* both pulled the film down into the machine and simultaneously rotated the shutter with bevel gears at *f* and *f'*. [United Kingdom patent 21,381, *Improvements in Chrono-photographic Apparatus adapted for the Projection of Positives upon a Screen*, 17 March 1896 under International Convention from France, Fig. 2, detail.]

☛German patent 93190, *Schnellseher mit spiralig auf eine Trommel aufgewickeltem Bildstreifen*, to Aktien-Gesellschaft S. Bergmann & Co. in Berlin, for a peep-show device powered by an electric motor, where 672 images are wound spirally on a large drum and presented to an individual viewing ocular set in front of a rotating shutter.

☛German patent 93599, *Bildtrommel-Leitspur für Schnellseher der durch Patent Nr. 71339 geschützten Art*, to Aktien-Gesellschaft S. Bergmann & Co. in Berlin, for a self-rewinding accessory to the Demenÿ Chronograph [German patent 71339] where the film is carried spirally wound on a drum.

March 18:

French patent 254,883, *Mécanisme de traction intermittente pour l'entrainement des bandes chronophotographiques, pour la photographie et les projections*, to Jules Carpentier in Paris for an intermittent mechanism for the registration of a band of chronophotographs for both photography and projection.

91 On 1 January 1897, Le Lieure replaced his Cinématographe with an Edison Vitascope. By 29 January 1897, Le Lieure's storefront had become the 'Museo Foto-Elettrico' and offered a performance of Roentgen X-rays, admission 1 Lira; the Lumière Cinématographe with eight films, admission 50 Cents; the panorama 'Il Giro del Mondo', admission 40 Cents; and a magic lantern performance of apparitions and spirits called 'Grotta di Lourdes', admission 25 Cents. A combination ticket for the three latter spectacles was available for 1 Lira.

92 It was a Joly-Normandin projector that was in operation on 4 May 1897 when fire broke out at the benefit for the Societé Charité Maternelle in a temporary structure in rue Jean Goujon just off the Champs Elysées, in Paris, killing 120 French socialites in the worst disaster yet to befall the cinema, known around the world as the Charity Bazaar fire. The fire was not caused by the highly inflammable nitrate film or the film projector, rather, the oxygen-ether limelight of the Molteni lantern used for illuminating the show, a model ironically called 'Sécuritas', had suddenly gone out. When the projectionist and his assistant struck a match to relight the lamp, ether gas had spread throughout the projection booth, and their ill-considered attempt to relight the lamp caused a massive explosion and the subsequent fire.

March 19:
Theatrograph of Robert William Paul owned by magician David Devant opens at Egyptian Hall, Piccadilly, London. Devant bought one of Paul's first machines, and added it to his magic shows two days before Paul himself opened to the public at the Olympia Theatre (see below). Devant served as an informal agent for Paul's apparatus, introducing it especially to his colleague magicians. By November he advertised that he owned three of Paul's machines, and he had appeared in several of Paul's films, including *The Mysterious Rabbit*, *The Egg Laying Man*, and *Objects Produced From Paper*. Devant initially used Edison films also purchased from Paul in his shows, but by August 1 was both himself using and advertising for sale a considerable number of titles from magician Georges Méliès, whose films and equipment he represented in England.[93]

Films included: *Band Practice*, *Highland Dancers*, *Serpentine Dancer*, *Boxing Cats*.

March 20:
Lumière Cinématographe demonstrated for an invited audience at the K. K. Lehr- und Versuchanstalt für Photographie, Vienna, by Eugène Dupont, a native of Lyon who was active in Vienna as a French trade representative.

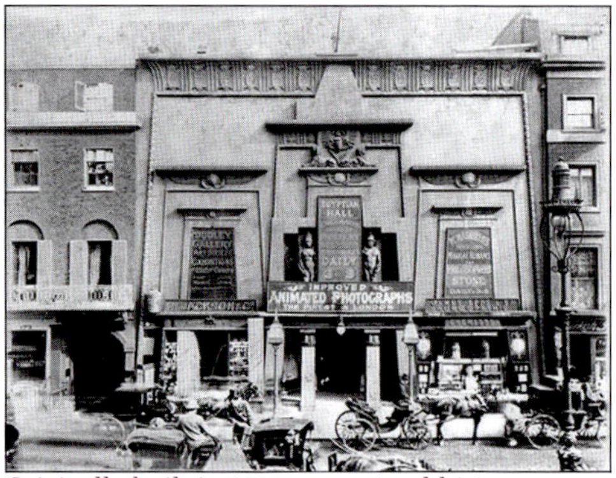

Originally built in 1812 as a natural history museum, the distinctive Egyptian Hall facade designed by Peter Frederick Robinson, seen here c1900, hosted many public entertainments before being demolished in 1903. [Museum of London, unknown photographer, c1900.]

March 21:
Kinetic Lantern of Birt Acres opens at 2 Piccadilly Mansions, near the intersection of Piccadilly Circus and Shaftesbury Avenue, London. The showings were in a storefront converted by Acres into a movie house called The Kineopticon. Admission sixpence. Destroyed by fire on 10 June 1896 and not re-opened.

Films included: *A Carpenter's Shop; A Visit to the Zoo; A Boxing Match*; *German Emperor Reviewing Troops; The Derby of 1895; Rough Sea at Dover.*

☛Theatrograph of Robert William Paul opened by Paul in a side hall called the Palmarium at the Olympia, London. A temporary structure of corrugated iron fixed to wooden studs was built for the shows, with fixed seats for 100 people. A separate enclosed platform for projection was raised eight feet from the floor and the light source used electricity.[94]

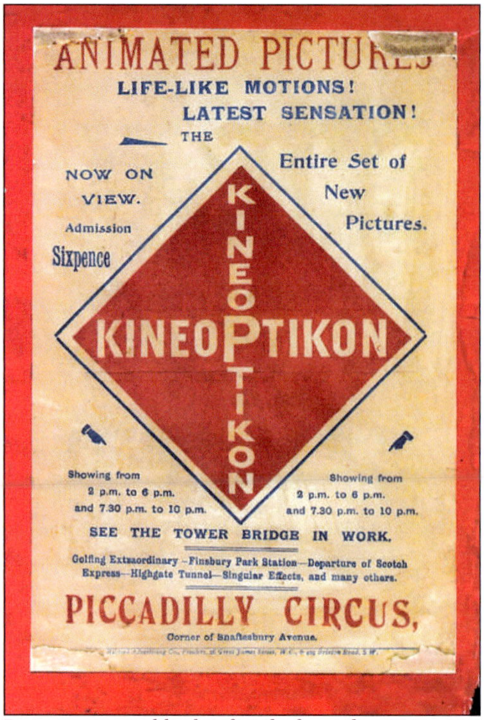

Poster preserved by his family from the Birt Acres Kineopticon exhibitions in Piccadilly, London, spring 1896. [Richard Birt Acres and Alan Birt Acres, via Deac Rossell.]

Films included: *Boxing Contest*, *Skirt Dancer*, *Comic Singer*, *Trilby*, *Egyptian War Dance*.

☛Lumière Cinématograph exhibited at a grand charity festival in aid of Congolese children at the Grand Theatre in Ghent, Belgium. Commentary on the films was provided by the Ghent lawyer A. Goderus. Performances were given on Saturday evening [March 21], Sunday afternoon and evening [22], and Monday evening [23].

Films included: a gardener gardened, a boat leaving port, an amusing party at cards, the exit of workers at a factory, the demolition of a wall.

93 Sometime in July, Devant expanded his activities with the Theatrograph by beginning to give evening performances in private homes for a fee of £25. In Germany, Karl Pahl likewise recalled giving many performances in private homes [in 1897] at prices from 120.- Marks to 250.- Marks per evening. This is a practise largely unrecorded in the literature, or in interviews, but one that is fully consistent with the long traditions of magic lantern showmen. It should be assumed that this was a relatively common practise in the first years of moving pictures.

94 On the morning of 21 March, the busy Paul demonstrated the Theatrograph for the management of the Palace Theatre, Shaftesbury Avenue, London. This was possibly before a live audience, but the management did not book his apparatus.

March 22:
Paul Theatrograph, called for this exhibition an Animatographe, gives a private evening show to the management of the Alhambra Theatre, London.

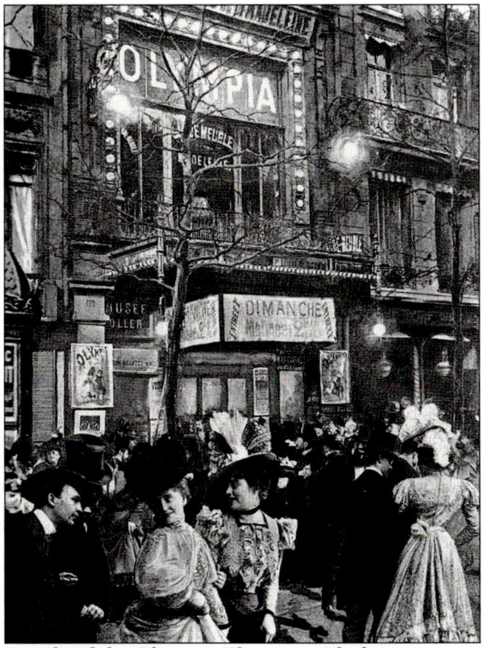

Facade of the Olympia Theatre, with the entrance to the Musée Oller just to the left of centre. [Jean-Jacques Meusy, *Paris-Palaces, ou le temps des cinemas (1894–1918)*. Paris, 1995: CNRS Editions, p. 37.]

☛Lumière Cinématographe opens at the Olympia Theatre, 28 Boulevard Capucines, Paris by Clément Maurice, who ran this show simultaneously with his presentations at the Grand Café, 14 Boulevard des Capucines. The new projection space was a former restaurant that became part of the Musée Oller and had its own entrance on the Boulevard. The shows ran until 23 July when they were replaced by the Cinographoscope of the Pipon brothers.

March 23:
Lumière Cinématographe opens at the circus in Reims, France, for two days.

March 25:
Paul Theatrograph, called the Animatographe for this exhibition, opens to the public at the Alhambra Theatre, Leicester Square, London. When Peter Newbould, a part-time inspector for the London County Council made a surprise visit to the Alhambra on 7 October 1896 after a clergyman's complaint, he found nothing untoward, but noted that Robert Paul was operating his Theatrograph at the site.

Films included: *Nautch Dancers, Female Contortionist, Beer Time in a Carpenter's Shop, Boxing Kangaroo, Rough Sea, Scientific Boxers, Lightning Cartoonist Sketching Bismarck.*

March 26:
Gray Latham and Eugene Lauste film *Bullfight* in Mexico City for the Eidoloscope, a 'continuous picture' lasting more than ten minutes.

☛Unidentified apparatus, advertised as a Cinematographe, opens at the Palace Theatre, Newcastle-upon-Tyne, commencing regional film shows in Britain. The screenings ran until April 9. This was possibly a Kinetographe de Bedts; Edison Kinetoscope films were shown.

Films included: *Highland Fling, Acrobat, Man Playing with Dog, Girl Doing Handstand, Boxing Cats, Scotch Reel, Wrestling Dogs, Bartholdi the Contortionist, Nautch Dancers.*

March 27:
Thomas Alva Edison sees his newest 'invention' for the first time when a private screening is given for him of the Phantoscope of Thomas Armat and C Francis Jenkins, about to be debuted in public as the Edison Vitascope.

☛Lumière Cinématographe opens in the mezzanine of the house at Kärntnerstraße 45, entry at Krügerstraße 2, Vienna, by Eugène Dupont. By Easter (April 4), the 'living photography' had become the sensation of Vienna. Shortly after the opening, the program began to change every Friday, and by April 27 Dupont was exhibiting local views, including traffic in front of the Kärntnerstraße, the central fire brigade, and others. Admission 50 Kreutzer. In July, with two other film shows running in the city, the admission price dropped to 30 Kreutzer.

Films included: *Der Concorde-Platz in Paris, Bubis Früstuck, Die Schmiede, Schiffspromenade, Das Meer, Die Eisenbahn.*

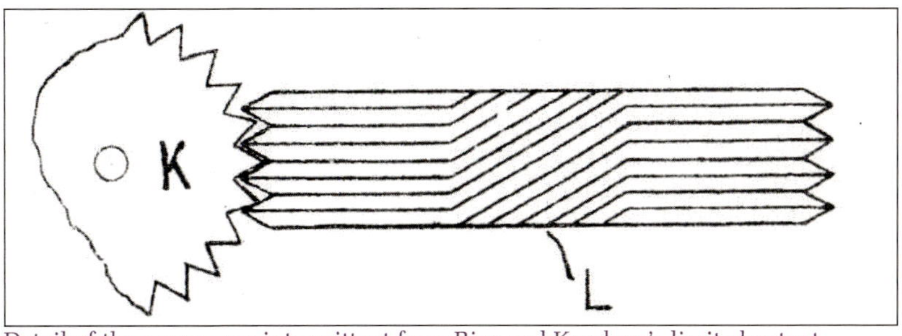

Detail of the worm-gear intermittent from Rigg and Kumberg's limited patent which only claimed improvements to the intermittent and to a brake system for the feed roller. [United Kingdom patent 6731, *Improvements in Kinematographs, Kinetographs and like Apparatus*, 27 March 1896, Fig. 4.]

☛British patent 6731, *Improvements in Kinematographs, Kinetographs, and like Apparatus*, to John Henry Rigg and Ernest Othon Kumberg, for their Kinematograph projector. Independently built and powered by an electrical motor, the apparatus used a drunken screw intermittent driven from the motor shaft acting on a grooved star wheel, and was the third projector in public use in Great Britain in 1896.[95]

March 28:
Kineoptikon of Birt Acres opened by T. Moore Howard at the Empire Variety Theatre, Newcastle-upon-Tyne.[96]

Films included: *Dancers, Boot Black, Boxing Dogs.*

☛Latham Eidoloscope opens to the public at the Everson Building, 110 South Salina Street, Syracuse, New York, by D. C. Porter. The screenings ran from 10 a.m. to 10 p.m. daily, for three weeks. Ten kinetoscope films were spliced together to make a continuous program running for 12 minutes. Hearing about the screening, Edison announced a boycott of the Latham brothers for their unsanctioned use of the kinetoscope subjects, and his lawyers planned a lawsuit.

March 29:
Lumière Cinématographe demonstrated for the Photographic Circle [al Circolo fotografico], via Principe Umberto 30, Milan, and later at the Teatro Milanese, it's first appearance in the city. The operator was Giuseppi Filippi, who had obtained the machine from the concessionaire Vittorio Calcina.

Films included: *Maréchal-ferrant, Enfants aux jouets, Una Marina, Débarquement.*

☛Lumière Cinématographe is added to the second half presentation of Le *Royaume des femmes* at l'Eldorado theatre in Paris. The shows lasted for five weeks, and formed a second part of the spectacle, given at 22 hours. After 16 April, the operator of the Lumière establishment showed films on the Cinématograph every afternoon from 2 pm to 6 pm at an admission of 1 F. Given the spacious theatre, this was the first showing of the Cinématographe that was not physically cramped.

March 30:
Lumière Cinématographe opens to the public at the Teatro Milanese, corso Vittorio Emmanuele 15, Milan, Italy, running until 6 July. Admission 1 Lira; on April 10 the price dropped to 50 Cents, with officials, soldiers and workers 25 cents, accompanying children free.

Films include: *Salti d'ostacoli per Corazzieri; Ciclisti e Cavalieri a Milano; Il Cav. Ferravilla al Caffé; Una novicata a Milano; I Lancieri alla Rivista; Acrobati les Ibremas; Il Carnevale di Venezia; La Squadra Italiana in Sardegna; Demolizione di un muro; Pompieri de Milano, Manouvra; Passeggiata di Automobili Milano; Ladri sui tetti; Serenata interrotta; Funerali di Felix Faure; La Ballerina.*

☛French patent 255,164, *Appareil pour photographier des scènes animées avec bandes pelliculaires dit Phototrope*, to Jules Carpentier for a device for photographic animated scenes with film strips called the Phototrope.

☛Lumière Cinématographe opens at the café conc Eldorado, Boulevard de Strasbourg, Paris.

☛Lumière Cinématographe opens at the Salon Margherita in Naples, Italy. The shows ran until 23 June.

April 1:
Lumière Cinématographe demonstrated for Kaiser Franz-Joseph I at the French Embassy, Vienna, Austria.

April 2:
Unidentified apparatus opens at the Théâtre Isola, 39 Boulevard des Capucines, Paris, by Vincent and Émile Isola. This was most likely the apparatus later sold by the brothers as the Isolatographe, a machine patented by Louis Charles on April 20 as F255,702 and, coincidentally, identical to the apparatus of Méliès, Korsten, and Reulos patented in France on 4 September 1896. Isola advertised many films in colour, including a dance by Loïe Fuller, to distinguish his theatre on the crowded boulevard of exhibitions.

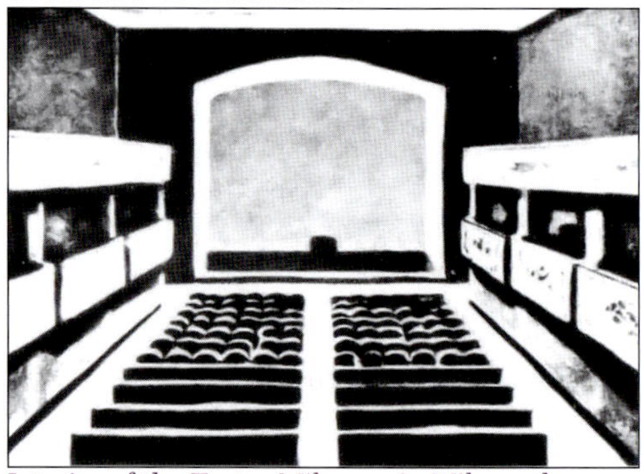

Interior of the Teatro Milanese in Milan, where the first Italian performances of the Cinématographe Lumière were given. [Aldo Bernardini, *Cinema muto italiano. Ambiente, spettacoli e spettatori 1896/1904.* Rome, 1980: Editori Laterza, p. 34.]

95 French patent 255,467, application 11 April 1896, *Perfectionnements apporté à la constructiondes kinématographes, kinétographes et autres appareils analogues.*

96 Richard Brown states that this show was 'using a projector made by Paul' . See *The Lumière Cinématographe. The first six months in England*, p. 30. Actually, T. M. Howard, of Walthamstow, was about this time involved with Birt Acres, and travelled widely with the Acres Kineoptikon.

April 3:
Thomas Alva Edison hosts a press conference and screening of the Vitascope at his laboratory in West Orange, New Jersey. This was the re-named Phantoscope of C. Francis Jenkins and Thomas Armat, as improved by Armat. "No one was more pleased at the success of his work than the great inventor himself", wrote the *New York Journal* on 4 April. "Wrapped in a big overcoat which hung to his heels and rose to his hat brim, he walked about the cold room chuckling and joking with the men who had done so much to make his work what it is...." This press showing of the new 'Edison' machine generated widespread newspaper comment across the country as only larger newspapers with wire service connections were invited, in a publicity coup by the machine's promoters, Raff and Gammon.

☛French patent 255,317, *Système d'appareil servant à enregistrer et à reproduire simultanément les scènes animées et les sons*, to Auguste Baron and Frédéric Bureau, for their Chronophotographe, a system capable of registering and reproducing animated scenes and sound. A projector and a phonograph were driven by the same electrical motor, with synchronization provided by an electrical alternator. The mechanical sound and picture system was not successful.[97]

April 4:
Lumière Cinématographe opens at the Salone Margherita of Carlo and Igino Marino, Naples, Italy, continuing until 25 May, on a variety bill that includes the Family Benedetti, acrobats; the eccentric French comedian Bloquelle; the singer Baronessa Milford and Herman the snake man.

☛The English magazine *Black and White* publishes in their women's pages on this date an early fictional reference to moving pictures, in the anonymous story *Diary of a Daughter of Eve*, in which the cinematograph is described as "just another passing fashion".

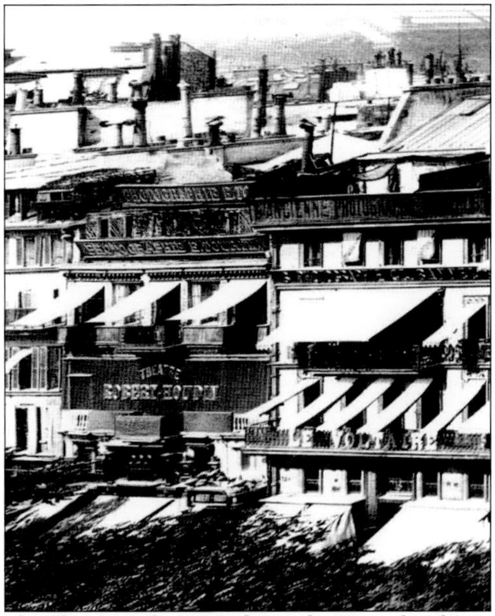
The Theatre Robert-Houdin at the time of Méliès' ownership and before the fire of 1901. [Jacques Malthête and Laurent Mannoni, *Méliès. Magie et Cinéma*, Paris, 2002: Paris musées, p. 79.]

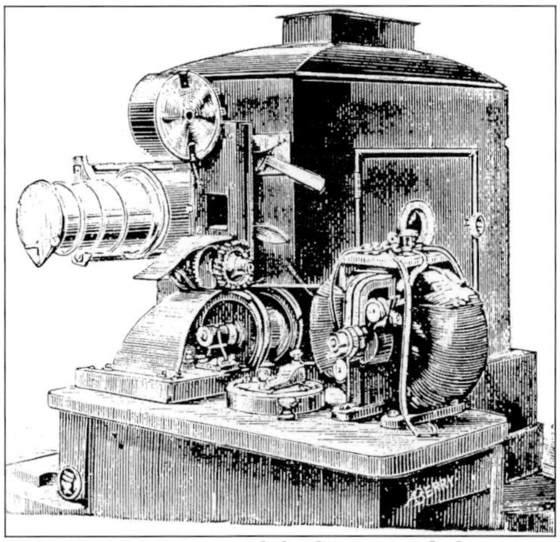
The Rigg Kinematograph had an extended run at the Royal Aquarium, with shows twice daily until the end of the year. [John Barnes, *The Beginnings of the Cinema in England*. London / New York, 1976: David & Charles / Barnes & Noble Books, p. 131.]

April 5:
Georges Méliès begins regular film showings at his Théatre Robert-Houdin in Paris, using a French projector, most likely a design of Louis Charles that was being sold by fellow magicians the Isola brothers and often called an Isolatograph in the literature. Méliès at the same time bought a Paul Theatrograph through magician David Devant in London, which he promptly turned into a camera so that he could begin making his own films. Initially, he used both Robert Paul and Edison Kinetoscope films in his screenings.

April 6:
Bioskop of Max and Emil Skladanowsky opens at the Cirkus Variete music hall in Kristiana, Norway, through 3 May, again using their Wintergarten programme. For this tour through Scandinavia and The Netherlands, which began with this engagement, the Bioskop was presented as a single act, without their dissolving view programme.

Films included: *Italienischer Bauerntanz*, *Komisches Reck*, *Akrobatisches potpourri*, *Das boxende Känguruh*, *Jongleur*, *Kammarintzky* [russischer Nationaltanz], *Ringkamp Greiner – Sandow*, *Apotheose*.

97 Auguste Baron was an inventor with a small laboratory in Asnières-sur-Seine who became interested in the cinema when a friend asked him to repair an 'Edison Mutoscope' [*sic*.]. Frédéric Bureau was the financial administrator of the Olympia in Paris, who was interested in and supportive of Baron's sound/film experiments. On 3 June 1896 the two also took out a patent on a mechanical system for perforating photographic films (French patent 256,926). Bureau died in 1896, but Baron continued his researches, and had perfected a new apparatus by 1898 (French patent 276,628 of 4 April 1898), and several short films were made for him in a specially equipped studio at Asnières by cameraman Felix Mesguich.

☛Kinematograph of John Henry Rigg and Ernst Othon Kumberg opens at the Royal Aquarium, Westminster, London, a device with a 'drunken screw' intermittent movement and a restraining brake on the top film spool to retard its unwinding. This was the fourth film projector to be publicly exhibited in Great Britain, and the third English projector. It was available on the open market by the end of the year.

☛Unidentified apparatus called Edison's Cinématographe opens at the People's Palace, Bradford.

Films included: *Barber's Shop*, *Dentist's Surgery*, *Blacksmith's Forge*, *Regimental Band*, *A Contortionist*, and two titles called *Skirt Dancer*.

April 7: Paul Theatrograph, operated by Edwin Rousby, a Budapest electrician, joins the Circus Parish of Hugo Herzog in Madrid, a troupe including acrobats, clowns and equestrians.

☛French patent 255,383, *Nouveau système d'appareil optique destiné au tirage photographique et à la projection des objets animées*, to Alexandre Salle and Élie Xavier Mazo for their Héliographe, using film 20mm wide and a film path with toothed sprockets. The intermittent was provided by a Saint André's Cross gear.

April 8:
Robert William Paul exhibits a color film on his Theatrograph, at the Alhambra Theatre, Leicester Square, London. The film was hand-painted over a period of one month with the aid of a microscope, by Edward Henry Doubell, a painter of magic lantern slides for the Royal Polytechnic Institution, Regent Street, and was called an "Eastern dance" in the press.

☛Isolatographe of Louis Charles opens at the Salle des Capucines, 39 Boulevard du Capucines, Paris, organized by magicians Émil and Vincent Isola. The Salle des Capucines was directly across the street from the Salon Indien of the Grand Café.[98]

April 10:
Kineopticon demonstated by Birt Acres at a meeting of the Cardiff Photographic Society in Cardiff, Wales. Acres used limelight illumination instead of electricity, and he apologised for the dim illumination and the density of his gelatine films on frosted Blair stock, but the demonstration, the first cinema showing in Wales, was enthusiastically received.

Films included: *Men Playing Cards*, *The German Emperor Reviewing His Troops*, *The Derby*, *Rough Sea at Dover*.

April 11:
French patent 255,467, *Perfectionnements apportés à la construction des kinématographes, kinétogaphes et autres appareils analogues*, to John Henry Rigg and Ernst Othon Kumberg for improvements in the construction of kinématographs, kinétographs and other similar apparatus.

April 13:
Unidentified apparatus, advertised as a Kinetoscope, opens at the Gaiety Palace of Varieties, Birmingham. The films shown were Robert Paul films, and the apparatus was likely a Theatrograph.

Films included: *Grenadier Guards Band*, *Boxing Cats*, *A Contortionist*, *Serpentine Dance*, *Scotch Reel*, *Umbrella Dance*, *Blacksmith's Shop*.

April 16:
Lumière Cinématographe demonstrated in Cologne, at the canteen of the Stollwerck factory, the chocolate manufacturers who ultimately contracted for the German rights to the French apparatus.

☛Unidentified apparatus, advertised as 'photographie animée', opens at the Salle Poirel, Galerie Nord, Nancy, France, for four days.

April 17:
Lumière Cinématographe shown to Kaiser Franz Joseph I at Eugène Dupont's exhibitions in Kärntnerstraße 45, Vienna.

April 18:
Watson Motorgraph is booked for the Palace Theatre, Cambridge Circus, London, in an agreement signed by manager Charles Morton. The contract specified a run of four weeks at £100 per week; the precise dates of the exhibitions are unknown, but the Motorgraph

98 Most of the literature cited in the Sources identifies this apparatus as a Kinématograph de Bedts, but now that Louis Charles's affiliation with the Isola brothers is known, it is much more likely that it was a machine built by Charles. Émile and Vincent Isola, born at Blida, Algeria, were machinists whose love of magic and growing passion for conjuring brought them to Paris, where they purchased the Théâtre des Capucines, according to legend with the help of a wealthy patroness whose dying son they had entertained. It became the Théâtre Isola, featuring their own magic shows, and competed with the Théâtre Robert-Houdin. The brothers later directed the Parisiana, the Olympia, and then bought and directed the Folies Bergère, which they turned into a great music hall, booking imaginative and substantial variety acts from all over Europe. [The famous nude shows were later added to the program of the Folies by the nephew of the subsequent managers, M. and Mme. Lallemand.] Like Georges Méliès, the Isola brothers were present at the first showing of the Lumière Cinématographe at the Salon Indien. Adept mechanics, they were selling their own projection equipment by late April for use in Berlin, Vienna, Brussels, Moscow and elsewhere.

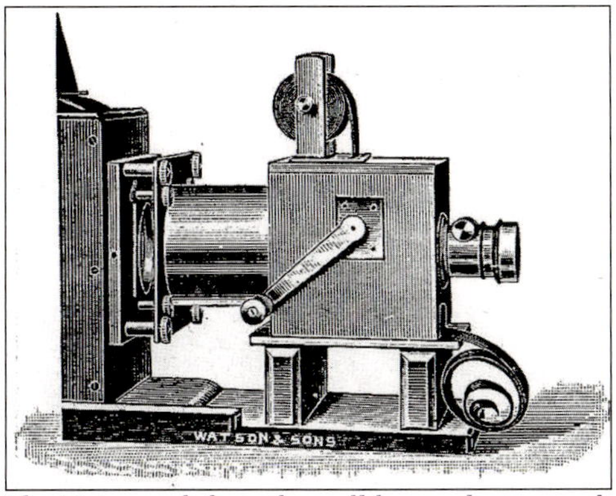

The Motorgraph from the well-known lantern and optical firm of Watson and Son, London, was a light and portable apparatus in wide use in 1896. [Henry Hopwood, *Living Pictures*. London, 1899: The Optician & Photographic Trades Review, p. 156.]

was running for the public on May 9. The manufacturers, Watson & Sons, were dealers in photographic and lantern equipment founded in 1837 and produced at least three models of lightweight, efficient cinematographs for sale.

April 19:
Lumière Cinématographe opens at 17 rue Esquermoise, Lille, France. The screenings ran through July 27.

April 20:
Lumière Cinématographe opens in a house at 12 Augustiner Platz, between Heumarkt and Neumarkt, Cologne, with a matinee performance for invited guests. The exhibitions ran over six weeks, at least until the end of May. Admission 50 Pfennig for 6 films. The exhibition was advertised as an "invention in the field of Chronophotography" in the *Kölner Stadt-Anzeiger*.[99]

Films included: *Feierabend in einer Fabrik, Brechen der Wagen an einer Klippe, Einfahren eines Schnellzuges in einen großstädschen Bahnhof, Carneval in Nizza, Ladung eines überseeischen Dampfers, Idyll im Zoologischen Garten.*

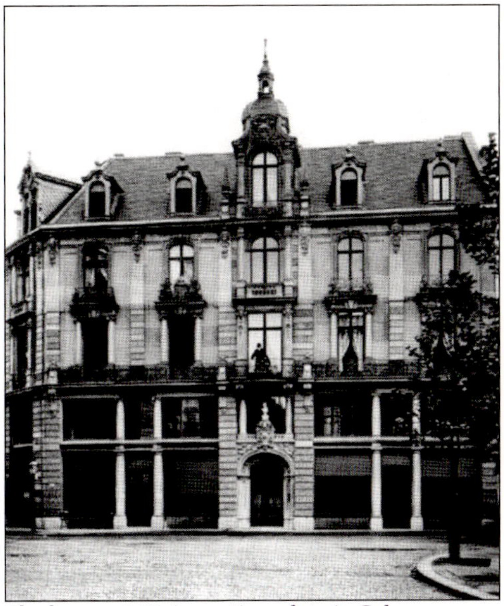

The house at 12 Augustinerplatz in Cologne where the Lumière Cinématographe opened on 20 April 1896. [Christa Aretz and Irene Schoor, *Köln im Film. Filmgeschichte(n) einer Stadt.* Köln, 2004: Hermann-Josef Emons Verlag, p. 21.]

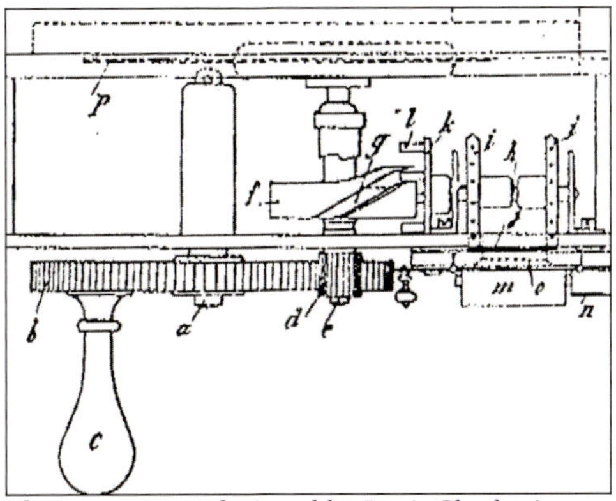

The intermittent designed by Louis Charles in spring 1896 and sold by the Isola brothers as the Isolatographe. The helical screw *g* acts on four posts *l* on the circular plate k which drives the sprocket *i, i* holding the film.
[French patent 255,702 of 20 April 1896, *Nouveau mode de commande de la pellicule dans la photographie animée*, fig. 2.]

☛Unidentified apparatus, advertised as a Cinematograph, opens at Dan Lowney's Star of Erin Theatre of Varieties (now the Olympia), Dublin, Ireland, for one week. The illumination was weak, and the showing unsuccessful.

Films included: *Grand Boxing Match, Scene in a Barbershop, Serpentine Dancer, Boxing Cats, Grand Marching Band.*

☛French patent 255,702, *Un nouveau mode de commande de la pellicule dans la photographie animée*, to Louis Henri Charles for his projector with an unusual helical screw intermittent. Sold by the magicians Vincent and Émile Isola and often called the Isolatographe, this important early apparatus was used in Berlin, Paris and elsewhere, and its design was identical to the much later patent of Georges Méliès, Lucien Korsten and Lucien Reulios.

April 21:
British patent 8418, *Improvements in connection with the projection of photographs of animated subjects*, to Jacob Bonn in London, for a cine projector with a movement similar to that of Max Skladanowsky, using an intermittent gear wheel fixed to the driving sprocket motivated by a worm gear mounted on a sliding axle shuttled back and forth by a stud in a camshaft groove.

99 The first three films are identified as *Sortie de l'Usine Lumière à Lyon*, *La Mer*, and *Le Train*. On 23 May 1896 the Cologne *Stadt-Anzeiger* carried an advertisement for new Cologne subjects added to the program, including *Arrival of a train at the Cologne railway station* (Ankunft eines Eisenbahnzuges auf dem Kölner Houptbahnhofe) and *Workers leaving a Cologne Factory* (Feierabend einer Kölner Fabrik).

April 22:
Lumière Cinématographe demonstrated at the Café Riche, Passage Injalbert, place de la Comedie, Montpellier. The audience was press and invited guests at the Exposition Général et Nationale de Montpellier.

☛Lumière Cinématographe opens at the Crystal Palace, Sydenham, England, returning for additional exhibitions on July 13 and August 31.

☛Lumière Cinématographe opens at its fourth location in Paris, at the Grands Magasins Dufayel, the huge department store at 13, Boulevard Barbès (26, rue de Clignancourt, 18e). Located in a working-class district of northern Paris, away from central department stores like Le Bon Marche, Printemps, and others, Dufayel's establishment served nearly 2 million customers, who bought furniture and household goods on credit. Dufayel's store enlarged to include a concert hall, theatre and Winter Garden, where Dufayel offered science demonstrations, free lectures, films, and performances to attract his clientele. The film screenings lasted at least three years and were a popular calling-card of the firm.

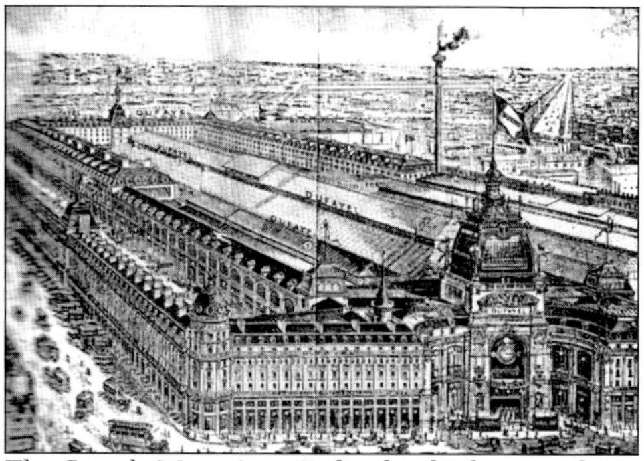

The Grands Magazines Dufayel, which opened in 1890 and provided regular cinematograph shows from April, 1896, was a focal point of the working-class neighbourhoods of northern Paris, and a centre of community activities.
[Jean-Jacques Meusy, *Paris-Palaces ou le temps des cinémas (1894–1918)*. Paris, 1995: CNRS Éditions, p. 35.]

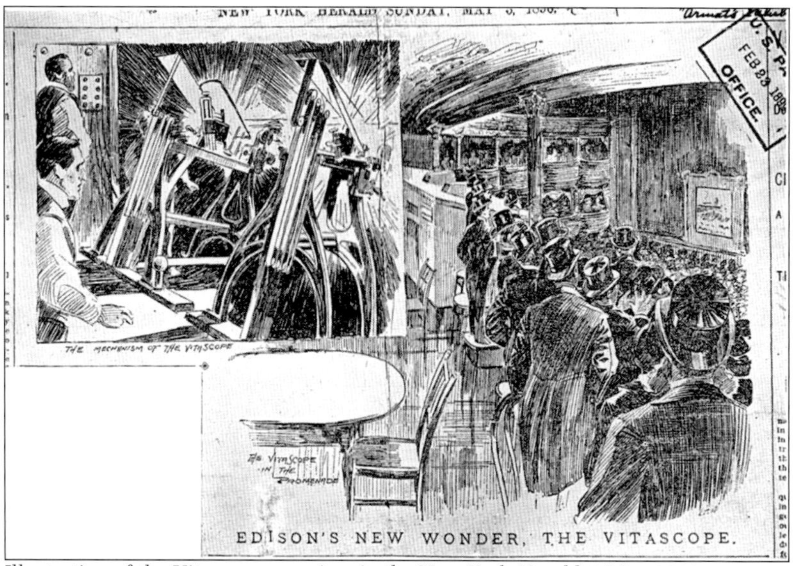

Illustration of the Vitascope premiere in the New York *Herald*, 6 May 1896, showing the film mounted on spools and a portion of the auditorium.
[Terry Ramsaye, *A Million and One Nights*. New York, 1926: Simon and Schuster, opposite p. 234.]

April 23:
Edison Vitascope, the re-named and improved Phantoscope of Thomas Armat and C. Francis Jenkins, opens with a gala event at Koster and Bial's Music Hall, Herald Square, New York City. Under the management of Norman Raff and Frank Gammon, the contract specified a fee of $800 per week for four months. Edison's name, reports of the Lumière sensation in Europe, and an intense publicity campaign all ensured a high profile event. Two projectors were used with 20-foot loops of film arranged over rollers similar to the Kinetoscope; each film was shown repeatedly to the audience, covering the interval needed to re-thread a new subject onto the alternate machine. For

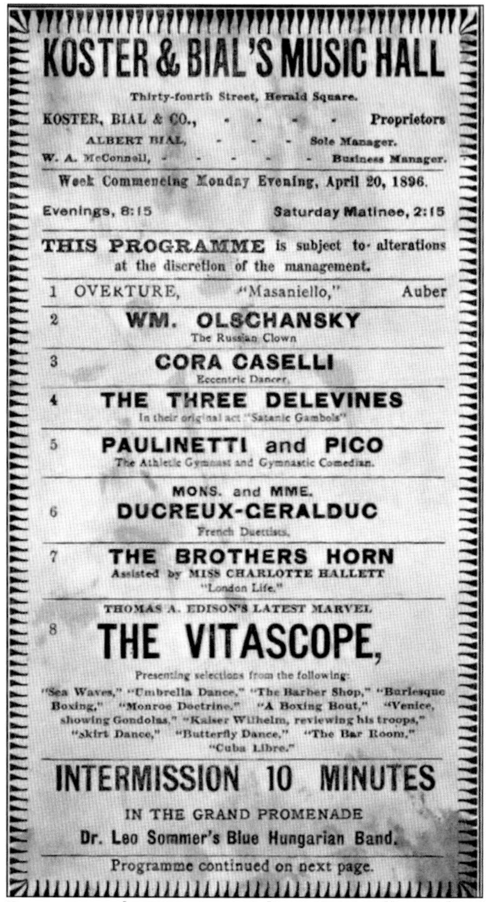

KOSTER & BIAL'S MUSIC HALL

Thirty-fourth Street, Herald Square.

KOSTER, BIAL & CO., ... Proprietors
ALBERT BIAL, . . . Sole Manager.
W. A. McConnell, ... Business Manager.

Week Commencing Monday Evening, April 20, 1896.

Evenings, 8:15 Saturday Matinee, 2:15

THIS PROGRAMME is subject to alterations at the discretion of the management.

1 OVERTURE, "Masaniello," Auber

2 WM. OLSCHANSKY
The Russian Clown

3 CORA CASELLI
Eccentric Dancer.

4 THE THREE DELEVINES
In their original act "Satanic Gambols"

5 PAULINETTI and PICO
The Athletic Gymnast and Gymnastic Comedian.

6 MONS. and MME. DUCREUX-GERALDUC
French Duettists.

7 THE BROTHERS HORN
Assisted by MISS CHARLOTTE HALLETT
"London Life."

8 THOMAS A. EDISON'S LATEST MARVEL
THE VITASCOPE,
Presenting selections from the following:
"Sea Waves," "Umbrella Dance," "The Barber Shop," "Burlesque Boxing," "Monroe Doctrine," "A Boxing Bout," "Venice, showing Gondolas," "Kaiser Wilhelm, reviewing his troops," "Skirt Dance," "Butterfly Dance," "The Bar Room," "Cuba Libre."

INTERMISSION 10 MINUTES
IN THE GRAND PROMENADE
Dr. Leo Sommer's Blue Hungarian Band.

Programme continued on next page.

Programme for Koster & Bial's Music Hall, week of 20 April 1896, announcing the Vitascope premiere performances.
[Terry Ramsaye, *A Million and One Nights*. New York, 1926: Simon and Schuster, opposite p. 236.]

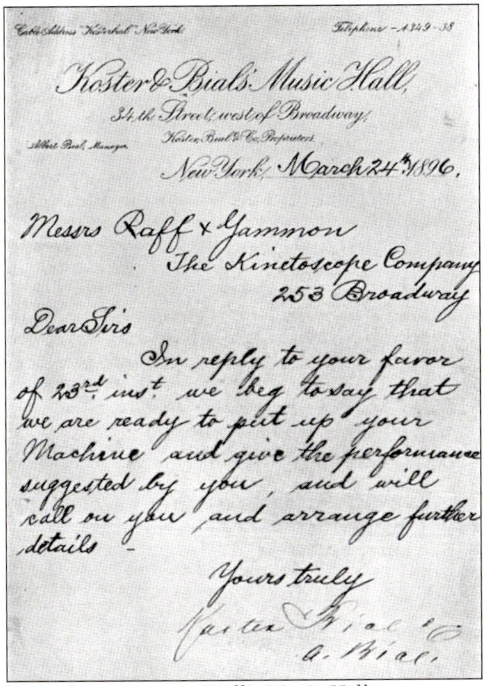

Cable Address "Kosterbial" New York — Telephone – 1349 – 38

Koster & Bials' Music Hall,
34th Street, west of Broadway,
Koster, Bial & Co. Proprietors.
Albert Bial, Manager.

New York, March 24th 1896.

Messrs Raff & Gammon
The Kinetoscope Company
253 Broadway

Dear Sirs
In reply to your favor of 23rd inst. we beg to say that we are ready to put up your Machine and give the performance suggested by you, and will call on you and arrange further details

Yours truly
Koster & Bial & Co
A. Bial.

Letter from Koster & Biall's Music Hall confirming the engagement of the Vitascope for the following month.
[Terry Ramsaye, *A Million and One Nights*. New York, 1926: Simon and Schuster, opposite p. 232.]

the first week of the engagement Thomas Armat was the operator of the machines.

Films on the opening program included: *Umbrella Dance*, which was hand-colored; *The Barber Shop*, *Walton and Slavin*, burlesque boxers from the play *1492*; *The Milk White Flag*, the finale of the first act; *The Monroe Doctrine*, specially produced for the debut; *A Rough Sea at Dover*; and *Serpentine Dance*, also hand-colored.

☛Lumière Cinématographe opens to the public at the Café Riche, Passage Injalbert, at the Exposition Général et Nationale, Montpellier. Admission 1 Franc, children (under 10) and military half price. On June 21 admission was reduced to 50 Centimes. The screenings continued until 29 November.

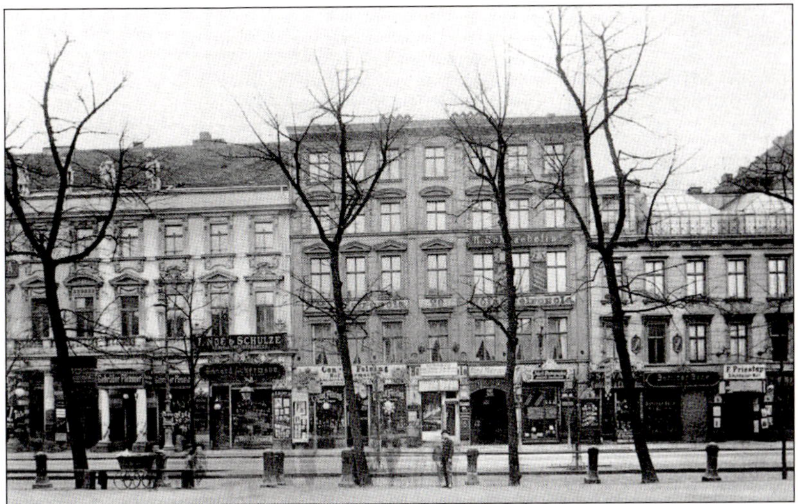

Unter den Linden 19 to 21 about 1901, where the early film theatre opened in a side hall of the restaurant at No. 21. [Michael Hanisch, *Auf den Spuren der Filmgeschichte. Berliner Schauplätze*. Berlin, 1991: Henschel Verlag, p. 63.]

☛Lumière Cinématographe returns to Reims, France, opening in a hall at the Casino, rue de l'Etape. The operator was Bordéra and the screenings ran until May 7.

April 25:
Press preview for the film exhibitions at 21 Unter den Linden, Berlin, the first standing cinema in the city, which used a side hall of the restaurant Wilhelmshallen at 21 Unter den Linden, Berlin, exclusively for film showings. The project was organized by the Deutsche Kinematographische Gesellschaft, whose principals were Baron von Prittwitz, Baron von Goldberger, the banker Marsop, councilman Saloschin and the journalist Leo Leipziger. The facility was managed by Herr Kuchel and projection was by the electrician Karl Pahl from the firm of Lehmann & Mann. The group had purchased a projector from Vincent and Emil Isola in Paris, which was long established in the literature as an Isolatographe, but was actually a machine designed and patented by the French mechanic Louis Henri Charles. Launched with great excitement and publicity, the theatre at 21 Unter den Linden immediately had difficulties and the admission price of 1.- Mark dropped in two days to 50 pfennig. The unsuccessful theatre was then sold on 24 May to a Russian businessman named Jussop [or Gussem?], who installed Gustav Schönwald as manager, but it remained unsuccessful. On 21 September 1896 the business was again sold, this time to Oskar Messter, who saw newly installed apparatus there made by Max Gliewe, including a five-sided Maltese Cross movement, and took over the Gliewe design for his own company.[100]

100. Max Gliewe was associated with the optical construction firm of Gliewe and Kügler in Berlin, and had designed his five-sided Maltese cross projector independently of Oskar Messter. As Gliewe prepared his fifth and sixth machines for sale, which he evidently never patented, Messter notified Gliewe that he was infringing Messter's Gebrauchsmuster, which Messter had applied for but which had not yet been granted. The two then came to an agreement that Gliewe's apparatus would be supplied only to Messter's company, with the exception of an order for 50 Gliewe projectors that had already been received from the British firm of Haydon & Urry, 353 Upper Street, Islington, London. It is most likely that this

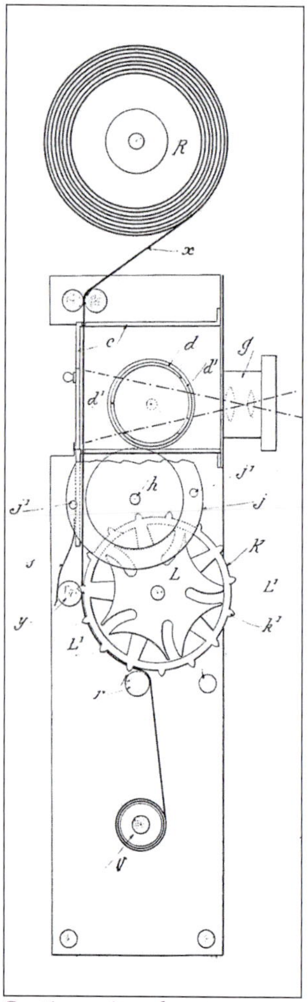

Contisouza's early patent showing his 5-sided Maltese Cross intermittent with its slightly curved entry slots. [French patent 255,937, *Appareil photographique à bande sensible continue pour la fixation et la reproduction des scènes animées*, of 28 April 1896, Fig. 1.]

☛Lumière Cinématographe demonstrated at the Salle des fêtes de l'hotel de Ville, Saint-Étienne, France, for the Société de Photographie, four days before it opened to the public for 11 weeks.

☛Lumière Cinématographe previewed at the Ancien Café de l'hotel d'Espagne, Place de la Republique 4, Rouen, France, for the Mayor and notables of the city by Paul Lambin and Daniels, who had purchased the concession for the city. Lambin was the owner of a local shop dealing in artist's supplies and photographic supplies; Daniels remains obscure. The Cinématographe opened to the public the next day, 26 April, admission 1 Franc, children and military 50 centimes. The screenings remained open until October, in parallel with a major exposition of French and Colonial industry and culture.

☛Lumière Cinématograph opens at the Etablissement de Phototypie on Grammaryestraat in Antwerp, Belgium. The hall was owned by Jos Maes, chairman of the Antwerp chapter of the Association Belge de Photographie. The screenings ran every half-hour from 10am until 11pm, and continued until early June.

April 26:
Kinematograph of Louis Charles, often called an Isolatographe, opens to the public in a side hall of the restaurant Wilhelmshallen at 21 Unter den Linden, Berlin, after its press preview on the 25th (see above). One review called the projections "essentially an improvement and perfection of the Anschütz Schnellseher". The exhibitions ran until at least mid-1897.

Films included: a serpentine dancer in colour; three Can-can dancers; two different street scenes of Paris life; a steamship at sea; a brawl in an English pub; boxers in a ring with their seconds, timekeeper and audience; bathing scenes at the seaside; a blacksmith shop.

April 27:
Paul Theatrograph opens at the Canterbury Theatre of Varieties, Westminster Bridge Road, London.

☛Paul Theatrograph opens at the Paragon Theatre of Varieties, Mile End Road, London.[101]

☛Georges Demenÿ demonstrates his new model Phonoscope for Léon Gaumont, now adapted by Demenÿ and his associate Léopold Réne Decaux into a combination camera and projector with regularly perforated film running on sprocket rollers, but still with a beater intermittent movement.

April 28:
French patent 255,937, *Appareil photographique à bande sensible continue pour la fixation et la reproduction des scènes animées*, to Pierre-Victor Continsouza for his combined camera and projector with a five-sided Maltese Cross intermittent, made by Gabriel Lepée. This is the first appearance of the name 'Maltese Cross' in a cinematograph patent. The compact vertical apparatus had a cylindrical rotating shutter placed behind the lens,

order was the origin of the Eragraph projector which Haydon & Urry offered in Britain from 1897 (possibly late 1896). A tentatively identified Eragraph Model No. 1 in the Barnes Collection includes the appropriate 5-sided Maltese cross intermittent, as does a complete Eragraph Model No. 2 in the Science Museum, London. Haydon & Urry submitted patent applications for both machines, which received provisional protection only and were never published (No. 3572 of 10 February 1897 and No. 20,296 of 3 September 1897, respectively). On 1 November 1900 the Messter workshop, formerly Bauer & Betz, combined with Gliewe & Kügler to become the Vereinigte Mechanikerwerkstätten GmbH, which built all of the apparatus for Messters Projektion GmbH until 1914.
The original Louis Charles projector from Unter den Linden 21 survives in the collection of the Deutsches Museum in Munich, donated by Oskar Messter. Both the projector by Louis Charles and his patent (F pat 255,702 of 20 April 1896) are identical to the later patent and projector of Lucien Korsten, Georges Méliès and Lucien Reulos (F pat 259,444 of 2 September 1896). It is unknown how the French patent office issued the later of the two patents, and equally unknown what relationship, if any, linked the two machines and their underwriters.

101 Beginning in June, 1896, the Paul Theatrograph was also exhibited at the Proms concerts throughout their summer season, under a contract made between impresario Robert Newman and magician David Devant, an early presenter of and agent for the Theatrograph. Shows were given during the concert interval in a small room adjacent to Queen's Hall, and at the end of the concert, around 10.30 pm, an additional presentation was given for an extra 6p admission. See *My Life in Music*, by Henry J. Wood (London, 1938: Gollanz).

pierced by two opposed rectangular openings.[102]

☛Lumière Cinématographe opens in the Panoptikum at Friedrichstrasse 65a, 1st floor, at the corner of Mohrenstrasse, Berlin. The house itself was filmed specially for the shows (Lumière Cat. No. 219), which lasted until the end of May. Entry 50 Pfennig for about 10 films.

Films included: a Paris marketplace with all its bustle, a train entering a station with its passengers debarking, children bathing at the seashore, waves rolling towards the audience.

☛Unidentified apparatus, advertised as a Cinématographe or Kinétographe, opens at the Café Riche, Nantes, France, by Désiré and Joseph Russi. The screenings ran through May 10.

☛Unidentified apparatus, advertised as a Kinétographe, opens at the café-concert Le Moulin Rouge, 406 rue Jules Lecesne, Le Havre, France, by the showman Mutel.

April 29:
Lumière Cinématographe opens at the Royal Hotel in Budapest, Hungary, during the Millennial Exhibition, a large world's fair intended to show off the modern city.

April 30:
Lumière Cinématographe opens at passage Sainte-Catherine, Saint-Étienne, France. The showings ran through July 20.

May 1:
Lumière Cinématographe opens at the Exposition Nationale, Palais des Fees, Geneva, organised by François-Henri Lavanchy-Clarke. 170 sessions were given through 18 October 1896. Along with 'Living Photographs', the Palais directed by Lavanchy-Clarke and sponsored by 'Sunlight' soap included a presentation of 'Swiss Fairy Legends' and a 'Magic Arcade'. The Kinetoscope and Kinetophone were shown at the Edison Pavilion of the Exhibition. The Lumière operator Alexandre Promio photographed several scenes at the Exhibition, including *Der Wasserfall*, *Arabischer Umzug*, *Ägyptischer Tanz*, *Dorffest* and *Rückkehr in den Stall*, before travelling through Switzerland to take views of Zermatt, Montreaux, and Lausanne, amongst others.

Films included: *Arivée d'un train en gare*, *La Demolition d'un mur*, *La Mer à Ciotat*, *Une Partie des cartes*, *Une Querelle de bébés*, *Vos du village Negrée* (this last title shot at the Exposition).

☛Lumière Cinématographe opens at the Société des Amis des Arts, 2 avenue Victor-Hugo, Aix-en-Provence.

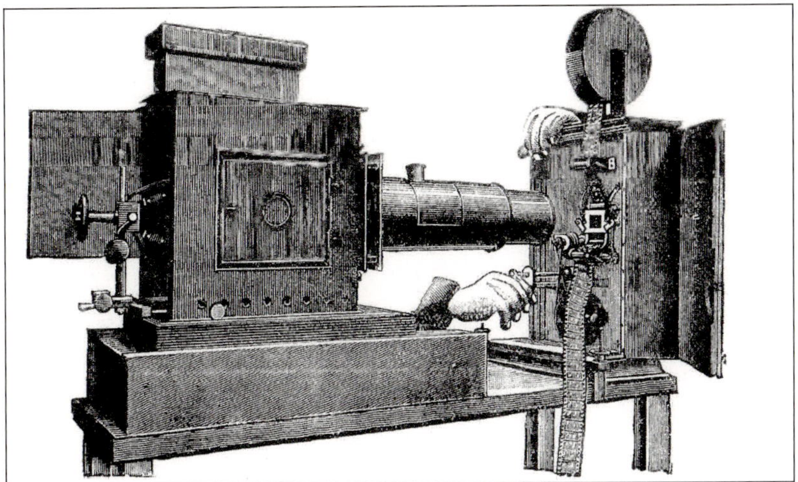

The Mouvementographe of Joseph Zion, an early machine on the French market in 1896. [Eugene Trutat, *Photographie Animée*, p. 93.]

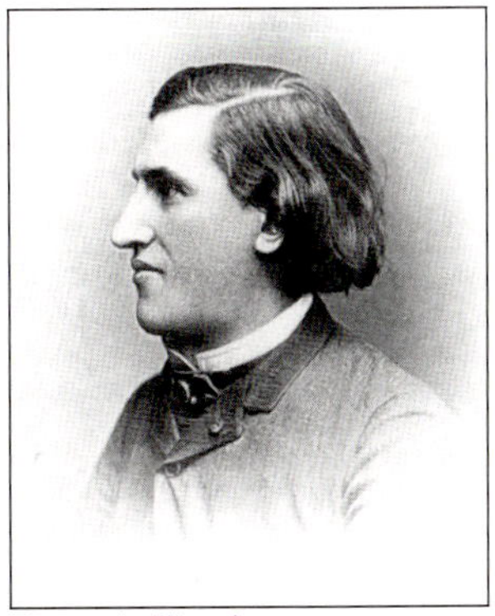

François-Henri Lavanchy-Clarke in 1896. [*Paul Meier-Kern, Verbrecherschule oder Kulturfaktor? Kino und Film in Basel 1896–1916*. Basel 1993, Helbing & Lichtenhahn, p. 23.]

☛Lumière Cinématographe opens in Treptower Park, at the Edison Pavilion of the Berlin Trade Fair, by the Deutsche-Automaten-Gesellschaft Stollwerck & Co., now the German

102 The wheel that motivated the intermittent had two pins on its surface, a feature retained in production models. As originally drawn, the five-sided Maltese Cross had unusual curved slots, evidently in an attempt to gain tangential entry for the motivating pins. These would have made it difficult to run the machine in reverse, and would necessitate a pin slightly smaller than the slot; in later models a proper straight-sided five-branched Maltese movement was used. Continsouza machines were either copied or purchased by H. O. Foersterling in Berlin beginning in early summer 1896 as his own Kinematograph or Biomotograph, and by R. J. Appleton & Co. of Bradford, England as the Cieroscope. It was also copied in a slightly modified form by the Paris firm of Clément & Gilmer as their Vitagraphe, which copies were probably sold in England by J. W. Rowe & Company in London as the Pictorialograph in 1897. Continsouza later became for many years the major equipment supplier for Pathé, manufacturing the Reporter camera, the classic projector l'A. B. R., and many other items. By 1914 his Etablissements Continsouza employed a thousand workers, and sold cameras, projectors, amateur cine equipment and electrical accessories throughout Europe and Russia.

concessionaires for the apparatus and who also had the German rights to the Edison Kinetoscope which they exhibited simultaneously. In August, the Edison Pavilion burned to the ground during a projection, but was rebuilt "in the shortest time" with all attractions, including the Cinématographe, restored for the duration of the trade fair.[103]

☛French patent 256,036, *Appareil photographique die Mouvementoscope*, to Joseph Zion for his Mouvementoscope, an apparatus with a modified worm intermittent, where a six-branched star wheel bears on a helical groove in a nut fixed to the driving axle of the machine.

☛Georg Bartling exhibits his own projector, called Kinematograph, at the Berlin Trade Fair through October 15. An exhibitor and mechanic, Bartling later worked with Johannes Nitzsche in Leipzig and manufactured projectors through the 1930s.

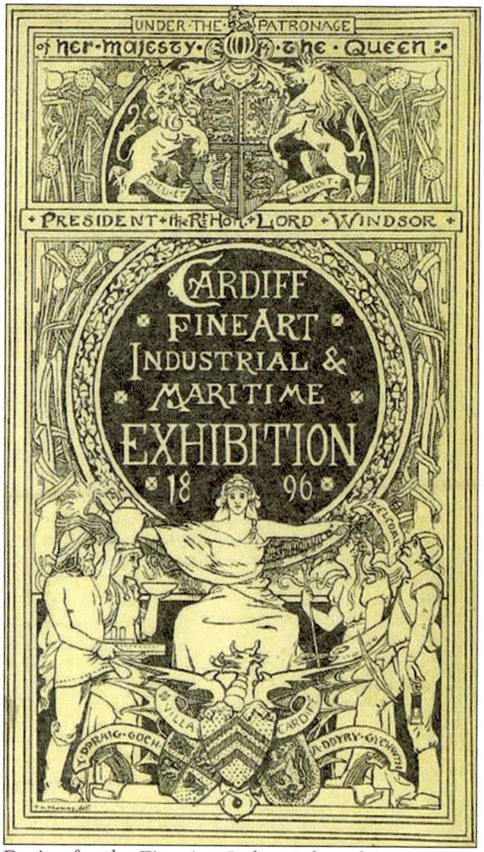

Design for the Fine Art, Industrial, and Maritime Exhibition in Cardiff, Wales, 1896, where one million persons visited during the six months of the exhibition. [From *Cardiff, an Illustrated Handbook*, 1896 (Western Mail).]

☛Edison Kinetoscope opens in an automat exhibition of the Deutsche Automaten-Gesellschaft (DAG) in a decorated mezzanine of the building at Georgstrasse 34, not far from the Café Kröpke in Hanover. Five kinetoscopes were in use. The owner of the building was the banker Wilhelm Basse, and the agent for the DAG was cigar dealer and manufacturer Theodor Lahmeyer.

May 4:
Kineopticon of Birt Acres opens at the St. James's Theatre, Manchester, exhibited only at matinee performances.

May 4 (Julian Calendar):
This date appears in many accounts of early cinema activity in Russia, as the date of the first appearance of the Lumière Cinématographe in St. Petersburg. See 17 May below (in the Gregorian Calendar as used throughout Europe and the USA, and in this chronology) for information about this event.

May 5:
Kineopticon of Birt Acres demonstrated for an invited audience at the Fine Art, Industrial, and Maritime Exhibition in Cathays Park, Cardiff, Wales. The Kineopticon was publicly exhibited from the next day, and Acres filmed at the Exhibition on June 27 (see below) and in August.

Demonstration films included: *The Derby*, *Rough Seas at Dover*, *The German Emperor Reviewing his Troops*, *Beertime in a Carpenter's Shop*, *Arrest of a Pickpocket*, and scenes of 'lightning' cartoonist Tom Merry.

May 6:
French patent 256,140, *Appareil pour la reproduction chronophotographique de la projection de scènes animées*, to Ambroise-François Parnaland for a combination camera and projector using film perforated with a reinforced central hole between fames and an unusual intermittent where short rods motivated by a central cam interrupt the rotation of two spinning circular disks each with three protrusions. This was the third chronophotographic device of the Parnaland brothers, but the first capable of both taking and reproducing movement.

May 6 (Julian Calendar):
This date is given frequently as the date of the first projection of the Lumière Cinématographe in Moscow, Russia, and is the correct date in the Julian Calendar, which Russia did not abandon until 1928. See 19 May, below, for information on this event in the Gregorian

103 Also exhibiting at the Berlin Trade Fair was the firm of Bartling & Comp. of Leipzig, who had built a projector for Edison-width films, designed and built by Georg Bartling. Two models were offered, one with an electrical lamp house that was ready for immediate delivery, at a cost, complete, of 2,000 Marks, and one with limelight which was ready for sale in August 1896 at a cost, complete, of 1,600 Marks. In 1898 Georg Bartling designed another projector with the locksmith and metalworker Johannes Nitzsche, one of his employees, which led to the founding in Leipzig of the firm of Nitzsche in 1903, offering many models of projector over the next decades. The firm was taken over by Zeiss Ikon AG of Dresden in 1924, but continued to offer machines under the Nitzsche name through the 1930s. See Nünthel 1999.

Calendar used throughout Europe and America, and in this chronology.

May 9:
Paul Theatrograph is given a preview screening at the Empire Theatre of Varieties, Johannesburg, South Africa, by magician Carl Hertz (pseudonym of Leib 'Louis' Morgenstern).[104]

May 10:
Unidentified apparatus, advertised as a Cinématographe opens at the Maison Savoye, Place Saint-Amour, Besançon, France, for one week.

May 11:
Lumière Cinématographe opens at the New Empire Theatre, Cardiff, organized by Felicien Trewey. The shows ran for two weeks, then returning for one week engagements beginning July 6, August 17, and December 14, and for two weeks beginning September 28.

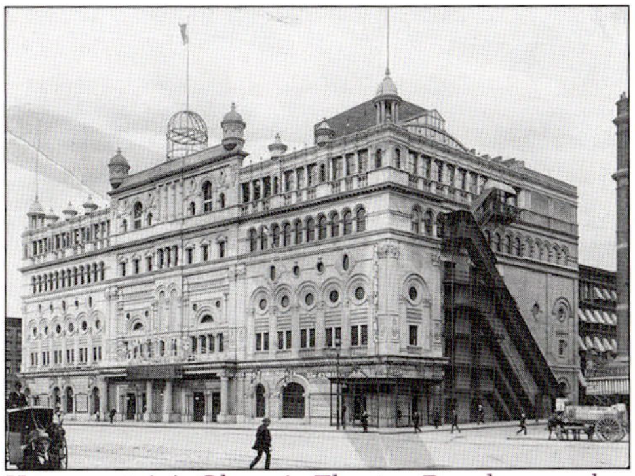

Hammerstein's Olympia Theatre, Broadway and 44th Street, New York City, built of Indiana limestone and opened in November 1895. [Wikimedia Commons.]

☛Paul Theatrograph opens to the public at the Empire Theatre of Varieties, Johannesburg, South Africa, as a presentation of magician Carl Hertz (pseudonym of Leib 'Louis' Morgenstern). Films included: *A Military Parade, The Sailors' Courtship, Street Scenes in London, A Trilby Dance, Highland Dancers.*[105]

☛Latham Eidoloscope opens at Hammerstein's Olympia Music Hall, New York City. Now with an intermittent movement added, the apparatus later also opened at the St. James Hotel near Herald Square, and in summer in a tent on Coney Island.

Films at the Olympia included: *Bullfight, Drill of the Engineer Corps, Whirlpool Rapids Niagara Falls, Fifth Avenue Easter Sunday Morning.*

☛Paul Theatrograph, advertised as an Animatografo, holds a private screening for the press and dignitaries at the Circo Parish in Madrid. The apparatus was presented by Edwin Rousby, and opened to the public on the following day.

☛William Heise, cameraman and filming supervisor for the Edison Manufacturing Company, takes Edison's new portable camera, finished on 6 May, to New York City, initiating the regular production of street scenes and scenic productions outside the Black Maria studio for the first time. *Herald Square*; *A Fountain in Central Park*; and *Elevated Railway Station, 23rd Street, New York* were all filmed on this day.

May 12:
Unidentified apparatus, advertised as 'photographie animée', opens at the Rouen Photo Club, 143 rue de la Republique, Rouen, France, for two days.

☛Edison Kinetoscope automat opens as part of an exhibition of about 60 automats by the Deutsche Automaten-Gesellschaft (DAG) in the Logengebäude at Sögestrasse 16, Bremen, Germany. The exhibition was under the direction of Paul Behrens, general agent of the Stollwerck company, the DAG, and the Deutschen Edison-Phonographen-Gesellschaft.

May 13:
The administration of the Musée Grevin in Paris reports the progress of Emile Reynaud in using his Photoscènographe to combine animated photographs with his painted bands at the Théâtre Optique: "M. Reynaud promises to be ready for presentation to the public by the end of June". In October 1895 with a horizontal film band copied from the apparatus of Étienne-Jules Marey, and by Spring 1896 with a vertical film band, the Photoscènographe took short films later colored and adapted by Reynaud for his Théâtre Optique. His first scene was photographed in April and ready in August 1896, the clowns Footit and Chocolat from the Nouveau Cirque acting a parody of *William Tell.*

☛Lumière Cinématographe demonstrated for the French Ambassador and various dignitaries at the salon of the Hotel Rusia, Carrera de San Jeronimo 36, Madrid, by Lumière operator Alexandre Promio. Public screenings commenced the following day in a basement room of the hotel.

104 Carl Hertz sailed for South Africa on the *SS Norman* on March 28, and gave a performance at sea on the trip. Lumière operator Marius Sestier sailed from Ceylon on the steamer *Polynesien* on 30 August 1896, and gave several exhibitions of moving pictures to the passengers on his way to Sydney, Australia. The great interest in animated pictures, the wide dispersal of Lumière operators, and the portablility of their equipment all argue for other, unrecorded, screenings at sea.

105 After this engagement, Hertz toured with his Theatrograph until 20 July 1896, through Praetoria, Kimberly, Bloemfontein, Pietrmaritzburg, Durban, King William's Town, and other cities in South Africa.

May 14:
The Columbia Phonograph Company signs a contract with C. Francis Jenkins to manufacture and promote the Phantoscope, which Jenkins claimed as his own invention. It becomes the first projection machine with an intermittent mechanism sold outright in America.

☛Charles Moisson and Francis Doublier film *The Coronation of Tsar Nicholas II* in Moscow, Russia, with a Lumière Cinématographe. Seven films were taken. Two days later, at the ceremony of the presentation of the new Tsar to the Russian people, the crowd of a half-million people waiting to see the Tsar and receive a present of a bit of cake, candy, a sausage and a goblet with the Tsar's monogram panicked, and over 5,000 people were killed. Films taken on this occasion were confiscated, along with the Cinématographe itself, and never seen again. No word of the carnage reached the Russian press.

☛Skladanowsky Bioskop opens at the theatre De Harmonie in Groningen, The Netherlands, during a fair, running through 20 May. Films included: *Italienishcer Bauerntanz, Komisches Reck, Boxende Känguruh, Jongleur, Kammarintzky, Ringkampf Sandow-Greiner, Apotheosis (Gebrüder Skladanowsky, Erfinder des Bioscops).*

☛Lumière Cinématographe opens in the east corner of the Salle Poirel, Nancy, France. The screenings ran through June 21.

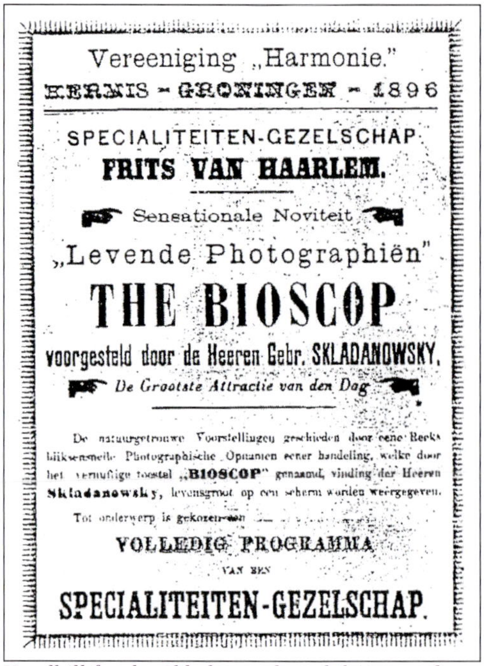

Handbill for the Skladanowsky exhibition at the Groningen fair in 1896.
[Joachim Castan, *Max Skladanowsky, oder der Beginn einer deutschen Filmgeschichte*. Stuttgart, 1995: Füsslin Verlag, p. 95.]

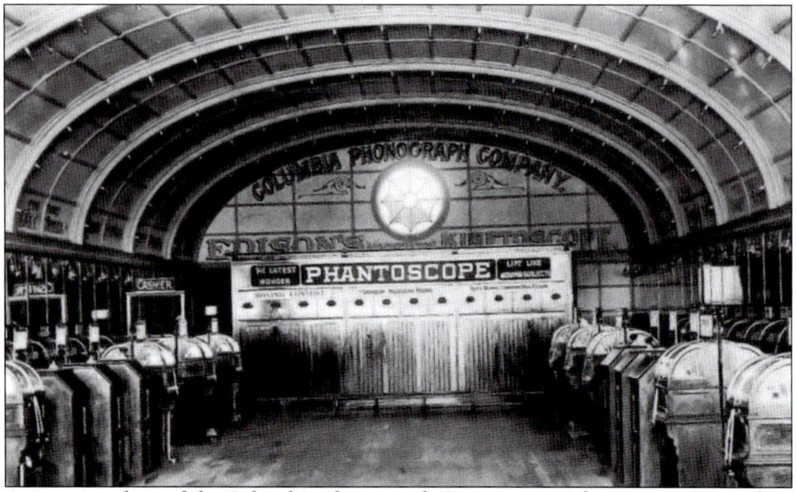

Automat parlour of the Columbia Phonograph Company in Atlantic City, NJ, with the Jenkins Phantoscope projector installed for 12 viewers at a time.
[Charles Musser, *The Emergence of Cinema*, p. 161 (Franklin Institute).]

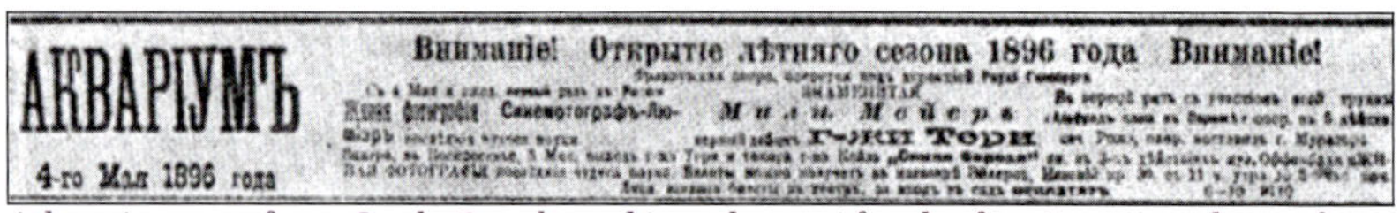

Advertisement from *Sankt-Peterburgskie vedomosti* for the first Lumière show of Charles Moisson and Francois Doublier in Russia at the Aquarium Theatre in St. Petersburg, showing the date in the Julian calendar.
[Bengt Idestam-Almquist (Robin Hood), *Rysk Film*. Stockholm, 1962, p. 15.]

May 15:
Lumière Cinématographe opens to the public at the Hotel Rusia, Carrera de San Jeronimo 36, Madrid, by Alexandre Promio, for the festival of San Isidro, whose slogan was "marvels of the new times". Admission 1 Peseta.

☛Lumière Cinématographe opens at a second venue in Rouen, France, at the Exposition. The showings ran through October 15.

May 16:
An anonymous short story published in the magazine *Pick-Me-Up,* pp. 109-10, on this date features the Lumière Cinématographe. Two people, thinking they are strangers, encounter each other in the darkened Empire Theatre in Leicester Square during the cinema show, only to find when the lights go up that they already know each other.

☛Lumière Cinématographe demonstrated for the press at the Lesser Free Trade Hall, Manchester, overseen by Madame Trewey representing the British concessionaire Felicien Trewey.

May 17:
Lumière Cinématographe opens in the pleasure garden of the Aquarium, a summer theatre in St. Petersburg, Russia, its first appearance in the country. The films were shown before the third act of the play *Alfred-Pasha in Petersburg*. From 19 May, regular screenings were organized in a hall at 46 Nevsky Prospect.[106]

Films included: *Arrivée d'un train en gare, Querelle enfantine, Partie d'écarté, Baignade en mer.*

☛Lumière Cinématographe opens in a side room of the Théâtre in Chartres, France, for the fête des Sauveteurs d'Eure-et-Loire, organized by Alexandre Promio, for two days.

May 18:
Edison Vitascope opens at B. F. Keith's Boston vaudeville house and runs as the principal attraction for twelve weeks. This is the first of more than a dozen openings following the 23 April New York City debut, as the Edison Manufacturing Company, who made the machines by agreement with Raff & Gammon, had considerable difficulty in providing finished projectors, incurring much wrath from states' rights concessionaires eager to exploit the new sensation. The Vitascope was replaced by the Lumière Cinématographe on 10 August.

☛Clément & Gilmer Vitagraphe opens in the minstrel show of Moore & Burgess, St James's Hall, Westminster, London. Available in early 1896, this apparatus had a tubular shutter with diametrically opposed openings, and was in principle a plagiarism of the design of Pierre-Vincent Continsouza.[107]

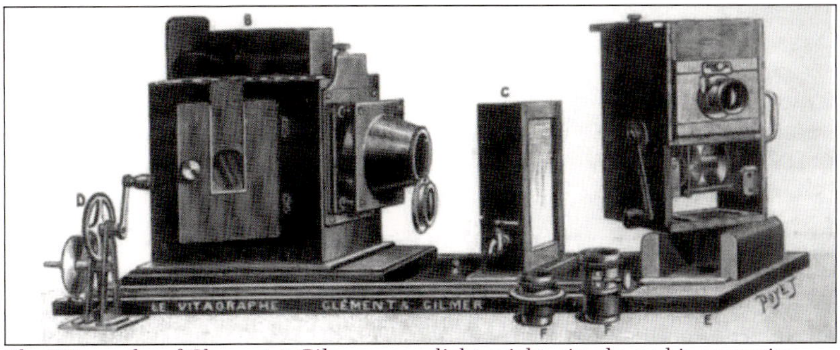

The Vitagraphe of Clement & Gilmer was a lightweight, simple, and inexpensive apparatus which was on the market quickly in 1896, here seen with its lamp house, and a water-filled condenser. At the left a film rewinding accessory and at the right a selection of lenses.
[John Barnes, *The Beginnings of the Cinema in England*, p. 201.]

☛Lumière Cinématographe opens at the Empire Theatre, Birmingham, organized by Felicien Trewey. The shows ran for two weeks, returning for one week on August 31, and again on October 26.

☛Lumière Cinématographe opens to the public at the Lesser Free Trade Hall, Manchester, as an independent exhibition. Madame Trewey oversaw the exhibitions, repesenting the Lumière concessionaire Felicien Trewey, with lecturer Harry Vernon commenting on the films and their special features. The shows ran for four weeks, admission 1*s*. The shows seem not to have been particularly well attended.

May 19:
Lumière Cinématographe opens at 46 Nevski Prospect, St. Petersburg, by the operators Marius Perrigot and Francis Doublier.

☛Unidentified apparatus, advertised as a Cinématographe Américain, opens in the Alcazar auditorium, rue de Godrans, Dijon, France, by the showman Tondu. The screenings ran through June 1.

☛Lumière Cinématographe opens at the Solodovnikov Theatre in Moscow, by Raoul Gunsbourg, an employee of the Russia concessionaire Camille Cerf.

May 20:
Unidentified apparatus, advertised as a Kinématographe Edison, opens at 13 rue du Chapeau-Rouge, Nantes, France, by the exhibitors Carlet, Royé and Hamon. The screenings ran through June 21.

May 21:
Skladanowsky Bioskop opens at the Arena on the Boerenwetering, behind the Rijksmuseum in Amsterdam, The Netherlands, on a Music Hall program organized by Frits van Haarlem.

Films included: *Italienishcer Bauerntanz, Komisches Reck, Boxende Känguruh, Jongleur, Kammarintzky, Ringkampf Sandow-Greiner, Apotheosis (Gebrüder Skladanowsky, Erfinder des Bioscops).*

☛Edison Vitascope opens in Hartford, Connecticut.

106 For those interested, thanks to Yuri Tsivian, the appropriate source for the Russian pioneers such as Timtschenko, Lubimov, Freidenberg, Samarski and Akimov, is the book by Ippolit Sokolov, *Istorija Izabretenija Kinematografia* (Moscow, 1960), which I have not been able to obtain.

107 In late Spring this apparatus went on tour in England with Moore & Burgess during the temporary closing of the St. James's Hall for redecorating.

☛Unidentified apparatus, advertised as an Animatograph, opens at the charity bazaar Cyclopia in Dublin, Ireland, by August Rosenberg of Newcastle-on-Tyne. Running for the week of 19–26 May, Cyclopia was a huge endeavour on behalf of the merging of two Dublin eye hospitals, and included a Dutch village with stallholders in costume, a water chute, X-ray demonstrations and more. The Animatograph used Edison films, and may have been an apparatus by Robert Paul.

Films included: *Zaro, the Tumbling Clown*; *Interior of a Whiskey Saloon*; *Death of Svengali* (Trilby); *The House on Fire*; *The Boxers*; *Scene from Comic Opera*; *Justice in the Far West*; *The Village Smithy*; *The Dentist's Chair.*

May 22:
Unidentified apparatus, advertised as a Kinétographe, opens at 47 rue Alsace-Sorraine, near the town dump, in Toulouse, France. The screenings ran through June 5.

May 23:
Edison Vitascope opens in Atlantic City, New Jersey.

☛Lumière Cinématographe opens at 14 rue Lafayette, across from the Théâtre des Variétés, near the Café des Américains,

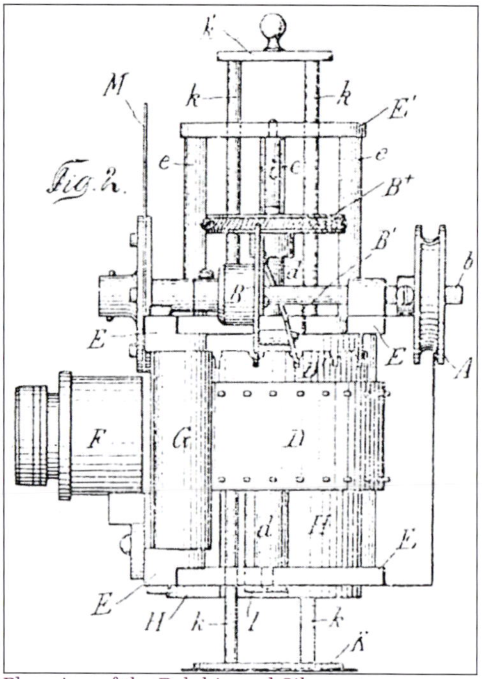

Plan view of the Dalphin and Silvan stereo camera and projector of May, 1896.
[Swiss patent 11755, *Appareil perfectionné pour l'exp0sition à la lumière de rubans pelliculaires sensibilisés et pourla projerction de séries d'images pohotographiques tirées sur fubans pelliculaires* of 23 May 1896, Fig. 2.]

Toulouse, France. The screenings ran through September 15.

☛Swiss patent 11755, *Appareil perfectionné pour l'exposition à la lumière de rubans pelliculaires sensibilisés et pour la projection de séries d'images photographiques tirées sur rubans pelliculaires*, to E. Dalphin and C. Sivan in Geneva, for a reversible camera and projector for anaglyphic stereoscopic films.

May 24:
Lumière Cinématographe opens in the festival hall of the Société Industrielle in Lille, France, for two days.

☛Unidentified apparatus, advertised as a Photographoscope, opens at the Café Monestié, Place du Capitole, Toulouse, France, by the showman Cornu. The screenings ran through June 10.

☛Unidentified apparatus, advertised as an Animetographe, opens in Barcelona, Spain, by a travelling showman. On May 29 it was announced that his equipment had arrived damaged, and the screenings were suspended.

☛Skladanowsky Bioskop opens at the Circus Variété in Amsterdam, as one part of a variety company's programme. A local review thought "living pictures that are reproduced on a screen, certainly was new and interesting".

Films included: Films included: *Italienishcer Basuerntanz, Komisches Reck, Boxende Känguruh, Jongleur, Kammarintzky, Ringkampf Sandow-Greiner, Apotheosis.*

☛The cinema at Unter den Linden 21, Berlin, is sold to the Russian Jussup (Gussem?).

May 25:
Lumière Cinématographe opens at 11 – 14 Kaiser-Wilhelm-Straße, Hamburg, Germany, running in an industrial exhibition of automated machinery organized by Stollwerk & Co. Four thousand people turned up for the show, and security guards had to be called to regulate the sale of tickets. The shows lasted into 1897.

☛Edison Vitascope opens at Keith's Bijou Theatre, Philadelphia, Pennsylvania, where it would run until replaced in late July by the second Lumière Cinématographe to reach America, which in turn ran in the theatre for nineteen weeks.

May 26:
Paul Theatrograph, called an Animatographe, opens in the Theatre at the Zoo, Moscow, Russia.[108]

108 Robert Paul's Theatrograph was momentarily named the Animatographe for its exhibition at the Alhambra Theatre in Leicester Square, London, but the name appears again in many foreign exhibitions of the apparatus, as here. The completely re-designed projector that Paul himself labelled

May 28:

Latham Eidoloscope opens at the Detroit Opera House, Detroit, Michigan, operated by T. L. Diggens. The Opera house manager, Whitney, had purchased the rights to Latham's improved apparatus with an intermittent movement, but business was slow and "the machine is still far from perfection". The shows ran for four weeks, until the Edison Vitascope opened in the same location (See July 1, below). The Eidoloscope then moved to a summer park in Detroit.[109]

☛Lumière Cinématographe previewed at the Casino in Grenoble, France.

☛British patent 11,639, *An improved apparatus for securing, or exhibiting in series, records of successive phases of movement*, to John Nevill Maskelyne, Junior, for his camera and projector using continuously moving film and a series of rotating and fixed lenses as an intermittent, called the Mutagraph. The device was an attempt to reduce flicker on the screen, and came from the imaginative mind of an experienced mechanic and magician who had devised many of his own stage illusions, which occupied the Egyptian Hall, London, from 1873. The Mutagraph was apparently never put on the open market, but was used regularly at the Egyptian Hall from an indeterminate date, probably sometime in 1897, and was also in use at the Woolwich Arsenal for rapid filming of ballistic projectiles until at least 1905.[110]

☛Edison Vitascope opens in New Haven, Connecticut.

May 29:

Unidentified apparatus, advertised as a Cinématographe Américain, opens at the mall of the marketplace at Saint-Vincent Square, Orlèans, France, for the Foire du Mail, by Jacques Inaudi. The apparatus was probably a Cinétograph by Louis Charles, and the screenings ran through 17 June.

☛Lumière Cinématographe opens to the public at the Panorama of the Alps, avenue de la Gare, Grenoble, France. The screenings ran through 1 July.

May 30:

Unidentified apparatus, advertised as a Cinématographe, opens at 2 place de la République, Rouen, France. The showings ran through October 24.

☛Lumière Cinématographe opens at the Sala Sivori in Genoa, Italy. The shows ran until 2 August.

May 31:

Lumière Cinématographe opens in the first floor of 24 rue Nationale, Tours, France, by the operator Vallin.

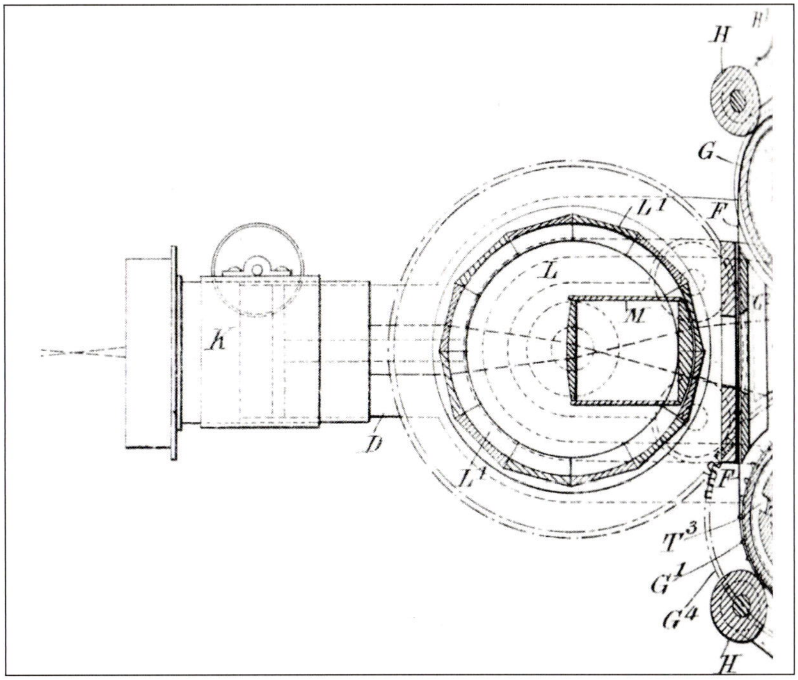

Maskelyne's 'lens drum' (L), placed between the continuously running film (F) and the projection lens (K). An outer drum (L) of concave lenses (L^1) rotated around a fixed inner tube holding two convex lenses (M) and optically corrected the images on the moving film, in a manner vaguely similar to the optics of the Reynaud praxinoscope. [US Patent 11,639, *An Improved Apparatus for Securing, or Exhibiting in Series, Records of Successive Phases of Movement*, of 28 May 1896, Fig. 1, detail.]

the Animatographe was not introduced to the market until Autumn 1897, so all 1896 exhibitions were accomplished with his Theatrograph in one of two models: Mark 1 or Mark 2, as John Barnes has called them.

109 At about this time, due to financial difficulties, the Lathams were forced to sell their business and patents to the Eidoloscope Company, which was dominated by the expanding photographic interests of E. & H. T. Anthony & Co., of New York. It is possible that this exhibition, and those following to the end of the year, were organized through Anthony.

110 The full patent specification was delivered on 1 March 1896. German patent 100559. The machine is not at all like Jenkins' rotating multilens camera of 1894. Somewhat similar devices can be found described by W. Stroud, British patent 4461 of 1898, and by Huet and Daubresse in United States patent 721,954. See also F. Paul Liesegang, 'Konstruktionstypen des Kinematographen,' in *Physikalische Zeitschrift*, 9. Jg., Nr. 22, p. 744.

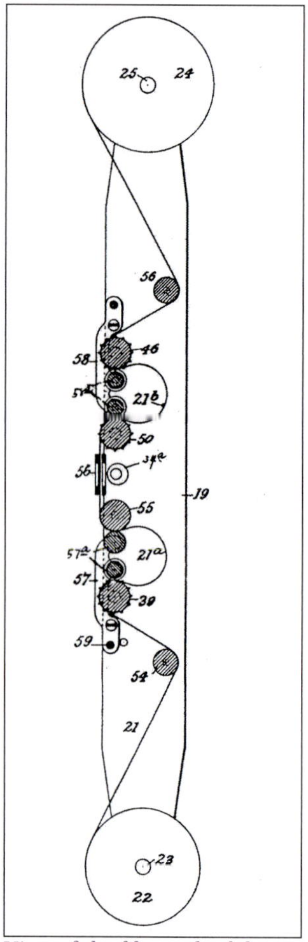

View of the film path of the Eidoloscope in the US patent, showing the 'Latham Loop' at 21a and 21b, much modified from the UK patent of 3 March 1896.
[United States patent 707,934, *Projecting-Kinetoscope*, Fig. 6.]

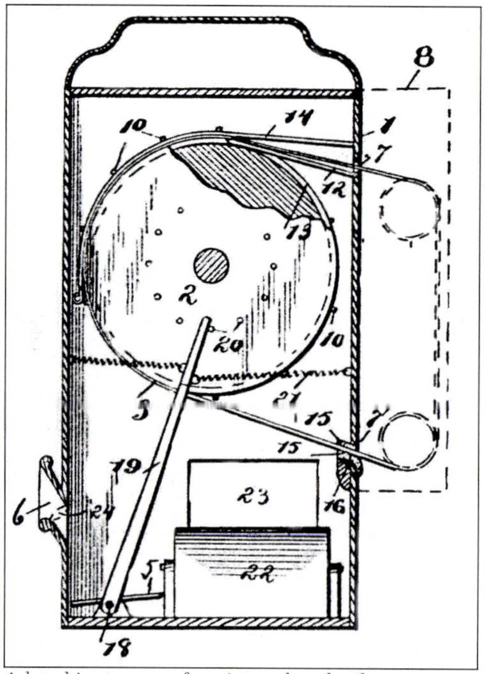

A late kinetoscope for picture bands: the oscillating mirror is at the bottom (5) to the right of the viewing port (6), and is moved by the spring-loaded long lever (19) striking pins on the rotating drum (20). The bands could be of any length, as indicated by the dotted magazine (8). A stereo version was also proposed.
[United States patent 588,916, *Kinetoscope*, of 1 June 1896, Fig. 2.

June 1:
United States patent 707,934, *Projecting Kinetoscope*, to Woodville Latham for the Eidoloscope, the apparatus developed with Eugene Lauste and W. K. L. Dickson which had been operable for well over a year, and had been sold to various showmen, including Vandergrift and D. C. Porter. Although the patent was applied for on this date, it was not issued until 26 August 1902, from which date it was a key document in much infringement litigation over the 'Latham Loop' until overthrown in the lawsuit against the Motion Picture Patents Company on 24 August 1912.[111]

☛Lumière Cinématographe opens at the Empire Theatre, Edinburgh, organized by Felicien Trewey. The shows ran for two weeks, returning for one week on both July 27 and September 21.

☛US patent 588,916, *Kinetoscope*, to Willard G. Steward and Ellis F. Frost for their kinetoscope-type apparatus using a simple oscillating mirror intermittent to reflect to the viewing aperture images running vertically around a large central drum, a sort of re-arranged praxinoscope. Although there is no recorded commercial development of an idea which appeared at a very late date, the patent is interesting both as an indication of the still very fluid state of apparatus development, with no genuinely dominant practise established, and also as a clear attempt to avoid the very widely drawn Edison patents, evidenced in the tentative and general descriptions of the film band, its perforations, and its motive power.[112]

June 2:
Harvard's Cinematoscope opens at the Star Theatre of Varieties, Liverpool. According to

111 It is curious that the application for this US patent is so late, not only following the British (No. 4841 of 3 March 1896, above), and the French (No. 255,171 of 31 March 1896), but also well after many public exhibitions and even several sales of the machine. Even the title of this patent, *Projecting Kinetoscope* is a bit old-fashioned by mid-1896, adding weight to the thought that Latham had been prepared much earlier to patent his apparatus but was somehow hesitant about taking out a US patent, even though that was the greatest potential protection for his machine, his 'loop', and his company. The undercapitalization and financial struggles of Latham and his Lambda Company cannot have been the decisive factor, as obtaining a patent was not inordinately expensive in the US and the company had already gone to the trouble of obtaining, at a distance, both British and French patents. Perhaps distance was here the primary factor. When Latham held a press conference for the Eidoloscope on 21 April 1895, its first public demonstration, an enterprising reporter for the *New York Sun* called Thomas Edison to ask his views on the new marvel and Edison's dismissive remarks ended with a threat to sue if any screenings continued (see above). Did Latham patent his work last in the US, and very late, because of a fear of attracting the lion's attention, in spite of the advantage of priority and protection with an earlier patent? Did he apply for patents three months earlier in Europe, where he was not active, to see what reaction this would provoke from the Edison organization? If so, this would be one of the earliest signs of Edison's power – or potential power – to inhibit and surpress developments in motion pictures, a power that would later be exercised to the fullest with the formation of the Motion Picture Patents Company.

112 The patent is weakened by these attempts, even though Steward and Frost propose correct optical and mechanical principles. They also avoid sprocket rollers, proposing alternative means of tensioning the film band on the drum in both feeding and take-up operations, and make no effort to describe how a long length of images, also proposed, would actually be stored and its pathway maintained. Interestingly, they further suggest that their mirror movement, used as an open device without an enclosing cabinet, could be applied to the close observation of any moving object, like machinery, causing it to have the appearance of standing still when seen in the reflector, as a kind of primitive timing stroboscope.

Cecil M. Hepworth, who examined Fred Harvard's now lost machine, it was very similar to a Wrench Cinematograph. Harvard's machine, used widely by him for regional shows in England, was variously advertised as Harvard's Animatoscope, Cinematoscope, or Cenematoscope.

June 3:
British patent 12,128, *Improvements in apparatus for making or exhibiting zoëtropic and similar pictures*, to Theodor Reich of Vienna, working in London, for a camera and projection apparatus using an intermittent claw mechanism and film 42mm wide perforated on both sides. The device was viable, but Reich did not get the light source correct and his apparatus burst into flames during a demonstration for potential investors; he returned to Vienna without developing the apparatus further.

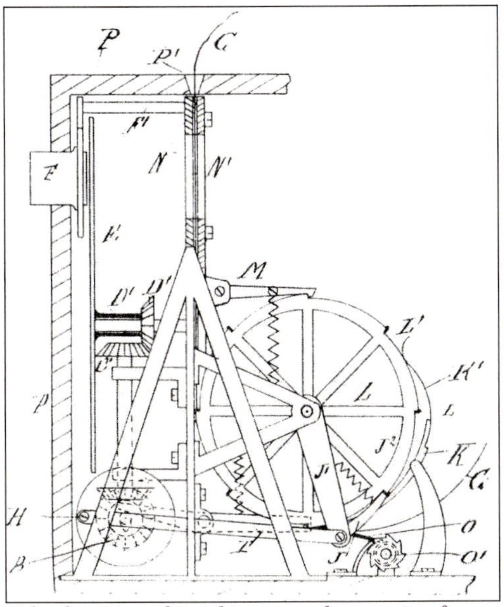

Side elevation of Reich's unusual apparatus for 42mm wide film, which ran over a wide roller (L) moved intermittently by a series of pawls and ratchets mounted below the projection lens (F). [United Kingdom patent 12,128, *Improvements in Apparatus for Making or Exhibiting Zoëtropic and Similar Pictures*, of 3 June 1896, Fig. 2.]

☞Robert William Paul films *The Derby* at Epsom.

☞Lumière Cinématographe opens at 11 rue Thiers, Troyes, France.

June 4:
Unidentified apparatus, advertised as a Cinématographe, opens at 123 rue Saint-Jean, Caen, France, for 13 weeks.

June 5:
Unidentified apparatus, called a Kinétographe d'Edison, gives a private demonstration at the principal theatre in Barcelona, Spain. It evidently did not open at the theatre.

Two films were shown: *Boulevards de Paris avec voitures en mouvement* and *Des gens qui marchent.*

June 6:
Lumière Cinématographe opens at the restaurant Zlatni Krst (Golden Cross), in the centre of Belgrade, Serbia, by the Lumière operator André Carré, assisted by the mechanic Jules Guérin. On 16 June, a special projection was given for King Alexander Obrenovi and the Queen Mother, Nathalie. Admission 1 Dinar, children and military ½ Dinar. The showings ran for 25 days from 4pm to 7pm, with Sunday hours from 9pm to midnight. This event is sometimes cited as May 25, using the Julian Calendar.

Nine films were shown, including *Arrivée d'un train en gare; Baignade en mer; Démolition d'un mur; Marseille, la Bourse; Enfants aux jouets; Paris, Champs-Élysées; Querelle enfantine.*

☞Lumière Cinématographe, along with the Edison Kinetoscope and phonograph, exhibited in the industrial hall of the Exhibition for Electrical Technology and Arts and Crafts in Stuttgart, Germany, presented by Director Wörnle of the Deutsches Automaten Gesellschaft (DAG), aided by Heinrich Mayer, the agent of the DAG for south Germany. The queen of Württemberg attended on the opening day, and the King of Württemberg followed on 24 June, with the Herzogin Wera and the Princesses Elsa and Olga seeing the film of the coronation of the Czar of Russia on 13 July. The public presentations ran every half hour from 9am until 10pm daily, for an admission price of 50Pfg. From 7 July the entry price was reduced on specific weekdays to 25 Pfg., and a higher price was charged from 21 July in the evenings (7pm to 10pm) for ten views of the Russian Coronation. The presentations ran until the exhibition closed on 5 October.

☞Lumière Cinématographe opens at the charity bazaar of a musical society in Mâcon, France, for two days.

☞Cinographoscope of Alexandre and Jules Pipon opens in a hall at the north-

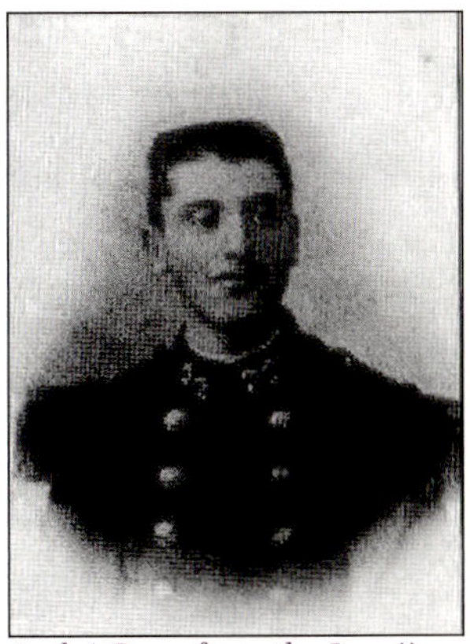

André Carre from the Lumière factory in Lyon was active as a Lumière operator in Turkey, Serbia, Roumania and Croatia. [Michelle Aubert and Jean-Claude Seguin, *La Production cinématographique des Frères Lumière*, p. 407]

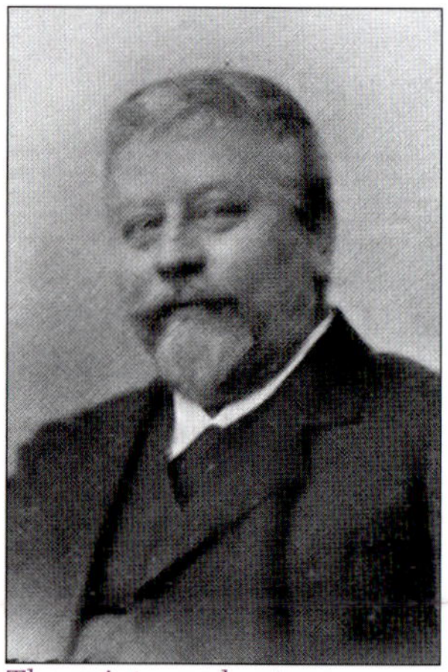

The painter and entrepreneur Lauritz Vilhelm Pacht about 1888. [Danish Film Institute.]

west corner of the terrace at the Casino Frascati, Le Havre, France. The screenings ran through August 2.

☛Phototachygraphe Sanson opens in Rouen, France, by Raoul Grimoin-Sanson.

☛Edison Vitascope opens in a storefront in Providence, Rhode Island, for three weeks.

June 7:

Birt Acres Kineopticon opens in a wooden pavilion in front of the unfinished new City Hall in Copenhagen, organized by Vilhelm Pacht, a well-known painter and entrepreneur who ran a panorama in the city and presented phonograph shows, dioramas, optical illusions, and wax figures. Admision 50 Øre, children 25 Øre. The Danish Royal Family visited the show on June 10. The pavilion was destroyed by fire in the night of June 18, attributed to an act of revenge by an electrician Pacht had fired. Upon receipt of a new apparatus from Acres, the showings resumed on June 30. As a novelty and curiosity amongst his many attractions, Pacht continued to show his Kineopticon on occasional dates through 1899. This showing is widely, but incorrectly, established in film histories as given on a Lumière Cinématographe. See endnote.[113]

☛Lumière Cinématographe opens at 26 rue Saint-Esprit, Clermont-Ferrand, France, for seven weeks.

☛Lumière Cinématographe returns to Chartres, France, at the former warehouse of the Loëns shop, rue de Marché-à-la-Filasse, for two weeks.

☛Unidentified apparatus, advertised as a Kinematograph with 'original Edison-scenes,' opened by August Fuhrmann at his Kaiserpanorama exhibition 'Cairo,' concurrent with the Berlin Trade Fair, but separately located. Fuhrmann advertised in the Trade Fair catalogue (Spezial-Katalog V, Chemie-Photographie-Wissenschaftliche Instrumente) his specialties for Dioramas, Sciopticons and other instruments along with Kinetoscopes and Kinetophones and the unnamed projector is likely to have been an Edison Vitascope.

June 8:

Edison Vitascope opens in Buffalo, New York; Meridien, Connecticut; and San Francisco, California, at the Orpheum Theatre where it remained for three weeks.

June 9:

French patent 257,089, *Appareil pour la reproduction chronophotographique et la projection de scènes animées*, to Ambroise-François Parnaland for a second camera and projector using a claw intermittent movement with his centrally perforated film. This device with its subsequent modifications (of the shutter on 6 August 1896, of the movement on 7 November 1896 [see below], and of the inter-

113 Many available film histories consider this not only the first film showing in Denmark, which it was, but also the introduction of the Lumière Cinématographe to Denmark, which it was not. As far as I can trace the historiography, Jacques Rittaud-Hutinet included Vilhelm Pacht as a Lumière operator/concessionaire in *Le cinéma des origines* (1985; p. 235) on the basis of the work of Jean Béranger, *La grande aventure du cinéma suédois* (1960), who stated that Pacht had purchased a machine from the Lumière brothers on a visit to Paris in April, 1896, and who based his assumption of Lumière apparatus both on the early writing of Ove Brusendorff (1939–41) and on the prominence given in contemporary Copenhagen news reports (*Politiken*, 8 June 1896, for example) of the effectiveness of Pacht's showing of a film of a train entering and then departing a station, which seems to indicate a Lumière film. Rittaud-Hutinet summarized Béranger's information on Pacht in *Le cinéma des origines*, and then repeated it in *August et Louis Lumière. Les 1000 premiers films* (1990; p. 231). This misinformation continues to turn up widely in French literature, for example in Philippe d'Hughes, *Almanach du cinéma, Vol. 1, des origines à 1945* (1992; p. 26).
But Pacht's trip to seek out the new sensation of motion pictures included stops in Berlin and London as well as Paris. Upon his return, Pacht advertised his showings as presenting the 'Kinoptikon', which hints at Birt Acres's Kineopticon, although cinema nomenclature in 1896 was by no means settled. The historian Marguerite Engberg, in her early article 'De Forste Danske Filmforevisninger' in *Kosmorama*, No. 33, February 1958, p. 136, suggests the name was invented by Pacht for its similarity to the 'Panoptikon' on the nearby Vesterbrogade. Gunnar Sandfeld in Den stumme Scene (1966; pp. 10-11) mentions no specific apparatus. Erik Nørgaard in *Levende billeder i Danmark* (1971; p. 20) notes that the Lumière connection is false stating that the Danish Filmmuseum curator Arne Krogh believes the apparatus was English. After further research by Krogh, Marguerite Engberg (*Dansk stumfilm 1 - De store år*, 1977; p. 13) also concluded that the apparatus and films were 'films of Birt Acres and on an Acres projector that he [Pacht] had just brought with him from London'. Rune Waldekranz agrees in *Filmens historia, del 1: Pionjärtiden 1880–1920* (p. 210): 'The projector and films, which Pacht had acquired on his visit in London, came from the English pioneer Birt Acres.' Hauke Lange-Fuchs in his *Birt Acres* (1987, pp. 75–79) comes to the same conclusion, quoting as well Sigurd Evensmo (*Det store Tivoli*, Oslo, 1967, p. 18) as identifying two of the films Pacht exhibited as Birt Acres films, *The Derby and Rough Sea at Dover*.
There is now a further source on Pacht's second machine, which opened on 30 June 1896 after the fire. This replacement was ordered through Acres, who charged his Kineopticon supplier, R. W. Munro Ltd., with a quick extra machine. [R. W. Munro, Works Order Book, October 1895 - January 1896, (June 1896), where an order for two "projecting machines as before, complete" was suddenly stricken out with a "3" replacing the "2".] Pacht's second machine being from Acres supports the evidence that his first was also from the British pioneer. This was an interesting exhibition for Acres; certainly he had the ability to supply a new machine very quickly, and Pacht was able to use it in public on a sporadic basis in his various shows for the next three years. In February 2022, Casper Tybjerg suggested in *Kosmorama* No. 281, based on his new analysis of the films shown by Pacht, that the apparatus in use was a Theatrograph of Robert W. Paul. Based on my experience with this *Chronology*, I remain skeptical of this conclusion but Tybjerg makes several good points and therefore the case remains open at the time of writing.

mittent again on 6 March 1897) is the basis of a successful machine manufactured for both professionals and amateurs.

☛French patent 257,067, *Méchanisme à périodes de marche et d'arrêt applicable aux appareils photographiques projecteurs et à tous autres appareils*, to the Pathé Company for an apparatus with an intermittent movement applicable for photographic projection. The intermittent was derived from one patented by George Willliam de Bedts on 14 January (see above) and the true author of the patent was Henri Joly.[114]

☛Lumière Cinématographe opens in the theatre of the spa Maatschappij Zeebad in Scheveningen, The Netherlands. The concession was taken directly by the management of the spa, and ran throughout the season.

June 10:
Vitagraphe of Clément & Gilmer, Paris, opens at Victoria Hall, Hoe Street, Walthamstow, England, for one night on tour with the Moore & Burgess minstrel show.[115]

☛Lumière Cinématographe reopens on the promenade on the south bank of the river, to the right of the statue of Lamartine, in Mâcon, France. The shows ran through July 13.

June 11:
Kineoptoscope of Cecil Wray, called a Cinetograph, opens in Bradford, England, by the Scientific Entertainment Company of Matlock Bath.

☛Chronophotographe Demenÿ opens in the Central-Sälen, Munich, advertised as 'living photography'. The showings were organized by G. A. Brunnarious & Co., Chronophotograph Lebende Photographien, of Vienna, who had applied to the Munich police headquarters for permision to undertake the projections using a machine by Georges Demenÿ.

☛Skladanowsky Bioskop opens in the pantomime theatre (Pfauenbühne) at the Tivoli Gardens in Copenhagen, running through the month of July. Admission 10 Øre.[116]

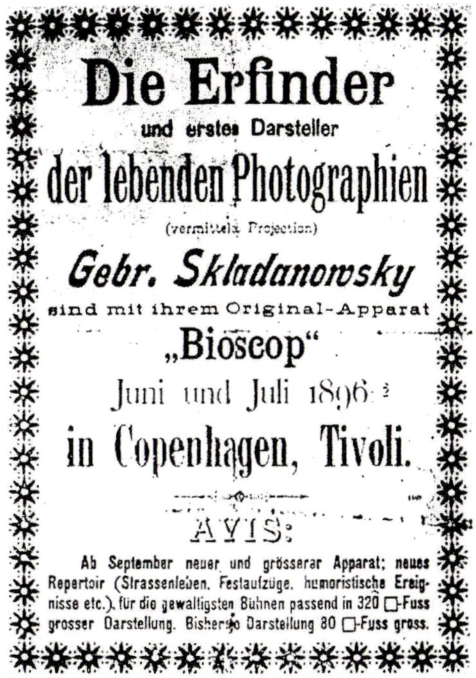

Handbill for the Skladanowsky Bioskop in Copenhagen, June and July 1896.
[Joachim Castan, *Max Skladanowsky*, p. 95.]

Films included: *Italiensk Bondedans*, *Udført af to Born*, *Brothers Milton komisk Reck*, *Boxende Kænguruh*, *Jongler-Produktioner*, *Makkarintzky*, *Russisk National-dans*, *Brydekamp mellem Gruner og Sandow*, *Brødrene Skladanowsky Bioscopets Opfindere*.

June 12:
The Queen of Spain attends a showing of the Lumière Cinématographe in Madrid, organized by Lumière operator Alexandre Promio.

☛French patent 257,178, *Chronophotographe perfectionné réversible projecteur*, to Étienne-Jules Marey for his reversible Chronophotographe which could serve as both camera and projector. Still using 90mm wide unperforated film, the apparatus retained Marey's basic design, modifying the pressure intermittent with an improved cam regulator, and adding a flexible guide before the take-up film spool

114 Laurent Mannoni, in *Le grand art de la lumière et de l'ombre*, p. 405, gives a most vivid illustration of the absolute frenzy of the young world of the cinema in late Spring 1896, which was experiencing a flood of developments that would continue throughout the year: on the day of 9 June 1896, the French patent office in Paris received new applications from representatives of Pathé at 2.00 p.m., from the Benoist & Berthiat Company at 3,00 p.m. (for their projector the Héliorama), from the future founder of Eclair, Ambroise-François Parnaland at 3.20 p.m., (for a reversible camera), and from Adolphe Kohn at 3.40 p.m., (for a projector).

115 There is also a recorded performance of this apparatus in September at the Argyle Theatre of Varieties, Birkenhead.

116. There is an unusual text in an advertisement for this exhibition in *Der Artist*, reproduced in Erik Nørgaard, *Levende billeder i Danmark*, p. 22. The first part of the advertisement is a normal one for such an exhibition, reading in various sized types: "The Inventors / and first presenters / of living Photographs / (by means of projection) / Brothers Skladanowsky / are with their Original Apparatus / 'Bioskop' / June and July 1896 in Copenhagen, Tivoli". Then in very small type at the bottom of the advertisement, under the heading "Advice", the following paragraph is appended, which not only undercuts the presentation currently advertised above, but also gives a unique clue to contemporary exhibition practise: "From September, newer and better Apparatus: new Repertoire (Street Scenes, Festive Acts, Humourous Occurrences, all Originally Taken). But the huge stage is fitted for portrayals of 320 square feet. Representations until now have been 80 square feet in size." These later September screenings at the Tivoli are nowhere recorded in the literature.

to absorb the intermittent tension on the film.

☛Lumière Cinématographe opens in the Barras auditorium of the former Marty mansion in Agen, France.

June 13:
Lumière Cinématographe opens in the Salon Margherita, Gall. Umberto I, Naples, Italy, through June 23.

Films included: *Aquarium*; *(Le) grandiose feste di Belfort*

☛Lumière Cinématographe opens to the public in the Börsensaal of the Gewerbehalle at the Exhibition of Electrical Technology and Arts and Crafts, Stuttgart, Germany. More than 100,000 persons saw the show before its end on 5 October. On some days special barriers were installed to control the crowds and protect the projection booth; the scheduled presentation of physics lectures in the Börsensaal led to occasional cancellations of the screenings, which was "very unpopular with the public". Admission 50 Pfennig.

☛Unidentified apparatus, advertised as an Omnéographe, opens at the Variété Théâtre, Kinderspielgasse 14, Strasboug, France, for two weeks.

☛Lumière Cinématographe opens at 6 rue Jean-Cacques Rousseay, Nantes, France, for six weeks.

☛Unidentified apparatus, probably a Cinétographe Werner, opens at the Fête de Neuilly by Adreien Delille, in Neuilly-sur-Seine, France, for three weeks.

June 14:
Unidentified apparatus, advertised as a Kynématographe, opens in the central pavilion of the Casino, Calais, France, by the operator Bresson. The showings ran through August 6.

☛Lumière Cinématographe opens in the rue du Casino, Vichy, France, for six weeks.

☛Unidentified Kinématographe, probably by G. W. De Bedts, advertised to open in the first-floor annex of the café Tortoni, Boulevard Amiral Courbet, in Nîmes, France. The hall had its own separate entrance on the ruelle Salamandre. Technical difficulties delayed the opening until June 22 (below).

June 15:
Oskar Messter delivers to the Russian showman Rogulin his first practical film projector. Messter's solution to intermittent projection came after he was asked to supply a new condensor lens for a Paul Theatrograph Model 2 by an exhibitor named Kreutzer, who had an engagement at the Wintergarten Theatre. Messter's first experimental machine had a seven-sided Maltese Cross gear like Paul's, but for Rogulin he supplied a single-blade shutter and five-sided Maltese Cross built by the mechanic Horn with a lamphouse bought from Rundorf. Rogulin had advanced part of the purchase price of 1945 Marks and Messter travelled to London to buy Edison films from Maguire & Baucus for the machine. Through the end of 1896 Messter would sell 64 projectors.[117]

☛Edison Vitascope opens in Baltimore, Maryland; Bridgeport, Connecticut; New London, Connecticut; and St. Louis, Missouri, where it was presented immediately after the opera *The Bohemian Girl*, and could be watched either from an outdoor garden or from inside the theatre.

☛Lumière Cinématographe opens at the Empire Theatre, Newcastle, organized by Felicien Trewey. The shows ran for one week, returning again for one week on August 3 and October 19.

☛Harvard's Cinematoscope opens at the Tivoli, Leicester. Fred Harvard was the manufacturer and exhibitor of this machine similar to a Wrench Cinematograph.

June 18:
Paul Theatrograph opens at the Real Coliseu de Lisboa, in the Rua da Palma, Lisbon, Portugal, as the Animatographo Rousby, a presentation of the Budapest electrician Edwin Rousby. The operators in Lisbon were different from those Rousby used in Madrid, with better reviews a consequence. Operators in Lisbon were the actor Francisco dos Santos and the electrician and photographer Manuel María de Costa y Veiga. Films were mostly Edison and Paul titles. Admission 100 Réis.

117 The family firm of scientific and medical instrument makers was founded in 1859 by Eduard Colmar Messter. The firm also supplied specialized optical equipment for stage and variety artists. After the 26-year-old Oskar Messter took over the company, he began in late 1895 to experiment with X-ray equipment. Rogulin, a performer from Moscow, had bought X-ray apparatus from Messter in April, 1896, so he was a repeat customer when he contracted for Messter's first projector on 3 June 1896. Rogulin also re-ordered films from Messter in July and October 1896. Nothing more is known of him.
According to Messter's account books, one projector was delivered in June, 1896, 5 in July, 5 in August, 15 in September, 10 in October, 13 in November and 15 in December. Of these, 8 went to Austria, 6 to Italy, 4 to Russia, and one each to Belgium, Bulgaria, Sweden and Hungary. The remaining 42 were sold in Germany, with the possible exception of one delivered in Germany but meant for The Netherlands. Showmen who bought early Messter cine equipment included the brewery director Schalkau from Mittelhufen, near Königsberg; the actor Schiller from Brünn; the Swiss patent lawyer Kühn; the Brazilian Klein; and the brothers Haak in Stuttgart (two machines).

For the final performance on 15 July, Rousby mounted a grand 'adieu to Lisbon' showing of 30 films.

Films included: *Dança Guereira Pela Troupe Cingalesa, Chineses Fumando ápio, Bailes Parisienses no Carnaval, Uma Oficina de Serralharia, A Célebre Chanteuse Armand'Ary, O Famoso Atirador Buffalo Bill, Baile Egipcio, A Ponte nova em Paris.*

☛Edison Vitascope opens in Portland, Maine; Bergen Beach, New York; and Scranton, Pennsylvania.

June 20:
Cinégraphoscope of Alexandre and Jules Pipon opens at the Fête du Neuilly by the travelling exhibitor Tresel, running through 13 July. This was the second moving picture show at the fair.

☛Lumière Cinématographe opens in the Edison Pavillion at the Exhibition of Saxon Arts and Crafts in Dresden, Germany, by the Deutsch-Oesterreichischen Edison-Kinetoskop Compagnie (DOEKCie), managed again by the actor Richard Ehrhardt. The operator of the apparatus was Jean Lauvernier from Lyon, and the shows ran until 27 September.

June 21:
Edison Kinetoscope opens at 289 Washington Street, Portland, OR, in a saloon run by Joseph Watson, for one week. Six extended machines showed the six rounds of the Corbett – Courtney fight.

June 22:
Lumière Cinématographe opens at the Café-Concert of Charles Aumont during the annual fair at Nishni-Novgorod, Russia. The young journalist Maxim Gorky writes in the local newspaper, "The thirst for such strange, fantastic sensations as it gives will grow even greater, and we will be increasingly less able and less willing to grasp the everyday impres-

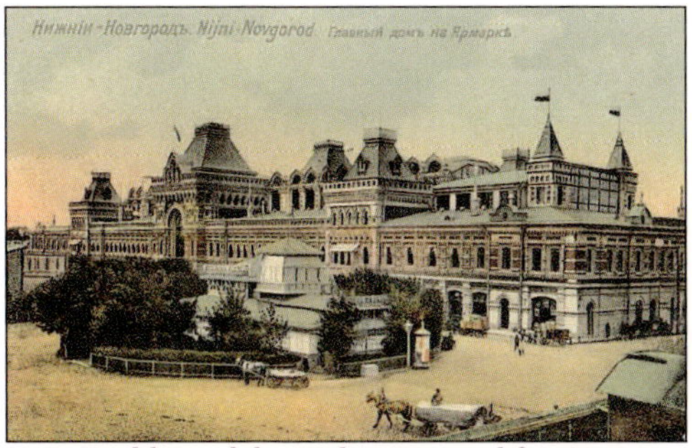

Main Building of the Nishi Novgorod fair in 1903. Dating to the 16th century, the fair sold half of the export goods produced in Russia, attracting large crowds and many entertainers. [Wikimedia Commons.]

sions of ordinary life". Gorky acknowledged that the new films might be "applied to the general ends of science", but was aware that such high purposes were not "to be found at Aumont's where vice alone is being encouraged and popularized".

☛Latham Eidoloscope opens in Boston for one week, shown between the acts of the play *The Yankee Cruiser.*

☛Unidentified apparatus, advertised as a Cinématographe, opens at the industrial exhibition in Moullins, France, for four days.

☛Lumière Cinématographe opens at the Empire Theatre, Sheffield, organized by Felicien Trewey. The shows ran for two weeks and returned for two more weeks on September 7.

☛Unidentified apparatus, advertised as the Cameramatographe, "the marvellous scientific invention similar to the Cinématographe", opens at Oswald Stoll's Panoptikon in Cardiff, Wales, operated by the ventriloquist and pioneer projectionist Lt. Walter Cole. When Felicien Trewey returned to the Empire Theatre in July with his Lumière Cinématographe, Stoll had two film shows running in the city.

Films included: *Butterfly Dance of Loïe Fuller*, a comic boxing match, views of Hampstead Heath.

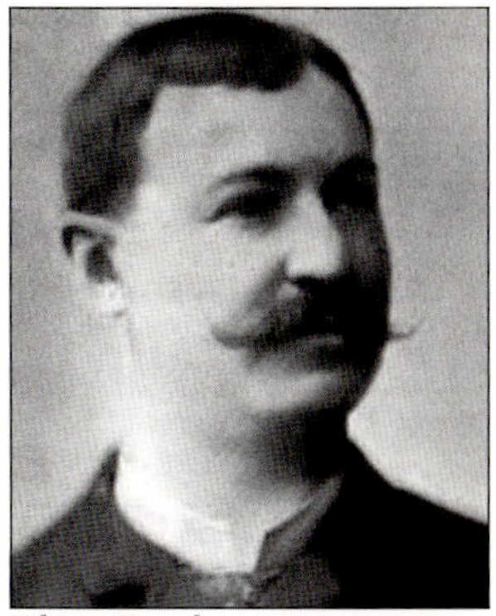

Edwin Rousby was a vaudeville performer and musician (real name Sandör Rosner) from Hungary who traveled widely in the Iberian Penninsula with the Paul Theatrograph. [victorian-cinema.net/rousby]

☛Unidentified apparatus, advertised as a Kinématographe Edison, opens at the Grand Café Tortoni on Boulevard Amiral Courbet, in a hall on the first floor with its own entrance on ruelle de la Salamandre, Nimes, France, by M. Leclerc. The apparatus was probably made by G. W. De Bedts in Paris, and the opening was announced for 14 June, but various technical difficulties delayed the presentation until the 22nd. Further technical problems after this premiere continued until 26 June, when the shows continued without difficulties until 9 July. Admission 1 Franc, with four shows per day at 6, 8, 9, and 10 p.m. From July 3, shows ran every half-hour from 4 p.m. and the admission dropped to 50 Centimes. The apparatus then left for Béziers, where it was installed at 23 des Allées Paul Riquet.

Films included: four views of Paris, *Opéra*, *Madeleine*, *Halles Centrales*, *Champs Elysées*; *La Bourse de Marseille*; *La Danse Serpentine* with Loïe Fuller; *La voiture des chèvres*; *L'arrivée d'un train en gare*; *Le Bain d'une Parisienne, son déshabillé*; and the end of the fourth act of *Madame Sans-Gêne*.

☛Edison Vitascope opens at Coney Island, Brooklyn, New York.

☛Edison Vitascope opens at the 1,544-seat Frothingham Theatre in Scranton, Pennsylvania, where it was augmented by a comedian and a vaudeville show, for six days. O. E. Jones, the theatre's business manager, had sub-leased rights to the apparatus for two counties in Pennsylvania.

June 24:
Lumière Cinématographe opens at the Eden Café, rue Aubert, Epinal, France. The screenings ran through July 5.

June 27:
Lumière Cinématographe press screening in Montréal, Canada, by Lumière operator Louis Minier and his assistant Louis Pupier.

☛Birt Acres films the Prince of Wales, Queen Alexandra, the Princesses Victoria and Maude, Lord and Lady Windsor, and Cardiff's Mayor at the fine Art, Industrial, and Maritime Exhibition in Cathays Park, Cardiff, Wales.

☛Lumière Cinématographe demonstrated for the press in advance of its opening at Keith's Union Square Theatre in New York on the 29th June.

June 28:
Lumière Cinématographe opens at Pilstorp's Summer-Theatre in Malmo, Sweden, which was turned in to a film theatre giving 16 performances a day, through September 27. The exhibition was arranged by the Dane Harald Limkilde, director of the Koncert-palæet in Copenhagen, and operated by the Swedish photographer C. V. Roikjer. The showings were concurrent with an industrial exhibition.[118]

☛Lumière Cinématographe opens to the public at the Palace Theatre, Montréal, Canada, by Lumière operator Louis Minier and his assistant Louis Pupier, running for two months. Local views were also produced during the run.[119]

☛Edison Vitascope opens at the West End summer amusement center in New Orleans, Louisiana, by William T. Rock and Walter Wainwright, to whom Raff & Gammon sold the local concession. The screenings alternated with Paoletti's Concert Band, and ran nightly at 8.30 and 10.00 p.m. through 25 July.

Films included *Skirt Dance* (Cissie Fitzgerald), *The Blacksmith Shop*, *The Kiss* (May Irwin and John Rice), *Milk White Flag – first Act*, *The Waves* (Dover, England).

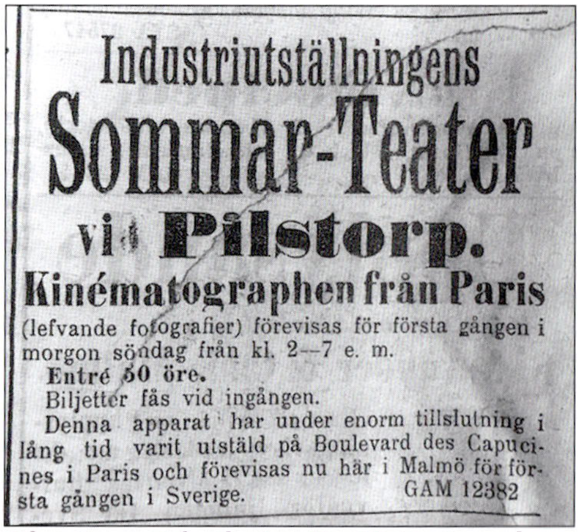

Advertisement for the Lumière Cinématographe in Malmo, its first appearance in Scandinavia. [Martin Andersson, https://www.sydsvenskan.se/2016-06-28/nar-filmen-kom-till-sverige]

☛Lumière Cinématographe opens in the Societetshuset in Helsinki, Finland, by a Russian Lumière operator.

☛Cinomatograph of Alexandre and Jules Pipon opens at the Foire St.-Jean on the Boulevard du Mail in Amiens, France, by the Cottrelle brothers. The screenings ran until 24 July.

June 29:
Lumière Cinématographe opens at Keith's Union Square Theatre, New York City, the first appearance of the apparatus in the United States. The Lumière company signed an exclusive agreement with the Keith Orpheum Circuit, which became the first promoters of the machine in America. A lecturer, Lew Shaw, interpreted the pictures for the audience, and Charles Hurd ran the concession for the Keith circuit. The Cinématographe ran for 23 consecutive weeks, often to standing room only crowds.

Films included: *The Gardener and the Bad Boy*, *Washing Day in Switzerland*, *A Dip in*

118 Limkilde had originally planned to bring the Lumière Cinématographe to Copenhagen, [according to a conversation of the author with Marguerite Engberg, October 1994], but decided instead to open in Malmo when the opportunity of running concurrently with the industrial exhibition there arose. As a result, oddly, the Lumière Cinématographe seems never to have appeared in Copenhagen. See also 7 June 1896 (Pacht) and the entry's accompanying note.

119 Minier and Pupier then went to the Toronto Industrial Exposition, returning to Montréal for the Industrial Exposition in that city, before setting off on a tour of the main cities of Quebec. The Lumière Cinématographe reopened at the Palace Theatre under the hand of Felix Mesguich, on his way back to Paris after working in the U.S., and then returned a third time to the Palace with Lumière operator M. Prosper, who had taken over the Montréal Exposition screenings from Minier.

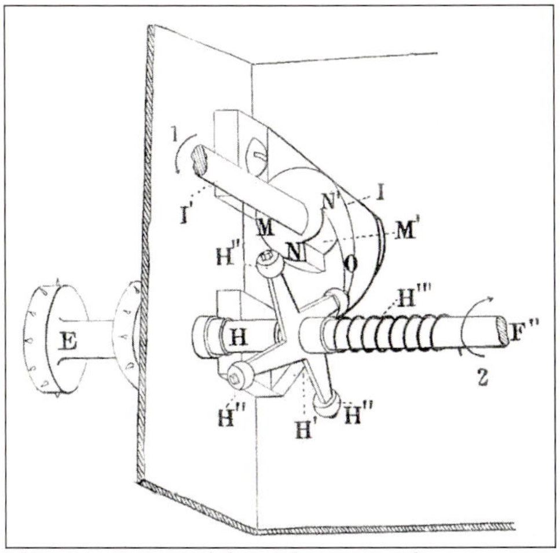

The intermittent of the Héliocinégraphe: rotating counterclockwise, the spur M and its projection M[1] pokes the four-star wheel H, H[1], H[11], moving the sprocket at left one frame at a time.
[Eugène Trutat, *La Photographie animée*, Paris 1899, p. 92.]

the Sea, *Hyde Park London*, *The Cascade (Geneva Exposition)*, *The Messers. Lumière at Cards*, *The Arrival of the Mail Train*, *Charge of the Seventh Curiassers.*

☛Unidentified apparatus, advertised as a Cinématographe, opens in the concert hall in Le Mans, France, for four weeks.

☛French patent 257,582, *Appareil destiné aux photographies animées, dénommé l'Héliocinégraphe*, to the Perret and Lacroix Company for their Héliocinégraphe, a simple machine using toothed sprockets and a four-branched star wheel intermittent, which motivated a large toothed cylinder over which the film was threaded and which was intended to handle the film gently, reducing damage to the sprocket holes.

☛Unidentified apparatus, advertised as a Scénimatographe, opens in the market at Place Michel-Montaigne, Périgeux, France. The screenings ran through September 5.

☛Cinéphotographe of Lépée opens at the Fête de la Braderie on the Place de la République in Lille, France, by the travelling exhibitor Robert Colin. His Grand Théâtre Cocherie remained at the fair until 29 September.

☛Edison Vitascope opens at the 1,200-seat Grand Opera House in Wilkes-Barre, Pennsylvania, for one week. The shows were organized by O. E. Jones, a theatrical business manager from Pennsylvania who had obtained rights to the machine for two counties. Seats were 10 cents, 20 cents and 30 cents for the evening show and 10 cents for children and 20 cents for adults at the matinees.

June 30:
Lumière Cinématographe opens at the theatre Eden Mointagne Russe in Livorno, Italy. The screenings ran through 12 September.

☛UK patent 14,455, *Improvements in Kinetoscopic Projecting Apparatus*, to George Richards for a device where the film was driven by two sprocket wheels, above and below the aperture gate and motivated by a drunken screw intermittent. This was similar to the arrangement already in use in the Rigg Kinematograph and the dispute over the two designs was settled by the Comptroller-General of patents in Rigg's favour.

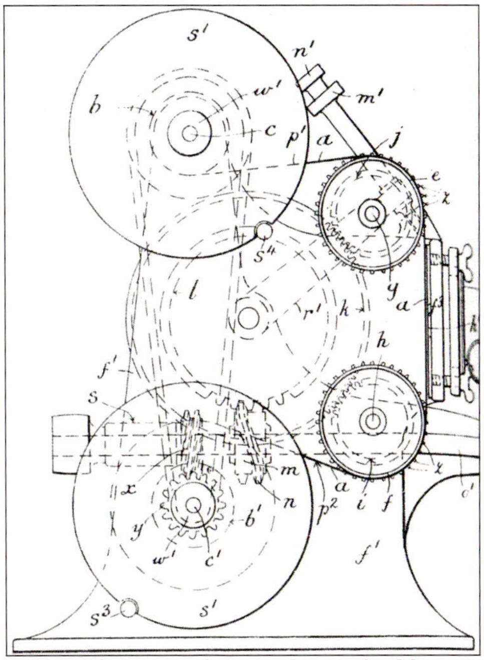

In Richards' patent, the central gear wheel *l* is moved intermittently by the drunken screw at *m* and *n* and in turn moves two sprocket wheels above and below the aperture at *g* and *h*.
[United Kingdom patent 14,455, *Improvements in Kinetoscopic Projecting Apparatus*, of 30 June 1896, Fig. 1, detail.]

July 1:
Edison Vitascope opens in Asbury Park, New Jersey; and in Cleveland, Ohio, where there was no vaudeville presented in summer and Saengerfest Hall was rented by the franchisee A. F. Riesner, who engaged his own small vaudeville company. Musical numbers by the Chicago Marine Band alternated with the film projections, to cover the time needed to re-thread the projector.

☛Lumière Cinématographe opens at the Teatro Milanese, Milan, Italy, for four weeks.

☛Lumière Cinématographe opens in a hall with its own entrance on place du Rolliement, on the first floor of the Café du Théatre, Angers, France. The showings ran until 6 August.

☛Lumière Cinématographe opens in the large hall of the Café Tortoni, Le Havre, France, for two days.

☛Edison Vitascope opens at the Detroit Opera House, Detroit, Michigan.

July 2:
Lumière Cinématographe moves to the first floor above the café of the Mille. Colonnes, 13 place Grenette, Grenoble, France, as show-

ings ended at the Panorama of the Alps. The screenings ran through July 29.

☛Unidentified apparatus, advertised as a Scénimatographe, opens in Montpellier, France.

☛Unidentified apparatus, advertised as a Cinéphotographe, probably an apparatus by Lépée, opens at the New Alcazar, Tours, France, for three days.

☛Cinematographe Joly-Normandin opens in Liège, under the name of Cinematographe parisien, by the editor V. George-Bragner, likely a pseudonym for Henri Piston, a journalist with the French satirical paper *Gil Blas*. The screenings ran until 4 August. The apparatus returned to Liege in September and October after other shows in Belgium.

Films included: *Enfants jouant au bois de Vincennes*, *Vue de la Marne prise à Joinville-le-Pont*, *Un dîner de famille*, *L'Avenue de l'Opera à Paris*, *Le Jardin d'Acclimatation à Paris*, *Deux minutes en wagon*, *Arrivée d'un train en gare*, *Le Jardinier (vue novelle)*, *La leçon de bicyclette*, *Sortie de N. D. des victoires à Paris*, and *Quadrille excentrique du Moulin-Rouge*; *Un dîner de famille*; *Deux minutes en wagon*; *Vue de la Marne prise à Joinville-le-Pont*.

July 3:
Unidentified apparatus, variously advertised as a Cinétographe, Cinématographe, Cénélographe, or Cynétographe, opens at 2 rue de la Terrasse, in one corner of the place de la République, in the former shop of M. Delpeyrat, Limoges, France. The screenings ran through 19 July.

☛Cinégraphoscope of Alexandre and Jules Pipon opens in a hall at the Eldorado, Place de la République and rue du Proc-Epic, Le Mans, France. The screenings ran for three weeks.

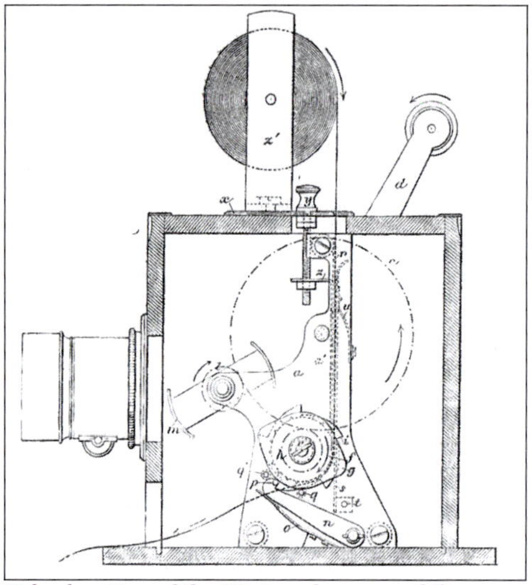

Side elevation of the Cinégraphoscope of the Pipon brothers, also known as the Cinographoscope or the Lapiposcope, showing the ratchet-and-pawl intermittent movement of the apparatus popular on French fairgrounds. [Eugène Trutat, *La Photographie animée*, Paris 1899, p. 89.]

July 4:
Unidentified apparatus, advertised as a Cinématographe, opens at 25 rue Victor-Hugo, Boulogne, France, for four weeks.[120]

☛Unidentified apparatus, advertised as a Cinétographe, opens at the Foire St-Jacques on the Place Sérocourt in Bourges, France.

☛Latham Eidoloscope opens in a storefront in Providence, Rhode Island, replacing an Edison Vitascope which had been exhibiting there for three weeks.

July 5:
Edison Vitascope opens at the Orpheum Theatre, Los Angeles, California, for two weeks.

☛Edison Vitascope opens at John D. Hopkin's South Side Theatre in Chicago, Illinois, where it remained for twenty consecutive weeks.

July 6:
Unidentified apparatus, advertised as a Vivomatógrafo, opens in a salon at calle Florida 344, Buenos Aires, Argentina, by the impresario Enrique de Mayrena (or Magnerans) with a special screening for the press. The daily screenings that followed were available from 11.30 through 23.30, and ran through the end of August, with a programme of new films after 12 August. Lumière films were shown.

Films included: *Llegada de un tren a la estación*; *Las vistas del mar*; *Plaza de la Vendome, Paris*; *Hyde Park de Londres*; *Puente de Blackfriant, Londres*; *Combate de box*. From 12 August: *Llegada de un batteau-mouche en el Sena*; *Trafalgar Square – Londres*; *Danza egipcia*; *Dúo acrobático*; *Escena en un café*; *Baile del Moulin Rouge*, *Hyde Park*, *Les Halles*, *Jugadores de naipes*, *El graben en Viena*; *Boulevard Haussman*; *El regador reegado*; *Serpentina con colores*; *Coronación del zar Nicolás*.

☛Thomas Blashill, chief architect for the London County Council, accepts the plan to build a Theatrograph building at Earl's Court for their forthcoming Indian exhibition organized by Imre Kiralfy. Responding to correspondence of 8 June 1896, Blashill authorized the construction of a small "brick buiding situated on the north side of the Panorama building", consisting of "a small hall 26ft. 6 ins. By 21 ft. with a superficial area of 556 ft. and a seating accommodation for 54 persons. On

120 The Boulogne debut of the Lumière Cinématographe was prior to this date through an apparatus travelling with a circus.

the south side is a small ante-room through which the public are admitted to the hall, and on the other side of the room, is a room which is not at present used for any purpose". The exhibitor, apparatus, and films accommodated by this space are unknown.

July 7:
Lumière Cinématographe demonstrated for the Czar and Czarina with the Imperial Court, St. Petersburg, Russia, by Alexandre Promio.

☛Unidentified apparatus, called a Kinematograf, opens in the Koncertpalæet, Copenhagen, Denmark, by exhibitor Charles Marcel. Although advertising a Paris cinématographe, Marcel showed only Kinetoscope films, evidently prints actually made for the Kinetoscope as the images were poor and unclear, and the show was severely criticized by the local press. As a result the showings lasted only two days.

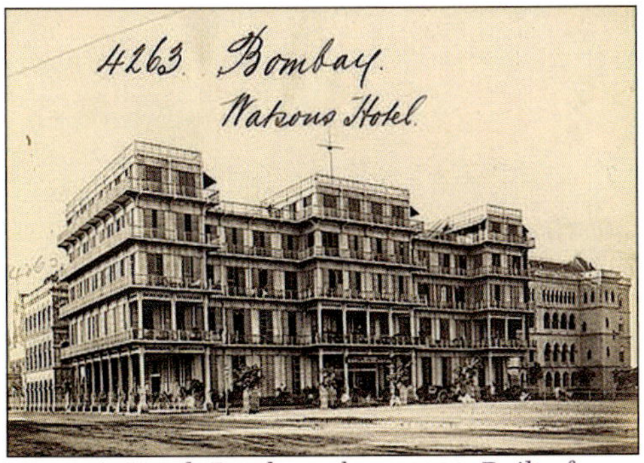

Watson's Hotel, Bombay, about 1890. Built of English materials in 1867–69, the iron frame building still stands but in poor condition and is now occupied by flats and businesses. [Wikipedia, 19th century postcard, public domain.]

☛Lumière Cinématographe opens at Watson's Hotel, Bombay, India, by Lumière operator Marius Sestier, a Lyonnais chemist and Lumière agent who was employed to take the Cinématographe to India and Australia.

☛Maxim Gorky publishes a short story, 'Revenge' in the *Nizhny Novogrod Newsletter* in Nizhny Novogrod, Russia. Watching the Lumière film *Repas de bébé*, a prostitute becomes depressed by seeing on the screen the kind of family life she will never enjoy.

July 8:
Lumière Cinématographe opens at 57 rue de Ouvidor, Rio de Janiero, Brazil.

Films included *Sapeurs pompiers*, *Danse du ventre*, *Combat de coqs*, *Arrivée du train*, *Scène intime*.

☛Lumière Cinématographe opens at the Café Massy, rue Poitevin, Arras, France.

☛Lumière Cinématographe opens at the Café Marguerite, rue Mayenne, Bourges, France. The showings ran through July 30.

July 9:
Lumière Cinématographe opens at the Casino, Vichy, France, for two days concurrently with showings of the Lumière apparatus at the Theatre.

☛Lumière Cinématographe opens at the Teatro Minerva in Venice, Italy. The shows ran through 28 August.

July 11:
Demenÿ Chronophotographe opens at Carl Gabriel's Panoptikum, Neuhauserstraße, Munich, Germany. Admission 1 Mark, children and military half price. The exhibition was arranged by Eugène Dupont, the Lumière representative in Vienna, who initially refused Gabriel a Cinématographe but then sold him the Demenÿ apparatus and also provided him with an operator.

Films included: *Ein Herausbrausender Eisenbahnzug*, *Eine Schlangendompteuse*, *Ein Kettensprenger*, *Das Aufziehen der Hauptwache.*

☛Cinéphotographe of Lépée opens at the fair in Rochefort-sur-Mer by the travelling exhibitor Henri Chabot. His Thêatre Chabot ran until 30 July.

☛Edison Vitascope opens at the Teatro Baralt in Maracaibo, Venezuela, by the entrepreneur Luis Manuel Méndez, who had purchased rights for Venezuela and Colombia from Raff & Gammon in New York. Manuel Trujillo Durán, a local photographer, operated the machine.

Films included: *The Monroe Doctrine*, *Serpentine Dance*, *Sioux Ghost Dance*, *Umbrella Dance*, others.

☛Unidentified apparatus, advertised as a Cinetografo and possibly a Kinétographe of Méliès, Korsten and Reulos, opens at the Teatro Fenice in Trieste, Italy, by the Milanese impresario Giovanni Cantagalli from Milan. This first day was an invitational show for the press, with the public opening on July 12. Lumière films were used. The screenings ran until 23 August.[121]

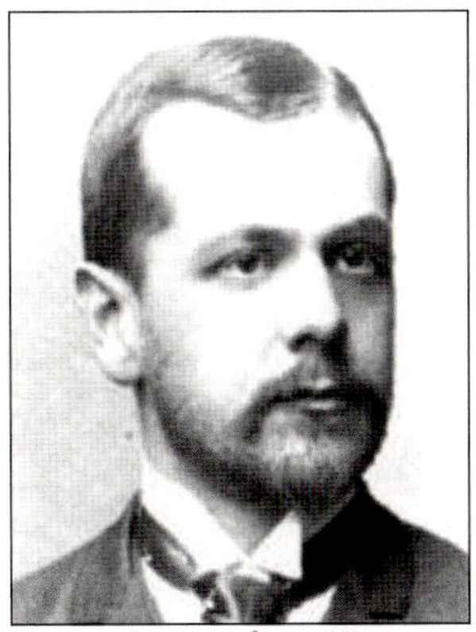

Eugène Dupont from Vienna, a pioneering agent and entrepreneur in cinema [victorian-cinema.net, public domain]

121 The Cronofotografo of Georg Hengl from Vienna was the second film show to reach Trieste, in January, 1897. The Lumière Cinématographe arrived at the Teatro Fenice on 16 June 1897.

Films at the press demonstration included: *Forgerons, Dance sur scène, l'arrivée d'un train à la Ciotat, Baignade en mer, Place de l'Opéra.* Three additional films were added when the show opened to the public, including *Une sortie d'église, Carneval à Nice,* and *Modella.*

July 12:
Cinéphotographe of Lépée, called a Sinéphotographe, opens in La Roche-sur-Yon by the exhibitor Eugène Chabot. His Théâtre Chabot ran until 18 July.

July 13:
Lumière Cinématographe opens at the Crystal Palace, London. The long run at the Regent Street Polytechnic had just closed, and the machine and films were transferred to South London, running at least through August.

☛Lumière Cinématographe opens at the Empire Theatre, Swansea, Wales, organized by Felicien Trewey. The shows ran for one week, returning for one weak on each of 10 August and 12 October.

July 14:
Lumière Cinématographe opens at the Bombay Novelty Theatre, Bombay, India, by Lumière operator Marius Sestier. The screenings lasted until 15 August, admission 1 Rupee.

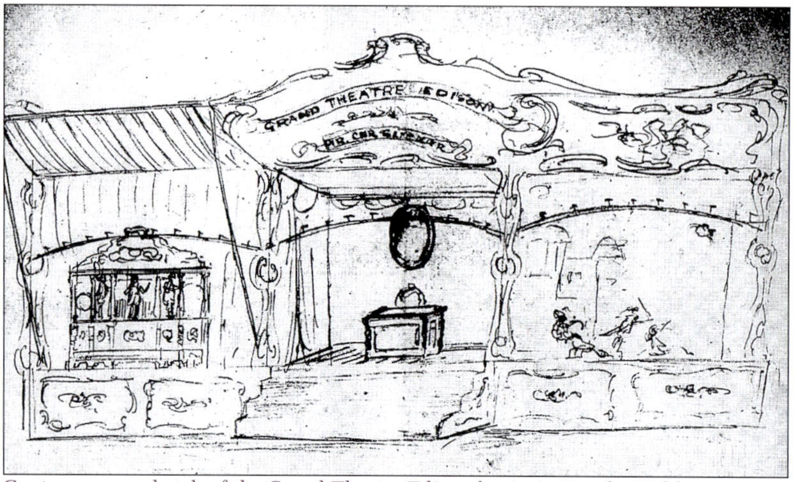

Contemporary sketch of the Grand Theatre Edison by A. A. Van der Velde. [Harm Nijboer and Asing Walthaus, *George Christiaan Slieker, 1861–1945*, Leeuwarden, 1995, p. 28.]

July 15:
Foersterling Biomatograph, called Edison's Ideal, opens in the Grand Théâtre Edison of Christiaan Slieker on the Wilhelminaplein in Leeuwarden, The Netherlands. This was the first travelling movie show in The Netherlands. Slieker advertised his apparatus as "Edison's Ideal, Living Pictures ... Discovered by the Messrs. A. and L. Lumière". Admission to the front, 50 Cents [20 seats] and to the rear, 25 Cents [96 seats]. A former showman of panoramas and other entertainments, Slicker quickly moved to Alkmar, Nijmegen, and other Dutch cities.[122]

☛Lumière Cinématographe opens in a new space at the side of the Maison Binda, avenue Alsace-Lorraine, Bourge-en-Bresse, France. The shows ran until July 30.

☛Lumière Cinématographe opens at the Casino in Karlovy Vary, western Bohemia (now Czech Republic), for one week. The screenings were organized by Goldschmidt, an agent for Eugène Dupont, the Lumière concessionaire. Admission 1 Gulden (two Austrian Crowns), except on Wednesdays and Sundays when the price was discounted to 50 Kreutzer. Each film began with a still image on screen, which subsequently began to move.

122 H. O. Foersterling & Co. Of Liepzigerstraße 12, Berlin, was amongst the first companies in Europe to offer projection equipment for sale in 1896, advertising in the trade journal *Der Comet* as early as 2 May. Their machine weighed 50 kg complete and was offered as particularly good for travelling showmen. They offered a full outfit including films for a price of 1250 Marks, at a time when a Messter Kinematograph sold for 2000 Marks. The machine they offered was copied from Pierre-Victor Continsouza in Paris. While Foersterling was active in the film business for only a few short years, disappearing from view in 1901, his apparatus was used widely across northern and central Europe before that date.
Importantly, more than just selling their equipment, the firm created and packaged with their apparatus an advertising and promotional concept which was used by showmen along with their machine in a clever attempt to associate their presentations of the Foersterling apparatus with that of the leading manufacturers of the day, particularly Lumière, Edison, and Messter, while at the same time not quite infringing directly on the copyrights or trademarks of those companies. Many exhibitors at this time in both the large cities and in the countryside devised a wide variety of strategies to associate themselves with Lumière or Edison, especially if they were not using a genuine Cinématographe or Vitascope. The most common of these strategies was simply re-naming the machine in their advertisements, which is one practise that has led to such a confusing array of nomenclature in early cinema. But Foersterling originated the first centrally-devised campaign to deliberately 'position' their apparatus in relation to the most widely known and heralded equipment no matter whom the individual operator was, regardless of the specific location in which he was exhibiting, and no matter what country he was working in. The Foersterling promotional concept was successfully used across many national borders in Europe and, equally, across language barriers, by a number of separate showmen. It is the first known presentational campaign of the young new medium.
All entries in this chronology but one noting the use of the H. O. Foersterling & Co. Kinematograph were previously either unidentified or mis-identified by authors writing local or national histories of early cinema. In their early sales literature, Foersterling also called their projector the Biomatograph, a name advertised only to the trade.

Films included: *La sortie des usines, Le déjeuner de bébé, Arrivée d'un train à La Ciotat, La partie d'écarté, Maréchal Ferrant, Baignade en mer*, others.

☛Kinematograph of R. Lechner & Co. opened in Vienna by the local photographic manufacturer. The program included films of the coronation of the Czar in Moscow, street scenes in both Moscow and Vienna, and a serpentine dance in color.[123]

July 17:
Paul Theatrograph opens at the Teatro-Circo Principe Real in Porto, Portugal, as the Animatographo Rousby. The variety program included comedians and Spanish dancers; the show opened two days after closing in Lisbon, as a presentation of Edwin Rousby. Lumière films were shown.

Films included: *Desembarque na Foz, Uma Queimada no Campo, A Praça da Concórdia, O Derby, Os Bombeiros, Una Gegata em Henley, Um Vapor no Canal de Calais, Recreios Infantis, O Ferrador, O Grande Canal de Veneza, Os Cavalos Saltadores, O Boulevard do Italianos, O Atelier Fotográfico, Uma Disputa.*

☛Unidentified apparatus, advertised as a Cinéphotographe, opens in a room with its own entrance to the street on the first floor of the Café Continental, Nantes, France, for one week.

July 18:
Unidentified apparatus opens in the Casino in the Church Square of the Bohemian spa Mariánské Lázn (now Czech Republic).

Films included: *The Umbrella Dance, Burning of the Maid of Orleans, A Card Game, A Boxing Match, Life and the Bustle of the Opera Place in Paris, The Central Food Market in Paris, The Serpentine Dancer (Mlle. Loïe Fuller of Paris).*

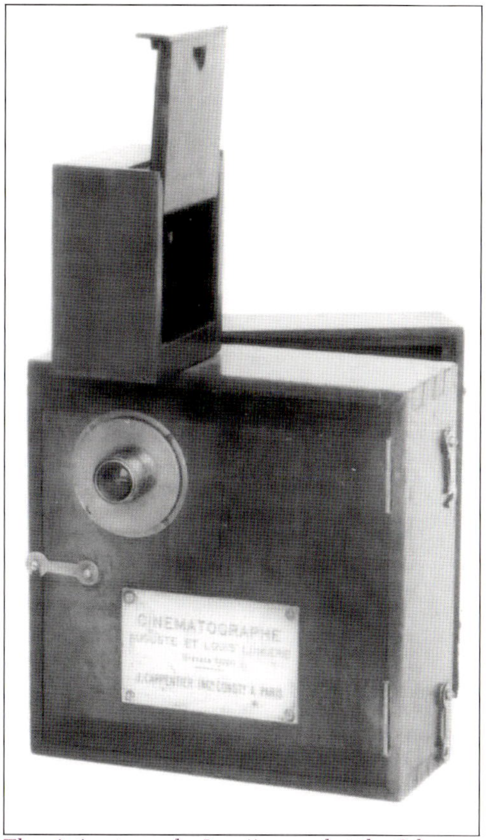

The cinématographe Lumière used at the Odeon Theatre in Buenos Aires, which survives in the collection of the Museo Municipal del Cine. [Guillermo Caneto, et. al., *Historia de los Primeros Años del Cine en la Argentina, 1895–1910*, Buenos Aires, 1996, p. 27.]

☛Cinographoscope of Alexandre and Jules Pipon opens at 28 rue Gambetta, Saint-Étienne, France, for three weeks.

☛Unidentified apparatus, advertised as a Kinematograf Edisona, opens in the Resursy Obywatelski, at Krakowskim Przedmieciu 64, Warsaw, Poland. The stately columned suburban mansion was a meeting place of the elite of the city. The apparatus was most likely a Biomatograph of H. O. Foersterling and Co., Berlin.

☛Edison Vitascope opens in Winnipeg, Canada, by Richard A. Hardie, who had travelled throughout Manitoba in 1892 with an Edison phonograph.

☛Lumière Cinématographe opens in the Salón Rouge on the calle 25 de Mayo, Montevideo, Uruguay. The screenings ran until January 1897.

Films included: *vistas en que aparecen el mar, el derrumbe de un muro, el almuerzo de un bebé, la salida de los obreros de una fábrica.*

☛Lumière Cinématographe opens at the Odeon theatre in Buenos Aires, Argentina, operated by the journal editor Eustaquio Pellicer and organized by the theatre's impresario, Francisco Pastor. Unusually, Pellicer is said to have bought the Cinématographe and 25 films in Paris for 4000 Francs at the request of Pastor.[124]

Films included: *El taller de herrería; Niños en el Jardin de las Tullerías; La salida de operarios de una fábrica; La Plaza de la Ópera; El interior de una estación de ferrocarril; La Plaza de la estación de San Lázaro.*

123 Earlier in July, a new sensation had opened in Vienna, the Aschanti Village in the Tiergarten; the organizer was Lyon native Ferdinand Gravier, who shortly after the opening added film screenings to his attraction with another Cinématographe. In the same month of July the first apparatus was offered for sale in Vienna, by the manufacturer R. Lechner, who advertised both cameras and projectors called 'Kinematograph' for sale. He also offered the Cinétographe of the Werner brothers of Paris for sale.

124 The Cinématographe used for these performances is now in the Museo Municipal del Cine in Buenos Aires.

July 19:
Paul Theatrograph opens at the Empire Theatre, Middlesbrough, by James Fioni, for three weeks.

July 20:
Lumière Cinématographe opens at the Empire Theatre, Newport, Wales, organized by Felicien Trewey. The shows ran for one week, returning for an additional week on 24 August.

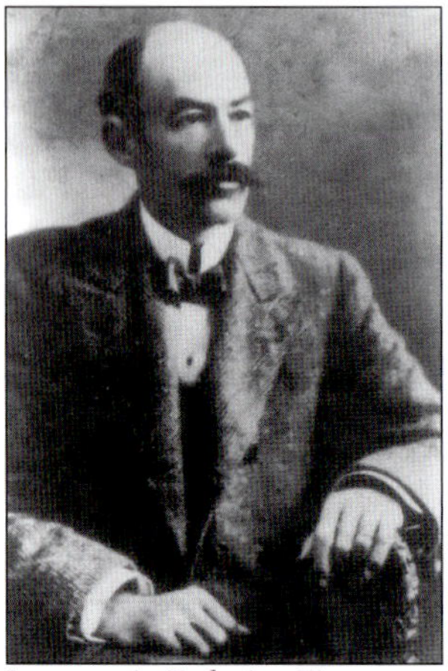

Impresario Federico Figner, who introduced both the Edison Kinetoscope and the Vitascope to Buenos Aires, Argentina. [Guillermo Caneto, et. al., *Historia de los PrimerosAños del Cine en la Argentina, 1895–1910*, Buenos Aires, 1995, p. 29.]

☛Edison Vitascope opens at Ontario Beach, Rochester, New York, by E. M. McLaughlin.

☛Demenÿ Chronophotographe opens at the Teatro Gerolamo in Milan. The screenings ran through 3 August.

☛Edison Vitascope opens at calle Florida 168 in Buenos Aires, Argentina. The impresario Federico Figner organized the screenings, which were held in conjunction with his six Kinetoscopes and demonstrations of X-rays.

July 21:
Edison Vitascope opens at West End Park, Ottawa, Canada. Originally a promotion for the Ottawa Electric Railway, this hugely successful show organized by Edison's agents George and Andrew Holland, and hosted by travelling magician and showman John X. Green, was extended for months and attracted up to 1,600 persons a night.

☛Birt Acres, assisted by Cecil M. Hepworth, gives the first Royal Command Performance of moving pictures on his Kineopticon, when a program is screened at Marlborough House on the eve of Princess Maud's wedding. The show included footage of the Prince and Princess of Wales, and the Princesses Victoria and Maud at the Cardiff Exhibition. One film caught the Prince of Wales scratching his head, and when later shown publicly caused a major furore in the press, with Acres called a "photographic fiend".

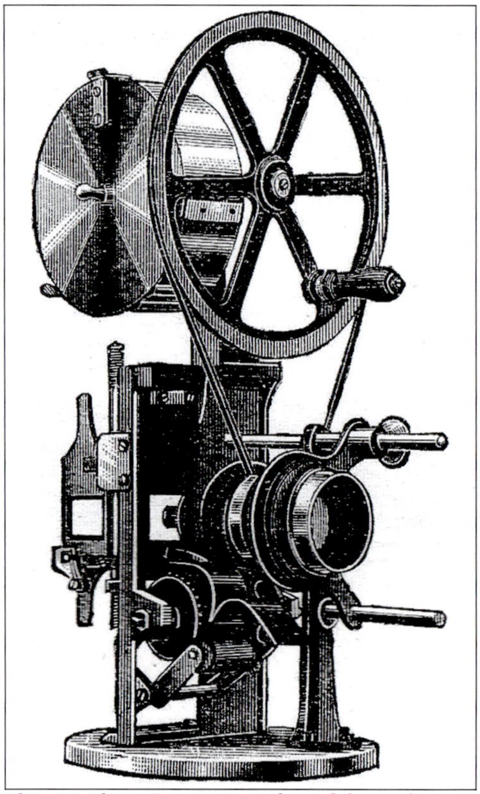

The Rosenberg Cinematograph, widely used in the United Kingdom. [Henry Hopwood, *Living Pictures*, London 1899, p. 163.]

☛British patent 16,080, *Improvements in or relating to apparatus for taking, viewing, or projecting photographic images in rapid succession*, to William Routledge, Augustus Rosenberg, and William MacDonald for Routledge's projector and camera called the Kineoptograph, later also appearing as Rosenberg's Cinematograph. A popular machine, it remained on the market for several years.

☛Unidentified apparatus, advertised as a Paris Cinématographe, opens in the Kristallsalon of the Victoria Theatre, Tivoli Gardens, Stockholm, by Charles Marcel. The shows ran through 31 July and Edison Kinetoscope films were shown; the exhibition was not considered successful, and the apparatus was replaced by the Skladanowsky Bioskop on August 1.

July 22:
Birt Acres films the wedding procession of Princess Maude and Prince Carl of Denmark, from the lower end of a sparsely decorated St. James Street, London.

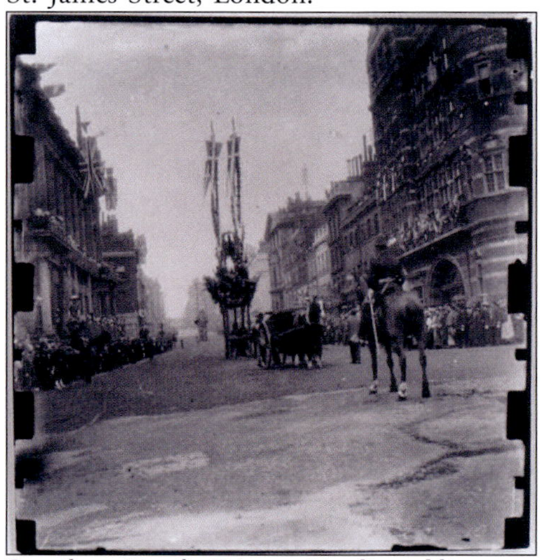

Crowds waiting for Princess Maud's wedding procession at St. James Street, London. Photograph by Birt Acres on a Frena still camera prior to operating his Kinetic Lantern.[Birt Acres photograph, 1896, Collection Deac Rossell.]

July 23:
Cinographoscope of Alexandre and Jules Pipon opens at Place de la Halle aux Blé, Rennes, France, by the travelling exhibitor Tresel. The showings lasted until 11 August.

☛Cinographoscope of Alexandre and Jules Pipon opens at the Musée Oller, 28 Boulevard des Capucines, Paris. The Cinographoscope ran until April 1897, when it was replaced by the Biographe français of Léar (Albert Kirchner), which then ran through the end of October 1897. The Musée Oller was wholly contained within the Olympia Theatre, but had its own separate entrance on the Boulevard.

☛Unidentified apparatus, advertised as a Vidamotógrafo, opens at Avenida No. 32, Donostia-San Sebastian, Spain, as the first cinema show in the Basque country.

Films included: *La coronación de zar en Muscú*

July 25:
Unidentified apparatus, advertised as Le Kinematograph de Paris, opens in the Casino in Karlovy Vary, western Bohemia (now Czech Republic). The shows occupied the same room where the Lumière Cinématographe was exhibited earlier in the month. Admission 50 Kreutzer, children 20 Kreutzer.

Films included: *The Arrival of a Train*, *The Serpentine Dancer* [in color], street scenes of Paris, others.

July 26:
Chronophotographe Demenÿ opens to the public at the Teatro Gerolamo, piazza Beccaria 8, in Milan, Italy. The shows ran daily through 9 August.

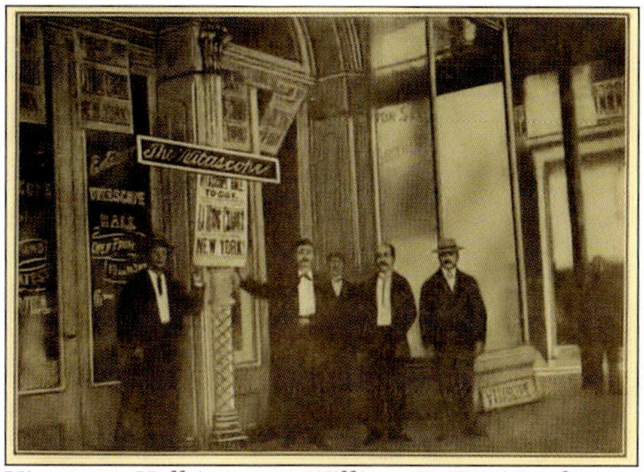

Vitascope Hall in 1896. William T. 'Pop' Rock is standing at the right, Walter Wainwright is one of the two men to his left.[1896 photograph, published in *Moving Picture World*, July 1916. Photographer unknown.]

☛Edison Vitascope re-opens at the Academy Theatre in Milwaukee, Wisconsin, by M. M. Hixon and J. H. Wollam, as part of a bill including a variety company and a dramatic company performing the play "Uncle Dan'l", presented twice daily at 2 and 8 p.m. Admission 10, 20, 30 Cents. Hixon and Wollam were a doctor and a mechanic, respectively, from the small town of Dupont, Ohio, who had bought the exhibition rights to the state of Wisconsin from Raff & Gammon. Their shows ran two weeks in Milwaukee, returning for another two weeks in September and one in November. The opening engagement was advertised as "First Milwaukee exhibition wizard Edison's preternatural invention, the Vitascope".

☛Edison Vitascope opens at 623 Canal Street, New Orleans, Louisiana, in a storefront renamed Vitascope Hall, by William T. Rock and Walter Wainwright. The pair had exhibited the Vitascope the previous month at the West End summer park. Rock had bought the Louisiana rights from Raff & Gammon for $1,500. The screenings ran through September 30. Admission 10 Cents.[125]

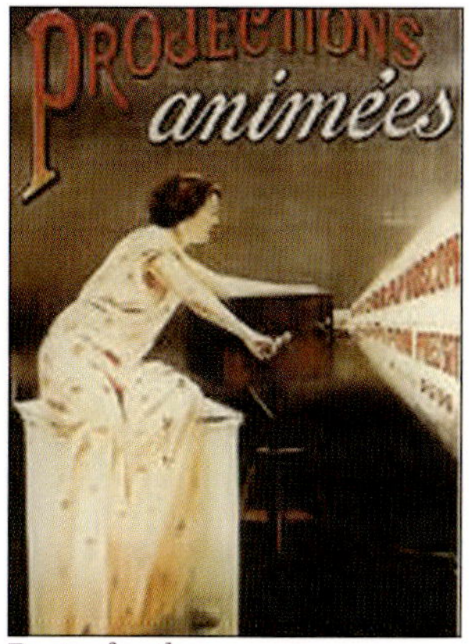

Poster for the Cinographoscope of the Pipon Brothers. [http://cinematographes.free.fr/pipon]

☛Lumière Cinématographe opens in Kansas City, Missouri.

July 27:
Lumière Cinématographe opens at Keith's Bijou Theatre, Philadelphia, Pennsylvania, replacing an Edison Vitascope. The apparatus, which was the second Lumière machine to reach America, remained in continuous exhibition at this theatre for nineteen weeks.

July 28:
Lumière Cinématographe opens at the Theatro Odeon, Buenos Aires, Argentina, by the Lumière operators Max Glücksmann and Eugène Py.

125 A number of promotions accompanied this run. From 29 August through 30 September a coupon for free admission to any child accompanied by an adult ran in the local paper. From 12 August different programs of films were advertised for morning and evening screenings. Although there was frequent mention of the crowds and the success of the screenings in the local newspaper, Wainwright and Rock clearly had to work for it; they had advertised their states' rights for sale back on 3 July: "Vitascope State Rights and Territory for Sale. Engagements, etc., For particulars apply Wainwright & Rock, 923 Canal Street".
In 1897, William T. 'Pop' Rock joined with J. Stuart Blackton and Albert J. Smith to form the Edison Vitagraph Company, which in 1898 became the American Vitagraph Company, one of the most important early American film production firms. Rock was President and handled film sales and exhibitor relations, while his partners made the films. Walter Wainwright became Vitagraph's special London agent, supplying the newest British and Continental productions for distribution by Vitagraph in the United States.

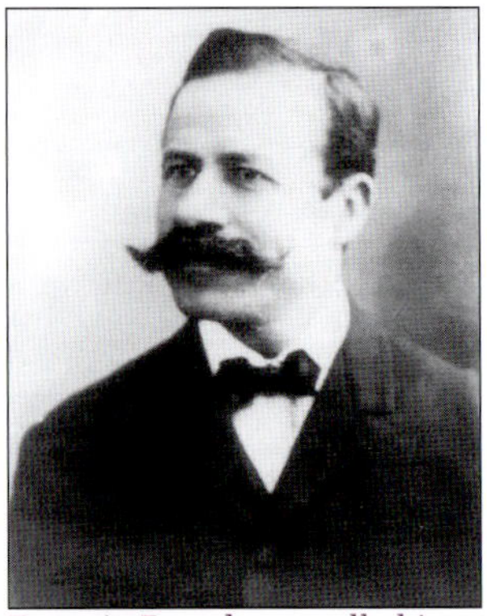

Eugenio Py, who travelled in Argentina with a Lumière Cinématographe from 1896 to 1901, before becoming a theatre owner. [Guillermo Caneto, et. al., *Historia de los Primeros Años del Cine en la Argentina*, Buenos Aires, 1895–1910, 1995, p. 36.]

☛Cinographoscope of Alexandre and Jules Pipon opens in the market fair, Boulevard du Mail, Amiens, France, by the brothers Cottrelle. The screenings ran through 24 August.

July 31:
Unidentified apparatus, called a Cinétograph, opens in the Stadt-Casino, Basel, Switzerland. The showings ran through 6 August; admission 1 Franc, children 50 Cents.

Films included: *Les pompiers (Sauvetage), Bateaux sur la Seine, Danseuse Serpentine, Leçon de bicyclette, Buffalo-Bill, Le Nègre danseur, Les Halles de Paris, Le Sacre du Czar, Couronnement de la Rosière, Homme serpent, Promenade au Bois de Boulogne, Arrivée de Chemin de fer.*

☛French patent 258,523, *Appareil pour tirer et projeter des photographies de scènes animées*, to Joseph Zion and Eugène Gautier for their Mouvementographe, a combination camera and projector using a drunken screw intermittent and a 120° shutter linked directly to the crank axis.

August 1:
The Théâtre Robert-Houdin in Paris advertises for the first time a special motion picture show 'made by the direction of the Théâtre', i. e., Georges Méliès.

☛Lumière Cinématographe opens at 21 ruc Carnot, Poitiers, France.

☛Paul Theatrograph opens in the Small Salon of Bern's variety hall, Stockholm, Sweden, where the music hall singer Annette Teufel, the 'Viennese Soubrette', was the main attraction. The film shows were given by an Englishman from Berlin.

☛Cinématographe Joly-Normandin opens in the dance hall, rue du Casino, Royan, France, for four weeks, using films of Eugène Pirou.

Films included: *L'arroseur arrosé; Assaut de boxe entre deux champions de Joinville; Une séance de boxe; Jardin d'acclimatation; Leçon de bicyclette; Sortie de l'église Notre-Dame-des-Victoires; Champs-Elysées près de l'arc de l'Étoile; Quadrille au Moulin-Rouge; Séance de canne.*

☛Unidentified apparatus, probably a Biomatograph or Edison's Ideal by Hermann O. Foersterling, presenting 'Living American life-size photographs', opens in the private Helenów entertainment park in Lódz, Poland. The exclusive park had high entrance fees that attracted only the merchants and elite of the city as its patrons, and on 19 August the show moved to the more popularly attended Weaver's Guild in the city center. The shows used Edison films and ended on 24 August.

Films included: *A Fire in Chicago, Oriental Dance in the Harem, A Barbershop Scene, Sioux Indian War Dance*, and *Streets of Large Cities with the Multicolor Crowd.*

☛Lumière Cinématographe opens at 16 avenue Victor-Hugo, Valence, France, for two weeks.

☛Skladanowsky Bioskop opens at the Kristallsalon of the Victoria Theatre in the Tivoli Gardens, Stockholm, Sweden. The screenings ran until 15 September. On 2 and 3 August the Skladanowskys began shooting their second series of films with their second camera, which used a Maltese Cross intermittent, in front of the Novilla House and in Djurgärden in Stockholm, using professional actors from the theatre company, but as this camera used

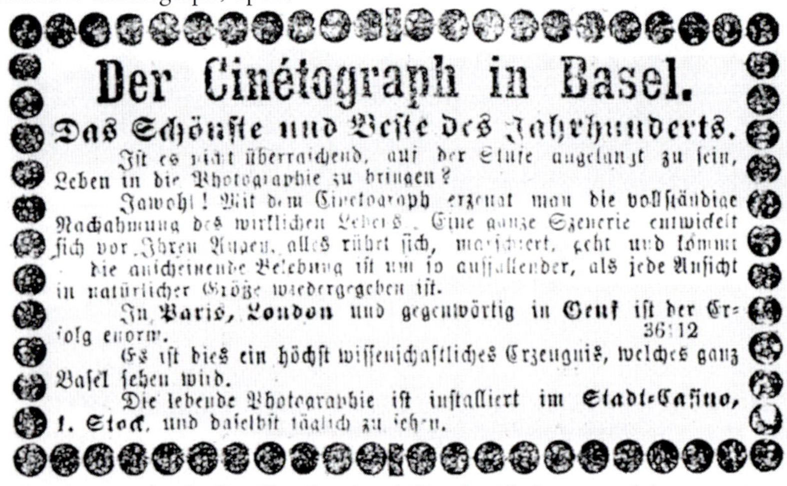

Advertisement for the first film showings in Basel, with the name of the apparatus in its headline.
[*Nazional-Zeitung*, 31 Juli 1896, from Paul Meier-Kern, *Verbrecherschule oder Kulturfaktor? Kino und Film in Basel 1896–1916*, Basel, 1993, p. 11.]

63mm wide film (Eastman negative film of 126mm width cut in two) the new films could not be used on the Bioskop projector until later in the year when a new model was built.[126] Films shown were again the Wintergarten programme of November 1895.

Films included: *Italienishcer Bauerntanz, Komisches Reck, Boxende Känguruh, Jongleur, Kammarintzky, Ringkampf Sandow-Greiner, Apotheosis (Gebrüder Skladanowsky, Erfinder des Bioscops).*

☛Lumière Cinématographe opens at the photographic studio Maurice, in Biarritz, France, in the Basque country. Due to the traditional gathering of European aristocracy in the resort, a special screening was arranged on 26 August of the films of the coronation of the Czar in Russia.

Films included: *Llegada de un tren, Demolicion de un muro.*

August 2:
Paul Theatrograph opens at the Teatro Filodrammatici, Milan, Italy, advertising some films in color. The shows ran through 20 August but received a poor review in the local paper, *La Sera*, which suggested the theatre was very large, and the images were too small.

☛Lumière Cinématographe opens in Aix-les-Bains, France.

☛Lumière Cinématographe opens at Bastille Day celebrations held at the Tivoli del Eliseo, Mexico City, as the closing attraction on a long bill of festivities. The operators were Fernand Bon Bernard, holder of the Lumière concession for Mexico, Venezuela, the West Indies and Guiana, and his technical director, Gabriel Veyre.[127]

☛Cinématographe Joly-Normandin opens in Rethel, France, for three weeks by André Milhès, using films of Eugène Pirou.

Films included: *Arrivée et départ d'un train de la banlieue de Paris; Défilé d'artilleurs; Une nourrice; Une rue de Vienne; Le train en gare; Danse serpentine; Les plongeurs soudanaise; Le Brûlers d'herbes; Les Laveuses; L'Ombrelle qui tourne.*

August 3:
Unidentified apparatus, advertised as a Paris Cinématographe, opens in Sundvall, Sweden, by Charles Marcel, for three weeks.

☛Paul Theatrograph, called Animatograph, opens at the Bijou Opera House, Minneapolis, MN. The gala opening organized by Theodore L. Hays used English films, including *Persimmon Winning the Derby Race*. The operator was George D. Strong.[128]

August 5:
Cinematographe Joly-Normandin opens at the Restaurant du Cercle in Spa, Belgium, under the name of Cinematographe parisien, by the editor V. George-Bragner, likely a pseudonym for Henri Piston, a journalist with the French satirical paper *Gil Blas*. The screenings ran for two weeks, and Queen Marie-Henriette and Princess Clémentine received a private screening during the run.

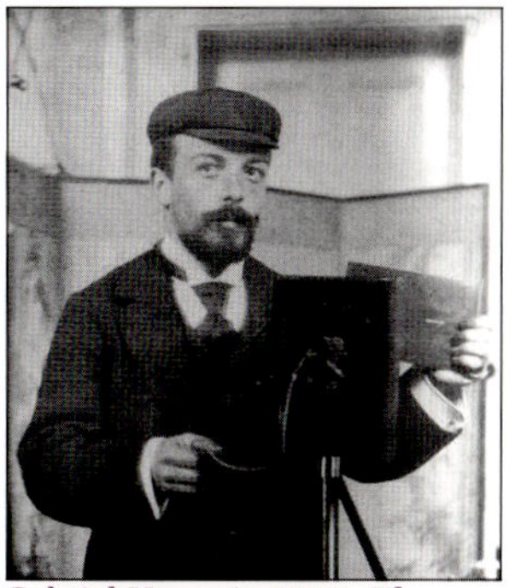

Gabriel Veyre in 1898. The Lumière operator, a chemist from a small village south of Lyon, was active in Mexico, central America, Canada, Japan and China. [Philippe Jacquier and Marion Pranal, *Gabriel Veyre, Opérateur Lumière*, Lyon, 1996, p. 107.]

August 6:
Lumière Cinématographe demonstrated for an invited audience including President Porfirio Díaz, his family and friends, and members of his Cabinet, at the President's residence in the Castle of Chapultepec, Mexico City, organized by Lumière operators Gabriel Veyre and Fernand Bon Bernard.

☛Unidentified apparatus, advertised as a Kinetografo, opened by Manuel Galindo and the company Eliseo-Express in the Calle de los Jardines, Bilbao, Spain. Advertisements for this grand show began three days

126 The last performance of the Skladanowsky Bioskop was on 30 March 1897, the day Max Skladanowsky's trade license expired. Applying for a new licence from the authorities in Berlin, where he had moved from the suburb of Pankow, Skladowsky was refused a license as the city bureaucrats considered there were already too many film licenses in circulation. No exceptions could be made. Skladanowsky thus also has the dubious, and once again forgotten, distinction of preceding Georges Méliès, D. W. Griffith, and others as the earliest cinema pioneer abandoned and discarded by the fast-growing film industry he helped launch.

127 Sources differ on the name of Lumière concessionaire Bernard, some calling him Fernand Bon Bernard, and others naming him C. J. van Bernard.

128 Strong, a veteran artist with travelling shows, later entered the film business and was known as 'Dad' or 'Daddy' Strong. After this opening, he recalled using the Paul apparatus "in a little old building next door to Sawyer's saloon on Nicollet Avenue ... [where they] could squeeze 200 people at a time in that old place, but it was a continuous show – continuous from 10 o'clock in the morning until 10, 11, 12 o'clock at night, just as long as they'd keep on coming". See Kane, Lucile M., and John A. Dougherty, 'Movie Debut: Films in the Twin Cities, 1894–1909', in *Minnesota History*, Vol. 54, No. 8 (Winter, 1995), pp. 347.

earlier, as the Kinetografo was the star attraction of an 'artistic-recreational museum' containing dioramas, an Edison phonograph, photographs, and other attractions. The machine broke down on opening day, which was attributed to the operator 'not previously having tried' his apparatus. New films were shown every day, with the morality of some pictures being criticized as scenes "that can happen in another country freer than ours". The spectacle then travelled around villages on the Bay of Biscay.

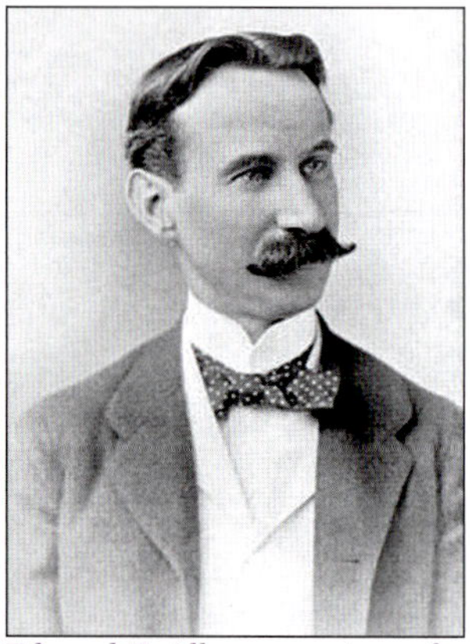

Edward F. Albee, a partner of B. F. Keith and a major Vaudeville impresario, about 1894. [Wikipedia Commons. Public Domain.]

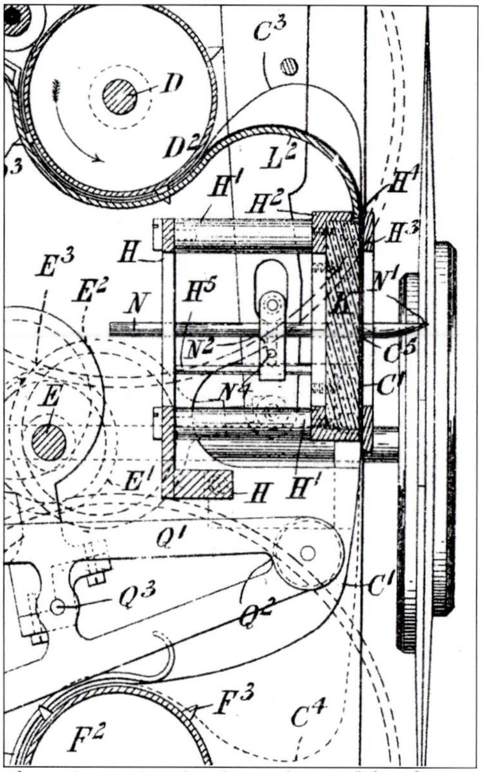

The reciprocating claw intermittent of the Blair apparatus, in this case not just pulling down on the film but also acting as a simple pin registration to hold the film precisely during its time at the aperture. The pins are at N, with the tapered end at N^1 and the film runs from C^3 to C^1. [United Kingdom patent 17,505, *Improvements in or relating to Photographic Cameras or Film-exposing Apparatus*, of 7 August 1896, Fig. 2, detail.]

August 7:

British patent 17,505, *Improvements in or relating to photographic cameras or film-exposing devices*, to the European Blair Camera Company and Thomas Henry Blair for a combination camera and projector called the Vivontoscope, which used a claw intermittent run from an eccentric, and had tapered steadying pins to hold the film precisely during its exposure in the gate.[129]

August 8:

Lumière Cinématographe opens in Sao Paulo, Brasil.

☛Cinématographe Werner opens in the pub Korte Hoogstraat, Boven Passage, Amsterdam, The Netherlands. Organized by Michel and Alexis Werner, the screenings ran for three weeks. Music was provided by Edison's Phonograph; admission 50 Cents. Special matinee performances for children were given on Wednesdays, admission 25 Cents.[130]

☛Lumière Cinématographe opens in a hall on the Place de l'Hôtel de Ville, Angoulême, France, where the Banque National de Paris is now situated. The screenings lasted through 19 October; admission 1 Franc.

☛Unidentified apparatus, advertised as Photographies animées, opens at the Champ de Foire in Boulogne-sur-Mer, France.

129 Two earlier British chronophotographic equipment patents from the Blair company are No. 12,458 of 27 June 1895, and No. 13,284 of 16 June 1896. A history of the work and inventions of Thomas Henry Blair and his Blair Camera Company, the important European Blair Camera Company has yet to be written. Although Blair was hotly competitive with the Eastman Dry Plate Company in the manufacture of mass-market box and folding cameras in the 1890's, Blair's importance here is as a successful early manufacturer of flexible celluloid-based film stock that was practical for motion picture work. W. K. L. Dickson of the Edison laboratory changed to Blair film stock almost exclusively for motion picture experiments in 1892, due to the superior quality and consistency of their material after experiencing many delays and technical problems with Eastman celluloid films. Blair ultimately developed a semi-translucent, frosted-surface stock especially suited for use in the Edison Kinetoscope, where the film image was viewed by transmitted light from underneath the running film, and Blair provided all of the film stock for Kinetoscope viewing prints.

European Blair was the first company to offer flexible celluloid stock in England, and provided film to Robert W. Paul, Birt Acres, and many other pioneers in the U. K. and on the Continent, including the Lumière company. With the introduction of film projection, however, Blair was unable to manufacture a satisfactory clear-based film stock: in use, his emulsion quickly separated from the celluloid base. The American company also suffered management changes in late 1895; as a result, the Edison Manufacturing Company shifted all of its film stock purchases to Eastman Kodak in mid-September 1896. Meanwhile, Blair's folding cameras experienced difficulties in the market, as they had produced designs which, while optically fine, had to avoid infringing on Eastman-controlled camera patents. By the end of the century, the Blair Camera Company and its associated concerns were in deep financial trouble, and George Eastman successfully concluded an arrangement in early 1900 with their financial backer, Darius L. Goff, a textile manufacturer in Pawtucket, Rhode Island, to purchase all of the Blair photographic interests for shares of his new concern, Kodak, Limited. Part of the final contract stipulated that T. H. Blair remain out of all business connected with photography for a span of years, and the exploitation of the Vivontoscope ceased as a result.

130 The Werner brothers returned to Rotterdam in early 1897 with a set of films of the Czar visiting Paris, *Intocht van het Zcarenpaar te Paris*.

☛Cinéphotographe Lépée opens at a fair in Abbeville, France, by the exhibitor Robert Colin. His Grand Théâtre Cocherie ran for four days until 5 August.

☛Lumière Cinématographe opens in Ravenna, Italy, for four days.

August 9:
Unidentified apparatus opens in the Moor Hall of the Grand Hotel, Brno (Brünn), Moravia (now Czech Republic), by showman Albert Schiller from Vienna. Only Kinetoscope films were shown, and the screenings ran until 23 August.

Films included: *A Scottish Dance*, *At the Barber's*, *On the Beach*, *The Umbrella*, *A Duo of Dancers*, and a fictional scene of a fireman saving the occupants of a burning house.

☛Cinéphotographe of Gabriel Lépée opens at the market in Tours, France, by showman Eugène Chabot, for two weeks.

☛Lumière Cinématographe opens at the Teatro Minerva in Venice, by Giuseppi Filippi.

August 10:
Lumière Cinématographe replaces the Edison Vitascope at B. J. Keith's Boston Theatre and runs for 22 weeks, the third Cinématographe to reach America. Although theatre manager E. F. Albee complained that the Vitascope had been doing poor business in the prior several weeks, this change was part of Keith's exclusive arrangement with the Lumière Company.

☛Paul Theatrograph opens at the Grand Theatre, Stockton, Britain, by James Fioni, for three weeks.

August 11:
Unidentified apparatus opens at the Hsu Gardens, Shanghai, China, as part of a variety bill that included a magician, an acrobat, and a juggler with fireworks.[131]

☛Jenkins Phantoscope opens at the Great Northern Roof Garden in Chicago, USA, intensifying its competition with the exclusive Vitascope presentations of John D. Hopkins at his vaudeville theatre. Hopkins's screenings were already undermined by a nearby Phantoscope exhibition in a phonograph parlor, but this second Phantoscope exhibition was a failure. As Hopkins wrote, "one of our electricians was engaged to run it — so you understand the rest".

August 12:
UK patent 17,881, *Improvements in cinematographs*, to Alfred Wrench for the Wrench Cinematograph projector, which in the excellence of its performance was a serious rival to the Paul Theatrograph. It was a combination lantern slide and film projector with a double ratchet and pawl intermittent movement, and a barrel shutter behind the film aperture, offered for sale at the low price of £36. The apparatus was on the market

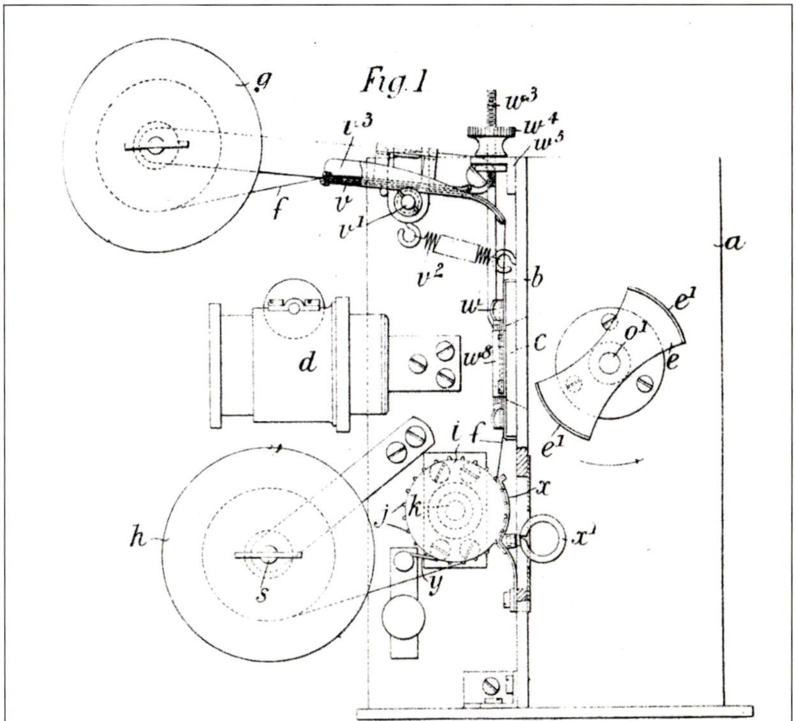

Side elevation of the Wrench projector, with its distinctive barrel shutter (e, e^1) at the right. [United Kingdom patent 17,881, *Improvements in Cinematographs*, of 12 August 1896, Fig. 1.]

131 Jacques Rittaud-Hutinet in *Le cinéma des Origines*, p. 54, says this was a Lumière Cinématographe. Jay Leyda, in *Dianyang*, traces the known itineraries of the Lumière operators in Asia and says it was not possible for a Lumière agent to have been in Shanghai at the time of the presentation. The shows were advertised twice in Shanghai. In general, the first motion pictures reached Asia later than the period covered by this chronology. But I cannot resist noting, at the least in a footnote, the introduction of moving pictures to Korea. The first showing in Seoul took place in a barn in October, 1898, where a 100-foot strip of film was shown to advertise the products of the Anglo-American Tobacco Company. According to F. Parrish in 'Korea's Motion Picture Industry', in *Free World*, Vol. 16, No. 8, n.d. [c. 1966], p. 37, patrons were offered two cents each to watch the film. According to Y-I Lee in *The History of Korean Cinema: Main Currents of Korean Cinema* (Seoul, 1988), p. 19, patrons were expected to pay for admission with ten empty cigarette boxes, or a piece of nickel.

almost simultaneously with the application for its patent and was made in considerable numbers, supplying exhibitors both across the UK and on the Continent.[132]

☛Paul Theatrograph opens as the Animatographo Rousby at the Teatro Aliança, Espinho, Portugal, by Edwin Rousby.

☛Unidentified apparatus, advertised as a Cinétographe Edison, opens at the small auditorium of the exchange in Mulhouse, France, for one week.

☛Henri van Muyden [Gorgibus], publishes his short story 'Cabozet à l'Exposition' in the Swiss magazine *Le Papillon*, p. 130. Written in slang, Cabozet tells a friend about his trip to the Geneva exposition, where one of the entertainments is a cinematograph.

August 13:
Unidentified apparatus, advertised as a Cinématographe, opens at 11 rue de la République, Narbonne, France, by the showman Olier.

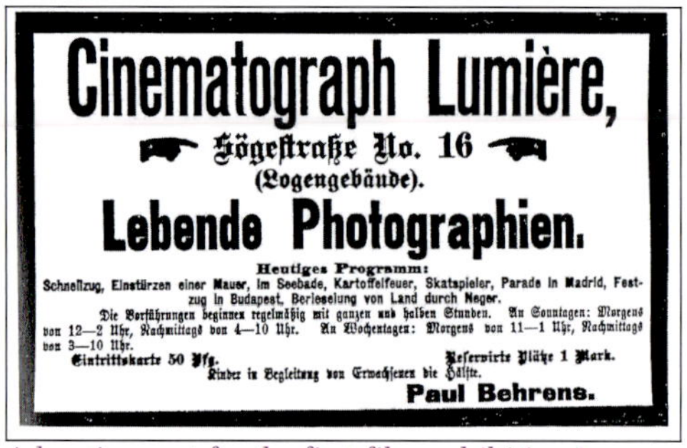

Advertisement for the first film exhibition in Bremen, organized by Ludwig Stollwerck's local agent Paul Behrens.
[Bremen Courier, August 1896, from Dorothea Breitenfeldt and Jutta Reinke, "Kinderjahre des Films in Bremen", in Joachim Steffen, Jens Thiele and Bernd Poch, Hrsgs., *Spurensuche. Film und Kino in der Region*, Oldenburg, 1993, p. 109.]

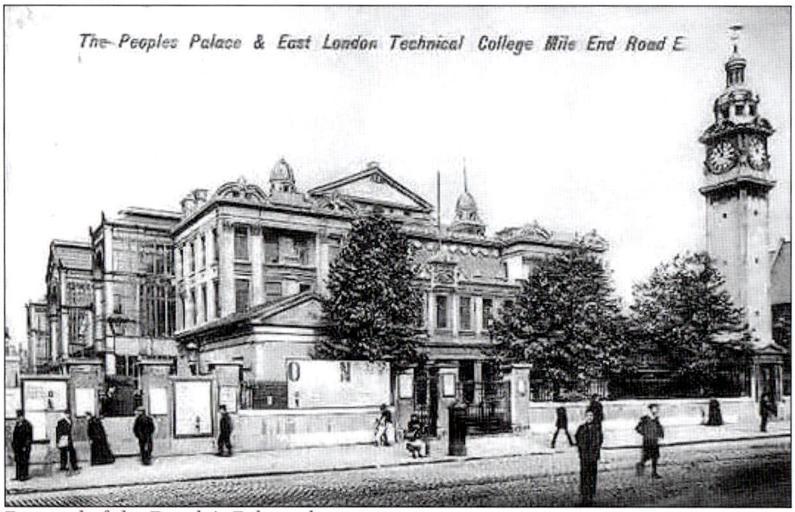

Postcard of the People's Palace about 1900.
[Philip and Harold Mernick, at www.http/mernick.org.

☛Lumière Cinématographe opens at 4 cours Gambetta, Tarbes, France. The screenings ran through 23 August.

August 14:
Lumière Cinématographe demonstrated for an invited audience of 1500 press and opinion makers in the mezzanine of the apothecary Calle de Plateros 9, Mexico City, by Lumière operators Gabriel Veyre and Fernand Bon Bernard.

Films included: *Liegada de un tren*; *Montañas rusas*; *Una carga de coraceros*; *Jugadores de ecarté*; *La comida del niño*; *Salida de los talleres Lumière en Lyon*; *El regador y el muchacho*; *Demolición de una pared*; *Bañadores en el mar*; *Comitiva imperial en Buda Pest*; *Disgusto de niños*; *Quemadores de yerbas*; *Una plaza de Lyon*.

☛Lumière Cinématographe returns to the Casino, Vichy, France, for two days.

August 15:
Lumière Cinématographe opens in the Logengebäude 'Friedrich Wilhelm zur Eintracht', Sögestraße 16, Ecke am Wall, Bremen, Germany, by the Stollwerck representative Paul Behrens, with an invitational press screening. Public showings began the next day and lasted three months through 22 November, with the program changed about twelve times, showing six to ten separate titles in each program. Screenings were every half hour from 11am to 1 pm and 3pm to 10 pm, for an admission of 50 Pfennig. At the outset reserved seats were 1 Mark, and from 3 November a booklet of ten tickets was 3.50 Marks. The showings ran until 30 November.

☛Paul Theatrograph opens as the Animatographo Rousby at the Teatro-Circo Saraiva

132 For example, it was the Wrench Cinematograph that became the first motion picture projector offered in 1896 by the well-established firm of magic lantern and photography suppliers Eduard Liesegang of Düsseldorf, founded in 1854. The apparatus was on sale as a combination still (lantern slide) and animated film projector. Liesegang continued to offer the Wrench machine, under their own marque, until 1899. The cost, including lantern, limelight burner and film works, was initially 850 Marks. From 1897 Liesegang began to build their own machines to the same design (possibly under license?), before introducing their own models of combined still and animated projectors in 1900. The Wrench machine was also sold by the firm of Unger & Hoffmann of Dresden, from late 1896.

de Carvalho in Figueira da Foz, Portugal, as a presentation of Edwin Rousby.

☛Lumière Cinématographe opens to the public in the mezzanine of the apothecary Calle de Plateros 9, Mexico City, through early October, by Lumière operators Gabriel Veyre and Fernand Bon Bernard. Screenings commenced every half hour and films changed frequently. Admission 50 centavos to see eight films. At the end of August special gala performances were arranged at an admission of 1 Peso to see 12 films. On 27 September admission was reduced to 25 centavos. Veyre began taking local views in mid-August.

☛Unidentified apparatus, advertised as a Cinematographo Libório, opens at the Teatro D. Amélia in Rua António Maria Cardoso, Lisbon, Portugal, by Z. Bermudes. Although the apparatus was likely from an English builder, either a Wrench Cinematograph or an early Motorgraph from Watson & Sons, voluminous press comment on the opening, even when comparing it to Rousby's competing Theatrograph, spoke only the names of Edison and Lumière, and their triumphant invention of 'living pictures'. The two week engagement opened with a one-act comedy, followed by the Cinematographo, and finished with another one-act comedy. A Haberer mechanical orchestra played in the intervals between the films. Films from Georges Méliès and Robert W. Paul were shown.

Films included: *O Trapeiro*, *Corrida Cómica*, *Noite Terrivel*, *Desfilar do Regimentoi*, *Dança Serpentina*, *Chegada do Comboio Expresso a Joinville*, *Coroação de Rosière*, *O Queimar das Folhas*, *Corrida de Cavalos Em Londres*, *Saida do Cortejo Real*, *Marlborough House*, *O Casamento ... da Princesa Maud*, *Egando as Flores*, *Maskelyne*, *O Mar na Costa da Normandia*, *A Avenida de Westminster*.

☛Cinégraphoscope of Alexandre and Jules Pipon opens in the place d'Armes, La Rochelle, France, by the showman Briand. The screenings ran through 20 September.

☛Lumière Cinématographe opens in the courtyard of the former prison, by the embankment, in Sables-d'Olonne, France.

☛Lumière Cinématographe opens at the market in Saint-Germain-Lembron, France.

☛Unidentified apparatus opens for the birthday celebrations of the Tivoli Gardens, Stockholm, Sweden, by Sophus Madsen, a variety artist who later became a well-known exhibitor.

☛French patent 257,257, *Appareil chronophotographique réversible à Images continues*, to Georges Demenÿ for a camera and projector with a continuously moving film band and two lenses, derived from dissolving magic lantern practise. The double-projector avoided flicker on the screen by no longer having dark intervals during the change of image. Demenÿ also intended the device for stereo projection.

☛Acres Kineopticon opens in the Queen's Hall of the People's Palace, Mile End Road, London, England, by exhibitor T. C. Hayward. Two performances were given, at 7.30 and 9 p.m., on a bill with the Thames Iron Works Military Band. The Kineopticon returned to the People's Palace for the week beginning 24 August.

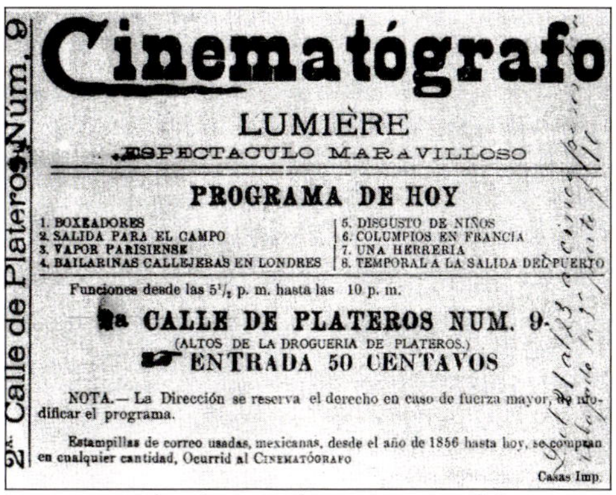
2ª Calle de Plateros Núm. 9

Cinematógrafo

LUMIÈRE

ESPECTACULO MARAVILLOSO

PROGRAMA DE HOY

1. BOXEADORES
2. SALIDA PARA EL CAMPO
3. VAPOR PARISIENSE
4. BAILARINAS CALLEJERAS EN LONDRES
5. DISGUSTO DE NIÑOS
6. COLUMPIOS EN FRANCIA
7. UNA HERRERIA
8. TEMPORAL A LA SALIDA DEL PUERTO

Funciones desde las 5½ p. m. hasta las 10 p. m.

2ª CALLE DE PLATEROS NUM. 9.

(ALTOS DE LA DROGUERIA DE PLATEROS.)

☛ ENTRADA 50 CENTAVOS

NOTA.— La Dirección se reserva el derecho en caso de fuerza mayor, de modificar el programa.

Estampillas de correo usadas, mexicanas, desde el año de 1856 hasta hoy, se compran en cualquier cantidad, Ocurrid al CINEMATÓGRAFO

Casas Imp.

Programme for the initial appearance of the Lumière Cinématograph in Mexico City. [Aurelio de los Reyes, *Filmografìa del cine mudo mexicano 1896–1920*, Mexico City, 1984, p. 18.]

Films included: *Sea Waves at Dover*, *Golfing Extraordinary*, *Tom Merry Sketching Gladstone*, *Tom Merry Sketching Salisbury*, *Boxing Match*, *Highgate Tunnel*, *Henley Regatta*, *The Arrest of a Pickpocket*, *Broadway - New York*, *Prince and Princess of Wales at Cardiff*.

☛Lumière Cinématographe opens at the fair in Valence, France, by the showman Albert Blanc. The show ran until 6 September.

August 16:
Fire breaks out in the Edison Pavilion at the Berlin Industrial Exhibition during a performance of the Lumière Cinématographe. Due to the quick action of Baumeister Bauer, who quieted the crowd of 150 persons, the only injuries were to the hands of the French operator Galey and his assistant Heinz, who carried the projection apparatus to safety. The Pavilion burned to the ground. Damages were assessed at 6000 Marks, and screening resumed in the rebuilt Pavilion on 30 August.

☛Lumière Cinématographe opens to the public in the mezzanine of the apothecary Calle de Plateros 9, Mexico City, by Lumière operators Gabriel Veyre and C. J. van Bernard. Admission 50 Centavos. Advertised as having astounded President Díaz, President Fauré of France, the German Emperor and the Czar of Russia, the screenings attracted a very heterogeneous audience, but even so a formal-dress society performance was announced for Thursday, 27 August "to accommodate the requests of many families".

Films included: *Disgusto de niños, Las Tullerias de Paris, Carga de Coraceros, Demolición de una pared, Elregador y el muchacho, Jugadores de Ecarté, Llegada del tren y Comida del niño.*

☛Foersterling Biomatograph, called Edison's Ideal, opens as the third moving picture show in Berlin, in a specially-erected hall in the Königs-Garten, to the right of the garden veranda, Leipzigerstrasse 136. Construction of the hall seemingly delayed the opening from 9 August, and Foersterling personally demonstrated his apparatus on Sunday, 23 August. Admission 25Pf., Children 10Pf. The showings ran through 6 September. Films were advertised as never before seen in Berlin.

☛Edison Vitascope opens at Elitch's Garden Theatre in Denver, Colorado.

☛Jenkins Phantoscope opens at Manhattan Beach in Denver, Colorado.

August 17:
Edison Vitascope opens in Albany, New York, shown between the acts of a play presented by the Corse Payton Company.

☛Lumière Cinématographe opens in the old post-office building in Brooklyn, New York, moving on 1 November to a larger storefront across from Association Hall.

☛Paul Theatrograph demonstrated to an invited audience at the Melbourne Opera House, Melbourne, Australia, in a midnight screening given by magician Carl Hertz (pseudonym of Leib 'Louis' Morgenstern).

August 18:
Lumière Cinématographe opens in the cellar pub Zum Einhorn at Georgenstrasse 34 (near Baringstraße), Hanover, Germany. The screenings ran every half-hour from 11am to 1pm and 4pm to 10pm, admission 20 Pfennig with children and military free. The admission price was raised to 25 Pfg. on 18 October, and to 30 Pfg. on 25 October. Screenings moved to the main automat exhibition in the mezzanine of the building on 1 January 1897, and ended on 13 January, due to fire damage to the building.

☛Lumière Cinématographe opens in Odessa, Russia, by Lumière operators Marius Chapuis and Decorps.

August 19:
Unidentified apparatus, advertised as a Photobioscope, opens at 18 rue des Marchands, Blois, France.

☛Cinematographe Joly-Normandin opens at the Globe Theatre in Verviers, Belgium, under the name of Cinematographe parisien, by the editor V. George-Bragner, likely a pseudonym for Henri Piston, a journalist with the French satirical paper *Gil Blas*. The screenings ran for a single week, and returned to Verviers at the end of September.

August 20:
French patent 259,045, *Reproduction simultanée des mouvements et des sons dans les projections de scènes animées*, to August and Louis Lumière for an apparatus for the simultaneous reproduction of image and sound during the projection of animated scenes.

☛Lumière Cinématographe opens in the auditorium of the coliseum, avenue de la République, Beauvais, France.

August 22:
Paul Theatrograph, advertised as "the great London sensation, the Cinématographe", opens at the Melbourne Opera House, Melbourne, Australia, by magician Carl Hertz on a bill including an English vocalist, a comedian, a baritone, an Australian song and dance man, minstrels, and dancers. Promoted by Harry Rickards, the screenings lasted a month, with Hertz showing both films of Robert W. Paul and Kinetoscope films he had purchased in South Africa. Hertz dubiously recorded that he painstakingly converted Kinetoscope films to Paul's perforations by laboriously pasting over the original sprocket holes and then cutting new holes in the film, but this is showmanly piffle, as Paul's film perforations were precisely the same as those of the Kinetoscope. Hertz also projected his Kinetoscope films, intended for reproduction at about 30 or 40 frames per second, at the ordinary projection speed of about 16 frames per second, eliciting much press comment on the slowed motion of several of his subjects.[133]

Films included: *Rough Seas at Dover*, *Death of Svengali* (from *Trilby*), *Westminster Bridge*,

133 A week after Hertz left Melbourne to continue his tour, Rickards opened another Paul Theatrograph at the Empire Theatre of Varieties using the operator Baxter, "from Paul's London workshops", with a new group of Paul films. Films included: *G. H. Chirgwin, the 'White Eyed Kaffir'*; *London Railway Scene; The English Derby, 1896*; *Henley Regatta, 1896*; *Devant, Conjuror*; and *London Street Scenes*.

London Street Scene, *Kimpton Park Races*, *A Military Review*, *Boxing Cats*, *Gaiety Co. Ballet*, *Negro Dancers*, *Serpentine Dance* [by a dog], *Sword Combat on Horseback*, *Burlesque Boxing Match*, *Rush Hour Record on London Bridge*, *The Sailor's Courtship*.

☛Cinographoscope of Alexandre and Jules Pipon opens at place Duguesclin in Saint-Brieuc, France.

☛Unidentified apparatus, advertised as Cinématographe Animé, opens at a fair at La Plaine, facing Rue Saint-Savournin, in Marseilles, France, for six days.

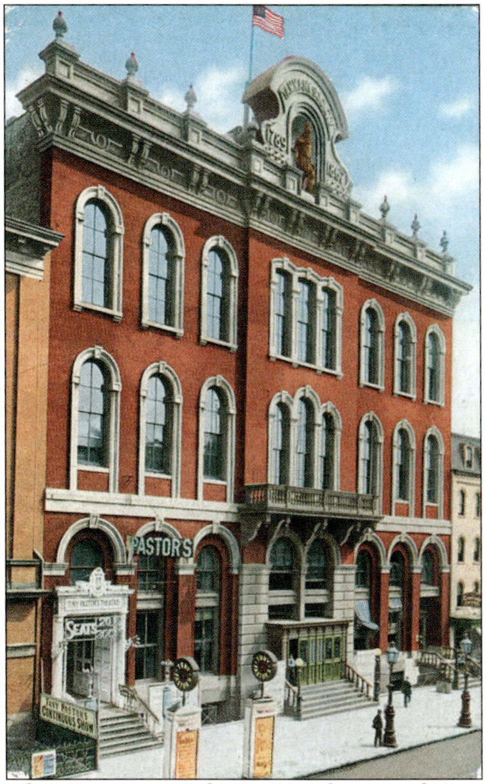

When Tony Pastor's theatre moved uptown from The Bowery to 14th Street in New York City in 1881, it occupied space at the southern end of Tammany Hall by taking over the lease of the Germania Theatre.
[Postcard c1895, Tony Pastor Collection, Harry Ransome Center, University of Texas.]

August 23:
Lumière Cinématographe gives a private screening of local views on the subject of Mexico, including films taken at the Military College, for the President of Mexico, General Díaz and his family, at his official residence, the Castillo de Chapultepec, Mexico City.

☛Unidentified apparatus, advertised as a Kinétographe, opens at the Foire aux Pains d'Epices in Royan, France.

August 24:
Acres Kineopticon opens at Tony Pastor's Theatre in New York City, running until 17 October. The apparatus was represented in the U.S. by A. Curtis Bond.

☛Paul Theatrograph opens at the Palace Theatre, New Brighton, England, by itinerant exhibitor William Dower, for one week.

☛Acres Kineopticon, advertised under the name Royal Cinematoscope, opens at the Metropolitan Theatre, London, by showman Lewis Sealy. The re-naming of this apparatus, used only by Sealy, was due to the exhibition of Acres's films of the Royal family taken at Marlborough House. Sixteen or seventeen films were shown.

August 25:
Lumière Cinématograph opens in Santiago, Chile.

August 26:
Unidentified apparatus, advertised as the Animatographo Portuguez Pinto Moreira, opens at the Teatro Principe Real, Porto, Portugal, by the 'distinguished electrician' Francisco Pinto Moreira. Twenty-one performances were given through 6 September, with twenty films on the final program.[134]

Films included: *Dança Serpentina*, *Banho de Diana*, *Os Nadadores*, *A passagem de um piquete mixto de cavalaria e enfantaria*, *Uma Praia de Banhos*, *Uma cena de lavadeiras*, *Uma praia*, *O desfile dum regumento de cavalaria*, *Disputa na margem do rio*, *O Comboio*, *Um Boulevard de Paris*, *Uma dança escocesa*.

☛Cinématographe Joly-Normandin, advertised as Cinématographe parisienne, opens in the foyer of the theatre in Metz, France, for two weeks, by Madame Paul Deshayes, using films of Eugène Pirou.

Films included: [*Arrivée d'un train*]; *L'arroseur arrosé* [as *Le Jardinier*]; *La leçon de boxe*; *Avenue de l'Opéra*; *Sortie de l'église Notre-Dame-des-Victoires à Paris*; *Bain d'une parisienne; L'Avenue des Champs-Elysées (à Paris)*; *Une Quadrille au Moulin-Rouge à Paris*; *Un dîner*; *Panorama (trois minutes en chemin de fer)*.

☛Lumière Cinématographe opens at the Pavillion Gambari in Bergamo, Italy.

August 27:
Lumière Cinématographe opens at the Teatro Brunetti, and then at the Teatro del Corso, Bologna, Italy, through 4 September, accompanying the pantomime of Mario Costa, *La storia d'un Pierrot*, as part of the touring company of Jole Cantini's presentations of

134 This unknown apparatus was again frequently called a Lumière Cinématographe in the press, and the machine was widely rumored to have been purchased from the Lumière brothers by Pinto Moreira, but the equipment remains unknown.

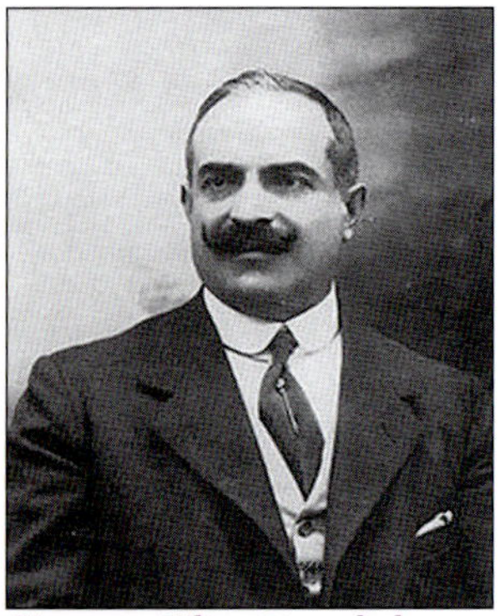

Giuseppe Filippi traveled throughout Italy with a Lumière Cinémnatographe until 1901, when his exhibitions moved to South America.
[Wikipedia Commons.]

artistic and scientific shows. Cantini had an agreement with the Italian concessionaire for the Lumières, Vittorio Calcina, who supplied the apparatus and its operator, Giuseppe Filippi.

Admission 50 Cents, ten cents more than the usual price at the theatre. The screenings ran until 4 September.

☛Paul Theatrograph returns to the Real Coliseu, Lisbon, Portugal, presented by Edwin Rousby. On 29 September, Rousby began showing a special program of Portugese Views photographed by Henry William Short for Robert W. Paul, later exhibited in London from 22 October as "A Tour in Spain and Portugal". 143

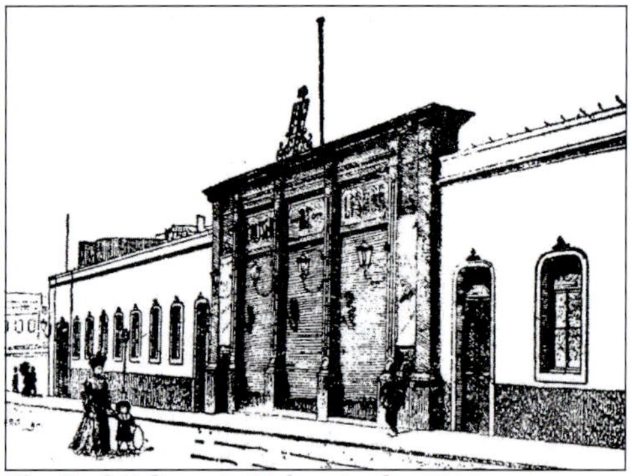

The Real Coliseu in Lisbon in the 1890s.
[Antonio J. Ferreira, *A Fotografia Animada em Portugal 1894–1895–1896–1897*. Lisbon, 1986: Cinemateca Portuguesa, p. 30.]

performances of 67 different films were given through 15 January 1897.[135]

☛Edison Vitascope demonstrated at the Criterion Theatre, Sydney, Australia, to an invited audience of theatrical professionals by Joseph Macmahon.

August 29:
French patent 259,399, *Nouvelles combinaisons d'optique supprimant toute intermittence dans l'éclairement des tableaux photographiques dits mouvementés (chrono-photographies) et permettant de réduire considérablement le nombre des épreuves positives*, to Louis Ducos du Hauron for an apparatus with a continuously moving film band where exposure is made through a synchronously moving circle of lenses, for example 32 objectives, both moving past a stationary opening. This patent is a revival of Ducos du Hauron's original suggestions in patents of 1 March and 3 December 1864, which lapsed at the time because he was unable to pay the patent fees. By mid-1896 the idea was fully obsolete; it is his proposals of the 1860s that were an imaginative and bold step for their time towards the realization of the cinema.

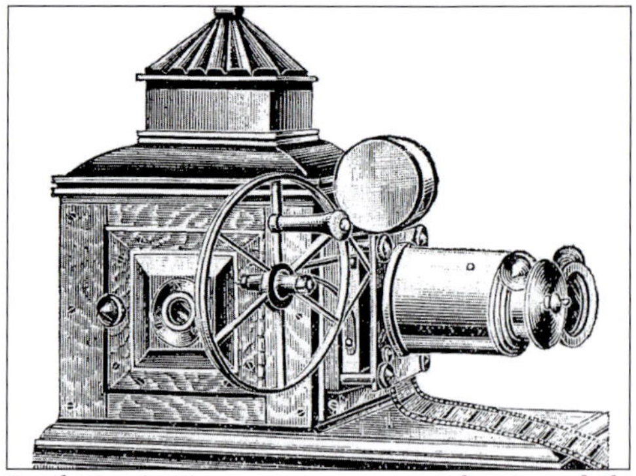

Cecil Wray's Kineoptoscope mounted as intended in the slide stage of a magic lantern, 1896.
[John Barnes, *The Beginnings of the Cinema in England*, London, 1976, p . 145.]

☛Lumière Cinématographe opens at place Michel-Montaigne, Périgeaux, France.

☛Unidentified apparatus, advertised as a Scénimatographe, opens at the Foire de Septembre, Place Michel Montaigne, in Périgeaux, France. The shows ran through 8 September.

August 30: Unidentified apparatus, advertised as a Cinetografo, opens at 10 piazza della Borsa in Trieste, Italy, organized by the local impresario Vittorio Mazzoni. The screenings ran until 12 September, and were accompanied by an unidentified graphophone, advertised as a Grafofono Edison.

August 31:
UK patent 19,181, *Improvements in apparatus for exhibiting kinetoscopic or zoetropic pictures*, to Cecil Wray for his Kineoptoscope projector, a compact apparatus intended to fit into the slide stage of a standard optical lantern, or magic lantern, in the same manner as a mechanical lantern slide. The projector was inexpensive, popular, and widely marketed as Riley's Kineoptoscope, after its main distributor, Riley Brothers of Bradford.

135 On 3 November 1898, the pioneer cameraman and inventor Henry William Short received British patent 23,158 for his Filoscope, a flip-book device encased in a small pocketable metal sheath. The 176 numbered photographs in each Filoscope, which gave a few seconds of animated pleasure to the user, were primarily taken from Robert. W. Paul films or from Short's own films (also often for Paul) and today form an important resource for surviving film excerpts of the earliest period. The elusive H. W. 'Harry' Short introduced his friend Paul to George Georgiades and George Trajedes when the pair were looking for someone to make replica Kinetoscopes for them, sparking Paul's interest in the cinema. Short also later introduced Paul and Birt Acres, who joined in a fateful, brief alliance in Spring 1895, making the first English moving pictures.

☛Edison Vitascope opens at Robinson's Musee, 81 Yonge Street, Toronto, Canada, organized by travelling showman Ed Houghton. Admission to the Musee was 10 Cents, and to the films, which were shown on the Wonderland floor which exhibited wax figures, an additional 10 Cents. The showings ran through 16 October.

☛Paul Theatrograph opens at the Empire Theatre, Paisley, UK.

September 1:
Lumière Cinématographe opens at the Toronto Industrial Exhibition, Toronto, Canada, as part of a grandstand show organized by one of the exhibit's managers, H. J. Hill. Admission 25 Cents, children 10 Cents. Hill purchased rights to exhibit in Ontario, plus two additional machines, and installed the Cinématographe on 23 October, at 96–98 Yonge Street, opposite the Robinson Musée, running through December.

Films included *The Derby and Everything About It* and *Henley Regatta*, two films of Robert W. Paul, and the six-part *Coronation of the Czar*, a Lumière title.

☛Chronophotographe Deménÿ opens at the Foire aux Sabots in Saint-Nazaire, France, by Ernest Grenier, previously an exhibitor of phonographs, mutoscopes and a kinetoscope. The shows ran until 6 October.

☛Cinéphotographe of Lépée opens at the Foire aux Sabots in Saint-Nazaire, France by Alphonse Toussaint. The shows ran until 4 October.

☛Cinéphotographe of Lèpée opens at the Foire de la l'Angevine on the quai de Viaduc in Laval, France, by C. J. Lépée. The shows ran until 7 October, and moved on to Lorient in mid-October..

September 2:
Unidentified apparatus, advertised as a Kinetographe Edison, but more likely a Kinétographe of G. W. De Bedts, opens at the Esplanade, for the Fête de la Broderie in Lille, France, by Joseph Henin. The screenings ran until 12 September.

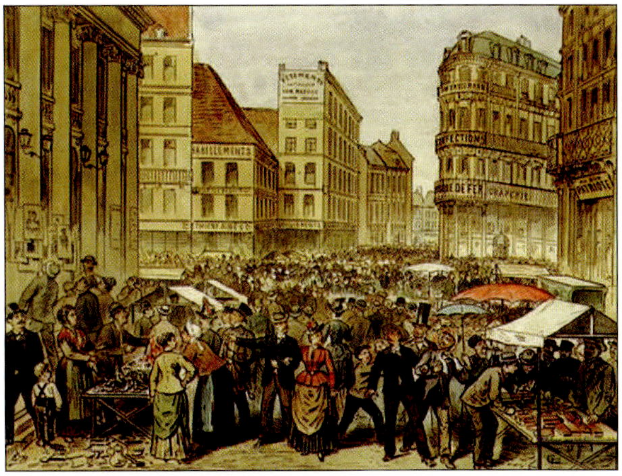

The longstanding annual clearance sale in the Saint-Saveur district of Lille, an attraction of the fair on the Champ de Mars, seen here in a print from 1885. [Unidentified lithograph, Lille Municipal Archives]

☛Unidentified apparatus, advertised as a Cinematógrafo and probably a Lumière Cinématographe, opens at the Circo Coruña in A Coruña, Galicia, Spain. The first day included an invitational press screening organized by Srs. Pedregal and Ramos, and the operator was most likely R. Blasco. The exhibition lasted until 13 September.

September 3:
Demenÿ Chronophotographe opens in the Stadt Panoptikum, Kohlmarkt 10, Vienna, Austria, by Louis Veltée, along with his wax figures. Veltée, the son of a fireworks manufacturer, later opened the first film production company in Austria along with his daughter Louise Kolm, who became a leading Austrian actress, and her husband Anton Kolm, an established photographer. Admission 20 Groschen, children half price.

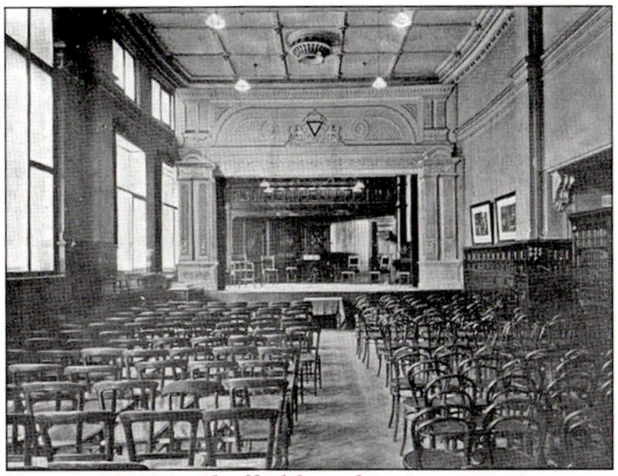

Fargate YMCA, Sheffield, auditorium interior, c1900.[Sheffield City Council, Picture Sheffield.]

☛Unidentified apparatus, advertised as a Cinématographe, opens at the Eden Theatre, Vichy, France, for two days.

☛Cinématographe Lumière opens at the Foire aux Sabots in Saint-Nazaire, France, for two days.

September 4:
Lumière Cinématographe opens at the Teatro Milanese, Milan, Italy, through 1 November.

Films included: *[L']inaugurazione del monumento a Vittorio Emanuele (Milano).*

☛Edison Vitascope opens at 64 South Street, Rochester, New York, by the former Manhattan merchant Edmund McLoughlin and Arthur Frothingham, who purchased New York State rights to the Vitascope from Raff & Gammon. The ex-

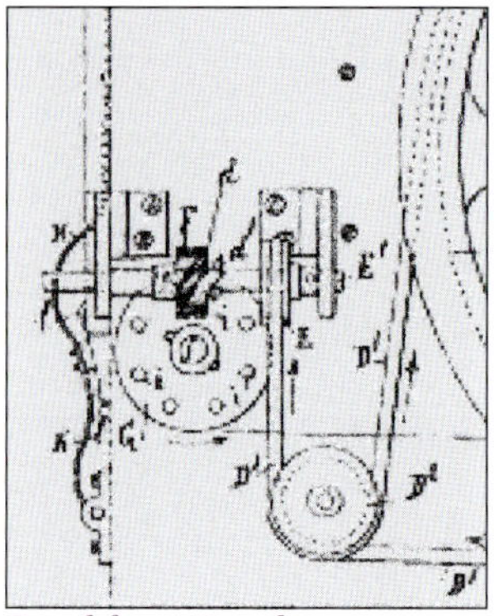

Detail from French patent 259,444 of Korsten, Méliès and Reulos, showing the same drunken screw intermittent system used by Louis Charles in April 1896. [French patent 259,444, *Appareil destine à prendre et à Projecter les photographies animées*, Fig. 3, detail.]

hibitions lasted four weeks. The partners opened in Buffalo later in the month, and in Utica in late December for a five-week run.

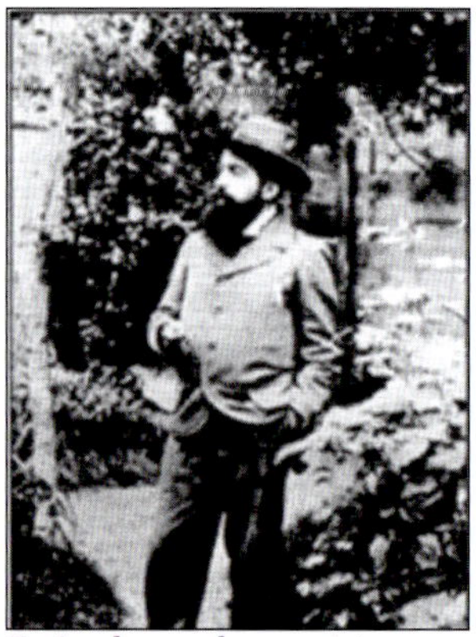

Trained as a pharmacist, Constant Girel became a Lumière operator and worked in Germany, Switzerland, France, Italy, Vietnam and Japan. [Michelle Aubert and Jean-Claude Seguin, *La Production cinématographique des Frères Lumière*, p. 410.]

☛Acres Kineopticon opens in the Lecture Hall of the Fargate Y.M.C.A in Sheffield, England, by H. Jasper Redfern, a local photographer. Exhibitions twice daily at 3pm and 8.30pm were accompanied by demonstrations of Röntgen's X-rays for a premium admission of 1s, reserved seats 2s. The shows ran until 2 October and used films of Birt Acres.

Films included: [*the recent Royal wedding, the reception at Marlborough House, the Derby (the start, the race and the crowds on the course afterwards), a boxing match, a railway train, and a lightning cartoonist at work with his pencil*].

☛French patent 259,444, *Appareil destiné à prendre et à projeter les photographies animées*, to Lucien Korsten, Georges Méliès, and Lucien Reulos for their Kinétographe. The compact machine was available for sale in August, 1896, including the offer of films made to order. The first Star Film catalogue includes several films, Nos. 28-35, shot in the area where Georges Méliès vacationed in July 1896, around Le Havre and Trouville, but the films were probably not shot with this camera. The patent is a close copy of an earlier French patent by Louis Charles which has only recently come to light, and Méliès' relationship to this earlier work by Charles remains a mystery, as does the issuance of this patent by the French authorities.[136]

September 5:

Unidentified apparatus, advertised as a Kinétographe Américain, opens at the Casino in Lons-le-Saunier, France, for four days.

☛Lumière Cinématographe opens in Nîmes, France.

☛Unidentified apparatus opens in Pachuca, Mexico.

☛Lumière Cinématographe opens at the Teatro Andreani in Mantova, Italy, accompanying the pantomime *Histoire d'un Pierrot* as part of the artistic and scientific shows of the touring Jole Cantini show, for six days.

☛Lumière Cinématographe opens in the Stadtgartentheatre (city park theatre) in Karlsruhe, Germany. The city was in festive mode for the 70th birthday of Großherzog Friedrich von Baden on 9 September, with many visitors expected. The screenings ran from 9am to 10pm, for an admission of 50 Pfg., children and military half price. Screenings ended on 30 November, when the Cinématographe moved to an automat gallery.

September 6:

Unidentified apparatus, advertised as a Kinématographe, is running on the Esplanade at the Fête de la Braderie in Lille, France, by Joseph Hénin, for six days. The apparatus was likely made by G. W. de Bedts in Paris. Hénin's booth was 17 metres long, and had previously presented panoramas and stereoscopes.

September 7:

Lumière Cinématographe opens at the vaudeville house of Harry Davis in Pittsburgh, Pennsylvania, simultaneously with an Edison Vitascope show in another theatre. The screenings ran for twelve weeks.

☛Edison Vitascope opens in a theatre in Pittsburgh Pennsylvania, as part of the presentation of the play *The Sidewalks of New York*, simul-

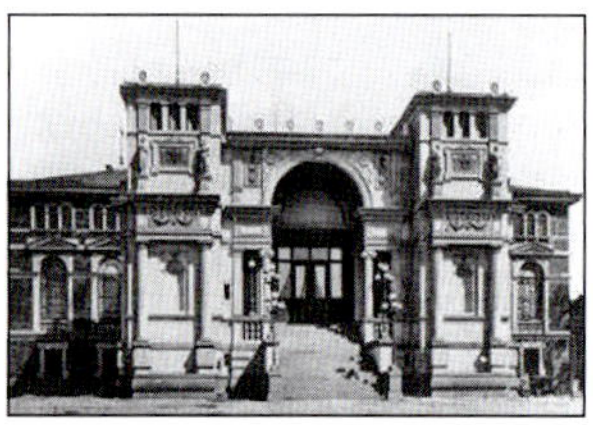

]The City Park Theatre was an exhibition hall 100 meters long, built in 1886 and demolished in 1913, where the first film shows in Karlsruhe were given. [Stadtwiki Karlsruhe.]

136. Additional French patents of 29 October 1898 and 19 June, 11 July, and 3 September 1899. Méliès founded the company Reulos, Goudeau et Cie., for the manufacture of cinema equipment. The Théâtre Robert-Houdin was later turned into a cinema, and was then torn down in 1923 for the construction of the Boulevard Haussman. Méliès' camera is now in the collection of the Cinémathèque française; according to Laurent Mannoni, who has carefully examined the machine, it is clearly adapted from the basic works of a Paul Theatrograph, so in fact it was probably with this adapted camera that Méliès took his first films in July, 1896.

taneously with a Lumière Cinématographe exhibition elsewhere in the city. The screenings ran for three weeks.

☛Lumière Cinématographe opens at Keith's Opera House in Providence, Rhode Island, for one week during the annual Rhode Island State Fair.

☛Paul Theatrograph, advertised as an Animatograph, opens in Washington, DC.

☛Edison Vitascope opens for one week at the Rhode Island State Fair in Providence, by the Rhode Island concessionaires, Barry, White and Hopkins.

☛Lumière Cinématographe opens with an invitation-only screening in the small hall on the first floor of the Concerthouse in Breslau, Germany. Seventeen Lumière films were shown in two sessions. The screenings opened to the public the next day for an admission of 50 Pfg. for adults and 30 Pfg. for children, running from 11am to 1pm and 3pm to 9.30pm. The operator was Constant Girel from Lyon. On 17 September the local newspaper reported on the large number of school classes at the screenings, which ended on 6 December after moving to a lower hall in the Concerthaus.

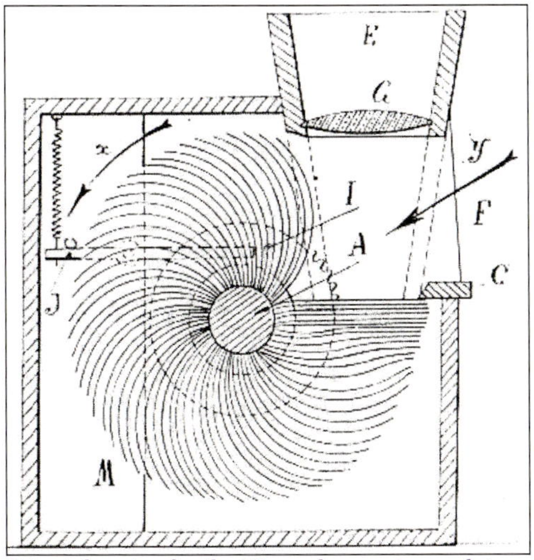

Patent drawing for the Kinora home viewer, later produced by Gaumont. The patent acknowledged the prior work of Herman Casler. [French patent 259,515, *Appareill de vision directe den épreuves chronophotographiques, dit: 'Kinora'*, Fig. 1.]

Septembcr 9:
Lumière Cinématographe opens in the banquet hall of the Hotel Didon, Périgueux, France, by the operator Chavanon. The screenings ran through 27 September.

September 10:
Lumière Cinématographe demonstrated for an invited audience at the Villa Reale, Monza, Italy, by the Lumière operator Pierre Chapuis, assisted by Giuseppi Filippi.

☛Unidentified apparatus, advertised as the Animatographo Portuguez Pinto Moreira, opens in Salamanca, Spain, by Francisco Pinto Moreira.

☛French patent, *Appareil de vision directe des épreuves chronophotographiques, dit Kinora*, to August and Louis Lumière for their Kinora, a miniature mutoscope / flip card viewer for directly viewing photographic images employing a reel of up to 640 small photographs printed onto paper from a motion picture negative. Originally intended to open up a home viewing market for the Lumière film catalogue, the viewers were produced in a wide variety of designs, from simple oak hand-turned models to an ornate mahogany clockwork apparatus for three simultaneous viewers.[137]

☛Foersterling Biomatograph, called Edison's Ideal, opens at Kaufmann's Variété in Berlin by Madame Olinka, for three days. The 'sympathetic' young blonde wife of a renowned imitator of animal voices, Herr Hubertus, Olinka had advertised her pending availability on the variété circuit with Foersterling's apparatus from early August, and this appearance launched her tour across Germany and the Netherlands.

Films included: dancing children, marching soldiers, street scenes, scenes in restaurants, dancing harem girls and Japanese women, a train arriving, a magician, and many others.

September 11:
Lumière Cinématographe opens at the Teatro de Corso, Bologna, Italy, for two days to 12 September.

137. United States patent 591,858; British patent 23,183 of 19 October 1896, in the name of B. J. B. Mills (on behalf of A. & L. Lumiere). After an initial wave of popularity in the last years of the century, the Kinora had a revival in the period from 1908. Film industry pioneer Charles Urban handled the device in England, and supplied films from several sources in Kinora format, as well as providing commissioned studio portraits (from 1904). Interestingly, metal Kinora reel cans from c. 1905 and later are stamped "Patent A. and L. Lumière and E. B. Koopman". Elias B. Koopman was a financial partner of Herman Casler and principal of the American Biograph and Mutoscope Company, inventors and makers of both flip-card mutoscopes and the Biograph 68mm film camera and projector. At some point the British Mutoscope and Biograph Company took over sale and production of the Kinora from the Lumières, clearly indicating a hitherto unexamined association between these two pioneering film companies.
Other small-format flip-card viewer apparatus of various constructions include: British patent 14,917 of 17 November 1886 to A. A. Melville (living picture book]; 20,136 of 11 September 1896 to A. A. Melville (flip book); Austrian patent 3926 to Ph[illip] Wolff; United States patent 667, 635 to W. S. Simpson (Mutoscope); British patents 13,143 and 26,722 of 1898 to Charles Raleigh (mutoscope); United States patent 822,438 to H. Eldredge & C. Doty (stereo hand mutoscope); French patent 352,701 to E. R. Law (stereo mutoscope); United States patents 721,261 and 722,393 to W. P. Warren (mutoscope); British patent 925 of 18 March 1868 to J. B. Linnett (flip book); United States patent 258,164 of 1882 to H. Van Hoevenbergh (flip book); French patent 256,039 of 1 May 1896 to Watilliaux and Claparède (flip book); British patent 8,572 of 3 April 1897 to J. O'Neill and R. McNally (flip book); British patent 22,763 of 5 October 1897 to A. B. Langham (mutoscope); British patent 23,158 of 3 November 1898 to Henry W. Short (pocket mutoscope).

☛United Kingdom patent 20,136, *A New Device by which the Leaves of Picture and other Books may be Turned Over in a Regular Manner*, to Arthur Andrew Melville for a U-shaped metal clip to be used in flip books. This continues Melville's interests in flip books and updates his patent of November 17, 1886 (see above). The drawings use an illustration of athletes jumping hurdles.

September 12:
Unidentified apparatus, advertised as a Cinematographo Edison, opens at the Palazzo Ceci e Rosi in Florence, Italy. The screenings ran until 30 November.

☛Cinematographe Joly-Normandin opens at L'Aigle Impérial in Bruge, Belgium, Belgium, under the name of Cinematographe parisien, by the editor V. George-Bragner, likely a pseudonym for Henri Piston, a journalist with the French satirical paper *Gil Blas*. The screenings ran for five days.

September 13:
Lumière Cinématographe opens at the Teatro Brunetti, Bologna, Italy, for four days to 16 September.

☛Unidentified apparatus, advertised as 'photographie animée', opens in a hall on the first floor of the Café Bussy, Place du Lycée, rue du Commerce, Nevers, France, for one week.

☛Unidentified apparatus opens in Lvov, Poland.

☛Edison Vitascope opens in Cincinnati, Ohio.

☛Unidentified apparatus, advertised as a "new kinematograph", opens in the first floor of Ohlauerstrasse 12, Breslau, Germany.

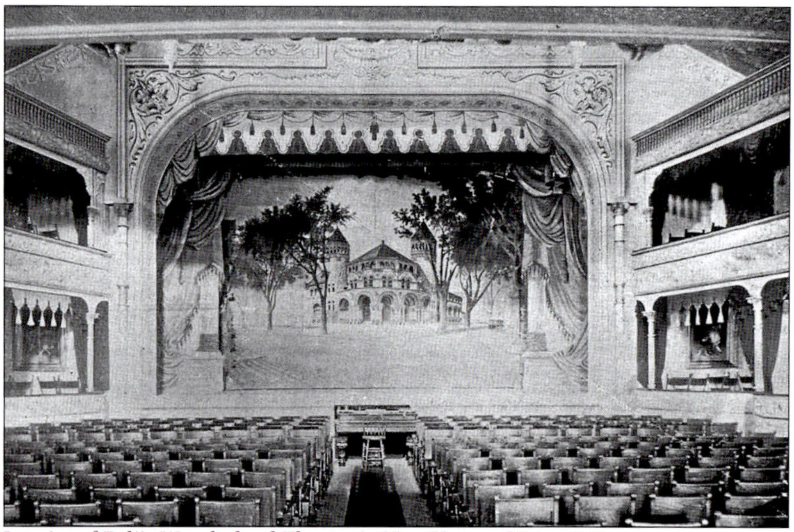

Interior of Poli's Wonderland Theatre in New Haven, CT in 1895. [WWW.cinematreasures.org]

September 14:
Casler / Dickson Biograph of the American Mutoscope Company has its first public screening at the Alfin Theatre, Pittsburgh, for one week as the closing number of a variety bill built around strongman Eugene Sandow. The week it was in Pittsburgh it was one of three different cinema presentations running in the city. Called the Mutopticon on this tour with Sandow, it would not be advertised as the Biograph until 12 October.

Films included: *Rip's Toast* [or *Rip's Toast to Hudson and Crew*], *Stable on Fire*, *A Hard Wash*, *Trilby and Little Billee*, *Li Hung Chang at Grant's Tomb*, and views of Sandow as well as three scenes from *Rip Van Winkle*. The same films were used in the Philadelphia, Brooklyn and New York Opera House exhibitions.

☛Lumière Cinématographe opens in Chicago.

☛Lumière Cinématographe opens at the Wonderland Theatre, New Haven, Connecticut, where manager Sylvester Z. Poli recorded an attendance of 122,607 people over three weeks, or "an average of nearly 6,000 a day, which undoubtedly surpasses any theatrical attendance recorded in the history of New Haven".

September 17:
Paul Theatrograph opens at the Tivoli Theatre in Sydney, Australia, by magician Carl Hertz (pseudonym of Leib 'Louis' Morgenstern), booked by the variety entrepreneur Harry Rickards.[138]

September 18:
Lumière Cinématographe demonstrated to an invited audience at Goodman's Lyceum Theatre, Sydney, Australia, by Lumière operator Marius Sestier. The audience included members of Parliament, Lieutenant-Governor Sir

138 After this engagement manager Rickards shifted the Paul Theatrograph to his other touring companies, evidently because Hertz received a percentage of the boxoffice income and was making considerably more money than his manager. The Newbury-Spada Company exhibited a Paul Theatrograph in Ballarat and Hobart during December 1896, and the Cunard Family Entertainers used one in Brisbane in May, 1897. Hertz did not exhibit films for the rest of his tour in Australia, and when he reached the Theatre Royale in Adelaide at Christmas, 1896, he was billed below Marius Sestier's Lumière Cinématographe. Hertz returned to Australia in late 1897 and toured with films of Queen Victoria's Jubilee.

Frederick Darley, and members of the diplomatic corps.

September 19:
Unidentified apparatus, advertised as a Kinefotografo and most likely a Paul Theatrograph, opens in via Macquedo (now Maqueda) 483, facing the Teatro Massimo, Palermo, Italy, running through 30 November.

Films included: *L'entrada di un vapore in un porto, La piazzza della Repubblica a Parigi, Monelli che raccolgono monete sulla spiaggia di mare a New York, La via Piccadilly a Londra, La passeggiata velocipedistica a Hyde-Park a Londra, L'arrivo du un treno, Le lavandaie, La cuoca* [comic scene], *Un domamtore di cavalli, Una ballerina* [in color], *I pompieri di Parigi che salvano due ragassi da un incendio, Una banda militare, Lo sbarco di passeggeri da un vaporino sul Tamigi, Il gran derby d'Epson 1896, Il carosello Ilgabinetto di un dentista americano o Dentista americano.*

☛Lumière Cinématographe opens at the Teatro Reinach in Parma, Italy, accompanying the pantomime *Histoire d'un Pierrot* as part of the artistic and scientific shows of the touring Jole Cantini show, for ten days.

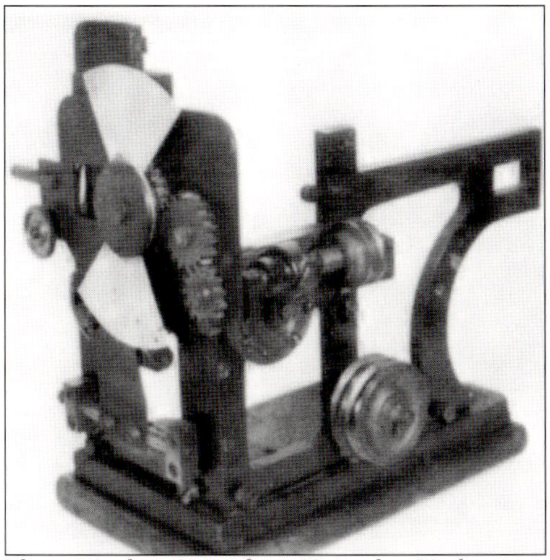

The original projector from Unter den Linden 21, an apparatus designed by Louis Charles and sold as an Isolatographe, preserved through Oskar Messter's donation to the Deutsches Museum, Munich. [Deutsches Museum, Munich.]

Films include: *Piazza del Duomo (Milano), Il fabbro, Bagni Sudanesi, Useita dalla Cattedrale di Colonis, Il giardiniere, Manovra di corazzieri Francesi, Capelle multiforme, L'Arrivo d'un treno.*

☛Oskar Messter takes over the cinema at Unter den Linden 21, Berlin, Germany. This was a major step in his expanding career in cinema which would ultimately lead to both the formation of the UFA empire and the preservation of pioneer apparatus from Unter den Linden 21.

September 20:

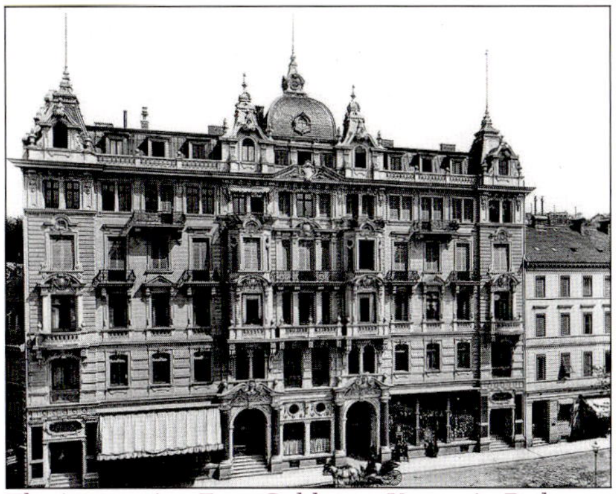

The impressive Zum Goldenen Kreutz in Baden Baden was completed from plans by Wilhelm Vittali in 1893 with apartments above ground floor shops. The restaurant was on the left side of the building seen here two years after its completion. [Unknown photographer, 1895. Wikimedia Commons.]

Cinématographe Joly-Normandin opens as Cinématographe Joly in Charleville, France, by André Milhès, using films of Eugène Pirou.

Films included: *Jardinier arroseur*; *Dispute du cocher et de son client*; *Enfants au bois*; *La bicycliste; La Mer à Dieppe*; *Place de l'Opéra*; *Baignade des Soudanais*; [*Le pochard entêté*]; *Sortie de Notre-Dame-des-Victoires.*

☛Lumière Cinématographe returns to Odessa, Russia, opening at the Russian Theatre, by Lumière operators Marius Chapuis and Decorps.

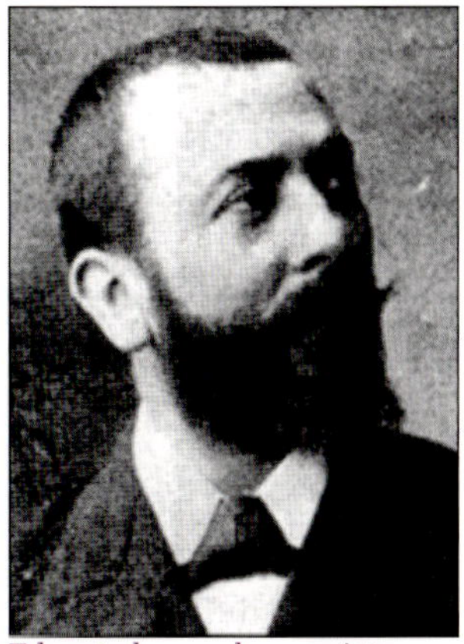

Educated as a pharmacist, Marius Sestier became a Lumière operator in India and Australia. After returning to Lyon, he commercialized the pharmaceutical products devised by Auguste Lumière. [Michelle Aubert and Jean-Claude Seguin, *La Production cinématographique des Frères Lumière*, p. 415.]

☛Edison Vitascope opens in Louisville, Kentucky.

☛Lumière Cinématographe opens in the rear dining room of the restaurant Zum Goldenen Kreutz in Baden-Baden, Germany, with screenings every hour from 2pm until 10pm, for an admission of 50 Pfg. for adults and 25 Pfg. for children. Although the screenings were to end "irrevocably" on 30 September, they seem to have continued, and when the restaurant was sold to a new owner, the Cinématograph was to be seen "for a few more days" due to public demand.

☛Unidentified apparatus opens at the refurbished Folies Parisiennes at 29 rue de

Flandre, Paris, under the management of Paul Ruez. The 900-seat local theatre had a good audience, and the unnamed 'Photographies animées' ran for three-and-a-half months, until 22 December.

September 21:
The Casler / Dickson Biograph opens at Gilmore's Auditorium, Philadelphia, for one week as part of a variety bill headed by strongman Eugene Sandow.

☛Paul Theatrograph opens at the Empire Theatre, Barrow in Furness, England, by James Fioni.

☛Paul Theatrograph opens at Rowley's Empire, Huddersfield, England.

☛Lumière Cinématographe opens in Ruelle, France.

☛Edison Vitascope opens in Washington, DC, as the final act with a minstrel show at the Bijou Family Theatre.

September 23:
Cinographoscope of Alexandre and Jules Pipon demonstrated in a gallery of the Olympia Theatre, Paris, for the director of the Musée Grevin, Gabriel Thomas, and his administrative council, by M. Bouilleau. The administration of the Musée was considering a cinematic attraction for the theatre, but their verdict was that the

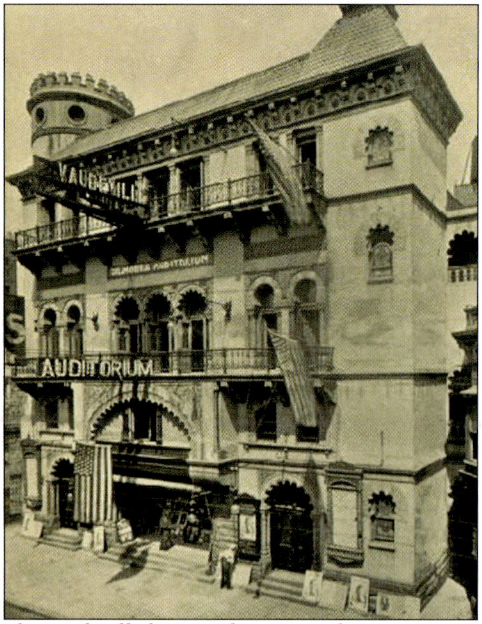

The vaudeville house Gilmore's Auditorium in Philadelphia in 1899.
[Irvin R. Glazer Theatre Collection, Philadelphia Athenaeum.]

Pipon apparatus showed no advance over the Lumière Cinématographe.

☛Cinéphotographe Lépée opens at the Foire St-Michel on the Boulevard de la République in Nîmes, France, by the showman Datigny. The shows ran until 13 October. The local press considered these shows, on an apparatus designed by Victor Continsouza and manufactured by C. J. Lépée, to be superior to the prior visit of a de Bedts Kinématographe in June.

September 24:
Cinématographe Joly-Normandin opens as Cinématographe perfectionné, système Joly, in Commentry, France, using films of Eugène Pirou.

Films included: *Le jardinier ou l'arroseur arrosé*; *Assaut de boxe entre deux champions de Joinville*; *Défilé d'un régiment (musique en tête)*; *Enfants jouant dans un bois avec d'autres personnes*; *Quadrille excentrique au Moulin-Rouge*.

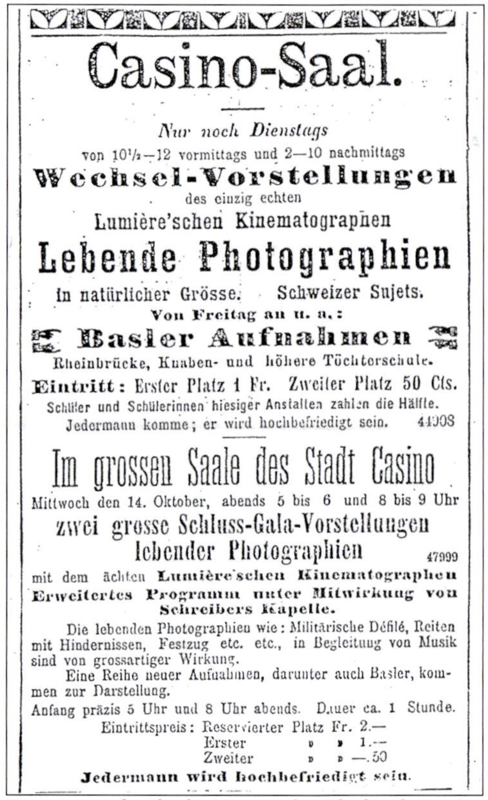

Casino-Saal.

Nur noch Dienstags
von 10½–12 vormittags und 2–10 nachmittags
Wechsel-Vorstellungen
des einzig echten
Lumière'schen Kinematographen
Lebende Photographien
in natürlicher Grösse. Schweizer Sujets.
Von Freitag an u. a.:
Basler Aufnahmen
Rheinbrücke, Knaben- und höhere Töchterschule.
Eintritt: Erster Platz 1 Fr. Zweiter Platz 50 Cts.
Schüler und Schülerinnen hiesiger Anstalten zahlen die Hälfte.
Jedermann komme; er wird hochbefriedigt sein. 44008

Im grossen Saale des Stadt Casino
Mittwoch den 14. Oktober, abends 5 bis 6 und 8 bis 9 Uhr
zwei grosse Schluss-Gala-Vorstellungen
lebender Photographien 47999
mit dem ächten **Lumière'schen Kinematographen**
Erweitertes Programm unter Mitwirkung von Schreibers Kapelle.
Die lebenden Photographien wie: Militärische Défilé, Reiten mit Hindernissen, Festzug etc. etc., in Begleitung von Musik sind von grossartiger Wirkung.
Eine Reihe neuer Aufnahmen, darunter auch Basler, kommen zur Darstellung.
Anfang präzis 5 Uhr und 8 Uhr abends. Dauer ca. 1 Stunde.
Eintrittspreis: Reservierter Platz Fr. 2.—
Erster » » 1.—
Zweiter » » —.50
Jedermann wird hochbefriedigt sein.

Programme for the last Lavanchy-Clarke shows in October, indicating local views of Basel and Switzerland.
[*National-Zeitung*, 13 October 1896, via Paula Meier-Kern, *Verbrecherschule oder Kulturfaktor? Kino und Film in Basel 1896–1916*, p. 31.]

September 25:
Lumière Cinématographe opens in the small auditorium of the Stadt-Casino, Basel, Switzerland, by François-Henri Lavanchy-Clarke. For a 'Gala Final Projection' on October 14 the screenings moved to a larger hall in the Casino where films were shown to the accompaniment of music played by Schreiber's Band. Lavanchy-Clarke showed his advertising films for Sunlight Soap throughout the engagement. Admission: first seats, 1 Franc; second seats, 50 Cents, schoolboys and schoolgirls from local schools, half price.

September 26:
Lumière Cinématographe opens at No. 11, pass. Aycinema, Guatemala City, Guatemala, organized by Arnold Tobler.

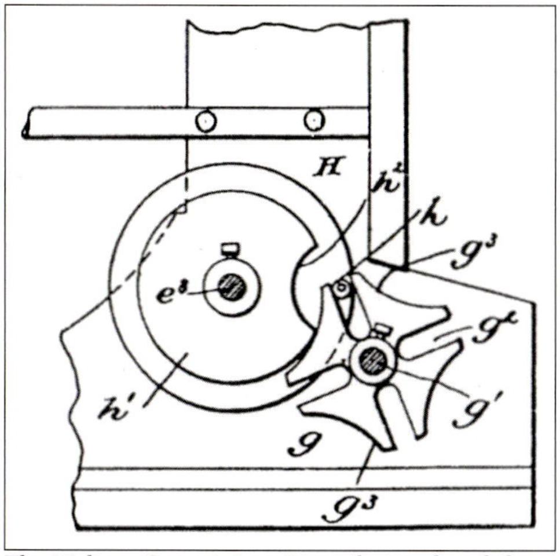

The Maltese Cross intermittent that replaced the beater movement of Thomas Armat's Vitascope in his US patent 578,185. [United States patent 578,185, *Vitascope*, of 26 September 1896, Fig. 6.]

☛United States patent 578,185, *Vitascope*, to Thomas Armat for improvements to the Vitascope, including its use as a camera when appropriately enclosed. The major change to the projector is the substitution of a four-sided true Maltese Cross intermittent for the former beater movement. Minor alterations were also made to the tensioning device in the film gate and to the size of the sprocket wheels.

☛Edison Vitascope opens in Brisbane, Australia, by Joseph and James Macmahon, running through 10 October.

☛British patent 21,381 to Henri Joly for *Improvements in Chrono-Photographic Apparatus adapted for the Projection of Positives upon a Screen*. This was Joly's basic apparatus and refers to his French patent 254,836 of 17 March.

☛Wordsworth Donisthorpe writes a letter to the editor of *Electricity*, published in the issue of 2 October, in which he reveals the inspiration for his pioneering work in moving pictures as the Zoetrope and the Wheel of Life. "When the Kinesigraph first came into my head a Zoetrope was in my hands", wrote Donisthorpe, "One of the pictures was a boy turning somersaults ...".

☛Edison Vitascope press screening organized by William Finkenstein on the ground floor of the Hotel Humboldt (now Hotel Francés) on Maestranza, Guadalajara, Mexico, opening to the public on the following day.

September 27:
Foersterling Biomatograph, called Edison's Ideal, opens in the Centralhallen-Theatre, Hamburg, Germany, by the travelling exhibitor Madame Olinka.[139]

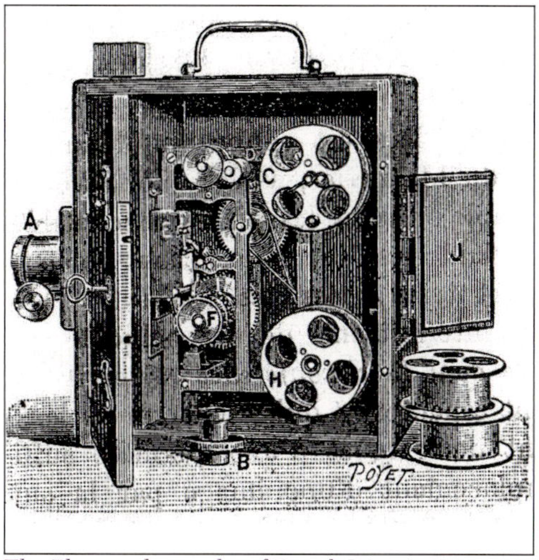

The Phototachygraphe of Raoul Grimoin-Sanson, an early Maltese Cross apparatus, but far from the first one as Grimoin-Sanson later claimed. [G-Michel Coissac, *Histoire du Cinématographe*, Paris, 1925, p. 276.]

☛Lumière Cinématographe opens at via del Corso 393, Rome, Italy, running through 5 October.

☛Unidentified apparatus, advertised as a Cinématographe, opens at the former Café Bonin in the place du Palan, next to the church of Notre-Dame, Châteauroux, France, by the showman Leclerc. The showings ran through 18 October.

☛Cinéphotographe Lépée opens at a fair on the Place Divette in Cherbourg, France, by the showman Lagneau in his Théâtre Salon des Sciences, for three weeks. Lagneau had a long career on the fairs, selling his cinematograph booth only in 1912.

☛Phototachygraphe of Grimoin-Sanson opens at the Café Canterbury in Liege, Belgium, by Raoul Grimoin-Sanson himself and his brother-in-law Allard. The screenings were held in conjunction with the local fair. [this date may have been September 22]

Films included: *Le Négus à l'exposition de Rouen*, *Un défilé de gymnastes*, *Le lac et les cygnes*, *Les chevaux et les chiens à l'exposition russe*, *La place de la Madeleine à Paris*, *Les fontaines de la place de la Concorde*, *Un train arrivant en gare d'Auteuil*.

139 Madame Olinka, the only woman travelling exhibitor with a widely recorded career to be found in this chronology, presented her 'living photographs' from around September 1896 until at least the summer of 1900. She was active in northern Germany in early Autumn 1896, and in The Netherlands later the same year. She turns up again in Posnan, Poland, in May 1898, and then again in Germany in the city of Halle, in May 1900. Her presentations were mostly in variety theatres, where she was booked as a separate act through her husband, Herr Hubertus, in Breslau. Until about spring 1900 she announced, presented, and described each film from the front of the state in stentorian tones, which one reporter found "very original and strange." She is described in reviews as young, blonde, dressed in a saucy silk dress, and carrying a riding crop in her left hand. As late as 1900 she was described as using an Edisongraph projector, which could very well still have been her original Foersterling-supplied equipment.

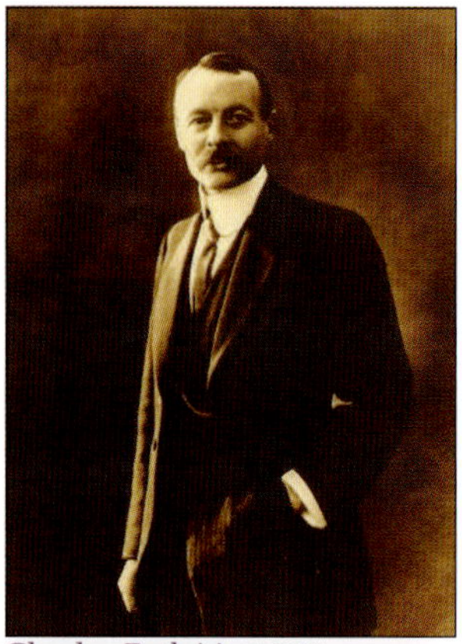

Charles Pathé in 1919. [*Moving Picture World*, June 1919.]

September 28:

Charles Pathé founds the Société Pathé Frères on a capital of 40,000 Francs with his brother Emile. Charles Pathé, an exhibitor of phonographs on the fairgrounds, had been active in the film business since October 1895, when he began to sell counterfeit Kinetoscopes made by Robert W. Paul in London. By early May 1896 he offered a projector called the Eknétographe Pathé, later called the Kinétographe, on the burgeoning market. This apparatus was possibly a machine designed by Henri Joly, with whom Charles Pathé had recently, and nastily, broken up, or it was possibly a copy of a projector by George William de Bedts. The Société Pathé Frères would quickly evolve into numerous daughter companies around Europe, and become the largest vertically integrated film company on the Continent.

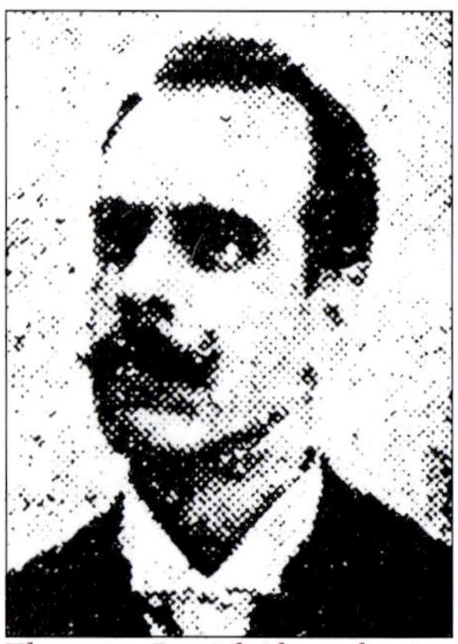

The actor Daniel Alves about 1896. [Antonio J. Ferreira, *A Fotografia Animada em Portugal 1894–1895–1896–1897*, Lisbon, 1986: Cinemateca Portuguesa, p. 100.]

☛Casler / Dickson Biograph opens at the Columbia Theatre, Brooklyn, New York, for one week, where it was again called the Mutagraph and was in support of the same variety show featuring Eugene Sandow.

☛Unidentified apparatus, advertised as a Kinematographe, opens at the Theatre Royal, Montréal, Canada, as the last act on a variety programme. Admission 10, 20, 30, 50, and 75 Cents. The apparatus was possibly a machine by Rigg.

☛Lumière Cinématographe opens at 237 Pitt Street, Sydney, Australia, the first auditorium solely devoted to showing films, organized by H. Walter Barnett and C. B. Westmacott, both prominent society photographers with Falk's Studios in Sydney, who were in partnership with promoter J. C. Williamson and Lumière operator Marius Sestier. The large screen was surrounded by a richly moulded frame, and the films were occasionally accompanied by an orchestra from the nearby Lyceum Theatre. The screenings continued until 27 October. Admission 1 Shilling. Australia's first locally produced film, of a crowd disembarking from the Manly ferry *Brighton*, taken by Barnett and Sestier on 25 October, was shown at the last screening.[140]

☛Lumière Cinématographe opens at the town theatre, Auxerre, France, for two days.

☛Paul Theatrograph, advertised as an Animatograph, opens in Baltimore, Maryland.

September 30:

Paul Theatrograph, called an Animatographe, opens at 2223 St. Catherine Street, Montréal.

☛Unidentified apparatus, advertised as the Sombratographo Alves, opens in the Belém marketplace, Lisbon, Portugal, as a presentation of the Teatro Bijou Infantil, a children's theatre founded in 1893; organized by the actor Daniel Alves.

☛Lumière Cinématograph opens in a storefront in Lower Town Saint- Roch, Quebec City, Canada, by F. A. Jackson, who had purchased rights to exhibit the machine in the province. He undertook the standard Lumière operator routines, giving an advance press preview, inviting local dignitaries, and giving shows for school children. Jackson spent four weeks at this location, and then moved to another storefront in Upper Town for his last two weeks in Quebec City before moving on to the towns of Trois Rivières and Sherbrooke before the end of the year.

☛Lumière Cinématographe opens at the Teatro Ristori in Verona, Italy, for five days.

October 1:

Foersterling Biomatograph, called Edison's Ideal, opens in the Victoria Salon, to the left of the ground floor, at Leipzigerstrasse 134, Berlin, Germany. The show advertised 'always' new pictures, changing daily, and the

140 Falk Studio technician Arthur Peters built a developing drum in Sydney for use with local productions, so at least some of Sestier's work was not sent back to Lyon for processing, as the dates of the taking and exhibition of his Derby films also confirm. By March 1897, Marius Sestier's library of Lumière films, both imported from France and locally taken, had grown to 270 titles, providing him with supplies for extremely varied exhibition programs.
Beginning on 2 November the Salon Lumière was taken over by Goodman of the Lyceum Theatre and C. B. Westmacott, who installed an unknown British projector, but the exhibitions were a failure and the enterprise closed at the end of the week. Film screenings returned to 237 Pitt Street on 7 November; see below.

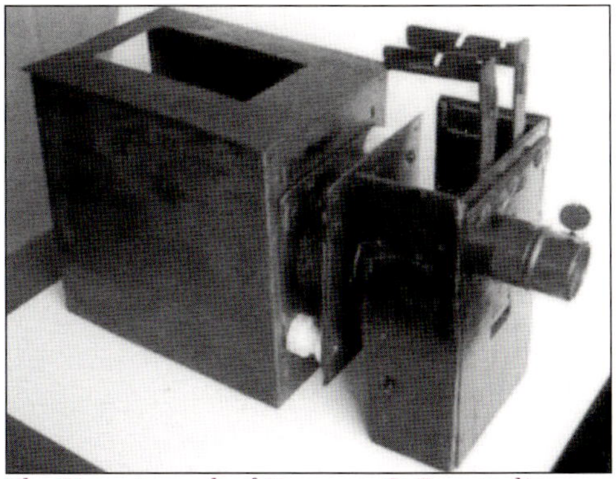

The Biomatograph of Hermann O. Foersterling with its original lamphouse. [Harm Nijboer & Asing Walthaus, *George Christiaan Slieker, 1861–1945. De eerste bioscoopondernemer in Nederland* (Leeuwarden, 1995: Uitgeverij Perio), p. 61.]

shows ran through 7 November. Admission 50 Pf., children and military half-price.

October 2:
Foersterling Biomatograph, called Edison's Ideal, opens at the variety theatre Kaiserkrone, Kiel, Germany, on a bill with humorist Bernard Marx. Although the initial advertisement hints that this was a Lumière Cinématographe by saying that the Kinematograph was seen "for the first time at the Berlin industrial exhibition", the second advertisement of the show called it Edison's Ideal and the third Edison's Kinematograph. The Lumière apparatus opened in Kiel on 1 November (see below) under Stollwerck management.

☛Lumière Cinématographe opens at 28 Boulevard Victor Hugo in Nimes, France. Admission 50 Centimes. Because an unidentified Cynématographe, or Cinéphotographe had opened for the festival of St. Michel a few days earlier in the Champ de Foire, Boulevard de la République, the announcements for this show emphasized that this was the "true" Lumière Cinématographe, and early screenings were reserved for notables of the town. Eight films were shown for an admission of 1 Franc. At the request of the mayor and religious leaders, over 400 tickets were distributed to students of both state and church schools late in the run. The screenings lasted until 8 November.

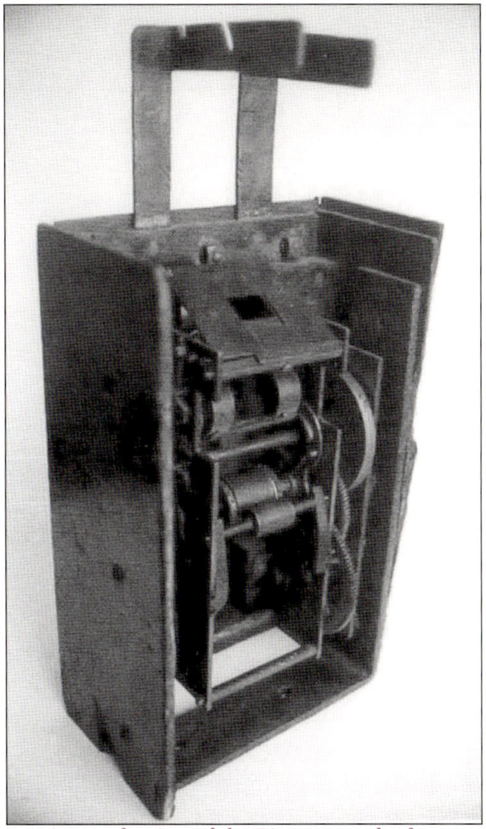

Interior mechanism of the Biomatograph of Hermann O. Foersterling, showing its clear similarity to the work of Bunzli and Continsouza. [Harm Nijboer & Asing Walthaus, *George Christiaan Slieker, 1861–1945. De eerste bioscoopondernemer in Nederland* (Leeuwarden, 1995: Uitgeverij Perio), p. 61.

☛Cinématographe Joly-Normandin opens in Mézières, France, by André Milhès. Films included: *Descente du train.*

October 3:
Unidentified Kinematographe, possibly a Rigg, opens at the Toronto Opera House, managed by Ambrose J. Small. As both the Opera House and the Theatre Royal in Montréal were owned by Jacobs & Sparrow, it is likely they used the same machine.

☛Foersterling Biomatograph, called Edison's Ideal, opens on the Theresienwiese at the Oktoberfest in Munich, by showman Jean Dienstknecht from Hamburg.[141]

☛Cinographoscope of Alexandre and Jules Pipon opens at 9, rue passage du Logis-du-Roi, the former hall of the Café de la Tour, Amiens, France, by the brothers Cottrelle. The shows ran for two weeks.

☛Unidentified apparatus, most likely a Cinématographe Joly-Normandin, opens in the grande salle of the Olympia Theatre, Paris, accompanying a Spanish operetta, *La Gran Via.* Admission 1 F, with 25 places reserved daily for officers, sub-officers and soldiers from the Army of Africa when in their impeccable uniforms. The shows ran until March, 1897.

Films included (many in colour): *Le coucher de la mariée*, *Deux peuples*, *La Baignade des Nègres*, *La Loïe Fuller*, *Les Grandes Eaux de Versailles.*

October 4:
Foersterling Biomatograph, called Edison's Ideal, opens at the Wilhelm Theatre, Görlitz, Germany, by Madame Olinka.

Films included: comical street pedestrians, a children's party, passing Cavalry, a train entering a station with debarking

141 Jean Dienstknecht later opened the first film distribution company in Munich.

passengers, a lively scene in a bathing house.

☛Lumière Cinématographe opens at the Teatro Storchi in Modena, Italy, accompanying the pantomime *Histoire d'un Pierrot* as part of the artistic and scientific shows of the touring Jole Cantini troupe.

☛Foersterling Biomatograph, called Edison's Ideal, opens in the gymnasium of a German sports association in Ústi nad Labem, Bohemia (now Czech Republic). The showings lasted three days and were badly received, according to the *Aussiger Anzeiger*, because the travelling showman used coal gas for illumination, which produced a weak light.[142]

Films included *A Chase in a Room*, and *Miss Foy, The Serpentine Dancer* (in color), plus a film of a merry-go-round and its waving spectators.

☛Unidentified apparatus opens in the Big Hall of the Linden Tree Hotel in Moravská Ostrava, Bohemia (now Czech Republic).

☛Demenÿ Chronophotographe opens in a photography studio, passage de la Comédie, across from the Theatre, Amiens, France, by Léon Caron. The shows ran for six weeks.

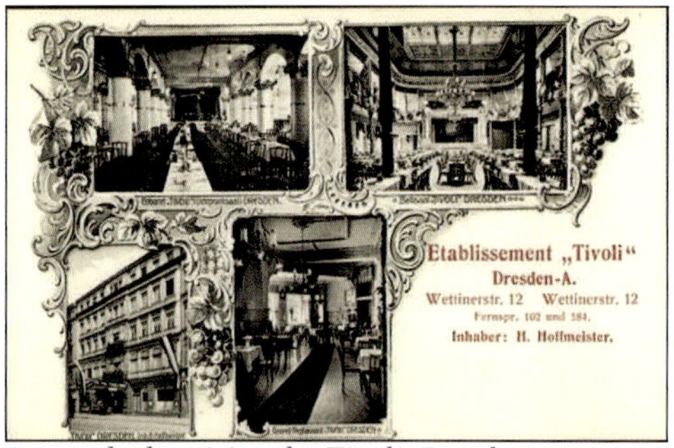

Postcard advertising the Tivoli, Dresden, c1902 showing the facade, the ballroom, the restaurant, and a function room. [www.altesdresden.de]

☛Lumière Cinématographe opens in a "specially outfitted" lower Salon of the Tivoli at Wettinerstrasse 12, Dresden, Germany. Screenings ran from 2.30pm until 10pm daily, on Sundays 11am to 1.30pm and 3pm to 11pm. Three separate programmes ran consecutively each day. The operator was Jean Lauvernier from Lyon, who offered freelance projections through the Dresden theatrical agent Marby after this showing closed. The screenings ran until 31 March 1897.

October 5:
Unidentified apparatus, advertised as a Cinematografo, opens in the Caffè-concerto L'Orfeo, alleria Margherita in the via Depretis, Rome, Italy, as part of a musical pantomime presented by the Bozza brothers.

☛Casler / Dickson Biograph, opens at the Grand Opera House, New York City. Still called a Mutopticon, this weeklong engagement to 12 October concluded its tour with the Sandow vaudeville show.

☛Unidentified apparatus, advertised as a Centograph ("a French machine"), opens in Baltimore, Maryland.

October 6:
Foersterling Biomatograph, advertised as Das Ideal Edison's, opens at Karlstrasse 28 opposite the Circus Renz and near the Friedrichstrasse train station in Berlin. Screenings ran from 10am to 11pm daily, and continued through at least 15 November.

October 7:
Lumière Cinématographe opens in the Rater Saal of the Königsbau, Stuttgart, Germany, immediately upon its closing at the end of the Exhibition of Electrical Technology, running from 10am to 10pm. The opening program presented eight films of the Imperial Congress in Breslau, and the screenings ended on 15 November.

☛Unidentified apparatus, advertised as a Cinefotografo, and likely a Cinéphotographe by C. J. Lépée, opens at the Teatro Filarmonico in Verona, Italy, for one month.

☛According to *La France* on this date, customers of the elite restaurant Du Louvre, 21 cours de l'Intendance, in Bordeaux, France, could attend free sessions of the cinematographe every evening during dinner. This practise lasted until about 1908, and is one of the rare traceable instances of a relatively widespread attempt by restaurants and clubs to use the new moving pictures to attract clients.

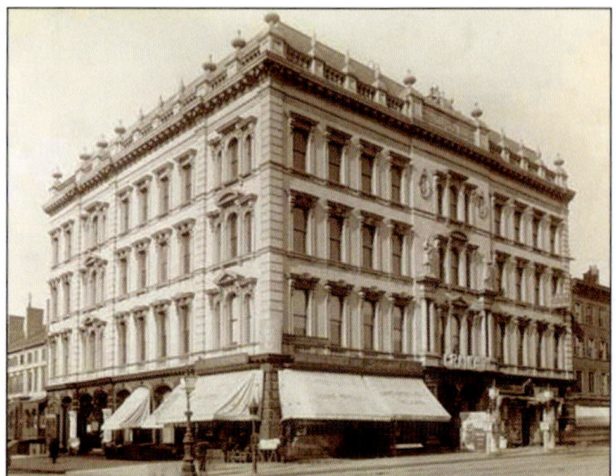

The Grand Opera House, corner of 8th Avenue and 23rd Street, New York City, in 1895. Built in 1868 with an auditorium holding 1800 people, the building was demolished in 1960. [Photograph by the Byron Company, Wikimedia Commons, public domain.]

142 The same German exhibitor opened at Cheb, in Bohemia, in early December. His showings there were interrupted because of a faulty part, but resumed four days later upon receipt of a spare from Berlin. The unknown showman toured several more towns in Bohemia, including Teplice (c. 21–31 October), Jablonec (c. 4-6 November), and Trutnov (end of November).

October 8:

Foersterling Biomatograph opens at the cultural and sports club Kola, in Zagreb, Croatia, organized by the photographers Masinger and Breyer. Advertised as "Edisonov Ideal", the shows ran for eleven days. The operator and owner of the cinema apparatus was Samuel Hoffmann.

☛Lumière Cinématographe opens in the dance hall Démeusy, 7 boulevard des Vosges, Belfort, France.

☛Edison Vitascope gives a free exhibition to the public in an improvised hall in the central garden of the Alameda, Mexico City. According to a report in *El Nacional*, picturesque views were shown and colored advertisements were projected to pay for the event, which was possibly a publicity activity of the local Edison agency.

☛Foersterling Biomatograph, called Edison's Ideal, opens in Van der Bruggen Straat at the annual fair in Nijmegen, The Netherlands, by travelling exhibitor Christiaan Slieker. The shows were reviewed enthusiastically as "Lumière's Cinématographe" by the local paper.

☛Unidentified apparatus, advertised as a Cinétographe and possibly an apparatus either from Pathé or the Werner brothers, opens in the grand hall of the café of M. Loubier in Oran, Algeria. Although M. Antheaume is named as the proprietor of the apparatus, it turns up a few days later in Tlemcen (see below) as an attraction of M. Poordy.

Films include: *La danse du ventre*, *Le boulevard*, *L'arrivée d'un train*, *Le salon de coiffure*, *Un chahut au Moulin Rouge*, and two films representing the Tsar of Russia in France.

October 9:

Foersterling Biomatograph, called Edison's Ideal, opens in Litomerice, Bohemia (now

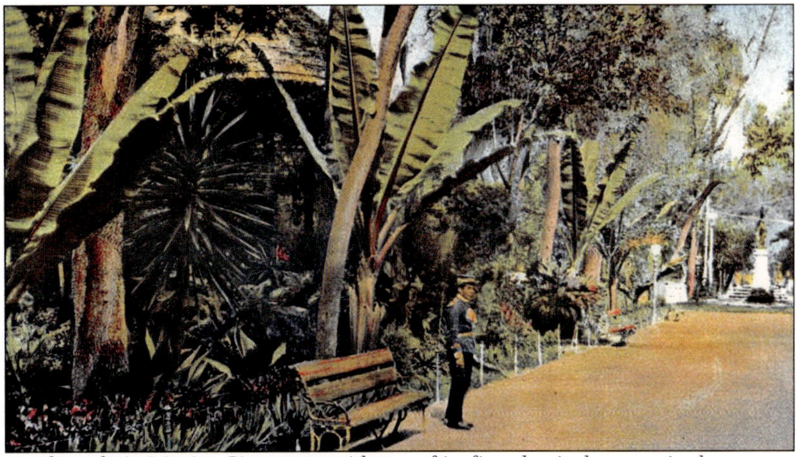

La Alameda in Mexico City c1900 with one of its five classical statues in the background. Established in 1592, the park has been a centre of public events in the city for centuries, including promotional cinema screenings in 1896.[Lithographed vintage postcard, detail. Public domain.]

Czech Republic), by the Oeser brothers, as part of their travelling Electric Theatre, which included performances of "electricity, optics, mechanics, magnetism, physics and Oriental magic". The Biomatograph was exhibited with their giant electric phonograph.[143]

☛An unusual advertising campaign for travelling Lumière Cinématographe shows in Ontario appeared on this date in the *Toronto Star*, as local rights holder H. J. Hill advised potential audiences in surrounding small towns to not be deceived by imitations, while his show continued its run in Toronto. "Don't be misled by cheap imitations", he declared, noting that after Christmas his apparatus would appear in "All important towns north and East of Toronto. Wait for it." His machines later visited Oshawa, Peterborough, Orilla, Cornwall and other towns.

☛Cinématographe Joly-Normandin opens on the Boulevard Charlemagne in Oran, Algeria. The date of the opening is uncertain here, but it is clear that by 14 October both the Joly-Normandin apparatus and a Cinétographe (see above) had been operating in Oran for several days. Local newspapers twice wrote comparisons of the two shows, broadly favouring the Joly apparatus but also conceding that the Cinétographe had corrected some early failures of illumination. On 18 October this show moved to the Boulevard Séguin, in the Salon-Exhibition occupied by M. Naux, where the shows ran from 5 to 7pm and from 8.30 to Midnight. There was also a fierce competition in terms of the films offered as both shows ran until the end of the month.

Films include: *Les forgerons*, *La corvée de neige*, *L'arroseur arrosé*, *La baignade des nègres dans le lac du Champ de Mars*.

☛Unidentified apparatus, advertised as a Kinematograph and accompanied by a Graphophone, opens

143. This apparatus was formerly identified as made by Oskar Messter. Following this exhibition, the Oeser brothers took their Foersterling Biomatograph to Brno in early November, remaining at the Garden Hall of the Silver Eagle Inn in Eagle Street until 16 November. They then exhibited in Olomouc, Šternberk, Jihlava and Svitavy before the end of 1896.

in the first floor room of the public house 'Zum Kalb' at Ebrachergasse 2, Würzburg, Germany. The rented accommodation was renamed the 'Edison-Salon,' and admission was 50 Pfg., children and military half price. A journalist who attended the screenings recalled many years later that 'many higher officers and gentlemen from the first circle visited the show and gave their full attention to the scenes.' The exhibition ran through 4 November.

Films included: a street scene in Moscow, the Tsar, Russian farmers with laden troikas drawn by small horses, a gardner watering his garden surprised by a mischevious young boy.

October 10:
Cinéphotographe of C. J. Lépée opens in Sables-d'Orlonne, France.

☛Unidentified apparatus, advertised as a Cynématographe, opens in the Kleberplats, Strasbourg, France, for one week.

☛Unidentified apparatus opens at the Foire St-Michel on the Cours de la République in Le Havre, France, by the showman Gallici-Loramus, for one week.

☛Unidentified apparatus, advertised as a Cinefotografo, and likely a Cinéphotographe of C. J. Lépée, opens at the beer hall Pavone in Trento, Italy, for two days.

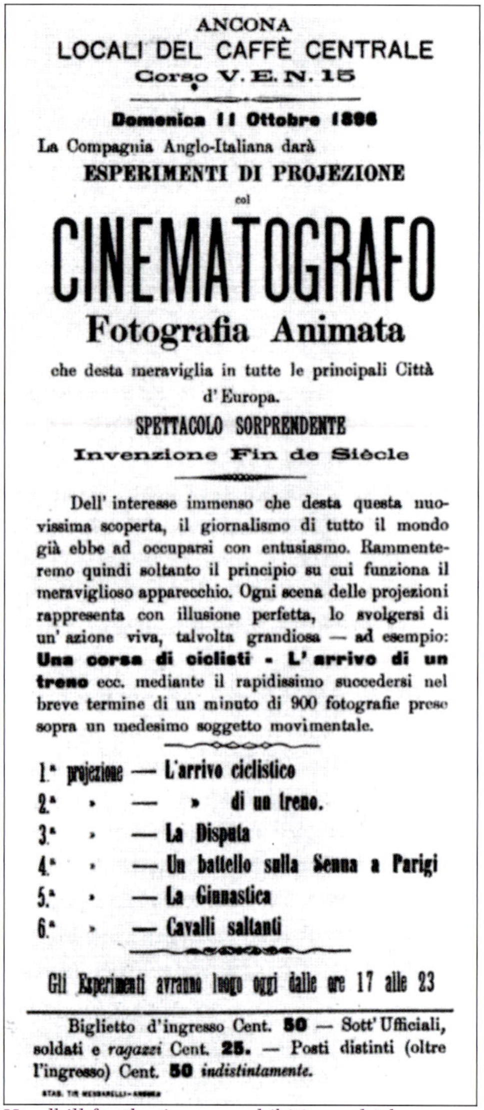

Handbill for the Ancona exhibition, which was called "Projection Experiments" as late as October 1896. Since the organizer was the Edison agent for Italy, the show was likely an Edison Vitascope. [Aldo Bernardini, *Gli ambulanti*, Gemona 2001: La Cineteca del Friuli, p. 156.]

October 11:
Cinématographe Joly-Normandin opens as Cinématographe Eugène Pirou at the Grand Café de la Paix, 12 Boulevard de Capucines, Paris, not far from the Lumière exhibition on the same street. Pirou was an active Paris photographer who became a prominent early film exhibitor and filmmaker with the Joly apparatus, distinguished by its use of five perforations per frame instead of the four used by Edison. In November Pirou opened a second Paris exhibition at the Maison Doisteau, 86 rue de Clichy, under the name Cinématographe Eugène Pirou-Normandin. He maintained his exhibition into 1897, no doubt encouraged by the production of some risqué films like *Le coucher de la mariée* (The Bride goes to Bed) and *Bain de la parisienne* (The Bath of a Parisienne) that were later reproduced by many others.

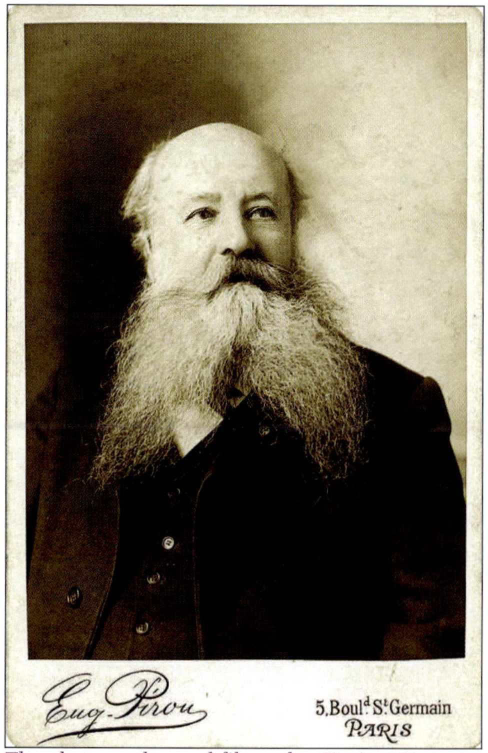

The photographer and filmmaker Eugène Pirou in a self-portrait from 1906. [Wikimedia Commons. Public domain.]

Films included: *Arrestation d'un ivrogne*; *Charge oblique* [de cavalerie]; *Départ des souverains russes pour Versailles; Sortie de la M. Daumont de LL. MM. Avec M. Le président de la République se rendant à Versailles; Farce de chambrée à la caserne*; *(Le) plongeon des soudanaise*; *Le coucher de la mariée (de Melle Louise de l'Olympia)*; *Départ de l'ambassade pour l'église russe; Dispute de cocher; Menuet Louis XV; Bain de la parisienne; Arrivée du président de la République à l'ambassade; Défilé du cortège du tsar; Les hommes-réclame du coca des Incas; Noël en Alsace; Passage d'un défile. 27⁰ Dragons; Pioupiou et Nounou; Place de la Madeleine; Charge du Régiment en ligne; Sauts d'obstacles au Camp de Satory; La tentation de Saint-Antoine.*

☛Unidentified apparatus, advertised as "Edison's living photographs", opens in the Kaisersaal of the restaurant Deutscher Kaiser, Königstraße 41, Lübeck, Germany, continuing until 4 November. The pauses between films were filled with phonograph records, or by a speaker, and there were sound effects to the films, as noted in the local paper: "The Kaiser's speech at the opening of the North/East Sea Canal, with its three hammer-blows, was very effective and could be heard clearly throughout the hall". Admission 50 Pfg., children 25 Pfg. The inclusion of two (at least) Birt Acres films indicates this could have been an Acres Kineopticon exhibition, or one of a Foersterling Biomatograph.

Films included (some in colour): a serpentine dance, bathers at the beach, arrival of a train, a parade of soldiers in Berlin, the Kaiser arriving to open the Kiel canal.

☛Unidentified apparatus, advertised as a Cinematographo, Fotografia Animata, opens at the Caffè Centrale, Corso V. E. N. 15, in Ancona, Italy, by Edison's agents the Anglo-Italian Commerce Company. Admission 50 Cents; officials, soldiers and children, 25 cents; reserved places, 50 Cents above admission..

Films include: *L'arrivo ciclistico, L'arrivo di un treno, La Disputa, Un battelle sulla Senna a Parigi, La Ginnastica, Cavalli saltanti.*

October 12:
Casler / Dickson Biograph opens at Hammerstein's Olympia, New York City, with a special event organized as a political rally for the Republican Party. This date is frequently incorrectly cited as the first public exhibition of the Biograph.

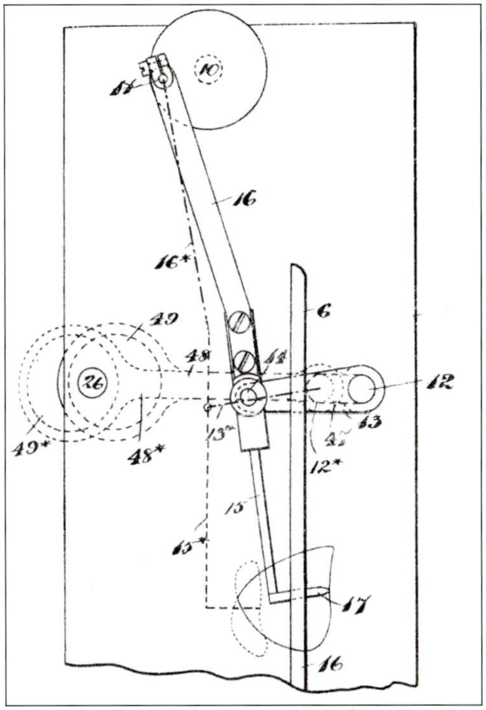

The sophisticated pin intermittent of Newman and Guardia, which provided for significantly more time for each frame of the film to rest in the projection gate. The rotating shaft 10 provided the up-and-down motion of the pins 17 engaged with moving the film, but instead of a half-and-half rest and movement, the additional eccentric at 49 and 49* moving on shaft 48 was arranged so that the claw engaged the film only every other rotation, thus accomplishing 75% rest to 25% movement. [United Kingdom patent 22,707, *Improvements in Kinematograph Apparatus*, of 13 October 1896, Fig. 6.]

Films included: *Empire State Express*, and films of William McKinley, the future President then running for office, on his front porch in Canton, Ohio.

☛Unidentified apparatus, advertised as a Kinematographe, opens at Cook's Opera House, Rochester, New York, for three days.

☛Paul Theatrograph opens at the National Palace, Croydon, England.

☛Unidentified apparatus, advertised as a Cinefotografo, and likely a Cinéphotographe of C. J. Lépée, opens at the beer hall Dante in Trento, Italy, for one week. It had clearly moved on from the establishment Pavone in the same city, where it ran on 10 and 11 October.

October 13:
Edison Vitascope, advertised as an Edison Kinematograph, opens at the Auckland Opera House, Auckland, New Zealand on a bill with Charles Godfrey's Company. The operators were 'Professors' Hausmann and Gow.

Films included: *Train in Full Motion, Sea Bathing, Electric Trams, Merry-go-Round's, Dancing Girls, London Streets*, others.

☛British patent 22,707, *Improvements in kinematograph apparatus*, to Arthur Samuel Newman and Newman & Guardia Co. for a Kinematograph projector using a sprocketless friction feed and a claw intermittent movement. This was A. S. Newman's second design (the first was not patented or manufactured) and came to market in 1897 in an improved form, matching the standards of this well-regarded firm of photographic manufacturers.

☛Unidentified apparatus opens in a hall at the rear of the Gambrinus Hotel, Moravská Ostrava, Bohemia (now Czech Republic). The showings were supplemented by a phonograph which played military marches, opera arias, and a Mexican waltz in the intervals while the films were changed.

October 14:
Cinématographe Joly-Normandin opens in Compiègne, France.

October 15:
Paul Theatrograph is demonstrated to the Scientific Society of Gloucester by the ventriloquist and conjurer Hercat, who often advertised his shows as 'Hercat's Life-endowed Photographs' or 'Hercats Cinematographe'.

☛Acres Kineopticon opens at Chesterfield Memorial Hall, Sheffield, by H. Jasper Redfern, using films of Birt Acres. The films were again accompanied by demonstrations of the Röntgen X-rays. Admission was 6d, 1s and 2s for the 8pm show that ran for four days.

☛Edison Vitascope opens at the Teatro Garibaldi in Padova, Italy, as an accompaniment to the pantomime *Histoire d'un Pierrot*. The travelling company Jole Cantini has switched suppliers of its moving picture act, leaving the Lumière concessionaire Vittorio Calcina and moving to the Edison agents the Anglo-Italian Commerce Company, who supplied the apparatus, the films, and the operator, Ugo Perfetti.

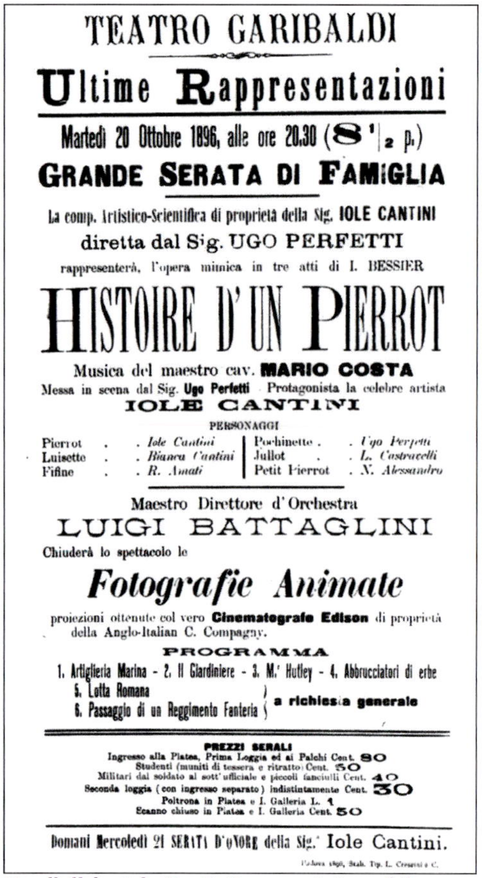

Handbill for Jole Cantini's presentation of the Edison Vitascope as an accompaniment to his theatrical show *Histoire d'un Pierrot*, October 1896.[Aldo Bernardini, *Cinema Italiano delle Origini: Gli ambulanti*, Gemona, 2001: La Cineteca del Friuli, p. 71.]

Films include: *Artiglieria Marina*, *Il Giardiniere*, *M. Hutley*, *Abbrucciatori di erbe*, *Lotta Romana*, *Passaggio di un Reggimento Fanteria*.

October 16:
US patent 574,851 *Kinetographic Camera*, to J. H. Joly for his basic reversible camera and projector, referring to his French patent of 16 March.

☛Unidentified apparatus, advertised as a Cinematografo Edison and likely a Vitascope, opens at the Pavillion Ariosto in Reggio Emelia, Italy, for six days.

October 17:
Foersterling Biomatograph, advertised as "Edison's Ideal", opens at the hall of the restaurant Germania at 31 Limbecker Straße, Essen, Germany, for two weeks.

☛Unidentified apparatus, advertised as a Kinematographe, demonstrated to an invited audience in a lounge at the Black Horse Hotel, Prague, Bohemia (now Czech Republic), by the Prague optician and mechanic Adolf Oppenheimer, who represented his screenings as organized by the fictitious Imperial and Royal Court Optician A. Rosenthal of the French Société de tableaux vivants d'Edison à Paris. Six films were shown.

Films included: *Military Riding School*, *The Coronation of the Tsar in Moscow*, *Laundresses Bleaching Linen*, *Life in the Swimming Baths*, *The Arrival of an Express at a Railway Station*, *The Bustle of the Place of the Republic in Paris*.

☛Unidentified apparatus, advertised as a Cinegrafoscopio and possibly a Cinographoscope of Alexandre and Jules Pipon, opens at the Caffè-concerto Olympia in Rome, Italy, for four days.

☛Unidentified apparatus opens at the Edison-Ausstellungs-Salon für Lebende Photographie (gen. Kinematograph) in the Victoria House, corner Seestrasse and Ringstrasse, Dresden, Germany. Managed by Richard Ehrhardt, screenings ran from 11am to 1pm and 3pm to 8pm for an admission price of 50Pfg. The last notice of this exhibition was on 29 December 1896.

October 18:
Unidentified apparatus, advertised as the Sombro-Animatographo Alves, opens at the Teatro da Vila, Alhandra, Portugal, by the actor Daniel Alves.

☛Unidentified apparatus, advertised as a Kinematographe and as "Edison's newest phenomenal invention", opens to the public in a lounge of the Black Horse Hotel, Prague, Bohemia (now Czech Republic), by the local optician and mechanic Adolf Oppenheimer of Pikop Street 26. Demand for tickets was so great that extra showings were added after the first week. Admission, 40 Kreutzer, children half price. From 1 November reserved seats cost 80 Kreutzer. Oppenheimer never registered his screenings with the local police, as required, because he considered them publicity for his optical shop, and not commercial entertainment. He gave no exhibitions outside Prague. The shows ran until 17 January 1897, and at the gala final performance of 12 films each spectator received a small cutting of film as a souvenir. Oppenheimer advertised his apparatus for sale in Prague on 21 February 1897.

October 19:
Edison Vitascope previewed privately at the Theatre Royal, Adelaide, Australia, by St. Hill and Moodie, operators for the Macmahon brothers.

☛Lumière Cinématographe opens in the theatre at Nikolaiev, Russia, by Lumière operators Marius Chapuis and Decorps.

☛Lumière Cinématographe opens in the Salon del Liceo de Varones of the former Collegio Leon XIII, calle de Alhóndiga, 8, Guadalajara, Mexico, through 15 November and returning again on 27 November, by operators Gabriel Veyre and Fernand Bon Bernard. Admission 25 centavos.

☛Unidentified apparatus, advertised as a Cinematographo Edison, opens at the Teatro Varietà in Trento, Italy, for one day.

☛Unidentified apparatus opens in the coffee house Merkur, on Judenberg in Augsburg, Germany, admission 1 Mark. The screenings lasted only 15 minutes each, but "were very well visited".

Films included: the arrival of a train at the station; street scene with pedestrians, wagons and bicyclists.

October 20:
Edison Vitascope opens to the public in a Cine Salon in a former shop in King William Street, Adelaide, Australia, by St. Hill and Moodie, operators for the Macmahon brothers, running through 10 November.

☛Unidentified apparatus, most likely an 'Edison's Ideal' Biomatograph from Hermann O. Foersterling, opens at the Wilhelmstheater in Danzig, Germany (now Gdańsk, Poland) by the pharmacist Paul Kräusslich, running until 31 October. The Danziger Zeitung reported that the presentation was of the highest interest, with the figures shown about one-third life size. The following year Kräusslich was active in Scandinavia with his Biomatograph, ultimately settling in Norway where he was a pioneer travelling exhibitor in towns across the north.

Fims included: a serpentine dance, street scenes in Paris, two fencers, a rowing scene, and three Japanese dancers (in color).

October 21:
The Cinographoscope Company of New York is formed by Charles G. S. Baker, William C. McGarth, and a former Vitascope Company employee, Charles H. Webster. Their Cinographoscope projector was advertised for sale two weeks later. Webster then joined with Edmund Kuhn to create the International Film Company, which sold dupes of Edison subjects and their own original films in November, with the company's Projectograph apparatus inexpensively on the market by December.

☛Unidentified apparatus, advertised as a Cinématographe, opens at the fair of St. Michael, place Danton, Le Havre, France, by the showman Gallici-Loramus, for one week.

☛Cinématographe Joly-Normandin opens as a Cinématographe in Autun, France, for four days.

Films included: *L'Invogne*; *Dispute entre cocher et client*; *Le Forgeron*; *Le coucher de la mariée*; *Menuet Louis XV*; *Ballet chinoise*; *L'Incendie; Place de la Madeleine*; *Quadrille d'avenir*.

☛Unidentified Cinegrapho Edison opens at Riv. Margherita 2 in Treviso, Italy, for 10 Days.

October 22:
Foersterling Biomatograph, advertised as Edison's Ideal, opens at the Barfüsserplatz market square in Basel, Switzerland, by the travelling showman Georg Bartling.

☛Lumière Cinématographe demonstrated for an invited audience at the Court of Saxony Hotel on the corner of Hybernská Street and Senovázná Street, Prague, Bohemia (now Czech Republic), by Hermann Arlet, representing the Lumière concessionaire from Vienna, Eugène Dupont. The exhibition hall was decorated with exotic flowers and illuminated by three electric bulbs; four rows of seats faced a canvas screen of twenty square meters. The projector was located behind a heavy curtain supplied with three small glass windows.

Films included: *The Demolition of a Wall, The Arrival of a Train at a Railway Station, A Boat Leaving Port, Workers Leaving the Lumière Factory in Lyon, Life in Swimming Baths on a Beach, Cavalry Manoeuvres, The Coronation of the Tsar and Tsarina in Moscow, Children Playing with Toys, Breakfast at the Lumière's, Two Wrestlers, A Waterer Watered, The Caught One.*

☛Unidentified apparatus, advertised as a Cinématographe, opens at 6 rue Rouget-de-Lisle, Lons-le-Saunier, France, for five days.

☛Edison Vitascope opens in a small hall of the local Edison agency in Mexico City, Mexico, where it was exhibited with the Kinetoscope, Kinetophone, and X-ray demonstrations. Earlier in the month, the Vitascope had opened at the Theatre Orrin, but suffered technical problems, which were never solved and the limited screenings were unsuccessful.

☛Unidentified apparatus, advertised as an Alétoscope Ponti, opens at the Foire St-Romain, Boulevard Beauvoisine, in Rouen, France. The apparatus was possibly an Aléthoscope of Paul Mortier. The screenings ran through 14 November.

☛Lumière Cinématographe opens in La Spezia, Italy.

October 23:
Lumière Cinématographe opens to the public at the Court of Saxony Hotel, Prague, Bohemia (now Czech Republic), by Hermann Arlet, representing the Lumière concessionaire Eugène Dupont. The program of seven films changed weekly, each film opening as a static image on the screen before changing into movement. Showings were given from 10 a.m. to 9 p.m. daily, admission 30 Kreutzer, children 10 Kreutzer.

☛Unidentified apparatus, advertised as a Cinématographe, opens at the Foire d'Octobre in the Allée Sud, in Bordeaux, France. The shows ran until 17 November.

☛Unidentified apparatus, advertised as a Chronophotographe, opens at the Foire d'Octobre in Bordeaux, France. The shows ran until 17 November.

☛Lumière Cinématographe opens at the Teatro Guillaume in Brescia, Italy.

October 24:
Edison Vitascope opens at the Teatro Minerva in Udine, Italy, as an accompaniment to the pantomime *Histoire d'un Pierrot*, by the travelling company Jole Cantini who have switched from Lumière apparatus. The shows ran for four days.

☛Unidentified apparatus opens in Maribor, Slovenia, by travelling showman Charles Crassé from Graz, owner of the machine.

☛Lumière Cinématographe opens at the Casino, Lons-le-Saunier, France, by operator Gaudichon, for five days.

☛Lumière Cinématographe opens at the Teatro Malibran in Venice, Italy, for one day.

☛Lumière Cinématographe opens at the Teatro Communale in Venice, Italy, for four days.

☛Unidentified apparatus, advertised as a Cinefotografo and likely a Cinéphotographe of C. J. Lépée, opens at the Teatro Sociale in Riva del Garda, Italy, for three days.

October 25:
Lumière Cinématographe opens at the Alpineum, corner of Rue du Vieux-Billard and Avenue du Mail, Geneva, Switzerland, by showman Maurice Andréossi, immediately at the end of the Exposition Nationale just as François-Henri Lavanchy-Clarke's concession on the Cinématographe terminates. Andréossi, a professional photographer and entrepreneur, had previously presented the moving Diorama "Alpineum" and panoramic projections of the Alps and historical subjects in this space. He travelled to Lyon and used his 'Latin charm' to purchase a Lumière Cinématographe, previously not for sale, directly from the Lumières for 2000 Francs,

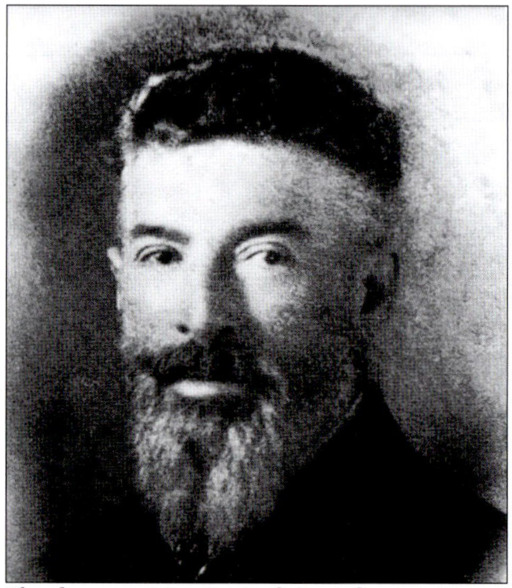

The showman Maurice Andréossi about 1900. [Hervé Dumont, *Geschichte der Schweizer Films*, Lausanne 1987: Schweizer Filmarchiv / Cinémathek suisse, p. 20.]

plus a collection of films for another 4000 Francs. The theatre closed 13 May 1899.

Films included: *Les chasseurs à cheval*, *Les Fêtes Franco-Russes de Paris*, *Fêtes de Breslau*, *La Place de la Concorde*, *Scène du village Suisse*, *La Tsarine avec Felix Faure*, *Les Turcos*, *Voitures de gala avec le Tsar*.

☛Marius Sestier and his associate H. Walter Barnett shoot the first film made in Australia, *Arrival of the ferry Brighton at Manly*, on their Lumière Cinématographe. The film was exhibited two days later at their Salon Lumiere in Sydney.

☛Foersterling Biomatograph, called Edison's Ideal, opens at the Flora Variety Theatre, Amstelstraat 26, Amsterdam, The Netherlands, by Madame Olinka.

☛Lumière Cinématographe returns to Boulogne, France, opening at the municipal circus, place F. Sauvage, by the operator Planchon, for two days.

☛According to a report in the newspaper *El Universal*, patrons of an Edison Vitascope exhibiting in Juárez, Mexico, who had travelled across the border from El Paso, Texas, to see the show returned home very annoyed because of the incompetence of the operator of the machine.

☛Cinématographe Joly-Normandin opens as Cinématographe perfectionné, système Joly, in Grenoble, France, using many films of Eugène Pirou.

Films included: *Départ pour Versailles*; *La Baignade des Soudanais au Champ-de-Mars;* *L'agent et le pochard*; *Sortie d'une église*; *Arrivée de M. Le président à l'ambassade*; *Défilé du cortège*; *Débarquement du tsar et de son cortège à Cherbourg*.

October 26:

Paul Theatrograph opens at the Empire Theatre, Cardiff, Wales, and is also re-engaged at the Empire Theatre, Northampton and the Empire Theatre, Middlesbrough. Newspaper reports of the Cardiff engagement noted an additional film showing Queen Street was "of special interest to the audience, many of whom were delighted to find someone they know".[144]

☛Cinématographe Perfectionné of Alexandre and Jules Pipon opens at the Melbourne Cine Salon, 221 Collins Street, Melbourne, Australia, by A. J. Perier, sales manager of the photographic supplies company Baker & Rouse, and Gustav Neymark. The shows ran through 9 November, admission 1 Schilling. The *Sydney Bulletin* commented: "The entertainment consisted of 16 views displayed in a very small frame, very little better, as works of photography, than those which Rickards includes in his variety entertainment".

Films included: *Grand National Steeplechase 1896*; *Coventry Bicycle Race*, *Parisian Street Life*, *Soudanese Diving*, *A Pleasant Surprise*, *Buck Jumping*, *Finish of the Grand Prix of Paris 1896*, *Arrival of the Paris Express* [and its departure], *Military Exercises*.

October 27:

Lumière Cinématographe opens in the foyer of the Music Hall of the Stadt-Casino, Basel, Switzerland, by Wilhelm Hof, who had rented the apparatus from François-Henri Lavanchy-Clarke, holder of the Swiss Lumière franchise. The screenings ran through 13 November, and included films of Basel and Switzerland.

☛Foersterling Biomatograph, advertised as Edison's Ideal, opens on the Grünenkamp in a booth at the free marketplace of the Neustadt, Bremen, Germany, by showman Jean

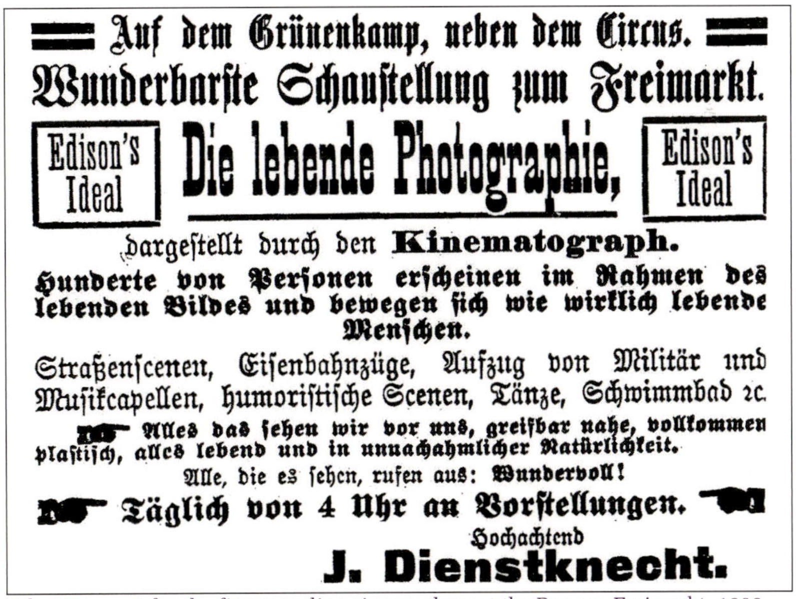

Advertisement for the first traveling cinema show at the Bremen Freimarkt, 1896. [*Bremer General-Anzeiger*, 24 October 1896, via Fritz Peters, *Freimarkt in Bremen*, p. 113.]

144 The first appearance in Wales of the Paul Theatrograph was in early October at the Public Hall, Morriston, organized by the London exhibitor William Dower.

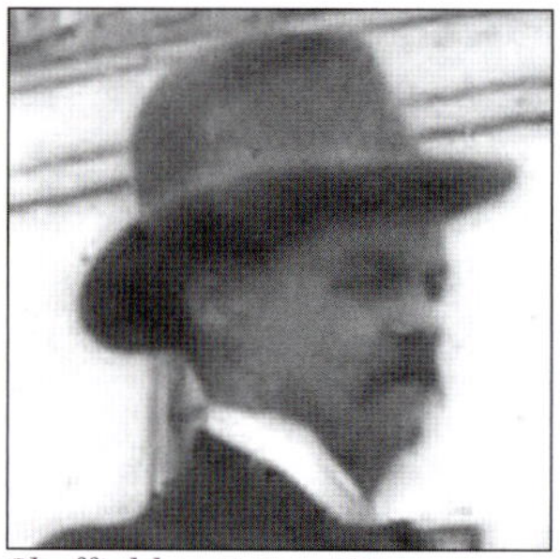

Sheffield optician H Jasper Redfern exhibited his Acres Kineopticon and made many local views for the next decade, before focusing on medical research. [www.victorian-cinema.net]

Dienstknecht from Hamburg.

October 28:
Edison Vitascope opens in Wellington, New Zealand, by Australian showman James Macmahon.

October 29:
Lumière Cinématographe opens at Dan Lowney's Star of Erin Theatre of Varieties, Dublin, Ireland, this time with Felicien Trewey himself operating the apparatus, although Lowney is reputed to have persuaded Trewey to come to Dublin for much less than his normal rate. The show was successful and ran through 14 November.

☛Acres Kineopticon opens at the Drill Hall, Rotherham, by H. Jasper Redfern, for three days. Films by Birt Acres were again accompanied by demonstrations of Röntgen's X-rays, as well as the ventriloquist Monsieur Delure. The 8pm shows were priced at 6d, 1s and 2s, with 'early doors 3d and 6d extra.'

☛Lumière Cinématographe opens at the Teatro Ristori in Verona, Italy, for three days.

October 30:
Oskar Messter receives his first order for a film camera, from the Köhler brothers in Hamburg. The finished machine was delivered at the end of November. Messter's first cameras were simply projector mechanisms, with slight alterations to the shutter and film gate, that were fully enclosed in light-tight cabinets.

☛Cinéphotographe Lépée opens at the Foire de la Toussaint in Le Mans, by showman Lagneau, in his Théâtre Salon des Sciences. The shows ran until 25 November.

October 31:
Casler / Dickson Biograph opens at Koster & Bial's Music Hall, New York City, after closing at Hammerstein's Theatre.

☛Lumière Cinématographe opens at the Teatro Sociale, Mirandole, Italy, by Enrico and Italo Pacchioni. Additional shows were given on 1 and 8 November. Pacchioni was independent of the Lumière organization, and travelled throughout nothern Italy giving shows with his machine.

☛Edison Vitascope opens at the Melbourne Athenaeum, Melbourne, Australian, by Joseph and James Macmahon, for one week. Both Edison and Paul films were shown.

☛Lumière Cinématographe opens at the Princess Theatre, Melbourne Australia, by Harry Barnett and Marius Sestier as part of the third act of the Japanese fantasy pantomime *Djin-Djin*, promoted by J. C. Williamson. On the afternoon of this opening, Barnett and Sestier had filmed three pictures of the VRC Derby at the Flemington racecourse: *Derby Day: The Betting Ring*; *The Running of the VRC Derby*; and *Lady Brassey Presenting Blue Ribbon to Derby Winner 'Newhaven'*. The exhibitions at the Princess Theatre ran until 20 November.

☛Edison Vitascope opens at the Teatro Rossini in Venice, Italy, accompanying the pantomime *Histoire d'un Pierrot* of the Jole Cantini touring company, for two days.

☛Lumière Cinématographe opens to an invited audience of the city's elite in the mezzanine room of a building at Bürgermeister Smidstrasse 83, in Bremerhaven, Germany. The evening screening was in conjunction with the opening of an automat exhibition of the Deutsche Automaten-Gesellschaft. The Cinématographe opened to the public the next day, under the management of Capt. Hechtel. Screenings ran from 5pm to 10pm every half hour, with eight pictures shown for an admission of 50 Pfg. The apparatus was said to come directly from Lyon, and was operated by Monsieur Jay, who was praised for his "extraordinary competence" as one of the best Lumière operators. Screenings ended on 16 May 1897. The apparatus itself was sold to Capt. Hechtel on 27 January 1897, and sold by him again in August to C. A. Blunk, who used it during the annual Bremen Freimarkt.

November 1:
The Lumiére company opens the Lumière Agency at 13 East 30th Street, New York City, and begins to lease their machines and sell states rights in the apparatus, marking the end of the exclusive arrangement for U. S. exploitation of the Lumière Cinématographe by the Keith vaudeville circuit.

☛Lumière Cinématographe opens on the first floor of Holstenstrasse 11, Kiel, Germany, running from 10 in the morning until 11 p.m. in the evening. Admission 30 Pfennig, children and military enlisted men only, half price. This permanent installation was in the Stollwerck automat-hall, or wholesale facility, at the Zacherl pub across from the City Hall, which itself was "admission free" as the advertisement noted.

☛Lumière Cinématographe opens in the hall of the Vienne Union, rue de la République, Vienne, France, by the operator Trabuc. The screenings ran through 27 November.

November 2:
Casler / Dickson Biograph opens at Ford's Opera House, Baltimore, Maryland.

☛Lumière Cinématographe opens at the Wonderland Theatre, Rochester, New York, running for 17 weeks.

November 3:
Unidentified apparatus opens in Celje, Slovenia, by travelling showman Charles Crassé from Graz.

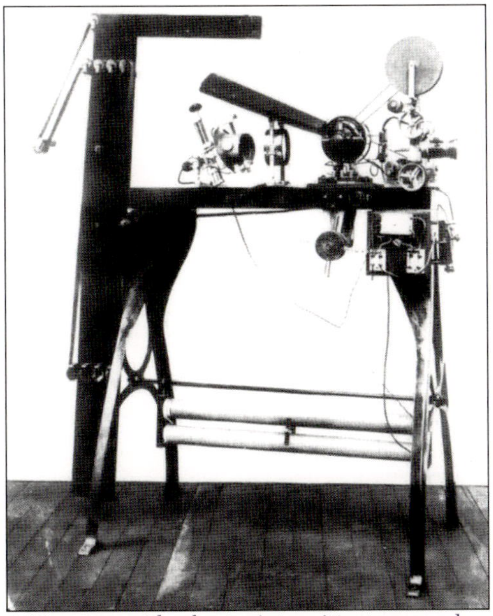

A Vitascope with a beater intermittent arranged as a spoolbank projector, efficiently organized on its wide back panel.
[Edison National Historic Site.]

☛Marius Sestier and H. Walter Barnett take ten films of the Melbourne Cup at Flemington, Australia, with their Lumière Cinématographe.

☛Cinéphotographe Lépée opens at the salle de l'Alcazar Roussillonnais, Perpignon, France, by the showman Datigny, for three days. The show reopened on November 8 at the fair in the Promenade des Platanes, remaining through 28 November.

☛Foersterling Biomatograph, called Edison's Ideal, opens at the Varieté music hall in the Karlin quarter of Prague, Bohemia (now Czech Republic). Technical difficulties delayed the opening from Sunday, November 1, and Varieté director Rudolf Tich evidently replaced the apparatus almost immediately with an Edison Vitascope operated by the American George Kemp and assisted by the Varieté's electrician Josef Hoffmann. The screenings on the Vitascope ran until the end of November.[145]

☛Lumière Cinématographe opens at the Politeama Garibaldi in Treviso, Italy, by the Salvi brothers, accompanying their mechanical marionette show. The screenings ran until 8 November.

November 4:
Edison Vitascope opens at the Teatro Niccolini in Florence, Italy, accompanying the pantomime *Histoire d'un Pierrot* of the Jole Cantini touring company.

November 5:
Unidentified apparatus, advertised as a Cinématographe, opens at the Toussoun Bourse in Cairo, Egypt. Films were screened every half hour from 5pm until 11pm, with programme changes on November 13 and 26. Advertisements ended on December 17.

November 6:
Unidentified apparatus opens in an empty pub near the workers' quarter Segeroth, north of the center of Essen, organized by the bicycle dealer Louis Bogdan. The films were accompanied by military music played on a phonograph. Admission to the best seats, 50 Pfennig, to the rest, 30 Pfennig; children half price. Three weeks later a travelling showman opened another unidentified apparatus in Essen.

Films included: *The Czar in Paris.*

☛Cinographoscope of Alexandre and Jules Pipon opens in the hall of the grain exchange, Vannes, France, for two weeks.

☛Unidentified apparatus opens in the hall of the Messers. Hapke at the Wiener Café, Weenderstraße, Göttingen, Germany. The

145 Further details are needed to properly identify this screening. The great detail of the description of the projection set-up reported clearly applies to an Edison Vitascope, yet the advertisement for the exhibition reproduced by Zdenek Štábla is an absolutely classic Foersterling design, conforming in every particular to the promotional campaign Foersterling established for his apparatus and which had been used by this date by a dozen showmen in a half-dozen countries, a campaign begun at a date well before the Vitascope had reached any city in Europe. The technical difficulties delaying the opening are also consistent with other Foersterling reports; certainly "the biggest screening surface in Prague" was unsuitable for this apparatus. As director Tich saw both the inadequacy of the equipment and a strongly positive public reaction to animated pictures, it would have been equally consistent with the practise of the day that the apparatus would have been replaced by another machine and another operator overnight, if one was available. I believe that it is this second machine that was a true Edison Vitascope, for which Štábla provides a great amount of fascinating detail in his article – including the description of spool-bank projection of films in loops, the use of three machines, and the information that the operator, Hoffmann, covered the threaded film loops with a wetted sheet to soften the films and make them more flexible in their passage through the Vitascope's beater mechanism. There is no indication elsewhere in Europe that any Foersterling exhibitor had the financial or showmanly substance to mount a multiple-projector exhibition over an extended period of time at a location in a major city.
George Kemp advertised two Edison Vitascopes for sale in Prague on 29 November, taking the third to his shows in Plze; he then disappears from Bohemia.

shows ran for five days, admission 50 Pfennig for 6 films.[146]

☛Unidentified apparatus, advertised as a Cinematografo, opens at the Viennese beer hall in Imola, Italy.

November 7:
Lumière Cinématographe demonstrated for an invited audience including the mayor and members of the city council at the charity home, via Po 33, Turin, Italy, at a one-day conference on "cronografia – fotografia" led by Professor E. Louvet-Gay. The Cinématographe was the only apparatus demonstrated.

Films included: *Giuochi infantili, Fabbro-ferrair, Entrata dello Czar al Kremlino, Barco e bagni di mare, Bagni di Diana, Corazzieri (manovra di sciabola), Ciclisti e cavalieri a Londra, Arrivo del treno.*

☛Edison Vitascope opens in High Street, Christ-Church, New Zealand, at a Cinematographe Salon, operated by Australian showman James Macmahon.

☛Demenÿ Chronophotographe opens in the Salon Cinematographe, 237 Pitt Street, Sydney, Australia, by the Macmahon Brothers, running until early 1898. The premises had previously been used by Maurice Sestier's Lumière Cinématographe.

Films included: *Paris: the Avenue de L'Opera*; *French Swordsmen's Duel*; *Arrival of a Paris Train*; *Animals at a French Zoo*; *Stevan Plats, Vienna*; *Waves at Dieppe*; *Living Statuary*; *Batteries of the Royal Artillery*; *Dancer: La Loïe Fuller* (in color).

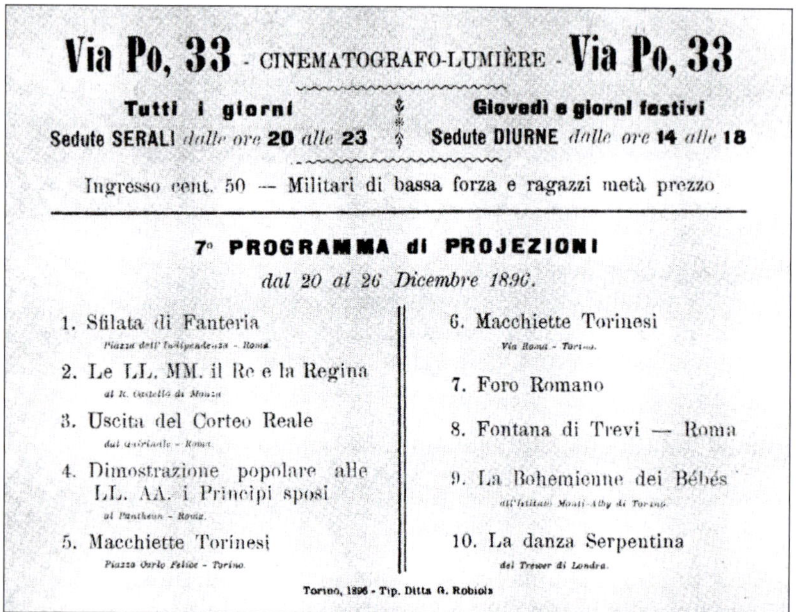
Via Po, 33 - CINEMATOGRAFO-LUMIÈRE - Via Po, 33

Tutti i giorni
Sedute SERALI *dalle ore* 20 *alle* 23

Giovedì e giorni festivi
Sedute DIURNE *dalle ore* 14 *alle* 18

Ingresso cent. 50 — Militari di bassa forza e ragazzi metà prezzo

7° PROGRAMMA di PROJEZIONI
dal 20 al 26 Dicembre 1896.

1. Sfilata di Fanteria
2. Le LL. MM. il Re e la Regina
al R. Castello di Monza
3. Uscita del Corteo Reale
dal Quirinale - Roma
4. Dimostrazione popolare alle LL. AA. i Principi sposi
al Pantheon - Roma
5. Macchiette Torinesi
Piazza Carlo Felice - Torino
6. Macchiette Torinesi
Via Roma - Torino
7. Foro Romano
8. Fontana di Trevi — Roma
9. La Bohemienne dei Bébés
10. La danza Serpentina
del Trewer di Londra

Torino, 1896 - Tip. Ditta G. Robiola

Programme for the Lumière Cinématographe shows in Turin, here for the week of December 20–26th. [Aldo Bernardelli, *Cinema muto italiano. Ambiente, spettacoli e spettatori 1896/1904*, p. 43.]

☛Addition to French patent 257,089 of June 9 of Ambroise-François Parnaland, modifying the claw mechanism of his camera and projector to allow the use of square perforations on either side of the film image, one per frame. Parnaland's perfected equipment was available from early 1897; he was later co-founder of the French film company Eclair, formerly the Parnaland Company.[147]

☛Edison Vitascope opens in the Illusion Showroom of Wladyslaw Krzeminski, Lódz, Poland. Krzeminski presented slide shows, magic tricks and curiosities of nature including an eight-fingered hand and a stuffed two-headed dog. Earlier in 1896 he added the Edison phonograph to his attractions. Krzeminski, with his younger brother Antoni, became the first Polish travelling cinema showman, exhibiting widely across Poland and Russia from March, 1900.

☛Unidentified apparatus, advertised as a Cynématographe, opens at the home of M. Hérault, rue du Poids-du-Roi, near the rue Denis-Papin, Blois, France.

☛Demenÿ Chronophotographe opens at 11 rue de l'Esplanade, Séte, France, for two weeks.

November 8:
Lumière Cinématographe opens to the public at the former charity home, via Po 33, Turin, Italy, running until 31 December. Admission 50 Cents, children and military half price.

☛Cinematografo Edison, probably a Vitascope, opens at the Teatro Nazionale, Bologna, Italy, through 12 November. Admission 25 Cents.

146 The *Göttinger Tageblatt* reported on 5 December 1896 that the exhibition had returned with new films, and an "improved Kinematograph" which could be highly recommended.

147 The apparatus was further modified on 6 March 1897 with changes to its intermittent movement, and on 28 February 1899 to allow either of two sets of claws to engage the film: one for Parnaland's original central perforations and the other for his new side perforations. Clément-Maurice later showed the famous Phono-Cinéma-Théâtre films for the Paris Exposition of 1900 on a borrowed Parnaland apparatus.

☛Cinéphotographe Lépée opens at the Foire St-Martin on the Promenade des Planates in Perpignan, France, by the showman Datigny. The shows ran until 28 November.

November 9:
Magniscope of Edward Hill Amet opens at the Duquesne Theatre, Pittsburgh, Pennsylvania. Manufactured by the Amet Talking Machine Company, the apparatus weighed only 70 pounds and was intended for easy touring. Theatre manager John D. Hopkins replaced an Edison Vitascope with this apparatus, and he replaced the same apparatus with the Amet machine at his Chicago vaudeville house in mid-November.

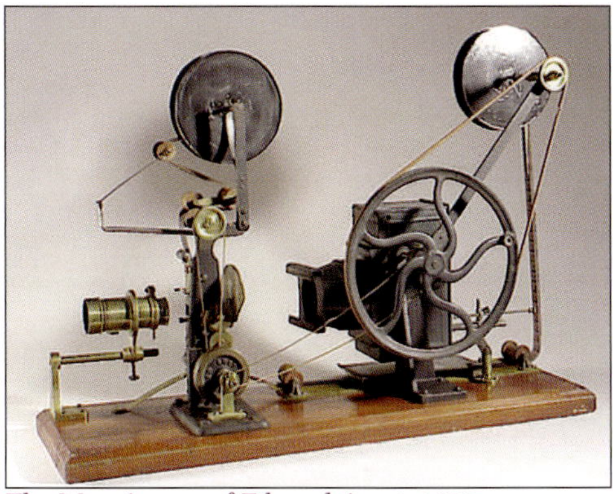

The Magniscope of Edward Amet, 1896. [Museum of Science and Industry, Chicago.

☛Lumière Cinématographe opens in Louisville, Kentucky.

☛Lumière Cinématographe opens at the Teatro di Serravalle in Vittorio Venito, Treviso, Italy, for three days.

November 10:
Lumière Cinématographe opens at Aleestraße 40 (today Heinrich-Heine-Allee), Düsseldorf, Germany, by the Deutsche Animatographen-Gesellschaft, exhibiting from 10 a.m. to 1 p.m. and from 4 p.m. to 10 p.m. daily.[148]

☛Kinétographe de Bedts, advertised as the Kinetographo Portuguez Paz dos Reis, opens at the Teatro Principe Real, Porto, Portugal,

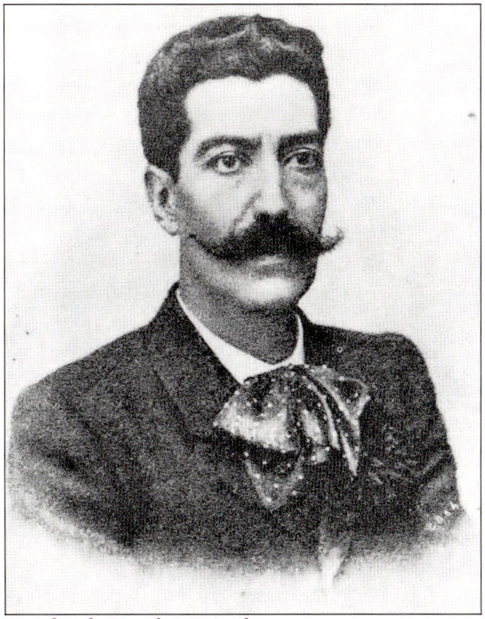

Aurelio da Paz dos Reis about 1896. [Antonio J. Ferreira, *A Fotografia Animada em Portugal 1894–1895–1896–1897*, Lisbon, 1986: Cinemateca Portuguesa, p. 108.]

by Aurelio da Paz dos Reis and F. Bastons, Jr. The program included seven Portuguese titles and five foreign views.

☛Cinématographe Joly-Normandin opens as a Cinématographe parisienne in Beaune, France, for nine days.

Films included: *L'Invogne*; *Les Soudanais au Champ-de-Mars*; *Déshabillé de la mariée*; *Dispute entre cocher et son client*; *Menuet Louis XV; Ballet chinoise*; *Quadrille d'avenir*.

☛Unidentified Cinematografo Edison opens at the Teatro Partenope in Naples, Italy.

November 11:
Lumière Cinématographe opens at 2 place Charles-Albert, Nice, France. The showings ran until 30 April 1897.

☛Unidentified apparatus opens at the Foire St-Martin on the Place d'Austerlitz in Sainte-Menehould, France, by the showman Charles Koenig, who also exhibited a phonograph.

☛Edison Vitascope opens at the Museo foto-electrico Le Lieure in Rome, Italy, organized by Edison's representatives in Genoa, the Anglo-Italian Commerce Company and projected by their employee Corrado Vandi. The screenings ran until 6 January 1897.

November 12:
Lumière Cinématographe opens at the Teatro Minerva, Udine, Italy, through 19 November.

☛Unidentified apparatus, advertised as a Movitographe, opens in the conference hall of the Maison Appy, 62 rue Gioffredo, Nice, France. The showings ran through 24 December.

☛Cinématographe Joly-Normandin, advertised as a Cinématographe Perfectionné, opens in the Passage Sainte-Catherine, Saint-Etienne, France, for five days, using films of Eugène Pirou.

Films included: [*L'arrivée du train*]; *Les chargeurs de décombres*; *Le Forgeron; Les enfants au jardin d'acclimatation*; *La leçon de bicyclette*; *Bain d'une mondaine*; *Le ballet de Li-Hung Tchang*; *Le tsar au Champs Elysées*.

☛Unidentified apparatus, advertised as a Cinétographe and likely by the Werner brothers, opens at the theatre in the town hall of Tlem-

148 A Joly apparatus, "well known as the best system", was exhibited in Düsseldorf at Schadowstrasse, corner of Wagnerstrasse, daily from 11 a.m. to 1 p.m. and 2 p. m. to 9 p.m., from 19 January 1897.

cen, Algeria, by M. Poordy, the 'celebrated engineer and electrician.' The screenings ran for one week, and accompanied a magician and prestidigitator called Professor Marga.

☛Films include: *La ferme, Le buveur de bière, Le rémouleur, Partie de Soute-mouton, Salon de coiffure, L'arroseur, Le Tsar au bois du Boulogne, Le quadrille de Grille d'Égout* (en couleur), *Place de la République à Paris.*

November 13:
Cinématographe Deményÿ-Gaumont opens at the Foire St.-Martin on the Champ de Mars, Angers, France, by Ernest Grenier in his Théâtre Électrique. The shows ran until 30 November.

November 14:
Lumière Cinématographe opens at the town theatre in Cracow, Poland, with a program similar to that used at the Grand Café in Paris. The Lumière operator was Eugène Dupont, who found theatre reformer and intendant Tadeusz Pawlikowski enthusiastic about combining theatre performances with the Cinématographe. The shows ran through 13 December.

☛French patent 2629, *Nouvel appareil pour l'obtention et la projection animée*, to Pierre-Victor Continsouza and René Bünzli for an improved cinema apparatus in which a glass plate is substituted for the film band; the plate is moved intermittently and the photographs taken in a spiral form on the plate. The inventors predicted the end of film strip cinematography. Particularly noteworthy in this patent, however, was a superbly drafted four-spoke Maltese Cross movement. Continousza later supplied apparatus for Pathé Frères.[149]

☛Foersterling Biomatograph, called Edison's Ideal, opens at the Arts and Sciences building, The Hague, The Netherlands, by Madame Olinka, where it was the main attraction of a Gala Soirée Artistique that included a comic, an impersonator, a singing ensemble and other acts.

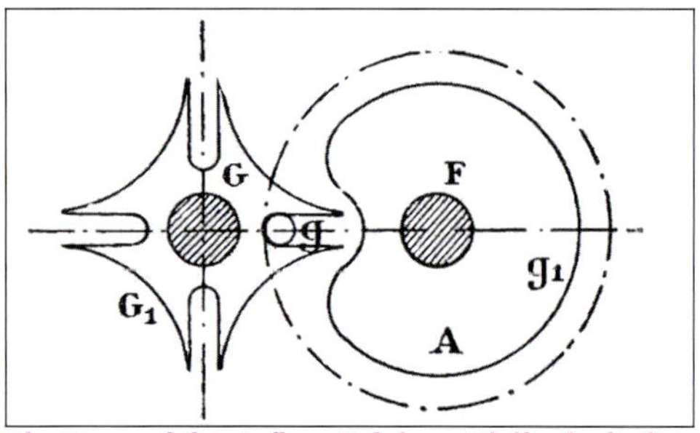

The irony of this influential, beautifully-drafted four-branched Maltese Cross intermittent is that it was in a patent for a glass plate cinematograph. [G.-Michel Coissac, *Histoire du Cinématographe*, p. 285.]

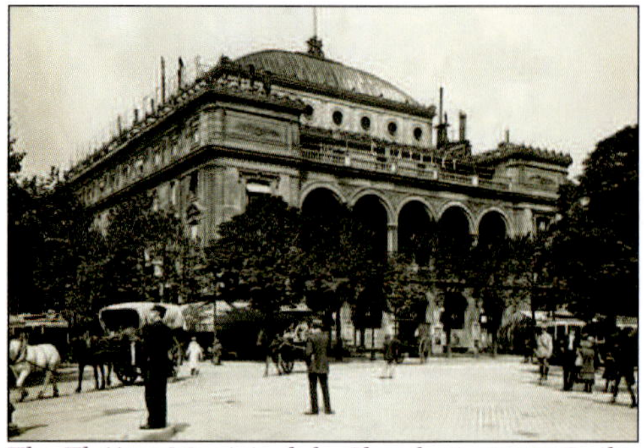
The Théâtre Municipal du Chatelet in 1917. Built in 1862 for an equestrian show, the theatre has served Parisians a wide variety of delights, none more prominent than the run of *Around the World in 80 Days* by Jules Verne and Adolphe d'Ennery which appeared for 64 (non-consecutive) years and over 2000 performances. [Photograph by Charles Joseph Antoine Lansiux, Musée Carnavalet, Paris.]

☛Demenÿ Chronophotographe opens in the large marriage room of the city hall, Le Havre, France, by exhibitor Léon Gaumont. The screenings ran for two days.

☛Unidentified Cinematografo Edison opens in the Café-chantant Alhambra in Milan, Italy. The screenings ran until 24 December.

☛Demenÿ Chronophotographe opens at the Théâtre Municipal du Châtelet, place du

149 Various inventors and manufacturers continued to offer new glass plate cinematographic apparatus until about 1910, mostly intended for home or amateur use. In part, the appearance of these machines was a continuing evidence of the strength of magic lantern culture: the machines were extensions of the lantern world, with its image-on-glass technology, its individual showmen, its parlour entertainments, and its use of small church and community halls for projection. They could not imagine, or compete within, the cinema culture which was already showing to ever larger audiences in bigger halls with a longer projection throw aided by more powerful arc lights. Just as the glass-plate apparatus used a non-flammable image carrier that was thoroughly familiar to the more advanced amateur photographer, another part of the appeal of this technology was its price. It was estimated in 1912 in Germany, for example, that a glass plate for the Bettini Plattenkinematograph held 576 images, or the equivalent of about 11 meters of 35mm film. At 80 Pfennig the meter, a celluloid film negative cost 8.80 Marks, and the equally long positive print doubled the price to 17.60 Marks, while a glass plate for the Bettini apparatus cost about 15 Pfennig, with the requisite positive making a total cost of 30 Pfennig for the equivalent amount of screen playing time. It was on such dramatic economic savings that the dreams of many inventors rested.
One of the most interesting early glass-plate cinematographs was patented by Leonard Ulrich Kamm in London on 17 March 1898, appearing on the market a year later. The Kamm apparatus was also patented in Germany, Nr. 120967, on 23 October 1900. The Kammatograph had an ingenious and smooth-running mechanism, with a crank driving a broken worm gear directly on the notched rim of the glass plate holder; the plate held 550 images arranged in a spiral. The central axis of the glass plate itself drove a helical screw arrangement to the rear of the machine which moved the entire plate toward the crank side of the machine, keeping the images properly lined up with a fixed lens equipped with a before-the-lens shutter.
Other equipment of this type included the Spirograph of Henry W. Joy (British patent 14,493 of 1907), an engineer with Urban Pictures Industries in New York City, whose plate was made of cellulose 10 ½ inches in diameter and holding the equivalent of about 13.8 meters of 35mm film, and the Plattenkinematograph of the Bettini brothers (United States patent of 15 June 1897) with a square plate 1.30 meters long and 130mm wide holding 3456 images.

Châtelet, Paris, as the central effect in a revival of the 1845 fairy spectacle *La Biche au bois*, in four acts and 30 scenes. The Demenÿ Chronophotographe projected a ballet scene on the theatre's curtain that consisted of over 1000 hand-coloured images prepared for Léon Gaumont by Jacques Ducom, the former projectionist for Lumière at the Boulevard du Capucines. The spectacle received more than 80 performances at the 3,400-seat Châtelet well into 1897.

November 15:
Lumière Cinématographe opens at the Teatro Contavalli, Bologna, Italy, added to G. Galliani's local theatre company production of the comedy *Tourna in scena I pisuneint* by Testoni. Admission 60 Cents; the screenings ran for two weeks.

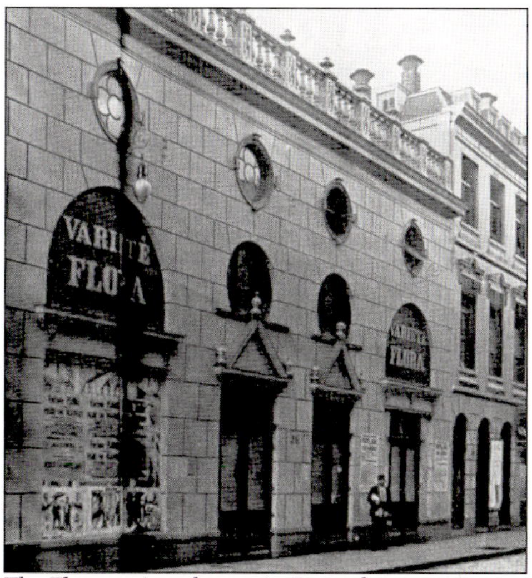

The Flora variete theatre in Rotterdam c1900, twice host to Madame Olinka's film screenings. The building burned down completely in 1902. [Karel Dibbets and Frank van der Maden, *Geschiedenis van de Nederlandse Film en Bioscoop tot 1940*. Weesp, 1986: Het Wereldvenster, p. 24–25.]

☛Lumière Cinématographe opens in the lobby of the Bains de la Poste, 18 rue de la République, Avignon, France, for three weeks.

Cinématographe Joly-Normandin opens as Cinématographe Eugène Pirou in Ghent, Belgium. The shows included many Pirou films of the visit of the Russian Tsar to France.

Films included: *Départ des souverains russes avec M. Le Président de la République pour Versailles*; *(Le) plongeon des soudanaise*; *Le coucher de la mariée; Départ de l'ambassade pour l'église russe*; *Arrivée du président de la République à l'ambassade; Visite du président de la République française à l'ambassade russe à Paris*; *Défilé du cortège du tsar*.

November 16:
Casler / Dickson Biograph opens in Chicago, accompanying Palmer Cox's Brownies.

☛Unidentified apparatus opens in a hall of the hotel Stadt Wien, Ljubljana, Slovenia, by travelling showman Charles Crassé, for one week. Throughout his trip in Slovenia, Crassé showed Lumière films, but also one film of Georges Méliès, *Une bonne farce – le chifonnier*.[150]

☛Foersterling Biomatograph, called Edison's Ideal, opens in the Flora Variety Theatre, Coolsingel 24, Rotterdam, The Netherlands, presented by Madame Olinka. The screenings ran through 30 November.

☛Lumière Cinématographe opens at the City Club, a social meeting point for the city's upper class, in Tiflis (Tblisi), Georgia.

☛Edison Vitascope opens in Atlanta Georgia, where it concluded each presentation of the Florence Hamilton Company, a theatrical troupe presenting a different play each night.

☛Unidentified apparatus, advertised as an Animatograph, opens at the Swan & Edgar department store, corner of Regent Street, London, by Lewis Sealy. Two performances were given daily, at 11.30 a.m. and 4.00 p.m. The apparatus was most likely an Acres Kineopticon, which Sealy used both before and after this date. Birt Acres films were used.

Films included: *Scrambling Urchins*, *Brighton Beach*, *Cycling in Hyde Park*, *The Derby*, and views of the Royal Wedding.

November 18:
Foersterling Kinetograph opens at 66 Mauer-Strasse, Berlin, near Leipzigerstrasse. Here Foersterling opened a kind of multi-media exhibition for all of his "Precision apparatus", prominently advertising an "Electrical-Edison- Theatre" along with exhibitions of the newest kinetograph and graphophone. The shows ran from 11am to 1pm and again from 4pm to 10 pm, with a "combined entry" price of 50pf, children and military half-price. The shows ran at least until 31 December.[151]

150 The same Charles Crassé made the first films shot in Yugoslavia, which were screened in Belgrade beginning on 6 March 1897. The films included: *Polazak Kralja Aaleksandra Obrenovi iz dvora u Sabolnu crkvu* (Départ du roi Alexancre Obrenovi de la cour pour la cathédral), *Tramvajska stanica na Terazijama* (La Station de tramway de Terazije), *I\laenje radnika iz fabrike duvana* (La Sortie de la manufacture de tabac), *Kalemgdanska šetnja* (Promenade à Kalemegdan).

151 It is an intriguing prospect that this Edison-Electric-Theatre was, in fact, the Siemens 'Little Theatre' that had been exhibited by Arthur Schwartz of the Electrical Wonder Company at the Chicago World's Fair. Schwartz was by now back in Germany, had re-entered the photographic industry, and may have been associated with Foersterling. The Theatre was described in a later advertisement of Foersterling as a mountain landscape in the Alps on a miniature stage where sunrise, thunderstorms, hail, lightning, rainbows, the moon and stars were represented. See Goergen 1998, 81.

November 19:
Unidentified apparatus, advertised as a Theatroscope, opens at 58 St. Laurent, Montréal, Canada.

☛Unidentified apparatus, advertised as a Cinématographe, opens in the Grand Foyer of the Théâtre, Versailles, France, where it was presented in the interval.

☛Unidentified apparatus, advertised as "animated photographs in natural colors", opens in the Eagle Hall of the Grand Hotel, Maria Street, Prague, Bohemia (now Czech Republic), by the Frenchman Emile Joffé, who had been working as a photographer in Prague. The screenings were accompanied by an Edison phonograph which reproduced both music and sound effects for the films, admission 25 Kreutzers, children 10 Kreutzers. The screenings ran until 8 December.

☛Cinématographe Joly-Normandin opens as Cinématographe perfectionné, système Joly, at 21 rue de l'Ecu, near the Café Glacier, Clermont-Ferrand, France. The shows used many films of Eugène Pirou, and continued through the end of the year.

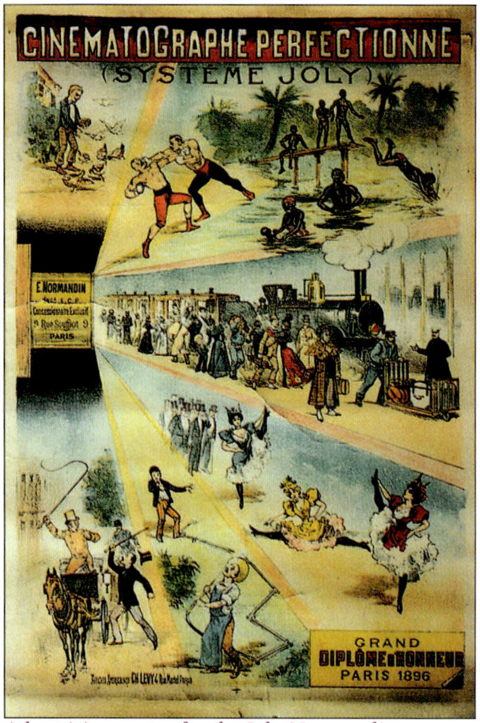

Advertising poster for the Joly-Normandin apparatus, 1896. [Jean-Louis Capitaine, *l'Invitation au Cinématographe*. Paris, 1993: Maeght Éditeur, n.p.]

Films included: *Le jardinier ou l'arroseur arrosé*; *Assaut de boxe entre deux champions de Joinville*; *Enfants jouant dans un bois avec d'autres personnes*; *Le travail des forgerons*; *Baignade des Soudanais au Champ-de-Mars à Paris*; *Sortie de l'église Notre-Dame-des-Victoires à Paris*; *Bain d'une parisienne*. 1. *Le déshabillé* 2. *Le entrée au bain*; *Quadrille excentrique au Moulin-Rouge*; *La boxe entre deux champions de Joinville*; *Le tsar au Panthéon*; *Le tsar au Champs Elysées*.

☛Cinématographe Joly-Normandin opens as Cinématographe Joly in Châlons-sur-Marne, France, using many films of Eugène Pirou.

Films included: *Le jardinier ou l'arroseur arrosé*; *Une séance de boxe*; *Dispute d'un cocher avec son client*; *Enfants au bois*; *Une leçon de bicyclette*; *Bain des Soudanais*; *Scènes d'ivrogne*; *Sortie de l'église Notre-Dame-des-Victoires*; *Le tsar au Panthéon*; *Bain de la Parisienne*; *Moulin Rouge*; *Scène de table*.

☛Lumière Cinématographe opens at the Villa Reale in Monza, Italy, for one evening.

November 20:
Unidentified apparatus opens at the caffé-concerto Alhambra, Milan, Italy, through 7 December.

☛Edison Vitascope opens at a Salon Cinematographe, a shop next to the Wains Hotel, Princes Street, Dunedin, New Zealand, under the direction of Australian showman James Macmahon. The local press reported "All this is very wonderful and also instructive, and the accompanying music is very much in advance of what one hears at side shows".

☛Lumière Cinématographe ends its engagement on a vaudeville bill at the Princess Theatre, Melbourne, Australia, operated by Marius Sestier. Parts of the Melbourne Cup films were previewed at a benefit in aid of the blind. At the same time in Melbourne the Edison Vitascope was at Atheneum Hall, and a Cinématographe Perfectionné was at 266 Collins Street.

November 21:
Unidentified apparatus opens for one day in the theatre at Pula, Slovenia, by Angelo Curiel of Trieste and his associate Max Karreiter. The showmen used the pseudonym Prof. Cav. De Horney, and called themselves 'Professor of physics at the Academy of Science in Madrid, etc.' The screening was technically unsatisfactory under a French operator, M. Madesny.

☛Kinétographe de Bedts opens at the Teatro de S. Geraldo, Braga, Portugal, by Aurélio da Paz dos Reis, where it was called Kinetographo Portuguez Paz dos Reis, for two days. Admission to first row front boxes, 2,500 Reis; side boxes, 2,000 Reis; second row front boxes, 3,000 Reis; side boxes, 2,500 Reis; third row boxes, 1,000 Reis; stalls, 500 Reis; upper orchestra, 300 Reis; front gallery, 240 Reis; numbered gallery, 200 Reis; and general admission, 100 Reis.

☛Lumière Cinématographe opens in the hall of the Vienne co-operative (Union), rue de la République, Vienne, France.

☛Edison Vitascope opens in Perth, Australia, by James and Joseph Macmahon.

☛Vitagraphé of Clément and Gilmer, Paris, was recently demonstrated by M. Eloss at a meeting of the Cardiff Photographic Society, Cardiff, Wales, according to a report on this date in the *South Wales Echo*.

☛Unidentified apparatus, advertised as a Cinématographe, opens at the theatre in Compiègne, France, for three days.

☛Cinématographe Joly-Normandin opens as Véritable cinématographe parisien in Mulhouse, France, by Bernheim-Wormser, using films of Eugène Pirou.

Films included: *Le coucher de la mariée*; *Bain d'une parisienne*; *Défilé complet du cortège du tsar*.

☛Lumière Cinématographe opens at the Politeama Ariosto in Reggio Emelia, Italy, for four days.

☛Unidentified apparatus, advertised as a Cinematografo Edison opens in Lugo, Italy.

☛Unidentified apparatus, advertised as a Cinématographe, opens at the Hotel Greif in Bolzano, Italy, for nine days.

November 22:
Lumière Cinématographe opens at the Teatro Comunale, Faenza, Italy, by Ernesto and Italo Pacchioni, for two days.

☛Unidentified apparatus, most likely the Animatographo Alves, opens at the theatre in Loures, Portugal.

☛Unidentified apparatus opens in Przemyl, Poland.

☛Casler / Dickson Biograph opens in St. Louis, Missouri, accompanying a show of Palmer Cox's Brownies.

November 23:
At Windsor Castle, the first film performance before a British monarch is given in the presence of Queen Victoria, for the tenth birthday celebrations of Prince Alexander. Two machines were used, a Paul Theatrograph and a special apparatus made by T. J. Harrison, whose wide-guage camera with eight round perforations per frame had taken views of the Royal family at Balmoral the previous month.

☛Latham Eidoloscope is incorporated into the fourth act of the play *Carmen* presented by the Rosable Morrison theatre company, using the Lathams' film *Bullfight*. Performances were 23 & 24 November in Atlanta, Georgia, and 11 December in Austin, Texas.

☛Paul Theatrograph opens at the Empire Theatre, Swansea.

☛Foersterling Biomatograph, called Edison's Ideal, advertised as "direct from Paris", opens in the rear hall of 89 Bismark Street, Posnan, East Prussia (now Poland), as a presentation of Michal Michalskiego.

November 24:
Lumière Cinématographe opens at the Criterion Theatre, Sydney, Australia, by Marius Sestier. The theatre was leased by Sestier and H. Walter Barnett. The film programme was unusually long, and included the premiere showings of the whole of the exhibitor's Melbourne Cup footage, as well as standard Lumière titles. Admission to the Dress Circle, 2 Shillings; Stalls, 1 Shilling; Family Circle, 6 Pence. Children Half price. The shows ran for two weeks.

Films included: *Cup Carnival Series: Arrival of Train, Hill, Platform*; *The Lawn near the Band Stand*; *Arrival of H. E. Lord Brassey and Suite*; *The Saddling Paddock*; *Finish of Hurdle Race, Cup Day*; *Weighing Out for the Cup*; *Finish of the Race*; *Lady Brassey Placing the Blue Ribbon on 'Newhaven'*; *Near the Grand Stand*; *Afternoon Tea under the Awning*; *'Newhaven', his Trainer* [W. Hickenbotham] *and Jockey Gardiner*. Also shown: *N. S. W. Horse Artillery at Drill, Victoria Barracks, Sydney*; *Passengers leaving S. S. Brighton at Manley, Sunday Afternoon*; *A Baby's Quarrel*; *French Infantry on the March*.

November 25:
Unidentified apparatus, advertised as a Cinematografo Edison opens at the Teatro Mariani in Ravenna, Italy.

November 26:
French patent 261,650, *Système d'appareil pour projections circulaires animées, dit Cinématorama*, to Auguste Baron for his Cinématorama, a complex arrangement of ten cameras or projectors arranged in a circle to permit 360-degree filming or projection. Adapted by Raoul Grimoin-Sanson as the Cinerama [French patent 272,517 of 25 November 1897] the device was announced for the Paris Exposition of 1900, and marvellous engravings of its appearance are illustrated in many texts. However, recently examined financial documents reveal that the installation had so many financial problems that it never opened at the Exposition.

☛Paul Theatrograph opens at the Salon Margherita, Naples, Italy, for a few days.

☛Lumière Cinématographe opens at the theatre in Bar-le-Duc, France.

☛Cinématographe Joly-Normandin, advertised as a Cinématographe Perfectionné, is contracted to open at the Theatre Novendades, Barcelona, Spain, by the theatre's management.

November 27:
Unidentified apparatus opens at Lindemann's Restaurant, Am Sande, Lüneburg, Germany. Admission 50 Pfennig, children and military half price. Both Lumière and Méliès films were shown.

Films included: *Serpentinetänzerin*, *Vorbeimarsch eines Regiments vor dem Zaren in Paris*, *Oceandampfer auf dem Meere*, *Straßenscene*, *Place de la Republic in Paris*, *Die Ringer*, *Ankunft eines Eisenbahnzuges*.

☛Edison Vitascope opens at the Vladek Hotel, Plze, Bohemia (now Czech Republic), by Josef Hoffmann. On December 12 the local newspaper reported on a fire that broke out during the exhibition, caused when a fragment of glowing carbon dropped into a basket of film. Operator Hoffmann unsuccessfully tried to extinguish the flames, and when the basket exploded, he threw the burning films out of the projection enclosure and into the rear of the auditorium, causing panic amongst the 300 spectators present. The flames burnt themselves out quickly, and no injuries were reported, but only a good lawyer saved Hoffmann from a jail sentence.

☛Lumière Cinématographe returns to the apothecary at Calle de Plateros 9, Mexico City, Mexico, as Lumière operators Gabriel Veyre and C. J. van Bernard return from Guadalajara. The screenings ran until October 1897.[152]

November 28:
Kinétographe de Bedts opens as the Kinetographo Portuguez Paz dos Reis at the Theatro D. Alfonso, rua de Alexandre Herculano, Porto, Portugal, by Aurélio da Paz dos Reis. The entire program consisted of films taken by Paz dos Reis.

Films included: *Manobras de Bombeiros*, *Cortejo Ecesástico...*, *Feira de Gado na Corujeira*, *O Zé Pereira na Romaria de Sto. Tirso*, *Cinira Polónio dizendo uma cançoneta*, *Uma salva de artilharia na Serra do Pilar*, *A Feira de S. Bento*, *Chegada de um Comboio Americano a Cadouços*, *Jogo do Paum*, *Saida do pessoal da Fábrica Confiança*, A *Rua do Ouro (Lisboa)*, *Marinha no Tejo*, *Saida de Dois Vapores*.

☛Unidentified apparatus, advertised as the Projectoscópio Costa Veiga, opens at the Coliseu dos Recreios, Lisbon, Portugal, by exhibitor Manuel Maria da Costa Veiga.[153]

November 29:
Foersterling Biomatograph, called Edison's Ideal, opens in the garden of the Tivoli Park,

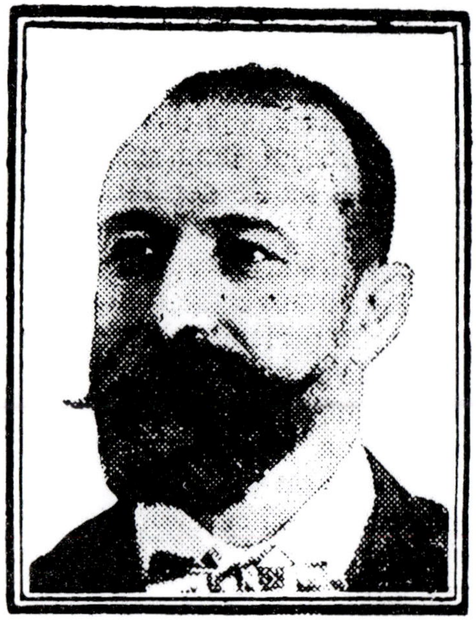

The exhibitor Manuel Maria da Costa Viega about 1896. [Antonio J. Ferreira, *A Fotografia Animada em Portugal 1894–1895–1896–1897*, Lisbon, 1986: Cinemateca Portuguesa, p. 124.]

corner of Wittevrouwensigel and Nachtegallstrat, Utrecht, The Netherlands, by travelling showman Christiaan Slieker. Forty-six people attended the first night, and the local paper reported that "the images were very small". Admission to the first rows, 50 Cents; for the rear, 25 Cents.

Films included: *Het vertrek en aankomst der treinen*, *De gezillige drukte te Parijs*, *Het Amsterdams zwembassin*, *Straatoveeltjes*, *Watervollen*, *Stadsgezichten*, *'t komen en gaan van sneltreinen*, *Landschappen*, *Rivieren door booten bevaren*, *Kluditge tafereeltjes*, *Een markt met groentevrouwen*, *Spelende knapen*.

☛Latham Eidoloscope opens at the Grand Opera House, New Orleans, Louisiana, accompanying Rosable Morrison's production

152 Gabriel Veyre and C. J. van Bernard left Mexico to return to France on 1 January 1897; as they left, their Lumière apparatus was sold to Ignacio Aguirre, who continued public screenings in the same location until October, 1897, when he left the area to travel to the provinces, reopening in Puebla. By the end of December, 1896, the Edison Vitascope had opened in Mexico City.

153 António J. Ferreira, in *A Fotografio Animada em Portugal*, p. 125, identifies this machine as an Edison Projecting Kinetoscope, or Projectoscope, which was available in the United Kingdom near the end of November 1896 (cf. Barnes, *The Beginnings of the Cinema in England*, p. 172). Charles Musser in *The Emergence of the Cinema*, p. 92, cites 30 November 1896 (see below) as the first US public engagement of the Projecting Kinetoscope. Perhaps this Lisbon engagement was for a Projectomotoscope of James Henry Lee, who had manufactured his apparatus to order since August 1896. Or perhaps this was one of the innumerable engagements on other apparatus linked only in advertising and promotion to Edison (and/or to Lumière). The timing seems a little early for it to have been the real Edison apparatus.

of *Carmen* by showing the Lathams' film of a bullfight as part of the last act of the play. The production ran through December 5.

☛Cinématographe Joly-Normandin, advertised as a Cinématographe perfectionné, opens in Saint-Etienne, France, using films of Eugène Pirou.

Films included: *Arrestation de l'ivrogne*; *Sortie de église; Quadrille Louis XV*; *La soupe à la caserne; L'arroseur arrosé*; *Enfants au bois*; *Les Forgerons; (Les) plongeurs soudanaise*; *Le prestidigitateur*; [*Les trois farceurs*]; *Déshabillé et coucher de la mariée*; *Mondaine au bain*; [*Combat à pied suivi de charge*]; *Les Hercules*; *Quadrille des Gommeux*.

☛Unidentified apparatus, advertised as a Kinetograph, opens at Münzstrasse 21, at the corner of Kaiser-Wilhelmstrasse, Berlin, Germany, by Max Mosich. Admission was 50pf for the 1st places, and 30pf for the second places. The "interesting projections" were combined with photographic lectures, and Mosich later (December 5) advertised these screenings as a promotion of his own sales of apparatus, films, and lamphouses.

☛Unidentified apparatus, advertised as a Cinématographe Edison, opens in a storefront behind Parliament in Athens, Greece, with an invitational screening for academics and journalists. Public screenings began the next day, from 9.30am to Noon, 2pm to 6pm, and 8pm to 10pm, with tickets for each half-hour session 2.20 Drachmas, later 2 Drachmas. Ten films were shown and the apparatus ran for about a month, with an estimated 400 shows.[154]

Films included: a serpentine dance, Japanese dancers, Paris street scenes, the arrival of a train, a parade of horsemen, riding instruction.

November 30:
Edison Projectoscope, or Projecting Kinetoscope, opens at the Bijou Theatre, Harrisburg, Pennsylvania, its first public engagement in the United States. This new machine was Edison's replacement for the obsolete Armat-Jenkins Vitascope, which had been overtaken by Amet's Magniscope and the International Film Company's Projectograph, among other updated machines now available to a growing market.

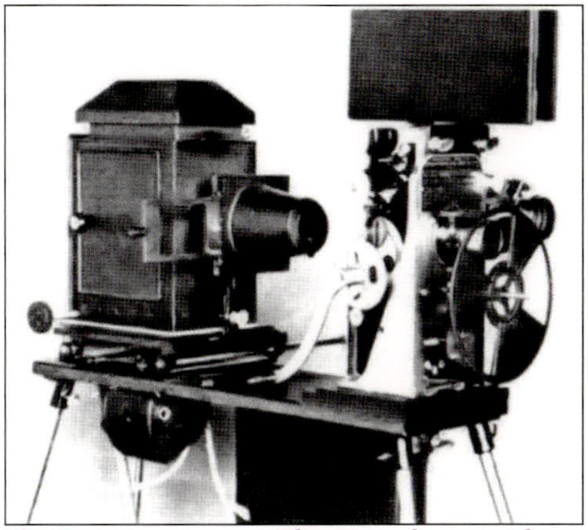
The Projectoscope was Edison's replacement for the ageing Vitascope and after prototype exhibitions in November 1896 was placed on the market in early 1897 at the price of only $100. [Edison National Historic Site, National Park Service.]

☛Casler / Dickson Biograph opens at Cook's Opera House, Rochester, New York, for one week, briefly interrupting a long run of the Lumière Cinématographe.

☛Casler / Dickson Biograph opens at Poli's Wonderland Theatre, New Haven, Connecticut. Several local views were made by W. K. L. Dickson over the ensuing weeks, including views of the New Haven Fire Department, the nearby Winchester Arms gun factory, the Yale football team at practice, and a group of comedies, photographed on 21 and 22 December on a stage erected behind the theatre.

☛Lumière Cinématographe opens at the fair of St. Martin, Sainte-Menehould, France.

☛Robert W. Paul submits to the Patent Office a completed specification for his British patent 4686 of 2 March 1896 (see above), making further modifications to his Theatrograph. The primary change was the addition of new continuous feed sprocket rollers above and below the double intermittent sprocket wheels to aid in properly tensioning the feed and take-up of the film, and an improved masking system for the film gate.

☛Casler / Dickson Biograph opens in Kansas City, Missouri, accompanying a show of Palmer Cox's Brownies.

Late November:
Magniscope of Edward Amet, advertised as an Ametomagnoscope, opens at the Duncombe's New Opera House in St. Thomas, Ontario, Canada, by the venue's owner, Thomas H. Duncombe, who had previously exhibited a Lumière Cinématographe at the opera house. Duncombe bought the Magniscope, renamed it, and exhibited it for the next five months in at least 23 locations in 18 towns across Ontario, returning to his principal business when the novelty of exhibiting films wore off.

154 From newspaper descriptions and the films, it is possible that this apparatus was a Foersterling Biomatograph. The links to Edison apparatus (and films) cited by Psoma are unconvincing.

December 1:
Paul Theatrograph exhibited at the Assembly Rooms, Cheltenham, England, as part of a concert program of the Cheltenham Cricket Club, under the patronage of the Mayor and other local notables. Exhibited again on December 3.

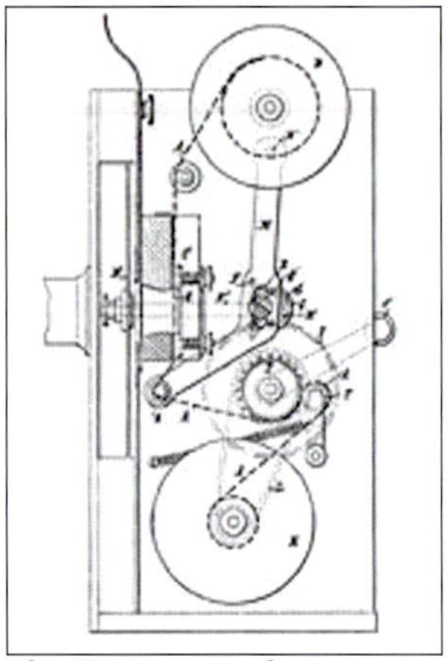

The Cinématographe Parisienne of Georges Mendel most likely had a brief life as Mendel was more of a retailer than a manufacturer, and the same name was applied in 1897 to an apparatus of Raoul Grimoin-Sanson. [http://cinematographes.free.fr/mendel.]

☛Messter Kinetograph opens at the Hansa Theatre, Hamburg.

☛Edison Vitascope opens at the Pilsner Hof [Plzeňský Dvûr] Hotel in Plzeň, Bohemia (now Czech Republic), by the American travelling exhibitor George Kemp.

☛French patent 261,771, *Appareil pour la photographie et la projection des scènes animées dit Le Cinématographe Parisien*, to Georges Mendel for his combination camera and projector called the Cinématographe Parisien. A Paris photographic dealer, Mendel expanded to offer cinema apparatus from several manufacturers and later filed a number of patents for synchronised sound projection using phonograph technology developed by Henri Joly.

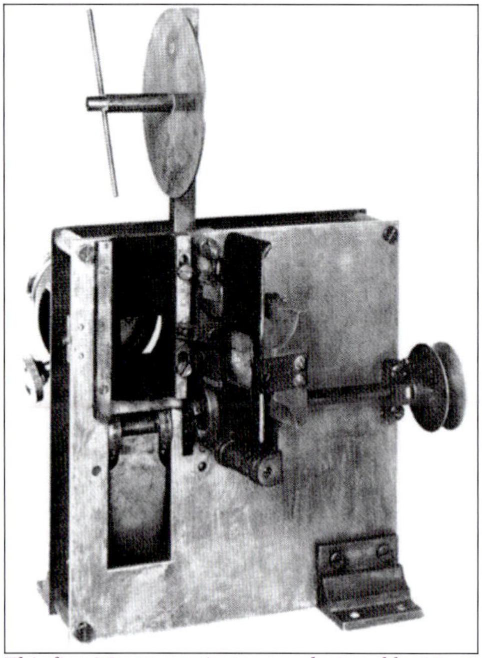

This first Messter projector was designed by Max Gliewe and was practically identical with the Eragraph projectors Gliewe supplied to the London firm of Haydon & Urry. The tips of the five-sided Maltese Cross intermittent can just be seen at the right of the lower sprocket, with the disk retainer for the films clearly visible above. [Herbert Tümmel, *Deutsche Laufbildprojektoren, Ein Katalog*. Berlin, 1986: Stiftung Deutsche Kinemathek, p. 132.]

☛Cinéphotographe Lépée opens at a fair on the Quai de Limoges in Saumur, France, by the showman Lagneau in his Théâtre Salon des Sciences, for one week.

☛Unidentified apparatus opens in the Christmas Market at the Berlin Meßpalast, 110 Alexandrinenstrasse, by Max Mosich and Keßler. The shows ran through 31 December. Increasing attendance caused the administrators of the marketplace to institute a policy of a 20pf admission after 4pm from 21 December. Visitors to the Christmas Market could redeem this admission price with evidence of a purchase from stallholders, or purchase of a ticket for an amusement on site. By Christmas Day, 16,360 admission tickets had been sold, and about 15,000 had been redeemed. Of the redeemed admission tickets, over 10,000 were due to stallholder purchases, while 1173 were on account of the anatomy museum, 1120 the children's chute, 927 the torture chamber, 850 the wild animals, 651 the Panopticon, 627 the carousel (which was always full), 625 the puppet theatre, 546 the kinematograph, and 486 the illusion.

☛Cinématographe Joly-Normandin opens in the auditorium of the Theatre of Novelties, Café Monserrat, in Sisi-bel-Abbès, Algeria, by M. Vernet. The screenings ran through 13 December.

Films include: *Pochard and Mastroquet*, *L'arrivée à Paris de L.L.M.M. Impériales de Russie*, *La Baignade des Nègres au Champ de Mars* [*Baignade des Soudanais*], *Un Leçon de Bicyclette*, *Dispute entre Cocher et Client*, *Les Forgerons*, *Chargement de Décombres*, *Cortège du Tzar à Paris*.

☛Lumière Cinématographe moves from the Stadtgartentheatre to an automat hall at Kaiser Wilhelm-Passage 23, Karlsruhe, Germany. The hours at first were on 5pm to 9pm, but quickly changed to 10am to 1pm and 3pm to 9pm. On 10 December the admission dropped from 50 Pfg. to 40 Pfg., and the screenings ended on 14 December.

☛Messter Kinematograph opens at the Apollo-Theatre, 218 Friedrichstraße, Berlin, Germany. The popular Berlin stage presented variety acts, reviews, and sometimes operetta. Messter not only showed his own films at the Apollo, but shortly began to photograph the theatre's stars in its Concert Garden. The apparatus was advertised as the Kosmograph, and was offered for sale as the "Apollo, Model

1896". It used a five-sided Maltese Cross intermittent and disk plates for the supply and take-up film reels. It drew substantially on designs of Messter's collaborator Max Gliewe. The shows ran at least until 31 December. The shows received strong approval in the press, with the films praised for their clarity in projection, although one journalist thought Madame Olinka's presentations were sharper, if somewhat smaller on the screen.

Films included: waves on a Baltic Sea beach, a train entering a station, a quadrille at the Moulin Rouge, and from 21 December the 'sensation' *Endlich Allein*.[155]

December 3:
Lumière Cinématographe opens in Hartford, Connecticut.

☛Unidentified apparatus, advertised as an Edison-Theatre, opens at Friedrichstrasse 85, next to the Café Bauer, Berlin, Germany. Admission was 30pf for screenings that ran from 10am to 10.30pm daily.

December 4:
Animotoscope of Lyman H. Howe opens at the YMCA in Wilkes-Barre, Pennsylvania, sponsored by the Bible Study Club of the First Baptist Church. This was the first engagement of Howe's self-built machine, in his home town. A touring phonograph concert showman, Howe became a major touring film exhibitor and travel lecturer over the next decade; he toured throughout the 1896-97 theatrical season with his Animotoscope, a rough copy of the Edison Vitascope distinguished by its large reel for feeding the Edison films Howe used, necessary since he spliced the films together and showed them consecutively in two groups with an intermission. Reserved seats 50 Cents; general admission, 25 Cents.

Films included: (First series) *Bowling Green, New York City*; *The Haymakers at Work*; *Mounted Police Charge in Central Park, New York City*; *Runaway Horse, Central Park, New York City*; *Boys Chased Off Dock in Hudson River and Rescued*; *The Morning Bath*; *Irwin-Rice Kissing Scene*. (Second series) *Feeding the Doves*; *Tub Race*; *Responding to the Alarm of Fire*; *Fireman at Work, the rescue*; *Burning stables and rescue of horses*; *Watermelon Contest*; *Lone Fisherman*; *Old Ocean off Manhattan Beach after a severe storm*.

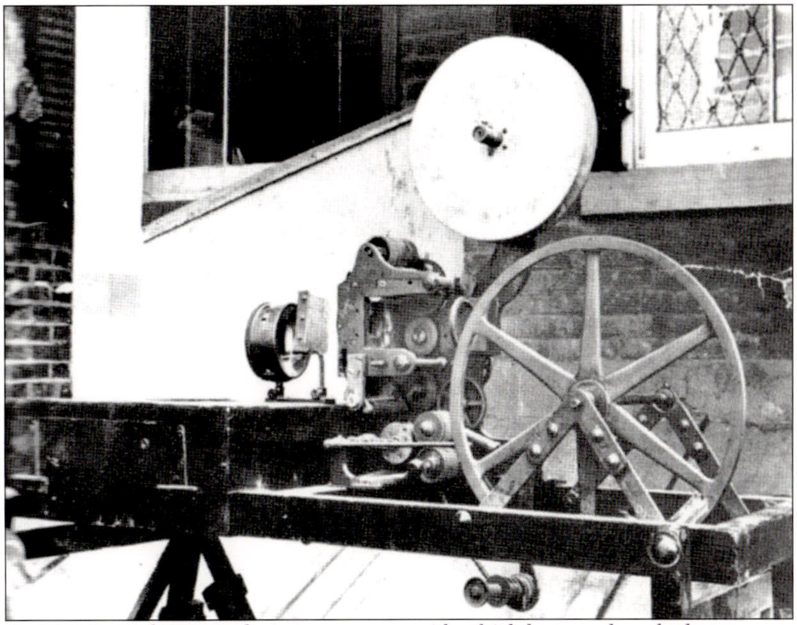

Lyman Howe's home-made Animotoscope, with which he toured on the lecture circuit in 1896 and 1897. [Charles Musser, with Carol Nelson, *High-Class Moving Pictures. Lyman H. Howe and the Forgotten Era of Travelling Exhibition, 1880–1920. Princeton*, 1991: Princeton University Press, p. 51.]

December 5:
Unidentified apparatus, advertised as a Cinematografo Edison, opens at the Teatro Filodrammatico in Trieste, Italy, for four days, by the local journalist and theatrical agent Angelo Curiel and his partner Max Karreiter, who together used the pseudonym Professor Cav. De Horney.

December 6:
Lumière Cinématographe opens in Cannes, France.

☛Unidentified apparatus, advertised as a Cinématographe, opens in the market at Place Saint-Jacques, Dieppe, France, for two weeks.

☛Cinématographe Demény-Gaumont opens at a fair on the Place des Armes in Alençon, France, by Ernest Grenier in his Théâtre Électrique, for one week.

☛Unidentified apparatus, advertised as an Anamatagraph, opens at the Bijou Variety Theatre in Toronto, Canada, by J. Ausman. The shows ran through Christmas, and then Ausman took his machine on tour to smaller towns north of Toronto in 1897.

155 *Endlich Allein* was Messter's re-labelling of Eugene Pirou's provocative French film *Le coucher de la mariée*.

☛Casler / Dickson Biograph opens at J. H. Moore's Wonderland Theatre, a vaudeville house, in Detroit, Michigan, for six weeks, when it was replaced by a Lumière Cinématographe, advertised as "Finer Than the Biograph". The Lumiére apparatus ran for five weeks, and then was itself replaced by a return engagement of the Casler / Dickson Biograph for four weeks, now advertised as "The Greatest Animated Picture Machine".

☛Lumière Cinématographe opens at the Politeama Pestapevar in Forli, Italy.

December 7:
Paul Theatrograph opens at the Royal Theatre, Halifax; the Royal Theatre, Bournemouth; the Grand Theatre, Bolton; the Oxford Theatre, Middlesbrough; and the Palace Theatre, Plymouth. All in England.

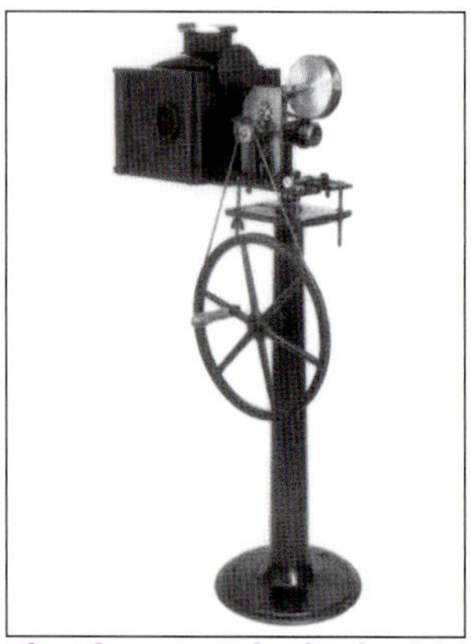

The Theatrograph of Robert W Paul, well-constructed, sturdy, and widely used in 1896. [John Barnes, *The Beginnings of the Cinema in England, Volume 1, 1894–1896*. Exeter, 1998: University of Exeter Press, p. 52.]

☛Lumière Cinématographe opens at the Rheinischen Hof of the Herrn Schladitz, port of Wilhelmshaven, Germany, by the Stollwerck representative Paul Behrens. Admission 50 Pfenning. The shows ran through 17 December.

☛Cecil Wray demonstrates moving pictures to the Photographic Society, Bradford, England, most likely on his Kineoptoscope projector (see 31 August, above). The films used were Edison Kinetoscope subjects.

Films included: *Eating Water Melons for a Wager, The Kiss.*

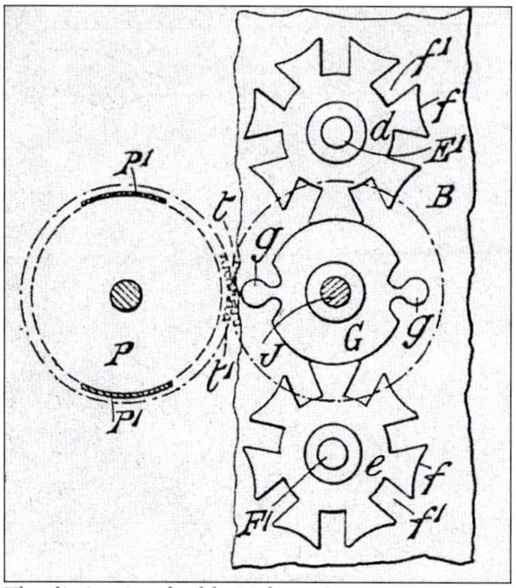

The distinctive double Maltese Cross intermittent with seven arms used in early Theatrograph projectors. In theory, this design moved two sprockets on either side of the film gate simultaneously, thus reducing strain on the film, but in reality the movement was very stiff and it was quickly replaced by a single intermittent using a loop of film.
[United Kingdom patent 4686 of 2 March 1896, *Improvements in Appartus for Projecting Kinetoscope Pictures on the Screen*, Fig. 3.]

December 8:
Paul Theatrograph, advertised as an Animatographe, opens in the Bijou Theatre of Robertson's Musée, 81 Yonge Street, Toronto, Canada, replacing the Edison Vitascope (see 31 August, above). This time the apparatus was shown on the main floor in the more prestigious variety hall of the Musée.

☛Foersterling Biomatograph, called Edison's Ideal, opens in the Markthalle, Oldenburg, Germany, by the Hamburg showman Friederich Georg Gröning, remaining until 20 December. With the showing of *The Arrival of the Czar in Paris*, Gröning played military music on a phonograph as an additional attraction.[156]

☛Unidentified Cinematografo Edison opens at the Salone Sammicheli in Verona, Italy, for five days.

December 9:
Demenÿ Chronophotographe demonstrated for the Photographic Club at Anderton's Hotel Tavern, 162–5 Fleet Street, London, England, the first time the apparatus is seen in Great Britain. It was demonstrated again the following afternoon at the Empire Theatre.

☛Lumière Cinématographe opens in a shopfront at 478 George Street, Sydney, Australia, by H. Walter Barnett and Marius Sestier. The shows were run by Barnett through 6 March 1897, while Sestier went to Adelaide to give additional shows.

December 10:
US patent 611,591, *Consecutive-view apparatus*, to Herman Casler for an improved projector with an improved feed and take-up mechanism. The principles of the apparatus were similar to his earlier patents of 26 February 1896, but here the intermittent gripper

156 The apparatus was not well received by the local paper, in contrast to the Lumière Cinématographe. It used limelight as a light source, which gave a less satisfactory picture throughout the show than the Cinématographe's electrical lamp. This could have been due to the inexperience or inattention of the operator. The images of the Foersterling machine were also described as blurry. After this engagement travelling showman Fredrich Georg Gröning began a tour throughout Ostfriesland, freed from the need for electrical power, and exhibited his apparatus in Aurich, Wilhelmshaven, Norden, Emden, and Leer.

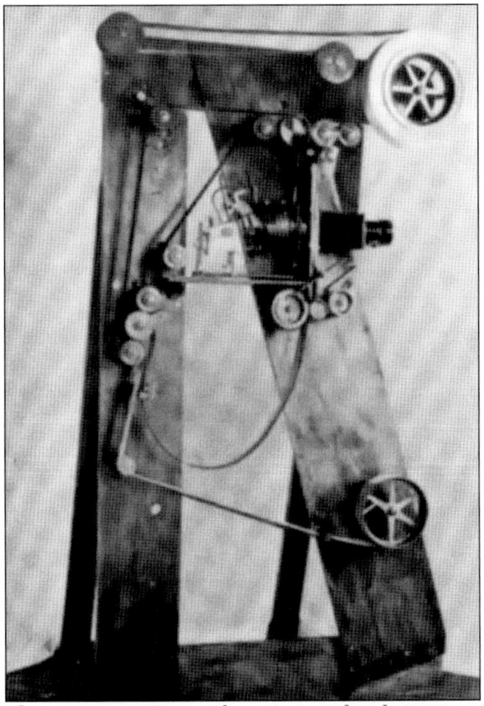

This prototype Biograph projector of early 1896 from Casler's own album is the source for the patent drawings in US 611,591.
[Gordon Hendricks, *The Beginnings of the Biograph*, illus unpp.]

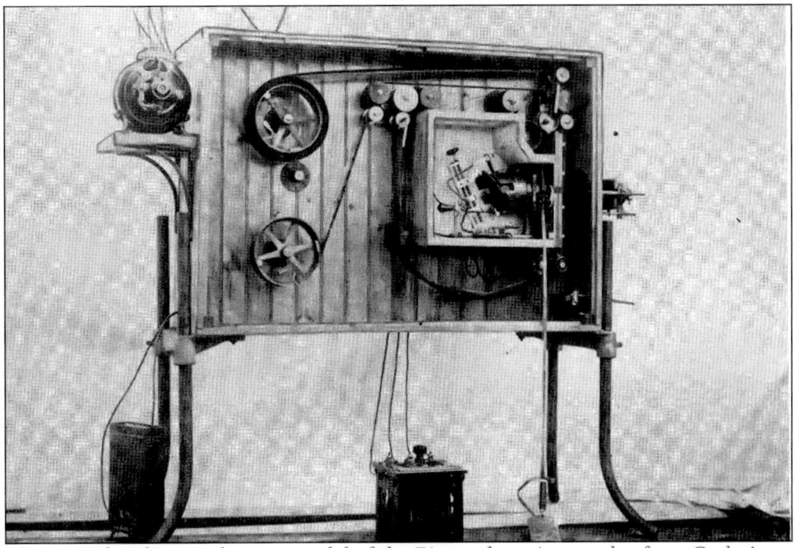

The more familiar production model of the Biograph projector, also from Casler's album. [Gordon Hendricks, *The Beginnings of the Biograph*, illustrations unpp.]

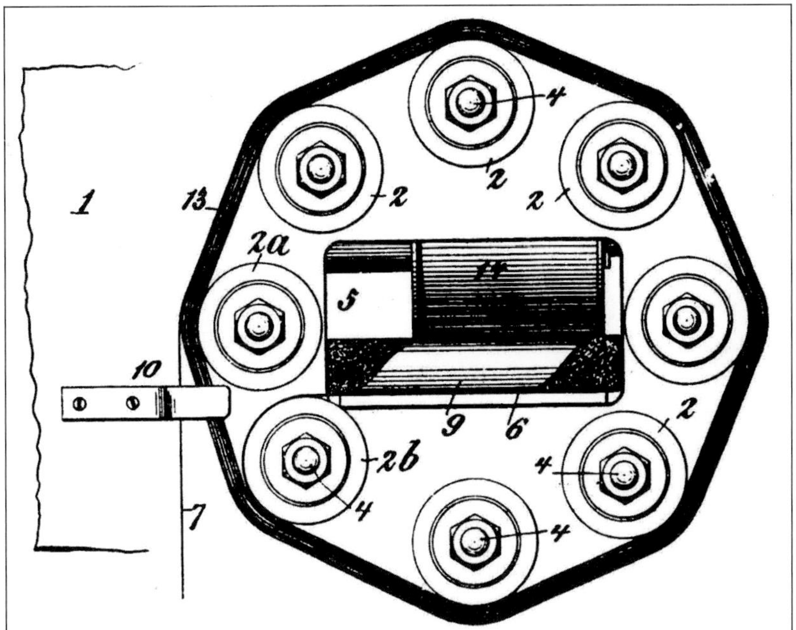

Casler's innovative film reel, where film was drawn from the centre (at 6) into the projector and then rewound after use around the outside of the reel (from 7) very similar to the modern 'cakestand' reels used in multiplex cinemas.
[United States patent 617,435, Fig. 1.]

is driven constantly, and it is both the feeding reel and the take-up reel which are adjustable through a friction disk speed control. Casler also proposes the use of feed and take-up reels with very large open centers that would slip over his fixed, mechanically integral projector reels, allowing longer films to run through the machine. Both the Biograph camera and the accompanying projector ran at higher speeds than the Edison and Lumière apparatus, at first 40 and then nearer 30 frames per second, producing high quality images on large screens in projection. Early projectors used a 25 ampere Colt hand-feed arc lamp with 3/8-inch carbons; the huge size of the Biograph projector as frequently illustrated comes from Casler's habit of enclosing the light source inside an asbestos-lined compartment fully within the mechanism, with the giant box then also enclosing the rest of the film feed and take-up pathway and reels. The Biograph system was not sold on the open market; instead, like the Lumière equipment initially, it was used only by specially trained operators either working directly for the American Mutoscope and Biograph Company or hired by lessee theatres.

☛US patent 611,590, *Web-Feeding Mechanism*, to Herman Casler for a single-reel film feeding and take-up apparatus, as well as an improved intermittent mechanism, for motion picture projectors. In the new feeding mechanism, a single driveshaft operated an array of upper and lower sprockets and tensioning wheels which drew an endless band of film of any length from the inside of a supply reel mounted horizontally above the projector, and then rewound it on the outside of the same horizontal wheel. The improvement to the broken roller friction intermittent, which was operated by the same driveshaft, was essentially a framing device provided by a friction connection to the intermittent sprockets where the driveshaft bore on a flat disk; an adjustment was provided where the driveshaft could be made to move closer to the circumference of the disk (thereby, faster) or closer to its axis (slower), thus keeping the images precisely registered as they ran through the gate of the projector.[157]

☛US patent 617,435, Reel, to Herman Casler for a special film reel where a continuous length of film was drawn from the inside of the reel into a projector for exhibition and was then rewound on the outside of the reel. This was an accompaniment to Caslers US patent 611,590 for a new style of feeding mechanism for the Biograph projectors.

☛Lumière Cinématographe moves from the Collegio Leon XIII to the Teatro Humboldt, Guadalahara, Mexico, through December 20, by operators Gabriel Veyre and Fernand Bon Bernard.

☛Lumière Cinématographe opens in Milwaukee, Wisconsin.

☛Unidentified apparatus opens at the Club du cercle musicale Apollon in Smyrna, Greece (today Izmir, Turkey).

December 11:
Lumière Cinématographe opens at the Teatro del Corso, Bologna, Italy, thorugh 20 December. The shows accompanied a production of the Zacconi-Pilotto theatre company; admission 1 Lira.

☛Jenkins Phantoscope opens at the Théâtre Français, Montréal, Canada, promoted as "Edison's latest invention" in much the same style Jenkins frequently used in the U. S.

☛Unidentified apparatus, advertised as a Movitographé, opens in Nice, France. Films included: *Cortège de Tsar* (in color), *Coucher de la Parisienne*, *Danseuses du Moulin-Rouge*.

☛Unidentified apparatus, advertised as a Cinématographe and likely a Demenÿ-Gaumont apparatus, opens at the fair of St. Martin, Angers, France, by the showman Ernest Grenier.

☛Unidentified apparatus, advertised as De Echte Edison's Kinematograph, opens as one number on a variety program at the theatre in Utrecht, The Netherlands, by J. Thiele. Admission to the first seats, 1 Guilder, to the rear, 60 Cents. The showings began two days late due to a defect in the apparatus, but were nonetheless poorly reviewed in the local press. 46 people attended the opening performance; the showings lasted five days.

December 12:
Paul Theatrograph opens at the Theatre Royal, Hobart, Tasmania, Australia, as part of the presentation of the Newbury-Spada touring theatrical company.

☛Oskar Messter and the engineer G. W. Betz receive five "Gebrauchsmuster", or "smaller patents" covering improvements and design changes in their projection apparatus. The precise contents can today no longer be determined.[158]

☛Unidentified apparatus, advertised as a Nouveau Cinématographe, opens in the first

157 In concept and in many technical details, this continuous-feed mechanism is remarkably identical with modern "platter", or "cakestand" projectors, which also use a single-reel endless film band horizontal feed and take-up system. In its own time it was certainly an important step towards finding a way to project longer films, and towards decreasing the horrendous wear to which films were subject in the projection apparatus of 1896-97. Since the Biograph ran at a higher frames-per-second rate than other equipment, its early films were normally some 230 feet long. Casler specifically intends his subtle framing adjustment for a gripper or broken roller intermittent, as used in the Biograph projector, to overcome inconsistencies in the manufacture and processing of flexible celluloid films. Although exact image registration with a friction roller intermittent was always especially troublesome, Casler states that it was impossible to predetermine the distance between the centers of successive frames of the film since "it varies in different films, in the same film at different times, and even in different portions of the same film at any one time, by reason of the uneven expansion and contraction of the film in drying and under differing atmospheric conditions". Since the physical and mechanical qualities of celluloid film in the late 1890s are among the least recorded and examined elements of the invention of motion pictures, as it is perhaps the least retrievable aspect of film history a century later, both Casler's statement and the device he patented to overcome the problem are significant evidence that the quality of the film band itself might have a greater bearing on the success or failure both of individual showings and of some pieces of specific apparatus than is normally credited.

158 The "Gebrauschsmuster" was neither a Trademark nor a Patent, as sometimes cited in the literature, but a way of protecting how something looked, or appeared; in English it is sometimes called a "petty patent". It gave some protection to processes and designs, while a full German patent was reserved for major, fundamental inventions of new devices and operating principles. Messter and Betz had clearly been preparing material for some time before this flurry of applications; in general, most patent/trademark application dates vary from the actual development

floor of the Café du Palas, Nimes, France, The upstairs room had its own entrance on the rue Régale. The showings emphasized local views; admission 50 Centimes. The screenings ran through the holidays until early 1897.

Films included: *l'arrivee d'un train à Saint Cézaire*; *Une partie de Mazet*; *La mer au Grau du Roi*; *L'Arche de Noë, chemin d'Avignon*.

☛Unidentified apparatus, advertised as a Cinématographe, opens at a fair on the Grand Place in Montreuil-sur-Mer, for three days.

☛Unidentified apparatus, advertised as a Cinématographe Géant, opens in Louvain, Belgium, by Charles Schram. The small theatre, or kiosk, was eleven metres long and five metres wide. From 1897 Schram, a travelling photographer, exhibited on fairs across Belgium, the Netherlands, and France.

December 13:
Unidentified apparatus, advertised as a Kinematograph, opens in the Hotel de Russie, Karlovy Vary, Bohemia (now Czech Republic), by the Prague photographer Emil Joffé.

☛Cinématographe Parisien of Georges Mendel opens at the meeting hall of M. Soulat, place du Marché-au-Blé, Châteauroux, France, by the showman Mergault, for two weeks.

☛Cinéphotographe Lépée opens at the Foire d'Hiver on the Place Bretagne, Nantes, France, by the showmen Lagneau and Louis Vernassier in their Théâtre Salon des Sciences. The shows ran until 15 February 1897.

December 14:
Paul Theatrograph, advertised as the Vitamotograph, opens at Sadler's Wells Theatre, London, England; another Theatrograph opened at the Empire Theatre, Burnley, England, for its fifth visit; yet another returns to the Assembly Rooms, Cheltenham.[159]

☛Appleton's Cieroscope opens at the Mechanic's Institute, Bradford, England, for a one-week engagement. The Cieroscope was a combination camera, printer, and projector made by R. J. Appleton & Co. of Bradford. Offered on the open market from February, 1897, at a cost of £15 15s (or £17 17s with W. Wray's special cinematograph lens), it was not patented in England, and quite probably was a re-badged Vitagraphe from the firm of Clément & Gilmer in Pais.

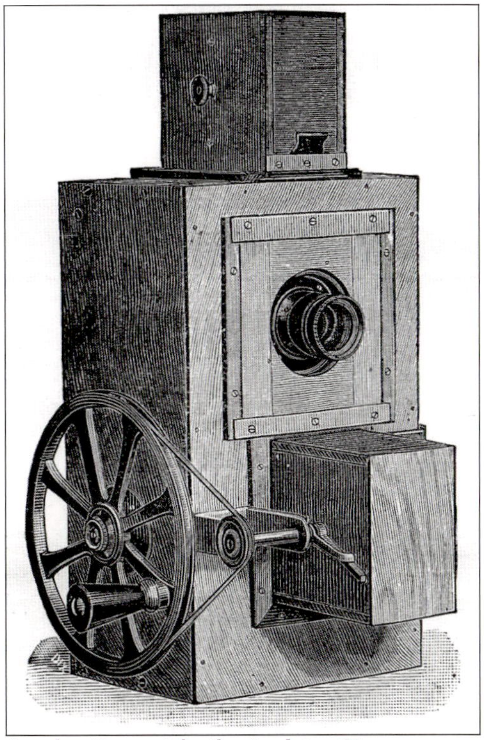

An advertisement for the Appleton Cieroscope. [Henry Hopwood, *Living Pictures*, p. xxi.]

☛Lumière Cinématographe opens at the photography shop of the Napoléon brothers, Avenue Santa Monica, Barcelona, Spain. Admission 1 Peso.

Films included: *Joueurs de Cartes*, *Arrivée d'un Train*, *Baignade en Mer*, *La sortie de l'Usine Lumière à Lyon*, *Senyor enredat*, *Carro de transport pujani una costa*, *Attention à la peinture*, *La Galatea* (in color).

December 15:
Unidentified apparatus, advertised as a Cinématographe, opens at 22 rue de Paris, Le Havre, France, by the showman Bonain.

☛Cinématographe Joly-Normandin opens in the Ständehausstrasse 1 at the Wiener Café, Hanover, Germany, arranged by the owner of the café, Julius Weichelt.

December 16:
British patent 28,799, *Improved appliance for taking, projecting and printing animated photographs*, to John William Leslie Naish of Edinburgh, for a Cinematograph with a claw intermittent driven by a triangular eccentric and an off-center shutter behind the lens. The apparatus also featured a second optical path-

of apparatus: Messter's 1897 Thaumatograph, at least his fourth projector model, was advertised for sale only in early 1897, but the trademark application for its name was submitted on 19 December 1896.

159 At this time, Robert Paul had at least five Theatrograph exhibitions running concurrently in London alone. In a 1936 address to the British Kinematograph Society, Paul described his early exhibitions by saying, "At this period the purchasers of many of my projectors worked them personally. Though we did our best to train lanternists and limelight operators to use the machine properly, their results were sometimes indifferent. Therefore I attended in the evenings at many of the London music halls, the times of showing being carefully arranged in advance. This helped to maintain the reputation of the projector. I drove, with an assistant, from one hall to another in a one-horse brougham, rewinding the films during the drive."

way mounted above the mechanism which allowed slides, other images, or titles to be projected on the screen while a film in the projector was replaced. This machine was not marketed publicly until 1897.

☛Unidentified apparatus opens at the caffè-concerto Alhambra, Milan, Italy, running through 21 December.

☛Unidentified Cinematografo Edison opens in Como, Italy.

☛Cinématographe Joly-Normandin opens at the auditorium of the museum in Tlemcen, Algeria, by M. Vernet, for three days.

Films include: *La leçon de bicyclette, Le voyageur et le coucher, l'ivrogne, La baignade, Le pochard et le mastroquet, L'arrivé du tsar à Paris.*

December 17:
Kinétographe of Méliès and Reulos opens in Orizaba, Mexico, by showman Carlos Mongrand, according to a report on this date in *El Reproductor*. The screenings had no success, because "the families were in no mood for amusement".

December 18:
Lumière Cinématographe opens in Bordeaux, France.

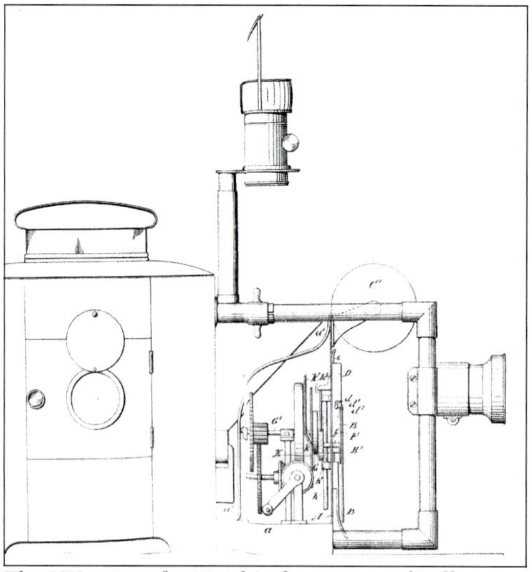

The UK patent for Naish's device specifically included the option of projecting either films or lantern slides.
[United Kingdom patent 28,799, Fig. 1 detail.]

☛Unidentified apparatus, advertised as an Edison-Theatre, opens at Stolzenburg's Festsälen, Neuendorfer Strasse 91, Berlin. The screenings were combined with phonograph exhibitions and took place hourly from 3pm until 9pm. Admission was 50pf for the first places, 30 pf for the second, with children and military half-price.

December 19:
Lumière Cinématographe screened for an invited audience of donors to the charity hospital at via Po 33, Turin, Italy.

Films included: *Bal d'enfants, Roi et Reine d'Italie, Monza.*

☛Lumière Cinématographe opens at Janssen's Konzerthaus, Jever, Ostfriesland, Germany, by Paul Behrens, running until 22 December. Behrens charged an extra 10 Pfennig admission for this show, raising his price to 60 Pfennig for the engagement.[160]

☛Cinématographe Joly-Normandin reopens (or possibly continues) in Rethel, France, by André Milhès, using many films of Eugène Pirou.

Films include: *Dispute du cocher et de son client; Enfants au bois; La bicycliste maladroite;* [*Le pochard entêté*]; *Sortie de Notre-Dame-des-Victoires.*

☛Cinématographe Joly-Normandin opens as Cinématographe système perfectionée Joly in Aubenas, France, by Léopold Courthial, using many films of Eugène Pirou.

Films included: *Les Forgerons; Place de la République à Paris; Baignade des Soudanais;* [*Scène d'ivrogne*]; *Le tsar au Panthéon; Quadrille des Gommeux.*

☛Lumière Cinématographe opens at the Teatro Ristori in Verona, Italy, by the Salvi Brothers, accompanying their mechanical marionette show.

December 20:
Lumière Cinématographe opens at via del Corso 393, Rome, Italy, running through 31 December. Admission to the front seats, 1 Lira, to the rear seats 50 Cents, military and children half price.

Films include: *Giardino delle Tuilleries a Parigi, Danza Giavanese, Berlino -Hallesches Thor, Il viaggiatore e i ladri, Le Feste di Parigi, Arrive delle LL. MM. Le Czar a la Czarina e del presidente Signor Felix Faure, Un reggimento di Dragoni, Ritorno dei Sovrani dalla Chiese Russa.*

☛The Star Film logo of Georges Méliès appears for the first time, in an advertisement in *L'Industriel Forain*, noting the gold medal awarded to the Kinétographe at the Exposition du travail of 1896.

☛Cinematographe Normandin-Joly opens in a newly established theatre for "Living Photographs" at Ständehausstraße 1, Hanover,

160 Travelling showman Behrens was here evidently engaging in the common early practice of "preparing" local newspapers for his shows by kindly providing them with rave reviews of his equipment and of the audience response to it. Author Bernd Poch carefully documents similarities between articles in the *Norddeutsche Volksblatt* of 6 December and the *Jeversches Wochenblatt* of 18 December discussing Behrens's shows and a story in *Der Komet* from the previous 20 June. See Bernd Poch, "Viel Geld mit wenig Mühe", in Detlef Hoffmann and Jens Thiele, eds., *Lichtbilder-Lichtspiele. Anfänge der Fotografie und des Kinos in Ostfriesland* (Marburg, 1989: Jonas Verlag), pp. 319–320.

Germany. A gramophone concert was part of the attraction.[161]

☛Cinématographe Joly-Normandin opens as Cinématographe Eugène Pirou in Ghent, Belgium.

Films included: *Le coucher de la mariée.*

☛Cinématographe Deményÿ-Gaumont opens at the Foire de Noël, Lisieux, France, by Ernest Grenier in his Théâtre Électrique for three days.

☛Lumière Cinématographe opens in Kansas City, Missouri.

☛Lumière Cinématographe opens in Cincinnati, Ohio.

December 21:
Casler / Dickson Biograph opens in Providence, Rhode Island.

December 22:
Lumière Cinématographe demonstrated for the Khedive Abbas II Helmy at his Koubbeh palace north of Cairo, Egypt, by Lumière concessionaire Henri Dello-Stoglio.

December 23:
Unidentified apparatus, advertised as a Kinematograph, opens in a rented shop at Nieuwendijk 71, Amsterdam, The Netherlands, by exhibitor Wilhelm Schmitz. On 10 February 1897, Schmitz gave a cinema exhibition to the Queen.

☛Lumière Cinématographe opens in a hall of the Maison Marannè, place de la Bibliothèque, on its return to Auxerre, France. The showings ran through 11 January 1897.

☛Cinématographe Joly-Normandin opens as Cinématographe perfectionné, système Joly in Evreux, France.

Films included: *Défilé complet du cortège Imperial.*

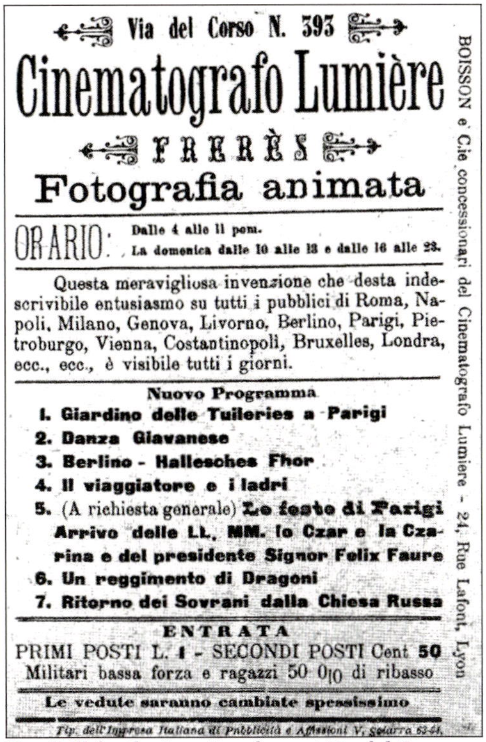
Via del Corso N. 393

Cinematografo Lumière

FRÈRÈS

Fotografia animata

ORARIO: Dalle 4 alle 11 pom. La domenica dalle 10 alle 13 e dalle 16 alle 23.

Questa meravigliosa invenzione che desta indescrivibile entusiasmo su tutti i pubblici di Roma, Napoli, Milano, Genova, Livorno, Berlino, Parigi, Pietroburgo, Vienna, Costantinopoli, Bruxelles, Londra, ecc., ecc., è visibile tutti i giorni.

Nuovo Programma

1. Giardino delle Tuileries a Parigi
2. Danza Giavanese
3. Berlino - Hallesches Fhor
4. Il viaggiatore e i ladri
5. (A richiesta generale) Le feste di Parigi Arrivo delle LL. MM. lo Czar e la Czarina e del presidente Signor Felix Faure
6. Un reggimento di Dragoni
7. Ritorno dei Sovrani dalla Chiesa Russa

ENTRATA

PRIMI POSTI L. 1 - SECONDI POSTI Cent 50
Militari bassa forza e ragazzi 50 0|0 di ribasso

Le vedute saranno cambiate spessissimo

BOISSON e C.ie concessionari del Cinematografo Lumiere - 24, Rue Lafont, Lyon

Handbill for the Lumière show at Via del Corso, which describes the "wonderful invention" as arousing "indescribable enthusiasm" in a dozen cities across Europe and is now to be seen every day in Rome. [Aldo Bernardelli, *Gli ambulanti*. Gemona, 2001: La Cineteca del Friuli, p. 81.]

☛Unidentified apparatus, advertised as Le Beau Salon du Cinématographe, opens at the Foire de Décembre in Béziers, France. The shows ran through 6 January 1897.

☛Edison Vitascope opens in Lexington, Kentucky.

☛Edison Vitascope returns to the Teatro Sociale in Este, Italy, accompanying the pantomime *Histoire d'un Pierrot* as part of the touring show Jole Cantini's presentations and under the auspices of Edison's representatives the Anglo-Italian Commerce Company in Genoa.

☛Cinématographe Joly-Normandin opens in

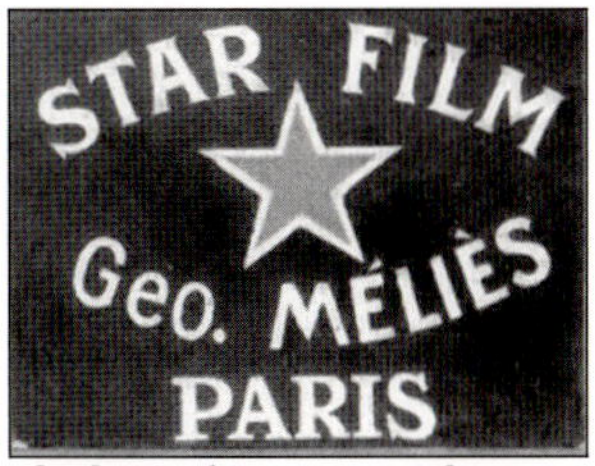

The logo of Georges Méliès' film production company, which would be seen around the world.
[David Robinson, Méliès, *Father of Film Fantasy*, p. 26.]

Mostaganem, Algeria, for three days, by M. Vernet. The apparatus then went on to the town of Mascara in January 1897. One film is described in the local press, a train emerging from a tunnel with passengers embarking and debarking at a station.

☛Lumière Cinématographe returns to Wilhelmshaven, Germany, for a single day after Paul Behrens negotiates with the Kartellkommission that their employees will pay a reduced admittance of 30 Pfg.

December 24:
Lumière Cinématographe privately demonstrated at the Theatre Royale, Adelaide, Australia, by Lumière operator Marius Sestier, now in partnership with Australian actor Wybert Reeve. The apparatus used for this show was the third Cinématographe to reach Australia.

161 The *Hannoversche Tageblatt* of 22 December 1896 identified this exhibition as "lebende Photographien von L. Normandin (System Toly), clearly a misnomer for the Cinématographe Normandin-Joly, as the old form of writing the capital "J" with a top crossbar across the vertical stroke of the "J" was easily misread. Someone unfamiliar with the equipment could most easily mistake this for a "T" and have created the only appearance in film history of the "System Toly". The question of the exhibitor of the apparatus remains open: is "L. Normandin" another misprint for Ernst Normandin, who bought Joly's patent and manufactured the equipment, or was L. Normandin a relation of Ernst Normandin?

Trademark of the workshop of Messter & Betz, which after a series of mergers and buyouts ultimately evolved into the empire of Universum Film AG (UFA). [Prof. Dr. Albert Narath, *Oskar Messter*, p.15.]

December 25:
Unidentified apparatus opens as the Animatographo Portuguez Pinto Moreira, at the Teatro Sá de Miranda, Viana do Castélo, Portugal, by Francisco Pinto Moreira.

☛Unidentified apparatus, advertised as a Cinématographe, opens in an "American Theatre" at the Foire Hivernale on the Place du Champ de Foire in Beauvois, France. The showings ran through 14 January 1897.

☛Unidentified Cinematografo Edison opens at the Teatro Comunale in Lugo, Italy.

December 26:
Lumière Cinématographe opens in a hall at the Valand Exposition, Göteborg, Sweden, by the German showmen Ornaz and Buchau. Beginning in early February 1897, they would travel with their program through the Swedish provinces, including Borás, Skövde, Örebro, Norrköping, Uppsala, Falun, Gävle, Söderhamm and Västeràs.

☛Lumière Cinématographe opens at the Theatre Royal, Adelaide, Australia, by Marius Sestier and Wybert Reeve, running until 29 January 1897.

December 27:
Unidentified apparatus, advertised as the Cynématographe Leroy opens at the Maison Donnadieu, Allée Paul-Riquet, on the corner of the avenue de Besson, Béziers, France, for four days.[162]

☛Lumière Cinématographe opens at the Solostzov Theatre, Kiev, Russia, by Lumière operators Marius Chapuis and Paul Decorps.

☛Unidentified apparatus, advertised as a "nouveau cinématographe" opens in a room above the Café Itier du Palais, Boulevard de l'Esplanade, Nîmes, France.

☛Amet Magniscope opens in Detroit, Michigan.

☛Cinétograph of the Werner brothers or of Pathé, under the direction of M. Poordy opens at the Grand Café Glacier in Bougie, Algeria, for two days. The screenings were again accompanied by the magician and hypnotist Professor Marga, who also performed a memory act with his 'incomparable subject,' Mlle Blanche. Unusually, the local newspaper describes the apparatus and work of Georges Demenÿ in its short notice, perhaps in an attempt by M. Poordy to associate himself with the Joly-Normandin apparatus which was travelling simultaneously through many of the same small towns.

Films include: *A régiment en marche*, *Une scène de lutte*, *Les laveuses sur la Seine*, *Le buveur de bière*, *Défense d'afficher*, *La partie de saute-mouton.*

December 28:
Casler / Dickson Biograph opens in Philadelphia, Pennsylvania.

December 29:
Edison Vitascope opens in Utica, New York.

☛Edison Vitascope opens at the Teatro Giardino in Cesena, Italy, as a presentation of the dramatic company Bonfiglioli.

December 30:
Cinématographe Joly opens in the amphitheatre of the botanical garden, Evreux, France, for two days.

☛Cinématographe Joly-Normandin opens as the Cinématographe Pirou, in the spring garden of the Municipal Casino, Nice, France. The screenings ran until the end of April, 1897.

December 31:
Unidentified apparatus opens as the Chnimatographo Sanz at the Coliseu dos Recreios, Lisbon, Portugal, as a presentation of Arsénio Sanz. This machine could have been a Rigg Kincmatograph, or possibly onc madc by Gyngell.

Films included: *A Caravana do Jardim de Aclimatação de paris*, *O Transatlântico Normandie Saindo do Havre*, *Uma Lição de Equitação*, *Os Sudaneses no Campo de Marte*, *Baile Japonês*, *O Mundo às Avessas*, *Miss Fuller – Dança Serpentina.*

☛Oskar Messter and G. W. Betz establish the trademark (Warenzeichen No. 23,538) of their firm of O. E. Messter and G. W. Betz. The engineer Betz, of the company Bauer & Betz, Berlin, worked closely with Messter at the end of 1896 and through 1897, designing and manufacturing various models of projectors and cameras for both amateurs and professionals.[163]

162 Jacques and Marie André, in *Une saison Lumière à Montpellier*, p. 157, note 1, say that a Cinématographe Leroy opened in Béziers in November, so perhaps this was a return visit. Also in November, a Cinématograph Demenÿ opened in Béziers.

163 This was Messter's first separate film manufacturing company. They advertised cameras, projectors, and films for sale. In 1898 Messter took over the firm of Bauer & Betz, and G. W. Betz joined the Deutsche Mutoskop- und Biograph-GmbH, where he became the first head of the Photographic Department.

PART 2: CITATIONS TO DATES

1833

January 20: Wachelder 2006, 100-02; Robinson 1991, 8-12.

April 24: Schuster & Strasser 1998, 134-38; Wachelder 2006, 108-12.

1834

January: Horner 1834, 36-40.

1841

January 27: Anon. 1841, 62-4; Rossell 2005a, 530.

February 19: Anon. 1841, 62-4; Rossell 2005a, 530.

1843

February 12: Mannoni, Pesenti Campagnoni, & Robinson 1991, 326-28.

1845

Sitzungs-Berichte... 1853, 482-85; Kurzel-Runtscheiner 1938, 40-65; Debler 2001, 307-9; Kaldy-Karo 2001, 180-83.

1847

January 3: Debler 2001, 304-9; Kaldy-Karo 2001, 185-91.

January 16: Debler 2001, 298-3904; Kaldy-Karo 2001, 180-5; *Allgemeine Theatrezeitung*,1847.

March 7 or 8: Kaldy-Karo 2001, 197.

March 22: Kaldy-Karo 2001, 197-8.

June 5: Kaldy-Karo 2001, 199; *Münchner Morgenblatt* 1847, June 21.

1848

March 4: Kaldy-Karo 2001, 203.

March 5: Kaldy-Karo 2001, 203.

1852

May 22: Gosser 1977, 86-7; Mannoni, Pesenti Campagnoni, & Robinson 1991, 329-31.

November 12: Herbert 2008, 445-6; Gosser 1977, 88-90.

1853

April 21: *Sitzungs-Berichte....*1853, 482-85; Kurzel-Runtscheiner 1938, 40-65; Debler 2001, 307-9; Kaldy-Karo 2001, 206-7.

July 12: Georg Dill, watercolour of family demonstration, signed and dated in the drawing 12 July 1853, Historisches Museum, Hannover, uncatalogued.

1855

January 18: *Sitzungsberichte .....* 1855, 463-6.

1860

February 27: UK patent 537, *Improvements in Apparatuses for Exhibiting Photographic, Stereoscopic, and other Pictures, Models, Figures, and Designs*, application February 27. Issued August 27; Thomas 1964, 12.

May 22: UK patent 1260, *Improvements in Thaumatropes or Phenakistoscopes*, application May 22, issued November 20.

1861

February 5: US Patent 31,357, *Exhibiting Stereoscopic Pictures of Moving Objects*, issued February 5, 1861; McCosker 1941, 404-6; Gosser 1977, 103-5.

June 8: UK patent 1457, *A Photographic Apparatus, having for Object to Reproduce the Successive Phases and Shiftings of a Motion*, application 8 June 1861. Issued 28 November 1861; Coe 1981, 40.

June 24: *Sitzungsberichte...*1861, 84.

1862

June 13: Herbert 2017, 182n5.

1864

March 14: Transactions of the Royal Scottish Society of Arts 1862-64, 171-3; Herbert 2017, 182n4.

1865

August 31 – September 3: Grüson 1893, 511-13; Brichta 1952, 113.

1867

March 6: UK patent 629, *An Improved Mode of and Means for Producing Optical Illusions*, application 6 March 1867. Issued 7 June 1867.

April 23: US patent 64,117, *Toy*, issued 23 April 1867.

1868

March 18: UK patent 925, *Improvements in the Means of Producing Optical Illusions*, application 18 March. Issued 14 September; Rossell 2005, 40-1; Gethmann 2005, 8-9.

March 27: UK provisional protection 1049, *Improvements in the Means of Method of Producing Optical Illusions*, application March 27. Not issued.

1869

August 10: US patent 93,594, *Optical Instrument*, issued 10 August 1869; Herbert 2001, 46; Gosser 1977, 137-8; Peter Domankiewicz, communications of 07-06-2019.

1870

February 5: Peter Domankiewicz, *Was the Phasmascope a Phantoscope Phantasy? Henry Heyl and Moving Pictures*. Privately circulated (2019) and intended for publication soon. [In error: every historian writing before 2019, including myself.]

March 16: Peter Domankiewicz, *Was the Phasmascope a Phantoscope Phantasy? Henry Heyl and Moving Pictures*. Privately circulated (2019) and intended for publication soon. [In error: every historian writing before 2019, including myself.]

1876

July: Herbert 2017, 37-8.

November 9: Provisional UK patent 4344, *Improvements in Apparatus for Taking a Succession of Photographic Pictures and for Exhibiting Such Pictures*. The submission was never carried to a full specification.

1878

June 11: http://www.stephenherbert.co.uk/muychron02a.htm [Chronology 1876-78]; Hendricks 1975, 243.

June 27: US patent 212,865, *Improvement in the Method and Apparatus for Photographing Objects in Motion*, application 276 June 1898. Issued 4 March 1879.

July 11: US patent 212,864, *Improvement in the Method and Apparatus for Photographing Objects in Motion*, application 11 July 1898. Issued 4 March 1879.

1879

January 25: Haas 1976, 120.

June 28: Haas 1976, 120.

1880

January 16: http://www.stephenherbert.co.uk/muybCOMPLEAT.htm [Chronology 1880]; Hendricks 1975, 115; Herbert 2004, 115.

March 21: Hendricks 1975, 115; http://www.stephenherbert.co.uk/muybCOMPLEAT.htm [Chronology 1880].

May 4: Hendricks 1975, 115; Haas 1976, 120; http://www.stephenherbert.co.uk/ muybCOMPLEAT.htm [Chronology 1880].

May 5: Hendricks 1975, 115; Haas 1976, 120; http://www.stephenherbert.co.uk/ muybCOMPLEAT.htm [Chronology 1880].

1881

August 31: US patent 279,878, *Method of and apparatus for Photographing Changing or Moving Objects*, application 3d1 August 1881. Issued 19 June 1883.

September 26: Haas 1976, 130; Hendricks 1975, 135.

November 3: http://www.stephenherbert.co.uk/muybCOMPLEAT.htm [Chronology 1881]; Mannoni 1994, 295.

November 26: Hendricks 1975, 136; Haas 1976, 130.

December 14: Haas 1976, 130; http://www.stephenherbert.co.uk/muybCOMPLEAT.htm [Chronology 1881].

1882

February 11: http://www.stephenherbert.co.uk/muybCOMPLEAT.htm [Chronology 1882].

March 6: Hendricks 1975, 141; http://www.stephenherbert.co.uk/muybCOMPLEAT. htm [Chronology 1882].

March 13: Haas 1976, 132-3; Hendricks 1975, 140-1; http://www.stephen herbert.co.uk/muybCOMPLEAT.htm [Chronology 1882].

March 16: Hendricks 1975, 141; http://www.stephenherbert.co.uk/muyb COMPLEAT.htm [Chronology 1882].

March 18: Hendricks 1975, 141; http://www.stephenherbert.co.uk/muyb COMPLEAT.htm [Chronology 1882].

April 4: Hendricks 1975, 141;http://www.stephenherbert.co.uk/muyb COMPLEAT.htm [Chronology 1882].

April 5: Hendricks 1975, 141; http://www.stephenherbert.co.uk/muyb COMPLEAT.htm [Chronology 1882].

April 7: US patent 258,164, *Optical Toy*, application April 7, issued May 16.

May 24: US patent 259,950, *Optical Toy*, application 24 May 1882. Issued 20 June 1882.

June 5: *Liverpool Mercury*, June 6, 1882, issue 10735, 6; Hendricks 1975, 141; Herbert 2004, 119.

June 8: *Liverpool Mercury*, June 9, 1882, issue 10738, 6; Herbert 2004, 119.

July 30: Herbert 2004, 120 [In error: Hendricks 1975, 149]

October 19: Herbert 2004, 120; Haas 1976, 142; Hendricks 1975, 149.

October 23: Herbert 2004: 120-21; Hendricks 1975, 149.

November 17: Herbert 2004, 121; Hendricks 1975, 149.

November 28: Herbert 2004, 121; Haas 1976, 142; Hendricks 1975, 149. Haas 1976, 154, reproduces a ticket for this lecture.

December 22: Herbert 2004, 121; Hendricks 1975, 149. Haas 1976, 154, reproduces a ticket for this lecture.

1883

January 9: Haas 1976, 143; Hendricks 1975, 149. Haas 1976, 154, reproduces a ticket for this lecture.

February 12: Haas 1976, 143; Hendricks 1975, 149; Herbert 2004, 121-2.

February 13: Hendricks 1975, 149 & 152; Herbert 2004, 122.

February 15: Haas, 1976, 143; Hendricks 1975, 149; Herbert 2004, 122.

February 16: Hendricks 1975, 149; http://www.stephenherbert.co.uk/muyb COMPLEAT.htm [Chronology 1883].

August 7: Hendricks 1975, 153-4; Haas 1976, 146.

September 20: Haas 1976, 143-4; [In error: http://www.stephenherbert.co.uk/muyb COMPLEAT.htm [Chronology 1883]; Hendricks 1975, 154].

November 9: http://www.stephenherbert.co.uk/muyb COMPLEAT.htm [Chronology 1883].

November: Hendricks 1975, 152.

1884

February 8: Hendricks 1975, 154; http://www.stephenherbert.co.uk/muyb COMPLEAT.htm [Chronology 1884].

August: Braun 1992, 411n15; http://www.stephenherbert.co.uk/muyb COMPLEAT.htm [Chronology 1884]; Hendricks 1975, 163.

1886

November 2: US patent 376,247, *Method of and Apparatus for Producing Animated Pictures of Natural Scenery and Life,* application 2 November 1886. Issued 10 January 1888.

November 4: *Boston Medical and Surgical Journal*, 25 November 1886, pp. 502-3. With thanks to John Barnes for this reference.

November 17: UK patent 14,917, *An Improved Toy or Picture Book*, application November 17. Issued September 16; Gethmann 2005, 14-5.

1887

March 19: Rossell 2001, 73-4; Liesegang 1926, 47; Liesegang 1986, 50.

Mid-June: Rossell 2001, 74-5; Liesegang 1940, 70; *Photographische Mittheilungen* 1887/88, 103.

September 20: *Photographisches Archiv*, 1887, p343; Rossell 2001, 75.

September: Haas 1976, 155; http://www.stephenherbert.co.uk/muyb COMPLEAT.htm [Chronology 1887].

October 3: Rossell 2001, 75; *Photographischen Correspondenz*, Vol. 24 (1887), Nr. 326, 472-3.

October 10: Rossell 2001, 75; *Photographischen Correspondenz*, Vol. 24 (1887), Nr. 326, 472-3.

December: Haas 1976, 155; http://www.stephenherbert.co.uk/muyb COMPLEAT.htm [Chronology 1887].

December: Haas 1976, 155; http://www.stephenherbert.co.uk/muyb COMPLEAT.htm [Chronology 1887].

1888

January 10: UK patent 423, *Improvements in the Method of and Apparatus for Producing Animated Photographic Pictures*. Application 10 January 1888. Issued 16 November 1888.

January 11: French patent 188,089: Schmitt 1996, 20.

February: Rossell 2001, 75.

February 25: Spehr 2008, 75-77; Hendricks 1961, 4 – 14; Hendricks 1975, 175; Haas 1976, 177.

February 27: Spehr 2008, 75-77; Hendricks 1961, 4 – 14; Hendricks 1975, 175; Haas 1976, 177.

April 23: Haas 1976, 154, where a ticket for the lecture is reproduced; http://www.stephenherbert.co.uk/muyb COMPLEAT.htm [Chronology 1888].

June 21: Hass 1976, 154, where a ticket for the lecture is reproduced; http://www.stephenherbert.co.uk/muyb COMPLEAT.htm [Chronology 1888].

July 14: German patent 46561, *Selbsteinkassirender Schaustellungsapparat*, application July 14. Issued April 3, 1889; Rossell 2005b, 566.

December 1: French patent 194,482, *Appareil dit Théâtre optique*, to Emile Reynaud. Application 1 December 1888. Issued 14 January 1889. Additions of 6 January 1889 and 26 August 1889; Auzel 1992, 46; Sadoul 1946b, 55-61.

Late 1888: Rossell 2001, 77; *Bulletin de la Société Francaise de Photographie*, Vol. 4 (1888), 303-4.

1889

January 22: Domankiewicz 2019, 3-5. [in error: Coe 1962, 28-9]

February 8: British patent 2295, *Improvements in Apparatus for the Production of Optical Illusions.* Application 8 February 1889. Issued 11 January 1890; Hecht 1993, 217, No. 326A; Liesegang 1986, 52.

February 9: Haas 1976, 167; http://www.stephenherbert.co.uk/muyb COMPLEAT.htm [Chronology 1889].

February 23: Jenkins 1975, 128-131.

Mid-March: Haas 1976, 167; http://www.stephenherbert.co.uk/muyb COMPLEAT.htm [Chronology 1889].

March 22: *The Morning Post* (London), March 25, 1889, issue 36433, p. 3; *The Morning Post* (London), March 6, 1889, issue 36417, p. 5; Haas 1976, 167; http://www.stephenherbert.co.uk/muyb COMPLEAT.htm [Chronology 1889]; *The Pall Mall Gazette*, 23-03-1889, issue 7493, 6.

March 23: *The Standard* (London), March 21, 1889, issue 20186, 4.

April 9: Gosser 1977, 182 & n8; Mitry 1967, 35; Ackerman 1930, 61-2 & 89-90. [In error: Pinel 1992, 49]

☛Jenkins 1975, 128.

May 2: *The Morning Post* (London), May 2, 1889, issue 36466, p.4; Haas 1976, 167; http://www.stephenherbert.co.uk/muyb COMPLEAT.htm [Chronology 1889].

May 8: Haas 1976, 167; http://www.stephenherbert.co.uk/muyb COMPLEAT.htm [Chronology 1889].

May 9: Haas 1976, 167; http://www.stephenherbert.co.uk/muyb COMPLEAT.htm [Chronology 1889].

June 15: Slide 1989, 227.

June 19: Haas 1976, 167; http://www.stephenherbert.co.uk/muybCOMPLEAT.htm [Chronology 1889].

June 21: UK patent 10,131, *Improved Apparatus for Taking Photographs in Rapid Series*, application 21 June 1889. Issued 10 May 1890; Hendricks 1961, 133; Chanan 1980, 91; Domankiewicz 2019, 5-6. [In error: Mitry 1967, 61; Zglinicki 1979, 198, but correct on p. 204; Mitry 1976, 14; Coe 1962, 29.]

July 26: *The North-Eastern Daily Gazette*, July 26, 1889, ni, np.

August 10: *Philadelphia Photographer*, 1889, p. 337; *Wilson's Photographic Magazine*, 17 August 1889, p. 674; *Baltimore Deutsche Correspondent*, 9 July 1889, 1.

August 15: UK patent 12,921, *Improvements in the Production and Representation of Instantaneous Photographic Pictures*, application 15 August 1889. Issued 15 November 1890; Herbert 2017, 73.

☛*Photographisches Wochenblatt* (Berlin), 1889, 304-5, 328, 387.

August 18: Liesegang 1986, 55; Coe 1992, 43; Hecht 1993, 224, No. 340A; Donisthorpe's letter to *BJP* 12 March 1897 is in Hecht, 297, No. 423A. See also Coe 1960; Gosser 1977, 180ff. [In error: Zglinicki 1979, 228]

August 19: Spehr 2008, 144. See also 142-7.

August 21: Haas 1976, 167; http://www.stephenherbert.co.uk/muyb COMPLEAT.htm [Chronology 1889].

August 21: *The Pall Mall Gazette*, August 21, 1889, issue 7621, 7.

August 27: Jenkins 1975, 131-2.

September 5: Kaiserliches Patentamt, Patentschrift 53840, application 5 September 1889, issued 10 October 1890.

September 12: Haas 1976, 167; http://www.stephenherbert.co.uk/muyb COMPLEAT.htm [Chronology 1889].

September 17: Haas 1976, 167; http://www.stephenherbert.co.uk/muyb COMPLEAT.htm [Chronology 1889].

October 2: Haas 1976, 167; http://www.stephenherbert.co.uk/muyb COMPLEAT.htm [Chronology 1889].

October 28: *The Sheffield and Rotherham Independent*, October 28, 1889, issue 10973, 1.

November 7: Haas 1976, 167; http://www.stephenherbert.co.uk/muyb COMPLEAT.htm [Chronology 1889].

November 9: Haas 1976, 167; http://www.stephenherbert.co.uk/muyb COMPLEAT.htm [Chronology 1889]. http://www. stephenherbert.co.uk/ mLECTURES.htm. University Museum, Oxford.

November 15: *Rossell 2001, 77; Scientific American,* Vol. LXI, No. 20, 16 November 1889; *Bulletin de la Société française de Photographie* (Paris), 89, 310.

November 16: Hecht 1993, 228, No. 340Q; *Scientific American*, Vol. LXI, No. 20, 16 November 1889, cover & 310.

November 21: Haas 1976, 167; http://www.stephenherbert.co.uk/muyb COMPLEAT.htm [Chronology 1889].

November 27: Haas 1976, 167; Coe 1962, 125; http://www.stephenherbert .co.uk/muybCOMPLEAT.htm [Chronology 1889].

November 28: *The York Herald*, November 28, 1889, issue 12010.

December 2: Haas 1976, 167; http://www.stephenherbert.co.uk/muyb COMPLEAT.htm [Chronology 1889].

December 12: Haas 1976, 167; http://www.stephenherbert.co.uk/muyb COMPLEAT.htm [Chronology 1889].

Late December: *Science. A Weekly Newspaper of All the Arts and Sciences.* (New York), Vol. XV, No. 366, 86.

1890

January 8: *Liverpool Mercury*, January 9, 1890, issue 13106, p. 6.

January 16: Rossell 2001, 78-9; *Photographisches Wochenblatt* (Berlin), Vol. 87, 96.

☛Rossell 2001, 78; *Photographisches Wochenblatt* (Berlin), Vol. 87, 96.

January: Liesegang 1940, 61-2; Rossell 2001, 78-9.

February 3: Herbert 2004, 127; http://www.stephenherbert.co.uk/muyb COMPLEAT.htm [Chronology 1890].

February 11 and 13: Herbert 2004, 128; *The Belfast News-Letter*, issue 23273, p. 4; *The Belfast News-Letter*, Issue 23275, 4.

February 12 and 14: Herbert 2004, 129; *Freeman's Journal & Daily Commercial Advertiser*, February 8, 1890, p. 9.; *Freeman's Journal & Daily Commercial Advertiser*, February 13, 1890, np.

February 17: Herbert 2004, 129.

February 25: Liesegang 1986, 54; Domankiewicz 2019, 6; *Photographic News*, 1890, Vol. 34, p. 157-9, 183; Spehr 2008, 105-11.

February 26: Herbert 2004, 129; http://www.stephenherbert.co.uk/muyb COMPLEAT.htm [Chronology 1890].

March 8: UK patent 3730, *Improvements in or applicable to Photographic Cameras*, application 8 March 1890. Issued 10 January 1891**;** Coe 1992, 35. [In error: Coe 1981, 58]

March 12 and 14: Herbert 2004, 129; *Birmingham Daily Post*, March 11, 1890, issue 9894, p. 4; *Birmingham Daily Post*, March 13, 1890, issue 9896, 5.

March 15: *The New York Times*, 16 March 1890.

March 26: UK patent 4704, *Improvements in Cameras for Photographing Objects in Motion***,** application 26 March 1890. Issued 28 February 1891; Liesegang 1986, 55; Coe 1992, 45; Hecht 1993, 235, No. 351R; Gosser 1977, 193 & 193n16, 182-194.

☛Hecht 1993, 234, No. 351J; Hendricks 1961, 171.

March 31: UK patent 4978, *Improvements in Toys, Shades, and Advertising Devices, and in Methods of Actuating or Exhibiting the same*. Application March 31, 1890. Issued February 28, 1891.

April 7: Hendricks 1961, 84-92, esp. p. 91-2; Spehr 2008, 180-82.

April 10: *Photographische Mittheilungen*, 1890, p21, reporting on the meeting of the Photographische Verein of 11 April 1890.

April 21 & 22: Rossell 2001, 79-8; Eder 1891, 35 – 40; Kieninger 1995, 77.

Late April: Kieninger 1995, 77; Rossell 2001, 80; Liesegang 1940, 75.

May 9: http://www.stephenherbert.co.uk/muybCOMPLEAT.htm [Chronology 1890].

June 26: *Photographic News* 1890 v34 509-510; *Photographic Journal* 1933 v37, 77-78.

September 16: Coe 1992, 41-2. Coe in haste transposes the direction of Le Prince's trip: he was already in Dijon, and took a train towards Paris. For a book-length study with a full biography and many carefully imaginative speculations, see also Christopher Rawlence, *The Missing Reel, The Untold Story of the Lost Inventor of Moving Pictures* (London, 1990: William Collins & Sons).

September 30: Hecht 1993, 235, No. 351R.

October 1: Jenkins 1975, 147.

October 3: Coissac 1925, 587; Hecht 1993, 235, No. 351N; Frizot 1984, 104-6. [In error: Pinel 1992, 50]

October 8: Zglinicki 1979, 186; Burger 1987, 25.

☛ *The Bristol Mercury & Daily Post*, October 11, 1890, issue 13234, 5.

October 13: Herbert 2004, 130; http://www.stephenherbert.co.uk/muybCOMPLEAT.htm [Chronology 1890].

October 20: Herbert 2004, 130; http://www.stephenherbert.co.uk/muybCOMPLEAT.htm [Chronology 1890].

October 21: *Photography* v2 1890 p. 707; *British Journal of Photography* 1890 v37 716.

October 28: Herbert 2004, 130; http://www.stephenherbert.co.uk/muybCOMPLEAT.htm [Chronology 1890].

☛ Schmitt 1996, 22.

November 3: Coe 1992, 32-3.

November 7: *The Bristol Mercury and Daily Post*, 16 September 1890, issue 13212, p. 8.

November 9: German patent 58 166, *Vorrichtung zur Erzeugung und Vorführung von Augenblicksbildern*, Application 9 November 1890, issued 11 August 1891.

November 11: US patent 452966, *Method of Producing Instantaneous Photographs*, Application 11 November 1890, granted 26 May 1891.

November 15: German patent 60285, *Stroboskopischer Apparat (Schnellseher)*,application 15 November 1890 Issued 19 December 1891.

November 27: *Photography* Dec 4 1890 p. 771. [In error: Coe 1962, 98.]

☛ Herbert 2004, 130-1; *The Dundee Courier & Argus*, November 7, 1890, issue 11650, 1; *The Dundee Courier & Argus*, November 25, 1890, issue 11665, 1.

December 4: http://www.stephenherbert.co.uk/muybCOMPLEAT.htm [Chronology 1890].

December 8 and 9: http://www.stephenherbert.co.uk/muybCOMPLEAT.htm [Chronology 1890].

December 12: *Liverpool Mercury*, December 11, 1890, issue 13394, 1.

December 16: *The Blackburn Standard & Weekly Express*, December 20, 1890, issue 2862, 6.

December 17: http://www.stephenherbert.co.uk/muybCOMPLEAT.htm [Chronology 1890].

1891

January 9: Burger 1987, 25.

January 24: http://www.stephenherbert.co.uk/muybCOMPLEAT.htm [Chronology 1891].

February 27: http://www.stephenherbert.co.uk/muybCOMPLEAT.htm [Chronology 1890].

March 9: Fraenkel 1956, 373; Zglinicki 1979, 176-9; Hecht 1993, 240 No. 361C.

March 22: German patent 59390, *Aufnahme- und Projections-Apparat für bewegliche Objecte*, application 22 March 1891. Issued 17 October 1891; Forch 1913, 55; Hecht 1993, 238, No. 357A. [In error: Zglinicki 1979, 229, has an incorrect patent number]

May 20: Hendricks 1961, 111-112; Musser 1991, 31; Spehr 2008, 200-1.

July 18: Letter of Ottomar Anschütz to Siemens & Halske, 28 August 1891, Siemens Archiv, file LN238.

July 27: Hecht 1993, 245, No. 362S.

August 8: *Tagesanzeiger* (der Internationale Elektrotechnische Ausstellung), Nr. 85, 8 August 1891; Hoffmann, 1995, 21.

August 24: Liesegang 1986, 57; Hendricks 1961, 130-37; Musser 1990, 238-9.

December 6: Zglinicki 1979, 222.

1892

February 12: Coissac 1925, 587; Liesegang 1986, 60; Card 1967, 106.

March 3: Coissac 1925, 587; Liesegang 1986, 56; Frizot 1984, 148. See also Coe 1992, 55; Gosser 1977, 200-201. British patent: Hecht 1993, 255, No. 374K. [In error: Mitry 1967, 53]

April: Letter of Ottomar Anschütz to Siemens & Halske plus their reply, 9 April 1892, Siemens Archiv, file LN238.

April 16: http://www.stephenherbert.co.uk/muybCOMPLEAT.htm [Chronology 1892].

April 18: http://www.stephenherbert.co.uk/muybCOMPLEAT.htm [Chronology 1892].

May 2: Braun 1992, 173; see also pp. 170-74. [In error: Frizot 1984, 121; Deac Rossell, *Chronology 1995*, 124. Unclear on this point is Coe 1992, 33.]

May 3: Siemens & Halske, summary invoice to Ottomar Anschütz, 31 July 1892, Siemens Archiv, file LN239; Zander invoice, Siemens & Halske to Ottomar Anschütz, 17 June 1892, Siemens Archiv, film LN238.

June: Letters of Ottomar Anschütz to Siemens & Halske of 1 August 1892 and 31 October 1892, Siemens Archiv, film LN239.

June 5: German patent 66346, *Kontrolvorrichtung für Selbstverkäufer*, application 5 June 1892. Issued 19 December 1892; Siemens Archiv, file LN238.

June 13: Siemens Archiv, file LN238.

July 21: Letter of Ottomar Anschütz to Siemens and Halske, 30 June 1892, Siemens Archiv file LN239 and shipping notice, Siemens and Halske, 21 July 1892, Siemens Archiv, file LN238.

September 1: Letter of E. Zander to Siemens and Halske, 1 September 1892, Siemens Archiv, file LN239; letter of E. Zander to Siemens and Halske, 29 September 1892, Siemens Archiv, file LN238; Rossell 2016, 155. In error: F. A. Talbot, *Moving Pictures, how they are Made and Worked* (1912 & 1923) and Terry Ramsaye, *A Million and One Nights* (1926), both of whom have dated this exhibition after the appearance of the Edison Kinetoscope rather than before.

September 24: US patent 525,991, *Series Photographic Camera*, application 24 September 1892. Issued 11 September 1894; 'Der älteste Kinematograph, von Max Mayer, München', mss. In Oskar Messter files, Bundesarchiv-Filmarchiv, Berlin, folder 87 (old numbers).

September 29: letter of E. Zander to Siemens and Halske, 29 September 1892, Siemens Archiv, file LN238; Rossell 2016, 155.

October 10: letter of E. Zander to Siemens and Halske, 29 September 1892, Siemens Archiv, file LN238; Rossell 2016, 155.

Mid-October: *Western Electrician*, 15 October 1892, Vol. IX, No. 16, 15 October 1892, 200-1.

October 28: Auzel 1992, 54; see also 46-66, 75.

November 19: Jenkins 1975, 444 & 134-159.

November 12: Public Record Office, Kew, London [now the National Archives], file BT31/52134

December 14: UK patent 23,042, *Improvements in Coin Freed Apparatus for Exhibiting Optical Illusions*, application 14 December 1892. Issued 25 November 1893.

December 19: *The Pall Mall Gazette*, 20 December 1892, i8658; *The Sheffield and Rotherham Independant*, 22 December 1892, i11964, 6 [reprinted from *The Daily News*, London].

December 20: Liesegang 1986, 56; Coe 1992, 55-6; Loiperdinger 1990, 25.

Further Anschütz Schnellseher exhibitions with four machines in Boston, Massachusetts.

1893

January 13: US patent 509,362, *Toy*, application 13 January 1893. Issued 28 November 1893.

March 1: US patent 509,841, *Photographic-Camera Shutter*, application 1 March 1893. Issued 28 November 1893.

☛US patent 517,539, *Camera*, application 1 March 1893. Issued 3 April 1894; Spehr 2008, 290-4; Coe 1978, 61.

March 11: *Reynolds's Newspaper*, 19 March 1893, i2223.

March 21: *The Morning Post* (London), 21 March through 1 April 1893.

March 24: *The Morning Post*, 31 March 1893 through 29 December 1894; *The Standard*, 1 May 1893 through 31 May 1895; Public Record Office, Kew, London [now the National Archives], file BT34/886/37536; Crystal Palace programme, 25 April 1893 (Richard Brown Collection).

April 11: http://www.stephenherbert.co.uk/muybCOMPLEAT.htm [Chronology 1893].

April 15: Electrical Wonder Company prospectus, 15 April 1893, Siemens Archiv, file LN239.

April 27: German patent 74 792, application 27 April 1893, issued 28 April 1894; *Photographisches Jahrbuch*, Jahr 1895, p. 599.

May 1: Electrical Wonder Company brochure, Cinémathèque Française.

May 9: Spehr 2008, 295-7; Hopwood 1899, 73; Liesegang 1986, 57; Hendricks 1966, 36-38; Musser 1990, 72; Musser 1991, 35-6.

May 10: http://www.stephenherbert.co.uk/muybCOMPLEAT.htm [Chronology 1893].

June 17: Braun 2010, 229-30; http://www.stephenherbert.co.uk/muybCOMPLEAT.htm [Chronology 1893].

June 30: French patent 231,232. Application 30 June 1893.

June 26: Spehr 2008, 297-9 & 305-7; Hendricks 1966, 9-10.

June 29: Coissac 1925, 587; Frizot 1984, 107-110. [In error: Hecht 1993, 263, No. 386L has a very misleading description of this patent.]

October 10: Coissac 1925, 587; Coe 1992, 57; Forch 1913, 41; Confèderationi Suisse Bureau Fédéral de la Propriété Intellectuelle Exposé d'Invention No. 7703, 11 December 1893. [In error: Liesegang 1986, 58; Mitry 1976, 15, has an incorrect patent number]

November 3: Bernard & Gunthert 1993, 208 & 220.

November 6: Bernard & Gunthert 1993, 208 & 220.

December 8: UK patent 23,670 of 1893, *Apparatus for Exposing Successive Photographic Plates, and for Exhibiting Magic Lantern and other Slides*, application December 8, issued February 10, 1894.

December 14: UK patent 24,0321, *An Improved Musical Toy*, application 14 December 1893. Issued 20 October 1894.

December 27: Coissac 1925, 587; Liesegang 1986, 60.

1894

February 25: Zglinicki 1979, 213-14; Ceram 1965, 144-45; Sadoul 1946, 174; Gosser 1975, 228-29. [In error: Mitry 1967, 63; Mitry 1976, 15; Pinel 1992, 62, 68, & 97.]

March 6: Hendricks 1966, 56-60; Musser 1990, 75.

April 14: Hendricks 1966, 56-60; Musser 1990, 81.

May 17: Hendricks 1966, 60; Musser 1990, 81.

June 1: Hendricks 1966, 60; Musser 1990, 81.

June 14: Programme of the Camera Club Conversazione, 14 June 1893 (Courtesy Barnes Collection).

June 15: Musser 1990, 82-4.

July 6: Hecht 1993, 271, No. 395T; Hendricks 1966, 51.

July 8: Hendricks 1966, 62.

July 16: Brown & Anthony 2017, 5-6. [in error: Talbot 1912, 33-4; Ramsaye 1926, 138; and many others.]

July 27: Coissac 1925, 588; Liesegang 1986, 58; Coe 1992, 57; Hecht 1993, 268, No. 394D. [Pinel 1992, 62-3 cites the date of the French patent correctly but fails to note the improvement was included in earlier patents in Germany and the United Kingdom.]

August 4: US patent 539,799, *Lantern for Bicycle-Riders*, application 4 August 1895. Issued 28 May 1895.

August 9: Hendricks 1966, 62.

September 7: Hendricks 1966, 100-109.

September 18: Mesa 2014, 18; Caneto, et. al. 1996, 21-3.

October 1: Mitry 1963, 31; Mannoni 1993a, 50-53; Mannoni 1996, 18. [In error: Deslandes 1963, 84.]

October 5: Sadoul 1964, 9 & 148.

October 6: Hendricks 1966, 61 & 63.

October 9: Remshardt 2004, 456-7; Hollyman 1983a, 239; Ramsaye 1926, 97.

October 18: Barnes 1976, 188, as corrected in Barnes 1983, 238; Brown & Anthony 2017, 6.

November 3: Idestam-Almquist 1962, 584.

November 6: German patent 85791 *Projektionsapparat für stroboskopisch bewegte Bilder*, application 6 November 1894. Issued 7 March 1896; Hecht 1993, 271, No. 396; Coissac 1925, 588; Köcke 1966, 344-5.

November 10: Hendricks 1966, 62-64; Hollyman 1983, 188.

November 11: Barnes 1992, 159ff.

November 12: Spehr 2008, 375-6.

November 21: US patent 549,309, Mutoscope, application 21 November 1894. Issued 5 November 1895; Hendricks 1964, 9; Liesegang 1986, 58; Musser 1990, 145; Rossell 1999, 79-81.

November 24: US patent 536,569, *Phantoscope*, application 24 November 1894. Issued 26 March 1895; Liesegang 1986, 59; Hecht 1993, 271, No. 395U.

November 25: Zglinicki 1986, 59; Köcke 1966, 346; Rossell 2001, 119-21. See also Coe 1992, 36-7.

November 26: Hendricks 1966, 63-4.

November 29 & 30: Traub 1940, 34; Rossell 2001, 121-22.

November 30: Long 1993, 38-9.

December 3: Kane & Dougherty 1995, 344-5.

December 5: Mannoni 1993a, 53.

December 12: Liesegang 1986, 59; Hecht 1993, 271, No. 395V; United States patent 560,800, application 12 December 1894, issued 26 May 1896.

December 13: Hendricks 1966, 65-6.

December 16: Nørgaard 1973, 20.

December 17: Berry 1994, 18; Brown & Anthony 2017, 139.

December 27: Maden & Dibbets 1986, 13; Briels 1971, 7-10.

☛Hecht 1993, 268, No. 394F.

☛UK patent 25,100, *Improvements in Kinetoscopes*, application 27 December 1894. Issued 26 October 1895; Brown and Anthony 2017, 68-71 & 159-62.

December 28: Sadoul 1964 , 148.

☛Ferreira 1986, 13-17.

1895

January 1: Auzel 1992, 58-59.

January 3: Barnes 1976, 143.

January 6: Kane & Dougherty 1995, 345.

January 14: Kane & Dougherty 1995, 345.

January 20: Hendricks 1966, 66.

February 4: Waldekranz 1976, 362.

February 5: Long 1993, 39.

February 13: Liesegang 1986, 60; Coissac 1925, 588. Lens: Seeber 1979, 141.

February 22: Zglinicki 1986, 59; Köcke 1966, 346; Coe 1992, 37. [In error: Fraenkel 1956, 374].

February 26: Musser 1990, 145; Spehr 1999, 24.

March 1: Spehr 1999, 24-5.

March 2: Hendricks 1964, 8 – 15, esp. 13-14; Musser 1990, 145.

March 6: Ferreira 1986, 21-23.

☛Brown 2012, 411.

March 9: US patent 540,545, *Series Photographic Camera,* application 9 March 1895. Issued 4 June 1895. See also: Rossell 1998, 109-10; Rossell 2013, 19-22.

March 11: Convents 2000, 46-7.

March 13: Buache & Rial 1964, 73.

March 16: Long 1993, 39.

March 20: Henningsen 1990, 56.

March 22: Fescourt, et. al. 1932, 65; André & André 1997, 76; also, Mannoni 1993a, 56; April 1895 issue of the *Bulletin of the Photo Club of Paris,* quoted by Mannoni 1994, 393-4.

March 23: Wit 1986, 11.

March 25: Liesegang 1986, 61; US patent 546,093, application filed 25 March 1895, issued 10 September 1895.

☛Gosser 1988, 2.

March 29: Barnes 1976, 19-21; Hendricks 1966, 133-4.

March 30: Barnes 1976, 202 & 21.

☛French patent 246,246 *Appareil pour projections de photographies instantanées de scènes animées sur bandes pelliculaires, dénommé cynégraphe, issued 30 March 1895*; Coissac 1925, 588. Camera: Coe 1978, 126 & 150. [In error: Mitry 1967, 80].

☛Liesegang 1986, 60; Mannoni 1994, 473. [In error: Sadoul 1964, 14, 148].

April 1: Rossell 1998, 112; Zglinicki 1979, 213; *American Photographic Times,* July 1896, pp. 330-1.

April 2: Spehr 2008, 370-1 & 310-11.

April 17: André & André 1997, 76.

April 18: Loiperdinger 1990, 5.

April 21: Musser 1990, 94; Pratt 1973, 20 [In error: Mitry 1967, 65]

☛Bernardini 1980, 15.

May 1: Loiperdinger 1999, 305.

May 4: Musser 1990, 94-6.

May 5: Ros-Vilella 1979, 165.

May 6: Sadoul 1964, 149.

May 11: Rossell 2001, 122; Siemens Archiv file LN239.

May 16: Totenberg 1990, 24.

May 18: UK patent 9881, *Improvements in Means for Viewing a Series of Pictures for the Purpose of Obtaining from same an Appearance of Movement,* application May 18, issued April 18, 1896; Hendricks 1966, 165-67 & 169; Brown 2012, 411.

May 19: Mannoni 1996, 18-19.

May 20: Liesegang 1986, 62; Musser 1990, 94-96; Spehr 1999, 25. [In error: Pratt 1973, 20; Ramsaye 1926, 134.]

May 21: Loiperdinger 1999, 67 & 300.

May 23: Herbert 2017, 105 & 197n13.

May 25: Coissac 1925, 588; Liesegang 1986, 58; Coe 1992, 57-8.

May 27: UK patent 10,474 *Improved Apparatus for Enabling Photographic Images to be Taken, Projected, or Viewed in Rapid Succession*, application 27 February 1895. Issued 2 May 1896; Liesegang 1986, 61; Barnes 1976, 26-7; [In error: Mitry 1967, 69 & 83; Bessy & Duca 1948, 24; Mitry 1976, 16; Pinel 1992, 71].

May 29: Barnes 1976, 27-9. [In error: Ceram 1965, 171].

☛Rossell 2001, 122; Wagner 1972, 14.

May 30: Martinez 1992, 23-4.

June 1: Genovese 1984, 52-3.

June 2: German patent 92809, application 2 June 1895. Issued 29 July 1897. See also: Rossell 1998, 109-10; Rossell 2013, 18-25.

June 10: André & André 1997, 76; Bessy & Duca 1948, 41. [In error: Fescourt, et. al. 1932, 65].

June 11: Long 1993, 39.

June 12: Bessy & Duca 1948, 41; Fescourt, et. al. 1932, 65; Chardère 1987, 113-115; Rittaud-Hutinet 1985, 27-30. [In error: Mitry 1976, 16].

June 13: Mitry 1976, 89.

June 18: Mannoni 1993a, 54-5; Coissac 1925, 588.

June 19: Long 1993, 39.

June 20: Barnes 1976, 57.

☛Lange-Fuchs 1987, 28.

June 28: Long 1993, 39.

July 1: Rossell 2001, 122; Siemens Archiv file LN239.

July 5: Letamendi 1998, 199-202.

July 11: Fescourt, et. al. 1932, 65; André & André 1997, 76; Rittaud-Huittenet 1985, 30; Traub 1940, 50.

July 20: Zglinicki 1979, 239-40; Narath 1970, 2-23; Castan 1995, 48-9 & 43-5. [In error: Mitry 1967, 69; Mitry 1976, 16].

August 5: Musser 1990, 146.

August 10: Mannoni 1994, 407.

August 13: Long 1993, 40.

August 22: Mannoni 1994, 386-7.

August 24: Loiperdinger 1999, 55.

August 25: German patent 92247, *Vorrichtung zur Aufnahme und Projektion von Reihenbildern*, application 25 August 1895. Issued 12 June 1897; Lange-Fuchs 1987, 70.

August 26: Musser 1990, 99; Pratt 1973b, 15; Pratt 1973, 21.

☛French patent 249,875, *Un nouvel appareil chronophotographique*, issued 26 August 1895; Liesegang 1986, 61; Coissac 1925, 467 & 588; Mitry 1976, 90. [In error: Zglinicki 1979, 229].

August 28: Liesegang 1986, 62; Musser 1990, 101-103; Hecht 1993, 274, No. 397A. [In error: Mitry 1976, 15].

September 2: Long 1993, 40.

September 6: US patent 579,882. Application 6 September 1895. Issued 30 March 1897; Musser 1990, 508, note 11.

September 7: Long 1993, 42.

September 21: Chardère 1990, 57.

September 22: Musser 1990, 147.

September 26: Wit 1986, 11.

September 27: Long 1993, 42.

September 29: Musser 1990, 103; North 1973, 28; Hendricks 1961, 69 & 135; Gosser 1988, 2.

October 13: Mannoni 1996, 20-1.

October 16: http://www.stephenherbert.co.uk/muybCOMPLEAT.htm [Chronology 1895].

October 18: http://www.stephenherbert.co.uk/muybCOMPLEAT.htm [Chronology 1895].

October 24: Barnes 1976, 37 – 40; Mitry 1963, 35.

October 29: Musser 1990, 104; Ramsaye 1926, 196.

November 1: Lichtenstein 1990, 312-24; Grusser 1965, 25.

☛Lichtenstein 1990, 312-24; Grusser 1965, 25. [In error: Bessy & Duca 1948, 22; Mitry 1976f, 16, has an incorrect patent number].

November 8: Liesegang 1986, 57 & p. 61; Coissac 1925, 588; Hecht 1993, 275, No. 402E; Mitry 1967, 82.

☛Long 1993, 42.

November 10: Rittaud-Hutinet 1985, 30-32; Sadoul 1964, 149; Convents 1984, 16; Convents 2000, 74-8.

November 11: Bernardini 1980, 203; Coissac 1925, 597.

November 12: Rittaud-Hutinet 1985, 32; Convents 1984, 16.

November 13: Convents 1984, 16; Convents 2000, 74-8.

November 14: US patent 584,228, Mutoscope, application 14 November 1895. Issued 8 June 1897.

☛US patent 584,311, *Mutoscope,* application 14 November 1895. Issued 8 June 1897.

November 16: Mitry 1963, 35; Fescourt, et. al. 1932, 65; Sadoul 1964, 149.

November 25: Musser 1990, 104; Hecht 1993, 305, No. 438J.

☛Kane & Dougherty 1995, 346.

November 29: Long & Sowry n.d. (1995), 1.

December 7: US patent 560,367, *Apparatus for Exhibiting Successive Photographs*, application 7 December 1885. Issued 19 May 1896; Rossell 2001, 99-101.

December 18: Musser 1990, 104; Gosser 1988, 4-5.

December 20: Henningsen 1990, 56-7.

December 21: Fraenkel 1956, 374; Totenberg 1990, 24.

December 23: Pratt 1973, 21; Musser 1990, 100.

☛Loiperdinger 1999, 92-3.

December 27: Spehr 2008, 410; Mannoni 1994, 401.

December 28: Chardère & Borgé 1985, 94-105; Mannoni 1994, 423-6; Sadoul 1964, 34-8.

December: Wlaschin 2008, 218.

1896

January 1: Genovese 1984, 53.

January 5: Goergen 1998, 13.

January 8: German patent 93745, *Serien-Apparat mit rotirendem Camera-träger*, application 8 January 1896. Issued 1 September 1897.

January 10: Coissac 1925, 588; Schmitt 1996, 25; Hecht 1993, 291, No. 415F. See also Mannoni 1994, 417ff.

☛Brown 1993, 15(a), Table II.

January 14: Barnes 1976, 62-5. See also Brown 1993, 15(a), Table II. [In error: Zglinicki 1979, 229; Liesegang 1986, 61.]

☛Coissac 1925, 275-6 & 588; Schmitt 1996, 25; Hecht 1993, 291, No. 415F; Card 1967, 107.

January 15: Musser 1990, 109-111.

☛Barnes 1976, 65.

☛Mannoni 1994, 418.

January 20: Musser 1990, 100; Pratt 1973, 21; Pratt 1973a, 39.

January 22: US patent 571,496, *Kinetoscope*, application January 22, issued November 17.

January 25: Rittaud-Hutinet 1985, 34 & 51.

☛Chardère & Borgé 1985, 104-5.

February 17: Mitry 1976, 16; Sadoul 1946, 112; Forch 1913, 97-8.

February 19: UK patent 3777, *A New or Improved Means for Giving intermittant Motion to a strip of Film for Taking or Exhibiting Photographs*, application 19 February 1896. Issued 13 February 1897; Barnes 1976, 108.

☛US patent 673,992 *Vitascope*, application 19 February 1896. Issued 14 May 1901; Hecht 1993, 289, No. 412E; Armat 1967, 19-20.

February 20: Barnes 1983, 245; Barnes 1976, 93; Barnes 1998, 90 – 102. Films: *Lightning*, Vol. IX, No. 228, 27 February 1896, p. 1.

☛Barnes 1976, 65, 84-5. Note: Brooker 2013, 152 & Weeden 2008, 102-4.[In error: Mitry 1976, 83 & 85; Rittaud-Hutinet 1985, 51; Zglinicki 1979, 219 & 224; Ceram 1965, 152 & 185; Bessy & Duca 1948, 51; Coissac 1925, 185.]

February 21: Barnes 1976, 89; Barnouw 1981, 50-4; Weeden 2008, 104; Brooker 2013, 152-3.

February 25: Coissac 1925, 274; Mitry 1976, 16; Mannoni 1993, 13.

February 26: US patent 629,063, *Kinetographic Camera*, application 26 February 1896. Issued 18 July 1899. Liesegang 1986, 66; Musser 1990, 146; Rossell 1999, 81-93.

☛US patent 666,495, *Consecutive-view apparatus*, application 26 February 1896, issued 22 January 1901; Rossell1999, 93-7. [In error: Liesegang 1986, 66.]

February 28: Barnes 1976, 93-5. [In error: Mitry 1967, 83.]

☛Brown 1993, 15(a), Table II.

☛Rittaud-Hutinet 1994, 6.

February 29: Rittaud-Hutinet 1985, 51.

☛Fletcher 2001, 71.

March 1: Rittaud-Hutinet 1985, 51.

☛Rittaud-Hutinet 1994, 6.

☛Castan 1995, 93-4; Zglinicki 1979, 74. [In error: Castan 1995, 92]

☛Berneau 1988, 18. [In error: Rittaud-Hutinet 1985, 51; Coissac 1925, 185.]

March 2: British patent 4686, *Improvements in Apparatus for Projecting Kinetoscope Pictures on the Screen,* application 2 March 1896. Issued 23 January 1897; Liesegang 1986, 65; Barnes 1976, 49.

☛French patent 254,394, *Cinographoscope Pipon Frères*. Application 2 March 1896, issued 28 March 1896; Schmitt 1996, 25.

March 3: US patent 707934, *Projecting-Kinetoscope*, application 1 June 1896. Issued 26 August 1902; Liesegang 1986, 62; Hecht 1993, 288, No. 409G, &. 276, No. 404A/1; Musser 1990, 134. [In error: Mitry 1967, 65.]

March 5: Coissac 1925, 276-8 & 589; Mitry 1967, 80; Card 1967, 107. Convents 2000, 97. [In error: Bessy & Duca 1948, 24.]

☛Coissac 1925, 274-5; Mitry 1976, 16; Mannoni 1993, 13.

March 6: Rittaud-Hutinet 1994, 6.

March 7: Brown 1993, 18. [In error: Mitry 1976, 16.]

March 9: Barnes 1976, 90, see also 89-92; Barnes 1983, 238.

March 12: Maden & Dibbets 1986, 15-17; Briels 1971, 11-16; de Klerk 1999, 6. [In error: Rittaud-Hutinet 1985, 51.]

☛Bernardini 2001, 153.

March 13: Bernardini 1985, 72 & 87; Bernardini 1980, 23, 26-7.

March 17: Coissac 1925, 589; Mitry 1976, 90; Mitry 1967, 82-3.

☛German patent 93190, *Schnellseher mit spiralig auf eine Trommel aufgewickeltem Bildstreifen*, application March 17, 1896. Issued August 9, 1897.

☛German patent 93599, *Bildtrommel-Leitspur für Schnellseher der durch Patent Nr. 71339 geschützten Art.*

March 18: Coissac 1925, 589.

March 19: Barnes 1976, 65, 117 – 121; Barnouw 1981, 54-8.

March 20: Loiperdinger 1990a, 38; Bleier-Brody 1966, 22; Bleier-Brody 1960, 27-8.

March 21: Barnes 1976, 66-70.

☛Barnes 1976, 96; Fletcher 2001, 71.

☛Convents 2000, 91-2.

March 22: Brown 1993, 21.

☛Meusy 1995, 30.

March 23: Rittaud-Hutinet 1994, 6.

March 25: Barnes 1976, 96 – 100, esp. 99; Fletcher 2017, 8. [In error: Mitry 1967, 83; Mitry 1976, 17.]

March 26: Musser 1990, 134.

☛Manders 1991, 6-7; Brown 1993, 30.

March 27: Musser 1990, 115-6.

☛Fritz 1981, 13-4; Bleier-Brody 1960, 28.

☛UK patent 6731, *Improvements in Kinematographs, Kinetographs, and like Apparatus*, application 27 March 1896. Issued 27 June 1896; Brown 1993, 27; Barnes 1976, 130-3.

March 28: Brown 1993, 30.

☛Keim 2008, 11-13; Pratt 1973, 21; Musser 1990, 100.

March 29: Bernardini 1980, 34; Bernardini 1985, 77 – 80; Bernardini 2001, 82d & 153.

☛Meusy, 1995, 30-1.

March 30: Bernardini 1980, 34 & 37.

☛Coissac 1925, 589.

☛Rittaud-Hutinet 1990, 236.

☛Bernardini 2001, 153.

April 1: Rittaud-Hutinet 1984, 51.
April 2: Meusy 1995, 31.
April 3: Musser 1990, 116; Ramsaye 1926, 228, Moore 2012a, 381-97.
☛Coissac 1925, 589; Hecht 1993, 290, No. 413D; Jossé 1984, 48-50.
April 4: Bernardini 1980, V1, 30-31 & 243.
☛Magic Lantern Society of Great Britain, *Newsletter* No. 35, p. 5.
April 5: Mannoni 2002, 122, 125-7, 129. [In error: Deslandes 1963, 26 & 91-2; Barnes 1976, 120; Frazer 1979, 34-5; Rossell 1995, 146; others.]
April 6: Goergen 1998, 14; Castan 1995, 94. Waldekranz 1976, 363; Lichtenstein 1990, 318.
☛Barnes 1976, 130-4.
☛Herbert 1994, 19.
April 7: Martinez 1992, 25-6.
☛Mitry 1976, 16; Coissac 1925, 178-9.
April 8: Barnes 1976, 113-4; Barnes 1998, 132-3; Barnes 1983, 245.
☛Deslandes 1963, 78, 80; Mannoni 1993, 15; Derval 1955, 7-8; Barnouw 1981, 48-50; Mannoni 1994, 427. [In error: Rittaud-Hutinet 1990, 236.]
April 10: Berry 1994, 22-3.
April 11: Coissac 1825, 589.
April 13: Herbert 1994, 20.
April 16: Loiperdinger 1990a, 32; Loiperdinger 1999, 135.
☛Rittaud-Hutinet 1990, 235.
April 17: Fritz 1981, 14.
April 18: Barnes 1976, 141-2.
April 19: Rittaud-Hutinet 1990, 232.
April 20: Loiperdinger 1990a, 32-4; Fischli 1990, 7-8; Loiperdinger 1999, 136-9.
☛Herbert 1994, 20; Rockett, Gibbons, & Hill 1987, 3
☛French patent 255,702, *Nouveau mode de commande de la paellicule dans la photographie animee*. Issued 20 April 1896; Mannoni 2002, 126-30.
April 21: Barnes 1976, 157.
April 22: André & André 1997, 150-1.
☛Barnes 1994, 19.
☛Meusy, 1995, 35-38.
April 23: Musser 1990, 109-118; Musser 1991, 60-4. [In error: Mitry 1967, 87; Ceram 1965, 156; Mitry 1976, 17.]
☛André & André 1997, 150-1.
☛Rittaud-Hutinet 1990, 237.
April 25: Zglinicki 1979, 312; Hanisch 1991, 62ff; Goergen 1998, 15-21, 25, 30.
☛Rittaud-Hutinet 1994, 6.
☛Poupion 1990, 32-5.
☛Convents 2000, 92-3.
April 26: Zglinicki 1979, 312; Hanisch 1991, 62ff; Goergen 1998, 15-21, 25, 30; Narath 1966, 12; *Vossische Zeitung*, Nr. 195, 26-04-1896, 1. Beilage, 'Lokales.'
April 27: Barnes 1976, 100.
☛Barnes 1976, 100.
☛Mannoni 1994, 411.
April 28: French patent 255,937, *Appareil photographique à bande sensible continue pour la fixation et la reproduction des scènes animées*, application 28 April 1896; Hecht 1993, 293, No. 415V; Coissac 1925, 279-80 & 590 [In error: Mitry 1967, 81.]
☛Loiperdinger 1990a, 34; Goergen 1998, 21-25. [In error: Rittaud-Hutinet 1985, 51.]
☛Rittaud-Hutinet 1990, 235.
☛Rittaud-Hutinet 1990, 232.
April 29: Štábla 1989, 204.
April 30: Rittaud-Hutinet 1990, 237.

May 1: Rittaud-Hutinet 1985, 51; Dumont 1987, 20; Buache & Rial 1964, 5-6 & 36.
Rittaud-Hutinet 1994, 5.
☛Loiperdinger 1990a, 34; Tümmel 1986, 27 & 143-6. [In error: Bessy & Duca 1948, 51; Coissac 1925, 185; Georgen 1998, 26-8.
☛Mitry 1976, 17; Coissac 1925, 280.
☛Georgen 1998, 26.
☛Loiperdinger 1999, 307.
May 4: Brown 1993, 32.
May 4 (Julian Calendar): Pozner 2006, 90; Deac Rossell.
May 5: Berry 1994, 23-4.
May 6: Mannoni 1993, 14-5.
May 6, Julian Calendar: Deac Rossell.
May 9: Barnes 1976, 124.
May 10: Rittaud-Hutinet 1990, 229.
May 11: Berry 1994, 25. [In error: Brown 1993, 31; Barnes 1994, 19; Rossell 1995, 149.]
☛Barnes 1976, 124. See also 122-24.
☛Musser 1990, 133-34; Musser 1999, 154.
☛Martinez 1992, 25-6; Folgar de la Calle 1989, 11; Letamendi 1998, 182-4.
☛Musser 1997, 202-4. [In error: Musser 1991, 64-6]
May 12: Rittaud-Hutinet 1990, 237.
☛Loiperdinger 1999, 306.
May 13: Auzel 1992, 66-7.
☛Martinez 1992, 33; Letamendi 1998, 182-4.
May 14: Musser 1990, 159.
☛Leyda 1983, 18-9.
☛Westra 1983, 12; Castan 1995, 95; Georgen 1998, 29.
☛Rittaud-Hutinet 1990, 235.
May 15: Martinez 1992, 35; Folgar de la Calle 1987, 11.
☛Rittaud-Hutinet 1990, 237.
May 16: Barnes 1992, 305; Wlaschin 2008, 218.
May 17: Rittaud-Hutinet 1985, 54-5; Pozner 2006, 90.
☛Rittaud-Hutinet 1994, 5; Jean-Claude Seguin-Vergara, 'La légende Promio', 97.
May 18: Musser 1990, 122; Musser 1999, 156.
☛Barnes 1976, 172-3.
☛Brown 1993, 3; Barnes 1994, 19.
☛Brown 1993, 32-3.
May 19: Rittaud-Hutinet 1985, 56; Leyda 1983, 17.
☛Rittaud-Hutinet 1990, 231.
☛Pozner 2006, 90 & 92.
May 20: Rittaud-Hutinet 1990, 235.
May 21: Briels 1971, 16-7.
☛Musser 1990, 122; Musser 1999, 156.
☛Condon 2012, 35-41.
May 22: Rittaud-Hutinet 1990, 238.
May 23: Musser 1990, 122.
☛Rittaud-Hutinet 1990, 238.
☛Swiss patent 11755, *Appareil perfectionné pour l'exposition à la lumière de rubans pelliculaires sensibilisés et pour la projection de séries d'images photographiques tirées sur rubans pelliculaires*, application 28 May 1896.
May 24: Rittaud-Hutinet 1990, 233.
☛Rittaud-Hutinet 1990, 238.
☛Ros-Vilella 1979, 165.
☛Georgen 1998, 31; Castan 1995, 95; de Klerk 1999, 7.
☛Georgen 1998, 31.
May 25: Totenberg 1990, 25; Loiperdinger 1990a, 36. [In error: Zglinicki 1979, 220.]

☛Musser 1990, 122 & 138-9; Musser 1999, 156.

May 26: Leyda 1983, 18-9.

May 28: Musser 1990, 133; Musser 1999, 156.

☛Rittaud-Hutinet 1994, 6.

☛UK patent 11,639, *An Improved Apparatus for Securing, or Exhibiting in Series, Records of Successive Phases of Movement*, application 28 May 1896. Issued 1 May 1897; Barnes 1976, 157; Lehmann 1911, 64-6; Forch 1913, 103-6.

☛Musser 1999, 156.

May 29: Rittaud-Hutinet 1990, 236; Hennion 2008, 47 & 52.

☛Rittaud-Hutinet 1990, 231.

May 30: Rittaud-Hutinet 1990, 237.

☛Bernardini 2001, 153.

May 31: Rittaud-Hutinet 1994, 6.

June 1: Musser 1990, 97.

☛Brown 1993, 31; Barnes 1994, 19.

☛US patent 588,916, application 1 June 1896. Issued 24 August 1897.

June 2: Barnes 1976, 74; Barnes 1983, 44.

June 3: UK patent 12,128, *Improvements in Apparatus for Making or Exhibiting Zoëtropic and similar Pictures*, application 3 June 1896. Issued 15 May 1897; Liesegang 1986, 65; Formann 1966, 34-5.

☛Barnes 1976, 28.

☛Rittaud-Hutinet 1994, 6.

June 4: Rittaud-Hutinet 1990, 230.

June 5: Ros-Vilella 1979, 165.

June 6: Tasic & Passek 1986, 13; Kosanović 1997, n. p.; Knezević 1994, 28; Kosanovic 2004, 5. [In error: Rittaud-Hutinet 1985, 51].

☛Loiperdinger 1990a, 36; Loiperdinger 1999, 303-4.

☛Rittaud-Hutinet 1994, 6.

☛Rittaud-Hutinet 1990, 232.

☛Rittaud-Hutinet 1990, 237.

☛Musser 1999, 156 & 162.

June 7: Lange-Fuchs 1987, 76-9; Sandfeld 1966, 10-11; Nørgaard 1973, 20. Royal Family: Idestam-Almquist 1962, 584; Engberg 1958, 136. [In error: Rittaud-Hutinet 1985, 51 & 235; Rittaud-Hutinet 1990, 231; Béranger 1960].

☛Rittaud-Hutinet 1990, 231.

☛Rittaud-Hutinet 1990, 231.

☛Georgen 1998, 26-8; Georgen 1998, 32.

June 8: Musser 1990, 122; Musser 1999, 156.

June 9: Mannoni 1993, 15; Mannoni 1996, 24-5.

☛Coissac 1925, 590.

☛Briels 1973, 25.

June 10: Barnes 1976, 173.

☛Rittaud-Hutinet 1990, 234.

June 11: Barnes 1983, 242, correcting Barnes 1976, 144.

☛Loiperdinger 1990a, 36.

☛Engberg 1977, 14; see also advertisement in Nørgaard 1973, 22. [In error: Georgen 1998, 31; Castan 1995, 95.]

June 12: Rittaud-Hutinet 1985, 51; Fraenkel 1956, 374; Sadoul 1964, 150.

☛Frizot 1984, 122-4.

☛Rittaud-Hutinet 1994, 5.

June 13: Bernardini 1980, 247; Bernardini 1985, 71, 78.

☛Loiperdinger 1990a, 36; Hofmann 1992, 219.

☛Rittaud-Hutinet 1990, 238.

☛Rittaud-Hutinet 1990, 235.

☛Hennion 2008.

June 14: Rittaud-Hutinet 1990, 230.

☛Rittaud-Hutinet 1994, 6.

June 15: Fraenkel 1956, 374; Jacobson 1993, 22; Ilger & Linke 1994, 96.

☛Musser 1990, 122 & 125; Musser 1999, 156.

☛Brown 1993, 31; Barnes 1994, 19.

☛Barnes 1976, 74; Barnes 1983, 44.

June 18: Ferreira 1986, 31-40 & 167; Soto 2007, 13n11.

☛Musser 1990, 122.

June 20: Hennion 2008.

☛Loiperdinger 1999, 305.

June 21: Labosier 2004, 287 – 88.

June 22: Leyda 1983, 20-1; Harding 1996, 5-6.

☛Pratt 1973, 22.

☛Rittaud-Hutinet 1990, 233.

☛Brown 1993, 31; Barnes 1994, 19.

☛Berry 1994, 25 & 487-8n30.

☛Lecointe 2004, 2-3; [In error: André & André 1997, 156-7.]

☛Musser 1999, 156.

☛Musser 1991a, 49.

June 24: Rittaud-Hutinet 1990, 231.

June 27: Lacasse, 1984, 6; Lacasse 1984a, 27.

☛Berry 1994, 23-4.

☛Musser 1999, 154.

June 28: Rittaud-Hutinet 1985, 51; Waldekranz 1976, 441n658; Idestam-Almquist 1962, 584; Engberg 1958, 136.

☛Lacasse 1984, 6; Lacassc 1984a, 27.

☛Breard 1951, 2-5; Musser 1999, 156.

☛Idestam-Almquist 1962, 584.

☛Hennion 2008.

June 29: Musser 1990, 137-9. [In error: Mitry 1967, 85; Rittaud-Hutinet 1985, 51; Ceram 1965, 152; Bessy & Duca 1948, 51; Mitry 1976, 17; Coissac 1925, 185; Pinel 1992, 83.

☛Rittaud-Hutinet 1990, 232.

☛Coissac 1925, 280; Kress 1912, 60.

☛Rittaud-Hutinet 1990, 236.

☛Hennion 2008.

☛Musser 1991a, 49.

June 30: Bernardini 2001, 153.

☛UK patent 14,455, *Improvements in Kinetoscopic Projecting Apparatus*, application 30 June 1896. Issued 22 August 1896; Barnes 1976, 133.

July 1: Musser 1990, 122 & 124; Musser 1991, 64 & 502n29; Musser 1999, 156.

☛Bernardini 1980, 247.

☛Rittaud-Hutinet 1994, 5.

☛Rittaud-Hutinet 1990, 232.

☛Musser 1999, 156.

July 2: Rittaud-Hutinet 1990, 231.

☛Rittaud-Hutinet 1990, 233.

☛Rittaud-Hutinet 1990, 238.

☛Blot-Wellens 2015, 18; Convents 2000, 94-5.

July 3: Rittaud-Hutinet 1990, 233.

☛Rittaud-Hutinet 1990, 232.

July 4: Rittaud-Hutinet 1990, 229.

☛Hennion 2008.

☛Musser 1999, 162.

July 5: Musser 1990, 122-3; Musser 1999, 156.

☛Musser 1999, 156; Musser 1990, 122-3.

July 6: Caneto et. al. 1996, 25-6; Mesa 2014, 18.

☛Fletcher 2017, 7.

July 7: Rittaud-Hutinet 1985, 56; Leyda 1983, 21.

☛Engberg 1958, 136; Engberg 1977, 14.

☛Barnouw & Krishnaswamy 1980, 3-5. [In error: Rittaud-Hutinet 1985, 51; Rittaud-Hutinet 1990, 229].

☛Wlaschin 2008, 218.

July 8: Rittaud-Hutinet 1985, 54; Serrano n. d., 2; Mesa 2014, 97.

☛Rittaud-Hutinet 1994, 5.

☛Rittaud-Hutinet 1990, 230.

July 9: Rittaud-Hutinet 1990, 239.

☛Bernardini 2001, 153.

July 11: Wolf & Kurowski 1988, 8.

☛Hennion 2008.

☛Serrano n. d., 1.

☛Bernardini 2001, 70 & 153; Kosanovic 1987, 137-8.

July 12: Hennion 2008.

July 13: Brown 1993, 26.

☛Brown 1993, 31; Barnes 1994, 19.

July 14: Barnouw & Krishnaswamy 1980, 3-5. [In error: Rittaud-Hutinet 1985, 51; Rittaud-Hutinet 1990, 229.]

July 15: Maden & Dibbets 1986, 18. Van der Maden incorrectly identifies this apparatus as a Messter Kinematograph.

☛Rittaud-Hutinet 1994, 5.

☛Štábla 1989, 205-6.

☛Rittaud-Hutinet 1990, 237.

☛Hendrykowska 1993, 15.

July 17: Ferreira 1986, 46 & 167; Rittaud-Hutinet 1990, 235.

July 18: Štábla 1989, 205 – 6.

☛Rittaud-Hutinet 1990, 237.

☛Hendrykowska 1993, 15.

☛Moore 2012, 62.

☛Lòpez 2015, 133; Mesa 2014, 345.

☛Lòpez 2015, 133; Caneto et. al. 1996, 26-8; Mesa 2014, 18-9.

July 19: Barnes 1976, 126-7.

July 20: Brown 1993, 31.

☛Musser 1999, 156.

☛Bernardini 2001, 153.

☛Lòpez 2015, 133; Caneto et.al. 1996, 28-31.

July 21: Morris 1978, 1-6.

☛Barnes 1976, 180-3.

☛UK patent 16,080, *Improvements in or relating to apparatus for taking, viewing, or projecting photographic images in rapid succession,* application 21 July 1896. Issued 19 June 1897; Barnes 1976, 135-6.

☛Deslandes 1966, 24; Idestam-Almquist 1962, 84; Castan 1995, 96.

July 22: Full-frame image in Deac Rossell Collection, gift of Richard Birt Acres, as identified by DR and Luke McKernan, 03-2016.

July 23: Rittaud-Hutinet 1990, 237; Hennion 2008.

☛Meusy 1995, 38.

☛Letamendi 1998, 186.

July 25: Štábla 1989, 204-5.

July 26: Bernardini 1980, 37-8; Bernardini 2001, 73.

☛Musser 1990, 114 & 125; Musser 1999, 156.

☛North 1973, 60; Musser 1990, 126; Breard 1951, 6-12.

☛Musser 1999, 156.

July 27: Woal 1994, 134; Musser 1990, 122; Musser 1999, 156.

July 28: Rittaud-Hutinet 1985, 54.

☛Rittaud-Hutinet 1990, 228.

July 31: Meier-Kern 1993, 10-12.

☛Kress 1912, 61.

August 1: Deslandes 1963, 92.

☛Rittaud-Hutinet 1990, 237.

☛Idestam-Almquist 1962, 85; Waldekranz 1986, 34.

☛Rittaud-Hutinet 1990, 237; Blot-Wellens 2015, 120.

☛Hendrykowska 1994, 206; Bizkupski 2013, 145.

☛Rittaud-Hutinet 1994, 6.

☛Hennion 2008, 52.

☛Waldekranz 1976, 363; Lichtenstein 1990, 320 & 318; Castan 1995, 96.

☛Letamendi 1998, 186.

August 2: Bernardini 1980, 38 & 247; Bernardini 2001, 138.

☛Rittaud-Hutinet 1994, 5.

☛Fullerton 2008, 96.

☛Blot-Wellens 2015, 119, 120.

August 3: Idestam-Almquist 1962, 84.

☛Kane, & Dougherty 1995, 346-7.

August 5: Convents 2000, 95.

August 6: Reyes 1987, 8; Fullerton 2008, 97-8.

☛Letamendi 1998, 199-205.

August 7: Barnes 1983, 44; Hastings 1927, 297; Musser 1991, 87; Ackerman 1930, 170.

August 8: Rittaud-Hutinet 1985, 54.

☛Donaldson 1980, 37.

☛Rittaud-Hutinet 1994, 5.

☛Hennion 2008.

☛Bernardini 2001, 153.

August 9: Štábla 1989, 206.

☛Rittaud-Hutinet 1990, 238.

☛Bernardini 2001, 82.

August 10: Musser 1990, 138-9; Musser 1999, 156.

☛Barnes 1976, 127.

August 11: Rittaud-Hutinet 1985, 54; Leyda 1972, 1.

☛Musser 1990, 160-1.

August 12: UK patent 17,881, *Improvements in cinematographs*, application 12 August 1896. Issued 7 August 1897; Barnes 1976, 139; Tümmel 1986, 113-4.

☛Ferreira 1986, 51.

☛Rittaud-Hutinet 1990, 233.

☛Wlaschin 2008, 218.

August 13: Rittaud-Hutinet 1990, 235.

☛Rittaud-Hutinet 1994, 6.

August 14: Reyes 1983, 81; Reyes 1987, 10; Fullerton 2008, 96-7; Mesa 2014, 207.

☛Rittaud-Hutinet 1990, 239.

August 15: Poch 1989, 318; Breitenfeldt & Reinke 1984, 109-110; Loiperdinger 1999, 306.

☛Ferreira 1986, 52.

☛Fullerton 2008, 96-7 & 99.

☛Ferreira 1986, 73 & 79.

☛Rittaud-Hutinet 1990, 232.

☛Rittaud-Hutinet 1994, 6.

☛Rittaud-Hutinet 1994, 6.

☛Idestam-Almquist 1962, 95.

☛Coissac 1925, 591; Hecht 1993, 289, No. 412B; Mannoni 1994, 467. [In error: Hecht 1993, 289, No. 412B has an incorrect date for this patent.]

☛Barnes 1976, 77.

☛Hennion 2008.

August 16: Zglinicki 1979; Loiperdinger 1990a, 34-6; Traub 1940, 51.

☛Reyes 1987, 10. [In error: Rittaud-Hutinet 1985, 54.]

☛Goergen 1998, 48 & 51; *Berliner Lokal-Anzeiger*, 18-08-1896, Nr. 385, Vergnügungen.

☛Musser 1999, 156; Musser 1999a, 248.

☛Musser 1999, 156.

August 17: Musser 1990, 125.
☛Musser 1990, 139; Musser 1999, 156.
☛Long 1993a, 41; Long 1993c, 2.
August 18: Aurich, Fuhrmann, & Müller 1991, 11-12; Loiperdinger 1999, 307.
☛Rittaud-Hutinet 1990, 236.
August 19: Rittaud-Hutinet 1990, 229.
☛Convents 2000, 95.
August 20: Coissac 1925, 592.
☛Rittaud-Hutinet 1994, 5.
August 22: Shirley & Adams 1983, 6; Reade 1970, 9; Long 1993a, 42.
☛Rittaud-Hutinet 1990, 237.
☛Hennion 2008, 53.
August 23: Reyes 1987, 11.
☛Hennion 2008, 53.
August 24: Musser 1990, 161-2.
☛Barnes 1976, 126.
☛Barnes 1976, 75-6.
August 25: Lòpez 2015, 133.
August 26: Ferreira 1986, 93, 95, 168-9.
☛Rittaud-Hutinet 1990, 233; Blot-Wellens 2015, 117.
☛Bernardini 2001, 153.
August 27: Bernardini 1980, 40-41 & 243; Bernardini 2001, 70 & 153.
☛Ferreira 1986, 53, 62, 70.
☛Long 1993a, 39; Long 1993c, 2.
August 29: Forch 1913, 8; Mannoni 1994, 241-6; Hecht 1993, 289, No. 412A.
☛Rittaud-Hutinet 1994, 6.
☛Hennion 2008, 53.
August 30: Bernardini 2001, 104 & 153.
August 31: UK patent 19,181, *Improvements in apparatus for exhibiting kinetoscopic or zoetropic pictures*, application 31 August 1896. Issued 12 June 1897; Barnes 1976, 143-5.
☛Morris 1978, 7-8.
☛Barnes 1976, 128.
September 1: Morris 1978, 8-9 & 277n19; Moore 2012, 65.
☛Rittaud-Hutinet 1990, 238; Hennion 2008, 32 & 52.
☛Rittaud-Hutinet 1990, 238; Hennion 2008, 52.
☛Hennion 2008, 53.
September 2: Hennion 2008, 53.
☛Folgar de la Calle 1989, 15-18.
September 3: Bleier-Brody 1966, 22; Fritz 1969, 22; Bleier-Brody 1960, 32.
☛Rittaud-Hutinet 1990, 239.
☛Hennion 2008, 53.
September 4: Bernardini 1980, 243 & 247; Bernardini 2001, 153.
☛Musser 1990, 126-7.
☛*Sheffield and Rotherham Independent*, 5 September 1896; Walsh 2014, 97-8.
☛Schmitt 1996, 30 [in error: Coissac 1925, 592; Deslandes 1963, 92]
September 5: Rittaud-Hutinet 1990, 233.
☛Rittaud-Hutinet 1990, 235.
☛Reyes 1983, 108.
☛Bernardini 2001, 70 & 153.
☛Loiperdinger 1999, 308.
September 6: Hennion 2008, 30.
September 7: Musser 1990, 139; Musser 1999, 156.
☛Musser 1999, 156.
☛Musser 1999, 156.
☛Musser 1999, 156 note i.
☛Musser 1999, 162.
☛Loiperdinger 1999, 308.
September 9: Rittaud-Hutinet 1990, 236.
September 10: Bernardini 1980, 243; Rittaud-Hutinet 1990, 233; Bernardini 2001, 82 & 153.
☛Ferreira 1986, 96.
☛Mannoni 1994, 473; Herbert 1991, 104-9.
☛Goergen 1998, 53, 47.
September 11: Bernardini 1980, 243; Bernardini 2001, 153.
☛UK patent 20,136, *A New Device by which the Leaves of Picture and other Books may be Turned Over in a Regular Manner*, application 11 September 1896. Issued August 7, 1897.
September 12: Bernardini 2001, 153.
☛Convents 2000, 95.
September 13: Bernardini 1980, 243; Bernardini 2001, 153.
☛Rittaud-Hutinet 1990, 235.
☛Hendrykowska 1993, 40.
☛Musser 1999, 156.
☛Loiperdinger 1999, 309.
September 14: Hendricks 1964, 34 & 39; Musser 1990, 150.
☛Musser 1990, 139; Musser 1999, 156.
September 17: Long 1993b, 37; Long 1993c, 2. [In error: Shirley & Adams 1983, 7; Wasson 1964, 2.]
September 18: Long 1993b, 37; Long 1993c, 2.
September 19: Genovese 1984, 53-4.
☛Bernardini 2001, 70 & 153; Castan 1998, 56. [In error: Koerber 1994, 35; Hanisch 1991, 74.]
September 20: Blot-Wellens 2015, 119-20.
☛Rittaud-Hutinet 1990, 236.
☛Musser 1999, 156.
☛Loiperdinger 1999, 309.
☛Meusy 1995, 40.
September 21: Hendricks 1964, 43-4.
☛Barnes 1976, 127-8.
☛Barnes 1976, 128.
☛Rittaud-Hutinet 1994, 6.
☛Musser 1999, 156 & 166.
September 23: Vanessa Schwartz and Jean-Jacques Meusy, 'Le Musée Grevin et le cinématographe. L'histoire d'une rencontre', in *1895*, No. 11, 35.
☛Hennion 2008, 37 & 52; Lecointe 2004, 3.
September 24: Blot-Wellens 2015, 121-22.
September 25: Meier-Kern 1993, 12-15.
September 26: Rittaud-Hutinet 1990, 54; Mesa 2014, 200.
☛Armat 1967, 19-20; United States patent 578,185, application filed 26 September 1896, issued 2 March 1897. [In error: Hecht 1993, 289, No. 412E.]
☛Long 1993b, 39; Long 1993c, 2.
☛British patent 21,381, application 26 September 1896, accepted 11 September 1897.
☛Herbert 2017 30.
☛Fullerton 2008, 101 & 111n67.
September 27: Donaldson 1983, 27.
☛Bernardini 1980, 243 & 247; Bernardini 2001, 153.
☛Rittaud-Hutinet 1990, 230.
☛Rittaud-Hutinet 1990, 230.
☛Hennion 2008, 35 & 52.
☛Convents 2000, 98 & 373.

September 28: Mannoni 1994, 402-5; Mannoni 1996, 23-5. [In error: Mitry 1976, 82]

☛Hendricks 1964, 44; Musser 1999, 156.

☛Morris 1978, 277n26.

☛Shirley & Adams 1983, 7; Wasson 1964, 2; Reade 1979, 3; Reade 1970, 9; Long 1993b, 37-8.

☛Rittaud-Hutinet 1994, 5.

☛Musser 1999, 155.

September 30: Morris 1978, 10.

☛Ferreira 1986, 101.

☛Moore 2012, 65.

☛Bernardini 2001, 153.

October 1: Goergen 1998, 61.

October 2: Lange-Fuchs 1987, 78. [This apparatus was previously unidentified.]

☛André & André 1997, 158-161; Lecointe 2004, 4.

☛Blot-Welllens 2015, 119.

October 3: Morris 1978, 277n25.

☛Loiperdinger 1990a, 38. [This apparatus was previously identified as a Lumière Cinématographe.]

☛Rittaud-Hutinet 1990, 228.

☛Meusy 1995, 40.

October 4: Donaldson 1983, 27; Goergen 1998, 66.

☛Bernardini 1980, 243; Bernardini 2001, 70 & 153.

☛Štábla 1989, 206-7.

☛Štábla 1989, 207.

☛Rittaud-Hutinet 1990, 228.

☛Loiperdinger 1999, 305.

October 5: Bernardini 1980, 81; Bernardini 2001, 153.

☛Musser 1990, 150; Musser 1999, 156.

☛Musser 1999, 155.

October 6: Goergen 1998, 65.

October 7: Loiperdinger 1990a, 44; Loiperdinger 1999, 304.

☛Bernardini 2001, 153.

☛Berneau 1988, 20.

October 8: Tasic & Passek 1986, 13; Kosanović 1988, n. p. [This apparatus was previously unidentified.]

☛Rittaud-Hutinet 1994, 5.

☛Reyes 1983, 91.

☛Briels 1971, 30-32.

☛Seguin 2015-18, Oran.

October 9: Štábla 1989, 207.

☛Moore 2012, 66.

☛Seguin 2015-18, Oran.

☛Maier 2009, 17-9.

October 10: Rittaud-Hutinet 1990, 237.

☛Rittaud-Hutinet 1990, 238.

☛Hennion 2008, 52.

☛Bernardini 2001, 153.

October 11: Blot-Wellens 2015, passim; Mannoni 1996, 25-6.

☛Lange-Fuchs 1987, pp. 79-83; Schaper 1987, pp. 11-12.

☛Bernardini 2001, 153.

October 12: Musser 1990, 152; Hendricks 1964, 46. [In error: Zglinicki 1979, 231.]

☛Pratt 1973a, 40.

☛Barnes 1976, 128.

October 13: Shirley & Adams 1983, 281n2; Dennis 1993, 6; Long & Sowry n.d. (1995), 1.

☛UK patent 22,707, Improvements in Kinematograph Apparatus, application 13 October 1896. Issued 28 August 1897; Barnes 1976, 152-4; Barnes 1983, 38-40; Barnes 1983a, 108-111.

☛Štábla 1989, 207.

October 14: Rittaud-Hutinet 1990, 231.

October 15: Barnes 1976, 128.

☛*Sheffield and Rotherham Independent*, 15 October 1896.

☛Bernardini 2001, 72 & 153.

October 16: US patent 574,851, *Kinetic Camera*, application 16 October 1896, issued 5 January 1897.

☛Bernardini 2001, 153.

October 17: Hofmann 1992, 221. [This apparatus was previously unidentified.]

☛Štábla 1989, 207-8.

☛Bernardini 2001, 153.

☛Loiperdinger 1999, 305.

October 18: Ferreira 1986, 102.

☛Štábla 1989, 208-9.

October 19: Long 1993a, 39-40; Long 1993c, 2.

☛Rittaud-Hutinet 1990, 235.

☛Fullerton 2008, 101; Mesa 2014, 208. [In error: Reyes 1983, 81.]

☛Bernardini 2001, 153.

☛Baumer 1995, 25 & 33.

October 20: Long 1993b, 40.

☛Correspondence Andrzej Debski, 13 July 2015; Iverson 2014, 124-6; *Danziger Zeitung*, 21 October 1896.

October 21: Musser 1990, 167.

☛Rittaud-Hutinet 1990, 232.

☛Blot-Wellens 2015, 115.

☛Bernardini 2001, 153.

October 22: Meier-Kern 1993, 16.

☛Štábla 1989, 210-11.

☛Rittaud-Hutinet 1990, 233.

☛Reyes 1983, 82-3.

☛Hennion 2008, 53.

☛Bernardini 2001, 153.

October 23: Štábla 1989, 210-11.

☛Hennion 2008, 53.

☛Hennion 2008, 53.

☛Bernardini 2001, 153.

October 24: Bernardini 1980, 50; Jacob 1979, 78; Bernardini 2001, 72.

☛Tasic & Passek 1986, 13; Kosanovic 1988, n. p.

☛Rittaud-Hutinet 1990, 233.

☛Bernardini 2001, 153.

☛Bernardini 2001, 153.

☛Bernardini 2001, 154.

October 25: Dumont 1987, 20; Buache & Rial 1964, 9-13 & 36, 39.

☛Long 1993c, 2.

☛Donaldson 1983, 27.

☛Rittaud-Hutinet 1990, 230.

☛Reyes 1983, 168-9.

☛Blot-Wellens 2015, 122, 125.

October 26: Barnes 1976, 129; Berry 1994, 488n33.

☛Long 1993, 37-8; Long 1993a, 2.

October 27: Meier-Kern 1993, 16.

☛Breitenfeldt & Reinke 1984, 112.

October 28: Dennis 1993, 6; Long & Sowry n.d. (1995), 1.

October 29: Rockett, Gibbons, & Hill 1987, 4.

☛*Sheffield and Rotherham Independent*, 29 October 1896.

☛Bernardini 2001, 154.

October 30: Ilgner & Linke 1994, 110.
☛Hennion 2008.
October 31: Musser 1990, 152.
☛Livio Luppi 1896, 25-8; Bernardini 2001; 109 & 154.
☛Long 1993a, 40; Long 1993c, 2.
☛Long 1993b, 38.
☛Bernardini 2001, 72 & 154.
☛Loiperdinger 1999, 309-10.
November 1: Musser 1990, 139.
☛Lange-Fuchs 1987, 80.
☛Rittaud-Hutinet 1990, 239.
November 2: Musser 1990, 154; Musser 1999, 156.
☛Pratt 1973a, 40-2; Musser 1999, 156.
November 3: Tasic & Passek 1986, 13; Kosanović 1988, n. p.
☛Reade 1970, 9-10; Long 1993c, 2.
☛Rittaud-Hutinet 1990, 236.
☛Štábla 1979, 211-13.
☛Bernardini 2001, 126 & 154.
November 4: Bernardini 2001, 72.
November 5: *The Egyptian Gazette*, November 5, 1896, page 2. Advertising continued regularly until December 17.
November 6: Hofmann 1992, 221.
☛Rittaud-Hutinet 1990, 239.
☛Müller, Pamela, unpublished research of the Gesellschaft für Filmstudien, Hannover (1994).
☛Bernardini 2001, 154.
November 7: Bernardini 1980, 44-5 & 244.
☛Dennis 1993, 6; Long 1993c, 2.
☛Long 1993a, 40.
☛Mannoni 1993, 15.
☛Hendrykowska 1994, 207-8; Biskupski 2013, 146.
☛Rittaud-Hutinet 1990, 229.
☛Rittaud-Hutinet 1990, 238.
November 8: Bernardini 1980, 43, 46, 244 & 247; Bernardini 2001, 154.
☛Bernardini 1980, 42; Bernardini 2001, 154.
☛Hennion 2008, 53.
November 9: Musser 1990, 162.
☛Musser 1999, 156.
☛Bernardini 2001, 154.
November 10: Filminstitut der landeshauptstadt Düsseldorf 1982, 11.
☛Ferreira 1986, 109 & 113.
☛Blot-Wellens 2015, 115.
☛Bernardini 2001, 154.
November 11: Deslandes & Richard 1968, 29.
☛Hennion 2008, 32 & 52.
☛Bernardelli 2001, 61 & 140.
November 12: Bernardini 2001, 244; Jacob 1979, 79; Bernardini 2001, 154.
☛Rittaud-Hutinet 1990, 235.
☛Rittaud-Hutinet 1990, 237; Blot-Wellens 2015, 119.
☛Seguin 2015-18, Tlemcen.
November 13: Hennion, 2008, 32 & 52.
November 14: Hendrykowska 1993, 19; Pacewicz 1990, n. p. [p76].
☛Gosser 1977, 284-6; Hecht 1993, 293, No. 415V/1.
☛Donaldson 1983, 26.
☛Rittaud-Hutinet 1990, 232.
☛Bernardini 2001, 154.
☛Meusy 1995, 42-3.
November 15: Bernardini 1980, 42 & 244.
☛Rittaud-Hutinet 1994, 5
☛Blot-Wellens 2015, 164, 181; Convents 2000, 98-9.
November 16: Musser 1990, 155; Musser 1999, 156.
☛Tasic & Passek 1986, 13 & 43; Kosanović 1988, n. p.
☛Donaldson 1980, 37; Donaldson 1983, 26.
☛Radvanyi 1998, 43 & 35.
☛Musser 1990, 125.
☛Barnes 1976, 76-7.
November 18: Goergen 1998, 68-9.
November 19: Morris 1978, 10.
☛Rittaud-Hutinet 1990, 239.
☛Štábla 1989, 213-4.
☛Deslandes & Richard, 29.
☛Blot-Wellens 2015, 121.
☛Bernardini 2001, 154.
November 20: Bernardini 1980, 247.
☛Dennis 1993, 6; Long & Sowry n.d. (1995), 1.
☛Reade 1970, 9.
November 21: Kosanović 1998, n. p.; Bernardini 2001, 77.
☛Ferreira 1986, 114-5.
☛Rittaud-Hutinet 1994, 6.
☛Long 1993c, 2.
☛Berry 1994, 486n10.
☛Rittaud-Hutinet 1990, 231.
☛Bernardini 2001, 154.
☛Bernardini 2001, 154.
☛Bernardini 2001, 155.
November 22: Luppi 1979, 28; Bernardini 2001, 155.
☛Ferreira 1986, 103.
☛Hendrykowska 1993, 40.
☛Musser 1999, 156.
November 24: Reade 1970, 10-11; Long 1993c, 2.
November 25: Bernardini 2001, 155.
November 26: Coissac 1925, 592 & 595; Hecht 1993, 290, No. 413D.
☛Bernardini 2001, 155. [In error: Bernardini 1980, 244.]
☛Rittaud-Hutinet 1990, 229.
☛Ros-Vilella 1979, 165.
November 27: Strobel 1993, 13-4.
☛Štábla 1989, 218.
☛Reyes 1983, 81-2.
November 28: Ferreira 1986, 116.
☛Ferreira 1986, 125.
November 29: Wit 1986, 21-3.
☛Breard 1951, 16-18.
☛Blot-Wellens 2015, 115, 120.
☛Goergen 1998, 72, 75.
☛Théodosiou 2009; Psoma 2009, 8-9.
November 30: Musser 1991, 92.
☛Musser 1990, 155; Musser 1999, 156.
☛Musser 1990, 155; Musser 1999, 156.
☛Rittaud-Hutinet 1994, 6.
☛Barnes 1976, 49-50.
☛Musser 1999, 156.
☛Bernardini 2001, 155.
Late November: Moore 2012, 67.
December 1: Barnes 1976, 129; Ceram 1965, 217.
☛Narath 1967, 109.
☛Štábla 1989, 214 & 216.

☛French patent 261,771, *Appareil pour la photographie et la projection des scènes animées dit Le Cinématographe Parisien*, Application 1 December 1896.

☛Hennion 2008, 35 & 52.

☛Goergen 1998, 75, 82.

☛Seguin 2015-18, Sidi-bel-Abbès.

☛Loiperdinger 1999, 308.

☛Goergen 1998, 74-5, 77, 81. [In error: Narath 1967, 109; Tümmel 1986, 131, Hanisch 1991, 78.]

December 3: Musser 1999, 156.

☛Goergen 1998, 75.

December 4: Musser & Nelson 1991a, 50-3; Musser 1990, 167.

☛Hennion 2008, 52.

December 5: Bernardini 2001, 77 & 155.

December 6: Rittaud-Hutinet 1994, 5; Hennion 2008, 52.

☛Rittaud-Hutinet 1990, 231.

☛Hennion 2008, 32 & 52.

☛Moore 2012, 68.

☛Musser 1999, 156 & 165.

December 7: Barnes 1976, 129.

☛Poch 1989, 318.

☛Barnes 1976, 144.

December 8: Morris 1978, 8.

☛Poch 1989, 318.

☛Bernardini 2001, 155.

December 9: Barnes 1976, 175.

☛Long 1993b, 40.

December 10: US patent 611,591, *Consecutive-view Apparatus*, application 10 December 1896. Issued 27 September 1898; Rossell 1999, 97-101. [In error: Liesegang 1986, 66.]

☛US patent 611,590, *Web-Feeding Mechanism*, application 10 December 1896. Issued 27 September 1898; Rossell 1999, 97-101 & 105.

☛US patent 617,435, *Reel*, application 10 December 1896. Issued 10 January 1899; Rossell 1999, 105.

☛Fullerton 2008, 102.

☛Musser 1999, 156.

☛Théodosieu 2009 n.p.

December 11: Bernardini 1980, 42 & 244; Bernardini 2001, 155.

☛Morris 1978, 10.

☛Deslandes & Richard 1968, 29.

☛Rittaud-Hutinet 1990, 29.

☛Rittaud-Hutinet 1990, 228.

☛Wit 1986, 23.

December 12: Long 1993c, 2.

☛Narath 1966, 14.

☛André & André 1997, 161.

☛Hennion 2008, 52.

☛Convents 2000, 100-103.

December 13: Štábla 1989, 214.

☛Rittaud-Hutinet 1990, 230.

☛Hennion 2008, 35 & 52.

December 14: Barnes 1976, 103 & 129.

☛Barnes 1983, 111-114.

☛Ros-Vilella 1979, 165; Moix & Porter 1958, 36-7.

December 15: Rittaud-Hutinet 1990, 232.

☛Loiperdinger 1999, 307.

December 16: UK patent 28,799, *Improved Appliance for Taking, Projecting, and Printing Animated Photographs*, application 16 December 1896. Issued 12 June 1897; Barnes 1983, 154-5.

☛Bernardini 1980, 247.

☛Bernardini 2001, 155.

☛Seguin 2015-18, Tlemcen.

December 17: Reyes 1983, 145; Reyes 1987, 14.

December 18: Rittaud-Hutinet 1994, 5.

☛Georgen 1998, 77-8.

December 19: Bernardini 1980, 244; Bernardini 1985, 73 & 80.

☛Poch 1989, 319-20.

☛Blot-Wellens 2015, 119, 122.

☛Blot-Wellens 2015, 160, 174.

☛Bernardini 2001, 126.

December 20: Bernardini 1980, 27, 244, & 247; Bernardini 2001, 155.

☛Deslandes 1963, 92.

☛Aurich, Fuhrmann, & Müller 1991, 15.

☛Blot-Wellens 2015, 179.

☛Hennion 2008, 32 & 52.

☛Musser 1999, 156.

☛Musser 1999, 156.

December 21: Musser 1999, 156.

December 22: Rittaud-Hutinet 1985, 54.

December 23: Briels 1971, 21-2.

☛Rittaud-Hutinet 1990, 228.

☛Blot-Wellens 2015, 199.

☛Hennion 2008, 37 & 52.

☛Musser 1999, 156.

☛Bernardelli 2001, 61 & 72.

☛Seguin 2015-18, Mostaganem.

☛Loiperdinger 1999, 306.

December 24: Long 1993b, 40.

December 25: Ferreira 1986, 97.

☛Rittaud-Hutinet 1990, 229; Hennion 2008, 52.

☛Bernardini 2001, 155.

December 26: Waldekranz 1986, 34.

☛Long 1993b, 40-1.

December 27: Rittaud-Hutinet 1990, 229.

☛Rittaud-Hutinet 1990, 232.

☛Rittaud-Hutinet 1990, 235.

☛Musser 1999, 165.

December 28: Musser 1999, 156.

December 29: Musser 1999, 156.

☛Bernardini 2001, 70.

December 30: Rittaud-Hutinet 1990, 231.

☛Deslandes & Richard 1968, 29.

December 31: Ferreira 1986, 133.

☛Narath 1966, 15.

PART 3: BIBLIOGRAPHY

Anon. 1841, *Übersicht der Arbeiten und Veränderung der Schlesischen Gesellschaft für vaterländische Kultur*

Abel, Richard, ed. 2005: *Encyclopaedia of Early Cinema*. Abingdon: Routledge.

Ackerman, Carl W. 1930: *George Eastman*. London: Constable and Company Ltd.

——- *Allgemeine Theatrezeitung* 1847, Nr. 10.

André, Jacques, & André, Marie 1997: *Une saison Lumière à Montpellier*. Perpignan: Institut Jean Vigo.

Armat, Thomas 1967: 'My Part in the Development of the Motion Picture Projector', in Raymond Fielding, ed., *A Technological History of Motion Pictures and Television*. Berkeley: University of California Press.

Ariel, Pete 1981 - 89: *Ariel Ciematographic Register*, Vols. 1 - 4. Frankfurt am Main: Deutsches Filmmuseum.

Aubert, Michelle, and Jean-Claude Seguin 1996: *La Production cinématographique des Frères Lumière*. Paris: Bibliothèque du Film (BIFI)/Editions Mémoires de cinéma.

Aurich, Rolf; Fuhrmann, Susanne; & Müller, Pamela 1991: *Lichtspiel Träume, Kino in Hannover, 1896 - 1991*. Hannover: Gesellschaft für Filmstudien e.V./Stadt Hannover.

Auzel, Dominique 1992: *Emile Reynaud et l'image s'anima*. Paris: Editions du May.

Barnes, John 1976: *The Beginnings of the Cinema in England*. London: David & Charles

Barnes, John 1998: *The Beginnings of the Cinema in England*. 2nd Edition. Exeter: University of Exeter Press.

Barnes, John 1994: *Cinématographe-Lumière in the United Kingdom*. St. Ives: Archives of the Barnes Museum of Cinematography. Privately circulated.

Barnes, John 1983: *The Rise of the Cinema in Great Britain*. (The Beginnings of the Cinema in England 1894 - 1901. Volume 2: Jubilee Year 1897.) London: The Bishopsgate Press Limited.

Barnes, John 1983a: *Pioneers of the British Film*. (The Beginnings of the Cinema in England 1894 - 1901, Volume 3, 1898: The Rise of the Photoplay). London: Bishopsgate Press Limited.

Barnes, John 1992: *Filming the Boer War*. (The Beginnings of the Cinema in England 1894 - 1901, Volume 4). London: Bishopsgate Press, Ltd.

Barnouw, Erik 1981: *The Magician and the Cinema*. New York \ Oxford: Oxford University Press.

Barnouw, Erik and S. Krishnaswamy 1980: *Indian Film* (Second Edition). New York \ Oxford \ New Delhi: Oxford University Press.

Baumer, Ruth 1995: *Augen Blick mal. Optische Erfindungen von der Lochkamera zum Wanderkino, mit Beiträgen zur Kinogeschichte in Schwaben*. [= Schriftenreihe der Museen des Bezirks Schwaben, Band 11] Gessertshausen: Museumsdirektion des Bezirks Schwaben.

Berg-Ganschow, Uta, & Jacobsen, Wolfgang, eds. 1987: *...Film...Stadt...Kino...Berlin...*. Berlin: Argon Verlag/Stiftung Deutsche Kinemathek.

Bernard, Denis, & Gunthert, André 1993: *L'instant rêvé Albert Londe*. Nimes: Jacqueline Chambon-Trois.

Bernardini, Aldo 1985: 'Catalogue des films Lumière présentés en Italie (1896-1897)', in Guibbert, Pierre, ed., *Les Premieres ans du cinéma français*. Lyon: Institut Jean Vigo.

Bernardini, Aldo 1980: *Cinema Muto Italiano***.** Vol. 1: Ambiente, spettacoli le spettatore, 1896 - 1905. Rome: Editori Laterza.

Bernardini, Aldo 2001: *Gli ambulanti: Cinema italiano delle origini*. Udine: La Cineteca del Friuli.

Berneau, Pierre 1986: 'Les débuts de cinéma à Angoulême', in *1895***,** No. 1, September 1986.

Berneau, Pierre 1988: 'Les débuts du spectacle cinématographique à Bordeaux,' in *1895*, No. 4, pp. 18-32.

Berry, David 1994: *Wales and Cinema. The First Hundred Years*. Cardiff: University of Wales Press.

Bessy, Maurice, & Duca, Lo 1948: *Louis Lumière*. Paris: Editions Prisma.

Bizkupski, Lukasz 2013: *Mia Stoatra Kcji. Narodziny kultury masowej na przetomie XIX I XX wieku*. Lodz: Narodowe Centrum Kultury.

Bleier-Brody, Agnes 1960: 'Daten zur Urgeschichte des österreichischen Films', in *Theatre und Film. Referate und Diskussionsbeiträge*, Jahresband 1960 of *Film-Kunst*, Vienna: pp. 27-34.

Bleier-Brody, Agnes, ed.1966: *Gesichichte des Films in Österrich*. Vienna: Catalog der 6. Viennale.

Blot-Wellens, Camille 2015: *El Cinematógrapho Joly-Normandin (1896 - 1897)*. Madrid: Filmoteca Española.

Braun, Marta 1992, *Picturing Time. The Work of Etienne-Jules Marey (1830 - 1904)*. Chicago and London: University of Chicago Press.

Braun, Marta 2010, *Eadweard Muybridge*. London: Reaktion Books.

Breard, Sylvester Quinn 1951: *A History of the Motion Pictues in New Orleans, 1896 - 1908*. MA Thesis, Louisiana State University.

Breitenfeldt, Dorothea, and Reinke, Jutta 1984: 'Kinderjahre des Films in Bremen', in Staatsarchiv Bremen, eds., *Mach Dir ein paar schöne Stunden...Kino in Bremen*. Bremen: Staatsarchiv Bremen. Also in: Steffen, Joachim; Thiele, Jens; & Poch, Bernd; eds. 1993: *Spurensuche. Film und Kino in der Region*. Oldenburg: Bibliotheks- und Informationssystem der Carl von Ossietzky Universität Oldenburg.

Brichta, Jindøich 1952: "Purkynì a jeho pøinos k wnálezu kinematografu", in *Pøehled fotograficki a filmovì techniky*, sv5, è7-8: pp. 110-114.

Briels, Adriaan 1971: *De Intocht van de Levende Photographie in Amsterdam*. Amsterdam: Nederlands Filminstitut.

Briels, Adriaan 1973: *Komst en plaats van de Levende Photographie op de kermis. Een filmhistorische verkenning*. Assen: Van Gorcum & Comp. B. V.

Brooker, Jeremy 2013: *The Temple of Minerva. Magic and the Magic Lantern at the Royal Polytechnic Institution, London 1837 - 1901*. London: The Magic Lantern Society.

Brown, Richard 1993: *The Lumière Cinématographe. The first six months in England*. Bury: Privately circulated.

Brown, Richard 2012: "A new look at old history – the Kinetoscope: Fraud and market development in Britain in 1895", in *Early Popular Visual Culture*, v10, No4 (November 2012), pp. 407 - 439.

Brown, Richard and Barry Anthony 2017: *The Kinetoscope. A British History*. East Barnet: John Libbey Publishing Ltd.

Buache, Freddy, & Rial, Jacques 1964: *Les Débuts du cinématographe à Genève et à Lausanne, 1895 - 1914*. Lausanne: Cinémathèque Suisse (Documents de Cinéma 5).

Burger, Jürgen, ed.1987: *Perspektiven: Zur Geschichte der filmischen Wahrnehmung*. Daueraustellung 1: Vom Guckkasten zum Cinématographe Lumière. Frankfurt am Main: Deutsches Filmmuseum.

Caneto, Guillerrmo, et. al. 1996: *Historia de los Primeros Años del Cine en la Argentina*. Buenos Aires: Fundación Cinemateca Argentina. [Authors are included only on title page and not with individual chapters:

Guillermo Caneto, Marcela Cassinelli, Héctor González Bergberot, César Maranghello, Elda Navarreo, Alejandrta Portela, Susana Strugo]

Card, James 1967: 'The Historical Motion-Picture Collections at George Eastman House', in Fielding, Raymond, ed., *A Technological History of Motion Pictures and Television*. Berkeley: University of California Press.

Castan, Joachim 1995: *Max Skladanowsky, oder, der Beginn einer deutschen Filmgeschichte*. Stuttgart: Füsslin Verlag.

Ceram, C. W. 1965: *Archaeology of the Cinema*. New York: Harcourt, Brace & World.

Chanan, Michael 1980: *The Dream that Kicks*. London: Routledge & Kegan Paul.

Chardère, Bernard 1987: *Lumières sur Lumière*. Lyon: Institut Lumire/Presses Universitaires de Lyon.

Chardère, Bernard 1990: 'A la Ciotat, avec Antoine, Auguste, Louis et les autres', in *1895*, No. 7, pp. 53-66.

Chardère, Bernard, & Borgé, Guy and Marjorie 1985: *Les Lumière*. Lausanne/Paris: Payout Lausanne/Bibliothèque des Arts Paris.

Coe, Brian 1978: *Cameras, from Daguerreotypes to Instant Pictures*. Gothenburg: Nordbok.

Coe, Brian, *The History of Movie Photography*. Westfield, NJ, 1981: Eastview Editions.

Coe, Brian 1992: *Muybridge & the Chronophotographers*. London: Museum of the Moving Image.

Coe, Brian 1962: 'William Friese-Greene and the Origins of Kinematography', in *The Photographic Journal*, March 1962 (Part I) and April 1962 (Part II).

Coe, Brian 1960: 'Wordsworth Donisthorpe', in *Cinema Studies*, V. 1 No. 1, p. 51-4.

Coissac, G.-Michel 1925: *Histoire du Cinématographe, de ses origines jusqu'à nos jours*. Paris: Editions du 'Cinéopse'/Librarie Gauthier-Villars & Cie.

Condon, Denis 2012: '"Baits to Entrap the Pleasure-Seeker and the Worldling:" Charity Bazaars Introduce Moving Pictures to Ireland,' in Marta Braun, Charlie Keil, Rob King, Paul Moore and Louis Pelletier, eds., *Beyond the Screen: Institutions, Networks and Publics of Early Cinema*. New Barnet: John Libbey Publishing Ltd.

Convents, Guido 1984: 'L'apparition du cinéma en Belgique (1895-1918)', in *Cahiers de la Cinémathèque*, No. 41, Spring 1984, pp. 15-18.

Convents, Guido 1994: 'Motion picture exhibitors on Belgian fairgrounds', in *Film History*, Vol. 6, No. 2.

Convents, Guido 2000: *Van kinetoscoop tot café-ciné. De eerste jaren van de film in België*. Leuven: Universitaire Pers Leuven.

Coulson, Thomas 1956: 'Philadelphia and the Development of the Motion Picture', in: *Journal of the Franklin Institute*, 262 (July 1956), pp. 1-16.

Dagognet, François 1992: *Étienne-Jules Marey: A Passion for the Trace*. New York: Zone Books.

Debler, Werner H. A. 2001: *Leopold Ludwig Döbler, 1801 - 1864, Wiener Hoftaschenspieler und Zauberprofessor aus einem alten Schwäbisch Gmünder Geschlect*. Schwäbisch Gmünd: Einhorn-Verlag Eduard Dietenberger GmbH

Dennis, Jonathan, ed. 1993: *Aotearoa and the Sentimental Strine. Making Films in Australia & New Zealand in the Silent Period*. Wellington: Moa Films

Derval, Paul 1955: *The Folies Bergère*. London: Methuen & Co. Ltd.

Deslandes, Jacques 1963: *Le Boulevard du cinéma à l'époque de Georges Méliès*. Paris: Editions du Cerf.

Deslandes, Jacques 1966: *Histoire comparée du cinéma. Volume 1: De la Cinématique au Cinématographe 1826-1896*. Tournai: Castermann.

Deslandes, Jacques, & Richard, Jacques 1968: *Histoire Comparée du cinéma. Volume 2: Du cinématographe au Cinéma 1896 - 1906*. Tournai: Castermann.

Domankiewicz, Peter 2019: *William Friese-Greene and the Art of Collaboration*. Privately circulated.

Donaldson, G. N. 1980: 'Film in Rotterdam / de eerste Jaren', in *Skrien*, No. 98, July/August 1980, pp. 37-40.

Donaldson, G. N. 1983: 'Wie is Wie in de Nederlandse Film tot 1930: Olinka (Madame)', in *Skrien*, No. 127, May/June 1983, pp. 26-7.

Dumont, Hervé 1987: *Geschichte des schweitzer Films*. Lausanne: Schweitzer Filmarchiv/Cinémathèque Suisse.

Engberg, Marguerite 1958: 'De første danske filmforevisninger,' in *Kosmorama*, no. 33, February 1958, pp. 136 - 39.

Engberg, Marguerite 1977: *Dansk Stumfilm, Vol. 1*. Copenhagen, 1977: Rhodos Forlag.

Fell, John, ed. 1983: *Film Before Griffith*. Berkeley: University of California Press.

Ferreira, António 1986: *A fotografa animada em Portugal 1894-1895-1896-1897*. [Lisbon]: Cinemateca Portuguesa.

Fescourt, Henri, et. al. 1932: *Le cinéma des origines à nos jours*. Paris: Aux Editions du Cygne.

Fielding, Raymond, ed. 1967: *A Technological History of Motion Pictures and Television*. Berkeley: University of California Press.

Filminstitut der Landeshauptstadt Düsseldorf, eds. 1982: *Düsseldorf Kinematographisch: Beiträge zu einer Filmgeschichte*. Düsseldorf: Trietsch Verlag.

Fischli, Bruno 1990: *Vom Sehen im Dunkeln. Kinogeschichten einer Stadt*. Cologne: Prometh-Verlag.

Fletcher, Tony 2017: *Regulating the Cinematograph in London 1897 - 1906*. Streatham: Local History Publications.

Fletcher, Tony 2001: 'The London County Council and the Cinematograph, 1896 - 1900,' in *Living Pictures*, Vol. 1, No. 2, pp. 69-83.

Folgar de la Calle, Jose M. 1987: *El espectáculo cinematográfico en Galicia (1896 - 1920)*. Santiago de Compostela: Universidad de Santiago de Compostela Servicio de Publicationes.

Forch, Carl 1913: *Der Kinematograph und das sich bewegende Bild*. Vienna & Leipzig: A. Hartlebens Verlag.

Formann, Wilhelm 1966: *Österreichische Pioniere der Kinematographie*. Vienna: Bergland Verlag.

Fraenkel, Heinrich 1956: *Unsterblicher Film*. Munich: Kindler Verlag.

Frazer, John 1979: *Artificially Arranged Scenes. The Films of Georges Méliès*. Boston: G. K. Hall & Company.

[Fritz, Walter 1990]: *The early years of Cinema in Central Europe (1895-1914)*. Brussels: Fédération Internationale des Archives du Film (FIAF).

Fritz, Walter 1981: *Kino in Österreich: Der Stummfilm 1896 - 1930*. Vienna: Österreichischer Bundesverlag.

Fritz, Walter 1969: *Geschichte des österreichischen Films*. Vienna: Bergland Verlag.

Frizot, Michel 1984: *La Chronophotographie*. Beaune: Association des Amis de Marey et Ministère de la Culture.

Fullerton, John 2008: 'Creating an audience for the "Cinematographe": Two Lumière Agents in Mexico, 1896', in *Film History*, Vol. 20, No. 1, pp. 95 - 108.

Genovese, Nino 1984: 'Il cinema dell origini in Sicilia (1895 - 1898)', in *Bianco e Nero* No. 4, October/December 1984, pp. 49-80.

Gethmann, Daniel, Peter Gorschlüter, Ulrike Groos, and Christoph Benjamin Schulz, eds., *Daumenkino. The Flip Book Show*. Düsseldorf, 2005: Kunsthalle Düsseldorf / Snoeck.

Goergen, Jeanpaul 1998: *Das Jahr 1896. Chronik der Berliner Kinematographen (mit einem Ausblick auf das Jahr 1897)*. Siegen: Universität-Gesamthochschule Siegen (= Massenmedien und Kommunikation, Bd. 120/121)

Gosser, H. Mark 1977: *Selected Attempts at Stereoscopic Moving Pictures and their Relationship to the Development of Motion Picture Technology, 1852 - 1903*. New York: Arno Press

Gosser, H. Mark 1988: 'The Armat-Jenkins Dispute and the Museums', in *Film History*, V. 2, No. 1, pp. 1-12.

Grüson, P. 1893: "Einige Versuche mit der Wunderscheibe", in *Archiv für die gesamte Physiologie des Menschen und der Tiere*, v55, i9-10, (November 1893), pp. 508 - 20.

Grusser, Kurt 1965: *Die Entwicklung der Filmtechnik*. Potsdam-Babelsberg:

Deutsche Hochschule für Filmkunst, Abt. Lichtspielwesen (Leherbrief 8; Lehrmaterial für das Fernstudium).

Haas, Robert Bartlett 1976: *Muybridge, Man in Motion*. Berkeley/Los Angeles/London: University of California Press.

Hanisch, Michael 1991: *Auf den Spuren der Filmgeschichte: Berliner Schauplätze*. Berlin: Henschl Verlag.

Hannavy, John, ed., 2008: *Encyclopaedia of 19th Century Photography*. London/New York: Routledge.

Harding, Colin and Simon Popple 1996: *In the Kingdom of Shadows. A Companion to Early Cinema*. London: Cygnus Arts.

Hastings, Charles Edward 1927: 'Cinematic Beginnings', in *Moving Picture World*, 26 March, 1927, pp. 89-300.

Hecht, Hermann, [Ann Hecht, ed.] 1993: *Pre-Cinema History: An Encyclopaedia and Annotated Bibliography of the Moving Image Before 1896.* London: Bowker/Saur.

Hendricks, Gordon 1964: *The Beginnings of the Biograph*. New York: The Beginnings of the American Film.

Hendricks, Gordon 1961: *The Edison Motion Picture Myth*. Berkeley: University of California Press.

Hendricks,Gordon 1966: *The Kinetoscope*. New York: The Beginnings of the American Film.

Hendricks, Gordon, 1975: *Eadweard Muybridge. The Father of the Motion Picture*. New York: Grossman Publishers.

Hendrykowska, Malgorzata 1994, 'Film journeys of the Krzeminski brothers, 1900 - 1908', in *Film History*, Vol. 6, No. 2, pp.

Hendrykowska, Malgorzata 1993: *Sladami Tamtych Ciene: Film w kulturze polskiej przelomuy stuleci 1895 - 1914*. Poznan: Oficyna Wydawnicza Book Service.

Henningsen, Wiltrud 1990: *Die Entstehung des Kinos in Münster*. Münster: Sofortdruck Nath.

Hennion, Jean-Baptiste 2008: 'Éclairage sur l'année 1896. Éléments chronologiques relatifs à l'introduction du spectacle cinématographique sur le champs de foire français,' in *1895*, No. 54, fevrier 2008, pp. 29 - 55.

Herbert, Stephen 1989: 'Animated Portrait Photography', in *History of Photography*, Vol. 13, No. 1, January-March 1989, pp. 65-78.

Herbert, Stephen 1991: 'Kinora Living Pictures', in *Photo Historian* [U. K.], No. 95, Winter 1991, pp. 104-113.

Herbert, Stephen 1994: *When the Movies Began.... A Chronology of the world's film productions and film shows before May, 1896*. London: The Projection Box.

Herbert, Stephen, 2001: 'O. B. Brown,' in David Robinson, Stephen Herbert and Richard Crangle, eds., *Encyclopaedia of the Magic Lantern*. London: The Magic Lantern Society.

Herbert, Stephen, ed. 2004: *Eadweard Muybridge. The Kingston Museum Bequest*. Hastings: The Projection Box.

Herbert, Stephen 2008, "Duboscq, Louis Jules", in John Hannavy, ed., *Encyclopaedia of 19th Century Photography*, V. 1, pp. 445-6.

Herbert, Stephen 2017: *Industry, Liberty, and a Vision. Wordsworth Donisthorpe's Kinesigraph*. (Second Edition) Hastings: The Projection Box.

Hoffman, Detlef, & Thiele, Jens, eds. 1989: *Lichtbilder Lichtspiele. Anfänge der Fotografie und des Kinos in Ostfriesland*. Marburg: Jonas Verlag.

Hoffmann, Hilmar, and Walter Schobert, Hgs., 1995: *Lebende Bilder einer Stadt: Kino und Film in Frankfurt am Main*. Frankfurt a. M.: Deutsches Filmmuseum.

Hofmann, Paul 1992: 'Auf der Suche nach den Anfängen der Kinematographie im rheinisch-westfälischen Industriegebiet', in Lisa Kosok and Mathilde Jamin, eds., *Viel Vergnügen. Öffentliche Lustbarkeiten im Ruhrgebiet der Jahrhundertwende*. Essen: Verlag Peter Pomp/Ruhrlandsmuseum Essen.

Hollyman, Burnes St. Patrick 1983: 'The first Picture Shows: Austin, Texas, 1894 - 1913', in Fell, John, ed., *Film Before Griffith*. Berkeley: University of California Press, pp. 188-95.

Hollyman, Burnes St. Patrick 1983a: 'Alexander Black's Picture Plays', in Fell, John, ed., *Film Before Griffith*. Berkeley: University of California Press, pp. 236-43.

Hopwood, Henry Vaux 1899: *Living Pictures*. London: The Optician and Photographic Trades Review.

Horner, William George 1834: 'On the Properties of the Daedaleum, a new Instrument of Optical Illusion', in *The London and Edinburgh Philosophical Magazine and Journal of Science*, January 1834, v4, pp. 36–40.

Idestam-Almquist, Bengt 1959: *När filmen kam till Sverige*. Stockholm: P. A. Norstedt & Söners Forlag.

Idestam-Almquist, Bengt 1962: *Rysk Film. En konstart blir till.* Stockholm: Wahlström & Widstrand.

Ilgner, Christian, & Linke, Dietmar 1994: 'Filmtechnik - Vom Malteserkreuz zum Panzerkino', in Martin Loiperdinger, Sabine Lenk & Frank Kessler, eds., *100 Jahre Film. Oskar Messter, Filmpionier der Kaiserzeit.* Basel / Frankfurt am Main, 1994: Stroemfeld/Roter Stern (KINtop Schriften 2).

Iverson, Gunnar 2014: 'Performing New Media and the Creation of National Identity: Kräusslich and Köpke in Norway Before 1910,' in Kaveh Askari, Scott Curtis, Frank Gray, Louis Pelletier, Tami Williams and Joshua Yumibe, eds., *Performing New Media, 1890 - 1915*. New Barnet: John Libbey Publishers Ltd.

Jacob, Livio 1979: 'Quel Merviglioso Apparecchio. Cronaca della prime proiezione cinematografiche in Friuli', in *Griffithiana*, No. 3-4, July/November.

Jacobsen, Wolfgang; Kaes, Anton; & Prinzler, Hans Helmut, eds. 1993: *Geschichte des deutschen Films*. Stuttgart/Weimar: Verlag J. B. Metzler.

Jenkins, Reese V. 1975: *Images and Enterprise. Technology and the American Photographic Industry 1839 to 1925*. Baltimore and London: The Johns Hopkins University Press.

Jossé, Harald 1984: *Die Entstehung des Tonfilms. Beitrag zu einer faktenorientierten Mediengeschichtsschreibung*. Freiburg/Munich: Verlag Karl Alber.

Kaldy-Karo, Robert 2001: *Ludwig Döbler, genius des biedermeier*. Horitschon [Austria]: Verlag novum.

Kane, Lucile M., and John A. Dougherty 1995: 'Film in the Twin Cities, 1894 - 1909', in *Minnesota History*, Vol. 54, No. 8 (Winter, 1995), pp. 342 - 358.

Keim, Norman O. 2008: *Our Movie Houses. A History of Film & Cinematic Innovation in Central New York*. Syracuse: Syracuse University Press.

Kieninger, Ernst, and Doris Rauschgatt, eds., 1995: *Die Mobilisierung des Blicks, eine Ausstellung zur Vor- und Frühgeschichte des Kinos*. Wien: DVS-Verlag.

Klerk, Nico de 1999: 'A Few Remaining Hours: News Films and the Interest in Technology in Amsterdam Film Shows, 1896-1910', in *Film History*, Vol. 11, No. 1, pp. 5 - 17.

Köcke, Hans 1966: 'Ottomar Anschütz – ein Meister der Reihenbilder', in *Bild und Ton*, Heft 11, pp. 344-346.

Koerber, Martin 1994: 'Filmfabrikant Oskar Messter – Stationen einer Karriere', in Martin Loiperdinger, Sabine Lenk, & Frank Kessler, eds., *100 Jahre Film. Oskar Messter, Filmpionier der Kaiserzeit*. Basel/Frankfurt am Main: Stroemfeld/Roter Stern (KINtop Schriften 2).

Kosanović, Dejan 1997: 'Le prime proiezioni e le prime represe cinematografiche a Trieste nel 1896 e nel 1897', in *Griffithiana*, No. 29-30, September 1997, pp. 37-41.

Kosanović, Dejan 1988: *Il Cinema Muto in Jugoslavia 1896 - 1932*. Belgrade: Instituto Per il Cinema [Brochure prepared for Pordenone, 1988]

Kosanović, Dejan 2004: *A Short History of Cinema in Serbia and Montenegro. Part I: 1896-1945*. Belgrade: Jugoslovenska kinoteka/Direkcija FEST-a.

Knezević, Srdjan 1994: 'Le Cinématograph Lumière à Belgrade et à Zagreb en 1896-1897,' in *1895*, No. 16, pp. 27-33.

Kress, E. 1912: *Conférences sur la cinématographie*. Paris: Comptoir d'édition de 'Cinéma-Revue'.

Kurzel-Runtsacheiner, Erich 1938: "Franz Freiherr von Uchatius", in *Blätter für Geschichte der Technik*, Viertes Heft, Wien, pp. 40-65.

Labosier, James 2004: 'From the Kinetoscope to the Nickelodeon: Motion

Picture Presentation and Production in Portland, Oregon, from 1894 to 1906', in *Film History*, Vol. 16, No. 3, pp. 286 - 323.

Lacasse, Germain 1984: 'Cultural Amnesia and the birth of film in Canada', in *Cinema Canada*, No. 108, June 1984.

Lacasse, Germain 1984a: 'Des exploitants française au Québec, (1896-1906), in *Les Cahiers de la Cinémathèque*, No. 41, Spring 1984, pp. 27-30.

Lange-Fuchs, Hauke 1987: *Birt Acres. Der erste Schleswig-Holsteinische Film Pionier*. Kiel: Walter G. Mühlau.

Lecointe, Thierry 2004: 'Les premières années du spectacle cinématographique à Nîmes - 1895 - 1913,' in *1895*, No. 43.

Lehmann, H. 1911: *Die Kinematographie, ihre Grundlagen und ihre Anwendungen*. Leipzig: G. G. Teubner Verlag.

Lenman, Robin, ed. 2005: *The Oxford Companion to the Photograph*. Oxford / New York: Oxford University Press.

Letamendi, Jon, & Jean-Claude Seguin 1997: *Los Orígenes del cine en Álava y sus Pioneros (1896-1897)*. Donostia - San Sebastiàn / Vitoria-Gasteiz: Filmoteca Vasca/Euskadiko Filmategia / Ayuntamiento de Vitoria-Gasteia/ASTEIZKO Udala / Fundación caja vital kutxa/caja vital kutxa fundazioa.

Letamendi, Jon, & Jean-Claude Seguin 1998: *Los Orígenes del cine en Bizkaia y sus Pioneros*. Donostia-San Sebastian; Filmoteca Vasca-Euskadiko Filmategia.

Leyda, Jay 1972: *Dianyang. An account of films and the film audience in China*. Cambridge: MIT Press.

Leyda, Jay 1983: *Kino: A History of the Russian and Soviet Film*. Third Edition. London: George Allen & Unwin.

Liesegang, F. Paul 1926: *Zahlen und Quellen. Zur Geschichte der Projektionskunst und Kinematographie*. Berlin: Deutsches Druck- und Verlagshaus.

Liesegang, F. Paul 1940: *Ottomar Anschütz. Meister der Augenblicks- und Reihenphotographie, Meister der Reihenwiedergabe. Sein Leben, sein Werk, seine Bedeutung*. Unpublished. Mss. at Agfa-Photo-Historama, Muserum Ludwig, Cologne. Copy with the author.

Liesegang, F. Paul 1986, (Translated and annotated by Hermann Hecht), *Dates and Sources*. London: The Magic Lantern Society of Great Britain.

Lichtenstein, Manfred 1990: 'The Brothers Skladanowsky', in Paolo Cherchi Usai and Lorenzo Codelli, eds., *Prima di Caligari, Cinema Tedesco, 1895 - 1920*. Pordenone: Giovanni del Cinema Muto, pp. 312-25.

Loiperdinger, Martin 1990: 'Ludwig Stollwerck, premier concessionaire Lumière en Allemagne', in Martin Loiperdinger & Roland Cosandey, eds., *Des sous comme s'il en pleuvait. Quatre documents pour servir à l'histoire du Cinématographe*. Pordenone: Giovanni del Cinema Muto.

Loiperdinger, Martin 1990a, 'The arrival in Germany of the Cinématographe Lumière,' in *Prima di Caligari, Cinema Tedesco, 1895 - 1920*. Pordenone: Giovanni del Cinema Muto, pp. 30-49.

Loiperdinger, Martin, ed. 1994, *Oskar Messter - Filmpoionier der Kaiserzeit*. Basel / Frankfurt am Main: Stroemfeld / Roter Stern.

Loiperdinger, Martin 1999: *Film & Schokolade. Stollwercks Geschäfte mit lebenden Bildern*. Frankfurt am Main / Basel: Stroemfeld / Roter Stern

Long, Chris 1993: 'Australia's First Films: Facts and Fables', Part One: 'The Kinetoscope in Australia', in *Cinema Papers*, No. 91, March 1993

Long, Chris 1993a: 'Australia's First Films: Facts and Fables', Part Two: 'Projectors Reach Australia', in *Cinema Papers*, No. 92, April 1993

Long, Chris 1993b: 'Australia's First Films: Facts and Fables', Part Three: 'Local Production Begins', in *Cinema Papers*, No. 93, May 1993.

Long, Chris 1993c: 'Birth of Australian Cinema – Chronology', summary condensation of dates from the articles in *Cinema Papers*; privately circulated by Chris Long, beginning January 1993.

Long, Chris, and Sowry, Clive [n.d. (1995)], 'Birth of New Zealand Cinema – Chronology'. Summary of dates and research, privately circulated.

Lòpez, Ana M. 2015: 'Cine temprano y modernidad en América Latina,' in *Vivomatografías. Revista de estudios sobre precine y cine silente en Latinoamérica*. V1 No.1, Decembre 2015, pp. 128-170.

Luppi, Livio 1986: 'Prima proiezioni in Italia: Pacchioni a Mirandola', in *Immagine: Note di Storia del Cinema*. Nuova Series No. 20, Rome: Associazione Italiana per le Ricerche di Storia del Cinema.

Maden, Frank van der, & Dibbets, Karel 1986: *Geschiedenis van de Nederlandse Film en Bioscoop tot 1940*. Weesp: Het Wereldvenster.

Maier, Margit 2009: *Das Geschäft mit den Träumen. Kinokultur in Würzburg*. Würzburg: Verlag Königshausen & Neumann.

Manders, Frank 1991: *Cinemas of Newcastle. A comprehensive history of the cinemas of Newcastle upon Tyne*. Newcastle upon Tyne: City Libraries & Arts.

Mannoni, Laurent 1993: 'Ambroise-François Parnaland: Cinema Pioneer, Co-Founder of the Eclair Company', in *Griffithiana*, No. 47, May 1993.

Mannoni, Laurent 1993a, '1894-1895: les années parisiennes du Kinetoscope Edison', in *Cinémathèque* 3, Spring/Summer 1993.

Mannoni, Laurent 1994: *Le grand art de la Lumière et de l'ombre. Archéologie du cinéma*. Paris: Editions Nathan.

Mannoni, Laurent, Donata Pesenti Campagnoni, David Robinson 1995: *Light and Movement. Incunabula of the Motion Picture*. Pordenone: Le Giornate del Cinema Muto / Cinémathèque française - Musée du Cinéma / Museo Nazionale del Cinema.

Mannoni, Laurent, 1996: 'Repères biographiques sur Henri Joly, l'initiateur technique de Charles Pathé', in *1895*, No. 21 (1996), pp. 16-38.

Mannoni, Laurent 2002: '1896, les premiers appareils cinématographique de Georges Méliès', in: Jacques Malthête et Laurent Mannoni, eds, *Méliès. Magie et Cinéma*. Paris: Paris Musées.

Martinez, Josefino 1992: *Las primeros veinticino anos de cine en Madrid, 1896 - 1920*. Madrid: Instituto de la Cinematografia y de las Artes/Ministerio de Cultura.

McCosker, M. J. 1941: 'Philadelphia and the Genesis of the Motion Picture', in *The Pennsylvania Magazine of History and Biography*, v65, No4 (October 1941), pp 401-19.

Meier-Kern, Paula 1993: *Verbrecherschule oder Kulturfaktor? Kino und Film in Basel 1896-1916*. Basel: 171. Neujahrsblatt, herausgegeben von der Gesellschaft für das Gute und Gemeinnützige, in Kommission bei Helbing & Lichtenhahn.

Mesa, Héctor García, ed., 2014: *Cine Latinoamericano (1896 - 1930)*. Caracas: Centro Nacional Autónomo de Cinematografía [second edition]

Meusy, Jean-Jacques 1995, *Paris-Palaces, ou le temps des cinémas (1894-1918)*. Paris: CNRS Editions/afrhc.

Mitry, Jean 1963: *Filmographie Universelle, Volume 1: Index Historique des Techniques et Industries du film*; Paris: IDHEC.

Mitry, Jean 1967: *Histoire du Cinema: Art et Industrie. Vol. 1: 1895 - 1914*. Paris: Editions Universitaires.

Mitry, Jean, ed. 1976: *Le cinéma des origines. Les précurseurs, les inventeurs, les pionniers*. Paris: Cinéma d'aujourd'hui (nouvelle serie) No. 9.

Moix, Miquel Porter, & Porter, Guillemette Huerre de 1958: *La cinematografia catalana (1896 - 1925)*. Palma de Mallorca: Editorial Moll.

Moore, Paul S., 2012: 'Mapping the Mass Circulation of early Cinema: Film Debuts Coast to Coast in Canada in 1896 and 1897', in *Canadian Journal of Film Studies*, Vol. 21, No. 1, Spring 2012, pp. 58-80.

Moore, Paul S., 2012a: 'Advance Newspaper Publicity for the Vitascope and the Mass Address of Cinema's Reading Public', in André Gaudreault, Nicolas Dulac and Santiago Hidalgo, eds., *A Companion to Early Cinema*. Chichester: John Wiley & Sons (Wiley-Blackwell), pp. 381-95.

Morris, Peter 1978: *Embattled Shadows: A history of Canadian Cinema 1895–1939*. Montreal: McGill-Queens University Press.

[Müller, Pamela, et. al.], Unpublished research of the Gesellschaft für Filmstudien. Hannover (1994).

Musser, Charles 1990: *The Emergence of Cinema: The American Screen to 1907*. New York: Charles Scribner's Sons (History of the American Cinema, Volume 1).

Musser, Charles 1991: *Before the Nickelodeon: Edwin S. Porter and the Edison Manufacturing Company*. Berkeley: University of California Press.

Musser, Charles, and Nelson, Carol 1991a: *High Class Moving Pictures. Lyman H. Howe and the Forgotten Era of Travelling Exhibition, 1880 - 1920*. Princeton: Princeton University Press.

Musser, Charles 1997: *Edison Motion Pictures, 1890 - 1900. An Annotated Filmography*. Washington, D. C. & Pordenone, Italy: Smithsonian Institution Press & Le Giornate del Cinema Muto.

Musser, Charles 1999, 'Nationalism and the Beginnings of Cinema: the Lumière Cinématographe in the US, 1896-1897,' in *Historical Journal of Film, Radio and Television*, Vol. 19, No. 2, pp. 149-76.

Musser, Charles 1999a: 'Reading Local histories of Early Film Exhibition, Part II: Roger William Warren's "History of Motion Picture Exhibition in Denver, 1896–1911,"' in: *Historical Journal of Film, Radio and Television*, Nol. 19, No. 2, pp. 247-53.

Narath, Albert 1967: 'Oskar Messter and his Work', reprinted from the *Journal of the SMPTE*, volume 69, October 1960, in Fielding, Raymond, ed., *A Technological History of Motion Pictures and Television*. Berkeley: University of California Press.

Narath, Albert 1966: *Oskar Messter, der Begründer der deutschen Kino- und Filmindustrie*. Berlin: Deutsche Kinemathek e. V. Filmwissenschaftliche Schriften.

Narath, Albert 1970: *Max Skladanowsky*. Berlin: Deutsche Kinemathek Berlin.

Niver, Kemp R.1985: *Early Motion Pictures: The Paper Print Collection in the Library of Congress*. Washington, DC: The Library of Congress.

Nørgaard, Erik 1973: *Levende billeder I Danmark*. Copenhagen: Lademann Forlagsaktieselskab.

North, Joseph H. 1973, *The Early Development of the Motion Picture (1887–1909)*. New York: Arno Press. (Ph. D. Thesis, Cornell University, 1949).

Nünthel, Ralph 1999, *Johannes Nitzsche. Kinematographen & Films. Die Geschichte des Leipziger Kinopioniers, seiner Unternehmen und seiner Technik*. Leipzig: Sax-Verlag Beucha.

Pacewicz, Tadeusz 1990: 'An Outline of the History of Cinematography in Poland from its Inception to 1914,' in Walter Fritz \ FIAF, eds., *The Early Years of Cinema in Central Europe (1895 - 1914)*. Brussels: International Federation of Film Archives (FIAF).

Pinel, Vincent 1992: *Chronologie commentée de l'invention du cinéma*. Special issue of *1895*, Paris: Association française de recherche sur l'histoire du cinéma.

Poch, Bernd 1989: 'Viel Geld mit wenig Mühe: Wanderkino in Ostfriesland', in Detlef Hoffmann and Jens Thiele, eds., *Lichtbilder - Lichtspiele. Anfänge der Fotografie und des Kinos in Ostfriesland*. Marburg: Jonas Verlag.

Poupion, Olivier P. 1990: 'Les premières séances Lumière à Rouen (Avril-Octobre 1896)', in *1895*, No. 7, pp. 29-52.

Pozner, Valérie 2006: 'Gorki au cinématographe: "je étais hier au royume des ombres ..."', in *1895*, No. 50, Decembre 2006, pp. 89 - 113.

Pratt, George C. 1973: 'Firsting the Firsts', in Marshall Deutelbaum, ed., *Image on the Art and Evolution of the Film*. New York: New York Graphic Society.

Pratt, George C.1973a: 'No Magic, No Mystery', in Marshall Deutelbaum, ed., *Image on the Art and Evolution of the Film*. New York: New York Graphic Society.

Pratt, George C. 1973b [1966], *Spellbound in Darkness. A History of the Silent Film*. Greenwich, CT: New York Graphic Society.

Prodger, Phillip 2003: *Time Stands Still. Muybridge and the Instantaneous Photography Movement*. Oxford / Stanford CA, The Iris B and Gerald Cantor Center for Visual Arts, Stanford University, and Oxford University Press.

Psoma, Elene 2008: *Filmland Griechenland — Terra incognita: griechische Filmgeschichte zwischen Politik, Gesellschaft, und internationalen Impulsen*. Berlin: Logos Verlag.

Puttkamer, Jesco von 1992: 'Illustrierte Chronik zur Bewegungsdarstellung in der Photographie', in *Sprung in die Zeit*. Berlin: Berlinische Galerie Museum für Moderne Kunst Photographie und Architektur/Ars Nicolai.

Radvanyi, Jean, ed. 1998: *Le cinéma georgien*. Paris: Centre Georges Pompidou.

Ramsaye, Terry 1926: *A Million and One Nights*. New York: Simon & Schuster.

Rawlence, Christopher 1990: *The Missing Reel. The Untold Story of the Lost Inventor of Moving Pictures*. London: William Collins & Sons.

Reade, Eric 1979: *History and Heartburn - The Saga of Australian Film, 1896 - 1978*. Sydney: Harper & Row.

Reade, Eric 1970: *Australian Silent Films*. Melbourne: Lansdowne Press.

Remshardt, Ralf 2004: '"The Story and the Screen:" Alexander Black's Picture Plays and the Prehistory of the Cinema,' in *Princeton University Library Chronicle*, Vol. LXV, No. 3, Spring 2004, pp. 452-78.

Reyes, Aurelio de los 1986: *Filmografia del cine mundo mexicano 1896-1920*. Mexico, D. F.: Filmoteca UNAM.

Reyes, Aurelio de los 1987: *Medio Siglo de Cine Mexicano 1896 - 1947*. Mexico City: Editorial Trillas.

Reyes, Aurelio de los 1983: *Los Origenes del cine en México, 1896 - 1900*. Mexico, D. F.: Sep/80.

Reyes, Aurelio de los 2013: *Los orígenes del cine en México (1896 - 1900)*. Mexico D. F.: Fondo de Cutura Económica.

Rittaud-Hutinet, Jacques 1985: *Le cinéma des origines. Les Frères Lumière et leurs opérateurs*. Seyssel: Editions du Champ Vallon.

Rittaud-Hutinet, Jacques 1990: *Auguste et Louis Lumière: Les 1000 premiers films*. Paris: Philippe Sers éditeur.

Rittaud-Hutinet, Jacques 1994: 'Les premières projections publiques en France', in *La lettre du premiere siècle du cinéma*, No. 3, January 1994.

Robinson, David 1991: *Masters of Animation*. Pordenone: La Cineteca del Friuli (= *Griffithiana*, v43).

Rockett, Kevin; Gibbons, Luke; & Hill, John 1987: *Cinema and Ireland*. London: Croom Helm.

Ros-Vilella, Maria Teresa 1979: 'Introduction du cinéma en Catalogne', in *Le cinéma des premiers temps (1900-1906), Les cahiers de la Cinémathèque*, No. 29, Spring 1979.

Rossell, Deac 1995: '"...the new thing with the long name and the old thing with the name that isn't much shorter..." A Chronology of Cinema, 1889–1896', in: *Film History*, Vol. 7, No. 2 (Summer 1995), pp.115-178.

Rossell, Deac 1998: *Living Pictures. The Origins of the Movies*. Albany: State University of New York Press.

Rossell, Deac 1999: 'The Biograph Large Format Technology', in Luke McKernan and Mark van den Temple, eds, *The Wonders of the Biograph* (= *Griffithiana, La Rivista della Cineteca del Friuli*, Nos 66-70, 1999-2000), pp. 79-115.

Rossell, Deac 2001: *Faszination der Bewegung. Ottomar Anschütz zwischen Photographie und Kino*. Frankfurt am Main / Basel: Stroemfeld / Roter Stern (= KINtop Schriften 6).

Rossell, Deac 2005: 'The Magic Lantern and Moving Images before 1800', in *Barokberichte* (Salzburg) 40-41 (August 2005), pp. 686-693.

Rossell, Deac 2005a: 'Jan Evangelista Purkinje', in Robin Lenman, ed., *The Oxford Companion to the Photograph*. Oxford: Oxford university Press.

Rossell, Deac 2005b: 'Eberhard Schneider,' in Richard Abel, ed., *Encyclopaedia of Early Cinema*. London/New York: Routledge.

Rossell, Deac 2013: 'Chronophotography in the context of moving pictures', in *Early Popular Visual Culture*, V. 11, No. 1, February 2013, pp. 10-27.

Rossell, Deac 2016: 'Copycats: Anschütz Chronophotographs as Direct Source Material for Early Edison Kinetoscope Films', in *Film History*, 28.2, pp. 142-172.

Sadoul, Georges 1946: *Histoire générale du cinéma: Vol. 1: L'invention du cinéma, 1832-1897*. Paris: Éditions Denoël.

Sadoul, Georges 1946a: *Histoire générale du cinéma: Vol. 2: Les pionniers du cinéma, 1897-1909*. Paris: Éditions Denoël.

[Sadoul, Georges, & Reynaud, Paul 1946b], *Emile Reynaud, peintre de films*. Paris: Cinémathèque Française.

Sadoul, Georges 1964: *Louis Lumière*. Paris: Editions Seghers (Cinéma d'aujourd'hui No. 29).

Sandfeld, Gunnar 1966: *Den stumme Scene. Dansk biografteater indtil lydfilmes gennembrud*. Copenhagen: NYT Nordisk Forlag/Arnold Busck.

Schaper, Petra 1987: *Kinos in Lübeck. Die Geschichte der Lübecker Lichtspieltheater und ihrer unmittelbaren Vorläufer 1896 bis heute*. Lübeck: Verlag Graphische Werkstätten GmbH.

Schmitt, Frantz 1996: *Dictionnaire des Brevets Cinematographiques Français. Des origines à 1929*. Paris: Editions Prodiex.

Schuster, Peter, & Christian Strasser 1998: *Simon Stampfer 1790 - 1864. Von der Zauberscheibe zum Film.* Hallwang: Land Salzburg, Landespressebüro (= Schriftenreihe des Landespressebüros, Serie "Sonderpublikationen", Nr. 142 [= Nr 6, Salzburger Porträts])

Schwartz, Vanessa, & Meusy, Jean-Jacques, 'Le Musée Grévin et le cinématographe: l'histoire d'une rencontre', in *1895*, No. 11, pp. 19 - 48.

Seeber, Guido 1979, 'Der kinematographische Aufnahmenapparat. Seine Geschichte, seine Konstruktion und seine praktische Benutzung', [previously unpublished mss.] in Norbert Jochum, ed., *Das wandernde Bild: Der Filmpionier Guido Seeber*. Berlin: Stiftung Deutsche Kinemathek.

Seguin, Jean-Claude 2015-18: Groupe de réflexion sur l'image dans le monde hispanique, at www.grimh.org

Serrano, Arturo, n. d., *The Beginnings of the Cinema in Venezuela*. Caracas: n.p. Posted at *academia.edu*

Shirley, Graham, & Adams, Brian 1983: *Australian Cinema: The First Eighty Years*. Australia: Angus & Robertson Publishers and Currency Press.

——- Siemens Archiv, München (now Berlin), Charlottenburg Werke, files LN 238, LN239.

——- *Sitzungs-Berichte der mathematische-naturwissenschaftliche Klasse der kaiserlichen Akademie der Wissenschaften*, Wien 1853, 10. Band, 482-85.

——- *Sitzungsberichte der mathematische-naturwissenswchaftliche Klasse derkaiserlichen Akademie der Wissenschaften*, Wien, 1855, vol. 5, pp. 463-66.

——- *Sitzungsberichte der königlichen böhmischen Gesellschaft der Wissenschaft* 1861, p. 84.

Slide, Anthony 1989: *The International Film Industry. A Historical Dictionary*. Westport, CT: Greenwood Press.

Soto, Begoña 2007: 'Rethinking Boundaries. The first moving images between Spain and Portugal,' in Frank Kessler and Nanna Verhoeff, eds., *Networks of Entertainment. Early Film Distribution 1895-1915*. Eastleigh (UK): John Libbey Publishing.

Spehr, Paul 1999: 'Eugene Augustin Lauste: A Biographical Chronology,' in *Film History*, F. 11, pp. 18-38.

Spehr, Paul C. 2000: 'Unaltered to Date: Developing 35mm Film,' in: John Fullerton and Astrid Söderbergh Widding, eds, *Moving Images: From Edison to the Webcam*. Sydney: John Libbey & Company PTY Ltd., pp. 3 - 28.

Spehr, Paul 2008: *The Man Who Made Movies: W. K. L. Dickson.* New Barnet, Herts.: John Libbey Publishing, with Le Giornate del Cinema Muto, Pordenone.

Štábla, Zdenek 1989: 'The First Cinema Shows in the Czech Lands', in *Film History*, V. 3, pp. 203-221.

Steffen, Joachim; Thiele, Jens; & Poch, Bernd; eds. 1993: *Spurensuche. Film und Kino in der Region*. Oldenburg: Bibliotheks- und Informationssystem der Carl von Ossietzky Universität.

Strobel, Richard 1993: *Kinokultur: Filmtheatre in Lüneburg, 1896-1993*. Bardowich: Wissenschaftler Verlag Werner Faultsch.

Tasic, Zoran, & Passek, Jean-Loup, eds. 1986: *Le Cinéma Yougoslave*. Paris: Centre Georges Pompidou.

Théodosieu, Nikos 2009: 'Flash Back. Les pionniers du cinéma en Grèce', in *Desmos/Le Lien*, No. 32, *Regards sur le cinéma Grec*.

Thomas, David B. 1964: *The Origins of the Motion Picture*. London: Her Majesty's Stationery Office.

Toeplitz, Jerszy 1973: *Geschichte des Films, Vol. 1: 1895 - 1928*. Munich: Rogner & Bernhard.

Tötenberg, Michael 1990: *Filmstadt Hamburg*. Hamburg: VSA Verlag.

——- *Transactions of the Royal Scottish Society of Arts 1863-64*, Vol. 6, Appendix Q: Proceedings of the Royal Scottish Society of Arts, Eighth meeting, 14 March 1864. Edinburgh: Printed for the Society.

Traub, Hans, 1940: *Als man anfing zu filmen - die Erfindung der Kinematographie und ihrer Vorläufer*. Berlin: UFA-Buchverlag GmbH (Bd. II der Schriften der UFA - Lehrschau).

Tümmel, Herbert 1986: *Deutsche Laufbildprojektoren. Ein Katalog*. Berlin: Stiftung Deutsche Kinemathek.

Wachelder, Joseph 2006: 'Bewegte Bilder? Bewegte Scheiben! Die Wunderscheiben Joseph Plateaus und Simon Stampfers und ihre Rezeption', in Daniel Gethmann & Christoph B. Schulz, eds., *Apparaturen bewegter Bilder*. Münster: Lit Verlag (= Band 02, Schriftenreihe des Internationalen Zentrums für Kultur- und Technikforschung [IZKT] der Universität Stuttgart)

Wagner, Rüdiger 1972: "Die Anfänge der Kinematographie in Hamburg," in *Hamburger Filmgespräche IV*. Hamburg: Hamburger Gesellschaft für Filmkunde e. V.

Waldekranz, Rune 1986: 'La nascita del cinema in Scandinavia', in Paolo Cherchi Usai, ed., *Schiave biance allo specchio. Le origini del cinema in Scandinavia*. Pordenone, 1986: Edizioni Studio Tesi [reprinted from *Levende Bilder. De första biograferna*, Stockholm, 1955].

Waldekranz, Rune 1976: *Saföddes Filmen: Ett massmediums uppkomst och genombrott*. Stockholm: Svenska Filminstitutet/Norstedts Tryckeri.

Walsh, Peter 2014: 'Standards of Practice in Transition: the Showmanship of Jasper Redfern as It Emerged,' in Kaveh Askari, Scott Curtis, Frank Gray, Louis Pelletier, Tami Williams and Joshua Yumibe, eds., *Performing New Media, 1890-1915*. New Barnet: John Libbey Publishing.

Wasson, Mervyn 1964: *The Beginnings of Australian Cinema*. Melbourne: Australian Film Institute.

Weeden, Brenda 2008: *The Education of the Eye. History of the Royal Polytechnic Institution 1838 - 1881*. London: Granta Editions(= History of the University of Westminster, Part One)

Westra, Frans, & de Kam, Rob 1983: *Eene zeer interessante Vertooning...80 Jaar Bioscopie in Groningen*. Groningen: Stichting Uitgeverij Xeno.

Wit, Herman de 1986: *Film in Utrecht van 1895 tot 1915*. Ph. D. Thesis, Instituut voor Theaterwetenschap, Rijksuniversiteit Utrecht.

Wlaschin, Ken, with Stephen Bottomore 2008: 'Moving picture fiction of the silent era, 1895 - 1928,' in *Film History*, vol. 20, pp. 217-260.

Woal, Linda 1994: 'When a dime could buy a dream. Siegmund Lubin and the birth of motion picture exhibition', in *Film History*, V. 6, pp. 152 - 165.

Wolf, Sylvia & Kurowski, Ulrich 1988: *Das Münchner Film und Kino Buch*. Munich: Editions Achteinhalb/Lothar Just.

Zglinicki, Friedrich von 1979: *Der Weg des Films*. Hildesheim: Olms Presse.

Zglinicki, Friedrich von 1986: *Die Wiege der Traumfabrik*. Berlin: Transit Verlag.

Newspapers directly cited in Part II, Citations

Berliner Lokal-Anzeiger, 18 August 1896, Nr. 385, Vergnügungen.

Bulletin de la Société Francaise de Photographie, Vol. 4 (1888), p303-4; Vol. 5 (1889), p. 310.

The Egyptian Gazette, Cairo, 5 November 1896 through 17 December 1896. (Normally, page 2).

Liverpool Mercury, June 6, 1882, issue 10735, p. 6; June 9, 1882, issue 10738, p. 6; January 9, 1890, issue 13106, p. 6; December 11, 1890, issue 13394, p. 1.

Münchner Morgenblatt, 1847, June 21.

Sheffield and Rotherham Independent, October 28, 1889, issue 10973, p. 1; 22 December 1892, i11964, p6 [reprinted from *The Daily News*, London]; 5 September 1896; 15 October 1896; 29 October 1896.

Vossische Zeitung, Nr. 195, 26-04-1896, 1. Beilage, 'Lokales.'

PART 4: INDEX

Germany:

New Zealand:

Norway:

Poland:

Geographical Notes:

This index reports the names of cities and towns, and their national affiliations, as of the dates of entry, since this will in most cases reflect the language and culture of the cities and towns at the time events occurred. Two major wars in the Twentieth Century, as well as other political events and migrations, caused many cities and towns to change their national affiliations: the current affiliation of cities and towns in this index are as follows:

Bombay, India, officially became Mumbai in 1995.

Breslau, Germany, became a part of Poland in 1945 and is today named Wroc³aw.

Brünn, Moravia, is today known as Brno, Chechia.

Danzig, West Prussia, Germany, became a Free City at the end of World War I, and was annexed to Poland after the second World War and is today named Gdañsk.

Kiev, Russia, since 1991 has been the capitol of the independent state of Ukraine.

Kristiana, Norway, took its name from Christiana after a spelling reform in 1877, and in 1925 was re-named Oslo.

Moravská Ostrava, Bohemia, is today Ostrava, Czech Republic.

Nikolaiev, Russia, is today Mykolaiv, Ukraine.

Pressburg, Germany became Bratislava in 1919, and is today the capitol of the Slovak Republic.

Smyrna, an ancient Greek city on the Anatolian Penninsula, is today known as Izmir, Turkey.

Trieste, Austria's main port and shipbuilding centre, was annexed to Italy at the end of World War I.